FIFTH EDITION

WRITING, READING, AND RESEARCH

Richard Veit

Christopher Gould

John Clifford

The University of North Carolina at Wilmington

Allyn and Bacon

Boston   London   Toronto   Sydney   Tokyo   Singapore

Vice President: Eben W. Ludlow
Editorial Assistant: Grace Trudo
Executive Marketing Manager: Lisa Kimball
Editorial Production Service: Chestnut Hill Enterprises, Inc.
Manufacturing Buyer: Suzanne Lareau
Cover Administrator: Linda Knowles

Internet: www.abacon.com

Between the time Website information is gathered and published, some sites may have closed. Also, the transcription of URLs can result in typographical errors. The publisher would appreciate notification where these occur so that they may be corrected in subsequent editions.

Library of Congress Cataloging-in-Publication Data

Veit, Richard.
    Writing, reading, and research / Richard Veit, Christopher Gould, John Clifford. — 5th ed.
        p.   cm.
    Includes bibliographical references and index.
    ISBN 0-205-31881-9
    1. English language—Rhetoric.   2. Research—Methodology.   3. Academic writing.   4.
College readers   I. Gould, Christopher.   II. Clifford, John.   III. Title.
    PE1408.V45   2000
    808'.042—dc21
                                                    00-044748

Printed in the United States of America

10 9 8 7 6 5 4 3 2 1   RRD-VA   05 04 03 02 01 00

A Book Published before 1900

Nightingale, Florence. <u>Notes on Nursing:
What It Is, and What It Is Not</u>. New
York, 1860.

A Paperback or Other Reprinted Book

Horwitz, Tony. <u>Confederates in the Attic:
Dispatches from the Unfinished Civil
War</u>. 1998. New York: Vintage, 1999.

An Online Book

Irving, David. <u>Hitler's War</u>. New York:
Viking, 1977. 20 Jan. 2000 <http://www.
focal.org/books/hitler/HW.pdf>.

Robinson, Kenneth. <u>Beyond the Wilderness</u>.
Online Originals, 1998. 21 Dec. 1999
<http://www.onlineoriginals.com/
beyondsy.html>.

Wollstonecraft, Mary. <u>Vindication of the
Rights of Women</u>. 1792. <u>Project
Bartleby</u>. Ed. Steven H. van Leeuwen.
13 Feb. 2000 <http://www.bartleby.com/
144/index.html>.

A Book on CD-ROM or Diskette

Merritt, Frederick S., M. Kent Loftin, and
Jonathan T. Ricketts. <u>Standard
Handbook for Civil Engineers</u>. 4th ed.
CD-ROM. New York: McGraw, 1999.

An Article in an Encyclopedia or Other Reference Work

A well-known reference work:

Brandon, James R. "East Asian Arts."
<u>Encyclopaedia Britannica: Macropaedia</u>.
15th ed. 1998.
"Wellstone, Paul." <u>Who's Who in America</u>.
54th ed. 2000.
"Yodel." <u>The Shorter Oxford English
Dictionary</u>. 1973.

A lesser-known reference work:

Hames, Raymond. "Yanomamö." <u>South America</u>.
Vol. 7 of <u>Encyclopedia of World
Cultures</u>. Boston: Hall, 1994.

An electronic reference work:

"Latitude and Longitude." <u>Britannica
Online</u>. 28 Feb. 2000 <http://search.
eb.com/bol/topic?xref=7843>.
"Yokel." <u>Oxford English Dictionary</u>. 2nd
ed. CD-ROM. Oxford: Oxford UP, 1992.

SOURCES IN PERIODICALS AND NEWSPAPERS

An Article in a Magazine

Block, Toddi Gutner. "Riding the Waves."
<u>Forbes</u> 11 Sept. 1995: 182+.
Lynn, Jacquelyn. "Hidden Resources."
<u>Entrepreneur</u> Jan. 2000: 102-08.
Robinson, Ann. "Gifted: The Two-Faced
Label." <u>The Gifted Child Today</u>
Jan./Feb. 1989: 34-36.

An Article in a Journal

Pages numbered continuously throughout the volume:

Reese, Hayne W. "Some Contributions of
Philosophy to Behavioral Sciences."
<u>Journal of Mind and Behavior</u> 20 (1999):
183-210.

Each issue begins on page 1:

Green, Anna. "Returning History to the
Community: Oral History in a Museum
Setting." <u>Oral History Review</u> 24.2
(1997): 53-72.

An Article in a Newspaper

Constable, Pamela. "Afghan Hijack Drama
Ends Peacefully." <u>Washington Post</u> 1
Jan. 2000: A1.
Ranii, David. "New AIDS Drug Is Step Closer
to Approval." <u>News and Observer</u>
[Raleigh] 7 Nov. 1995: 1D+.
Kaufman, Leslie, and Saul Hansell. "Holiday
Lesson in Online Retailing." <u>New York
Times</u> 2 Jan. 2000, natl. ed.: sec. 3:
1+.

An Editorial

"Replace Unfair Tax Law." Editorial. <u>USA
Today</u> 28 Aug. 1995: 12A.

A Letter to the Editor

Sadler, David. Letter. <u>U.S. News & World
Report</u> 3-10 Jan. 2000: 7.

A Review

Bickerton, Derek. "Life without Father."
Rev. of <u>The Emperor's Embrace:
Reflections on Animal Families and
Fatherhood</u>, by Jeffrey Moussaieff
Masson. <u>New York Times Book Review</u> 2
Jan. 2000: 5.
Glenn, Kenny. Rev. of <u>Man on the Moon</u>
[film]. <u>Premiere</u> Jan. 2000: 20.
Rev. of <u>Going to the Territory</u>, by Ralph
Ellison. <u>Atlantic</u> Aug. 1986: 91.
Stearns, David Patrick. Rev. of <u>The Well-
Tempered Clavier</u>, by J. S. Bach [CD].
Angela Hewitt, piano. <u>Stereophile</u> Dec.
1999: 173+.

A Printed Article Reproduced Online

"Doctors Striving to Preempt Diabetes."
<u>Boston Globe</u> 1 Jan. 2000: A3. 15 Jan.
2000 <http://www.boston.com/
dailyglobe2/001/nation/Doctors_striving_
to_preempt_diabetes+.shtml>.

Eddy, Melissa. "Experts Worry about
Economic Collapse in Bosnia." <u>News and
Observer on the Web</u> 1 Jan. 2000. 2
Jan. 2000 <http://www.nandotimes.com/
24hour/nao/business/story/0,2257,
500148948-500180852-500736195-0,00.html>.

(continued on next page)

List of Works Cited (continued)

Mazurek, Robert Henry. "Under the Ice." Popular Science Jan. 2000: 28. ProQuest. 14 Feb. 2000 <http://proquest.umi.com>.

Yue, Lorene. "Economists Expect Federal Reserve to Leave Rates Unchanged." Detroit Free Press 20 Dec. 1999. Newspaper Source. EBSCOhost. 14 Jan. 2000 <http://www.epnet.com>.

A Printed Article Reproduced on CD-ROM or Microform

Diamond, Nina L. "Dolphin Sonar: A Biologist and Physicist Team Up to Find the Source of Sound Beams." Omni July 1994: 24. Popular Periodicals Standard. CD-ROM. NewsBank. Oct. 1995.

Sipe, Cynthia L., and Anne E. Roder. "Mentoring School-Age Children: A Classification of Programs." Public/Private Ventures Mentor Spring 1999. ERIC. Microfiche. ED 431 070.

An Article Published Online (Not Reproduced)

"Phythian, Nicholas. "Ivory Coast Calm, Deposed President Leaves." Reuters. Yahoo! News 26 Dec. 1999. 26 Dec. 1999 <http://dailynews.yahoo.com/h/nm/1999 1226/ts/ivorycoast_leadall_8.html>.

West, Alden. "Camping with Wolves." Dynamic Patterns 5 May 1999. 28 Jan. 2000 <http://www.dynamicpatterns. com/webzine/non-fiction/west_camping_ wolves.html>.

OTHER SOURCES

An Audio Recording

Dickinson, Dee. Creating the Future: Perspectives on Educational Change. Audiocassette. Minneapolis: Accelerated Learning Systems, 1991.

Mahler, Gustav. Symphony No. 7. Michael Tilson Thomas, cond. London Symphony Orch. CD. RCA Victor, 1999.

Shuster, George N. Jacket notes. The Poetry of Gerard Manley Hopkins. LP. Caedmon, n.d.

Computer Software

Atoms, Symbols and Equations. Vers. 2.1. Software. 18 Jan. 2000 <http://ourworld.compuserve.com/homepages/RayLec/atoms.htm>.

Twain's World. CD-ROM. Parsippany, NJ: Bureau Development, 1993.

A Film or Video Recording

All the Pretty Horses. Dir. Billy Bob Thornton. Screenplay by Cormac McCarthy. Sony, 2000.

The Classical Hollywood Style. Program 1 of The American Cinema. Prod. New York Center for Visual History. Videocassette. Annenberg/CPB, 1995.

The Little Foxes. Dir. William Wyler. Perf. Bette Davis, Herbert Marshall, and Dan Duryea. MGM, 1941. Videocassette. Embassy, 1985.

A Government Document

See "A Work Written by a Group or Government Agency" above.

A Lecture

Granetta, Stephanie. Class lecture. English 315. Richardson College. 7 Apr. 2000.

Kamenish, Eleanor. "A Tale of Two Countries: Mores in France and Scotland." Public lecture. Friends of the Public Library. Louisville, 16 Apr. 2000.

A Pamphlet

Golden Retriever Club of America. Prevention of Heartworm. N.p.: GRCA, 2000.

Who Are the Amish? Aylmer, Ont.: Pathway, n.d.

A Personal Interview

Keating, Robert. Personal interview. 14 Oct. 1999.

A Television or Radio Program

The Crossing. Dir. Robert Harmon. Screenplay by Sherry Jones and Peter Jennings. History Channel. 1 Jan. 2000.

Silberner, Joanne. Report on Internet drug sales. All Things Considered. National Public Radio. 28 Dec. 1999.

An Unpublished Essay

Tetirick, Eliza. "Giving Myself Credit: Should I Apply for a Credit Card?" Essay written for Prof. Richard Veit's English 102 class. Fall semester 1999.

An Unpublished Letter or E-Mail

Colbert, Stanley. Letter to author. 5 Mar. 2000.

Wilkes, Paul. E-mail to author. 29 Dec. 1999.

An Unpublished Questionnaire

Questionnaire conducted by Prof. Barbara Waxman's English 102 class. Feb. 2000.

Contents

To the Instructor

Writing, Reading, and Research, Fifth Edition, derives from the assumption that the three activities in the title are central to a college education. Every college student must be able to access information and ideas, analyze and synthesize them, and communicate the resultant knowledge to others.

What is more, writing, reading, and research are so closely and symbiotically related that they need to be studied together. We believe that the research paper should not be seen (as it often is) as just one among many isolated writing activities, noted chiefly for its intricacies of search protocols and citation formats. Research, in the broader sense we envision, includes activities both large and small. Every task involving sources is a research activity, whether it be reading a textbook, using a library, searching the Internet, asking questions, taking notes, or writing a summary and analysis in response to an essay-exam question. A text on research-based writing, as we see it, should reflect this inclusive definition of research, engaging students in its rewards and excitement and preparing them to do it well.

It follows that students need to develop the many skills involved in college research. Writing an essay based on library sources, for example, employs a wide range of skills that, in our experience, many first-year college students have not yet developed. Most basic of all is the need to read well. Students need to employ efficient strategies, to read with perception and understanding, to analyze and critique what they read, and to make productive use of the information and ideas that arise from their reading.

For these reasons, we believe that writing, reading, and research skills should be taught and practiced together. A composition course that prepares students for the actual tasks they will face in their college and professional careers can and should be a unified whole. That unity is the principle that informs this book.

Learning the skills of writing, reading, and research is a process that can be divided into successive stages. We have attempted to take a commonsense approach to this process by introducing concepts sequentially. Although each chapter has its own integrity, each also builds on the concepts developed in preceding chapters.

In general, the book's movement is from simpler to more complex tasks—from working with a single source to working with multiple sources, from basic reading strategies to analytical and critical reading, from paraphrase and summary to simple synthesis, and then to more advanced creative and synthetic writing skills.

We had many specific goals in writing this book:

- To broaden the traditional notion of undergraduate research
- To teach the process of college research in a practical sequence
- To blend the best features of a contemporary rhetoric text, an interdisciplinary reader, and a research guide
- To provide a book that instructors would find a serviceable teaching instrument and that students would find lively and readable, instructive as a text, and useful as a research handbook
- To illustrate writing activities with student examples and to show the processes the writers carried out to achieve their finished products
- To provide helpful and engaging exercises, frequent opportunities to write, and many occasions for discussion and critical interaction.

Changes in the Fifth Edition

In the preface to the fourth edition, published in 1997, we acknowledged the revolution that had occurred in research with the advent of computer-related resources. In the few years since then, the pace of the revolution has accelerated, and the degree to which college research now depends on—and benefits from—electronic media is greater by many times what it was just a few years ago.

Chapter 9 provides a thorough introduction to computer-related resources, including ways to find sources electronically and to access sources that are themselves electronic. Information on how to cite various electronic texts is provided in Chapters A and B of Part II, the reference handbook section. This information is made concrete for readers in the three sample student research papers provided in Chapters 8 and 14, which use a variety of electronic, as well as print, sources.

Citation information has also been updated for this edition to reflect changes introduced in the fifth edition of *MLA Handbook for Writers of Research Papers* (1999).

We have provided all new end-of-chapter readings, with a continued emphasis on cross-disciplinary and multicultural topics, freewritten responses, and collaborative inquiry.

Acknowledgments

We owe the greatest debt to our students, from whom we have learned most of what we know about teaching composition. In particular, we would like to thank the student writers who shared their notes and drafts with us and allowed us to use their papers and experiences in this book.

We would also thank the following reviewers, whose wise and thoughtful suggestions made an immeasurable contribution to this fifth edition: Niki E. Nolles/Red

Rocks Community College; Rebecca K. Rowley/Clovis Community College; Nancy M. Mocek/DeVry Institute of Technology—DuPage, Illinois Campus; and Barbara A. Fahey/Scottsdale Community College.

Finally, we acknowledge Eben Ludlow, vice president at Allyn and Bacon, and our friends and colleagues at the University of North Carolina at Wilmington.

R. V.
C. G.
J. C.

PART I

Writing, Reading, and Research

1 *Introduction to Writing, Reading, and Research*

Writing, reading, and research are among the most useful and important proficiencies you can cultivate in college and implement continually throughout your career. It stands to reason, then, that a course designed to teach, develop, and apply these proficiencies—the course you are now taking—is as valuable as any in the curriculum.

You may be skeptical. If you plan a career in forestry, for example, or in biology, theology, or accounting, the courses in your major field are probably the ones that appear most important to you. Yet almost every course listed in your college catalog presupposes that entering students have acquired certain kinds of knowledge and skills. The most essential skills of all—the ones most vital to your success in college and your career—are writing, reading, and research. You enjoy an enormous advantage if you are an articulate writer, an alert and insightful reader, and a resourceful researcher.

A college education must do more than pour facts into your head. It must teach you how to learn on your own. The sum of knowledge in any field is too vast and the world is changing too rapidly for an education that merely imparts information. Instead, an education worthy of the name must provide access to whatever you need to know, both now and after you graduate. It must prepare you to learn what other people have discovered in the past, to understand what you read today, to receive and adapt to tomorrow's ideas. It must train you to think, to acquaint yourself with other people's ideas and knowledge, to evaluate and adapt them, and to contribute new ideas and discoveries of your own. These are the skills of writing, reading, and research as we define them in this book. You can see why we consider them important.

The good news is that there is nothing mysterious, or even terribly difficult, about these skills. You are perfectly capable of acquiring them. For one thing, you have been reading and writing for years, and (whether you know it or not) you have been performing research all of your life, both in and out of school. For example, when you were deciding which college to attend, you probably researched the subject by examining college catalogs, visiting Web sites, consulting with your guidance counselor, talking with friends, or traveling to several campuses. In fact, if you found and read a catalog and then wrote for an application, you used all three skills.

The aim of this book is to develop and expand those skills to meet the needs of your college career. Writing, reading, and research are interrelated activities, so it makes sense to study them together. Doing research often involves finding what other people have written, reading it, and then writing in response. Even as you write, you must read and reread what you have written, deciding whether further research and rewriting are needed. And finally, what you have written about your research becomes someone else's reading.

Because these skills can be learned only through experience, *Writing, Reading, and Research* will give you considerable practice in using them. In addition, since they can be learned most easily in a progression, with one accomplishment building on others already mastered, this book is arranged in a reasonable, practical sequence. The purpose of this first chapter is to provide a brief introduction to these essential and interrelated activities.

WRITING

Unlike the skill of speaking, which we acquire early in childhood without formal instruction, we almost always learn to write in school, and it takes time and practice to become proficient at it. Writing is a complex process, involving many separate skills from the basics of handwriting and spelling to the subtler nuances of tone and organization. Most of us master the fundamentals easily enough, but we can never truthfully claim to have perfected our writing skills. The most illustrious writers, after a lifetime of accomplishment, continue to learn from experience and develop their craft. A college course in composition or a book like this can assist your development as a writer, but repeated practice will always remain the best teacher.

The essence of writing is *choice;* as writers we are faced with constant decisions. Even when we know exactly what we want to say (which most writers will admit rarely happens), we still face an almost infinite range of options about how to say it. We must decide on an overall strategy, choose the appropriate level of formality for our audience, find the best opening and closing, and determine which facts, arguments, or supporting material to include and which to omit. Even the selection of individual words involves choosing from an array of available synonyms.

In one sense, choice is a burden in that it makes writing more difficult. Writing is undeniably hard work, and not just for beginners. If anything, experienced writers are aware of even *more* choices available to them. Every writer is familiar with writer's block in one form or another: staring at the page or computer monitor and agonizing over what to say next. And although there are compensating periods when the right words seem to flow, the text that "writes itself" is unfortunately a myth. Experienced writers accept the difficulty and persevere through periods when writing gets arduous, knowing that eventually they will work through them. They have also developed their own strategies for creating and clarifying ideas and overcoming obstacles.

Fortunately, choice provides us with opportunities as well as obstacles. It is what makes writing an art, not just a competency. As writers, we are more than trained word mechanics turning out an assembly-line product. We are artists in the sense that we are able to use our imaginations, experiences, and talents to create, from the unlimited options available to us, works that are original and effective. Writing gives us the means to communicate whatever we wish in a way that is profound, or funny, or provocative, or highly persuasive. Despite, or perhaps because of, the hard work and hard choices involved in writing, the sense of achievement we derive from having created a work uniquely our own can be great and at times even exhilarating.

Writing Habits and Strategies

One characteristic of skilled writers is that they spend considerable time in the preliminary stages of writing—long before they produce a complete, polished draft. Everyone's writing practices differ, and one of your goals as a writer should be to discover the procedures that give you the best results. David Bartholomae, a professor of English at the University of Pittsburgh, is one professional writer who has developed a systematic routine for composing. In the following passage, Bartholomae describes part of that routine.*

> There are things that get in the way of my writing and things that I put in the path of my writing that are different now than they were when I was younger, but the essential resistance—both mine and writing's—remains.
>
> Writing gets in my way and makes my life difficult, difficult enough that I sometimes wonder why I went into this business in the first place. There is work that comes easier to me. Writing gets in my way, but when I write, I almost always put up barriers—barriers to show my sense of duty—to stand (like parentheses) in the way of writing. I feel, as a matter of principle, that writing should not go smoothly and that when it does, unless I'm writing a memo (but even there I try to plant buried jokes or unofficial countervoices), when it does go smoothly, it's not doing the work of a professional or showing proper respect for what Thoreau referred to as the "extra-vagrance" of things.
>
> I think of writing primarily as a matter of resistance. At the same time, however, I will quickly admit that I have developed habits and changed habits to make writing more efficient. I've learned to revise, I've learned to use a word processor, I've learned to develop a schedule and to find a place that can make regular writing possible. Writing still, often, makes me unhappy, makes me sick, makes me do things—like smoke, for instance—that disgust me. I have my habits and quirks and behaviors, like other writers, and I've learned

*From "Against the Grain" by David Bartholomae in *Writers on Writing* (T. Waldrep, ed.). New York: Random House, 1985. Reproduced with permission of The McGraw Hill Companies.

that thinking about them has helped me to put them to use, and I've learned that talking about them can help me speak with greater authority to my students. . . .

What are my habits and quirks? I revise a lot and, as a consequence, I push my students to do the same. I spend a lot of time letting a paper bounce around in my head before I start writing. I begin my papers always with *things,* never with ideas or theses. I begin, that is, with a folder full of examples, or two books on my desk that I want to work into an essay, or a paragraph that I cut from an earlier essay of my own, or some long quotations that puzzle me and that I want to talk about and figure out. . . . I like green pens, I never outline, I work with two yellow pads (one to write on; one for making plans, storing sentences, and taking notes). I've learned to do all these things and they are a part of who I am and what I do as I write, but they strike me as unimportant when weighed on the scales of the Western tradition.

I'm not just being snide here. I feel a sense of historic moment when I write—not that I'm making history, but that I am intruding upon or taking my turn in a conversation others have begun before me. I feel a sense of the priority of others. Some of them, I think, are great writers, some of them are my colleagues and contemporaries, some of them are my teachers, some of them are strangers or students. I feel a sense of historic moment when I write that I'll confess I never felt at marches and rallies and that I never feel at university committee meetings or other public occasions.

Notice how Bartholomae experiences the same self-doubts and insecurities that plague less-experienced writers. But through practice and reflection he has learned that such feelings are an unavoidable, even productive, stage in a predictable routine that almost always ends with an acceptable draft.

Many people mistakenly believe that proficient writers create polished essays in a single, effortless try. The truth is that even experts start out with vague, half-formed bits and pieces of an idea. Their thoughts are not focused or developed, certainly not expressed in language that they are ready to share with a reader. At this stage, your writing and that of the most accomplished authors are probably similar.

The chief difference between experienced writers and most first-year college students is that the former, like David Bartholomae, have learned through trial and error to break down the complexity of writing by approaching it in manageable stages, so that what starts out confused and awkward ends up, several stages later, as a polished essay or a crafted report. If you strive for early perfection in your writing, you are doomed to failure and frustration. Polish and clarity evolve over time through patient drafting and redrafting. That is the secret of professional writers. Writing is not any easier for them. But they have confidence in the routines they have developed. They know that if they are patient and persistent, then good ideas, graceful sentences, and even polished grammar will come. So they relax and settle down to the hardest part of writing—getting started.

In this book we assume that you already have had a course in college or high school that introduced you to the stages of the writing process. Even so, we think it useful to outline and review a composing sequence used by many seasoned writers. Your writing habits are not exactly like anyone else's, and every time you write, the circumstances vary. So be prepared to make adjustments when necessary. But remember there are no shortcuts to good thinking and clear writing.

Several times in this book, we present papers by college students written in response to assignments in their composition classes. In the following pages you will read a paper by Kristin Smith, a first-year college student, who responded to the following assignment. In addition, to illustrate the composing process that leads up to a finished paper, we have recorded the evolution of Kristin's paper from her first reading of the assignment through the proofreading of her final draft.

Writing from Observation   ASSIGNMENT

Research involves seeking out what you want to know and making discoveries. Later in this course you will engage in *secondary research,* so called because it involves your finding out what other researchers have already discovered. Library research is an example of secondary research. This paper requires some *primary research,* in which you discover information about the world firsthand, through direct observation.

Here is the assignment in brief: *Focus your attention on a certain place or activity, learn what you can about it through careful, persistent observation, and write about your discoveries in an interesting, informative paper.*

The following suggestions and guidelines may be helpful:

• Choose an organization, office, building, or outdoor locale where a particular activity takes place. Examples could include a homeless shelter, art gallery, university cafeteria, pet shop, singles bar, or police station.

• Select a place or activity that is new or almost new to you. If you choose a topic with which you are familiar, you will not be able to see it with fresh eyes and might take for granted or miss what an observant outsider could see. For this assignment, it is important that you observe and write as a *reporter,* not as a participant.

• Observe carefully what goes on there, particularly what might not be obvious to the casual observer. Note how people act, perhaps including how they respond to each other, their style of behavior, and the unspoken rules of the place.

• Adopt one of two styles of gathering data: Be an unobtrusive "fly on the wall," listening and watching others who are generally unaware of your presence. Or be an inquiring reporter, talking to people and asking questions.

- Return as often as necessary until you know your subject well. Take copious notes during or immediately after each visit.

- Write about the institution/activity and about your personal experience there. Report on what *you* see, and feel free to use the word *I* in reporting on your observations. You can discuss what you intended to find, what you discovered, and how your ideas changed or were reinforced by the experience.

- Do not spend much time on the obvious surface facts about the place. Do not tell your readers things they already know. Get behind the obvious and tell your readers what is really going on.

- Describe particular events that occurred during your observation rather than generalizations about what happens on typical days. Use specific details.

Submit your prewriting, notes, and preliminary drafts along with your polished paper.

The nature and requirements of this assignment will become clearer, first as you read Kristin's polished essay and then as you follow her progress through the stages that led to her final draft. Notice how the assignment calls for something beyond purely personal writing. By this, we mean that the instructor expected members of the class to draw upon sources other than just their own thoughts and past experiences; that is, they were expected to rely on direct observation and, possibly, an interview or informal survey. The procedure might involve visits to several locales or repeated observation of a single site.

Being a fair and open-minded observer does not require the writer to assume a completely detached, impersonal stance toward a topic. In fact, when you read Kristin's essay, you will find she became personally involved with what she was writing about, her observation of the emotional crisis center in a public hospital. The assignment calls for a type of writing that is not completely different from the personal essays Kristin had written previously in high school and college, nor from the more formal research-based writing she would do later in her composition class. Although the assignment does not call for a traditional research paper—the kind that cites library sources and uses formal documentation—it does involve a certain type of research. (Later chapters of this book explain various methods of research in greater detail.)

Audience and Purpose

Whenever we engage in any type of discourse—that is, whenever we converse, write a letter, give a speech, compose an essay, or participate in any other kind of transaction involving language—we adapt our words and style of delivery to our intentions. Imagine, for example, an overheard dialogue between a male and a female college student who have just met at a party. The conversation might consist of little more than the customary phrases of introduction, followed by some routine questions about hometowns, majors, interests, and tastes in music. Nevertheless, an astute observer will recognize in this dialogue certain subtle attempts to manipulate a familiar ritual for complex purposes. Each speaker is trying to discover the degree of their attraction to the other, to make a deliberate impression, and to advance (or perhaps to slow or even to end) the progress of a relationship. Like these two speakers, all of us, since early childhood, have become experienced in adapting language behavior to different situations. So it is when we write.

Two factors that all writers must take into account are ***purpose*** and ***audience.*** That is, they consider their reasons for writing and the persons they expect to read what they have written. These considerations affect a wide range of decisions involving language, because there is no single all-purpose style or method of writing that suits every occasion. To illustrate this point, consider the following excerpt from the Declaration of Independence:

> We hold these truths to be self-evident, that all men are created equal. . . .

Contrast it with this excerpt from H. L. Mencken's comic paraphrase "The Declaration of Independence in American":

> All we got to say on this proposition is this: first, me and you is as good as anybody else, and maybe a damn sight better. . . .

Both passages are widely admired, but, because they were written for different purposes and addressed to different audiences, they exemplify vastly different styles. In the original version, Thomas Jefferson hoped to justify American independence to the world and to persuade his fellow colonists of the rightness of armed rebellion. In contrast, Mencken wanted to amuse his readers while making a point about language; therefore, his writing is informal and humorous. Each style suits the writer's goals, but neither style would have been appropriate in the other situation, or for the assignment Kristin Smith received from her instructor.

Kristin's purpose and audience were defined by the assignment. She was expected to gather information and impressions that might benefit her or provide insight and to report her findings from a personal vantage point. In addition, she was to share any discoveries with an audience of classmates. She understood that her instructor wanted to simplify the task by having her address readers like herself. However, she could not entirely ignore the fact that her instructor—who would be reading and responding to her writing—was an important part of her audience as well.

With these considerations in mind, Kristin began her research and writing, the stages of which are traced in the following pages. As you read these next pages, you can judge how effectively she took into account the demands of her purpose and audience. Here is the final draft of Kristin's paper:

Kristin Smith

English 102

Prof. Ira Pilton

Throwing a Life Preserver

We were seated in a circle, and the woman directly across from me had the floor. In a monotone voice, she relayed the events of her day as I studied the fuzzy rabbit slippers adorning her feet. Her face, drained and colorless, indicated that she was the worst off today. She'd struggled to get out of bed, she half-whispered; brushing her teeth, showering, and dressing were almost unbearable.

Thirteen people were seated here tonight: some had just come from work; others had shuffled down the hallway from the supervised residence hall. All shared the same affliction-- they had battled or were battling severe depression. Although permitted to observe this meeting through the help of a friend who interns at the emotional crisis center, I had worried that I might not be welcome. However, the warmth and acceptance among members of the group were so evident that I felt unobtrusive and even comfortable. Always fascinated by the human mind and heart, and having more than one friend who has combatted depression, I was intrigued by what was going on around me.

Having seen <u>Awakenings</u> and <u>One Flew over the Cuckoo's Nest</u>, I expected the familiar Hollywood images, but I quickly realized that they do not apply to the center or its residents. No one was physically restrained; no one chanted incessantly or engaged in uncontrollable outbursts; no one was drooling or staring vacantly at the wall. Everyone there was [. . .] normal. A few were slightly disheveled and unkempt, but for the most part, we all just looked tired.

The meeting began with introductions and an affirmation of confidentiality. Although residents are the only ones required to attend meetings, any person formerly treated at the center is welcome. Therefore, not everyone was acquainted with each other, and, since curiosity is often unwelcome, no one asked who I was or why I was there.

A fashionably dressed woman, dripping expensive jewelry, displayed the logo of a local tennis club on a white polo shirt. A man in a business suit placed a laptop beside his chair, his cell phone resting atop the case. There were a few teenagers, probably not yet out of high school. Residents were dressed more casually, but none would have stood out in a crowded shopping mall or restaurant as someone needing mental therapy.

Three group leaders facilitated the discussion: a licensed psychiatrist, a nurse from the residence hall, and a social worker specializing in emotional crisis and mental illness. Everyone was given a chance to speak and encouraged to participate, offering suggestions and feedback to those who had the floor. This particular group was designed to teach coping skills to persons plagued by depression, either brought on by a personal crisis or unattributable to any clear cause. Most were coping with the aftermath of a catastrophe such as the death of a loved one, diagnosis of a terminal illness, divorce, or job loss. Although the events that provoked depression were as varied as the backgrounds of the individuals in the room, the emotional reactions were similar. Deep sadness, along with feelings of inadequacy and helplessness, overwhelmed these people's lives, causing some to spiral downward into an emotional abyss from which they could not escape without assistance.

The woman speaking, "Caroline," had recently been through a divorce, the climax of an abusive and destructive four-year relationship. She found herself without a home, a job, or even the support of her family, who had not condoned her marriage from the beginning. Alone and frightened, she began to lose all hope. The emotional breaking point came when her three-year-old son was killed in an automobile accident during the divorce proceedings. I began to see how someone considered "normal" in every sense of the word can suffer a disabling crisis and need assistance merely to function. "Caroline" looked like a woman you might see in church or at the supermarket. "Caroline" explained how she had lost interest in her friends and her hobbies, eventually refusing to even leave the house. One day she went into the garage, closed the door, started her car, and sat down beside the exhaust pipe. She had just wanted to sleep and not to wake up again. Reality had become too painful, and she longed to escape the anguish. "The thing about heartache," she explained, "is that there's nowhere to go that it isn't there." Though I wondered what turning point had led "Caroline" to seek help, I prudently resisted the impulse to ask.

Although "Caroline's" situation was heart-wrenching, I soon discovered that group interactions are not intended to arouse

Smith 4

pity or to account for every incident of personal history. At this point, the group moderators stepped in and brought the focus of discussion around to skills that "Caroline" could develop to head off the feelings of helplessness and hopelessness the next time they arose. They asked simple questions about sleeping and eating, routine activities that can be excruciatingly difficult for persons with depression. Others began to offer advice, the group coming alive with suggestions: "Call someone the next time you feel yourself slipping." "Make sure you go to group every week. Call your therapist." "Remember to take your medication for the time being." "Force yourself to do something active." As each voice chimed in, I realized the empathy and support radiating from the group as a source of strength. "Caroline" did not grasp onto any one suggestion as though it offered a solution to all her difficulties, nor did she quibble with the feasibility of each--as I have known healthier, more "normal" people to do. Instead, she listened intently, reassured by the expressions of deliberate and constructive support from her peers.

    After the meeting, I asked my friend how often victims of depression are "cured." She smiled almost sadly and said that depression is difficult to treat. Often, the most effective remedy is to learn techniques of coping with the residual feelings. A person who has internalized these techniques is less likely to sink into an episode of hopelessness. As yet medical science has learned so little about the human mind that any type of treatment for an emotional illness is just an attempt. "We throw them a life preserver," she said, "and hope that they reach for it."

The persons I observed are proof that hopelessness and depression can be overcome. Some came to the meeting to keep themselves afloat, while others wanted to save someone else from drowning in a sea of despair. They were there not just because they had all suffered depression, but because they all shared hope. Some of those in attendance seemed incredibly centered and calm. I spoke with one man after the meeting. He spoke freely, explaining the perspective he had gained from surviving his "low points." He was there to reassure others that low points do not last forever and that lessons learned at a price are often more valuable than those merely happened upon. "It's odd," he concluded, "but I'm thankful for all the trials life has brought me. They've made me who I am, and I know now that I can handle anything. I choose life every day."

Leaving the meeting that evening, I vowed to do the same.

Kristin's is only one of a wide variety of possible responses to the assignment on pages 7–8. It is a polished piece of writing, but it did not get that way at once. The following pages trace the stages of her research and writing that culminated in the essay you have just read.

Prewriting

It is much easier to begin drafting a paper when you already have some ideas about what you might want to say. Therefore, it makes sense, before you begin drafting, to carry out some procedures that can help you generate and discover ideas and get them in writing. These procedures include *brainstorming, mapping, freewriting, collecting data,* and *outlining.* Kristin Smith used all five techniques as a sequence to help her get started.

Brainstorming

Brainstorming is used by writers, business people, and scientists to help them unlock their thinking. It is a way of bringing to mind as many ideas about a topic as possible. Brainstorming not only provides raw material to work with; it also gets your creative juices flowing. You can brainstorm out loud or on paper. One way is to write down all the words or phrases about a topic that pop into your head, listing them down the page, one after the other as they occur to you. Don't judge them or worry about whether they're consistent with one another. Sometimes you have to go through three or four or even a dozen useless ideas before a good one comes along. The purpose of this technique is to let associations connect with each other in the mind, like rubbing sticks together to create a spark.

When Kristin's instructor presented the writing assignment on pages 7–8, he asked the class to brainstorm about possible topics for their paper. Here is an excerpt from the list that Kristin produced:

Campus
   —orientation
       meeting other students, fitting in
       placement tests
       picnic and other social events
       how do people change after leaving home?
   —classes
       professors versus grad students
       class sizes—easier to make friends in small classes?
       attendance policies—why only in some classes?
   —commuting versus living on campus
       possible effects on social life and grades
       staying in touch with friends from home (like Susan?)

Work
  —types of part-time work
    jobs that pay well (modeling, bartending)
    jobs that offer learning experiences (internships)
    jobs that provide public service (counseling)

Counseling
  dorm counselors
  literacy education (Sandy and Walt)
  crisis hot lines: rape, domestic violence, addiction, depression
  summer camp (Camp Friendship)

Kristin was writing down ideas as they came into her head, without rejecting anything as inappropriate, unworkable, or silly. She wrote quickly without worrying about punctuation or spelling. She was writing entirely for her own benefit, and some of the names and items on her list had meaning only to her. But you can see how her mind was working—and how brainstorming helped her thought processes gather momentum, with one idea triggering another. The list shows her train of thought, moving from campus life to commuting, then to part-time jobs, and finally to types of counseling, the eventual focus of her paper.

Mapping or Clustering

When you map your thinking, you try to make ideas concrete, to get them in black and white so you can look at them and see the relationship of one thought to another. You try to make a pattern of words and phrases that radiate out from a central thought. In doing this, writers are often surprised how the process of linking helps them discover other ideas. Sometimes the visual pattern itself can suggest the idea for the essay's basic organization. As in brainstorming it is best to jot ideas down quickly, without trying to decide whether each one is good or bad.

From her brainstorming, Kristin found herself focusing on various types of counseling, which she further explored in the map printed in Figure 1.1. Each of the types of counseling that she listed led to a variety of ideas, and in the process of filling out the map Kristin came up with several interesting ideas for the assignment. Some of the paths her mind took proved to be dead ends ("medications," for example), but others continued to be promising ideas. She considered psychotherapy, hospitalization, and the causes of depression. Also on her map was the idea of describing the operations of a support group, which for Kristin proved to be the most promising of all.

Freewriting

After an unfocused invention activity such as brainstorming or mapping, the best way to arrive at more focused ideas is to freewrite. Begin writing about your topic at a steady, comfortable pace, jotting down whatever comes to mind, and continue, without stopping, for a planned amount of time, perhaps five or ten minutes. Don't try to screen ideas; simply let them flow. Don't worry about spelling or repetition or punctuation or even making sense. You don't do

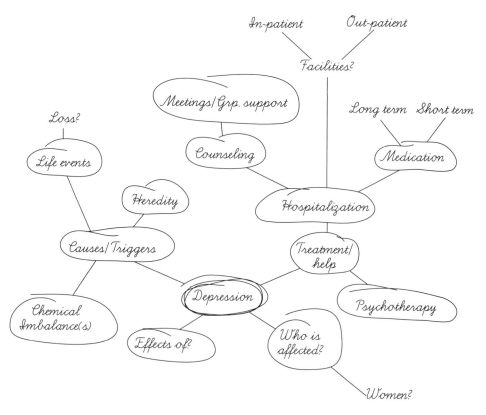

In-patient   Out-patient

Facilities?

Meetings/Grp. support

Loss?   Long term   Short term

Life events   Counseling   Medication

Heredity   Hospitalization

Causes/Triggers   Treatment/
                                        help

Chemical   Depression   Psychotherapy
Imbalance(s)

Effects of?   Who is
                   affected?

                                              Women?

Figure 1.1 Kristin Smith's Map

freewriting for others to read; you do it for yourself so you can think through your topic and come up with ideas to use later. Kristin's five-minute freewriting looked like this:

```
    How do you cope with the responsibility of answering a
hot line--so much at stake, so little time, need to stay
calm and organized.  Worst, having to deal with failure--I
know you can't solve everybody's problems, but there must
be some you can't even help, no matter how well trained
you are.  Can you get overwhelmed with pity, anger for
some--rape victims--and annoyed at others--alcoholics? I'm
interested in psychology, esp how people handle stress.
Some freak out, embarrass themselves, hurt other people,
feel guilt, become more stressed--spiral of shame.  Why
do people lose control?  Can they learn to manage it?
What do you say to someone in crisis?  Who calls hot
```

> lines--weak? strong? scared? How many calls are pranks?
> How can you tell? If I could listen in on a hot line, I
> might write about some of this. But could I listen in?
> Confidentiality is an issue. I wonder if I'd be allowed
> to observe. Maybe Jill could tell me. Since she interns
> at the hospital, she might put me in touch with someone.

This is a typical bit of freewriting—rambling, conversational, and honest. If it had been tightly organized, well planned, revised, and edited, it would not be authentic freewriting. Beginning with several possibilities in mind, Kristin used freewriting to give more focus to her thinking. As she freewrote, Kristen thought about calling her friend Jill, whose internship at the hospital had given her some experience with people in crisis. Later, when Jill suggested observing a group discussion at the emotional crisis center, Kristin arrived at the eventual topic of her paper.

Collecting Data

At this point in her project, Kristin called her friend who interned at the county hospital. After Jill suggested that she observe the emotional crisis center and provided the name and number of the director, Kristin scheduled a date and time. When she arrived at the center a few days later, she was not sure whether she should introduce herself and explain her purpose. Deciding to play it by ear, she was surprised when no one challenged her or seemed curious about who she was or why she was there. This worked to her advantage, since it enabled her to witness a typical meeting in which group members were no more guarded than usual. Although Kristin had brought a notepad and pen in her coat pocket, she quickly recognized that it would be inappropriate to take notes during the meeting. Instead, she waited until immediately afterward, writing a few notes in her car, then adding to them later when she reached home. Here are some excerpts from the notes she jotted down in her car:

> 13 people in group, various ages and occupations. Two
> teenagers, maybe 16 or 17, in jeans and t-shirts; look
> like they came here after school. Everyone looks tired,
> but otherwise fairly normal. No unusual mannerisms. Not
> what most people would expect--no one raving, talking to
> themselves, or tied up in a straightjacket. Group
> members who live in residence hall aren't as well dressed
> or carefully groomed. Woman with lots of jewelry--tennis
> club. Man in a business suit with laptop and cell
> phone. . . .
> The woman who held the floor was the most unkept--
> bunny slippers, poorly combed hair. But yet calm--dull
> voice, few facial expressions. Probably sedated. Told
> about difficulties with the most everyday kinds of
> tasks: getting up, brushing her teeth. The despair is

overwhelming at times. "The thing about heartache is
that there's nowhere to go that it isn't there." . . .
She says this without being dramatic or self-pitying. I
admire her strength and honesty at the same time that I
hurt for her.

Man in business suit: "It's odd, but I'm thankful for
all the trials that life has brought me. They've made me
who I am, and I know now that I can handle anything. I
choose life every day." . . .

Discussion leaders ask the woman how she's been
sleeping, what she ate for lunch. Group offers
suggestions for coping: "Call someone when you're
slipping." "Do something active even if you don't feel
like it." . . .

These excerpts—a small part of Kristin's notes—illustrate several different
types of note-taking:

- **Listing details.** Knowing that she would have to take notes as soon as possible after the meeting, Kristin forced herself to be observant and to pay particular attention to specific details. In her first two clusters of notes, she recorded the clothing and facial expressions of various group members.

- **Recording events.** In the second and third clusters, Kristin described the events she observed. Here she wrote in a type of shorthand without trying to record everything, knowing that she would flesh out this part of her notes as soon as she got home.

- **Interviewing.** Obviously Kristin could not interview participants in the group discussion. However, she did paraphrase many of their remarks and even managed to record two short quotations. She recognized the importance of getting their words and ideas into writing as quickly as possible, beginning with phrases that had left a particularly strong impression. Otherwise, she contented herself with a conscientious—though probably inexact—paraphrase of what they said as well as she could recollect it. If she had quoted or paraphrased persons who did not choose to remain anonymous, and if she had had the resources to cite them with greater accuracy, Kristin would not have been justified in taking this license. As it is, she used direct quotation very sparingly, only when the speaker's words were memorable and more telling than a paraphrase was likely to be.

- **Analysis.** Throughout her notes, Kristin recorded interpretations of what she observed. At one point she wrote, "Not what most people would expect—no one raving, talking to themselves, or tied up in a straightjacket," and later, "She says this without being dramatic or self-pitying. I admire her strength and honesty at the same time that I hurt for her." Analytical details like these are often the most valuable part of note-taking, since they record what you have learned. They can also help you discover a theme for your paper.

Outlining

Good notes furnish raw material for your paper, but at this stage that material is indeed raw. To incorporate it into your paper, you must *select* which parts you can best use (good notes typically contain two or three times as much data as the writer ultimately includes), and you must decide how to *organize* it. These are not separate steps, however, and many decisions about selecting and organizing are best made in the course of writing a draft. Most writers would not attempt a detailed outline of their final draft at this point, though many find it useful to draw up a very brief and broad outline before they begin a draft—if only to test a strategy for selecting and organizing their material. You should feel free as you write to alter your plan whenever you encounter new ideas or discover a better pattern of organization. Kristin Smith drew up this brief outline before she began her first draft:

> **Emotional Crisis Center**
>
> Opening: How I learned about the center and got access
>
> Depression as a disease—causes, effects, treatments, recovery (?)
>
> Group discussion
> > What I expected to see
> > What I really did see
> > > Residents versus former patients
> >
> > Caroline's story
> > Responses of group members
>
> Possibilities for overcoming the disease

Kristin's outline helped her get started on a first draft—a valuable impetus. But she was not a slave to this outline, and, as you have seen, she had departed considerably from it by the time she wrote the drafts reprinted on the following pages.

The First Draft

Having explored your topic in your mind and on paper through prewriting and having taken good notes, you have an important head start. You are now ready to begin a first draft. As you compose this draft, keep your prewriting plans in mind, but stay flexible. Since you are discovering ideas and since this is a first version, not the finished product, try not to worry yet about spelling or grammatical correctness. The time to put your paper into mechanically correct form is later, when you edit a revised draft. Pausing at this stage to check spelling or punctuation can be counterproductive if it interrupts composing. Unlike freewriting, a first draft should be composed in paragraphs, and ideas should be supported with examples, reasons, or illustrations.

After writing a first draft, Kristin edited and polished it. She then produced the following revision and had a classmate read and respond to it—a process called *peer review.* As you read the draft, notice her classmate's brief marginal comments and his longer remarks at the end.

Kristin Smith

English 102

Prof. Ira Pilton

                    Throwing a Life Preserver

        We were seated in a circle and the woman directly

across from me had the floor. In a monotone voice, she

relayed the events of her day as I studied the fuzzy

rabbit slippers adorning each of her feet. Her face

drained and colorless, she was the worst off today.

It had been a struggle to get out of bed, she half

whispered, and brushing her teeth, showering and

dressing almost unbearable.

Already I'm curious and engaged esp. in view of what your title implies

        There were thirteen people seated here tonight,

some had just come from work in their business attire,

some had just shuffled down the hallway from the

supervised residence hall. All shared one commonality--

they had battled or were battling severe depression. I

had gained admittance to this meeting through a friend

who interned here at the emotional crisis center of the

hospital, and I felt strangely unobtrusive and even

why, do you suppose?

comfortable within this group. Always having been

fascinated by the human mind and heart, and having

experienced more than one close friend combat

depression, I was extremely intrigued by what was going

on around me.

        Granted, I have seen <u>Awakenings</u> and <u>One Flew over</u>
<u>the Cuckoo's Nest</u> and harbored some Hollywood fabricated

ideas about what the residence hall would look like and how those in attendance would behave, but I quickly realized my conceptions to be exaggerated. No one was physically restrained, no one was incessantly chanting or having uncontrollable outbursts, and no one was drooling and staring vacantly at the wall. Everyone there was . . . normal. Some looked slightly disheveled and (unkept,) but for the most part, we all just looked tired.

[margin annotation: The contrast b/w lurid fiction and everyday reality encourages empathy]

[margin annotation: unkempt?]

The meeting had begun with an introduction of everyone in attendance and a promise of confidentiality. Not everyone knew each other, and so my presence was not brought into question. Residents were required to attend meetings, but anyone who had ever been treated in-patient or out-patient at the center was welcome.

[margin annotation: Did they assume that you were a former patient?]

There was a sharply dressed woman there, dripping expensive jewelry and wearing the logo of a local tennis club. A man wore a business suit, and at his side sat a laptop, his cell phone resting atop the case. There were a few teenagers there, probably not yet out of high school. Those from the residence hall were more casually dressed, but none could I have pointed to in a crowded mall or restaurant and distinguished as someone in need of mental help.

[margin annotation: on as shirt?]

Facilitating the meeting were three group leaders. A licensed psychiatrist, a nurse from the residence hall, and a social worker specializing in emotional crisis and

mental illness. Everyone was given a chance to speak
and encouraged to participate, offering suggestions and
feedback to those who currently had the floor. This
particular group was designed to teach coping skills to
those plagued by depression, either triggered by a life
crisis or simply for reasons unexplainable. (From my
studies and discussions with friends in the field, I
knew that depression can be hereditary and often has to
do with chemical imbalances within the brain.) Most of
those in the group had experienced a major catastrophe,
such as the death of a loved one, diagnosis of a
terminal illness, divorce or job loss.

This sentence seems digressive. Can you omit it, or am I missing a point that you're trying to make?

Although the events that provoked depression were as
varied as those in the room, the emotional reactions
were similar. Deep sadness, feelings of inadequacy and
helplessness, had overwhelming effects on these people's
lives, causing some to spiral further downward into an
emotional abyss from which assistance was inevitably
needed to escape.

The woman speaking was called "Caroline," and she had
recently been through a divorce, the climax to an
abusive and destructive four-year relationship. She
found herself without a home, a job, or even the support
of her family--they had not condoned her marriage from
the beginning. Alone and frightened, hope began to
elude her. The emotional breaking point came when her
three-year-old son was killed in an automobile accident

I can't imagine how anyone could endure this!

during the divorce proceedings. I began to see how
someone can be "normal" in every aspect of the word, yet
still suffer a life crisis and go through periods when
they need assistance to function. She looked like a
woman you might see in church or at the supermarket.
Unlike a broken arm or a bruised body, depression is
undetectable to the naked eye, yet as dangerous as any
other affliction. "Caroline" explained how she had lost

I don't quite follow this sentence.

interest in her friends and her hobbies. Eventually,
she had even lost any interest in leaving the house. One
day she went in the garage, closed the door, started her
car, and sat down beside the exhaust pipe. She had just
wanted to sleep, she said, and did not want to wake up
again. Reality had become too painful, and she just
wanted to escape the pain. "The thing about heartache,"
she went on, "is that there's nowhere to go that it
isn't there.

Did she explain how she found her way to therapy? Or is that beside the point here?

     Her story was heart-wrenching, but before I had a
chance to get completely caught up in the details, the
group moderators stepped in and brought the focus of the
discussion around to skills that "Caroline" could
develop to head off the overwhelming feelings of
helplessness and hopelessness the next time. They asked
simple questions like "How did you sleep last night?"
and "What did you have for lunch?" Someone who suffers
from depression will often find even these activities
excruciatingly difficult, and what others may consider

Should this information come earlier in this paragraph?

routine becomes an emotional battle of will for a victim
of depression. Other group members began to offer
advice, the group coming alive with suggestions: "Call
someone the next time you feel yourself slipping."
"Make sure you go to group every week. Call your
therapist." "Remember to take your medication for the
time being." "Force yourself to do something active."
As each voice chimed in, I realized the empathy and
support radiating from the group as a source of
strength.

How did Caroline respond to these suggestions?

Following the meeting, I asked my friend how often
people are "cured." She smiled almost sadly and said
that while depression is a disease that is difficult to
combat, there are coping techniques that can be learned
to deal more effectively with the residual feelings.
Once these methods are internalized, the chances of
sinking into an episode of hopelessness decrease. So
little is known about the human mind that any type of
treatment for any type of emotional illness is just an
attempt at best. "We throw them a life preserver," she
said, "and hope that they reach for it."

Maybe a transitional word (like "however"?) here?

Those attending the group that night were proof that
hopelessness and depression can be overcome. Some were
there to keep themselves afloat, while others wanted to
save someone else from drowning in a sea of despair.
They were there not because they had all suffered
depression, but because they all shared hope. Someone

of those in attendance seemed incredibly centered and
calm. I cornered one man after the meeting and began to
talk with him. He was very open, explaining the
perspective he had gained through surviving his "low
points." He was there to reassure others that low
points do not last forever and that lessons learned at a
price are often more valuable than those happened upon.
"It's odd," he explained, "but I'm thankful for all the
trials life has brought me. They've made me who I am,
and I know now that I can handle anything. I choose
life every day."

     Leaving the meeting that evening, I vowed to do the
same.

A positive way to end a paper on such a disturbing topic.

Kristin, I'm struck by your serious, respectful attitude toward such a sensitive topic. Because of the vulnerability of group members and the urgent need for confidentiality, allowing outsiders into a setting like this must carry risks. You've certainly justified the trust and confidence of your friend and whoever else helped to arrange your visit. Also, you contribute to efforts to dispel the stereotypes and shame that many people still associate with clinical depression. Because of those efforts, there are fewer barriers for people who need help.

The one question I have is whether your primary aim here is to inform readers about a misunderstood disease (its causes, symptoms, treatments, and so forth) or to depict a particular time and place in the course of therapy. (I'm not suggesting that those aims are incompatible, just asking whether one ought to receive priority.) I sense that you're more committed to depicting a time and place—since that's what we all seem to be doing with this paper assignment—and that makes a few of your sentences seem digressive. I've noted three of them, in paragraphs 6 and 8.

Peer Review

As you can see by comparing Kristin's editing draft with her final paper, she benefited from the careful review and helpful responses provided by Robin, her classmate. Most experienced writers are eager, even greedy, for this kind of feedback. By the time you have completed a draft that you are willing to submit for others to read, you have read it and reread it so often you can no longer view it objectively. A fellow student can help you see your paper through his or her eyes and enable you to gain a fresh perception of it.

A peer reviewer's principal task, then, is to give the writer a sense of how another reader will respond to the draft. When you read and comment on another person's writing, you should not think of yourself as an instructor or grader of the paper. Instead, try to be yourself and simply respond as honestly and helpfully as you can. Notice several important features of Robin's response to Kristin's draft:

• The longest comment is a final *holistic* response, one that reflects on the entire text—the intentions of the writer and her engagement of the reader—rather than commenting on isolated details. Robin is careful to provide two indispensable kinds of feedback in a few sentences: He tells the writer, truthfully but tactfully, what took place in his mind as he read the draft ("I'm struck by your serious, respectful attitude toward a sensitive topic. . . . You contribute to efforts to dispel the stereotypes and shame that many people still associate with clinical depression."), and he raises only one or two possibilities for revision ("The one question I have is whether your primary aim here is to inform readers about a misunderstood disease . . . or to depict a particular time and place in the course of therapy.").

• The respondent respects the writer's ownership of the draft: His comments are tentative rather than assertive. When he thinks a particular type of revision might be called for, he asks questions rather than issues directives ("Should this information come earlier in this paragraph?").

• The respondent remarks on positive features of the text without being dishonest or patronizing. He is supportive ("Already I'm curious and engaged. . . .") but lets the writer know where he has difficulties ("This sentence seems digressive. Can you omit it, or am I missing a point you're trying to make?").

• The respondent gives scant attention to lapses in style or mechanics. Occasionally, a reviewer may point out an error that could easily escape the writer's attention, but that is far less important now than the other kinds of help that can be provided. (Proofreading for awkward sentences and mechanical correctness will be an important concern later, and you may also enlist the assistance of an objective reader in carrying out that task.) Notice, however, that Robin did call Kristin's attention to the less-appropriate word *unkept* and suggested an alternative.

• Comments fall into several different categories: *proposals for revision* ("Maybe a transitional word here?"), *responses to the writer's strategies* ("The contrast between lurid fiction and everyday reality encourages empathy"), *descriptions of the reader's response* ("I can't imagine how anyone could endure this!"), and *requests for clarification or amplification* ("Did she explain how she found her way to therapy? Or is this beside the point?"). Although each type of comment can provide valuable help, those closer to the end of this list tend to be more useful in "opening up" the text for the writer and to keep her in charge of revising her own draft.

By far the most useful and influential comments that Robin wrote were those that encouraged Kristin to reexamine her overall aims ("The one question I have is whether your primary aim here is to inform readers about a misunderstood disease . . . or to depict a particular time and place in the course of therapy.") These comments, along with Robin's remarks at the end of her draft, helped Kristin realize that although knowledge about depression had influenced her perceptions of the emotional crisis center, her primary aim was not to report facts about the disease. In some cases, of course, factual information seemed necessary. For instance, in revising paragraph 9 of her first draft, Kristin felt she needed to explain that depressed people are often overwhelmed by routine daily tasks, because without that knowledge, some readers might consider the group's suggestions to "Caroline" misguided or insensitive. (In fact, Robin's marginal question about how "Caroline" responded to the suggestions may indicate such a misinterpretation.) Notice how Kristin incorporated the needed information less obtrusively in paragraph 8 of her final draft. Other details, such as the fact that depression is sometimes hereditary and can be brought on by chemical imbalances, seemed superfluous and could easily be omitted.

Rewriting

Careful, deliberate revision distinguishes the experienced writer from the novice. Experienced writers spend a large amount of time rereading, changing words, rearranging sentences and paragraphs, adding new material, and writing again. Some drafts require more revision than others.

A few things about revision hold true for almost any successful writer. First, you need feedback from an alert, objective respondent. You yourself can be that respondent, provided that you step back and view your work as a detached reader. After you have completed a draft, it is wise to let your paper sit (for a few days if possible, but at least overnight) so that you can see it from a fresh perspective. Some writers like to read their work aloud, either for themselves or for someone else. Some get ideas as they recopy or retype what they have written, since doing so forces them to read their work slowly and attentively. Frequently, however, the most valuable help can come from a trusted friend or classmate who reads your draft and offers suggestions. This is the kind of help that Kristin Smith received from her classmate during a peer-review session.

Of course, not all writers are alike, and different writers prefer different strategies for revision. Some prefer all-at-once revisions. They write a draft all the way through, and then they compose a revised second draft, then a third, and so on. Others engage in ongoing revisions, altering one sentence or paragraph again and again before moving on to the next. Kristin Smith probably falls somewhere in between. She composed her drafts on a word processor and made frequent changes as she went. But she printed out complete drafts at least five times and marked changes in pencil before entering them into the word processor. Here is how she revised one passage in her paper:

Although Caroline's   *I soon discovered that the*
~~Her~~ story was heart-wrenching, ~~but before I had a~~
purpose of a group is not to pity or interrogate the person who has the
~~chance to get completely caught up in the details,~~ the *floor.*

group moderators stepped in and brought the focus of *At this point,*

the discussion around to skills that "Caroline" could

develop to head off the overwhelming feelings of
                                        they arose
helplessness and hopelessness the next time. They
            about sleeping and eating
asked simple questions ~~like "How did you sleep last~~
            routine activities   *that can be*
~~night?" and "What did you have for lunch?"~~ ~~Someone who~~

~~suffers from depression will often find even these~~
                                for
~~activities~~ excruciatingly difficult, ~~and what others~~

~~may consider routine becomes an emotional battle of~~

~~will for~~ a victim of depression. Other ~~group members~~

began to offer advice, the group coming alive with

suggestions: "Call someone the next time you feel

As you can see by comparing Kristin's two drafts, rephrasing passages was only one of her strategies for revision. She also deleted a few passages entirely (for example, information about the causes of depression that appeared in the sixth paragraph or her initial draft), converted complete sentences into subordinate clauses (for instance, the third sentence of the ninth paragraph), and added a few details, like her description of Caroline's reaction to the suggestions of her therapy group.

Writers often reassess their basic goals during revision. They consider the readers they want to address, what they are trying to help those readers see or understand, and how they can provide more or better evidence to support their aims. Revision means *seeing again,* and often the best way to accomplish this is to look at your concluding paragraphs to see whether they reflect the same basic purpose as the earlier parts of your draft. Writers often discover a purpose as they compose a first draft, and it is not unusual for the ending of that draft to reflect an emerging theme more clearly than the beginning does.

Before completing her final draft, Kristin drew up another brief outline—one that better captures her paper's purpose:

Throwing a Life Preserver

1. Description of the setting
   a. What I expected to see
   b. What I really did see

2. Group discussion
   a. Structure and procedure
   b. Caroline's story
   c. Responses of group members

3. The effectiveness of treatment
   a. An objective appraisal
   b. Assessment of a group member

Editing and Proofreading

As the final step, you will need to go over your revision to edit and proofread it. At this point you try to polish by eliminating any confusing words or ambiguous phrases. You also carefully check spelling and punctuation. After editing and proofreading, you are ready to type your paper and give it one final reading for typing errors. If you have composed your paper on a computer word processor, use the spell-check feature to find errors, but be sure to give the printed paper a careful visual proofreading as well.

Discovering Your Own Writing Rules

Learning to write is sometimes compared to learning tennis, woodworking, or some other skill. Basically, such comparisons are valid and reassuring; all college students *can* indeed develop their writing abilities to the point of proficiency. However, writing differs from certain other skills—long division, for instance—in that writing involves very few rigid rules, and those few are mastered at an early age. (For example: Begin every declarative sentence with a capital letter and end it with a period.) Well-meaning advice-givers sometimes try to reduce writing to a set of supposed rules such as "Never open a sentence with the word *and*" and "Never use the words *you* and *I* in an essay." However, experienced writers not only find such dictates unreliable (they routinely disregard those just mentioned, for example) but also have learned that writing is seldom systematic, orderly, and predictable. That is not to say that their approach is haphazard. Knowing that trial and error is rarely an efficient approach to the complexity of the task, experienced writers rely instead on a repertoire of procedures, which includes brainstorming, mapping, freewriting, and other techniques described in the earlier pages of this chapter.

Throughout this book you will be introduced to procedures for approaching each stage of the writing process. Keep in mind that these procedures do not always work in the same predictable fashion for every writer. They will not lead you to a single correct response to the writing tasks included in this book, nor to those assigned by your instructor. What they will do is encourage you to experiment with techniques that experienced writers use to get past the moments of writer's block that everyone encounters from time to time. The only way to find out which of these procedures will help you under which circumstances is to engage in as many of them as possible, merely going through the motions at first if necessary. Over time, however, you should learn to rely on a few standbys that can minimize the anxieties brought on by the interplay of complex skills involved in writing, particularly writing for academic purposes.

 # READING

Reading is by no means a passive experience. It requires active participation. Without your involvement as a reader, the words on the printed page have no meaning. Only you can bring them to life. Your ability to interpret words, your knowledge of how sentences and paragraphs are put together, your past experiences with reading and with life, your current mood—all these work together to make your reading of an essay, a poem, or even a recipe different from anyone else's.

Interpreting Reading

No one can read exactly as you do. In some ways, reading is a very personal activity. When you read a book—even a book like this one—it is unlikely that anyone else will interpret it in exactly the same way that you do. In a class where most students have had similar experiences, responses will probably be similar, but they will not be identical. Since no one is an exact duplicate of anyone else, each person's reading experience will be unique.

The key to what you get out of reading is what you put into it. For example, if you bring an extensive background in music to the following passage, you will get much more from it than the average reader can:

> Although Schoenberg sometimes dreamed of serialism as a reassertion of German musical hegemony, he more commonly thought of it as a purely formalistic ordering device, and most American serialists share that view. So do the Soviets, with their crude denunciations of "formalism." But just as with psychoanalysis, dismissed by its opponents as a web of metaphors conditioned by time and place, serialism can be considered narrowly Viennese and, by now, dated. And not just dated and extraneous to an American sensibility, but out of fashion.
> —John Rockwell, *All-American Music*

Even if all the names and terms in this selection were explained, most readers would still find its meaning obscure. Actually the passage is neither difficult nor easy. The reader is the key here. To thousands of music experts, this passage is perfectly clear. But for those of us who do not bring the necessary meaning to it, very little emerges. Evidently, the passage is intended for a small, informed audience. If you were reporting on musical trends for a wider audience, you would not quote this passage. It demands too much of the average reader.

That is not to say that we cannot profitably read something that goes beyond what we already know and understand. Our purpose in reading is to do just that—to expand our knowledge and experiences. However, good writers are aware of their audience, and they modify their language accordingly. The author of the music passage was trying to reach only a musically sophisticated readership. Other authors, writing for a general audience, adjust their language for readers with varied backgrounds.

The following passage concerns a collection of unconventional musical instruments designed and built by visionary composer Harry Partch. The author of the passage, Allan Ulrich, is the classical music and dance critic for the *San Francisco Examiner,* a large daily newspaper. Ulrich is reviewing an exhibition of Partch's work for readers of the *Examiner*'s Sunday supplement:

> There are the visionaries and then there are the cranks. Somewhere in that wispy zone of shadow separating the two, in that spiritual limbo for which we lack a precise word, posterity has deposited Harry Partch (1901–74)—composer, instrument builder, philosopher, multiculturalist, great California-born creative maverick.
>
> The twenty-five instruments devised and constructed by Partch . . . reflect his obsession with the ancients, not merely in their names—Kithara I and Kithara II, Chromelodeon—but in his belief that they should affect an area beyond human consciousness. The enormous Marimba Eroica, individually hung Sitka spruce blocks laid over cave-like resonators the size of the piano, emits four low tones, the lowest of which is not audible to the human ear. That you can also feel Partch's music has no doubt endeared him to a younger generation; vibes and all that. . . .
>
> What the "Sounds Like Art" Festival should accomplish is to place Partch in some kind of context. He may have been one of the greatest American individualists; still, he has spawned a generation of composer-instrument makers who feel free to journey down their own paths. The Bay Area's Beth Custer and Matt Heckert, Los Angeles' Marina Rosenfeld and the German-born, Seattle-based artist who goes by the sole name of Trimpin will all add their distinctive constructions to this project.
>
> Here, perhaps, is where the Harry Partch legacy truly resides. Idiosyncrasy may have ventured, ever so timorously, into the mainstream of American music, but the current remains as unpredictable as ever.

Even a reader with little knowledge or interest in the study of music can derive some information from this passage. Although Ulrich introduces material that is new to most of us, he uses informal language and refers to familiar concepts, such as "vibes," that most adults can readily understand.

Successful reading depends on the reader's knowledge and skill as well as the writer's sense of audience. Reading emerges from what both writer and reader bring to the text. To be a good a reader, you must be alert, flexible, and open. If you are, reading can be as creative a process as writing—and as varied.

The expression "You find what you are looking for" makes good sense when applied to reading. When you read something just for information, you probably overlook such elements as style, tone, and metaphor. If a friend of yours accidentally swallowed a poison, you would immediately search the back of the bottle for the antidote. You would read rapidly, probably aloud: "Do not induce vomiting. Have the victim drink two quarts of fresh water." Needless to say, you would not comment to the victim about the style: "Hey, Louise, listen to these short, precise sentences!" Under the circumstances you just want information.

On the other hand, if you were asked to read and respond to the following poem, a *haiku* by the seventeenth-century Japanese poet Bashō, getting information would not be uppermost in your mind:

> *The ancient lagoon*
> *A frog jumps*
> *The splash of the water.*

These lines invite you to respond to images. You would not read them in hopes of advancing your knowledge of amphibian behavior or marine ecology. Someone experienced in interpreting poetry would respond differently than a novice, but each reader's response is personal and unique. One reader might be reminded of a childhood experience. For another reader, the images might create simply a sense of peace and beauty. Still another reader familiar with Zen Buddhism might have a more philosophical response. Such a reader might note the contrast between the poem's first line (an image of timeless stillness) and the second (a momentary action), and find in the last line, where the two contrasting images meet, an insight into an eternal truth. And someone totally unused to reading such an open-ended text might find it puzzling and useless.

Interpreting Reading

EXERCISE

As a test of what we have said, see how your responses to two very different passages compare with those of other readers. Reread the earlier paragraph about Harry Partch and write a sentence or two stating what you think is its main idea.

Now read the following *haiku* by another Japanese poet, Buson, and write an equally brief interpretation of it.

> *On the bell of the temple*
> *rests a butterfly,*
> *asleep.*

Do not hesitate to write down your own response to the poem, even if you feel it is probably not correct. In fact, most experts would say that a single "correct" interpretation of such a poem simply does not exist. For this exercise, trust your personal response.

Now compare your response with those of several classmates. Do they differ? Is there more agreement about the interpretation of the paragraph than of the poem? How do you account for such differences? Even with the Harry Partch paragraph, is there room for differences in response?

Responding to Reading

Just as with writing, we read for different purposes and in different ways. There is no single right way to read. When we encounter the short, precise sentences of a set of directions, our purpose is practical, because we want to know how to do something quickly and efficiently. We do not want to be startled or challenged. But when we pick up a poem or a short story, we want more than information; we want to get pleasure out of the way words and images are used. We want to be surprised. And if our own values and experiences are not engaged when we read literature, we are disappointed. These very different ways to read are at opposite ends of a continuum.

Most of the reading you will do in this text lies somewhere between the objective prose of how-to directions and the subjective language of poetry. It will require your intelligent participation. When you conduct research, you cannot read a source without being critically alert both to the information you read and to the author's attitude, purpose, and competence.

In addition to various exercises in writing, reading, and research, many chapters in this book conclude with a longer reading selection, followed by questions about your interpretations of the selection and about ideas that it raises. With most of the selections, you will be reading for multiple purposes. That will demand concentration and patience because, just as good writing involves revision, good reading often requires rereading.

When you respond to these readings, you will discover that you agree with your classmates about much of what you find there, but there will also be legitimate differences. As you read, you will form interpretations that other readers may not recognize. That is as it should be. We are all both alike and different—at the same time. Reading and writing demonstrate this fact.

The best way to respond to reading is to write about it. Writing stretches thinking by forcing us to connect one idea with another. And because it is visible, writing can help us see what we mean. It can also help us be clearer, more logical, more concrete. Freewriting is an especially useful form of writing about reading; when we freewrite, we respond openly, jotting down whatever we notice in our reading, whether a personal association, an observation on style, a restatement of what we think the author is getting at, or any other thought or feeling that comes to the tip of the pen.

EXERCISE | ## Responding to Reading

1. Here are five short reading selections. Read each passage carefully and then freewrite about it for five minutes. Remember, you create the rules for freewriting as you write (except for the basic rule that you should keep writing at your normal speed for a designated time).

   a. A sign posted in a clothing store reads:

      Kindly spare us the distress of refusing requests for refunds.

b. These personal ads were placed in a community newspaper that focuses on arts and entertainment:

M, 44, clean, sporty, original equipment, runs great, seeks F that needs a lift.

F, 28, black and glossy, seeks confidential WM, very giving, who's bound for whatever.

Mistress Marcy seeks playmate.

Ornery, self-sufficient, prof SWF, mid 40's, seeks man with integrity. If you're not honest, don't bother.

c. The following advertisement appeared among Help Wanted ads in a recent issue of the *Nassau Guardian,* the largest daily newspaper in the Bahamas:

The Firm Masterminds Historians, Scientists, Financiers, Philosophers, Senior Pastors, Bankers, Solicitors, Doctors (1998) Inc.
Wisdom / Reversals / Expulsions / Nulls & voids available via discernments laws & sciences/disengagements laws & sciences to discern / Expel / Call out / Shutdown / Reverse / Null & void / Secret or suspected child molesters / incestors / False pastors / mistressings / Homosexuality / Wife beaters & spousal batterers etc If you can establish just cause which is Mandatory! We cleanse homes / Marriages / Businesses / Churches. Rates are $750 to $2,500 per hour.

d. The following anecdote introduces a recent magazine article by Roger Shattuck titled "When Evil Is 'Cool.'" The article is preceded by this headnote: "Our culture, in particular the institution of the university, has contrived over the past few decades to transform sin into a positive: *transgression,* a term that, as used by postmodern critics, refers to an implied form of greatness."

Living alone in a Paris garret, an idle young bohemian meditated on the sudden, perverse spurts of energy that can interrupt a life of laziness and boredom. Such urges lead one to unthinkable acts—such as starting a forest fire or lighting a cigar next to a powder keg—just to see what will happen, to tempt fate.
One morning the young man awoke in a mood to perform such an outrageous act. Seeing below in the street a window-glass vendor, *un vitrier,* with his stock of panes in a pack on his back, he summoned the vendor to climb up the six stories to his garret. He asked for tinted glass, which the vendor did not have. In a rage the young man kicked the vendor back out into the staircase, where the tradesman almost stumbled under his heavy load. Then, watching from the balcony, the young man dropped a flower pot just as the vendor reappeared in the street, and thus broke his stock of glass to smithereens. This vicious prank might damn him, the young bohemian said to himself, but it also brought a moment of infinite bliss.

e. Originally published in the *Washington Post,* this editorial was reprinted as a syndicated column in daily newspapers throughout the United States.

GENIUS IN CHANGING NUMBERS

Gene Weingarten

[Some members of the United States Senate] want to skirt federal spending limits in next year's budget by releasing billions of dollars of this year's money the month after the fiscal year ends. When a *Washington Post* news story characterized this as adding a thirteenth month to the fiscal year, [they] bristled. For some reason, they think it makes them sound like wackos.

Well, not to me. [These senators] should stand proudly behind their thirteenth month. I think they're on to something here. In terms of creative problem solving, this idea smacks of genius.

In fact, similar reasoning could be used to solve all sorts of problems:

Global Warming

Switch to Celsius. The numbers are smaller. If the Earth's temperature rises 1/17th of a degree, who cares?

Guns in the Schools

Guns are not the problem, schools are the problem. We would have no guns in our schools if there were no schools. There's no need to eliminate education: we just have to rename the buildings. For example, Washington's Alice Deal Junior High School could be renamed Alice Deal Fat-Rendering Plant. Who would bring a gun to a fat-rendering plant?

World Hunger

No one would be technically hungry anymore if the World Health Organization issued new universal minimum recommended daily standards for a balanced diet.

Current standards for a typical adult male: 63 gm protein, 62 gm fat, 2,500 calories.

New standards: 2 gm protein, 1 gm fat, 12 calories.

Racism

Racists hate people who look different from themselves. All we have to do is eliminate this disparity. Studies in behavioral science have shown that witnesses at crime scenes tend not to distinguish one person in uniform from another; they see only the uniform. So we issue uniforms to all Americans.

I would suggest that men wear old-fashioned bellhop outfits, like the guy in the "Call for Philip Morris" ads. Women could dress as meter maids. (Men and women could not wear the same uniform, because then no one could tell them apart, and the species would die out.)

Not Enough Time in the Day to Get Everything Done

Add an hour to each day. The extra hour would come between 7:00 pm and 8:00 pm, and would be called seven-and-a-half pm. To avoid confusion, the half-hour would be called half-past-seven-and-a-half pm. After a few days, of course, it would start getting dark around noon, but you could easily remedy that problem by moving noon ahead one hour every day.

Children Seeing Too Much Sex and Violence on TV

Here we follow the lead set by our court system, which long ago figured out that the way to counteract an increase in juvenile crime was to lower the age at which a kid is considered an adult. So if too many children are watching sexy and violent stuff on TV, lower the age of majority. Then fewer children will watch. New age of majority: six. No five-year-old is going to watch *Sex and the City*.

Cynicism in the Newspapers

Change all by-lines to "By the Dalai Lama."

2. Exchange your freewrites with other members of the class. Are there differences in your responses? If so, how can they be explained? Why might different people respond in very different ways to these readings?

Reading Response Groups

Up to this point, we have portrayed reading as a process that engages individualism and independent thinking. Specifically, we have stressed the idea that readers actively *create* meaning rather than passively receive it from a "determinate" text—one that is supposed to elicit a single accurate interpretation that coincides with the author's intended meaning. Aiming to dispel the familiar notion that reading is simply a matter of retrieving information or ideas that writers have *put* in their texts, we have emphasized the *autonomy* of individual readers—their privilege to assign personal interpretations to what they read.

Granted that autonomy, a hypothetical reader might reasonably interpret the passage by Allan Ulrich on page 32 as a satirical jab at avant-garde music. To go a step further, let us suppose that some other reader viewed it as a parody of museum reviews—a mischievous hoax at the expense of literal-minded readers. While most people would find that a misguided response, a carefully selected group of like-minded readers might accept it as a creative, possibly productive, interpretation—though probably one that the author did not anticipate. Most reasonable people, however, would agree that there are limits. It is unlikely, for example, that any community of readers would acknowledge the possibility that Ulrich is denouncing modern art as a vehicle of bourgeois oppression. Such an interpretation is too eccentric to be supported persuasively.

The autonomy of individual readers, then, can be exaggerated. Like writing, reading is not a solitary act performed in total isolation. Instead, both writing and reading are *social* acts, and readers often benefit from the responses of their peers just as Kristin Smith did in writing her essay.

The following interaction among three experienced readers demonstrates the collaboration of a **reading group,** two or more individuals who share, often in writing, their personal responses to a text. Although reading groups come in various sizes, most are composed of three to six members. Your instructor may place you in a reading group and assign specific tasks, often called **prompts,** for you and your partners to address. (On the other hand, students enrolled in the same class can initiate groups of their own, and sometimes their collaboration can be spontaneous and unfocused.)

The following is a typical prompt designed to initiate discussion and collaborative response within a reading group. Take a moment now to read it, along with the essay to which it relates.

Freewriting

Read the article "A Short History of Love," which appeared in *Harper's,* a magazine of opinion that addresses current political and cultural issues. As you read, use your pencil to mark important or noteworthy ideas and any reactions or personal associations that come immediately to mind as you read. Keep this writing brief, using shorthand as much as possible, and try not to pause for more than a few seconds in perhaps three or four places at most. Then read the article again, this time looking more closely at the way Lawrence Stone presents the history of romantic love and draws conclusions from it. After you have completed both readings, freewrite for twenty minutes about the ideas in the article. In particular, consider whether or not you agree with the author's suggestion that there may be something dangerous and unhealthy in contemporary attitudes about love. Bring this freewriting to class next time, and be prepared to share it with other members of your reading group.

A Short History of Love

Lawrence Stone

Historians and anthropologists are in general agreement that romantic love—the usually brief but intensely felt and all-consuming attraction toward another person—is culturally conditioned. Love has a history. It is common only in certain societies at certain times, or even in certain social groups within those societies, usually the elite, which have the leisure to cultivate such feelings. Scholars are, however, less certain whether romantic love is merely a culturally induced psychological overlay on top of the biological drive for sex, or whether it has biochemical roots that operate quite independently from the libido. Would anyone in fact "fall in love" if they had not read about it or heard it talked about? Did poetry invent love, or love poetry?

Some things can be said with certainty about the phenomenon. The first is that cases of romantic love can be found in all times and places and have often been the subject of powerful poetic expression from the Song of Solomon to Shakespeare. On the other hand, as anthropologists have discovered, neither social approbation nor the actual experience of romantic love is common to all societies. Second, historical evidence for romantic love before the age of printing is largely confined to elite groups, which of course does not mean that it may not have occurred lower on the social scale. As a socially approved cultural artifact, romantic love began in Europe in the southern French aristocratic courts of the twelfth century, and was made fashionable by a group of poets, the troubadours. In this case the culture dictated that it should occur between an unmarried male and a married woman, and that it either should go sexually unconsummated or should be adulterous.

By the sixteenth and seventeenth centuries, our evidence becomes quite extensive, thanks to the spread of literacy and the printing press. We now have love poems, such as Shakespeare's sonnets, love letters, and autobiographies by women concerned primarily with their love lives. The courts of Europe were evidently hotbeds of passionate intrigues and liaisons, some romantic, some sexual. The printing press also began to spread pornography to a wider public, thus stimulating the libido, while the plays of Shakespeare indicate that romantic love was a concept familiar to society at large, which composed his audience.

Whether this romantic love was approved of, however, is another question. We simply do not know how Shakespearean audiences reacted to *Romeo and Juliet*. Did they, like us (and as Shakespeare clearly intended), fully identify with the young lovers? Or, when they left the theater, did they continue to act like the Montague and Capulet parents, who were trying to stop these irresponsible adolescents from allowing an ephemeral and irrational passion to interfere with the serious business of politics and patronage?

What is certain is that every advice book, every medical treatise, every sermon and religious homily of the sixteenth and seventeen centuries firmly rejected both romantic passion and lust as suitable bases for marriage. In the sixteenth century, marriage was thought to be best arranged by parents, who could be relied upon to choose socially and economically suitable partners. People believed that the sexual bond would automatically create the necessary harmony between the two strangers in order to maintain the stability of the new family unit. This assumption is not, it seems, unreasonable, since recent investigations in Japan have shown that there is no difference in the rate of divorce between couples whose marriages were arranged by their parents and couples whose marriages were made by individual choice based on romantic love.

In the eighteenth century, orthodox opinion about marriage began to shift from subordinating the individual will to the interests of the group, and from economic or political considerations toward those of well-tried personal affection. The ideal marriage was one preceded by three to six months of intensive courting by a couple from families roughly equal in social status and economic wealth; that courtship, however, took place only with the prior consent of parents on both sides. But it was not until the Romantic movement and the rise of the novel, especially the pulp novel in the nineteenth century, that society accepted a new idea—that it is normal and indeed praiseworthy for young men and women to fall passionately in love, and that there must be something wrong with those who fail to have such an overwhelming experience sometime in late adolescence or early adulthood. Once this new idea was publicly accepted, the arrangement of marriage by parents came to be regarded as intolerable and immoral.

Today, the role of passionate attachments between adults is obscured by a new development: the saturation of the whole culture—through every medium of communication—with the belief that sexuality is the predominant and overriding human drive, a doctrine whose theoretical foundations were provided by Freud. In no past society known to me has sex been given so prominent a role in the culture at large, nor has sexual fulfillment been elevated to such preeminence in the list of human aspirations—in a vain attempt to relieve civilization of its discontents. We find it scarcely credible today that in most of Western Europe in the seventeenth century, in a society in which people usually married in their late twenties, a degree of chastity was practiced that kept the illegitimacy rate—without contraceptives—as low as 2 or 3 percent. Today, individualism is given such absolute priority in most Western societies that people are virtually free to act as they please, to sleep with whom they please, and to marry and divorce when and whom they please. The psychic (and, more recently, the physical) costs of such behavior are now becoming clear, however, and how long this situation will last is anybody's guess.

Here I should point out that the present-day family—I exclude the poor black family in America from this generalization—is not, as is generally supposed, disintegrating because of the very high divorce rate—up to 50 percent. It has to be remembered that the median duration of marriage today is almost exactly the same as it was 100 years ago. Divorce, in short, now acts as a functional substitute for death: both are means of terminating marriage at a premature stage. The psychological effects on the survivor may well be very different, although in most cases the catastrophic economic consequences for women remain the same. But the point to be emphasized is that broken marriages, stepchildren, and single-parent households were as common in the past as they are today.

The most difficult historical problem regarding romantic love concerns its role among the propertyless poor. Since they were propertyless, their loves and marriages were of little concern to their kin, and they were therefore more or less free to choose their own mates. By the eighteenth century, and probably before, court records make it clear that the poor often married for love, combined with a confused set of motives including lust and the economic necessity to have a strong and healthy assistant to run the farm or the shop. It was generally expected that they would behave "lovingly" toward each other, but this often did not happen. In many a peasant marriage, the husband seems to have valued his cow more than his wife. Passionate attachments among the poor certainly occurred, but how often they took priority over material interests we may never know for certain.

Finally, we know that in the eighteenth century—unlike the seventeenth—at least half of all brides in England and America were pregnant on their wedding day. But this fact tells us more about sexual customs than about passionate attachments: sex began at the moment of engagement, and marriage in church came later, often triggered by the pregnancy. We also know that if a poor servant girl was impregnated by her master, which often happened, the latter usually had no trouble finding a poor man who would marry her, in return for payment of ten pounds or so. Not much passion there.

Passionate attachments between young people can and do happen in any society as a byproduct of biological sexual attraction, but the social acceptability of the emotion has varied enormously over time and class and space, determined primarily by cultural norms and property arrangements. We are in a unique position today in that our culture is dominated by romantic notions of passionate love as the only socially admissible reason for marriage; sexual fulfillment is accepted as the dominant human drive and a natural right for both sexes; and contraception is normal and efficient. Behind all this lies a frenetic individualism, a restless search for a sexual and emotional ideal in human relationships, and a demand for instant ego gratification.

Most of this is new and unique to our culture. It is, therefore, quite impossible to assume that people in the past thought about and experienced passionate attachments the way we do. Historical others—even our own forefathers and mothers—were indeed other.

The freewritten responses of one reading group appear below. They have been edited a bit to remove crossed-out words and phrases, spelling errors, and other distractions that the writers did not have time to correct.

Janet's Freewriting

The author wants us to think more critically about romantic love, perhaps even to view it as unnecessary. Too many of us assume that living without romantic love is to be deprived. Stone wants us to examine and question that assumption. He addresses readers familiar with Shakespeare and Freud and comfortable with terms like *orthodox opinion* and *ego gratification*. He assumes an audience already a bit cynical about romance and passionate love. I think the reader most receptive to Stone's ideas has lost any idealism about such matters and is willing to believe that passion is not necessary, maybe unhealthy, in long-term relationships. The essay is for people more likely to sneer at Valentine's Day than to search for just the right greeting card.

Stone's point is that passion, romance, and sexual fulfillment are less crucial to happiness than our culture conditions us to believe. He argues that poets and playwrights created romantic love and that Freud added the notion that sex is an overriding drive. The presumed need for passionate attachments has been constructed by a culture in which the individual comes first and the needs of the group are relegated to a distant second. Stone warns that addiction to romance places us at peril, and he lists the increase of sexually transmitted diseases, divorce, depression, and even mental illness among the results.

Stone supports his ideas with evidence from history, with particular attention to the mass publication of novels, the Romantic Movement, and the influence of Freud. There's a gradual change in tone as the reading progresses. After the first few paragraphs, I expected a scholarly, informative piece with no earth-shaking point to it. But by the time I was finished, I realized that Stone was kind of up on a soapbox. As the essay develops, I get the picture of an embittered prude manipulating history to argue against something he either doesn't want or can't have.

Alex's Freewriting

Stone asks readers to consider a cultural norm in a fundamentally different and unconventional way. The trappings of romantic love so permeate our daily lives that we assume there's something wrong with an adolescent or young adult who doesn't experience the feeling. So Stone asks us to set aside this conditioning for a moment and to entertain the idea that a thing we all "know" to be natural and proper really isn't. Also he wants us to see that there's something at stake. I'm not sure he wants to alarm us and alter patterns of behavior, but he does want us to think about the consequences of our beliefs and to get a debate going. I think he makes two important points. First, love may be a form of learned behavior. Second, because of historical developments (democracy and individualism, invention of mass media, Freudian psychology), romantic love has run rampant and poses certain dangers.

I think Stone is addressing a well-educated, broad-minded audience—the sort of people who subscribe to *Psychology Today*. Ironically, that type of reader, like the people who perpetuated the concept of romantic love prior to the eighteenth century, are an elite. An essay like this is probably leisure reading for such persons. I think Stone envisions a reader who prides herself on being an independent, tough-minded skeptic—someone who isn't taken in by bunk just because it's popular or "nice." An iconoclast, I guess you could say. I'm not sure Stone is *addressing* this type of audience so much as he is *conjuring it up*.

I see a contradiction in the evidence. In paragraph one, Stone mentions the uncertainty of "scholars" (psychologists?) about whether love is "culturally induced" or "has biochemical roots." If it's biochemical, then aren't historians and anthropologists mistaken in the view that Stone attributes to them? Or are psychologists less certain about this than scholars in other fields? Has Stone expressed himself poorly, or am I reading his first paragraph carelessly? Stone introduces more specific support in paragraph five, when he refers to the divorce rate in Japan. It's interesting, though, that he relies on emotionally charged language in his next-to-last paragraph, with words like *frenetic, restless,* and *demand.* This seems out of keeping with the rest of the essay, which sounds more scholarly.

The essay is chronologically ordered, tracing the history of romantic love. But beneath that, I see a question–answer approach. Stone opens with a problem or dilemma, and the first paragraph ends with two questions. The next paragraph opens with "Some things can be said with certainty," and Stone lists those things. Paragraph four then opens with "another question," and that question leads to two others. Paragraph five goes back to certainty, beginning with "What is certain is that. . . ."

Agnes's Freewriting

Stone reminds an audience of psychoanalysts of the history of romantic love. He assesses where we stand today, with tremendous social pressures for people to seek and insist upon sexual fulfillment. For me, the essay doesn't make clear whether Stone sees romantic love and sexual love as the same thing. Stone fails, probably on purpose, to give a detailed explanation of how "love" took the place of arranged marriages and how, through the "saturation of the whole culture," sexual gratification was encouraged, even idealized. The chips seem to go down when he examines the influences of Freud. Is he trying to discredit the Freudian theory of human sexuality, now taken for granted in some circles? (When he speaks of "relieving society of its discontents," he alludes to Freud's justification of neurosis, *Civilization and Its Discontents.*) Stone seems to say that we pay a heavy price for license and excess. Is he trying to upset the Freudians? to urge therapists to stress social values rather than individual desires as they guide their patients out of a self-induced wilderness?

Stone is speaking to a group of professionals interested in new ways of thinking about mental illness and its treatment. The allusion to *Romeo and Juliet* isn't so important, since every high schooler has read the play. The Troubadors are less familiar, but anyone who's heard of Bing Crosby or Perry Como has heard the term. So I think Stone is flattering his audience without really demanding much of them. It seems scholarly, but is it really? His tone is earnest, though bias slips in near the end. There's not a great deal of hard evidence. Frankly, I think this essay could be adapted for the *Parade* section of the Sunday paper with only minimal editing. After all, we're all interested in what makes us tick, and all the emphasis on the demons of instant gratification, license, and unfettered individualism would hit home with people trying to figure out what's gone wrong with their relationships. Why not say something about the psychic toll taken by adulterous liaisons or arranged marriages?

Although "A Short History of Love" is not an obscure or difficult text, each of these readers responded to it a bit differently. One obvious contrast involves the way they interpret the aims of the author. Janet sees Lawrence Stone as "an embittered prude manipulating history to argue against something he either doesn't want or can't have." Alex is more inclined to take the article at face value, simply as one writer's attempt to provoke thought and debate. Agnes seems annoyed, reading the text as an effort to display knowledge and flatter the reader's self-image.

Other important differences emerge. Alex is very analytical, examining the structure of the article—right down to the author's choice of specific words. Agnes makes reference to things outside the text (from the title of a book by Freud to the names of popular singers of the 1940s and 1950s). Janet falls somewhere in between: She makes a few personal associations (such as her reference to greeting cards) but also focuses on Stone's ideas and the order in which he presents them. In addition, both Alex and Agnes arrive at their interpretations by asking questions, interrogating the text and even examining their own responses to it.

Although other differences can be highlighted, the important point has been made: The personality, preoccupation, and thinking style of each reader influence the way he or she reads "A Short History of Love." This does not mean that any one of the three readings is better than the other two. On the contrary, it suggests that the best reading would be one that is informed and enriched by a consideration of all three perspectives. Such a reading would exploit the benefits of Janet's speculations about the author, Alex's close analytical reading, and Agnes's skepticism. This formidable array of talent and personal response is something that no single member of the group (nor any one of their classmates) possessed individually.

The sharing of freewritten responses is not always an end in itself. Instructors may also ask groups to address a particular issue or problem introduced by a reading. For example, Janet, Alex, Agnes, and members of other reading groups were presented with the following assignment when they came to class with their freewritten responses to "A Short History of Love":

Group Work

Read your freewriting aloud to the other members of your group. As your partners are reading, take note of any comment or observation that you find noteworthy, but be particularly alert to the following:

1. Do the members of your group feel that romantic love is governed more by culture or by biology?

2. Do they recognize an unhealthy preoccupation with romance, sex, and individualism in modern society? Do they share Lawrence Stone's sense of alarm and urgency?

3. Did anyone in your group connect what Stone calls "frenetic individualism" and the desire for immediate self-gratification to other areas of life?

After everyone has read, try to reach some consensus in regard to the following questions:

1. Has Lawrence Stone identified a serious social problem that needs to be addressed?

2. What would be the most plausible solution to the tensions analyzed in this article?

3. Does extreme individualism and the desire for self-gratification cause problems in other areas of life?

Be prepared to share your group consensus with the entire class.

Approaching tasks such as these, reading groups strive for consensus—or at least mutual understanding—rather than a single best, most authoritative answer. After Janet, Alex, and Agnes had read their freewritten responses aloud, all three discussed ideas and observations that affected them. For example, Alex remarked on Janet's belief that as Lawrence Stone gets further into his topic, he begins to sound more like a soapbox orator than a scholar. Alex connected that belief with something he had written about Stone's development—that "emotionally charged language" appears in the next-to-last paragraph of "A Short History of Love." Janet's observation thus helped Alex see the language in that paragraph in terms of a broader pattern. Janet, on the other hand, benefited from Alex's narrower focus on words in a specific segment of the text. Not only was her perception re-inforced by what Alex noted, but she also had supporting evidence for what had been only a vague impression about tone.

As the group proceeded to discuss each other's responses, a number of similar transactions occurred. Agnes took issue with Janet's and Alex's notion that Stone hopes to alter public behavior. She reminded her partners that Stone delivered his paper at an academic conference and that his primary audience was psychoana-lysts rather than a randomly selected group of single men and women. Acknowl-edging that they had lost sight of that fact, Janet and Alex modified their understanding of Stone's purpose. Later, Janet took note of her partners' doubts about Stone's authority in fields other than history and became more skeptical herself. All three group members continued their discussion for about fifteen min-utes, after which their instructor asked them to share their conclusions with the entire class.

At the end of this and following chapters, you are invited to work in reading groups, engaging in similar processes of collaborative response. When you do so, try to adopt the constructive approach exemplified by these three readers.

 # RESEARCH

Many students expect research to be an excruciating ordeal, and the idea of THE RESEARCH PAPER looms in student mythology as the academic equivalent of a root canal session at the dentist's office.

Fortunately, the myth is wrong. Research needn't be drudgery or an ordeal, al-though it can be both to those who go about it without knowing what they are doing or why. *Research* is nothing more than finding out what you need to know. If you are good at it—if you have learned some elementary research skills—it can be useful and satisfying; it even can be a pleasure.

You are already skilled in certain kinds of research. Right now, for example, if you wanted to find your dentist's telephone number, you could easily do so, even though your phone book contains thousands of names. You have research skills that enable you to find out what movies are showing on television tonight and how much local bicycle stores are charging for Raleigh mountain bikes. Research in college involves additional skills, which you will find no less useful and which you are fully capable of mastering. One aim of this book and of the course you are now taking is to help you become a competent college researcher. These same skills will continue to prove useful after you graduate.

Research can take any number of forms, from looking up the meaning of a word to conducting an opinion poll. Depending on what you want to find out, you might need to ask the opinions of experts, undertake fieldwork or laboratory experiments, interview eyewitnesses, analyze photographs, or observe the behavior of people who don't know they're being watched. This more observational type of research is the kind that Kristin Smith has used for her essay. Other research methods—ones we consider carefully in this book—involve written sources. You can discover general information in reference works such as encyclopedias and almanacs. More specific information and statements of ideas can be found in magazines, journals, pamphlets, and books. The college library collection and computer databases are two invaluable resources for college researchers.

When you like, you can use your research skills for your private benefit. For example, your knowledge of the library can allow you to research summer job opportunities for pharmacy majors or to find out which videorecorders are most reliable. One difference between such private research and the research you do as a college student is that the latter usually has a more public purpose. College research is often part of a larger project in which you share your findings with other scholars. Consequently, in order to communicate what you have learned as a result of your research, you will engage in *research writing.*

In short, any organized investigation can be called research, and any writing you do as a result—from poetry to scientific reports—can be called research writing. Research is important to your writing because you will not always know enough on your own. If you are writing about your own feelings, no research is needed; you are an expert already. But if the dating practices of a century ago are your subject, you will have to do research if you expect to produce anything worth reading. You owe it to your readers to produce writing that is informed and accurate. Research is essential to such writing.

Not all good writing, of course, is research writing. Your responses to the reading exercises on pages 34–37, for example, were probably based on reflection and personal opinion rather than on research. For the same reason, the following passage would not qualify as research writing:

> Marrying "early" before a career has caused a furor among my friends. . . .
> I've been accused of misrepresenting myself during college as someone trying to earn a MRS. degree rather than an education. When "feminist" friends hear that I am taking my husband's name, they act as if I'm forsaking "our" cause. One Saturday afternoon, a friend phoned and I admitted I was spending the day doing laundry—mine and his. Her voice resonated with such pity that I hung up.
> New York City, where we live, breeds much of this antagonism . . . [but] I've also experienced prejudice in my hometown in Colorado. At a local store's bridal registry, I walked in wearing a Columbia University sweatshirt and the consultant asked if I'd gone to school there. On hearing that I'd graduated ten months earlier, she explained that she had a daughter my age. "But she is very involved in her career," she added, presuming that I, selecting a silverware pattern, was not.
> —Katherine Davis, "I'm Not Sick, I'm Just in Love"

This personal account is well written and honest, but it does not involve research in the way that we mean it. It is a reflection; it does not make use of outside sources. And it is not the result of systematic inquiry. On the other hand, if Katherine Davis had used quotations and facts gathered from formal interviews with friends, had researched published scholarship about attitudes regarding marriage and family, or had cited the writings of prominent feminist authors, then that would change her method from reflection to research. This is what we mean by research writing—using sources beyond your personal thoughts in your essay.

EXERCISE | **Distinguishing Features of Research Writing**

Would you call Kristin Smith's essay "Throwing a Life Preserver" an example of research writing? Explain. Are any parts of that essay based on research? Would the essay become more convincing with additional research? If Kristin wished to incorporate more research into her essay, what kinds of research would you recommend?

 READING SELECTION

The following selection profiles an annual beauty pageant in the small community of Holly Ridge, North Carolina.

The Holly Pageant

LAVONNE ADAMS

1   Everything is ready. The fire trucks and ambulances have been moved outside, floors have been swept, chairs have been placed in orderly rows. At seven o'clock, the Holly Pageant is scheduled to begin.

2   Armed with a green metal cash box and a rubber stamp for the patrons' hands, I take my seat behind the folding table to the left of the front door. I watch as the girls and their parents arrive, chattering excitedly, arms laden with garmet bags, shoe boxes, makeup cases, curling irons. The mothers greet each other, size up the competition, push compliments from their tongues—"Oh, you look so pretty tonight!"—"What a beautiful dress!"—"I love what you've done to your hair!"

3   Barbara, one of the pageant organizers, arrives. She is in charge of acquiring the judges from the "Certified Judges List," a product of the judging seminars held every year in Raleigh. Each year, she assiduously sets the judge's table with a white tablecloth, glasses of water, and bowls of snack foods. Once the judges arrive, she ushers them into the radio room, where they remain sequestered until the pageant commences. She stands at that door, as anxious as a presidential body guard.

4   I have heard rumors of corrupt judges, bribed by overanxious mothers at other pageants, yet have been assured that these judges are not told the names of the contestants until they are handed the programs.

Barbara's four-year-old son runs up to her, yanks impatiently on her arm, whispers 5
something in her ear. She glances around anxiously, frowns as she takes his hand, then
disappears in the direction of the bathroom. The inner sanctum has been left un-
guarded. I take advantage of the opportunity. Unobtrusively, I walk toward the radio
room, cautiously turn the knob, ease open the door, and slip inside. The judges look
up, startled . . . perturbed. Once I explain why I am interested in talking to them, they
smile, settle back in their chairs, obviously relieved. They agree to let me interview
them after the pageant. I slip back outside.

The Holly Pageant is a tradition in this small North Carolina town, a social event 6
rivaled only by the yearly parish "reunion" at the town's largest Baptist church. The
Holly Ridge Volunteer Fire Department and Rescue Squad officially adopted the
pageant a few years ago, after a group of local citizens abandoned it. There was much
debate that night. Since I was a new member, I felt unsure of my local standing, so I
kept my mouth firmly closed. The other female members had stars in their eyes; the
men had dollar signs. "This," one of them declared, "could be financially rewarding."
He saw it as a means of breaking the endless cycle of barbecue dinners and bake sales.
He was proven right: the department cleared approximately $1,400 that first year.

The theme for this year's program is "Rock around the Clock." Mounted on the 7
wall directly opposite the front door is a large black and white poster featuring a cari-
cature of two "jitter-buggers," the male sporting a fashionable crew cut, the pony-
tailed female wearing a poodle skirt, bobbie socks, and saddle oxfords. The stage is
done in a 1950s motif, a reminder of an age of American innocence. Black 45-rpm
records and oversized red musical notes are plastered on the white walls. All the props
are surrounded with a gold tinsel garland, the kind used to decorate Christmas trees.
Everything is supposed to shine in the harsh white glare of the spotlights.

I hear music, applause, the introduction of this year's emcee, a popular local disc 8
jockey. The entertainment is beginning.

"Notice how carefully she walks—so ladylike," says the emcee. She is referring to 9
Tiny Miss contestant number two, who is carefully placing one patent-leather clad foot
in front of the other. With every step, her fluffy pink iridescent party dress shimmers.

The Tiny Miss contestants are three to five years old—there are four of them this 10
year. Glenda, another of the pageant organizers, told me that there was no contestant number one; she dropped out after the third night of practice—simply refused
to continue.

"It's time for our former Tiny Miss to present her portrait to Chief Duane Longo. 11
Duane?" calls out the emcee.

Traditionally, each of the outgoing queens presents the department with a framed 12
photograph—twinkling eyes, smile, and crown preserved for posterity. Duane walks toward the stage, bouquet of roses lying awkwardly across his left arm. Each footstep re-
sounds from the plywood platform that functions as the stage. The Tiny Miss Holly is
staring at his knee caps. He kneels. They look at each other uncertainly for just a moment, then swap the flowers for the photo. The little girl wraps her free arm around
his neck, briefly buries her face against his shoulder.

"Awww," I hear from a woman in the audience, "isn't that sweet!" 13

Duane leaves the stage a flattering shade of crimson. 14

The four Tiny Miss contestants return to the stage. One is hiding behind the 15
emcee; the rest are waiting expectantly, anxious smiles frozen on their faces.

"And your new Tiny Miss Holly is contestant number . . . three!" 16

The audience cheers, screams, whistles. A crown is placed upon a small head. 17

"When she grows up," the emcee tells the audience, "she wants to be a cheerleader." 18

19   I remember when they crowned last year's Tiny Miss Holly. One contestant, who stood to the winner's right, folded her arms across her chest, stamped her foot, eyebrows lowered over a fierce angry glare, bottom lip stuck out petulantly. For just an instant, I feared for the physical safety of the new little queen, afraid the other girl was going to hit her. As the twinkling crown was placed carefully upon the winner's blonde curls, her competitor burst into tears.

20   "How embarrassing for her mother," whispered a voice in the crowd.

21   There is a brief intermission. I see one of the defeated contestants standing next to the stage. She's surrounded by friends and family. Her father is talking softly to her as she hangs her head dejectedly. I move closer, catch the funereal terms of the adult voices as her parents pat her shoulder consolingly. "You looked real pretty, honey"— "You did a good job"—"You'll be ready for them next year."

22   The pageant continues with the introduction of the Little Miss contestants, ages six to nine, a bit older than the Tiny Miss contestants. These young girls appear on stage one at a time wearing incredible concoctions of satin, lace, taffeta, beads, and rhinestones: fairy tale visions from our youth. The women in the audience gasp, sigh, exclaim enthusiastically over the beauty of each dress. Contestant number one steps onto the stage wearing a stunning teal-green party dress, appliquéd with a combination of rhinestones, pearls, and sequins.

23   "Contestant number one," reads the emcee, "enjoys shrimping with her daddy."

24   I sit down in a chair recently vacated by one of the covey of visiting queens, winners of other local pageants. To my left sits a stately, composed woman who is scrutinizing the proceedings. I ask her if she is the mother of the queen whose seat I just appropriated. "No," she answers, pointing to yet another queen who is getting ready to entertain the crowd. "That's my daughter."

25   As we discuss pageants in general, I ask her about the cost of the clothing.

26   "You can't wear a sack, you know. This is based on more than talent and poise. You can put the most talented, beautiful girl up there, but if her dress is not competitive . . . well. . . ." She leaves the sentence unfinished, raises her eyebrows, looks at me knowingly. She then describes a dress she saw at another pageant: floor-length black velvet with white satin flowers, spaghetti straps, $15-a-yard rhinestone trim. Total cost, $2,500.

27   She points to the owner of that dress, who later entertains the crowd with a "Dixie/Battle Hymn of the Republic" medley. Tonight she is wearing a royal-blue sequined cocktail dress. I am disappointed that she has not worn the black gown, as I've never seen a dress that cost $2,500.

28   My curiosity piqued, I head backstage to track down the owner of the blue party dress. I walk into the combination meeting room and kitchen, now transformed into a massive dressing room, the smell of makeup, hair spray, perfume, and hot bodies hanging thick in the air. One teen contestant is in the kitchen area, practicing her tap routine on a sheet of plywood meant to protect the new linoleum floor, purchased with proceeds from last year's pageant. I look around the room, searching for that particular child, or rather that particular dress, in the confusion. I spot her on the far side of the room. As I work my way toward her, I dodge the hyperactive contestants and the tense chaperons who dress the girls and have them on stage at all the appropriate times. Once I catch up to her, I ask the woman I assume to be her mother, "If it's not too personal, would you mind telling me how much you spent on that dress?" I pause to gauge her reaction, then add encouragingly, "It's absolutely gorgeous."

29   To the mother's right stands a woman who has been acknowledged periodically throughout the evening as being instrumental in helping several contestants with both their dance routines and their hairdos. She is dressed in a pink lace, pearl-studded tea

gown, blonde hair and makeup flawless. The mother pauses uncertainly, looks to this woman for support.

"Why do you want to know?" the woman growls. A feral look comes into her eyes; her demeanor becomes aggressive, yet with an oddly defensive undertone.   30

I catch myself taking a step backward, totally unprepared for the hostility in her voice. I straighten my back, refuse to be intimidated, wonder if she thinks I'm a spy for a competitor. I explain, "I'm a writer. I'm working on a story."   31

I wait as she stares me up and down, then nods to the mother before once again turning her back on me.   32

"Three hundred and fifty dollars," states the mother.   33

While Glenda stressed that this year's parents have not been as competitive as those in years past, by the time you figure in the costumes and the dance lessons, it's about a $2,000 investment for each contestant. This year the pageant has a total of fifteen contestants.   34

Before the crowning of the new Little Miss, the former Little Miss makes her final appearance on stage. Tradition. With tears in her eyes, she waves farewell to her admirers. Well-wishers step forward with balloons and bouquets of flowers as a pre-taped message plays, "I want to thank God for giving me the opportunity to be Little Miss Holly . . . and Uncle Roger for letting me use his Corvette to ride in the parades."   35

My daughter says that several years ago the winner of the Little Miss competition wore her full-length dress to school the day after the pageant.   36

"And she wore her crown, too!" she adds emphatically.   37

"The sash?" I ask.   38

"Yep," she says. "Her daddy stayed with her all day. He even spread out napkins across her lap at lunch. And her friends had to hold up her skirts during recess because the playground was muddy and the grass was all wet. But she still climbed on the monkey bars."   39

We have another brief intermission, then the visiting queens go up on stage one by one to introduce themselves. Our newly crowned Tiny Miss and Little Miss are allowed to join the throng. When the Tiny Miss steps up to the microphone, she says, "Hi. I'm. . . ." She panics, has obviously forgotten what to say, looks around like a cornered mouse. "Mommy!" she calls out in a frightened voice. Her mother steps up to the stage with an indulgent smile and prompts her daughter. The little girl returns to the microphone and announces her name.   40

Glenda chuckles, "If that wasn't precious!"   41

Most of the older girls, the Pre-teens and the Teens, have been in pageants before. They're familiar with the routine, know all the ins and outs, understand how to play up to the judges, an art in itself.   42

Teen contestant number one, for instance, seems to be a house favorite. She does a clogging routine entitled "Texas Tap" that brings down the house. Her talent is undeniable, her exuberance contagious. I find myself smiling and clapping in time to the music along with the rest of the audience. Unfortunately, when it comes time for her prepared speech, this contestant forgets what she was going to say, stumbles verbally. She mumbles, "Oh God," then continues the best she can.   43

A young woman to my right shakes her head, turns to me and says with resignation, "She would have had a hard time, anyway. Her gown is red."   44

My face must reflect my bewilderment.   45

"With red hair?" she adds with implied significance.   46

Obviously, the contestant is unenlightened. Redheads don't wear red. *Faux pas.* One just doesn't do these things.   47

48   Some rules in the pageant circle are even more specific. Wearing black shoes with an evening gown is forbidden, as are hats, parasols, and elbow-length gloves. Rules are rules. I have heard that one mother, in another pageant, tried to add an extra row of lace to her daughter's socks. It was specified that only two rows of lace would be allowed. The pageant's organizers solemnly handed this mother a seam-ripper.

49   According to Glenda, this pageant has done away with collective judging, the commonly accepted practice of simultaneously lining up the girls on stage, having them turn, pose in front of the judges. "We don't want them compared to one another. They stand on their own merits."

50   Teen contestant number one does not win.

51   The pageant over, I weave through the departing crowd toward the radio room, anxious to talk to the judges. There is a long line. Accompanied by their mothers, each contestants is given the opportunity to discuss her performance with the judges, find out what cost her the competition, where she lost those valuable points. It is a quiet cluster.

52   To my left stands one of the winners. Her mother is not waiting with her, not monitoring her behavior. One of her friends walks by, teases, "Hey, you won this year. Why are *you* waiting to see the judges?"

53   The victor smiles, puffs out her chest with pride, swings her right hand up to her forehead. She nods toward the closed door. "I just want to tell them . . . (with a saucy salute) . . . thanks!"

54   A mother and her daughter, one of the defeated contestants, try to slip past unnoticed. Another mother looks up, asks, "Aren't you going to conference with the judges?"

55   "No, I'm afraid I might start crying," the first mother answers. Her daughter says nothing, but her eyes are red.

56   After a thirty-five minute wait, I am finally able to talk to one of the judges, a man named John. He's wearing a black tuxedo, sports a diamond stud in his ear, has a red carnation pinned on his lapel. He's a hairdresser, has done hair for lots of the pageants—that's how he got "hooked." Most of the judges, he explains, become involved when either friends or their own children enter a pageant. These judges don't get paid for their work; instead, they receive a small gift.

57   "Why do you do it, then?" I ask.

58   "I like to see the girls have a good time," he answers.

59   Every year I'm asked if I'm going to enter my two little girls in the pageant. Every year I say no.

60   "Mommy," asks my youngest, "don't you think I'm pretty enough to win?"

Freewriting

Freewriting helps you focus your thoughts and develop concrete ideas about what you read. Write a full page in your journal or notebook recording your reactions to "The Holly Pageant," along with any thoughts aroused by the essay. Write at your normal pace about whatever comes to mind. Because this writing is not intended for others to read, concentrate on putting your ideas on paper without stopping to polish your writing or correct errors. Although you are free to write any thoughts that relate to the reading, you may wish to respond to some of the following questions: Are you surprised or offended by anything in Lavonne

Adams's account of the Holly Pageant? How do you view the sponsors of the pageants and the parents of the contestants? If reading this essay brought to mind any personal experiences or observations connected with beauty pageants, how were they similar to or different from those of the author?

Group Work

A reading group can be two or more students who share ideas about their reading. For the group activities that follow reading selections in this book, you can be a member of either a fixed group or one whose membership changes from reading to reading. For this reading, group members should do the following: First, take turns reading your freewrites aloud to the group. Then discuss your responses to Adams's account of the Holly Pageant. Compare your own experiences and observations with those of the author. Finally, as a group, try to reach some consensus about the author's attitudes toward this particular pageant and toward beauty contests in general.

Review Questions

1. How did the Holly Pageant get started? Who sponsors it now?

2. The Holly Pageant includes four separate competitions. What is the age group and/or title for each?

3. List and explain the unwritten rules of the Holly Pageant.

Discussion Questions

1. Why would anyone other than the families and close friends of contestants attend the Holly Pageant? What seems to attract a larger audience?

2. Is Adams trying to make some larger point about American attitudes about beauty or competition? If so, why doesn't she state it explicitly?

3. How might sponsors or participants in the Holly Pageant view Adams's account of the pageant? Is there anything they would find unfair or exaggerated? How might they respond?

Writing

1. *Research:* In a dictionary, look up any of the following words that you are unfamiliar with:

    petulantly (¶19)   clogging (¶43)
    feral (¶30)   faux pas (¶47)

2. Interview a person who has helped to organize and plan or who has participated in any kind of local festival, celebration, or pageant. Use the information that you gather to support or dispute some of the impressions you developed from reading "The Holly Pageant."

ABOUT THE REST OF THIS BOOK

The chapters that follow in the first part of this book present an orderly program for developing your skills as a college reader, writer, and researcher. A number of chapters are concerned with reading, since an essential first step is to become a careful, perceptive reader. The early chapters are devoted to techniques and skills in reading for understanding. Later we introduce skills in reading critically and in writing analytically about a text. One area that receives special attention is reading argumentative writing and then writing to persuade others.

Our approach to research is systematic and consists of several steps. We first introduce important college skills that involve single sources, including paraphrase and summary. Those skills are then applied to working with multiple sources. The next step is to synthesize paraphrases and summaries of several readings.

We introduce you to various kinds of research, with particular attention to locating and using sources in the library. Our aim is to enable you to find almost any available information you are looking for. We show you how to compile information, select it, arrange and present it, and document it. In short, you will learn how to write research papers with skill and confidence.

The second part of this book, the Research Paper Reference Handbook, explains the formal conventions of research writing, including lists of works cited, parenthetical notes and footnotes, outlines, and typing requirements. In addition to the MLA style used in most composition classes, two alternative formats are also explained. For ease of use, conventions for lists of works cited and parenthetical notes are summarized in the Quick Reference Guides on the inside covers of the book.

We believe you will find this course rewarding and interesting. The activities you will engage in and the skills you will acquire are all eminently practical ones, and you will have ample opportunity to use them in the years to come. Being able to find the sources you are seeking, to read them perceptively, and to write clearly and articulately about what you have found can give you both a sense of power and a lasting satisfaction.

2 *Strategies for Reading*

One of the most important skills for a college student to learn is reading. That statement may surprise you. Of course you can read quite well already, since you are reading this page. But we mean what we say. Good reading involves some very sophisticated skills, just as good writing does, and all of us can continue to improve our reading and writing abilities throughout our lives.

■ INTERPRETATION

As you saw in Chapter 1, reading is much more than just recognizing the words on a printed page. It involves the ability to *interpret* what you read—recognizing the writer's intentions, perceiving what is implied but not stated, making connections between the ideas you read and other ideas you are aware of, and drawing conclusions. You already use sophisticated interpretive skills in your reading, as the following hypothetical example demonstrates.

Imagine that after having missed three meetings of your psychology class, you find in your mailbox the following communication from the Dean of Students' office:

> This is to inform you that this Office has been notified of your having reached the maximum number of absences permitted by the instructor of __Psychology 207__. In accordance with University Academic Policy, further absence will cause a lowering of your course grade and may result in your failing the course. This Office will continue to monitor your academic progress. Do not hesitate to contact us if we can be of any help to you.

You might draw this interpretation: First, the fact that you received a formal notification from the office of a campus official, rather than a friendly verbal comment from your teacher, alerts you to the existence of a problem. The formality of the language ("This is to inform you") and the impersonal style ("this Office has been notified," rather than "your teacher has told me") give you the sense that a formidable bureaucracy has its eye on you. You conclude somewhat uncomfortably that the university takes its attendance policy seriously.

Besides the actual warning about lower grades, you also note the more vague, implied threat ("This Office will continue to monitor your academic progress"), which is only partially eased by the more benevolent final sentence. You decide from your reading that it would be wise not to miss additional classes if you can help it.

The knowledge that you had when you began reading the notice enabled you to interpret it as you did. Your previous experience of schools and school officials, of policies and grades, and of the way people use language all led you to the particular meaning you derived from the notice. Of course not every reader would respond precisely as you do to such a note, but the point is clear—your mind is actively at work whenever you read. Good readers think all the time—recognizing, understanding, comparing, and evaluating the information they encounter.

EXERCISE

Interpretation

Imagine the following situation:

It is two weeks before election day. Mr. and Mrs. Brown, both in their late thirties, are walking with their five-year-old daughter through a shopping mall. Suddenly a man, smiling broadly, grabs Mr. Brown's hand and shakes it. On the lapel of his suit jacket is a large button that reads "Bean for State Senate." He says:

> Hi, folks, I'm Phil Bean. I hope you're having a pleasant afternoon. What a beautiful child you have! [*To the girl:*] Hi, sweetheart. Aren't you pretty! [*To the woman:*] She looks just like her mother. But you're too young—you must be her older sister. [*To both adults:*] Say, I'm a candidate for the state senate, and I hope I can count on your support. I'm not one of those professional politicians, but I think we need some everyday folks like you and me in the state government for a change, don't you? You can compare my background with my opponent's, and you won't find any drunken driving arrests in *my* past. Of course, I don't want to say anything bad about my opponent, who seems to be a young, well-meaning kind of fella. I'm sure smart folks like you can see what's what and you'll vote for me, Phil Bean. Have a nice day.

In a flash, he is off, grabbing another shopper's hand and introducing himself.

1. Take a few minutes to write your interpretation of what you have read. Do you learn anything about Phil Bean, beyond the explicit content of the remarks he makes to the Browns? What kind of impression does he make on you? Is that the impression he is trying to make? Specifically, what qualities do you find in him? Why do you think he says the things he does? Give specific examples.

2. Now think about why you were able to read the passage as you did. What previous knowledge and experiences allowed you to interpret it in that way? Would a visitor from a country with a different political tradition, such as Iraq or the Congo, be able to interpret Phil Bean's behavior and intentions as you did?

CONTEXT

It is difficult—in fact, nearly impossible—to read a text if you begin with no idea of what it is about. Suppose someone were to lead you blindfolded through the stacks of your college library, asking you at some random point to reach out and take any book off the shelves. You flip open the book, point your finger somewhere on the open page, and, when your blindfold is removed, try to read from that point. In all probability, it would be quite some time before the words would begin to make sense to you—if indeed they ever did. With no initial idea of the book's topic, with no knowledge of why or when or by whom the book was written, with complete ignorance of what preceded the passage you turned to, you would find yourself groping for meaning.

The fact is that in order to read any passage, from a comic strip to a textbook chapter, you have to have some expectation of what it is likely to be about. Otherwise, even the simplest words will make no sense. We have all had an experience in conversation similar to this one: Two friends, Nancy and Jerry, are discussing the rain clouds that loom threateningly in the western sky. Nancy's mind then turns to an upcoming softball game that she has planned, and she says, "I hope they'll all be able to come." Jerry, who is still thinking about the clouds, stares at her with a puzzled look. He cannot understand Nancy because he did not have the right context for her words. She spoke on one subject while he was expecting another.

Like conversation, reading requires you to put words within a *context*—a situation that gave rise to those words. Context includes the background information and experiences that make utterances comprehensible. For example, if you are reading the directions on the box of a frozen dinner, your knowledge of that context enables you to anticipate what you are likely to encounter. You have no trouble, then, understanding what is meant when you are told to "Preheat the oven to 375°." It is just the sort of thing that the context would lead you to expect.

Several elements go into making up the context of any passage you read. Imagine, for example, that you are reading the final chapter of a detective novel. The context that enables you to read and understand it includes the following:

1. Your knowledge of what it is you are reading. (If you aren't aware that it is a detective novel, you will not make much sense of it.)

2. Outside knowledge (your familiarity with terms you encounter, such as *homicide* and *motive,* and your expectation from past experience with detective novels that it will end with a solution to the crime).

3. Your having read the preceding passages. (The last chapter of the novel would be baffling to a reader who had not read the chapters that led up to it.)

All these elements allow you to anticipate what you are likely to find as you read. Without such a context, reading becomes impossible.

| **Analyzing Context**

1. As a test of our claim that it is all but impossible to read a passage without a context that allows you to anticipate what you might find, try this experiment:

   Read, if you can, the following passage:

   > . . . As the tellers passed along our lowest row on the left hand side the interest was insupportable—291—292—we were all standing up and stretching forward, telling with the tellers. At 300 there was a short cry of joy, at 302 another—suppressed however in a moment. For we did not yet know what the hostile force might be. We knew however that we could not be severely beaten. The doors were thrown open and in they came. Each of them as they entered brought some different report of their numbers. It must have been impossible, as you may conceive, in the lobby, crowded as they must have been, to form any exact estimate. . . .

   a. Are there any words in the passage that you do not know? What is the passage describing? What guesses about its subject did you make as you read it?

   b. Although its language is not especially difficult, it is likely that the passage did not make much sense to you, since you were deprived of the context that its readers would ordinarily have. If you had encountered the passage in its usual context, however, you would have known this information: The passage is an excerpt from a letter, written in 1831 by a well-known Englishman, Thomas Babington Macaulay. Macaulay was a Member of Parliament and, as earlier parts of the letter had made clear, he was present to vote in favor of the important Reform Bill. Macaulay and its other supporters had little hope that the bill would gain the more than three hundred votes it would need to be passed into law. Excitement grew as the clerks (tellers) began to count the two sides.

   Given this context, try again to read the passage. Is it clearer now? If so, why?

2. Imagine you have been asked to read the following process description as a test of your powers of recall. Here are the directions: Read it once, put it aside, and then write down as many specific facts as you can remember.

   > The procedure is actually quite simple. First you arrange things into different groups. Of course, one pile may be sufficient depending on how much there is to do. If you have to go somewhere else due to lack of facilities, that is the next step; otherwise, you are pretty well set. It is important not to overdo things. That is, it is better to do a few things at once than too many. In the short run this may not seem important, but complications can easily arise. A mistake can be expensive as well. At first the whole procedure will seem complicated. Soon, however, it will become just another facet of life. It is difficult to see any end to the necessity for this task in the immediate future, but then one can never tell. After the procedure is completed, one arranges the materials into different groups again. Then they can be put into their appropriate places. Eventually they will be used once more, and the whole cycle will then have to be repeated. However, that is part of life.
   > —John D. Bransford and Marcia K. Johnson, "Cognitive Prerequisites for Understanding"

   Although the vocabulary and sentence structure of this passage are simple, you probably faced difficulty recalling details. But suppose you had been provided the title, "Doing the Laundry." Is it likely you could have recalled more specific facts?

3. Now read the following narrative paragraph:

The Prisoner

Rocky slowly got up from the mat, planning his escape. He hesitated a moment and thought. Things were not going well. What bothered him the most was being held, especially since the charge against him had been weak. He considered his present situation. The lock that held him was strong, but he thought he could break it. He knew, however, that his timing would have to be perfect. Rocky was aware that it was because of his early roughness that he had been penalized severely—much too severely from his point of view. The situation was becoming frustrating; the pressure had been grinding on him too long. He was being ridden unmercifully. Rocky was getting angry now. He knew that his success or failure would depend on what he did in the next few seconds.

—John D. Bransford, *Human Cognition: Learning, Understanding and Remembering*

Now reread the paragraph, substituting the title "The Wrestler." Does the title alter your reading experience? Consider the following questions: Why is it possible to play with the meaning of this paragraph by changing its title? What would happen if the paragraph had a well-written topic sentence? From a reader's perspective, what is the value of a title or a topic sentence?

 ## STRATEGIES FOR UNDERSTANDING

As the preceding exercises demonstrate, familiarity with a context makes a passage easier to interpret. Since the context in which you place a text depends on your knowledge, as well as your experiences, values, opinions, and interests, two readers may not place a particular passage in precisely the same context and as a result will not interpret it in exactly the same way.

There are skills, however, that all good readers share. They are observant of context and seek clues to enrich it and to aid their understanding. In large part, these skills come from practice and experience. The more you read, the better reader you become. But it also helps if you are familiar with some of the principles and strategies of good reading. You can become a better reader very quickly with a little training.

Good readers routinely use several *reading strategies.* All of these strategies take additional time—and may therefore seem counterproductive at first—but they can save you a great deal of time in the long run, since they make your reading more alert and efficient.

Choosing the most appropriate and effective strategies is governed by your purposes in reading. Sometimes you read for entertainment; at other times, for information or ideas. Often you read for several reasons at once. Sometimes when you read, you accept the writer's authority and seek to understand and absorb what you read. At other times you read more critically, evaluating whether the writer's authority can be trusted and whether the ideas are worthy of acceptance. Chapter 7 presents strategies for critical reading. The focus of this chapter is on reading for understanding and information. Among the strategies that experienced readers find most important are these:

- Looking for clues in a text before you start to read it.
- Using the clues authors give you as you read.
- Reading with a pencil.
- Rereading if necessary.

Prereading Strategies

To read even the simplest passage, you have to be able to place it within a context and to anticipate what you are likely to find. The richer the context, the better you can anticipate and the easier your reading will be. It is to your advantage as a reader to discover in advance as much about your reading matter as you can. The strategy involved is simple: *Look over what you will read—quickly but alertly—before you begin to read it.*

Specifically, there are several clues to look for before you begin the actual reading, as the following situation demonstrates. Suppose you are reading an issue of *Newsweek* magazine and you come upon the "My Turn" article that appears on the facing page. What might you do before reading it (or even as you decide whether you want to read it)?

EXERCISE   **Finding Clues before Reading**

Before going any further, look now at the *Newsweek* article on the facing page and see what information you can gather about it *without actually reading its text.* What do you expect to be the topic of the article? What do you guess is the writer's point of view? What enabled you to make those assumptions?

Sources of Information

Good readers search for clues before they begin reading. Here are a few of the sources of information that will help you derive more meaning from your reading. While specific references are to the *Newsweek* article, being aware of and using these sources will improve all the reading you do.

Title

It may seem perfectly obvious to say that you should begin by reading the title, but a surprising number of students read assigned chapters and articles without paying any attention to their titles. In doing so, they miss an important source of information.

Surviving a Year of Sleepless Nights

Taking honors classes and getting straight A's made me a success. But it didn't make me happy.

By JENNY HUNG

NOW A HIGH-SCHOOL SENIOR, I still remember my freshman year with a shudder; it was the year my friends and I joked about as the "Year of Sleepless Nights." It wasn't that I had contracted a rare sleeping disorder or suffered from a bad case of insomnia that particular year; in fact, nothing could have been farther from the truth. I had done what many diligent students do: sacrifice precious sleep for the sake of academic success.

Don't get me wrong; my parents never mandated that I take all the honors classes I could gain admission to. No one told me to take three honors classes. No one, that is, except the little voice in my head that convinced me scholarly success was based upon the number of "H's" on my high-school transcript. The counselors cautioned me not to do it, students who had fallen into the trap before warned me against it and my parents just left it up to me. Through it all, I just smiled and reassured them, "Don't worry; I can handle it." The trouble was, I didn't have the slightest idea what lay ahead.

I soon found myself mired in work. For a person whose friends teased her about being a neat freak, I grew increasingly messy. My room and desk looked like my backpack had exploded. There was no time to talk to friends on the phone, not even on the weekends. Going to bed at midnight was a luxury, 1 a.m. was normal, 3 a.m. meant time to panic and 4 a.m. meant it was time to go to sleep defeated. Most days, I would shuffle clumsily from class to class with sleep-clouded eyes and nod off during classroom lectures. There was even a month in winter when I was so self-conscious of my raccoon eyes that I wore sunglasses to school.

My parents applauded my academic success, but hardly knew the price I paid for it. I vividly remember one night when my mother couldn't fall asleep. She kept going to bed and getting up again. Every

'There was even a month in winter when I was so self-conscious of my raccoon eyes that I wore sunglasses to school'

time I heard her get up, I'd turn off my light so she wouldn't catch me still awake. By 5 o'clock that morning, I was so sleepy that I didn't hear her footsteps as she shuffled down the hallway. When she saw the light under my door, she came in and demanded to know why I wasn't sleeping. That was when I knew I was defeated for the night. My mother frowned at me with concern, and I no longer had the strength or energy to resist the temptation to rest. I woke up two hours later and got dressed for school.

Despite the sleep-deprived state I constantly lived in, the A's kept coming home on my report card, and my homework was always turned in on time. I caught up on my sleep in what little spare time I could snatch on the weekends. I had created my own hell, and I was determined to endure until I could get myself out of it.

By the time my freshman year ended, I was rewarded for my hard work. My school held an academic assembly in May, and posters naming the top 10 students in each grade dangled from the ceiling. And there, on the top of the freshman list, I saw: "1.) Jenny Hung GPA: 4.43." The sight of my name on that list was gratifying after all the hard work I had poured into getting it up there, but it also made me think. Was that position really that important to me? Did I want to remember high school as nights without sleep and days of work? Sure, the weight of the medal felt good in my hand, but it didn't mean much. That I would remain at the top of that list was doubtful, and in the end, the paper of the poster was biodegradable. There can only be one valedictorian in each class, and that person usually has to work his fingers to the bone against fierce competition to claim that position. That life, I decided, was not for me.

When sophomore year came around, I chose my classes carefully. The honors classes didn't completely disappear from my transcript, but they weren't as plentiful as before. I found myself busy with all the extracurricular activities that began to fill up my days. My friends no longer thought of me as the outsider who slept through lunchtime gossip. I felt the joy of holding a yearbook I helped to create, and spent hours on the phone comforting a friend who had burst into tears over her dropping grades.

After all these experiences, I frown when I hear my classmates tell stories about their parents' pressuring them to do well in school. Sometimes I wonder if their parents understand what lengths their children go to so they can sport bumper stickers on their cars proclaiming MY CHILD GOES TO HARVARD! If that's the case, they need to learn what my parents and I have learned: academic success means nothing if your heart isn't into earning it, and in the end, books will always fail to teach you as much as life itself.

HUNG *lives in southern California.*

Titles of articles, chapter headings in books, and headlines of newspaper stories usually name the subjects they address, and they aid your reading by helping you anticipate what you are likely to find. We hope that the title of this chapter, "Strategies for Reading," led you to expect an explanation of how to get more from your reading. But not all titles are so plainly descriptive. Look at the *Newsweek* article and see what expectations you can derive from its title, "Surviving a Year of Sleepless Nights." The title probably succeeded in its intended purpose of piquing your interest, while the subtitle indicates that the article deals with the pressure to achieve that many academically gifted high school students feel.

Highlighted Quotations

Sometimes important passages will be excerpted and highlighted. These can provide clues to the central idea of the text. In the *Newsweek* article, for instance, a quotation from the text appears beneath the author's photograph in italic type: "There was even a month in winter when I was so self-conscious of my racoon eyes that I wore sunglasses to school." This clue allows most alert readers to predict that the article concerns the conflict between having enough time for study and meeting other basic needs. Along with the title, this quotation might also lead one to suspect that the author will confirm the widely held notion that most successful teenagers give priority to academic achievement over almost everything else.

The Author

With many works, knowing some information about the author can enrich your reading. If you recognize the author's name, you may be able to make some useful predictions. If, for example, you were to encounter an article entitled "Teenagers and Sex," you would form very different expectations if the author were the evangelist Pat Robertson than if it were Hugh Hefner, the publisher of *Playboy*. Professional titles, academic degrees, lists of other publications, or information about the author's occupation and accomplishments may give you clues about that person's point of view and expertise. Books frequently describe their authors on the flap of the dust jacket. Articles sometimes do so in a headnote before the article or in a footnote at the bottom of the first page or on the last page.

The *Newsweek* article is accompanied by a photograph of the author and followed by a one-sentence explanation of who she is. Since neither her name nor her face is familiar and the description indicates only that she lives in southern California, you may infer that the article concerns the personal experience of someone who is neither a professional writer nor a celebrity. However, her photograph suggests that Jenny Hung is in high school and that she is one of the many academically gifted children of Asian American families on the West Coast. That impression is reinforced by the study guides for the Scholastic Aptitude Test that line the bookshelf beside her desk. The trophies in the background may also suggest that the author has interests in nonacademic pursuits such as sports, acting, or music.

Past Experience

Sometimes prior reading can provide clues about what to expect. If you are a regular reader of *Newsweek,* you will recognize the "My Turn" column as a recurring feature of that magazine. Articles in this series are contributed by readers, not staff writers, and usually relate personal experiences or express opinions. This is further confirmation that this is a personal essay about the effects of extreme academic pressure on the physical health and emotional adjustment of high school students.

Section Headings

Scanning for headings and subheadings is especially valuable before reading a longer passage. One of the best and most important prereading strategies is to leaf quickly through a text for clues about the parts that make it up. Before beginning a book, examine its table of contents; before reading an article or chapter, page through it for headings and other clues. Having information in advance about a text's major ideas and organization can make your reading of it much more efficient. Although the *Newsweek* article has no subject headings, another reading that does can be found on pages 105–13.

Date of Publication

Knowing when a piece was written can help you evaluate it. When you are looking for information on advances in on-line marketing, for instance, it makes an enormous difference whether the source was written in 1995 or 2001. Knowing the date can also help place the author's viewpoint in perspective. Readers might respond differently to an article on the same topic as Jenny Hung's if it had been written two years earlier, prior to a series of high school shootings.

Length

Noting the length of an article or book chapter can give you an indication of how thoroughly the author's point will be developed. It also helps to know where you stand within that development as you read.

Bold Type, Illustrations, and Captions

You can find additional clues to the contents of a book chapter by briefly examining it before you read. Key words that name central concepts are often printed in bold letters. (Look for examples in this chapter.) Other major ideas are often illustrated in drawings and photographs and explained in their captions. Open a textbook that has illustrations and see what you can learn about any given chapter from looking at them.

With an article like the one we have examined, it takes only a few seconds of prereading to gather all this information. Prereading strategies amply repay the small investment of time you make to carry them out: your mind is receptive as you begin to read, your reading is made easier, and you can read more alertly and profitably.

Using Prereading Strategies

1. Read the article "Surviving a Year of Sleepless Nights," and determine the accuracy of the predictions you made using prereading strategies. Did these strategies enable you to read the article more efficiently?

2. Using as many prereading strategies as you can, explain what predictions you can make about the rest of this chapter and about the reading that begins on page 82.

Textual Clues

Good writers help their readers in several ways. They anticipate who their readers are likely to be, and then they write to be understood by them. They write clear sentences, using a vocabulary and style appropriate to the audience. They provide punctuation to signal when a pause in reading should occur or when one idea ends and another begins. Good readers, for their part, recognize and profit from the signals that writers give them.

It is always easier for us to read a passage if we have a reasonably clear idea of what it is likely to be about. In a variety of ways, authors allow us to anticipate their ideas. Even inexperienced writers provide readers with a number of signposts to help them, as the following paragraph from a student's paper on teenage drinking demonstrates:

> Another cause of drinking among teenagers is peer pressure. They are told, "Go ahead, it can't hurt you. After all, everyone else does it." Before you know it, they are drinking along with the rest of the crowd. Soon they are even drinking before class, at lunch, and after school. They now have a serious drinking problem.

This paragraph is from a rough draft and would benefit from additional development and revision. Even so, it demonstrates the kind of signposts that writers provide for readers. Previous paragraphs in the paper had discussed other reasons for teenage drinking. The first two words here, *Another cause,* are **signal words,** also called **transition words,** telling us that a further reason is be introduced. The entire first sentence acts as a **topic sentence** for the paragraph, announcing the paragraph's general subject. After reading it, we anticipate that the rest of the paragraph will explain further how this pressure works. The writer does just that, detailing the process of how teenagers develop a drinking problem through peer pressure, and she uses transition words or phrases like *before you know it, soon,* and *now* to show us that a sequence of stages is being described.

Notice also how your mind works as you read the following passage, in which the sentences have been numbered:

> 1 Scarfe was always a tyrant in his household. 2 The servants lived in constant terror of his fierce diatribes, which he would deliver whenever he was displeased. 3 One of the most frequent causes of his displeasure was the food they

served him. **4** His tea, for example, was either too hot or too cold. **5** The soup had either too much or too little seasoning. **6** Another pet peeve was the servants' manner of address. **7** God help the butler who forgot to add "sir" to every sentence he spoke to Scarfe, or the chauffeur whose tone was deemed not properly deferential. **8** On the other hand, when one of the more timid parlor maids would hesitate in speaking so as to be certain her words did not give offense, he would thunder at her, "Out with it, you stupid girl!"

  9 Scarfe's wife and children were equally the victims of his tyranny. . . .

Notice how each sentence in the passage creates a context for sentences to come and so allows you to anticipate them. In the analysis that follows, we have made some assumptions about how you, or any typical reader, might have responded to the passage. Take some time to examine the analysis carefully and see if you agree with it.

In your first reading of the Scarfe passage, very likely your mind worked in this way:

First, since sentence 1 makes a general statement, you respond to it as a **topic sentence.** In other words, you guess that Scarfe's tyranny is the **main idea** of the paragraph. It comes as no surprise that sentence 2 tells you a more specific fact about his tyranny—Scarfe terrorized his servants. After sentence 2, you might expect either to learn which other members of his household Scarfe terrorized or else to get still more specific information about his treatment of the servants. The latter turns out to be the case.

The author provides a helpful **signal phrase** in sentence 3, "one of the most frequent causes of his displeasure," to show you where the paragraph is heading. The words *one of* inform you that food is one among several causes of Scarfe's anger and suggest that you may be told about others. The author makes the relationship between 2 and 3 clear by **repeating key words:** *his displeasure* in 3 refers back to *he was displeased* in 2, and *they* in 3 refers to *the servants* in 2.

Sentence 4 likewise uses a signal phrase, *for example,* to tell you that it will provide an example of Scarfe's displeasure. Although sentence 5 lacks a signal phrase, you can recognize that it is similar in purpose to 4 because it is similarly phrased, also containing the words *either too . . . or too. . . .* Sentence 6 begins with a signal word, *another;* the phrase *another pet peeve* refers back to sentence 3, which described the first pet peeve. Since 3 was followed by examples, you can expect the same of 6, and in fact both 7 and 8 also give specific instances of "servants' manner of address." Sentence 8 begins with a signal phrase, *on the other hand,* which signals a change in direction; that is, the sentence offers an example that is in some way opposite from the example in 7. It says that servants could be criticized for being too deferential, as well as for not being deferential enough.

By using **topic sentences,** repeating **key words,** and providing **signal phrases,** writers give readers clues to make reading easier. Without having to think about it, an experienced reader will respond to these clues, make predictions, and read with greater ease and effectiveness as a result. Chapter 4 pays special attention to topic sentences. The remaining sections of this chapter are concerned with other reading clues.

Responding to Textual Clues

Only the first sentence (sentence 9) of the second paragraph is given in the passage about Scarfe. Make some predictions about the rest of that paragraph. Do you think sentence 9 is likely to be the paragraph's topic sentence? What would you expect the rest of the paragraph to be about? How is 9 related to the preceding paragraph? Does it contain any signal words or phrases linking it to the that paragraph?

2. Using your imagination to invent details, write the rest of the second paragraph, describing how Scarfe mistreated his wife and children. When you have finished, see what clues you provided to help your readers.

Transitions

Just as it is important for readers to recognize reading clues, it is also important for writers to provide them. *Signal words* make reading easier because they clarify the relationship between one sentence and another. It is for this reason that they are also called *transition words.* They help the reader see in which direction the ideas in a passage are moving. Relationships between sentences can be classified into several general categories. Four of the most important relationships, together with commonly used transition words for each, are listed below.

"And" Signals

And words signal movement in the same direction. They tell you that the new idea or fact will in some way be like the previous one. Here are the most common *and* signals:

and	similarly	furthermore	in fact	another
in addition	also	what's more	first	then
moreover	too	indeed	second	finally
likewise				

Example: Nixley's wisecracks got on his classmates' nerves. He *also* angered the teacher by snoring during the metaphysics lecture.

"But" Signals

But words signal a change in direction. They tell you that the new fact or idea will be different or opposite from the previous one.

but	however	on the other hand	still
yet	conversely	in contrast	instead
nevertheless	notwithstanding	the fact is	unfortunately
nonetheless			

Example: The doctor ordered Smedley to give up all spicy foods. *Nonetheless,* Smedley could still be found most nights by the TV set, munching happily on jalapeños and pickled sausages.

"For Example" Signals

For example words signal a movement from the general to the specific. They tell you that the new fact or idea will be a specific illustration of the previous general one.

for example	specifically	to illustrate
for instance	once	to begin with

Example: Pickleton is a splendid athlete. At a high school track meet, *for example,* she took firsts in both the low hurdles and the ten-kilometer race.

"Therefore" Signals

Therefore words signal a cause-and-effect relationship. They tell you that the new fact or idea will be the result of the previous one.

therefore	as a result	accordingly
consequently	hence	thus

Example: The Brunkin twins never remembered to set their alarm clocks. *As a result,* they were always late for their 8 o'clock statistics class.

Using Transitions

EXERCISES

1. The following passages are made difficult to read and sound choppy because signal words have been omitted. Supply signal words where you feel they would be useful to clarify relationships between sentences or to make the flow of the passage smoother.

   a. Colors are widely associated in people's minds with emotions. Red is traditionally associated with violence and anger. When people lose their tempers, they are said to "see red." Red has many positive associations. The poet Robert Burns wrote that his love was "like a red, red rose." Santa Claus is depicted wearing a red suit. Cheerfulness, as well as violence, is connected with red in our culture.

   b. We have taken it for granted that modern medicine is winning the war against contagious diseases. Fewer cases of malaria are reported each year. Smallpox has been eradicated. It comes as a shock to read that cases of venereal disease are rapidly increasing in number. New varieties have developed that are as yet incurable. No remedy for genital herpes is known to medical science. The traditional antibiotics that once cured gonorrhea are proving ineffective against new, fast-spreading strains. Doctors are hopeful that in time venereal diseases, like other epidemics in the past, will be conquered once and for all.

   Practically every sentence in these two paragraphs has either an *and, but, for example,* or *therefore* relationship to the sentence that precedes it and so could take a signal word. So many signals, however, would probably clutter the paragraph.

You have to decide where you will include them and where you will not. For each signal word you add, explain why you decided to use it.

2. Look at the article on pages 75–76, "Sorry, No Vacancies." What transition words do you find in it?

3. Find a passage from one of your textbooks that uses a variety of signal words. Write a brief commentary on how the author uses them to alert readers to transitions between ideas.

4. Examine the paragraph you wrote for exercise 2 on page 64. What transitional words and phrases have you provided to help your readers? Supply additional signals if they are needed.

Reading with a Pencil

College students frequently face two problems when they read for academic purposes: maintaining interest and getting the most from their reading. Staying alert is sometimes no small challenge. Probably every student has had the disconcerting experience of losing that struggle and drifting into a trance, with the eyes continuing to plod across the page long after the mind has wandered elsewhere. When concentration is a struggle, your reading is slow, unpleasant, and—worst of all—ineffective. Fortunately, there is a way of making your reading more efficient while maintaining your concentration: You can read better if you read with a pencil.

Two different activities are involved in reading with a pencil or a pen—*underlining* and *note-taking.* If the book is your own, you may wish to carry out both procedures in the pages as you read them. In underlining, you mark the main ideas and the most significant information. In note-taking, you summarize the author's ideas in your own words or write your own ideas and responses.

Reading with a pencil has several advantages. One is simply that it keeps your mind alert and active. By combining writing with reading, you bring a larger area of your brain into the activity. Reading with a pencil also forces you to respond more actively to a text. When your mind is searching for the author's main ideas and connecting them to personal experience and other reading, you become directly involved with the text. You are forced to think, and you find that you better understand what you are reading.

Besides increasing alertness, reading with a pencil creates a useful record that later can give you easy access to the information you have read. For example, if you have marked a textbook chapter with underlining and notes in the margin, you can review that material quickly and effectively before an exam just by consulting what you have marked. You don't have to reread everything, since you have already marked what you consider most important. Moreover, by reading the highlighted passages, you stimulate your memory and recall most of what you read and thought the first time through.

Just as no two people will read a book in exactly the same way, no two readers will mark a book in the same way either. This is true partly because people bring into their reading different kinds of experience; consequently, they respond in different ways to the same words and ideas. But even the same reader will respond to a passage in different ways, depending on his or her purposes in reading.

Annotating and Underlining for Recall

Let's assume, for example, that a student in an introductory psychology class is studying the ways a society determines what kinds of behavior it considers normal versus unusual or deviant. She is assigned a selection from her textbook, from which the following passage has been excerpted.* The student knows that she will be tested on the chapter's content; therefore, her goal is literal comprehension of important facts. Here is how she might annotate the passage:

Abnormality and Society

Defining Abnormal Behavior

1   When we ask how a society defines a psychological abnormality, what we are asking is where that society draws the line between acceptable and unacceptable patterns of thought and behavior. There are several different measuring sticks for acceptability, but perhaps the most used is the society's norms.

2   *Norm Violation.* Every human group lives by a set of *norms*—rules telling us what is "right" and "wrong" to do, and when and with whom. Such rules circumscribe every aspect of our existence, from our most far-reaching decisions down to our most prosaic daily routines.

3   Let us consider, for example, the ordinary act of eating. Do we eat whatever we want, wherever and whenever we want it? We do not. Eating is governed by norms as to what is "good for us" to eat, how often we should eat, how much we should eat, and where we should eat. Eating at a football game or at a rock concert is fine, but eating in church or at a symphony concert is not. Furthermore, there are rules as to when and where certain things can be eaten. Drinking wine with dinner is accepted practice; drinking wine with breakfast would be considered rather odd. Likewise, if a man lunches on stuffed squab in the bleachers at the ball park, his sanity or at least his virility may well be questioned by the fans seated around him; he is expected to eat a ball-park lunch— hot dogs and beer. Conversely, if he serves hot dogs and beer at a candlelit dinner party, his guests, expecting something closer to stuffed squab, will consider him either very daring or very ignorant.

4   Some cultures even have strict taboos governing the question of whom one can eat with. Certain tribes, for instance, prohibit eating in the presence of blood relatives on the maternal side, since eating makes one vulnerable to being possessed by a devil, and such devils are more likely to appear when one is in the presence of one's maternal relatives.

5   To outsiders, such norms may seem odd and unnecessarily complicated, but adults who have been raised in the culture and who have assimilated its norms through the process of socialization simply take them for granted. Far from regarding them merely as folkways, they regard them as what is right and proper.

norms are arbitrary yet most people assume they're "natural"

*From *Abnormal Psychology: Current Perspectives,* Fifth Edition, by R. R. Bootzin and J. R. Acocella. New York: Random House, 1993. Reproduced with permission of The McGraw-Hill Companies.

And consequently they will tend to label as abnormal anyone who commits serious violations of these norms.

6   In a small, highly integrated society, there will be little disagreement over norms. In a large, complex society, on the other hand, there may be considerable friction between different groups over the question of what is right and proper. For example, the Gay Liberation movement may be conceptualized as the effort of one group to convince the society as a whole to adjust its norms so that homosexuality will fall inside rather than outside the limits of acceptability. And it may be said in general that American society is in the process of broadening its definition of normality, so that fewer and fewer kinds of behavior are being classed as abnormal.

7   In a sense, the use of norms as a standard for judging mental health might seem inappropriate. <u>Norms</u> are not universal and eternal truths; on the contrary, as we have seen, <u>they change drastically across time and across cultures.</u> Therefore, they seem a weak basis for applying the label of abnormal to anyone. Furthermore, whether or <u>not adherence to norms</u> is an appropriate criterion for mental health, it might be called an oppressive criterion. Not only does it enthrone conformity as the ideal pattern of behavior, it <u>also stigmatizes the nonconformist.</u> For norms contain value judgments. People who violate them are not just doing something unusual; they are doing something wrong. <u>Yet despite these objections, norms remain the dominant standard for defining abnormality. Though they may be relative to time and place, they are nevertheless so deeply ingrained that they</u> *seem* <u>absolute, and hence whatever violates them automatically appears abnormal.</u>

Though oppressive and arbitrary, norms are the most common yardstick of conformity

Notice how the reader observed these guidelines to get more out of her reading:

GUIDELINES for Annotating and Understanding for Recall

• *Mark the most important ideas.* Let your underlining serve as an outline of the passage. Find the author's words that best express the main ideas and underline them. Usually that means underlining topic sentences and not underlining examples and other supporting material, unless they too are important.

Notice that the reader did not underline anything in paragraphs 3 and 4, which consist entirely of examples that illustrate a point made in paragraph 2. She did underline part of that earlier paragraph: a sentence that states the main idea of the entire passage:

Norm Violation. <u>Every human group lives by a set of</u> *norms*—<u>rules telling us what is "right" and "wrong" to do, and when and where and with whom.</u> Such rules circumscribe every aspect of our existence, from our most far-reaching decisions down to our most prosaic daily routines.

• *Don't underline too much.* Underlining nearly every sentence that you read defeats your purpose; it makes your underlining nearly useless for review. Be selective and highlight only the most important ideas and information. The amount of material you underline will depend on what you are reading. Some passages that contain many important ideas will be underlined heavily. Others that contain examples or background material may not be underlined at all. Let your judgment and common sense be your guide.

- *Mark with rereading in mind.* Find and underline the words of the author that best express the main ideas. You don't need to underline entire sentences. In fact, since you are interested in brevity, underline only those phrases that are needed to make the main idea clear to you when you reread them. Sometimes parts of two different sentences can be underlined and connected to form a single statement. This passage shows an example of selective underlining with rereading in mind:

> <u>Norms</u> are not universal and eternal truths; on the contrary, as we have seen, they <u>change drastically across time and across cultures.</u> Therefore, they seem a weak basis for applying the label of abnormal to anyone. Furthermore, whether or not <u>adherence to norms</u> is an appropriate criterion for mental health, it might be called an oppressive criterion. Not only does it enthrone conformity as the ideal pattern of behavior, it <u>also stigmatizes the nonconformist.</u>

When she reviews her textbook the night before her exam, the reader can quickly recall the main idea simply by reading the underlined words: "Norms . . . change drastically across time and across cultures. . . . [A]dherence to norms . . . also stigmatizes the nonconformist."

- *When the author's words are not convenient or clear, use your own.* If a passage is not phrased in words suitable for underlining, rephrase the main idea in your own marginal note. The reader of our sample passage wrote marginal notes to summarize ideas in paragraphs 5 and 7. Capsulizing important concepts in your own words is an aid to understanding what you read. When people talk about "writing to learn," one of the things they mean is that when students manage to translate difficult or unfamiliar ideas into their own language, their ability to understand and recall those ideas is enhanced.

- *Use special symbols to signal the most important passages.* Since some of the passages that you mark will be more important than others, let them stand out by drawing special symbols next to them in the margin. Stars, lines, exclamation and question marks, asterisks, and checks are only some of the marks you can use to make important passages stand out.

- *Mark only your own book.* Because no two readers think alike as they read, no one likes to read books that other people have marked. Writing in library books or books borrowed from friends is both a discourtesy and an act of vandalism. Use stick-on notes, or make photocopies of any borrowed materials that you want to mark. Of course, you are strongly encouraged to mark books that you own.

Reading with a Pencil

EXERCISE

The following article, published a few months before the "My Turn" column on page 59 appeared in *Newsweek*, takes a broader, more general look at pressures faced by high school students. Read the article once with the aim of placing Jenny

Hung's essay in context, judging whether her experiences are typical and whether they may be symptomatic of a larger problem. Then reread the article, this time annotating specific facts and concepts. Mark especially the passages that might help someone explain or better understand Jenny Hung's ideas and points of view.

The Truth about High School

*From Who's in Which Clique to Where You Sit in the Cafeteria,
Everyday Life Can Be a Struggle to Fit In*

Jerry Adler

It was one careless moment in the cafeteria that she now believes will haunt her forever, or at least until graduation, whichever comes first. Blond, smart, athletic, and well off, she must have thought she could get away with sitting down with a couple of gawky skaters from the fringe of high-school society, if only to interview them about hip-hop music for the school newspaper. She should have known that in high school, appearance outweighs motive by a hundred to one. There were giggles and stares, then loss of gossip privileges and exile from her seat at the center table next to the jocks. Now, a year later, recovered from a bout of anorexia as she tried to starve her way back into favor, she has found new friends. But the formerly cool sophomore, too humiliated to bear being identified, views her years in a West Coast high school as "hell."

It should come as no surprise . . . that teenagers can turn their social lives into a matter of life and death. Since the invention of high school, adolescents have been forming cliques and mentally ranking them—it is, says David Zinn, adolescent psychiatrist at Chicago's Beacon Therapeutic Center, excellent practice for an adult society "dominated by hierarchies." The relative positions of some groups have shifted over time, reflecting changes in adult society: jocks are, like their adult models, bigger than ever; cheerleaders are less exalted, perhaps because girls are now playing more sports themselves; while kids are still doing drugs, they've lost some of their demimonde glamor. In general, Zinn believes, high-school kids are more tolerant of differences than they were a generation ago. Minority kids, penetrating deep into the heartland, are less likely to be regarded as exotic freaks. But one of the biggest changes, says University of North Carolina pediatrician William Coleman, is driven by simple loneliness. As adolescents spend less and less time with their parents, cliques increasingly fill the emotional vacuum, and the high-school game of acceptance or rejection is being played for even higher emotional stakes.

Athletes enforce the social code at most high schools, which helps explain why they're usually at the top. "It's pretty common," says senior Lowell Crabb, a varsity football and baseball player at South Pasadena High, near Los Angeles, "to see jocks picking on the fat kid or the wimpy kid, or anybody who's different." Jocks were like that even in the old days, before their games were broadcast on the school's in-house cable channel, their teams were ranked nationally by *USA Today,* and big-city newspapers sent reporters around to interview them. Now Chicago psychiatrist Marc Slutsky believes their aggression is a response to the increased pressure they labor under. While schools have grown more and more concerned with nurturing students' academic self-esteem, athletics are becoming increasingly performance-driven and professional. "These kids get the least sensitive treatment," he says. "All that pressure on them saying 'don't screw up' gets displaced onto others."

Once high schools were divided simply into the in-crowd and everyone else. But as they have grown larger they have spawned a fabulous diversity of gangs, cliques, crews and posses. These include athletes and preppies and wanna-be gangsters; pot-smoking skaters and sullen punks; gays and nerds; and, yes, morbid, chalk-faced

Goths. Cliques proclaim their identities with uniforms that are surprisingly similar from coast to coast. Chinos and button-down shirts mark kids as preppies a thousand miles from Andover; baggy jeans signify hip-hop on a Laotian kid in Iowa no less than on a homeboy straight out of Bed-Stuy. Long before most people had heard of Columbine High School, the black trench coat was a potent symbol for kids in places like central Texas who would rather suffocate than conform to how the cool kids thought they should dress.

In contrast to a generation ago, cliques are much more likely to have both boys and girls in them, Zinn says, a development he traces to early exposure to sexual imagery on television. "Familiarity with the opposite sex comes much earlier now," he says. "You don't find as much mystery or excitement attached to it."

The lush diversity of cliques has made student life more democratic. "This isn't like a pyramid with one group on top," says Eva Greenwald, a senior at Oak Park and River Forest High School near Chicago, population 2,700. "Think of us as living in a lot of different bubbles." Conversely, in schools this size students can live not just apart from their peers, but almost unaware of them. Andrew, a senior athlete and honor student at Cal High School in Whittier, Calif., eats his lunch with his friends every day in the quad. After four years at Cal, "I have no idea what goes on in the cafeteria," he says. "I've actually never been in there."

Some students jealously guard their turf. At Glenbrook South High School, in the Chicago suburb of Glenview, the groups even take their names from their perches: the fashionable "wall people" who favor a bench along the wall outside the cafeteria, and the punkish "trophy-case" kids who sit on the floor under a display of memorabilia. When freshman Stephanie Hernandez sat at the wall one day last fall, she was ordered off the bench by a football player, and hasn't sat there since. "It's just a piece of plastic with holes in it, but they love it," she says. "OK, you can have your bench."

Must life be like this? Experiments in creating egalitarian high-school cultures have met with mixed results. The Paideia School, founded in 1971 as a liberal alternative to the white-flight academies springing up in Atlanta, sought to pre-empt jock culture by decreeing that every student had to be on a sports team. "I'm not a jock, I'm an athlete," says junior Will Arnold, a distinction that might seem superfluous for the captain of the Ultimate Frisbee team. This system has worked well, but it was tested last year when both the boys' and girls' basketball teams made it to the state finals, and hero-worship reared its unfamiliar head. "It can be seductive," headmaster Paul Bianchi says. "People like to see their names in the paper." Glenbrook South, home of the wall kids and trophy-case kids, makes an extraordinary effort at inclusiveness, offering something like seventy clubs and twenty-three sports and both regular and alternative student newspapers and theater groups. But still, says principal David Smith, there's no avoiding the fact that "adolescence is a tribal society. It's just the nature of the thing."

Fitting in is partly a matter of choice. Wearing black trench coats to school is not just a neutral fashion choice, but a way of flaunting one's indifference to the ruling cliques, which is precisely why the cool kids find it so infuriating. But fitting in is also a gift. To be popular, "either you have money, you look good or you play football," says Steve Walker, the gregarious captain of the football team at Merritt Island High School, fifty miles east of Orlando, Fla. Lacking those, you could try throwing a really great party, he says, but "other than that, I couldn't tell you, because I've been popular all my life. As long as I show up, the party's going to be OK."

In some ways, the system works, assigning kids the roles they're comfortable with. As an experiment one day last month, Lauren Barry, a pink-haired trophy-case kid at Glenbrook, switched identities with a well-dressed girl from "the wall." Barry walked around all day in the girl's expensive jeans and Doc Martens, carrying a shopping bag from Abercrombie and Fitch. "People kept saying, 'Oh, you look so pretty,' " she recalls. "I felt really uncomfortable." It was interesting, but the next day, and ever since, she's been back in her regular clothes. The lines drawn by teenagers are frequently unfair, often hurtful and generally enforced by physical and psychological intimidation. Which is why it's worth bearing in mind that high school only seems as if it lasts forever.

Annotating to Stimulate Response

Now let's look at a passage from a different kind of text, an essay by historian and novelist Wallace Stegner. In this case, the reader is enrolled in a course in American history. His instructor has assigned a collection of short readings, all concerned with the development of public lands in the Far West. Students will be expected to participate in a class discussion of those readings, to be followed by an essay exam that will test their ability to make connections—to recognize points of agreement and disagreement—among the authors of the assigned readings. The reader's marking of the text indicates that he is reading for more than just factual information:

1 — How many now?

Within the six Rocky Mountain states there lived in 1960 less than seven million people. They were densest in Colorado, at 16.9 to the square mile, and thinnest in Nevada at 2.6. Surprisingly, they were more urban than rural. Over half of Colorado's people were packed into the ten counties along the eastern face of the Rockies, the rest were scattered thinly across fifty-three counties. More than two thirds of Utah's population made a narrow dense band of settlement in the six counties at the foot of the Wasatch. The cause for this concentration is the cause that dictates so many aspects of Western life: water. As Professor Webb said, the West is an oasis civilization.

2 — Fewer than 3 per sq. mi.!

3 — Scarcity of water means population is concentrated in a few areas

Room, then—great open spaces, as advertised. In reality as in fiction, an inescapable fact about the West is that people are scarce. For comparison, the population density of the District of Columbia in 1960 was nearly 13,000 to the square mile, that of Rhode Island was 812, that of New Jersey 806, that of Massachusetts 654. By the criterion of space, California at 100 to the square mile had already in 1960 ceased to be West, if it ever was, and Washington at 42.8 was close to disqualification; but Oregon, thanks to its woods and its desert eastern half, was still part of the family at 18.4, which is less than half the density of Vermont.

5 — Calif. isn't "west", Fla. isn't "South." Stegner sounds like one of those writers who define what is and isn't Southern.

4 — Paradox: Lots of land but not much of it liveable

The natural resources of these open spaces are such as cause (heartburn) among corporations and individuals who wish the West were as open as it used to be, and were not watched over by so many federal bureaus. Now that the pineries of Wisconsin and Michigan are long gone, the Northwest holds our most valuable forests. Now that the (Mesabi) Range approaches exhaustion, Iron County, Utah becomes a major source of iron ore; the steel industry based upon Utah ore and limestone, and Utah, Colorado, and Wyoming coal is a first step on the road that led to Pittsburgh and Gary. It has been estimated that the Upper Colorado River basin contains a sixth of the world's known coal reserves. The oil shales of Utah and Colorado, already in experimental reduction in Parachute Canyon, lie ready for the time when petroleum reserves decline. The Rocky Mountains contain most of our gold, silver, lead, zinc, copper, molybdenum, antimony, uranium, and these, depending on the market of the moment, may produce

6 — Businessmen and developers suffer physically from their own greed.

7 — where's this?

8 — Natural resources of East and Midwest are depleted. Corporations now eye the West and its riches.

10 *Unusual word* *Erratic business cycles lead to "frenzies" and "panics"*

(frenzies) comparable with the gold rushes of last century. A few years ago, on a road across the Navajo Reservation near the Four Corners, I was stalled behind an oil exploration rig that had broken an axle fording Chinle Wash after a cloudburst. Behind me, in the hour I waited, stacked up fifteen or twenty cars and parts of three other exploration outfits. And who pulled the broken-down rig out and let us go on? A truck loaded with twenty tons of uranium ore. This on a road that only a little while earlier had been no more than ruts through the washes, ducks on the ledges, and periodic wallows where stuck travelers had dug and brushed themselves out of the sand.

9 *And now the steel industry is in decline. Does economic development set in motion an inevitable chain of events culminating in poverty?*

12 *Paradoxes: Sparsely populated but urban, great wealth but no water*

Enormous potentials for energy—coal, oil, shale, uranium, sun. But one source, water, has about exhausted its possibilities. The Rockies form the nation's divide, and on them are generated the three great western river systems, the Missouri, Columbia, and Colorado, as well as the Southwest's great river, the Rio Grande. Along those rivers and their tributaries most of the feasible power, reclamation, and flood-control damsites have been developed. Additional main-stem dams are not likely to recommend themselves to any close economic analysis, no matter how the dam-building bureaus promote them, and conservationist organizations in coming years can probably relax a little their vigilance to protect the scenery from the engineers.

11 *Precious minerals but no water*

—Wallace Stegner, *The Sound of Mountain Water*

In this case, the reader's annotations are a good deal more complex and diverse than those of the first reader, who was trying mainly to memorize facts and concepts. In fact, this reader's marginal notes fall into several different categories:

- *Summary.* Notes 3, 4, 8, and 11 differ little from the marginal notes attached to the passage from the psychology textbook. The reader is simply trying to recast Stegner's ideas into his own language.

- *Questions.* Questions help the reader identify the inevitable "gaps" in any selection—places that lead to confusion, places where the reader would like further details or explanation, places where the reader experiences doubt or reservation. In the first marginal note to the Stegner passage, for example, the reader wonders how much the population of the Rocky Mountain states has grown in the past thirty some years. Is Stegner's assessment, published in 1969, still valid? Did Stegner fail to foresee population shifts? Have natural barriers to settlement kept the region relatively immune to change through growth and development, as Stegner seems to have predicted?

- *Reactions.* A reader may react either to the ideas brought out in a passage or to the author's way of expressing those ideas (tone of voice, vocabulary, bias). Note 2 illustrates the first kind of reaction. This type of response can be a simple statement of agreement, disagreement, outrage, or whatever. For example, note 2 says little more than "Imagine that!" On the other hand, reactions become more complex when a reader calls on personal experience or makes connections with facts outside the writer's text. In note 5, the reader seems to be saying:

  Isn't it funny that Stegner should say that California, the westernmost of the 48 states, isn't "really" Western? It reminds me of how most people say that Florida, the southernmost state, isn't "really" Southern. Stegner sounds like an old-time native talking to an audience of outsiders and newcomers who don't know from Western.

Here the reader is drawing some conclusions about the relationship between himself (the "listener") and Stegner (the "speaker"). More importantly, the reader is consciously resisting the role of a passive listener, one who might accept uncritically a rather subjective interpretation of what constitutes "the West."

Notes 6 and 10 comment on vocabulary. Specifically, they point to Stegner's tendency to view corporate greed in terms of illness ("heartburn") and emotional disturbance ("frenzy"). In contrast to the natural splendor and abundance of the West, attempts to exploit its wealth are presented in terms of sickness and imbalance. Again, the alert reader is conscious of the writer's attempt to manipulate his interpretation or understanding of the subject.

• *Definitions.* Every reader, regardless of educational level, is likely to encounter an unfamiliar word or name from time to time. The often-heard advice to stop and look it up is not always practical, unless the word or name in question represents a key idea that keeps reappearing. Instead, most readers learn to make satisfactory guesses on the basis of clues provided by context. (Of course, this process is not likely to work with a passage that has a high density of unfamiliar vocabulary.) Although these guesses can help a reader comprehend a passage, it still is a good idea to mark unfamiliar vocabulary with a circle or question mark, returning later with a dictionary, encyclopedia, or almanac. In the case of note 7, the reader, not knowing where the Mesabi Range is located, guessed from clues provided in the preceding sentence that it was somewhere in the upper Midwest. Using a dictionary, he later discovered that the Mesabi Range is in Minnesota.

• *Extrapolations.* To *extrapolate* means to take a given set of facts or interpretations and to project or predict other facts and interpretations that are not given or available. For instance, a business executive, examining sales records for the past ten years, might wish to extrapolate from those figures how much sales should increase or decline in the next six months. Readers extrapolate when they take a writer's ideas and extend them, expand on them, or apply them to other situations that the writer overlooked, did not know, or failed to predict. In note 9, for instance, the reader points out that since 1969, the steel industry of Pittsburgh and Gary has suffered the same kind of economic decline as the one brought on by the depletion of coal and iron ore deposits in the upper Midwest. This leads the reader to extrapolate an idea about business cycles—an idea that is not stated (or even necessarily implied) by Stegner.

• *Inventories.* Sometimes readers detect recurring ideas, images, or patterns of language in a passage. Or, perhaps during a second reading, they detect connections among their own annotations. For example, when the reader connects Stegner's use of the words *heartburn* and *frenzy* to describe corporate behavior, he is beginning to make an inventory in his mind. Note 12 is an attempt to put another type of inventory into writing: The reader sees that Stegner describes the West through a series of paradoxes or contradictions.

Not every annotation you can make when reading with a pencil falls neatly into one of the categories listed above. However, the important thing to do whenever you read with a pencil is to record some of the thoughts and responses that pass through your mind as you experience the text. As readers become more proficient at the process, they often engage in a kind of conversation or dialogue with what they read. In the process, they become independent of rules, formulas, and categories of response.

Annotating a Passage   EXERCISE

Imagine that as a student in the same history course, you are assigned the following article, written thirty years after Stegner's essay. Read through the article; then read it again, annotating to stimulate response. Annotate the text in a way that would help you contribute to a class discussion and, perhaps, prepare you to make connections between these two readings on the same general topic.

Sorry, No Vacancies

Worried That Their Way of Life Is Threatened,
Rocky Mountain Residents Fight Growth

Christopher John Farley and Patrick Dawson

Greg Lopez gets lost when he drives around Parker, Colorado. And he's not from out of town—he's the mayor. Once a bedroom community, Parker is bursting with new streets and new residents—and is afflicted with a new sense of dislocation. From the steps of town hall, newly constructed grayish buildings can be seen spattered across a nearby hillside; at the town's outer limits, the wooden skeletons of half-built houses are strewed along the landscape. In five years, Parker's population has doubled, to ten thousand. Last February local voters reacted to the boom by passing one of the toughest antigrowth initiatives in the U.S., a measure requiring a unanimous vote of the town council before any new areas can be added to the town. "The people are alarmed," says Lopez. "They were tired of seeing earthmovers on Main Street. We're besieged by development."

Like the people of Parker, many Westerners feel under assault by settlers, vacationers and developers. . . . About a half-decade ago, Subarus full of Easterners and Range Rovers stuffed with Californians started trekking to the Rocky Mountain states. The refugees were tired of big-city life, traffic jams, crime, and shopping malls, so they moved to a new mecca, stretching from Montana to New Mexico, where the air was clean and the water was clear. It was paradise, except for the fact that it needed more strip malls, so those were promptly built. And pretty soon some of the friends and relatives of the settlers moved in, which meant a few more strip malls were required, not to mention houses and more roads. Before long, paradise started to look a lot like Toledo, Ohio. Or Los Angeles. Now many Westerners—led, perhaps peevishly, by the last wave of settlers—are fighting to slow development and stop the influx of new residents.

Many Western towns are tightening zoning codes, imposing construction moratoriums and limiting the number of building permits they issue. Moab, Utah, a desert town, has been overrun by spring breakers, mountain bikers, and other newcomers; in response, the surrounding county imposed a subdivision moratorium. The fight over growth in the West is sure to be intensified by the selection of Salt Lake City, Utah, as the host of the 2002 Olympic Winter Games, which will bring Olympic-size hype and a flood of tourists. "The Games will accelerate the environmental assault," says Alexis Kelner, co-founder of Utahans for Responsible Public Spending, a group against staging the Games locally. "The area can't take all the condos, hotels, and shopping centers that will now flow in."

In an era of military-base closings and budget cutbacks, it might seem perverse for any community to shut off economic growth. But many Westerners just don't want the pace of their lives to change. Cynthia Hall, who lives outside Albuquerque, New Mexico, cherishes her daily walks in the alfalfa fields on the outskirts of town. Last February she heard that a developer was under contract to buy 150 acres in the area and was seeking to have it annexed to the city so it could be commercially developed. Hall, along with a dozen neighbors, formed the Anderson Field Alliance to block the move and attempt to raise $8 million to buy and preserve the land, an effort that is stalled in city bureaucracy. In Douglas County, Colorado, a fast-growing Denver exurb, some locals have formed the Pinery Coalition to oppose a bid by the Great Gulf Group of Companies to build houses on a pine-studded local hillside and potentially raise the number of residences from 1,900 to 2,700. "My kids are already in full classes," frets Brenda Mason, a spokeswoman for the local homeowners' association. "There's no place for more children to go."

While the well-to-do worry about quality of life, low- and middle-income residents voice fears of being pushed out of boomtowns as the increased demand for housing sends prices to the sky. Growth critics imagine the West turning into a string of Vail-like resorts, where the rich play and others stay away. Denver's Roman Catholic Archbishop J. Francis Stafford wrote in a pastoral letter last fall, "We risk creating a theme park 'alternate reality' for those who have the money to purchase entrance, and around them sprawls a growing buffer zone of the working poor."

The problem is in striking a balance. In the early 1800s Jackson Hole [Wyoming] was merely a valley where fur traders put up their tents; in the past few years it has become a vanity address for stock traders and business tycoons to erect their second and third getaway homes. Since 1986 local housing prices in Jackson have risen 15 percent a year, while local wages increased only 5 percent annually—a trend that could force out the wealth-impaired. So town and county leaders enacted a development plan barring oversize "trophy" homes with more than eight thousand square feet of livable space.

Some residents believe the no-growth movement is futile and foolish. Says John Healy, a councilman in Parker: "The mind-set is 'I've got my five acres, so close the door.'" Gordon Mickelson, whose plans to develop 2,900 acres in Broomfield, Colorado, were thwarted by a local six-month suspension of planning hearings, says such measures could have dire consequences. "When you send a message of no growth, you're telling business, 'Don't come here.'"

Some towns, and a few wealthy, environmentally conscious citizens like actress Andie MacDowell, are signing over the rights to some of their property to nonprofit land trusts, thus ensuring that scenic vistas and traditional uses will be preserved. Last year the Montana Land Reliance helped set up thirty-nine such trusts, up from just eight in 1990. . . . Giving away land may prove to be the ultimate way of keeping it intact.

Keeping a Reading Journal

There are times when writing marginal notes may not be the most effective strategy. Perhaps you have borrowed a book from the library or from a friend, or you may want to expand the range of your responses to a particular reading (that is, write at greater length than you would be able to do comfortably in the margins of a book). On those occasions, a reading journal is a good way to foster the same type of active engagement with a text that takes place when you write marginal notes.

Consider how one reader commented on the following passage, the opening of Robert Pirsig's book *Zen and the Art of Motorcycle Maintenance*. The reader was taking a course in contemporary literature and selected Pirsig's book from a list of nonassigned readings. Asked to compose a paper that explains and develops her personal interpretation of the book, she decided to use a reading journal as a stimulus for personal reflection. First read the passage from the book and then observe the way that the reader reflected on that passage in a reading journal:

> *What follows is based on actual occurrences. Although much has been changed for rhetorical purposes, it must be regarded in its essence as fact.*
>
> I can see by my watch, without taking my left hand from the left grip of the cycle, that it is eight-thirty in the morning. The wind, even at sixty miles an hour, is warm and humid. When it's this hot and muggy at eight-thirty, I'm wondering what it's going to be like in the afternoon.
>
> In the wind are pungent odors from the marshes by the road. We are in an area of the Central Plains filled with thousands of duck hunting sloughs, heading northwest from Minneapolis toward the Dakotas. This highway is an old concrete two-laner that hasn't had much traffic since a four-laner went in parallel to it several years ago. When we pass a marsh the air suddenly becomes cooler. Then, when we are past, it suddenly warms up again.
>
> I'm happy to be riding back into this country. It is a kind of nowhere, famous for nothing at all and has an appeal because of just that. Tensions disappear along old roads like this. We bump along the beat-up concrete between the cattails and stretches of meadow and then more cattails and marsh grass. Here and there is a stretch of open water and if you look closely you can see wild ducks at the edge of the cattails. And turtles. . . . There's a red-winged blackbird.
>
> I whack Chris's knee and point to it.
>
> "What!" he hollers.
>
> "Blackbird!"
>
> He says something I don't hear. "What?" I holler back.
>
> He grabs the back of my helmet and hollers up, "I've seen *lots* of those, Dad!"
>
> "Oh!" I holler back. Then I nod. At age eleven you don't get very impressed with red-winged blackbirds.
>
> You have to get older for that. For me this is all mixed with memories that he doesn't have. Cold mornings long ago when the marsh grass had turned brown and cattails were waving in the northwest wind. The pungent smell then was from muck stirred up by hip boots while we were getting in position for the sun to come up and the duck season to open. Or winters when the sloughs were frozen over and dead and I could walk across the ice and snow between the dead cattails and see nothing but grey skies and dead things and cold. The blackbirds were gone then. But now in July they're back and everything is at its alivest and every foot of these sloughs is humming and cricking and buzzing

and chirping, a whole community of millions of living things living out their lives in a kind of benign continuum.

You see things vacationing on a motorcycle in a way that is completely different from any other. In a car you're always in a compartment, and because you're used to it you don't realize that through that car window everything you see is just more TV. You're a passive observer and it is all moving by you boringly in a frame.

On a cycle the frame is gone. You're completely in contact with it all. You're *in* the scene, not just watching it anymore, and the sense of presence is overwhelming. That concrete whizzing by five inches below your foot is the real thing, the same stuff you walk on, it's right there, so blurred you can't focus on it, yet you can put your foot down and touch it anytime, and the whole thing, the whole experience, is never removed from immediate consciousness.

—Robert Pirsig, *Zen and the Art of Motorcycle Maintenance*

Here are the annotations the reader wrote in her journal:

1. Well, the title is certainly interesting, and the author's note is amusing. Most writers probably aren't so quick to tell you that something may not be factual.

2. Funny how this starts off seeming *not* to be the sort of thing I'd choose to read: I'm not an outdoorsy person, and I've been on a motorcycle exactly once—thought I'd never walk again after 34 miles of it! I'm still attracted to this. Maybe it's guilt feelings, sitting in the car openly admitting that the scenery is OK but sort of dull after a while, something for seeing through windows. Maybe I'm not, as Pirsig suggests, old enough to appreciate it. I don't like to sweat—have a compulsion about being clean, and I'm none too secure about the idea of being inches from pavement that could skin me clean if I made one wrong move.

3. I like what he says about smelling things, though. The smell of lawns being watered, wet pavement, honeysuckle, the ocean, even rotting logs. I even like some city smells, like diesel fumes. I used to find the smell of Greyhound buses very exciting—the lure of adventure. I guess the motorcycle thing is similar, though maybe both Pirsig and I have been unduly influenced by movies. I did sort of enjoy my one and only ride on a cycle, but I've never felt safe about repeating the experience.

4. Pirsig seems to be hinting at something about safety and risk. He's riding with his son—surely he's no hotdogging type, you just don't risk your children that way. So the risk is something else. My boyfriend once suggested how wonderful it would be to spend the rest of your life sailing around the world. I thought not, since I was afraid of drowning, sharks, sunburn (too many movies again?). He added, "However long it might be." There are various kinds of risk, not all of them physical. It's sobering to think how attached I am to safety. I've certainly taken some risks in my life, though seldom physical.

5. I wonder if Pirsig is talking about this a bit when he says you become part of the scene instead of just an observer?

This response to reading lies at the opposite extreme from the notes and underlinings written in the psychology textbook. It is a highly personal response and a greatly elaborated one. Of course, neither of these extremes (nor anything in between) is necessarily better than the other. Partly, it is a matter of individual preference, but mostly it is a case of the reader's techniques being governed by her purposes for reading. The student responding to *Zen and the Art of Motorcycle Maintenance* is deliberately trying to record the personal impact of that book on her as a reader. She is doing so not because she is necessarily a more subjective, intuitive type of person than the first reader; rather, she is trying to meet the demands of an academic task that calls for a more personal type of response to reading.

The personal responses in this student's reading journal fall into several categories:

- *Reactions to details outside the immediate text.* In her first annotation, the student has attended to the author's prefatory note and reflected on the book's title. In doing so, she makes use of previous experiences as a reader.

- *Personal associations and recollections.* To some, this reader's second annotation may seem digressive and unrelated to the passage from Pirsig's book. However, one of the advantages of a personal journal—which is intended for the writer's own use, not the reading of others—is that a writer is free to explore ideas that are not always clearly connected. Sometimes surprising discoveries can occur.

- *Evaluations.* In her third annotation, the reader evaluates the effectiveness of Pirsig's writing before going on to another personal association.

- *Inferences.* In her fourth annotation, the reader begins to draw a conclusion about ideas brought forth in the passage. This type of response will be particularly useful later, when the reader tries to develop her thoughts in a more formal piece of writing intended for an audience of readers. Notice how the free play of seemingly irrelevant ideas in the earlier annotations appears to have primed the pump—to have led the reader spontaneously to draw an inference in the fourth annotation.

- *Speculations.* Making an inference often draws a reader into further reflection. In her fifth annotation, the reader extends and amplifies her ideas from the previous annotation.

No list of categories will exhaust the range of responses that can appear in a reading journal. Independent of rules and formulas, experienced readers learn to become inventive and even playful in their journals. However, if you have not used a reading journal before, you may want to try out some of the following suggestions or prompts:

- Select a quotation from the reading:
  –Explain it.
  –Apply it to your life.
  –Explain precisely why it is not clear.
  –Supply a concrete illustration for it.

–Rewrite it so it communicates better.
–Examine its unstated assumptions.
–Examine its logic/evidence.
–Argue with it.
–Examine its implications and significance.
–Study its style.

- Make a list of the words you did not know and their meanings.
- Take a long or complex unit (section or chapter) and boil it down to its key ideas or segments.
- Try to pin down definitions of key terms.
- Pick out several impressive sentences or images.
- Point out contradictions from place to place.
- Study relationships among facts, opinions, generalizations, and value judgments.
- Examine the treatment of opposing views. Are they mentioned? tolerated? refuted? respected? insulted?
- Examine the writing's structure.
- Discuss the sort of readers for whom the work seems intended.

A useful variation of the reading journal is the ***double-entry notebook.*** Here, the reader draws a vertical line down the middle of each page and writes journal entries in the left-hand column. Later, she can record responses to her own notes on the opposite side of the page. Many readers find the double-entry notebook an effective way to engage in reflection and critical analysis by opening up a conversation or dialogue with themselves as well as with the text. Here is how some of the annotations written in response to the passage from *Zen and the Art of Motorcycle Maintenance* might have looked if they had been recorded in a double-entry notebook:

Respond to the text in the left-hand column as you read.

Reflect on your responses later in the right-hand column.

1. I like what he says about smelling things, though. The smell of lawns being watered, wet pavement, honeysuckle, the ocean, even rotting logs. I even like some city smells, like diesel fumes. I used to find the smell of Greyhound buses very exciting—the lure of adventure. I guess the motorcycle thing is similar, though maybe both Pirsig and I have been unduly influenced by movies. I did sort of enjoy my one and only ride on a cycle, but I've never felt safe about repeating the experience.

The "nature" thing is really a diversion. Not sure why I think so, but I don't think he is going to be raving on about nature.

2. Pirsig seems to be hinting at something about safety and risk. He's riding with his son—surely he's no hotdogging type, you just don't risk your children that way. So risk is something else. My boyfriend once suggested how wonderful it would be to spend the rest of your life sailing around the world. I thought not, since I was afraid of drowning, sharks, sunburn (too many movies again?). He added, "However long it might be." There are various kinds of risk, not all of them physical. It's sobering to think how attached I am to safety. I've certainly taken some risks in my life, though seldom physical.

When he talks about being part of the scene, I also think of the idea that what's worth doing is worth doing well. The catch to that is, of course, that we can excuse any failure by saying, well, it wasn't worth doing.

3. I wonder if Pirsig is talking about this a bit when he says you become part of the scene instead of just an observer?

You hear people say that all the time— "it's stupid"—just because the outcome wasn't somehow satisfactory. There are a lot of people just going through the motions of things because they decide too quickly that the results *won't* be worth real involvement; so the bad outcome is predetermined.

In her double-entry notebook, this student has managed to sustain a dialogue between Pirsig's text and the personal associations that it arouses in her mind. Notice, for example, how the first annotation in the right-hand column carries the student from a purely personal reflection (found in the corresponding annotation in the left-hand column) back to an observation about Pirsig's text. The two following pairs of annotations, on the other hand, move in the opposite direction.

Successful college students learn to tailor their reading processes to meet varying purposes for reading. The different strategies presented in this chapter— annotating and underlining to recall specific facts and concepts, annotating to stimulate response, and keeping a reading journal—can help you regulate your reading processes, making them serve the needs at hand.

READING SELECTION

The following article, published in the *New Yorker,* reviews a controversial book about the history of American Indians in relation to environmental issues. Suppose that you are taking a course in environmental science and have been assigned this article as a course reading. The discussion topic for your next class is the history of environmentalism in the American West. With that in mind, read the article and, as you do, make entries in a reading journal.

Buffaloed

Was the Native American Always Nature's Friend?

NICHOLAS LEMANN

1   For more than a century, spiritually undernourished Americans of European descent have been looking longingly at Native American culture and discovering in it an implicit—and distinctly environmentalist—critique of their own civilization. The critique boils down to this: Indians respect the earth and all its creatures and live in harmony with them, and white people don't. Probably the best pop-culture example of this attitude was Kevin Costner's movie *Dances with Wolves,* but anybody who has children in elementary school will have encountered it without having had to ingest a media version. The romantic view of Indians as naturalists has grown-up intellectual adherents, too. *The Way of the Human Being,* by Calvin Luther Martin, a historian who has left his academic post at Rutgers and moved to the Adirondacks, is suffused with it. Martin tells us that the Western mind has a "severed intellect"—one that is "detached from deep participation with the earth." By contrast, "The remarkable courtesy rendered plants and animals by nonfarming, nonpastoral small-band societies revealed an approach to these beings that was profoundly different from the one my agricultural forefathers conjured up."

2   In *The Ecological Indian: Myth and History,* Shepard Krech III, a professor of anthropology at Brown, whose writing persona is that of a cautious, unbiased evidence examiner, sets out to—well, he'd say to evaluate the notion of an authentic Indian tradition that prefigures contemporary environmentalism. But demolish it would be more like it.

3   Krech's book is a series of summaries of the academic debates about how environmentally aware the Indians were, and much of its appeal lies in its delimited peek into historical and anthropological fracases that are fascinating in a small dose but would quickly become dreary if you had to spend your life trapped inside them. For example, in 1967 a "palynologist and geochronogist" named Paul Martin wrote an article accusing Indians of the Pleistocene era of having waged a Nazi-style "blitzkrieg" on large animals in the American West, which caused the extinction not only of species we've all heard of, like the woolly mammoth and the mastodon, but also, to quote Krech, of such creatures as "single-hump camels, stocky six-foot-long capybaras, five-hundred-pound tapirs, three-hundred-pound giant beavers, four-horned antelopes . . . bison-sized shrub oxen, and stag moose with fantastic multiple-palmated and tined antlers." Over the years, Martin's critics have come back with the theory that these species were killed off by asteroid showers and climate changes, not by Indians. Krech reviews the historical record, which is a tricky matter: for Martin's theory to be correct, the Pleistocene climate would have to have been cold enough to generate glaciation, causing the oceans to fall to the point where Indians could walk across the Bering Strait to get to their animal prey, but not so cold that it killed off the animals before the Indians could. Krech concludes, judiciously, that "it is safest not to rule out a role for Native Americans altogether."

Then there's the opposite Nazi-analogizing argument, made by David Stannard in   4
his 1992 book, *American Holocaust,* that many millions of Indians were indirectly killed
by Europeans through their destruction of the habitat and their introduction of new
and deadly diseases to which Indians had no immunity. Here everything depends on
the size of the Indian population in North America before Europeans arrived—whether
it was as big as eighteen million, a number Stannard adopted from the work of an anthropologist named Henry Dobyns, or something closer to what Dobyns's critics believe to be two million. (If those critics are correct, it means that there are almost no
missing people to account for: according to the first reliable estimates, there were still
two million inhabitants in North America in 1700, and the Dobyns school believes
that the bulk of the Indian casualties from European-borne diseases occurred in the
sixteenth and seventeenth centuries.) Again, Krech painstakingly guides us through
specific proved incidents of sudden mass death by disease, mostly smallpox and
measles, each grislier than the last, and finally rules that the aboriginal population was
between four and seven million, which means that the Indian death toll was much
lower than Stannard and Dobyns would have it. And Krech dismisses the idea that Europeans intentionally infected Indians.

He also points out that some reduction of the Indian population is probably at-   5
tributable to Indian customs that had nothing to do with Europeans, such as female
infanticide ("which had been widely practiced"), and to the exhaustion or the mis-
management of resources. Across the continent, Indians cleared forests by various
means, among them setting fires, in order to grow crops or to create propitious conditions for hunting. If the fires went out of control, or if tribes simply used up the
soil, wood, and game that supported them, they moved on, leaving the land barren.
At other times, tribes apparently rendered what were meant to be permanent settle-
ments uninhabitable. The Hohokam of central Arizona built up an amazingly extensive and sophisticated system of irrigation canals over a period of a thousand
years, then disappeared in the fifteenth century. The best-known student of their civilization, an archeologist named Emil Haury, has declared them to have engineered
a "nearly perfect adaptation to a desert homeland," but Krech isn't so sure. He believes that they may have unwittingly done themselves in by using up too much
wood and by irrigating the soil with river water that was so salty—the Hohokam
lived along the aptly named Salt River—that it gradually became impossible for crops
to grow.

■

Close to half of *The Ecological Indian* is devoted to a discussion of hunting practices.   6
Calvin Luther Martin, with his unshakable faith in Indian superiority, praises these
practices in his brief for Indian ecological awareness: hunter-gatherer societies never
began "systematically enslaving plants and animals" and turning them into "dumb
brutes and inert vegetables." Indians, Martin says, saw themselves and their prey as
possessing equal moral standing, and the act of killing for food as being encased in an
ethic of spiritual reverence. Krech, in turn, presents us—always in that careful tone of
his—with a great, great deal of Indian animal killing, casting doubt on the idea that
there was any moral code underlying it which the contemporary liberal mind would
find familiar and agreeable.

If there is one example of the ecological insensitivity of whites that everyone   7
knows, it is the vast slaughter of buffalo, which reduced the population of the animals from forty million in 1800 to nearly zero a hundred years later. Krech, startlingly,

presents the Indians as having been full participants in it. They regularly hunted buffalo by driving entire herds off cliffs, a practice that left the carcasses at the bottom
of the heap inaccessible and therefore wasted. They also hunted them just for such
delicacies and totems as their tongues, or their fetuses, or their heads, and left the rest
to rot in the sun. As a result, Krech tells us, "buffalo bones littered the prairies so
thickly that in places it was impossible to walk without rattling against their skeletons." Indians ate buffalo meat in almost absurdly copious quantities—more than five
pounds a day. And buffalo weren't the only species they helped endanger. They killed
so many deer that they nearly wiped them out in the South—not for purposes of sus-
tenance or ritual but to obtain skins that they could exchange with the Europeans for
guns and clothing. They were, Krech maintains, willing and enthusiastic participants
in this trade, not innocents corrupted by Western commercial values. Indians in the
north country killed millions of beavers to supply affluent Europeans with hats, and
Krech adds that the basic principles of resource management, such as the establishment of hunting territories and limits on killing, were more likely introduced into the
trade by the Hudson Bay Company than by Indians.

8   Is there just a hint of irony, the product of a not quite fully repressed urge to tease
sentimental glorifiers of Indians, underneath Krech's earnest and scrupulously fair
tone? Sometimes, as he rolls out the gruesome details, it seems that way, as in this passage quoting a white trader on the practices of the Mandan tribe, of Missouri:

> Some Indians preferred drowned buffaloes over all other types of food. McKenzie
> wrote, "When the skin is raised you will see the flesh of a greenish hue, and ready to
> become alive at the least exposure to the sun; and is so ripe, so tender, that very little
> boiling is required." Bottle-green soup made from it was "reckoned delicious" and
> the Mandan were so fond of "putrid meat" that they buried animals all winter and
> ate them in spring.

9   But Krech is more than just a conventional-wisdom overturner; he has a serious
larger point to make. It is his view that concepts like ecology, waste, preservation, and
even the natural (as distinct from the human) world are entirely anachronistic when
applied to Indians in the days before the European settlement of North America. The
Indians' belief system was not some traditional precursor of modern environmentalism but a product of animist religion. Their treatment of plants and animals was prin-
cipled, but by their lights then, not by ours now. Depletions of animal stocks were
often seen as a punishment attributable to hunters' deficiencies, rather than to their
too great success, the logic being that the Great Spirit would reward you for efficiently
killing lots of animals by creating more of them. There were also taboos against letting any animals escape from a hunt, because that would jinx the next one. And many
Indians believed in reanimation or in reincarnation, so the notion that killing animals in large numbers might lead to their extinction would have made no sense to
them.

10   The whole idea that North America was a wilderness existing in a state of ecological balance before the European explorers arrived strikes Krech as nonsense. "North
America was a manipulated continent," he says—manipulated by Indians, who had
been busily pursuing some combination of self-interest and religious belief for centuries. Krech also reminds us that the current state of scientific thinking is that "natural systems are not inherently balanced or harmonious" but instead exist in a state
of "long-term disequilibrium and flux." This was the case when the Indians were the
only humans here, and even when there were no humans here at all and the animals
grazed, forested, and killed on their own. America was never a natural paradise. Perhaps the most wickedly contrarian of all Krech's arguments is that when contempo-

rary Indians say that they, as he quotes one tribal leader, "have hunted and fished, in balance with nature, for more than 300 generations," their belief is not only incorrect but represents the unconscious adaptation of a stereotype invented by whites. "At first a projection of Europeans and European Americans," he writes, "it eventually became a self-image."

■

The endless, empty, and visually spectacular West has always been mythologized with particular speed and ferocity, and not just by Indians and their admirers. At the age of twenty-six, Buffalo Bill, the frontier scout and hunter, began a second career as a professional entertainer. He performed into his old age, reenacting his youthful exploits in burnished form for paying customers, who included appreciative Westerners as well as city slickers. It isn't unimaginable that Indians, too, were profoundly influenced by—or even had their sense of themselves shaped by—the myths of the West.   **11**

The obvious criticism of Krech's book is that he accepts the reliability of accounts by Europeans—explorers, soldiers, settlers, priests, traders—of Indians' customs and behavior. Can people in whom the idea of Indians as blood-thirsty savages was so deeply ingrained be trusted? Perhaps not, but Krech is careful to confine himself to firsthand reports, excluding generalizations and value judgments, and he supports them with archeological and scientific records and with material from Indian sources. Krech will surely be accused of being anti-Indian and anti-environmentalist, but what he really seems to be is anti-anachronist. The lesson of *The Ecological Indian* is not about Indians themselves so much as it is about the depth of the human need to see history through the lens of the present, and to avoid having to justify positions on their merits by locating them in a sanctified past.   **12**

Freewriting

Write for ten minutes about your thoughts as you read Nicholas Lemann's article. What do you learn from reading it? Does it influence your attitudes toward Native American history and culture? Does Lemann's point about Eurocentrism (seeing the folkways of non-European ethnic groups through the lenses of mainstream European-American culture), explained and developed in the last four paragraphs of his article, seem plausible? Can you apply it to common misperceptions of any other culture or subculture (for example, the cliques identified in "The Truth about High School," pages 70–72)?

Group Work

As freewrites are read aloud by each group member in turn, jot down notes whenever you hear ideas you wish to comment on or question. Discuss what you have written, taking note of similarities and differences in your responses. (For example, do you respond similarly to Lemann's ideas about Eurocentrism?) Do group members agree that cultural practices can be (or should be) discussed without reference to the ethical values of mainstream culture? (For example, can we discuss female infanticide without speaking in terms of right or wrong?)

Review Questions

1. How does Shepard Krech's book call into question attitudes toward Native American culture?

2. How does Lemann characterize Krech's persona (the voice or personality assumed by an author in a particular text)? What makes Lemann suspect that this persona may be ironic at times?

3. How have historians oversimplified the buffalo slaughter of the 1800s?

Discussion Questions

1. How does Shepard Krech—and how can any writer from the cultural mainstream of the United States—avoid the pitfalls of a Eurocentric perspective?

2. Other than in the film *Dances with Wolves,* where does one encounter the "romantic view of Indians as naturalists"? What do you suppose is the appeal of this view to European Americans?

3. What might be the appeal of Krech's argument to European Americans? Can you recognize any dangers in an uncritical acceptance of his argument?

Writing

1. Ask one of your college instructors to identify a subject of controversy or debate within his or her field of study. Write a clear, succinct, and objective summary of each point of view. You may wish to add your own assessment of the competing claims.

2. Krech's book takes what is often called a ***contrarian*** view of Native American cultural history—one that disputes widely held beliefs. Write a contrarian view of high school culture (challenging the one presented in "The Truth about High School," pages 70–72) or of beauty pageants (challenging the one presented in "The Holly Pageant," pages 46–50).

3. Choose an entry from your reading journal and develop it into a brief essay.

3 *Writing a Paraphrase*

When you *paraphrase* a statement, a passage, or a longer text, you recast its ideas in different words. College students are called upon to paraphrase almost daily. When you take notes during a class lecture, for example, you probably jot down the instructor's ideas in your own words. Likewise, an essay examination often involves restating material from lectures, reading, and class discussion. In fact, your ability to explain concepts in your own language is a crucial academic skill, since it allows you to demonstrate understanding of significant facts, inferences, and opinions.

PARAPHRASE AS A READING STRATEGY

Let's begin with the most informal, and probably the most common, type of paraphrase. Whenever they encounter an unfamiliar text, experienced readers immediately try to assign meaning to it. One way they do this is to paraphrase. Consider the following sentence from *Talking Power,* a book by Robin Lakoff, a prominent scholar in the field of language study:

> When it is important that language be forceful, we attempt to buttress it in some tangible ways.

A fluent reader might pause here, for less than a second, to interpret this sentence by mentally casting it in slightly different terms: "When words really matter, we try to back them up with something concrete." Sometimes, readers find it useful to write such interpretive paraphrases in the margins; other times, they simply read further to see whether their mental paraphrasing is correct. In the case of Lakoff's sentence, the accuracy of our paraphrase is confirmed by an illustration that follows in the same paragraph:

> Nowadays we often think of . . . oaths as mere words themselves, *pro forma* declarations. But they originated as dire threats. . . . The very words *testify, testimony* recall one ancient link between words and reality. They are derived from the Latin *testes,* its meaning the same as in current English. In swearing, the Roman male . . . placed his right hand upon his genitals; the implication was that, if he swore falsely, they would be rendered sterile.

Sometimes, a written paraphrase in the margins of a text proves useful later on. If, for example, you know that you must review material to prepare for an exam, a paraphrase of an important idea could be helpful. However, there are limits to how much you can write in the margins, as, indeed, there are limits to the amount of time you can profitably devote to paraphrasing, either in your head or on paper. And since a paraphrase, unlike a summary, restates every idea from its original source, a writer rarely paraphrases a passage longer than two or three contiguous sentences. Proficient readers, likewise, seldom recast sentence after sentence in their heads, even when they encounter difficult texts.

Take, for example, the following sentences, also from Lakoff's book:

> We are not mere passive recipients of manipulative communicative strategies. Orwell and other worriers ignore the truth, whether unpleasant or happy: we all manipulate language, and we do it all the time. Our every interaction is political, whether we intend it to be or not; everything we do in the course of a day communicates our relative power, our desire for a particular sort of connection, our identification of the other as one who needs something from us, or vice versa.

A common, but naive, bit of advice to someone who finds these sentences confusing would be to look up any unfamiliar words, thereby putting the passage into simpler language. Thus, a dutiful, though misguided, reader might spend five minutes with a dictionary in order to translate the first sentence as follows: "We are not inactive receivers of influencing talkative plans." The same industrious reader would learn that *Orwell* refers to George Orwell, a British novelist and essayist who lived from 1903 to 1950. All this effort provides little if any clarification. To make matters worse, the task becomes truly hopeless after the first sentence; since the vocabulary is now familiar to almost any literate adult, a dictionary provides no help at all.

Efficient readers, therefore, paraphrase sparingly. Often, they defer complete understanding for a few sentences, waiting to see if subsequent parts of the text provide help. Later in the paragraph from which we have just quoted, for example, Robin Lakoff says, "We are always involved in persuasion, in trying to get another person to see the world or some piece of it our way, and therefore to act as we would like them to act." Suddenly, the foregoing sentences become much clearer; Lakoff relieves most readers of the need to paraphrase preceding sentences.

This first type of paraphrase lies at one end of a spectrum on which we might place every act of reading and interpretation; more subjective types of response lie at the opposite end. When we want to explore our own responses and personal connections to a text, we read and write subjectively, less concerned with literal understanding of what the writer is trying to say. But when we want to try to get down exactly what a particular sentence or passage means, we paraphrase it. The figure below illustrates the spectrum of which we speak.

Responses to Reading

Objective	Subjective
Paraphrase	Personal response
(author's ideas)	(reader's ideas)

USING PARAPHRASE IN WRITING

Up to this point, we have treated paraphrase as a reading strategy—a way of understanding or coming to terms with concepts in academic texts. Whether performed mentally or recorded on paper, this private type of paraphrase is different from all others in one important way: It does not absolutely require an ***acknowledgment phrase*** (e.g., "according to Lakoff") or ***formal documentation*** (e.g., a parenthetical note keyed to a bibliographical entry). In other words, since this kind of paraphrase is not going to be read by anyone else, you are not obligated to identify its source explicitly. For example, were you to paraphrase the main points of this paragraph in a marginal note, you probably would not begin it with "Veit, Gould, and Clifford say that . . . " or end it with a note citing the authors' names and the page number.

Notice, however, that we qualify this advice: A private paraphrase—one that no one else is going to read—does *not absolutely require* acknowledgment and documentation. However, if you were to place such a paraphrase in a notebook or on an index card or on a photocopy that does not clearly identify the author, your failure to acknowledge and document the source could prevent any future use of the paraphrased ideas. If you ever wanted to use or even refer to those ideas in any kind of writing intended for other readers (including your instructor), you would have to relocate their original source and cite it appropriately. That would be necessary because every public use of paraphrase—every use involving one or more readers other than yourself—demands acknowledgment and proper documentation.*

One public use of paraphrase is to reword a difficult or highly technical passage for an audience unfamiliar with its concepts or terminology. Legal experts are often called upon to paraphrase complex or ambiguous texts such as contracts, court decisions, and legislation; in such cases, interpretation, as well as translation, is frequently involved. At other times, we may paraphrase an argument with which we disagree in order to demonstrate good faith and a willingness to listen. Finally, in research writing particularly, we paraphrase sources in order to cite important facts or information, to place a topic or issue in context, or to support an interpretation or opinion. The following sections of this chapter will consider these occasions for paraphrasing.

Before going on, however, we wish to emphasize one crucial point about paraphrasing for any purpose. Whenever you paraphrase, you must completely recast the phrasing of your source, using your own words and your own style. Simple word substitution does not constitute a legitimate paraphrase of another's language; neither does a mere rearrangement of word order. Suppose, for example, that you wanted to paraphrase the following sentence in an essay for your English

---

*The conventions of acknowledgement and documentation are discussed in subsequent chapters. In particular, the parenthetical note, a short annotation usually citing the source of paraphrased ideas or quoted words and the page(s) on which they can be found, is explained in Chapter 5. Although the scope of this chapter is confined to techniques of paraphrasing, the significance of proper documentation should not be overlooked or minimized.

class. The sentence is taken from the review of Walt Disney World by Manuela Hoelterhoff, writing for the *Wall Street Journal.*

The original passage

> I did not have a great time, I ate food no self-respecting mouse would eat, stayed in a hotel that could have been designed by the Moscow corps of engineers, and suffered through entertainment by smiling, uniformed young people who looked like they had their hair arranged at a lobotomy clinic.

An acceptable paraphrase might look like this:

An acceptable paraphrase

> Visitors to Disney World can expect unappetizing food, uncomfortable lodging, and mindless performances put on by cheery adolescents who all look alike.

On the other hand, the following sentence would not be an appropriate paraphrase because it merely tinkers with Hoelterhoff's sentence:

An illegitimate paraphrase

> You will not have fun; you will eat food unfit for human consumption, sleep in a hotel inferior to customary expectations, and endure performances by grinning teenagers who appear to have undergone brain surgery.

Whenever you write a paraphrase that others will read, as in a research paper, you are bound by certain rules of fair play. Specifically, you must completely recast material borrowed from your sources, using your own words and your own style. Failure to do so is ***plagiarism,*** an act of dishonesty. Unless you quote your source exactly (within quotation marks), readers will assume that the language they are reading is entirely your own. You must also give full credit for a source's contributions to your paper.

Upcoming chapters will provide more detail about the use of sources in research writing, including paraphrase and quotation, the citation of sources, and the avoidance of plagiarism.

Paraphrasing for a Different Audience

Writers are sometimes called on to paraphrase their own writing or the writing of others in order to make it clearer or more appropriate for a different audience.

For example, a passage written in an earlier century might need to be paraphrased for modern readers. A writer quoting Shakespeare, for instance, might feel the need to provide a paraphrase:

> "That which we call a rose," wrote the Bard, "by any other name would smell as sweet." His point is that we should not judge things by their names, since names do not alter the essence of those things.

The second sentence is a paraphrase of the first. Notice that it is more than a simple restatement of the author's words in other language. It if were, it would say something like: "A rose would be just as fragrant no matter what we called it." Instead, this paraphrase goes further and states the meaning behind those words—the meaning that Shakespeare left unstated.

As a second example, a scientist might report in a technical journal about a significant discovery she has made in genetic engineering. She would write her article in the technical vocabulary and style appropriate for her fellow scientists. Nonscientists, however, would probably be unable to read the article; and a news-

paper reporter describing that same discovery in a news story would need to paraphrase the scientist's words using less technical, everyday language.

Specialized and General Audiences

When you are writing for a specialized audience whose members share knowledge
about a particular field, it is appropriate to use the special language, or *jargon,* of
that field, even though that language is not comprehensible to outsiders. Browsing through the periodical section of your library will introduce you to a host of
magazines and journals written for specialized audiences. Articles in *Field and
Stream* assume knowledge of game animals and rifle scopes; *PC Computing* articles
take for granted that the reader knows the difference between RAM and ROM; and
the scholarly journal *Linguistic Inquiry* expects its readers to comprehend terms
such as *anaphoric dependencies* and *surface filters.* Each of us has special interests that
enable us to understand some articles and books that might be baffling to others.

Often in your research you will need to translate the specialized jargon of the
publications in which you find your information into clear, general English for
the nonspecialized readers you are addressing. Paraphrasing technical information so that it can be read easily by general readers is a skill that all college writers need to master.

Consider the following two passages about periodicity, the rhythmic behavior
observed in many plant and animal species. The first passage, from *Physiological
Zoology,* a scientific journal, is likely to present difficulties for most readers:

> Recent studies have provided reasons to postulate that the primary timer for   Passage for
> long-cycle biological rhythms that are closely similar in period to the natural a specialized
> geophysical ones and that persist in so-called constant conditions is, in fact, one audience
> of organismic response to subtle geophysical fluctuations which pervade ordi-
> nary constant conditions in the laboratory (Brown, 1959, 1960). In such con-
> stant laboratory conditions a wide variety of organisms have been demonstrated
> to display, nearly equally conspicuously, metabolic periodicities of both solar-
> day and lunar-day frequencies, with their interference derivative, the 29.5-day
> synodic month, and in some instances even the year. These metabolic cycles ex-
> hibit day-by-day irregularities and distortions which have been established to be
> highly significantly correlated with aperiodic meteorological and other geophys-
> ical changes. These correlations provide strong evidence for the exogenous ori-
> gin of these biological periodisms themselves, since cycles exist in these
> meteorological and geophysical factors.
> —Emma D. Terracini and Frank A. Brown, Jr., "Periodisms in Mouse 'Spontaneous' Activity
>   Sychronized with Major Geophysical Events"

If you were researching periodicity, you probably would derive enough information to get the gist of such specialized writing. But if you wanted to report that
information to readers unlikely to share your background and interests, you
would need to paraphrase what you discovered in plainer language. Consider how
Frank Brown, coauthor of the passage cited above, recasts some of the same information in another article, published in the less technical *Science* magazine:

> Familiar to all are the rhythmic changes in innumerable processes of animals
> and plants in nature. . . . These periodisms of animals and plants, which adapt

them so nicely to their geophysical environment with its rhythmic fluctuations in light, temperature, and ocean tides, appear at first glance to be exclusively simple responses of the organisms to these natural factors. However, it is now known that rhythms of all these natural frequencies may persist in living things even after the organisms have been sealed in under conditions constant with respect to every factor biologists have conceded to be of influence. The presence of such persistent rhythms clearly indicates that organisms possess some means of timing these periods which does not depend directly upon the obvious environmental physical rhythms. The means has come to be termed "living clocks."

—Frank A. Brown, Jr., "Living Clocks"

This rendering of facts is more accessible to the average educated adult. However, it still assumes the reader's interest in the particulars of scientific research—an assumption warranted by the author's awareness of who reads *Science* magazine. Notice how Frank Brown once again paraphrases these basic facts, this time adapting them to a still broader audience in an article published in the *Saturday Evening Post:*

One of the greatest riddles of the universe is the uncanny ability of living things to carry out their normal activities with clocklike precision at a particular time of the day, month and year. . . . Though it might appear that such rhythms are merely the responses of organisms to rhythmic changes in light, temperature or the ocean tides, this is far from being the whole answer. For when living things . . . are removed from their natural habitat and placed under conditions where no variations occur in any of the forces to which they are generally conceded to be sensitive, they commonly continue to display the same rhythms they displayed in their natural environment.

—Frank A. Brown, Jr., "Life's Mysterious Clocks"

In each of these three cases, writing is adapted to the needs of a particular group of readers. The first passage is directed toward professional scientists. There, the authors are careful to avoid assigning "agency"—telling who performed certain actions. Readers are told, for example, that "*recent studies* have provided reasons" and that "organisms have *been demonstrated* to display"; the authors avoid saying "*scientists* have provided reasons" or "*we and our colleagues* have demonstrated." Although writing that does not assign agency is usually harder to understand, scientists prefer that type of writing because it is thought to be more objective. The third passage, directed toward the readers of *Saturday Evening Post,* uses simpler vocabulary, like *living things* instead of *organisms,* and explains concepts like *controlled conditions,* which are defined as "conditions where no variations occur in any of the forces to which [living things] are generally conceded to be sensitive."

You may be wondering whether a writer ever paraphrases in language more formal than that of the original source. Because the results often sound peculiar, writers may do this when they want to create a comical effect. In "Politics and the English Language" George Orwell, for example, translated a passage from the Old Testament into political jargon. The passage, taken from *Ecclesiastes,* reads:

I returned and saw under the sun, that the race is not to the swift, nor the battle to the strong, neither yet bread to the wise, nor yet riches to men of understanding, nor yet favor to men of skill; but time and chance happeneth to them all.

In order to ridicule what Orwell calls "modern English," he paraphrased the passage as follows:

> Objective consideration of contemporary phenomena compels the conclusion that success or failure in competitive activities exhibits no tendency to be commensurate with innate capacity, but that a considerable element of the unpredictable must invariably be taken into account.

Orwell's aim is not to communicate the ideas and sentiments expressed in his source, but to show how a particular type of language makes those ideas and sentiments obscure and inelegant.

On the other hand, suppose you wished to paraphrase the following sentence from a magazine that targets an audience of gay readers:

> Chubby, fat, and obese queers suffer outcast status.

The word *queers,* usually a term of abuse, is offensive to most readers. (Since the author himself is homosexual, we assume that he does not intend it as such.) Also, words like *chubby, fat,* and *obese* are loaded with connotation—implicit meaning, as opposed to objective "dictionary" definition. Therefore, if our aim is objective reporting of ideas, an appropriate paraphrase might be the following:

> According to one observer, overweight homosexuals are shunned by other homosexuals.

Some might argue that we have unwisely recast the original sentence in euphemisms (polite equivalents for unpleasant or controversial words), because our paraphrase lacks the emotional impact of the original quotation. However, we believe that this is the best way to proceed under the circumstances.

Notice, too, the qualification, "According to one observer," which places distance between the source and the writer who paraphrased it. This seems appropriate in view of the fact that the statement is a controversial opinion, apparently based on personal experience or observation. Some textbooks draw a distinction between *informative paraphrases*—those that adopt the tone of a source, reporting facts and opinions as though they were the writer's own—and *descriptive paraphrases*—those that take a more detached stance, describing the source rather than presenting its views or information directly. Thus, an informative paraphrase of the foregoing sentence might begin as follows:

> Some books differentiate between informative paraphrases and descriptive ones. . . .

An informative paraphrase

A descriptive paraphrase, on the other hand, would open like this:

> Veit, Gould, and Clifford report that some books differentiate between informative paraphrases and descriptive ones. . . .

A descriptive paraphrase

Although the distinction between informative and descriptive paraphrase is valid, we do not emphasize it here, preferring to suggest at various points in this chapter how and when a writer might choose to adopt a more detached perspective toward a particular source. (This principle will be discussed also in Chapter 12.)

EXERCISES   Paraphrasing for a Different Audience

1. The following sentences come from another article about periodism, or "bio-logical clocks," the topic addressed in earlier excerpts. This passage, also by Frank Brown, was written for the *Biological Bulletin.* Try to paraphrase the sentences for a general audience, similar to the one Brown addresses in the article he wrote for the *Saturday Evening Post:*

    Much has been learned, particularly in recent years, as to the properties, including modifiability, of this endogenous rhythmicity. The fundamental problem, however, that of the timing mechanism of the rhythmic periods, has largely eluded any emi-nently reasonable hypotheses.

2. Recast the passage from Frank Brown's article in the *Saturday Evening Post,* adapting it to readers of *National Geographic World,* a magazine for children in elementary school.

3. Select a textbook from one of your advanced courses and copy out a passage that people who have not taken the course might be unable to understand. Paraphrase it so as to make it accessible to most readers.

4. The following referendum initiative appeared on ballots in the state of New Jer-sey. Write a paraphrase to assist voters for whom English is a second language:

    Should the "Jobs, Science and Technology Bond Act of 1984" which authorizes the State to issue bonds in the amount of $90,000,000.00 for the purpose of creating jobs by the establishment of a network of advanced technology centers at the State's public and private institutions of higher education and for the construction and improvement of technical and engineering related facilities and equipment as well as job training and retraining programs in high technology fields at these insti-tutions; and in a principal amount sufficient to refinance all or any such bonds if the same will result in a present value savings; providing the ways and means to pay that interest of such debt and also to pay and discharge the principle thereof, be approved?

Formal and Informal Writing

If you paraphrase a passage from *Saturday Evening Post* for the readers of *National Geographic World,* as you did in the preceding exercise, you write something that sounds different from the original. After all, the two versions are written for different purposes and for different audiences. Good writers have command of several styles and levels of formality, and they adapt their writing to specific occasions. Some documents, such as important official pronouncements, adopt a highly formal style. Informal notes to friends, on the other hand, are likely to use much more casual language. Between those extremes lies a whole range of stylistic levels. The examples that follow represent very different places along that range.

First is a passage from the Gospel of St. Luke as it appears in the King James version of the Bible, a translation undertaken by English scholars of the early seventeenth century, the age of Shakespeare:

> And it came to pass in those days, that there went out a decree from Caesar Augustus, that all the world should be taxed.
>
> (*And* this taxing was first made when Cyrenius was governor of Syria.)
>
> And all went to be taxed, every one into his own city.
>
> And Joseph also went up from Galilee, out of the city of Nazareth, into Judaea, unto the city of David, which is called Bethlehem; (because he was of the house and lineage of David:)
>
> To be taxed with Mary his espoused wife, being great with child.
>
> And so it was, that, while they were there, the days were accomplished that she should be delivered.
>
> And she brought forth her firstborn son, and wrapped him in swaddling clothes, and laid him in a manger; because there was no room for them in the inn.
>
> And there were in the same country shepherds abiding in the field, keeping watch over their flock by night.
>
> And, lo, the angel of the Lord came upon them, and the glory of the Lord shone round about them: and they were sore afraid.
>
> And the angel said unto them, Fear not: for, behold, I bring you good tidings of great joy, which shall be to all people.
>
> For unto you is born this day in the city of David a Saviour, which is Christ the Lord.
>
> And this *shall* be a sign unto you; Ye shall find the babe wrapped in swaddling clothes, lying in a manger.
>
> And suddenly there was with the angel a multitude of the heavenly host praising God, and saying,
>
> Glory to God in the highest, and on earth peace, good will toward men.
>
> And it came to pass, as the angels were gone away from them into heaven, the shepherds said one to another, Let us now go even unto Bethlehem, and see this thing which is come to pass, which the Lord hath made known unto us.
>
> And they came with haste, and found Mary, and Joseph, and the babe lying in a manger.
>
> And when they had seen *it,* they made known abroad the saying which was told them concerning this child.

The language of this passage is lofty and formal. Its vocabulary is elevated, even obscure in two or three instances; there are no contractions or colloquialisms (words or expressions more appropriate to informal conversation than to public speech or writing). Nevertheless, a good many, perhaps most, English-speaking Americans are so familiar with this account of the first Christmas that it presents no real difficulties for them. However, the following excerpt from *The Best Christmas Pageant Ever,* a play by Barbara Robinson, shows how the same biblical passage might confuse other native speakers of English. In this scene, the mother is directing a rehearsal for a Christmas pageant. The Herdmans—Ralph, Leroy, Claude, and Imogene—have never before attended a Christian worship service:

Mother: All right now *(finds the place and starts to read).* There went out a decree from Caesar Augustus, that all the world should be taxed . . . *(All the kids are visibly* *bored and itchy, except the HERDMANS, who listen with the puzzled but determined concentration of people trying to make sense of a foreign language.) . . .* and Joseph went up from Galilee with Mary his wife, being great with child. . . .

Ralph: *(Not so much trying to shock, as he is pleased to understand something.)* Pregnant! She was pregnant! *(There is much giggling and tittering.)*

Mother: All right now, that's enough. We all know that Mary was pregnant. *(MOTHER continues reading, under the BETH-ALICE dialogue),* . . . And it came to pass, while they were there, that the days were accomplished that she should be delivered, and she brought forth her firstborn son. . . .

Alice: *(to BETH)* I don't think it's very nice to say Mary was pregnant.

Beth: Well, she was.

Alice: I don't think *your mother* should say Mary was pregnant. It's better to say 'great with child.' I'm not supposed to talk about people being pregnant, especially in church.

Mother: *(reading)* . . . and wrapped him in swaddling clothes and laid him in a manger, because there was no room for them in the inn. . . .

Leroy: What's a manger? Some kind of bed?

Mother: Well, they didn't have a bed in the barn, so Mary had to use whatever there was. What would you do if you had a new baby and no bed to put the baby in? . . .

Claude: What were the wadded up clothes?

Mother: The what?

Claude: *(pointing in the Bible)* It said in there . . . she wrapped him in wadded up clothes.

Mother: *Swaddling* clothes. People used to wrap babies up very tightly in big pieces of material, to make them feel cozy. . . .

Imogene: You mean they tied him up and put him in a feedbox? Where was the Child Welfare?

To Alice, described by the author of the play as a "prim, proper pain in the neck," familiar words like *pregnant* show a lack of reverence in this particular context. Yet stage directions—the italicized comments that appear within parentheses—show that nothing of the kind was ever intended. Thus, the play introduces an important issue about language and paraphrase. As America becomes more and more culturally diverse, it becomes less and less appropriate to assume that any one phrasing of ideas or information is inherently better, clearer, or more appropriate than all others. Consider how the same chapter from the Gospel of St. Luke has been translated in a more recent version of the Bible:

At that time Emperor Augustus ordered a census to be taken throughout the Roman Empire. When this first census took place, Quirinius was the governor of Syria. Everyone, then, went to register himself, each to his own home town.

Joseph went from the town of Nazareth in Galilee to the town of Bethlehem in Judea, the birthplace of King David. Joseph went there because he was a descendant of David. He went to register with Mary, who was promised in marriage to him. She was pregnant, and while they were in Bethlehem, the time came for her to have her baby. She gave birth to her first son, wrapped him in cloths and laid him in a manger—there was no room for them to stay in the inn.

There were some shepherds in that part of the country who were spending the night in the fields, taking care of their flocks. An angel of the Lord appeared to them, and the glory of the Lord shone over them. They were terribly afraid, but the angel said to them, "Don't be afraid! I am here with good news for you, which will bring great joy to all the people. This very day in David's town your Savior was born—Christ the Lord! And this is what will prove it to you: you will find a baby wrapped in cloths and lying in a manger."

Suddenly a great army of heaven's angels appeared with the angel, singing praises to God:

"Glory to God in the highest heaven, and peace on earth to those with whom he is pleased!"

When the angels went away from them back into heaven, the shepherds said to one another, "Let's go to Bethlehem and see this thing that has happened, which the Lord has told us."

This particular version of the Bible uses more familiar words, like *pregnant,* in relating the Christmas story. Yet few educated adults would be likely to view it as a less reverent account.

Paraphrasing a Different Style   EXERCISES

1. The following parody of "Goldilocks," is written in the style of Kingsley Amis, a twentieth-century English novelist. You needn't have read Amis's work to gather that he is disdainful of middle-class snobbery and pretense.

Lucky Goldilocks

Anthony Brode

The three bears lived in a maddeningly neat house in a pimply suburb which straggled depressingly along the former by-pass of a small industrial town in the provinces. . . . [T]he bears had gone to a fiendish concert of clever-clever Bach concertos (which they called *concerti*) given by a group of nauseatingly highbrow little gnomes at the other end of town.

Goldilocks was hungry as usual and made straight for the dining-room, which was furnished in Tottenham Court Road* Jacobean with a horror-suite of sticky-looking chairs and a table with twisted legs like varnished barley-sugar. There were three plastic plates on the table, each containing a different type of American breakfast cereal.

Did she like the first sort? No in italics. Did she like the second? Far from it in capitals. Did she like the third? Not at all in 72-point Gill sanserif heavy upper and lower case. . . .

The bedroom, Goldilocks felt instinctively, was known to the Three Bears as the Boudoir. Everything was pink and frilly, and entering the room was like waking up inside a raspberry fondant.† She bounced up and down on the three beds in turn, and they gave out three different but equally depressing kinds of rachety groan.

---

*A suburban shopping district near London
†A thick, creamy sugar paste

At that moment there was a confused waffle of voices downstairs. They sorted themselves out into a bass voice which said, "Somebody's been eating my Crunchimunch," a contralto voice which said ("fluted" was the word of which Goldilocks instantly thought) "Somebody's been eating my Flaxibix!" and a nasty piping lisp which said "Thomebody'th been eating my Toathtieripth!" . . .

An uneven clumping noise grew louder and the bedroom door opened. . . .

"I'm sorry, Three Bears," she said earnestly, "but I was hungry and tired, so I came here. Please don't ask me any questions. . . ." Her voice faltered as she noticed that the Three Bears were wearing precisely the kind of clothes which irritated her most. One wore a nylon shirt and gaberdine trousers, the second a yellow satin dress and "sensible" shoes, and the third (or smallest and most repulsive) a frilly short skirt and white ankle-socks.

"Why weren't you at the concert?" said the nylon bear after a short pause.

"I . . . I wasn't invited," said Goldilocks wildly.

"You don't have to be invited," said the satin bear. "People just pop in."

Yes, it would be that sort of place, thought Goldilocks, and I'll bet when it was over they had meat-paste sandwiches and coffee made from something out of a bottle. "I'll bet when it was over you had meat-paste sandwiches and coffee made from something out of a bottle," she said.

"You mutht have been there," said the frilly bear in an accusing manner.

The nylon bear now spoke again. He was large and obviously accustomed to being listened to, and pitched his voice so that it carried right to the back of the hall. As the bedroom was very small, the effect was much the same as holding a competition for town criers in an airing cupboard.

"I feel it would be for the best," he boomed in a fruity central-office manner, "if you came heah to live with us and, ah, looked after the house. After all, you do appear to be somewhat at a larss."

Goldilocks made her Clement Atlee[‡] face and said nothing.

We would allow you three nights off a week to do folk-dancing," said the satin bear, "or, of course, pottery or woodwork classes if you prefer."

"And you could take me to ballet thchool in the afternoonth," piped the frilly bear.

Goldilocks gave a controlled but vibrant scream like an impatient locomotive and rushed away to the nearest public house for a game of darts and the double Scotch to which, according to a recently initiated economy campaign, she was not entitled until the following Tuesday week.

Compose a parody of another fable or of some equally familiar short text, adopting either the same voice or that of any writer with a fixation similar to Amis's disgust with people who put on airs.

2. Every poem expresses meaning in a unique way, and certainly in a way different from prose. For that reason, it is probably impossible to provide a faithful prose paraphrase of a poem. The experience of reading prose just isn't the same.

   Nevertheless, if you recognize that limitation, you will find that paraphrasing a poem causes you to think hard about its meaning and may help you gain a better understanding of it. Paraphrase the following poem by A. E. Housman (1859–1936). Make sure your paraphrase captures the meaning, not just of in-

---

[‡]British Prime Minister, 1945–51, and leader of the Labour Party

dividual words and phrases but of the poem as a whole. In other words, your paraphrase will present *your* interpretation of Housman's poem.

> **Loveliest of Trees, the Cherry Now**
>
> *Loveliest of trees, the cherry now*
> *Is hung with bloom along the bough,*
> *And stands about the woodland ride*
> *Wearing white for Eastertide.*
>
> *Now, of my threescore years and ten,*
> *Twenty will not come again,*
> *And take from seventy springs a score,*
> *It only leaves me fifty more.*
>
> *And since to look at things in bloom*
> *Fifty springs are little room,*
> *About the woodlands I will go*
> *To see the cherry hung with snow.*

Paraphrasing an Argument

One of the more difficult tasks you may face as a writer is paraphrasing, accurately and fairly, an argument with which you disagree. Nevertheless, the ability to do so helps to portray you as a person of good will and integrity whose views deserve to be taken seriously.

The need to paraphrase an argument with which you disagree may arise under various circumstances, but let's consider one of the most familiar. Suppose you want to refute a commonly held opinion. You may wish to begin by demonstrating that you understand, have considered, and respect that opinion. One obstacle can be your *personal commitments*. The following sentences appear in an essay by Paul McBrearty, who argues for the elimination of anonymous evaluation of college professors by their students:

> Anonymity in student evaluations virtually assures lowered academic standards and inflated grades. The pressures on teachers to *give* good grades so as to *get* good grades are severe, pervasive, unremitting, and inescapable.

The original passage

Though we happen to disagree with this argument, we would not consider the following to be an objective paraphrase of McBrearty's first sentence:

> Some college professors fear that students will use anonymous evaluations as a way of getting even for unfair grades.

Unacceptable paraphrase

What this paraphrase does is to *project* certain attitudes or views that are not clearly there. It implies that the writer condones arbitrary grading practices, when in fact he supports grading that is both demanding and fair.

Another obstacle to paraphrasing an argument accurately can be overdependence on familiar patterns or *schemas*. Schemas are recurrent structures that allow us to make predictions about what a writer or speaker is going to say next. Most of the time, schemas help us read and listen more efficiently. For example, the fourth sentence in the previous paragraph—"One obstacle can be your personal commitments"—leads most readers to expect that at least one other obstacle will be discussed in a subsequent sentence or paragraph. The danger, of course, is that a reader can take too much for granted and make a hasty assumption about what the writer is going to say. Consider, for instance, the second sentence taken from Paul McBrearty's essay:

The original passage

> The pressures on teachers to *give* good grades so as to *get* good grades are severe, pervasive, unremitting, and inescapable.

At first glance the following sentence might seem to be a fair paraphrase:

A hasty paraphrase

> Professors are tempted to bribe students with high grades.

Because we have heard this argument before, we might be tempted to conclude, upon reading the sentence cited above, that McBrearty is making the same claim. Later, however, he says:

The original paraphrase

> Whenever student evaluations are used in any way by administrators as a basis for the denial of promotion, retention, or salary increase, or for assigning a less-than-satisfactory rating to a faculty member, the faculty member is denied the constitutional right of due process if not permitted to confront what are in effect his or her accusers.

Although we still may not accept the validity of McBrearty's argument, we should recognize that he is not suggesting that his colleagues are offering bribes, but that they are responding to pressure in order to protect their jobs. Therefore, a much fairer paraphrase of this sentence would be:

A fairer paraphrase

> Professors fear that they will be penalized with poor student evaluations if they grade rigorously.

Sometimes, writers are called upon to paraphrase arguments that challenge not only their opinions, but also their personal values. On such occasions, the best strategy is to be explicit in attributing arguments to sources. Suppose, for example, a writer opposed to all forms of censorship needed to paraphrase the following argument from an essay by Barbara Lawrence titled "Four-Letter Words Can Hurt You":

The original passage

> Obscene words . . . seem to serve a similar purpose: to reduce the human organism (especially the female organism) and human functions (especially sexual and procreative) to their least organic, most mechanical dimension; to substitute a trivializing or deforming resemblance for the complex human reality of what is being described.

Such a writer might show that Lawrence's argument is incompatible with his own views by using what we have called a "descriptive paraphrase." In other words, he might precede his paraphrase with an ***acknowledgment phrase*** like "According to Barbara Lawrence" or perhaps one of the following alternatives:

Paraphrases acknowledging the author

> In an essay often cited by proponents of censorship, Barbara Lawrence argues . . .
>
> Barbara Lawrence presents an argument raised by feminists who wish to suppress pornography . . .

On the other hand, it probably would not be fair or appropriate to use a slanted or "loaded" acknowledgment phrase like "According to radical feminist Barbara Lawrence."

Earlier in this chapter, we spoke of the occasional need to paraphrase a source that uses language offensive to most readers. Another reasonable concern is how to paraphrase arguments that violate the fairly permissive boundaries of academic inquiry and conversation. While it is usually best to accord respect to persons with whom you disagree, occasionally you may encounter ideas so hateful that you feel compelled to express disapproval. A number of years ago, one of our students complained that he had found in the university library a publication that he considered insulting to homosexuals and religious minorities. In a letter voicing his indignation to the director of the library, this writer wanted to paraphrase some of the views expressed in the offending publication. The writer used judgmental phrases like the following:

> Here we find the familiar homophobic belief that . . .
>
> Overt anti-Semitism emerges later, when . . .

Judgmental paraphrases

Exactly when a writer is justified or wise in expressing judgments about paraphrased sources—or in deciding that a particular opinion is out of bounds and therefore unworthy of paraphrase—is a sensitive issue in the academic community. However, it is usually best to avoid judgmental citations unless there are clear and compelling reasons for their use.

Paraphrasing an Argument

EXERCISE

Try to paraphrase each of the following arguments, which appear in reading selections elsewhere in this book. Paraphrase only the argument, which appears in italic type; preceding sentences merely provide context.

   a. Early medieval Europe was a world in which persons of every level of intellectual cultivation accepted without question that the miraculous could weave like a shuttle in and out of everyday reality. We need to remember this and to resist the temptation to dismiss it out of hand as infantile credulity: *patronizing the past never helped anyone to understand it.*
   —Richard Fletcher, *The Barbarian Conversion*

   b. Stereotypes are sometimes seductive. . . . When women are told repeatedly that they are stupid, they may begin believing it. *Stereotyping can thus control, insidiously imprisoning its victims in constraining roles.*
   —J. Dan Rothwell, *Telling It Like It Isn't*

   c. Virtually every form of public speech in this country is government-subsidized. The print media enjoy a multimillion-dollar subsidy in the form of second-class mailing privileges. The government gives the broadcast media free access to the airwaves, a commodity worth billions. . . . *In light of the prevalence of government subsidies, if the state were free to deny funds to those whose speech it finds disagreeable, freedom of expression would be rendered meaningless.*
   —David Cole, "Constitution Protects Artists from Government Retaliation"

Paraphrasing in Research Papers

As we have said earlier in this chapter, research writing often paraphrases sources in order to cite important facts or information, to place a topic or issue in context, or to support an interpretation or opinion. In these cases, a writer must be especially careful to cite sources by name (usually in the form of parenthetical notes, which will be explained in Chapter 6).

Uses of paraphrase in research writing—particularly conventions of style and documentation—are explained in greater detail in Chapter 12. The following examples simply illustrate various contexts in research writing that might call for paraphrase.

Using Paraphrase to Cite Facts or Information

Suppose you are writing a research paper arguing that the United States should cut its consumption of beef in order to preserve the environment and alleviate world hunger. Using a direct quotation, you might open your paper as follows:

> In his recent book, *Beyond Beef: The Rise and Fall of the Cattle Culture,* Jeremy Rifkin cites the following facts:
>
> Some 100,000 cows are slaughtered every twenty-four hours in the United States. In a given week, 91 percent of all United States households purchase beef. . . . Americans currently consume 23 percent of all the beef produced in the world. Today, the average American consumes 65 pounds of beef per year. (154)

Using a quotation to cite facts

On the other hand, you might paraphrase the quotation to better effect. Consider this alternative:

Better: using a paraphrase to cite facts

> We are so addicted to beef that every week 91 percent of American families purchase it. Because of this dietary preference, our country lays claim to nearly a fourth of the world's supply. Individually, each of us devours 65 pounds of beef a year, requiring a daily slaughter of 100,000 cows (Rifkin 154).

Although it might have been easier simply to quote Rifkin, there is no compelling reason to do so. There is nothing particularly unusual about the words he uses; the basic facts he cites can be rendered just as effectively in your own words.

Using Paraphrase to Place a Topic or Issue in Context

Suppose curtailment of air conditioning during the summer months has been introduced as a conservation measure on your campus. Responding to outcries of opposition, you write an objective, carefully researched study of the consequences of this measure—both its savings and its drawbacks. In order to establish the need for such objective inquiry, you open your paper by addressing the commonly held notion that air conditioning has become an indispensable feature of everyday life. You might do this by paraphrasing the following passage from an essay by Frank Trippett:

The original passage

> [Air conditioning has] seduced families into retreating into houses with closed doors and shut windows, reducing the commonality of neighborhood life and

all but obsoleting the front-porch society whose open casual folkways were an appealing feature of a sweatier America. Is it really surprising that the public's often noted withdrawal into self-pursuit and privatism has coincided with the epic spread of air conditioning? Though science has little studied how habitual air conditioning affects mind or body, some medical experts suggest that, like other technical avoidance of natural swings in climate, air conditioning may take a toll on the human capacity to adapt to stress.

Your opening paragraph might look like this:

> Although most of us regard air conditioning as an unqualified blessing if not an absolute necessity, our dependence on it carries seldom-examined consequences. Author Frank Trippett enumerates some of these consequences. For one thing, air conditioning has impoverished Americans' notions of neighborliness by luring people away from their front porches and into rooms that are shut off from outside air. This seclusion may contribute to certain antisocial tendencies, such as self-absorption and extreme competitiveness. Also, Trippett suggests that while it remains only a theory, some scientists think that air conditioning may impair our ability to cope with stress (75).

A paraphrase

Notice that the source, Frank Trippett, has been identified at the beginning of the paraphrase rather than within the parenthetical note at the end. (The parenthetical note is retained, however, to identify the precise location of the ideas that have been borrowed—page 75 of the publication in which Trippett's article appeared.)

Using Paraphrase to Support an Interpretation or Opinion

Suppose that you are writing a paper arguing that the recording industry has grown too powerful. In the course of your research, you run across the book *Music for Pleasure* by Simon Frith, a scholar of popular culture. Frith argues that one consequence of the recording industry's power is the suppression of certain kinds of musical talent:

> The industrialization of music means a shift from active musical production to passive pop consumption, the decline of folk or community or subcultural traditions, and a general loss of musical skill. The only instruments people like me can play today are their CD players and tape decks.

The original passage

A paragraph in your research paper might open as follows:

> One consequence of the recording industry's power is the disappearance of musical talent. Simon Frith, a scholar of popular culture, has argued that the marketing of CDs has discouraged music-making by amateurs and has undermined regional and ethnic traditions, thus inhibiting the development and exercise of musical talent. Says Frith, "The only instruments people like me can play today are their CD players and tape decks" (11).

A paraphrase

There are two things to note in regard to this paragraph. First, when you paraphrase a source to support your opinion or interpretation, the chances are you will choose someone regarded as an authority. Therefore, it is likely that you will identify that source in an acknowledgment phrase rather than in a parenthetical note at the end. Notice, too, that the basis for regarding Frith as an authority—the fact that he is a scholar of popular culture—is mentioned as well. (Obviously, if your source were a universally recognized person like Albert Einstein or Hillary Clinton, you would not need to do this.) The other thing you may have noticed about this passage is that it contains a quotation as well a paraphrase. Since there really isn't any way to put the last sentence in words fundamentally different from Frith's—at least not without losing something—it is best to quote that sentence directly.

EXERCISE | **Paraphrasing in Research Papers**

Write a paraphrase of each of the following quotations—one that is appropriate to the situation at hand. Remember that you may choose to name the source before you start paraphrasing, or you may prefer to put the last name(s) of the source in a parenthetical note at the end, along with page number.

a. Enrolled in the art course Museum Studies, you have been asked to write a research paper that surveys current trends in developing exhibits. A paraphrase of the following quotation can illustrate the lengths to which curators are willing to go in order to create exhibits with popular appeal.

Source: A feature article by M. G. Lord, staff writer for the *New York Times;* the quotation appears on page 13A.

Quotation:
Librarians often kid about exhibiting the tchotchkes in their collections, but last spring the Beinecke Rare Book and Manuscript Library at Yale University actually did it. In a show called "Things," which closed earlier this month, were such unlikely artifacts as . . . the chamber pot used by Franklin Roosevelt when he was at Yale to receive an honorary degree.

b. Having seen an article about courses offered over the Internet, you decide to report on the possible effects of this trend in a research paper for the course Educational Media: Design and Production. A paraphrase of the following quotation can address the belief that face-to-face contact between students and professors is an indispensable aspect of university study.

Source: Andrew M. Rosenfield, a member of the Board of Trustees of the University of Chicago and co-founder of Unext.com, a company that plans to deliver an MBA degree program over the Internet. In the quotation, which appears on page 9 of an article by Rosenfield, the word *they* refers to future students who take courses without ever entering a university campus.

Quotation:
They will not have direct interaction, but what they will have is the wisdom of professors and pieces of their knowledge that are captured and scalable. And they will have supporting resources and mentors who are their guides.

c. You are writing a research paper on the rise of the labor movement in a course titled American Urban History. A paraphrase of the following passage can illustrate how the theories of Karl Marx may have echoed or influenced the attitudes of American industrial workers in the late 1800s.

Source: On pages 73–74 of a published manuscript, Marx defines *alienation,* a key term in his economic and political theories.

Quotation:
If the product of labour does not belong to the worker, if it confronts him as an alien power, this can only be because it belongs to some *other man than the worker*. . . . Thus, if the product of his labour, his labour *objectified,* is for him an *alien,* hostile, powerful object independent of him, then his position towards it is such that someone else is master of this object, someone who is alien, hostile, powerful, and independent of him.

GUIDELINES for Effective Paraphrasing

The general principles set forth in this chapter can be summed up in the following guidelines for effective paraphrasing:

- Paraphrasing involves a special kind of reading and response, appropriate when the occasion calls for close literal reading and accurate reporting.

- When you paraphrase a passage to make it suitable for a different audience, you should make appropriate adjustments in style, vocabulary, and degree of formality.

- When you paraphrase an argument, particularly one with which you disagree, you must be careful to be fair and objective.

- When you paraphrase a research source, you must completely recast the source's words in your own language and in your own style. Simple word substitution does not constitute a legitimate paraphrase of another's language; neither does the rearrangement of word order.

READING SELECTION

Brian Feagans, staff writer for a daily newspaper in Wilmington, North Carolina, spent several months following the lives of two homeless men known by their street names, Road Dog and Peg Leg. In the following article, Feagans reports some of what he learned.

On the Fringe

BRIAN FEAGANS

With a squirt of gasoline and the flick of a lighter, Peg Leg turned twigs to fire while   1
ranting about a store clerk who refused to fork over a free bag of ice.

"Wouldn't give a homeless man some frozen water," Peg Leg said, stoking the   2
campfire in the July swelter.

3   "What does it cost?—one cent, two cents. I'm gonna fix that. . . ."

4   The Vietnam veteran sliced vegetables as the faint hum of midnight traffic, softened by a forest of tall pines, floated in from a nearby intersection.

5   Shirtless and glistening with bug spray, Peg Leg was readying dinner in "the hooch," a dilapidated wooden shack he moved into in the spring. Supported by sturdy railroad ties, the two-room hut had two full walls, a porous metal roof and a dirt floor.

6   A moat of forty-ounce beer bottles assured no mosquito had to go far for the ideal habitat.

7   Peg Leg's new buddy, Road Dog, stayed quiet, pensive, brooding. A veteran of the streets, Road Dog had been sleeping in the hooch lately but still kept a tent in a wooded area across the street.

8   Road Dog, 39, puffed on a cigarette made from "ducks," or cigarette butts gathered from the ground. All you need is wrapping paper and time to pick out the shreds of tobacco still in them, Road Dog explained.

9   "We live on what other people throw away," he said.

10   The castaways included a dozen steaks and some bread from a Food Lion trash bin.

11   An early-morning dumpster-dive yielded the frosty slabs of meat, and Peg Leg kept them in a cooler with ice finally supplied by a regular worker who took over the late shift at Dodge's gas station. Unlike the other clerk, she knew Peg Leg's routine—how he helps bag the ice, wash employee cars and clean up now and then around the gas station.

12   Peg Leg threw a piece of grating on the fire, smothered the steaks with barbecue sauce, and plopped them into the smoky pit.

13   With a couple beers in their bellies, Peg Leg and Road Dog explained why they live in the woods.

14   They're survivors, not drug-addicted grifters trying to scrape up enough money for the next fix. They don't like homeless shelters—too many crackheads, too much fighting, not enough space.

15   That leaves the spotty woods on Wilmington's outskirts. It's close enough to land an odd job and scrape up discarded supplies. But it's still arm's length from a society that frowns on their lifestyle.

16   "I've been spit on," Road Dog said.

17   Their descriptions change with their moods.

18   Sometimes it's a lifestyle choice. Other times it's a transition period they want to leave behind.

19   But for the second half of this year—through trips to the beach, bloody fistfights, paying jobs, jail time, fires, church visits, and hospital trips—it was life on the fringe of Wilmington.

Looks Like We Made It

20   After downing the steaks and some "tramp stew," Dog and Leg kicked back and listened to some country music on their transistor radio.

21   Peg Leg's rounded sparring-partner nose spreads out into deep-set eyes, gaunt cheeks and square jaws. He stays fit by walking and biking and is strong for a man nearing fifty.

22   Though hobbled, Peg Leg never limps. He struts. Arms swing with hands cupped backward against a proud, chesty gait.

23   He talks in bursts, with a rich mix of down-home sayings and Black English vernacular.

24   In September, when asked if he ventured out during Hurricane Bonnie, Peg Leg said "Are you kidding? I was holed up like a Missouri tick, man. I know what time it is."

25   He grew up in West Virginia, "the seventh son of a seventh son" and the last of ten children.

His father and two brothers died within a five-month span when he was eight, a 26
turn of events he said devastated the family.

At eighteen, Peg Leg signed up for Vietnam. After the first tour, Peg Leg said he 27
came back home and found that no one understood him.

So he went for another round. 28

On his second tour, a three-day shootout in the jungle claimed part of his nineteen- 29
year-old body. His left leg had to be amputated just below the knee.

For his valor, he got a string of bullet wounds, a prosthetic leg and some memo- 30
ries "you ain't never gonna hear about."

The wartime demons come back at odd times. 31

In August, military police at Camp Lejeune stopped Peg Leg and some friends on 32
their way to the beach. At the sight of military fatigues, Peg Leg flipped out and spent
two days huddled in the woods.

"I broke down," he said, dropping the subject as tears welled up in his eyes. 33

"They'll never know what I've been through," he muttered outside of Dodge's one 34
night.

Peg Leg was once married. He has two teenage children and writes them regularly. 35

He doesn't like to talk about his past but says he's been no stranger to prison or 36
hard drugs.

While Peg Leg slings tidbits of his life through the air like splinters, Road unrav- 37
els his past like flaky pieces of bark, peeling away the years in awkward sections.

He speaks in riddles. 38

"I don't judge people," he said with a vast intonation that peaks mid-sentence. 39
"I've learned from my mistakes."

"But have they?" he asked moments later, eyebrows raised. 40

Little of his story came out as Leg chided him for his slow reactions. 41

"He'll just sit there thinking about something forever," then bring up a long- 42
discarded conversation, Peg Leg said.

Dog laughed, a deep guttural howl that left Leg shaking his head, annoyed. 43

Dog, ignoring his heckler, said he loves to sing and write poetry. 44

By 2:00 A.M. the summer heat had ebbed and candlelight-illuminated smoke was 45
rising from the doused fire.

Leg conceded Dog is a good singer, and the bickering turned into a pleasant fire- 46
side conversation about a new Alan Jackson song.

"It's a slow song," Leg said. " 'I'll go on loving you' or something. Man, it'll tear 47
your heart out—twice."

Dog hummed along with the radio, then sang a few lines committed to memory. 48

"Looks like we made it," he sang in unison with Shania Twain, eyes closed. "Look 49
how far we've come, my baby."

Leg reclined back from the foldout card table, and Dog was quiet for a moment as 50
the song continued.

"We might have took the long way. / We knew we'd get there someday." 51

"They said, 'I bet, they'll never make it,' " Dog chimed back in. 52

"But just look at us holding on. . . ." 53

The Hooch

Road Dog and Peg Leg met at Dog's in May. 54

"I just got through killing a beer," Dog recounted. 55

"I said, 'Hey man, what happened to you—you've got quite a limp. You been in a 56
war somewhere?' "

Leg pulled up his left pant leg and showed Dog the custom-made prosthetic re- 57
placing what Vietnam claimed three decades earlier.

58   "I went and got him a beer and that's how we kicked it off," Dog said.

59   They started hanging out and watching out for each other's safety among the other street characters at Wilmington's rough edges.

60   When Peg Leg's prosthesis rubbed the end of his leg raw, Road Dog helped nurse him back to health, fetching food and supplies.

61   When Road Dog got hit by a car months later, Peg Leg was there.

62   A friendship was born, and the hooch was home for both of them.

63   More Boy Scout retreat than ramshackle hut, the hooch has signatures of past visitors and the fittings of its most recent guests.

64   It has housed drifters and the downtrodden over the years on an undeveloped tract of private property nestled near the intersection of College Road and Market Street. No one has ever bothered Road Dog and Peg Leg there, except for the cops who rousted them out of bed and searched them after a nearby convenience store was held up, Peg Leg said, sipping a bottle of water after an early-August cleaning.

65   He got up early and finished the three-day task of moving beer bottles into a trash heap fifty yards away.

66   The hooch was clean, with fresh rake marks on the dirt floor.

67   Peg Leg's crutch hung down from one corner of a cloth four-by-six foot American flag. It faced a North Carolina flag nailed to a beam festooned with pots, pans, a saw, and toilet paper.

68   A buxom centerfold named Kayleigh fluttered above a stand-up gas station sign.

69   A large mirror used for shaving was propped against a tree outside. At head level, a toothbrush stuck out next to a jagged mirror fragment.

70   Road Dog had drawn the ire of Peg Leg by pinning jeans, shoe soles, socks, and underwear on two clotheslines outside the hooch.

71   "I didn't clean this mess out to look at this . . . damn dirty laundry," Peg Leg shouted over to Road Dog, who was still getting his bearings for the day.

72   Road Dog sat on a sleeping bag that had replaced the cushions of a green, ribbed corduroy couch in the hooch's darkest corner. He was ruing another daybreak roust by the cardinals, blue jays, and sparrows he feeds regularly.

73   "They'll know I'm up," he said. "They'll sit in the trees and start whistling at me."

74   Still sweating from the morning labor, Peg Leg mounted his bike and pedaled off to bag ice. Road Dog, polishing off a doughnut, decided he'd better check on his belongings left unattended across the street.

On the Road

75   Road Dog picked up his street name while hitchhiking near Denver.

76   A trucker was giving Road Dog yet another ride and was struck by how many times he saw him on his route along Interstate 80.

77   "He said 'Every time I turn around I see you running up the road like a dog,' " Road Dog said. " 'I'm gonna call you Road Dog.' "

78   The name stuck, and for good reason.

79   Dog's head is a series of potholes, lumps, and scars from past beatings. He's been on the wrong end of garden utensils, bullets, knives, fists, and boots.

80   His hand glides across the noggin like a blind man reading a familiar and painful history in Braille.

81   Dog was bludgeoned so badly with a hammer in San Francisco that he needed six months of therapy to learn how to walk again.

82   "When I came out, they said I was a walking miracle," Dog said, feeling the dents.

83   He pointed to a more recent scar over his left eyebrow.

A fellow worker on a sod job clubbed Road Dog with a shovel knocking him out cold in the spring.   **84**

He has gunshot wounds in his shoulder and thigh. He said one shot came from a bad drug deal and the other from trying to protect two women in crossfire.   **85**

While walking down the sandy path to his old tent in the woods, Road explained the latest mark—a puffy scab starting to flake away from the stubble on his face.   **86**

A car hit him while he was biking down College Road in the dark. He went careening onto the shoulder, and the car drove off, leaving him unconscious.   **87**

His tennis shoes slipped when he walked, loose without the laces that the ambulance crew cut away at the accident scene. Four days after the hit-and-run, he was still wearing green scrubs with the New Hanover Regional Medical Center logo.   **88**

Road Dog spent two years in the Army and attended college briefly in his home state of Illinois, but he says his life took a turn for the worse at age twenty.   **89**

Dog said he got mixed up in cocaine and the wrong crowd, a combination that led him to steal a car and a motorcycle. An auto theft conviction left him in prison for part of his early twenties, but Dog said he has had only minor brushes with the law in recent years.   **90**

Road Dog was engaged to be married five years ago, but when his fiancée was thrown in jail, he lost his grip and ended up on the streets, where he has been ever since.   **91**

He showed off the one loving mark on his body—a shoulder tattoo of Catrina the Indian Princess, a long-lost love from Arizona.   **92**

"Now she was special," he said. "A real baby doll."   **93**

Road Dog then noticed footprints in the sand leading to his "camp," where he still stores clothes, blankets, and books.   **94**

"The police were probably checking on me," he said. "They probably heard I was hit."   **95**

Tacks dotted a tree where passersby leave notes. A patch of shriveled plants marked his old garden of spearmint, herbs, lettuce, and tomatoes.   **96**

"I kind of miss it," he said. "I spent so much time out here."   **97**

Next to the giant pine was a burned American flag; its remains blanketed a rock-lined pit.   **98**

"I got to thinking how Americans act—not thinking about anyone who suffers," Dog said.   **99**

He added that the flag had touched the ground and was torn, making a burning compulsory.   **100**

Road Dog unzipped his old tent and checked on his library—the Bible ("I've read it three times"), a Jeff Gordon video, a poetry book by Alfred Noyes called *Watchers of the Sky,* and *Learning How to Deal with Adversity,* a self-help book by Charles Stanley.   **101**

Dog has been to the Gateway Church on Wrightsville Avenue a couple times and often talks about making another visit to a minister who has tailored his presentation to the homeless in the past.   **102**

"He said you can't expect them to go out there, living like they're living, and be perfect Christians," Dog said. "We drink to ease the pain. It keeps us in good spirits."   **103**

The Wall

The three-foot-high wall backstopping the Dodge's parking lot was the social hangout for Dog, Leg, and friends until the regular nighttime crowd got too large and store management broke it up.   **104**

Like a front porch away from home, it offered the entertainment of gas station customers, the rote of traffic at one of Wilmington's busiest intersections, and, of   **105** course, a beer shield. The management let Dog and Leg use the bathrooms for bathing, and they often used a nearby hotel shower.

106   With cardboard squares for cushions, the two buddies were the peanut gallery to the world. Each pass of a police car was met with Leg's hue and cry: "Five-O in the *house*." Dog pointed to each passing Harley-Davidson motorcycle and sported a grin.

107   Chuck, a new addition to Wilmington's street life, brought Road Dog a yellow Schwinn to replace the mangled hunk of metal left behind by the hit-and-run. Peg Leg dubbed it "Deathwish II."

108   Road Dog, sweating in the late August swelter, stood up every now and then to voice his pain. "I hurt so bad, he yelled out above the bustling nighttime traffic. "Why do I have to hurt so bad?" he asked before slowly taking a seat again.

109   Leg turned his attention to Chuck, now a good friend. He's got a wolflike beard and cheek ring. His wife had kicked him out of the house again, so it was a night on the streets.

110   Peg Leg was still suspicious.

111   "I don't trust no one with a house," he said so Chuck could hear.

112   Chuck chided Peg Leg a bit, calling him a name and grinning ear to ear. Peg Leg warned him to back off, then demanded a retraction.

113   "I'm going to straighten that . . . right now," he said.

114   With cat-like quickness he pounced on Chuck. Leg threw him to ground, locked him in with one hand and wailed away with the other. He got in three solid punches for each blow from Chuck, and the blood started flowing within seconds. Chuck raised his hands in surrender and Peg Leg backed off.

115   "OK, man, you win," Chuck said, smiling as blood gushed out of his nose.

116   By the time the dust had settled, Leg and Chuck were back on the wall chumming it up.

117   "Just had to lay down some ground rules," Leg explained. "We have rules out here, man."

Caged Dog

118   Dog complained to the guards as he emerged from the shouting voices and dark corridors of the New Hanover County Jail.

119   "You gotta do something about Cellblock D," he told the deputies.

120   "Shouting and hollering all night, I didn't get a wink in," he said. "Man. Uhmmm. They're animals in there. They're crazy."

121   Without $100 for bail, he spent three days in jail on a trespassing charge filed by Dodge's. It was crowded, so Dog had to sleep on the cement floor.

122   Word on the street was Dog had gotten drunk, yelled at some customers and didn't leave when store clerks asked him to. Dog said he wouldn't normally do something like that, but conceded he was too drunk to remember any details.

123   At midnight, he was just minutes from freedom. The jail clock was fifteen minutes slow, assuring Road Dog paid back his debt to society with a little interest.

124   He entered a Plexiglas purgatory between the cells and the waiting room.

125   There he traded an orange jumpsuit for a pair of still-damp cutoff jeans and a T-shirt. After Dog signed a release form, the deputy gave him his Jansport backpack and a manila envelope with personal items—two knives, some loose change, and a $5 bill.

126   "It's easier getting in than getting out, that's for sure," he said of the paperwork.

127   Light-footed but jittery, Road Dog took a deep breath, threw his backpack to the pavement, and rummaged for cigarettes, but they were too wet to light.

128   He was shaking.

That meant a must stop at the nearest twenty-four-hour convenience store to re-store his equilibrium.   **129**

Within ten minutes of getting out he had the first tastes of freedom—a pack of smokes and a Cobra forty-ouncer.   **130**

Back at the wall, Peg Leg was hanging out with the regular Dodge's crowd.   **131**

Dog wanted to join in but was apprehensive about returning to the scene of crime. He hovered on the other side of Market Street as the well-lubricated crowd yelled for him to come over.   **132**

Peg Leg was shouting out what a stupid drunk he was but still urging him to come back.   **133**

Dog approached timidly, his backpack slung to one side.   **134**

Jimi, a longtime friend who has done some street time with Road Dog, jumped up and gave his old buddy a big bear hug, lifting him off his feet slightly as he arched backward.   **135**

Peg Leg remained scornful. "You were yelling at customers like a damned fool," he said.   **136**

Then, abruptly, he hopped up and ambled over to his buddy.   **137**

"Give me a hug, Dog," Peg Leg said.   **138**

They embraced briefly and soon Leg's apprehension gave way to a smile.   **139**

He was back on the wall, trading stories about Road Dog and their own brushes with the law.   **140**

Jimi told of the time he slit his wrists, then showed the scrapes of rock bottom. He remembered how Dog rescued him from the woods and got him treatment.   **141**

"Dog's good people," he said. "He helps me, I help him. I love this man."   **142**

Peg Leg chimed in. "Ain't nobody gonna mess with Dog as long as I'm around," he said.   **143**

The Split

Two weeks passed, and Dog was recovering from another trip to the hospital.   **144**

His skull had another stamp—Peg Leg's fist.   **145**

Peg Leg said Road Dog had been drinking too much and needed "some fixing." Road Dog said Peg Leg was constantly hassling him, and the latest fight was the last straw.   **146**

He moved out of the hooch, back to his old camp, and pitched a brand new Spaulding tent given to him by a friend.   **147**

The split soon had a monetary figure: $18.32.   **148**

That was the cost of two new tires to replace the ones Dog slashed on Peg Leg's bike.   **149**

"It's nothing compared to the pain I went through," Dog said.   **150**

Peg Leg said he yelled out the debt figure to Dog one day, but his former friend just biked by and ignored him.   **151**

Other than a tooth that fell out when he bit into a ham, Road Dog said he's done all right since leaving the hooch.   **152**

The two kept tabs on each other through friends, but never hung out together.   **153**

By October, a hotel worker who heard Peg Leg's tire-slashing story shelled out the $18.32.   **154**

"You can tell Dog he's settled up," Leg said.   **155**

Peg Leg said he's glad to get rid of Road Dog, though he's reminded of his old buddy some mornings.   **156**

"Those . . . birds start hooting and hollering," he said. "They won't shut up until I throw 'em some bread."   **157**

The Fire Inside

158 *"Structure fully involved. (Unit) 695 extinguished."*

159   That was the Ogden Volunteer Fire Department's brief footnote to a blaze that engulfed the hooch Friday, November 13.

160   Peg Leg lost everything.

161   His charred bike frame was one of the few discernable items on the blackened earth. Charcoaled beams and a twisted pile of metal roofing marked what once was the hooch.

162   The afternoon fire claimed new chairs picked up in Raleigh and sections of blue tarp he had just installed to seal the walls for the winter.

163   Not missing the irony of a homeless man losing his home, Peg Leg kept his head up after the blaze.

164   "It's like getting a divorce," he said. "You start all over."

165   Peg Leg suspects another homeless man, a rival on the streets, torched the hooch.

166   A newfound job has softened the blow, however.

167   He has been bouncing between Wilmington and Raleigh with a roofing company he latched onto after Hurricane Bonnie.

168   "It feels good to work again, man," he said, cleanly shaven and flush with cash. "It feels real good."

169   He works twelve-hour shifts, toting ninety-pound shingle bundles up ladders and hammering them into place.

170   A co-worker is letting him stay at his house in Wilmington, but Peg Leg has spent much of November and December near Raleigh, where his boss has a trailer for employees.

171   On one rare day off from work, Peg Leg had a letter from his mother—whom he visited for the first time in years in the spring—tucked into his back pocket. He exchanges letters with her, his children, and old Vietnam buddies through a general mailbox at the Gateway church.

172   In high spirits, Peg Leg was abuzz with the news that his mother has a 1-800 number.

173   "Can you believe that . . . ?" he said. "Mama's got a hotline."

Down Time

174 It was the first fall-like day in October, and Road Dog had gotten a $14 haircut.

175   He saved up some money—his sign says "Homeless. Can You Help? God Bless You"—to help launch his new life in an isolated patch of woods on the other side of town.

176   "Not all my money goes to the drink," he said proudly, showing off his blue-green bike, some black corduroys, and a Paul Bunyan snap-button shirt.

177   A yellow plastic light-up toy that reads "BOO!" serves as a tail light just below the seat of the $90 Palisade.

178   "A boy in the park was checking it out the other day," he said. "He really got a kick out of it."

179   Road Dog had a lingering shiner—"I don't want to talk about it," he said—but said he had been drinking less.

180   His spirits were high as he walked his bike over a mat of pine needles to his freshly laid tent.

181   "Every man is like a lion. He needs his space."

182   "Space" for Road Dog is some time away from his friends on the street.

183   "I wanted to see what they were about," he said. "I took a chance. And what do I get? Beat up and run over."

Road Dog is looking forward to the winter. "I'm a woodsman," he said, breathing in the autumn air. "I think I made a wise choice coming out here. I've got some peace and tranquility."   184

Bobcats are his only companions.   185

"The bobcats won't leave me alone," he said of the animals that have gathered around his tent in the wee hours and howled.   186

"They sound so evil," he said. "It sounds like something from hell."   187

"These little critters, man, I'll tell you what. Uhhmm."   188

Pensive as always, Road Dog said he's worried that orange markers on trees signal coming development in the land leading from a nearby creek bed. He often laments the disappearance of green spaces in Wilmington.   189

"People think I'm crazy 'cause I live in the woods," he said. "My God, the Indians did it. I'm with nature. Everything I burn is already dead. I don't kill nothing but a couple spiders and yellowjackets. Let's turn the tables and see who's crazy."   190

A Home

It was the week of Christmas, and Road Dog was down on his luck.   191

A pizza delivery-car sideswiped him while he was riding his Palisade down Market Street. Days later, the bike was stolen when he parked it temporarily in front of a store.   192

Police gave Road Dog a warning for holding up traffic with his sign, and he was having trouble getting enough money to pay for food, particularly now that he avoids dumpster-diving. He got sick off food from a trash bin in September and has been wary of it ever since.   193

"I'm fed up," he said. "They should go find some real criminals."   194

Christmas Comes for Cyclops

Road Dog was seated at a picnic table at Hugh MacRae Park, listening to Christmas songs and country music on a transistor radio propped up on a beam. He hadn't slept all night and was sipping a beer in the abnormal December heat.   195

Using a knot in the wooden table as an eye, he had drawn Cyclops—the craven, one-eyed giant in Homer's Odyssey.   196

In an eighth-grade play, Road Dog played Cyclops.   197

"Ulysses tricked him," he said. "They got him drunk."   198

Road Dog paused for a while, with *White Christmas* blaring from the radio, and then completed his point: "A Cyclops with his eye poked out by Ulysses said, 'No man bothers me.' "   199

That morning, a driver speeding down College Road hit the curb and popped his tire.   200

"I told him, 'Look man, it's never too late to slow down,' " Road Dog said. "He said, 'OK, I hear you.' I have a lot on my mind right now. So does he."   201

Road Dog was talking more seriously about getting off the streets. He was planning to see his family—his mother, five sisters, and brother—in Illinois for the first time since Christmas 1995. Road Dog recalled last Christmas Eve, when he called his mother to wish her a merry Christmas.   202

"The first words out of my mother's mouth were, 'I was just going to bed,' " Road Dog said. "Can you believe that, to her son? I just hung up."   203

He planned to call her again Christmas Eve.   204

"I do still love Mama," he said. "She's had such tough times, and she's hard-headed like I am. Yeah, I'll call Mama."   205

Freewriting

Freewrite for ten to fifteen minutes about Peg Leg, Road Dog, and the other homeless people who congregate near Dodge's gas station and "The Hooch." You may write about anything you have learned or about any misconceptions that "On the Fringe" dispels. In particular, you might consider whether and how the people described in this article have adopted some of the characteristics and functions of a traditional family.

Group Work

Share freewrites within your reading group, having each member read aloud as others take notes. As you listen to each person read, jot down notes in two columns, listing positive and negative aspects of the relationships among Peg Leg, Road Dog, and the other homeless people described in "On the Fringe."

Review Questions

1. Why do Peg Leg and Road Dog refuse to seek out one of the homeless shelters that operate in their area?

2. How did Road Dog and Peg Leg become friends? What causes their estrangement?

3. How do Peg Leg and Road Dog maintain relationships with their families? How would you characterize those relationships?

Discussion Questions

1. What do you suppose are the attitudes of the author toward the individuals and the way of life he describes in "On the Fringe"? Are there any specific details in the text that reveal those attitudes? If not, what else might lead one to an impression of what those attitudes might be?

2. Given our knowledge about the backgrounds and circumstances of Peg Leg and Road Dog, is it fair, or even accurate, to refer to this reading as an article "about homelessness"? Is it logical to conclude that, because every individual is unique, no one can write an article about homeless people in the aggregate?

3. Newspaper articles are often called "stories," a term more commonly applied to fictional narratives that adhere to a familiar, conventional structure: a protagonist's struggle rises to a climax and is then resolved. What features of story structure appear in "On the Fringe"? (You might begin by looking for evidence of happy—or at least hopeful—endings in the sections titled "The Fire Inside" and "Christmas Comes for Cyclops.")

Writing

1. Since "On the Fringe" appeared in a local newspaper, it is more anecdotal and less analytical than articles in specialized journals or even news magazines

might be. Consult one or more of the following articles and write a brief comparison of the vocabulary, style, organization, and factual detail found in each source:

a. "Without a Home," by Dave and Melissa Guay, published in the May 1999 issue of *Parenting,* pages 86–91.

b. "Giuliani's Suppressed Report of Homeless Youth," by David Kihara, published in the August 24, 1999, issue of *Village Voice,* page 23.

c. "A Snapshot of Family Homelessness across America," by Ralph Nuñez and Cybelle Fox, published in the Summer 1999 issue of *Political Science Quarterly,* pages 289–97.

d. "Who Are 'the Homeless'? Reconsidering the Stability and Composition of the Homeless Population," by Jo C. Phelan and Bruce G. Link, published in the September 1999 issue of *American Journal of Public Health,* pages 1334–38.

2. Six months after "On the Fringe" was first published, the Veteran Affairs Committee of the U.S. House of Representatives conducted hearings to investigate homelessness among military veterans. Following is a short excerpt from the testimony of Cynthia A. Bascetta, Associate Director of Veterans Affairs and Military Health Care Issues:

Veterans constitute about one third of the adult homeless population in the United States on any given day. They form a heterogeneous group and are likely to have multiple needs. Many homeless veterans need treatment for medical or psychiatric conditions in addition to housing and other supportive services. Although many questions remain about how to treat homelessness, a series of research initiatives launched in 1982 and funded primarily by HHS suggests that effective interventions for the homeless involve comprehensive, integrated services. These initiatives also suggest that a range of housing, treatment, and supportive service options needs to be available to the homeless, and that flexibility is needed to appropriately match services to the individual needs of homeless people.

Although meeting the most basic needs of a homeless person for food, clothing, and shelter is a first step, it is rarely sufficient to enable a person to exit homelessness. Instead, progress in achieving housing stability requires comprehensive attention to the full range of a homeless person's needs. VA estimates that approximately one half of homeless veterans have a substance abuse problem, approximately one third have a serious mental illness (and of those, about half also have a substance abuse problem), and many have other medical problems. Some homeless veterans need assistance in obtaining benefits, managing their finances, resolving legal matters, developing work skills, or obtaining employment. Supportive services such as transportation or child care may also be needed. Problems in any of these areas can interfere with progress. . . .

Experts suggest that in terms of housing, the goal of homeless assistance programs should be stable residence in a setting that allows the highest level of independence each person can achieve. For some homeless veterans, independent housing and economic self-support are reasonable goals. But for others, including many seriously mentally ill homeless people, neither full-time work nor independent housing may be feasible. Instead, for these individuals, residence in a supportive environment, such as a group home, may be the most reasonable outcome. In addition, transitional housing may be necessary before a more permanent housing arrangement can be achieved. Thus, efforts to assist the homeless require a range of housing options (including emergency shelter as well as transitional and permanent housing); treatment for medical, mental health, and substance abuse problems; and supportive services such as transportation and case management. This spectrum of options is referred to as the continuum of care.

VA provides key services to homeless veterans through its mainstream health care programs. In addition, VA has established several programs specifically targeted to homeless veterans, providing veterans at some VA facilities services such as case management, work rehabilitation, or residential treatment for mental illness or substance abuse. Because it does not have sufficient resources to address all the needs of homeless veterans, VA has expanded its partnerships with community based providers. Thus, VA is working with other agencies to identify and prioritize gaps in service availability and to develop strategies for meeting those needs; that is, to develop a continuum of care for homeless veterans.

Citing details from "On the Fringe" and from Ms. Bascetta's testimony, write an essay arguing either that governmental programs offer a fair and reasonable safety net for homeless veterans like Peg Leg or that those programs are inadequate and out of touch with the needs of individuals.

4 *Reading for the Main Idea*

The reading strategies discussed in Chapter 2 have many purposes, one of the most important being to help you see, quickly and clearly, what the writer is getting at. Good readers always have one question before them as they read: What is this about? Or, in other words, what is the ***main idea*** of the passage? Being able to recognize, understand, and restate the main idea of a passage is a valuable skill that you will use in carrying out a variety of academic tasks, including library research.

Defining *main ideas* as a concept is not as easy as it may sound. Chapter 2 demonstrated how active readers *create meaning* when they experience a written text. Because people carry into their reading different backgrounds and personal histories, it seems improbable that any two readers will experience a long or complicated piece of writing (the novel *Moby Dick,* for example) in precisely the same fashion. In an effort to account for this diversity, one modern philosopher has declared that "every reading is a misreading." In the face of such views, you may ask how it is possible to determine anything like the main idea of a reading.

There is no easy answer to that question. However, it seems safe to say that the meaning of a written text does not belong entirely to the writer; nor does it belong entirely to the reader. Instead, the two, acting in collaboration, negotiate meaning. At least that's how reading operates under ideal circumstances. But in order for the processes of negotiation to work smoothly and predictably, both writer and reader must recognize and abide by certain established conventions. When you tried reading a passage in Chapter 2 that defied one of those conventions—it lacked an informative title—the collaboration between you and the writer broke down.

Basically, writers plant clues and signals, and readers respond to them in predictable and relatively uniform ways. This chapter focuses on some of these conventions. Your familiarity with them should help you hold up your end of the transaction between writer and reader.

GENERAL AND SPECIFIC STATEMENTS

If the main idea of any piece of writing were stated in a sentence, that sentence would be a ***general*** statement, much broader than the other sentences in the text, which are more ***specific.*** The difference between general and specific statements is an important one for readers to grasp. It can be demonstrated briefly with a few examples. Here are some words and phrases listed in order from the most general to the most specific:

most general   things
                        life forms
                        animals
                        mammals
                        humans
                        students
                        first-year students
                        members of Professor Filbert's comp class
most specific   Chip Holzclaw

Each term in the list is more specific, and therefore less general, than the one before it. As a category, each includes fewer members. The first term includes everything (every *thing*) in the universe, while the last includes only one single individual. Chip belongs to each category; his dog Jack belongs just to the first four; and Jack's flea collar is a member only of the most general category, things.

Some statements can also be arranged in order from most general to most specific:

- Some people have qualities not shared by everyone.
- Jo Ann has many exceptional traits.
- Most notable is her superhuman will power.
- She can stick to her diet no matter how great the temptation.
- Last week when I offered her a hot fudge sundae topped with real whipped cream for dessert, Jo Ann turned it down and ate half an apple instead.

Again, each statement is a more specific instance of the statement before it. Each bears a *for example* relationship to the one it follows, and the examples cover less and less territory. The last one is a very specific and **concrete** statement, one that presents a picture that you can visualize in your imagination—here describing a specific event at a specific time involving specific people. In contrast, the first one is a very general and **abstract** statement, one that calls up an idea but not any particular event that you can see with your mind's eye. Being aware of the difference between general, abstract statements and specific, concrete ones is essential for readers.

EXERCISES   ## General and Specific Categories

1. Arrange the following lists in order from the most general to the most specific:
    a. loafer
       foot covering
       casual shoe
       entity

 Mr. MacLennan's right shoe
 garment
 product
 shoe

b. The College of Arts and Sciences
 higher education
 Natural History of Intertidal Organisms 553
 The Marine Biology Option
 State University
 Department of Biology
 school
 Division of Physical Sciences

c. Mrs. Drumble lacks concern for her fellow creatures.
 Mrs. Drumble cuts off the tails of blind mice with a carving knife.
 Mrs. Drumble tortures rodents.
 Mrs. Drumble is a heartless person.
 Mrs. Drumble is cruel to animals.

d. Words can affect their hearers.
 Patrick Henry aroused sentiment for independence with his cry, "Give me
  liberty or give me death."
 Political oratory can be particularly stirring.
 Some statements provoke people's emotions.

2. For each of these items, supply two others: one that is more general and another that is more specific.
 a. chair
 b. circus performer
 c. Bert loves Felicia.
 d. Parents often urge their teenage children to do well in school.

 ## DEDUCTIVE AND INDUCTIVE ORGANIZATION

Within any passage, some statements are more general than others. Often the way
an author arranges general and specific statements is important. Notice, for example, that the sample passage on page 62–63, which you examined in Chapter 2,
contains four levels of generality. Here we have numbered those levels from 1 (the
most general) to 4 (the most specific) and arranged the sentences on the page with
more specific levels indented farther to the right:

 1 Scarfe was always a tyrant in his household.
  2 The servants lived in constant terror of his fierce diatribes, which he
   would deliver whenever he was displeased.
   3 One of the most frequent causes of his displeasure was the food
    they served him.
    4 His tea, for example, was either too hot or too cold.
    4 The soup had either too much or too little seasoning.

> 3   Another pet peeve was the servants' manner of address.
>> 4   God help the butler who forgot to add "sir" to every sentence he spoke to Scarfe, or the chauffeur whose tone was deemed not properly deferential.
>> 4   On the other hand, when one of the more timid parlor maids would hesitate in speaking so as to be certain her words did not give offense, he would thunder at her, "Out with it, you stupid girl!"
> 2   Scarfe's wife and children were equally the victims of his tyranny.

Notice that the most general sentence, at level 1, states the main idea of the entire passage—that Scarfe was a tyrant in his household. The two sentences at level 2 give examples of his tyranny. In the same way, sentences at level 3 present examples of statements made at level 2, and level-4 statements are examples of what is said at level 3. For the most part, then, sentences in the passage are arranged in a general-to-specific sequence.

Unlike the Scarfe passage, the explanatory paragraph you just read ("Notice that . . . ") is arranged in a specific-to-general order. Its first three sentences make specific statements, and then the last sentence sums them up in a general conclusion.

In general-to-specific, or *deductive,* passages, the writer first states the main idea in a general way and then demonstrates it with specific examples or explanations. In specific-to-general, or *inductive,* passages, the writer takes you through a sequence of discovery, with the main idea coming as a conclusion reached after the specific evidence has been presented.

Deductive arrangements are far more common than the reverse order, but probably few passages that you meet will be as neatly organized or as multileveled as the Scarfe example.

EXERCISES | ## Deductive and Inductive Passages

1. Decide whether each of the following passages is arranged in a deductive (general-to-specific) or inductive (specific-to-general) order.

   a. I need a woman who understands my obsessions and self-destructive tendencies; a woman who is smart and witty and self-reliant, who will indulge my taste in strange music and war movies, who can put up with my overbearing personality and my random acts of thoughtlessness and occasional petty cruelties, who will love me in spite of it all. And who will let me love her back for all her own idiosyncrasies and faults. I need Emma.
   —Clay Marshall, "Carnal Knowledge"

   b. The theme park is a metaphor for life. You wait and wait for those few moments when something actually happens. And some of those things, like some of the rides, are better than others. Sometimes it's pleasant, sometime's it's scary. Some things disappoint you. Other things make you giddy. And some things you just stand around and gawk at. But for the most part, you just hang out, waiting.
   —Jim Shahin, "Having Fun Yet?"

c. The seasonal beauty of a blueberry farm is wonderful. The red-leafed bushes of the fall by spring turn to shiny green, spattered with millions of pretty, little white flowers that give way in summer to heavy clusters of the tasty fruit. Yet every season brings a new phase of backbreaking, demanding work. Fall starts with the cultivation of the land between the rows by mowing and then fertilizing the bushes. In fall and winter there's the continual and necessary pruning process. In spring there's more fertilization and hand-herbiciding, and two colonies of bees (about forty thousand bees) per acre are brought in to pollinate the blossoms.
—Rebecca Gray, "Blue Heaven"

d. Walk into Gael Grande's math class and students are surrounded by their own eye-popping art work, designed using advanced mathematical principles that would stump many college grads. Next door, fourteen-year-old student Lynn Lee holds intricate, hand-built dioramas as she describes the role Martin Luther played in history, then fields a batch of theological questions from classmates. Over in Kailim Toy's history class, students are heatedly comparing Quebec's attempt to secede from Canada in 1995 to the South's desire to separate from the North during the Civil War. Home to some of the city's biggest student brains, the seven-year-old magnet center is a special school within a school located on North Hollywood High School's sprawling campus.
—Los Angeles Daily News

2. This paragraph from a student paper has sentences on several different levels of generality, but the pattern of arrangement is mixed. Discuss its use and arrangement of specific and general statements.

Outside pressures are often the cause of early marriages. Tom and Emily have been dating since junior high. She wears his class ring, and each of them is rarely seen without the other. They are such a familiar item that friends expect them to get married and talk of it openly. These expectations from their peers constitute an unspoken but real pressure on them to marry. They are also faced with pressure from their parents. Tom's mother is a close friend of Emily's, and they often discuss the wedding as if it were a certainty. Emily's parents have dropped several hints about her moving out of the house and of "making us grandparents." As a result of these pressures from peers and parents, Tom and Emily have announced their engagement to be married next June.

3. As was done with the Scarfe passage on pages 119–20, number the sentences in each of the previous passages to represent their levels of generality.

4. Write another version of the second paragraph of the Scarfe passage. Begin with the final sentence ("Scarfe's wife and children . . . "), and invent details for your sentences as needed. Make the sentences in your paragraph follow this organization for levels of generality: 2, 3, 4, 4, 3, 4, 4.

 THESIS STATEMENTS AND TOPIC SENTENCES

Sometimes, as several examples have demonstrated, writers condense the main idea of a passage into a single sentence. When one sentence states the main idea for an entire essay (or for any longer passage, such as a research paper or a book chapter), it is called a ***thesis statement.*** When a statement within an individual paragraph states its main idea, it is called a ***topic sentence.***

Identifying Topic Sentences

Not every paragraph you encounter in your daily reading will have a topic sentence (in fact, fewer than half of them will), just as not every longer passage will have an explicit thesis statement. When topic sentences and thesis statements do occur, however, they are among the most valuable reading clues; they help you see the writer's intentions and anticipate what is to follow. It pays to attend to them. Since a deductive arrangement is much more common than an inductive one, topic sentences appear most frequently at the beginnings of paragraphs, introducing and preparing for the supporting sentences that follow. Less often, they come after some preliminary statements, summing up or drawing conclusions from them. As you read the following paragraphs, see if you can identify their topic sentences.

> The effect of an ice age is dramatic. It does not just ice up the poles but drops temperatures everywhere around the world by about ten degrees centigrade. The world's wildlife gets squeezed into a band near the equator and even here life is hardly comfortable. The vast polar ice packs lock up a lot of the earth's water, disrupting rainfall and turning previously lush tropical areas into drought-stricken deserts.
> —John McCrone, *The Ape That Spoke*

> In the Medieval Glass of Canterbury Cathedral, an angel appears to the sleeping wise men and warns them to go straight home, and not return to Herod. Below, the corresponding event from the Old Testament teaches the faithful that each moment of Jesus's life replays a piece of the past and that God has put meaning into time—Lot turns round and his wife becomes a pillar of salt (the white glass forming a striking contrast with the glittering colors that surround her). The common theme of both incidents: don't look back.
> —Stephen Jay Gould, *The Flamingo's Smile*

The first paragraph opens with a topic sentence that is perfectly straightforward: *The effect of an ice age is dramatic.* Such a sentence is an aid to reading, since it signals what will follow: specific examples that illustrate the topic sentence—in this case, three dramatic consequences of an ice age. The second paragraph is arranged inductively and provides no such clues at the beginning. Its author begins with specific evidence: He describes the stained-glass depiction of two Biblical episodes. A topic sentence is presented as the final sentence, which draws a general conclusion from the evidence: the two scenes illustrate the same theme.

EXERCISE | ## Topic Sentences

1. Identify the topic sentences in each of the sample paragraphs in Exercise 1 on pages 120–21.

2. Identify the topic sentence in each of these passages:

a. Edward Bulwer, Baron of Lytton, wrote many memorable lines. You know the expression, "The chickens have come home to roost"? Bulwer coined it, though, being an honest man, he gave the Arabs credit. "The pen is mightier than the sword"? That's right: Bulwer wrote it. In fact, the expression is somewhat misused. Bulwer qualified it by saying, "Beneath the rule of men entirely great, the pen is mightier than the sword." The savvy baron knew full well that the pen occasionally loses. "There is no such word as 'fail' "? Bulwer again.
—George Canizares, "It Was a Dark and Stormy Night"

b. On the last night I sit up on the top deck 'til sunrise. The sea is like wet slate—multifaceted like a prehistoric arrowhead but constantly moving. The only light is in the fish-gutting area from where I can see a white slick of sea birds trailing back a quarter of a mile, feasting on guts. I understand what John Boy means when he said he could never go back to a normal life after this. It would be like returning to civil society after a war. When the sun comes up it is just the tiniest shade of colour on a background of more slate, like a faded Elastoplast on the sky. Every pore of my skin stinks of fish guts. This boat is a shithole in the midst of vast splendour.
—Martin Deeson, "Fishin' Impossible"

c. Think of the sarcastic use of the phrase "quote-unquote": "the mayor's quote-unquote dedication to duty" means the speaker doesn't think the mayor is very dedicated. . . . Or think of its gestural equivalent, the "air quote," or, in [Professor Marjorie] Garber's words, the "Happy Talk finger dance." These gestures often suggest "a certain attitude—often of wry skepticism—about the authority of both the quotation and the quotee," she writes. Some users call them "scare quotes," she says, suggesting Jacques Derrida's idea that the words quoted are "under erasure" or somehow deficient.
—Sarah Boxer, "In Fine Print, Punctuation to Puncture Pedants with"

 ## RESTATING THE MAIN IDEA

Identifying topic sentences is more than a mere exercise. It is important that you remember the point of what you have been doing. Good reading means recognizing what the writer is getting at; that includes seeing and understanding the main idea. When a topic sentence states the main idea very neatly for you, it is a valuable help. Sometimes, however, topic sentences are not as straightforward as they are in the preceding examples. Read the following paragraphs, keeping a lookout for each writer's main idea:

> Our files show that most men are unhappy with the state of their bodies. They would prefer to have the kind of torso that provokes ooohs and aahs from admiring women. They would like to have bulging biceps that will win the respect and envy of other men. They are seeking the feeling of pride and confidence that comes from possessing a truly well-developed physique. They want the kind of body that any man can build by subscribing to the Jack Harrigan Dyna-Fit Program.
> —An imagined magazine advertisement

Almost everyone has hitherto taken it for granted that Australopitheca [our female hominid ancestor who lived more than a million years ago], since she was primitive and chinless and lowbrowed, was necessarily hairy, and the artists always depict her as a shaggy creature. I don't think there is any reason for thinking this. Just as for a long time they "assumed" the big brain came first, before the use of tools, so they still "assume" that hairlessness came last. If I had to visualize the Villafranchian hominids, I'd say their skin was in all probability quite as smooth as our own.

—Elaine Morgan, *The Descent of Woman*

In the paragraph from the body-building ad, you might question whether the first or the last sentence should be called the topic sentence. A case can be made for either. The first sentence is a general statement, contending that most men are dissatisfied with their physiques. The remaining four sentences then restate that contention more specifically. On the other hand, the writer's main idea is not just to state this dissatisfaction but to imply a conclusion from it, namely that men (more specifically, the readers) should want to spend their money on the company's fitness program. Perhaps, then, the last sentence is more appropriately viewed as the topic sentence. Actually, since the main idea of the whole paragraph combines information from the first and last sentences, together with what you infer about the author's intentions, you could state the main idea in a concise general statement of your own: *Men who wish to improve their physiques should invest in the Harrigan Dyna-Fit Program.*

A similar question about the topic sentence arises with the paragraph about Australopitheca. Here the author's main idea is stated twice—first in the short second sentence and then again more concretely in the final sentence. But neither sentence expresses the entire idea of the paragraph, and so once again you could formulate your own statement of its main idea, perhaps like this: *Despite most people's assumption to the contrary, Australopitheca was probably no hairier than modern woman.*

Paragraphs with Implied Main Ideas

Many paragraphs have no explicit topic sentence. Often it is because they deal with several different ideas joined together for convenience, as in this example:

The first Mormon community was at Kirkland, Ohio, but in order to approach the Lost Tribes, it moved to a spot on the east bank of the Mississippi which the Prophet named Nauvoo. At first the Mormons were welcomed in Illinois, courted by both political parties, and given a charter that made Nauvoo practically an autonomous theocracy. The settlement grew rapidly—even faster than Chicago. It was at Nauvoo that Joseph Smith received the "revelation" sanctioning polygamy, which he and the inner circle of "elders" were already practicing. Although supported by Isaiah iv. 1, "And in that day seven women shall take hold of one man," this revelation split the church. The monogamous "schismatics" started a paper at Nauvoo; Smith caused the press to be broken up after the first issue; he and his brother were then arrested by the authorities for destruction of property and lodged in the county jail, whence they were pulled out by a mob and lynched. Brigham Young, who succeeded to the mantle of the Prophet, and to five of his 27 widows, directed retaliation, and for two years terror reigned in western Illinois. The Mormons were a virile, fighting people, but the

time had come for them to make another move, before they were hopelessly outnumbered.
—Samuel Eliot Morison and Henry Steele Commager, *Growth of the American Republic*

This paragraph narrates a series of events in the early history of the Mormon church, but no one sentence summarizes all of them.

Sometimes a single-topic paragraph does not need a topic sentence because the main idea can be easily inferred from the context. Here is an example of such a paragraph without a topic sentence:

> Thin soup served in a soup plate is eaten from the side of the spoon, dipped into the liquid away from you. Thick soup may be eaten from the tip and dipped toward you. Soup served in bouillon cups is usually sipped (silently) from the spoon until cool and then drunk—using one handle or both. Eat boneless and skinless fish with a fork, but to remove skin or bones it is necessary to use a knife. According to the best modern practice, you may cut a piece of meat and lift it at once on the fork in the left hand to the mouth while holding the knife in the right.
> —*Britannica Junior* (1956), "Etiquette"

If the authors had wanted to introduce this paragraph with a topic sentence, they would have written something like this: *Polite people follow certain rules of table etiquette when they eat.* But since the preceding paragraphs had described other examples of table manners, they felt that no topic sentence was needed here. Many times, however, topic sentences are useful. One of the mistakes often made by inexperienced writers is to omit such sentences when they would aid the reader.

Restating the Main Idea   EXERCISES

1. Being able to label a topic sentence when one occurs in a passage is useful, but the really important thing is to recognize the main idea of the passage. Remember that the two will not always coincide.

    For each of the following paragraphs, try first to identify a topic sentence. If no one sentence adequately states the author's main idea, write your own one-sentence statement of that idea. Then consider whether the readability of the passage would have been improved if the author had used your topic sentence. If so, should it go at the beginning, middle, or end of the passage?

    a. Inside Chicago's top-ranked Whitney Young High School, the posters started appearing last December. LET'S BE #1! GIVE IT 110%! Usually this sort of rah-rah propaganda supports the basketball team, but this campaign by the principal had a different aim: urging kids to score high on the Illinois Goal Assessment Program, a standardized test that students take in February. Tests are nothing new to the kids at Whitney Young—they already take three other batteries of standardized exams each year. But for a group of high-achieving eleventh graders, the pressure was just too much. These kids say real learning is being shoved aside as teachers focus on boosting test scores. Creative writing? Forget it. Instead, they say, teachers emphasize a boilerplate essay format that exam scorers prefer. So on February 2,

eight juniors purposely failed the social-studies portion of the test. The next day ten failed the science test. Then they sent a letter to the principal: "We refuse to feed into this test-taking frenzy."
—Daniel McGinn, "The Big Score"

b. There's a wall of honor at Frank W. Ballou Senior High, in Washington, D.C. Strange thing, though, nobody wants his name on it. The wall was intended to boost morale among the few students who were thriving in the violent, inner-city school. Unfortunately, anybody whose name shows up there runs a risk of getting beaten up. So Ballou's principal embarks on an even more ill-advised campaign. He offers rewards to students who get A's, holding assemblies and presenting $100 checks with much pomp in front of a jeering student body. . . . The principal is announcing the name of another winner, Cedric Jennings. No one answers. Cedric's a smart, proud kid, and at the moment he's hiding in a chem lab.
—Jeff Giles, "Inner City to Ivy League"

2. Suppose that the paragraph in part b in the preceding exercise had been connected to the paragraph in part a with this transitional sentence: "The scene at Frank W. Ballou High School in Washington, D.C., is a very different one." Try to compose a topic sentence that would summarize this longer paragraph.

3. In the following passages, topic sentences have been replaced by ellipses (. . .). Using context to discover the main idea of each passage, try to guess what the author's topic sentence might have been.

a. . . . Even before she tasted the hard-knock life of children's talent shows, [Britney] Spears was preparing for greatness. From age two she would hog the family bathroom, singing passionately into a hairbrush. "I was in my own world," she says. She made her stage debut at five, singing "What Child Is This" at her kindergarten graduation. "I found out what I'm supposed to do at an early age," she explains.
—Steven Daly, "Britney Spears"

b. Professor Fangle permitted Bushrod to enroll in his American literature class after the published deadline for adding courses—with the strict understanding that he would make up the work that other students had already completed. By the end of September, Bushrod still had not submitted any of this work. At the urging of his instructor, he scheduled an office conference to discuss the assignments and to agree upon a reasonable deadline for submitting them. However, he did not keep his appointment. By fall break, Bushrod had accumulated six more absences and failed three daily quizzes. Explaining that his return flight from Bermuda had been delayed, he was absent from class the day after fall break and thereby missed an opportunity to review material covered on the midterm examination, which he subsequently failed. At this point, Professor Fangle offered Bushrod the option of withdrawing from the course without a failing grade, but he rejected the offer indignantly. Although he submitted two analytical essays assigned during the second half of the semester, both were late. One of the essays dealt with an eighteenth-century French play, and the second plagiarized an article about Edgar Allan Poe published in a well-known literary journal. Confronted with this evidence, Bushrod became verbally abusive and threatened to assault his instructor physically. He refused to leave Professor Fangle's office until escorted away by the campus police. . . .
—Report from the chair of a grade-appeal committee to the dean of students

4. Like an inductive paragraph, which ends by stating a conclusion, many scientific experiments can be called inductive, in that they lead to a discovery. So too the following could be called an inductive exercise, which asks you to draw conclusions from your discoveries.

a. In books, magazines, or other texts, find one example of a paragraph that begins with a topic sentence and another of a paragraph that ends with a topic sentence. Transcribe (or photocopy) them both and bring them to class.

b. Examine an example of each of the following:
   - college-level textbook
   - novel
   - biography (book or essay about a person)
   - newspaper article
   - magazine article

   From each, select ten paragraphs at random and see how many (1) begin with a topic sentence, (2) end with a topic sentence, (3) have a topic sentence placed elsewhere, (4) have an implied topic sentence, or (5) have no unifying concept at all.

c. Now draw conclusions from your experiment: How easy was it to find topic sentences? When they occur, where are topic sentences more likely to be placed? Are certain types of writing more likely than others to make use of topic sentences? If so, why do you think that is? Are there any general conclusions that you can now draw about how writers use paragraphs?

Discovering Implications

As the preceding section demonstrated, in many paragraphs a topic sentence is implied rather than explicitly stated. Discovering the main idea is a task left for the alert reader. But it is only one of many such tasks. Writers leave many gaps in the meaning they intend to communicate, and they expect their readers to fill them in.

Even in everyday conversation, we do not always put everything that we mean into words. Consider, for example, the *implication,* the unspoken but intended meaning, in the following conversation between two students:

Aaron: I signed up for Professor Phrisby's Organic Chemistry class.

Caitlin: I hope you've got a large supply of caffeine tablets.

Without saying it in so many words, Caitlin is implying that Professor Phrisby's course is difficult and requires much studying into the late hours. For Aaron to understand her meaning, he must make connections, relying on his past experience with college life and with how people use language. A less sophisticated listener, such as an eight-year-old, might not be able to bridge the gap between what Caitlin says and what she actually means.

Being a sophisticated listener or reader demands skill at drawing inferences.* Not everyone will derive the same meaning in each circumstance. Sometimes the gaps in our messages are open to more than one interpretation. In the preceding

---

*The words *imply* and *infer* are often confused. A speaker like Caitlin who communicates an idea without stating it explicitly is *implying* an unspoken meaning. A listener like Aaron who understands the implication is *inferring* meaning. In other words, speakers imply and listeners infer.

example, Aaron was probably already aware of the reputation of Professor Phrisby's course and understood exactly what Caitlin meant. But someone else overhearing Caitlin's response might draw a different conclusion, inferring perhaps that Professor Phrisby's classes are boring and students have difficulty staying awake. Success in communication depends upon knowing your audience and adapting your message to allow them to draw the inferences you intend.

Writers rely on implication just as speakers do. Consider the following paragraph, taken from an essay about the bizarre treatment its author often receives as a result of his blindness:

> For example, when I go to the airport and ask the ticket agent for assistance to the plane, he or she will invariably pick up the phone, call a ground hostess and whisper: "Hi, Jane, we've got a 76 here." I have concluded that the word "blind" is not used for one of two reasons: Either they fear that if the dread word is spoken, the ticket agent's retina will immediately detach, or they are reluctant to inform me of my condition of which I may not have been previously aware.
> —Harold Krents, "Darkness at Noon"

The writer leaves it for us to infer from the passage that a "76" is an airline code for a blind passenger. He also assumes we will infer that the ticket agents whisper into the phone because they do not want people in the vicinity, including Krents himself, to hear their words. Earlier in the essay, Krents had written, "There are those who assume that since I can't see, I obviously also cannot hear." Having read that, a reader might infer that the whispering agents mistakenly believe that Krents will neither hear nor understand their words. The final sentence of the paragraph demands even more sophistication from readers in drawing implications. Krents probably expects his readers to infer a meaning that might be spelled out like this:

> The agents don't really believe they will go blind if they say the word, and Krents isn't sincere when he suggests that they do. The agents also can't really believe that Krents doesn't know he is blind. But as silly as those conclusions are, the real reasons for the agents' behavior are even more foolish: They apparently think of blindness as a condition too embarrassing to be spoken of to a blind person. They aren't giving Krents credit for having come to terms with his blindness or for being able to notice that they are evading the topic. Worse, they aren't even able to realize that a blind person is a human being with the same capacities of hearing and thinking as everyone else.

You can easily see that the passage, with its unspoken implications, is far more effective than if Krents had spelled out everything he meant. By causing us to think for ourselves and to draw conclusions, Krents has enlisted us as partners with him in the creation of meaning. That sense of partnership makes us all the more receptive to his purposes for writing. After reading his paragraph, you may have drawn the following more general conclusion:

> Perhaps I, the reader (now that I see the agents' behavior as foolish), should give some thought to how I treat blind people or others with disabilities.

Drawing inferences is an important part of reading, and good readers are as alert to meaning that is implied as to that which is explicitly stated.

Implications

1. What might you infer from the following bits of overheard conversation?

    a. **Library patron:** Do you know where I can find a life-size globe?
        Librarian: The only one I know of is currently in use.

    b. **Desk clerk** (to a man carrying a cocktail from the hotel bar into the lobby): Excuse me, sir, you're in Virginia.

2. Though the words in each of the following passages state a clear and explicit meaning, they don't explain everything that was on the author's mind. What inferences can you draw as you read each passage?

    a. The second anniversary of Princess Diana's death came and went on August 31, and even Britain barely noticed. The mourning machine has been sputtering for months. Plans for a statue of the princess near Kensington Palace appear to have been scrapped. The museum at Althorp, her ancestral home, is no longer a hot ticket. And the market for Diana books has dried up. "We don't even stock all the books coming out," says a biography buyer. At last, it seems, Diana is gone.
        —*Newsweek*, "Goodbye, Di"

    b. We live in a great nation—among the Christmas catalogs is one especially for dog owners, full of dandy things you can get for Bowser or Fido. I was perusing the item about the "Gourmet Bone Basket"—"He'll jump for joy when he sees the handwoven, bone-shaped basket brimming with over two pounds of the most popular dog treats"—when what to my wondering eyes should appear but the item immediately underneath the Christmas gift basket for your dog. "Hanukkah Bowl with Treats," in case your dog is Jewish. "Say Mazel Tov to the dog in your life! Elegant, silver-plated eight-inch bowl is filled with hand-decorated, all natural peanut butter treats: six Star of David cookies and a Menorah bone, plus a furry ball squeak toy." Now that I think of it, the poodle has shown distinct symptoms of being Jewish for years: She's incredibly smart, has a mordant sense of humor, and loves bagels.
        —Molly Ivins, "www.mollybooks.yea!"

    c. It is perfectly acceptable to spend lots of money on anything that is "professional quality," even if it has nothing to do with your profession. For example, although you are not likely ever to climb Mount Everest, an expedition-weight three-layer Gore-Tex Alpenglow-reinforced Marmot Thunderlight jacket is a completely acceptable purchase. You may not be planning to convert your home into a restaurant, but a triple-doored Sub Zero refrigerator and a $10,000 AGA cooker with a warming plate, a simmering plate, a baking oven, a roasting oven, and an infinite supply of burners is still a sensible acquisition.
        —David Brooks, "Conscientious Consumption"

A FURTHER COMMENT ON PARAGRAPHS

We should repeat and reemphasize our earlier statement that most paragraphs that you encounter in reading do not have straightforward topic sentences. In actual practice, the paragraph is a far less structured unit of thought than is often claimed. Most writers, most of the time, do not think in terms of paragraphs as they compose. They develop ideas as they write, and they use the paragraph break as a form of punctuation, sometimes to signal the start of a new idea or a change in direction, at other times to provide emphasis for dramatic effect. At still other times, long topics are divided rather arbitrarily into several paragraphs to give the reader a sense of pausing and to make the writing appear less formidable.

Eye appeal is frequently a factor in paragraphing. Essays written in a sprawling handwriting are likely to have (and need) more paragraph breaks than will more compact-looking typewritten essays. Newspapers, with their narrow columns of type, prefer shorter paragraphs than those found in books. Psychologists have discovered that readers find material easier to read when it is divided into short to medium-length paragraphs than when it is presented in long paragraphs.

For all these reasons, no two writers create their paragraphs in exactly the same way. Given a passage (such as either of those featured in the following exercise) from which all paragraph breaks have been omitted, it is likely that any two professional authors or writing instructors chosen at random will disagree about where the breaks belong.

EXERCISES | **Supplying Paragraph Breaks**

1. Paragraph breaks have been removed from the following passages. Decide where you would put them and indicate your choices using the paragraph symbol (¶). Remember that there are different yet appropriate responses to this exercise.

    a. Computing support for students is diversified and widespread across the university campus. Eight general-access microcomputer labs are operated on campus. There are also a number of departmentally-operated computer labs offering specialized, discipline-specific hardware and software. The central computer operates under Open VMS and offers access to statistical packages, language compilers, and electronic mail. A Cray supercomputer, located at the North Carolina Supercomputer Center in Research Triangle Park, is accessible through the campus network for appropriate and approved instructional and research activities. The university has a high-speed fiber optic campus data network which provides access to the Internet, central servers, departmental LANs, and the Randall Library on-line catalog. Each year, greater emphasis is being placed by the faculty upon student utilization of computing facilities. Every department on campus uses computing in some aspect of its daily activities. Students are expected to assimilate computing skills as an integral part of their campus life. Each student is provided with an e-mail account. This account will remain active as long as the student is enrolled at the university. All students are expected to abide by the rules and policies governing appropriate use of computing resources and facilities as stated in the UNCW Computing Resource Use Policy. For more information about computing at UNCW, contact the Office of Information Technology Help Desk, and visit our World Wide Web site at http://www.uncwil.edu/oit.
        —*Undergraduate Catalog,* University of North Carolina at Wilmington

b. What is different about group generalizations based on race? Generalizations that discriminate against blacks have been outlawed for obvious historical reasons. But what about group generalizations that discriminate in favor of blacks? How are they different from the group generalizations that are the warp and woof of everyday life? The answer cannot be that they are different simply because race is innate and immutable. So, according to its enthusiasts, is I.Q.—yet opponents of affirmative action generally wish to see the role of such innate characteristics (if not I.Q., then "merit" or "talent") enhanced, not reduced. The answer must be that race is such a toxic subject in American culture that it should not enter into calculations about people's places in society—even in order to benefit racism's historic victims. That is a respectable answer. But it understandably rings hollow to many blacks, who see this sudden and ostentatious anathema on racial consciousness a bit too convenient. Where was color blindedness when they needed it?
—Michael Kinsley, "The Spoils of Victimhood"

2. Compare your responses to the first exercise with those of your classmates. Was there general agreement about the number of paragraph breaks you supplied? Did you agree with the authors of the two passages (who, as it happens, presented them as six paragraphs and one paragraph, respectively)? What conclusions might you draw from the exercise?

 READING SELECTION

The following article describes a hoax perpetrated by H. L. Mencken, a famous American journalist and satirical author. Fred Fedler, who wrote the article, lists Mencken's prank among a long series of "media hoaxes" that have occurred over a period of nearly three hundred years. Fedler cites three defining characteristics of media hoaxes:

First, [they] are usually created to entertain—not cheat—the public. Thus, the hoaxes are a form of practical joking, but on a grand scale. Journalists who create the hoaxes never think of themselves as liars or cheats, nor even as fakers. Unlike criminals, they rarely intend to defraud the public: to gain some unfair or dishonest advantage. The journalists only want to amuse people: to give them something to talk and laugh about.

Second, as a part of the fun, journalists often admit that their stories are fictitious. While writing the stories, journalists include clues that reveal they are fictitious. But most readers are so excited by the stories' other details that they fail to notice—or understand—the clues. A day or two later, the journalists often publish a second story admitting that it was all a hoax. The journalists may explain why they created the hoax—and brag about its success.

Third, hoaxes . . . are sometimes unintentional . . . but the public is more gullible than most people realize.

This third characteristic applies particularly to Mencken's prank: the story appealed so much to the public that many people stubbornly refused to accept the author's acknowledgment that it was only a joke.

An Enduring Hoax

H. L. Mencken's Fraudulent History of the White House Bathtub

FRED FEDLER

1   A charming tale about the White House bathtub has become America's most enduring hoax. A Baltimore journalist created the hoax in 1917 and confessed, three times, that it was nonsense. Despite his confessions, the hoax continues to appear in respected publications. President Truman repeated the hoax, and all three television networks broadcast it. Even respected historians quote and reprint it.

2   The hoax persists because it is such a whimsical tale. Its author, H. L. Mencken, created the hoax for the fun of it, to distract Americans from the horrors of World War I.

3   Mencken's father owned a cigar factory in Baltimore and expected him to take it over. Instead, Mencken applied for a job with the Baltimore *Morning Herald*. Because he was young and inexperienced, its editor refused to hire him. He suggested, however, that Mencken might return now and then to see whether there were any stories for him to cover.

4   Other editors gave similar advice to young men looking for newspaper jobs. Many of the young men never returned. Others returned once or twice, then became discouraged because they were never given anything to do. Mencken reappeared at 7:30 every night for a month. At the end of the month, the editor sent him to a neighboring suburb, and he returned with a story about a stolen buggy. After that, he was given more assignments, then hired at a salary of $7 a week.

5   By the age of twenty-five, Mencken was the newspaper's editor-in-chief. In 1906, the newspaper was sold, and he became editor of the Baltimore *Sunday Sun*. He also began to write a column for the paper, and other newspapers reprinted it. Thus he became a national celebrity.

6   The *Sun* stopped publishing Mencken's column during the First World War, apparently because he favored the Germans (rather than the English or French). A friend at the *New York Evening Mail* asked Mencken to write a column for that paper, but warned him to avoid topics related to the war. The friend wanted Mencken to amuse, not offend, his readers.

7   One of Mencken's new columns insisted that New York should withdraw from the United States. Another column insisted that poetry was wicked and immoral. Mencken explained that all the columns—his verbal fireworks—were intended "to inject a little lighthearted fun into rather grim war days."

8   Mencken's most famous hoax appeared in the *Evening Mail* on December 28, 1917. His column, titled that day "A Neglected Anniversary," began: "On December 20, there flitted past us, absolutely without public notice, one of the most important profane anniversaries in American history—to wit: the 75th anniversary of the introduction of the bathtub into these states. Not a plumber fired a salute or hung out a flag. Not a governor proclaimed a day of prayer. Not a newspaper called attention to the day."

9   [Menken went on to assert that] the day had not been entirely forgotten, however. Eight or nine months earlier, a young surgeon connected with the Public Health Service in Washington had discovered the facts while looking into the early history of public hygiene. At his suggestion, a committee was formed to hold a banquet celebrating the bathtub's 75th anniversary. Before the plans were complete, Washington banned the sale of alcoholic beverages. Thus, the plans had to be abandoned, and the day passed wholly unmarked, even in the nation's capital.

Mencken added that the nation's first bathtub was installed on December 20,   **10**
1842, in Cincinnati, "then a squalid frontier town, and even today surely no leader in
culture." Cincinnati contained many enterprising merchants, and one of them, a man
named Adam Thompson, dealt in cotton and grain. Thompson often traveled to England and acquired the habit of bathing while visiting that country.

The English bathtub was a puny contrivance, little more than a glorified dishpan,   **11**
and people needed a servant to help fill and empty it. Thompson conceived the notion of improving the English tub, of devising one large enough to hold the entire
body of an adult male. Thompson also wanted to devise a new water supply: pipes
from a central reservoir, so people would no longer need a servant to haul water to the
scene.

In 1842, Thompson built the nation's first modern bathtub in his Cincinnati   **12**
home. Thompson had a large well in his garden, and he installed a pump to lift water
into his house. The pump, operated by six Negroes, worked much like an old-time fire
engine. Pipes carried the water to a cypress storage tank in the attic. Two other pipes
ran from the tank to the bathroom. One, carrying cold water, ran directly to the bathroom. "The other, designed to provide warm water, ran down the great chimney of the
kitchen and was coiled inside it like a giant spring."

The tub itself was made of mahogany by Cincinnati's leading cabinet maker. "It   **13**
was nearly 7 feet long and fully 4 feet wide. To make it water-tight, the interior was
lined with sheet lead, carefully soldered at the joints. The whole contraption weighed
about 1,750 pounds, and the floor of the room in which it was placed had to be reinforced to support it."

On December 20, 1842, Thompson took his first two baths in this luxurious tub,   **14**
a cold bath at 8:00 a.m. and a warm bath sometime during the afternoon. Heated by
the kitchen fire, the warm water reached a temperature of 105 degrees. On Christmas
Day, Thompson invited a party of gentlemen to dinner, showed them the tub, and
gave an exhibition bath. Four guests, including a French visitor, risked plunges into it.
The next day, all Cincinnati heard about it. Local newspapers described the tub and
opened their columns to violent discussions about it.

The opposition was bitter. Critics said the tub was undemocratic and unhealthy,   **15**
an "obnoxious toy from England, designed to corrupt the democratic simplicity." Doctors worried that bathing was dangerous, a possible cause of "phthisic, rheumatic
fevers, inflammation of the lungs, and the whole category of zymotic diseases."

The controversy spread to other cities. In 1843, Baltimore considered an ordinance   **16**
to prohibit bathing between November 1 and March 15. The ordinance failed by only
two votes. Virginia placed a tax of $30 a year on all the bathtubs installed in that state.
Four cities—Hartford, Providence, Charleston, and Wilmington—imposed special and
very heavy water rates upon citizens who installed bathtubs in their homes. In 1845,
Boston made bathing unlawful, except upon medical advice, but its ordinance was
never enforced and was repealed in 1862. Clearly, the Thompson tub was too expensive for most people. In 1845, the common price for installing one in New York was
$500. A Brooklyn plumber devised a zinc tub and, after 1848, all the plumbers in New
York were putting them in. Medical opposition soon collapsed. In 1859, the American
Medical Association held its annual meeting in Boston, and a poll of its members
showed that nearly 55 percent regarded bathing as harmless; 20 percent regarded it as
beneficial.

Millard Fillmore, the nation's thirteenth president, gave the bathtub recognition   **17**
and respectability. While still vice president, Fillmore visited Cincinnati and inspected
the original Thompson tub. Thompson had died, but the gentleman who bought his

home preserved its bathroom. Fillmore was entertained in the home, and biographers say he took a bath in the tub. Experiencing no ill effects, he became an advocate of the new invention. After becoming president, he instructed his secretary of war to seek bids for the construction of a bathtub in the White House. For a moment, his instructions revived the old controversy. Opponents complained that other presidents had gotten along without any such luxuries. Disregarding the clamor, Fillmore's secretary of war called for bids, then awarded the contract to a firm of Philadelphia engineers "who proposed to furnish a tub of cast iron, capable of floating the largest man."

18   Fillmore's bathtub was installed in 1851 and remained in the White House until the Cleveland administration, when it was replaced by the present enameled tub. President Fillmore's example broke down all the remaining opposition. By 1860, newspaper advertisements showed that every hotel in New York had a bathtub, and some had two or three.

■

19   Mencken thought that his hoax was so obviously fraudulent that no one would believe it. To his amusement, then to his consternation, and finally to his horror, he began to see the hoax reprinted, or its "facts" quoted, in other publications. In 1926, Mencken decided that his joke had gone far enough; thus, he confessed that the entire story was fictitious. He published the confession in his syndicated column and claimed that it appeared in thirty newspapers with "a combined circulation of more than 250 million." (That may have been a mistake or, more probably, another of Mencken's exaggerations. Today, all 1,650 of the nation's daily newspapers have a combined circulation of only sixty-four million, one-fourth the total Mencken attributed to the thirty newspapers that published his column.)

20   Mencken's confession, "Melancholy Reflections," appeared on May 23, 1926. It admitted that his story was "a tissue of absurdities, all of them deliberate and most of them obvious." At first, he said, he had regarded the hoax with considerable satisfaction. Some of the nation's most respected publications reprinted it as fact, and some readers asked for more information about the topic. Other readers sent him additional details that helped prove his story was true.

21   "But the worst was to come," Mencken continued. "Pretty soon I began to encounter my preposterous 'facts' in the writings of other men. They began to be used by chiropractors and other such quacks as evidence of the stupidity of medical men. They began to be cited by medical men as proof of the progress of public hygiene. They got into learned journals. They were alluded to on the floor of Congress. They crossed the ocean and were discussed solemnly in England, and on the continent. Finally, I began to find them in standard works of reference. Today, I believe, they are accepted as gospel everywhere on Earth."

22   Mencken said he was reluctant to reveal the truth because he would be criticized for it. The residents of Cincinnati had begun to boast that the bathtub industry started in their community, and Mencken feared that they would charge him with "spreading lies against them." Furthermore, "[t]he chiropractors will damn me for blowing up their ammunition. The medical gents, having swallowed my quackery, will now denounce me as a quack for exposing them. And in the end, no doubt, the thing will simmer down to a general feeling that I have once more committed some vague and sinister crime against the United States, and there will be a renewal of the demand that I be deported to Russia."

Mencken concluded that people dislike the truth, and that the people who try to   23
tell it become unpopular. Nevertheless, Mencken confessed: "All I care to do today is
reiterate, in the most solemn and awful terms, that my history of the bathtub, printed
on December 28, 1917, was pure buncombe. If there were any facts in it, they got there
accidentally and against my design."

Despite Mencken's confession, other publications continued to reprint his hoax.   24
So on July 25, 1926, he tried again. In an essay titled "Hymn to the Truth," he said
that, initially, he liked the hoax. "It was artfully devised," he explained, "and it contained some buffooneries of considerable juiciness. I had confidence that the customers of the *Evening Mail* would like it." Unfortunately, they liked it too well. "That
is to say," he continued, "they swallowed it as gospel, gravely and horribly. Worse, they
began sending clippings of it to friends east, west, north, and south, and so it spread
to other papers, and then to the magazines and weeklies of opinion, and then to the
scientific press, and finally to the reference books."

Mencken added that he had revealed the hoax's absurdities two months earlier,   25
on May 23. "I confessed categorically that it was all buncombe," he said. Thirty great
newspapers, including the Boston *Herald,* had published his confession. The *Herald*
placed his confession under a four-column headline on its editorial page. Next to his
confession, the *Herald* placed a cartoon labeled, "The American Public Will Swallow
Anything." Mencken complained that three weeks later—and in the same section—
the *Herald* reprinted his hoax "soberly, and as a piece of news."

Mencken's second confession continued: "What ails the truth is that it is mainly   26
uncomfortable, and often dull. The human mind seeks something more amusing, and
more caressing. What the actual history of the bathtub may be I don't know: digging
it out would be a dreadful job, and the result, after all that labor, would probably be a
string of banalities. The fiction I concocted back in 1917 was at least better than that.
There were heroes in it, and villains. It revealed a conflict, with virtue winning. So it
was embraced by mankind, precisely as the story of George Washington and the cherry
tree was embraced. . . ."

Finally, Mencken again concluded: "No normal human being wants to hear the   27
truth. It is the passion of a small and aberrant minority of men, most of them patho-
logical. They are hated for telling it while they live, and when they die they are swiftly
forgotten. What remains in the world, in the field of wisdom, is a series of long tested
and solidly agreeable lies."

In 1927, Mencken rewrote portions of his second confession, "Hymn to the   28
Truth," and reprinted it in a book. Thus, for a third time, Mencken admitted that his
story was "a tissue of somewhat heavy absurdities, all of them deliberate and most of
them obvious." Nevertheless, he estimated that at least nine-tenths of his reader believed it.

■

In 1926, a distinguished magazine, *Scribner's,* published an article about the history of   29
bathing. *Scribner's* explained that the nation's first presidents bathed in the Potomac
River, sometimes in the nude. President John Quincy Adams plunged in whenever the
weather was suitable, but it was a risky business. *Scribner's* explained that Adams left his
clothes lying on the river bank. When someone stole them, the president was forced to
send a boy to the White House for more. President Adams was also trapped in the Potomac by one of the nation's first female correspondents. Adams had refused to grant
her an interview, apparently because he disliked the notion of female correspondents.

Scribner's reported that the woman sat on President Adams's clothes and refused to let him wade ashore until he agreed to give her a story.

30   *Scribner's* added that other presidents continued to bathe in the Potomac "up to Millard Fillmore, who when he came into office caused the first bathtub to be installed in the White House." The magazine then repeated all Mencken's nonsense about the bathtub.

31   Even a newspaper in Mencken's hometown repeated the hoax. In 1929, the *Baltimore News* published a front-page column that said white enameled bathtubs were about to become obsolete and would be replaced by up-to-date tubs that came in more vivid colors. The column explained, "There are delicate blues and pinks for blonde beauties, green for red-haired belles, and more inflammatory tints for brunettes." After describing the new colors, the column added that a wealthy grain dealer in Cincinnati had installed the nation's first private bathtub but "was the subject of much ridicule and some bitter denunciation." Millard Fillmore saw the Cincinnati tub and had one installed in the White House, "bringing down upon his head the wrath of his political opponents."

32   Two years later, Arthur Train wrote *Puritan's Progress,* an informal account of the Puritans and their descendants, including "their manners & customs, their virtues & vices." On page 51, Train states that the first American bathtub "was, I am informed, made of mahogany and lined with sheet lead, and exhibited by its proud owner at a Christmas party in Cincinnati in 1842."

33   Mencken's story also fooled the *New York Times.* On August 4, 1935, the *Times* reported that tenants on the city's East Side were demanding the installation of bathtubs in their apartments. The paper then summarized the history of the bathtub, and its summary included Mencken's "facts" about the Cincinnati tub. . . .

■

34   In 1917, Mencken said he was celebrating the bathtub's seventy-fifth anniversary. Other journalists apparently noted the date. Twenty-five years later, on December 20, 1942, they celebrated the bathtub's one-hundredth anniversary. Since then, the story has continued to reappear, usually in January. President Fillmore was born on January 7, 1800, and journalists mention the bathtub in stories about his accomplishments as president.

35   Even President Truman repeated the story. Workmen remodeled the White House during the early 1950s, and everyone involved in the remodeling seemed to believe that President Fillmore installed the building's first bathtub. When reporters criticized President Truman's plans to add a balcony to the White House, Truman responded that there had been considerable opposition to the first bathtub, too.

36   *CBS Evening News* repeated the story in 1976. The *Baltimore Sun* immediately responded, "On the *CBS Evening News* last Wednesday, Roger Mudd reported on the graveside ceremonies for the anniversary of the birth of President Millard Fillmore 'best known for the compromise of 1850, the postage stamp, and the first bathtub in the White House.' " The *Sun* complained that Mencken's tale about the bathtub—"and the stuff about Cincinnati, too"—was nonsense.

37   The ABC and NBC television networks apparently made the same mistake. Thus Mencken's hoax was passed on to another forty-five or fifty million Americans.

38   A few publications, including the *Saturday Evening Post,* have tried to expose the hoax. On November 13, 1943, the *Post* reported that Adam Thompson may have invented the bathtub, but that H. L. Mencken invented Thompson. It explained that

Thompson and his tub were part of an unusually persistent hoax that Mencken per-petrated in 1917. It concluded: "Like some Frankensteinian monster, Adam Thompson has got completely out of his creator's control. Mencken has denied the truth of his yarn at least three times. Thompson continues to bob up in print just the same. He will undoubtedly keep right on doing so after this."

The *Washington Post* published another exposé on January 4, 1977, but realized **39** that it would also fail to stop the hoax. The paper predicted that its exposé "will not even slow it up, any more than a single grape placed on the railroad tracks would slow up a freight train."

The *Post* called Millard Fillmore a genuine patriot and an effective president, but **40** "the victim of one of the most charming myths in the nation's history." It added that no one knew the true story of the first White House bathtub. Moreover, it agreed with Mencken, who said that digging out the true story would be a dreadful job, and prob-ably less interesting than his hoax.

In fact, a magazine editor named Beverly Smith had dug out the true story twenty- **41** five years earlier. In 1952, Smith reported: "Never in 26 years of reporting had I run into such a baffling comedy of errors, fakes, and legends." The first evidence that Smith uncovered indicated that President Rutherford B. Hayes used the first White House bathtub sometime after 1877. Later evidence indicated that Andrew Jackson de-nounced the first White House bathtubs as undemocratic and removed them in 1829. Other evidence indicated that, by accident, H. L. Mencken was right: that President Fillmore installed the first White House bathtub.

After weeks of additional research, Smith concluded that the first presidents to oc- **42** cupy the White House—John Adams and Thomas Jefferson—may have had personal, portable tubs. Andrew Jackson spent $45,000 refurbishing the White House and clearly enjoyed "warm, cold, and shower baths." Thus, the most conclusive evidence indi-cated "that the first regular bath . . . was installed somewhere between 1829 and 1833 by the rough, tough, tobacco-chewing Tennessean, Andrew Jackson. . . ."

Jackson never told the American public about his bathtub, probably because bath- **43** tubs were still a luxury and would have tarnished his image. [His successor], Martin Van Buren, was defeated when he ran for re-election, in part because of his image as a dandy. Van Buren was "accused of turning the White House into a palace, drinking champagne and taking warm baths."

Despite Smith's revelations, respected historians and scholars continue to quote **44** Mencken's hoax. In 1973, Daniel J. Boorstin published *The Americans: The Democratic Experience.* Dr. Boorstin was director of the Smithsonian Institution, and his book was part of a three-volume study of U.S. history. Reviewers deemed his book "scholarly" and "generally excellent." But on page 353, Dr. Boorstin states, "In 1851, when Presi-dent Millard Fillmore reputedly installed the first permanent bath and water closet in the White House, he was criticized for doing something that was 'both unsanitary and undemocratic.' "

Another historian repeated the hoax in 1981, but with an unusual twist. Paul F. **45** Boller, Jr., author of *Presidential Anecdotes,* wrote that Mrs. Fillmore, not her husband, "installed the first bathtub in the Executive Mansion." Boller's publisher liked the story so much that he placed a picture of President Fillmore—seated in the tub—on the book's cover.

A paperback edition, published in 1982, corrected the error. It explained: "Even **46** his chief claim to fame—installing the first bathtub in the White House—is without foundation." Despite Boller's correction, his publisher kept Fillmore's picture on the book's cover.

■

47   Why has the hoax fooled so many readers? Mencken concluded that Americans like some lies more than the truth—that lies are often more interesting. Also, he wrote about obscure events that occurred seventy-five years earlier. Few readers knew anything about the topic, and none could easily check the details. Moreover, he wrote the hoax in a convincing manner, mixing fact with fiction and including details that impressed his readers. Thus his story was not a total fraud. He invented the Cincinnati merchant named Adam Thompson but also mentioned prominent Americans whom the public knew and trusted, including President Fillmore.

48   Attempts to expose the hoax failed because many of the people who read Mencken's first column failed to notice or read his retractions. Millions of other Americans saw his hoax reprinted elsewhere. Many of the other publications failed to reprint Mencken's confessions. As a result, Americans continue to believe and repeat his hoax.

49   While paging through old newspapers and magazines, Americans will continue to find copies of Mencken's hoax reprinted in them. Because the hoax is so amusing, some readers—even respected scholars—will believe, quote, and reprint it, thus passing the hoax on to another generation of Americans.

Freewriting

In your notebook, write for fifteen minutes about experiences and observations relating to pranks, practical jokes, and tall tales. You might start by listing some of the most familiar or outrageous examples that you can recollect. You might include legends attached to historical figures like George Washington and Abraham Lincoln, athletes like Babe Ruth, and other famous individuals. Finally, consider why so many people accept improbable stories or explanations of events (e.g., legends or urban myths) and whether you agree with Mencken's theory about why they persist in believing, even after a hoax has been exposed.

Group Work

Listen carefully and take notes as each freewrite is read aloud. Notice whether members of your group report similar experiences, observations, or examples and whether they express compatible opinions. What general explanations about legends and hoaxes (what causes them, what accounts for their popularity, why people refuse to relinquish them) can you agree upon?

Review Questions

1.   What was H. L. Mencken's self-professed motive for writing this and other facetious columns during this stage of his career?

2.   For what purposes did chiropractors and "medical men" appropriate and try to exploit the bathtub hoax?

3.   What have historians since been able to learn about how the White House got its first bathtub?

Discussion Questions

1. What is the main idea of this article? Is Fedler more concerned with describing the bathtub hoax or accounting for its persistence? Where does he use general statements to alert readers to his aims?

2. Locate two or three paragraphs that have topic sentences. Are these paragraphs arranged in a deductive or inductive order? Entire essays or sections of essays can be organized inductively or deductively. Is the arrangement of paragraphs 42–44 deductive or inductive?

3. Apparently Mencken disdained the gullibility of his readers. Do you sense that Fedler shares that attitude? Is he more, less, or equally judgmental? What does this tell you about his sense of audience?

Writing

1. After briefly relating a familiar myth or folk legend, try to account for its enduring popularity. Consider what basic human need it may satisfy, what troubling or confusing question or truth it may help people understand or come to terms with. It might help to consider the following two poems by Emily Dickinson:

Apparently with no surprise
To any happy Flower
The Frost beheads it at its play—
In accidental power—
The blonde Assassin passes on—
The Sun proceeds unmoved
To measure off another Day
For an Approving God.

■

Tell all the Truth but tell it slant—
Success in Circuit lies
Too bright for our infirm Delight
The Truth's superb surprise.
As Lightning to the Children eased
With explanation kind
The Truth must dazzle gradually
Or every man be blind—

2. In a short essay, assess the validity of Mencken's claim that "people dislike the truth, and that people who try to tell it are unpopular." Support or refute that claim with examples from history and literature as well as personal experience or observation.

3. Most families tell stories about themselves and repeat them over time, often revising, elaborating, and improving the narrative (i.e., making it more dramatic, more satisfying *as a story*). One writer, William Maxwell, says of such stories:

What we, or at any rate what I, refer to confidently as memory . . . is really a form of storytelling that goes on continually in the mind and often changes with the telling. Too many conflicting emotional interests are involved for life ever to be wholly acceptable [as a story with an engaging plot], and possibly it is the work of the storyteller to rearrange things so that they conform to this end, In any case, in talking about the past we lie with every breath we draw.

In a similar vein, essayist Joan Didion has confessed:

I have always had trouble distinguishing between what happened and what merely might have happened, but I remain unconvinced that the distinction, for my purposes, matters. The cracked crab that I recall having for lunch the day my father came home from Detroit in 1945 must certainly be embroidery, worked into the day's pattern to lend verisimilitude; I was ten years old and would not now remember the cracked crab. . . . And yet it is precisely that ficti- tious crab that makes me see the afternoon all over again, a home movie run all too often, the father bearing gifts, the child weeping, an exercise in family love and guilt.

Regardless of whether one agrees with Maxwell or Didion, their experience as writers and storytellers complicates notions of truth versus lie, discernment versus gullibility that Mencken, as well as most other people and accepts as axiomatic. Write an essay that contrasts these two points of view, relating them to the bathtub hoax, to a familiar legend, or to a family story that you are acquainted with.

5 *Writing a Summary*

A *summary* of a text or a passage is a shortened version of it. The writer of a summary keeps only the main ideas and essential information from the original, while eliminating most supporting details, such as the examples and illustrations. Many summaries are written to save readers time, but they can have other purposes as well, such as to focus readers' attention or to refresh their memories. Many of your textbooks, for example, conclude each chapter with a summary of contents designed to solidify what you have learned. Most scientific and technical articles begin with an *abstract,* a brief summary of their findings so you can see the point quickly and even decide if you want to read the text in its entirety.

As a student, you are no stranger to summary writing. A book report or "report on the literature" requires you to summarize the contents of one or more works. A lab report includes an abbreviated account of your experimental procedures and results. An argumentative paper, like a trial lawyer's case, may conclude with a forceful summation of the evidence you have presented. Although it may be less familiar to you now, one of the most extensive uses of summaries comes when you do research. You read articles and books filled with detailed information. Since you cannot tell your readers everything you have learned, you must decide what is most important and appropriate, and you record only that on your note cards. In fact, the entire research paper is by nature a summary, a carefully condensed and focused presentation of what you have discovered in the course of your investigation.

Whenever you read, your mind does something like summarizing: seeking out the main ideas, making connections between them (and connections with your other experiences), and creating a framework for efficient storage in your memory. You can assist that process when you write notes on your reading. For example, a student reading a textbook to learn how the human eye works might write this summary note in the margin:

Rods and cones in the retina encode images

In the human visual system the initial encoding of the image occurs in the *retina,* a layer of neural cells at the rear of the eyeball. The retina contains a two-dimensional layer of sensory cells, called *rods* and *cones,* which are sensitive to light. Each of these cells is capable of generating a neural signal when struck by light.

—Neil A. Stillings, "Vision," from *Cognitive Science: An Introduction*

A student's summary note in the margin

The textbook passage

Writing the note helps the student see the main point of the passage and re-member it.

 ## SUMMARY AND PARAPHRASE

Sometimes the reading notes that you write in the margins of your textbooks *paraphrase* passages, but the preceding brief note *summarizes* the original passage as well, since it omits many details, including the definitions of terms. As you will see, summary and paraphrase share similarities in both form and function. Before introducing those similarities, however, we need to consider two ways in which summary and paraphrase differ. First, unlike a paraphrase, a summary may quote a phrase or two, or even a short sentence, from the original source, provided that it is set off with quotation marks. Second, a summary involves decisions about what is most important and what can be left out. In the following passage, a British author writes about the processing and marketing of food products.

The original passage

> All these techniques, originating in the United States and vigorously mar-keted by American businessmen, have spread across the industrialised communi-ties of Europe. There have been several social consequences.
>   One of these has been a significant change in shopping habits. When food retailers still purchased their supplies in bulk—flour and sugar by the sack, tea in a chest, butter in a keg, and cheeses whole—the local store was a place of resort. It was a social centre as well as a distribution point. Standard articles, prepack-aged and preserved by canning or freezing in a large-scale modern factory, are distributed with more efficiency, even if with the loss of social intercourse, in an equally efficient large-scale supermarket. Hence it is reasonable to suggest that one of the effects American food technology has had on the character of Euro-pean society has been to accelerate the extinction of the general store on the street corner, of the specialised butcher, baker, greengrocer, and dairy and to substitute the supermarket. Great Britain, moving forward a decade behind the United States, possessed 175 supermarkets in 1958, 367 in 1960, and 4,800 in 1971.
> —Magnus Pyke, "The Influence of American Foods and Food Technology in Europe"

Notice the difference between a paraphrase and a summary of this passage. A student wishing to use the information from this passage in a research paper might paraphrase it as follows:

A paraphrased version

> New methods of processing and distributing food, developed in America and sold overseas, have brought social change to Europe. For one thing, many Euro-peans no longer shop for groceries as they did when stores bought large con-tainers of flour, sugar, tea, and butter and whole cheeses. In those days, the food store was a place to meet friends as well as to buy groceries. Though im-personal by comparison, today's supermarkets are more efficient, selling prod-ucts that come individually packaged from the factory, where they have been canned or frozen to keep them fresh. Consequently, American methods have led to the gradual disappearance of butcher shops, bakeries, produce markets, and dairy stores, all of which have been supplanted by supermarkets. The num-

ber of supermarkets in Britain, which is about ten years behind trends established in the U.S., grew from 175 in 1958 and 367 in 1960 to 4,800 in 1971 (Pyke 89–90).

The paraphrase changes the writer's language, but it retains all of his ideas, including examples and minor details. The following summary, on the other hand, presents only the most important ideas in a much shorter version:

> American innovations in the production and distribution of food have brought supermarkets to Europe. Once a neighborly "place of resort," the corner store has been supplanted by the more efficient, though less sociable, supermarket (Pyke 89–90).

A summary

Notice that the summary eliminates details and examples found in the paraphrase. Nevertheless, the summary provides a faithful account, taking into consideration the author's ideas and attitudes. You may have noticed also that this particular summary retains a phrase from the original source, placed in quotation marks.

A good summary, like a good paraphrase, makes the author's ideas clear, possibly even clearer than they are in the original. However, the writer of a summary has the advantage of being able to quote a phrase or short sentence from the source, provided that it is set off with quotation marks. Finally, you should notice that both the paraphrase and the summary acknowledge their common source with a parenthetical note.

Paraphrase and Summary

EXERCISE

A process for writing summaries appears in the next section of this chapter, but you already can summarize a passage whose main idea you recognize. The following excerpt from a book by historian Richard Fletcher explains how hagiography, stories about the lives of saints, contributed to the conversion of European pagans to Christianity. First paraphrase the passage; then write a brief summary of it. Both your paraphrase and your summary should be composed in your own language, although you may wish to quote a short phrase or two in the summary. Avoid making reference to the author's name, and end both paraphrase and summary with a parenthetical note: (Fletcher 10–11).

> Although hagiography came . . . in many different costumes its aim was consistently to edify—to hold the saint up as an example of godly living and holy dying, to spur listeners or readers to compunction and devotion. One means of edification which may cause disquiet to the modern readers was the recording of wonders and miracles worked by the saint. Early medieval Europe was a world in which persons of every level of intellectual cultivation accepted without question that the miraculous could weave like a shuttle in and out of everyday reality. We need to remember this, and to resist the temptation to dismiss it out of hand as infantile credulity: patronizing the past never helped anyone to understand it.

WRITING SUMMARIES

To summarize a single paragraph, the procedure is about the same as the one you practiced in the previous chapter when you created topic sentences for paragraphs whose main ideas were implied but not stated: *You can read the passage once or twice until its meaning is clear, put it aside, and then write a brief summary from memory.*

As the length of an essay increases, however, your ability to remember it decreases, and the process of summarizing becomes more difficult. Throughout your college career, you are going to be asked to write a variety of summaries. Some will be routine, such as the summary of a single brief essay; others will be more complex summaries of several essays or books. In any case, you will need a workable method that can help you create polished summaries with the most efficient use of your time and energy.

The following sequence of steps can save much time and frustration. As in all types of writing, time well spent in the preliminary stages pays off later on.

A Process for Summarizing Longer Passages

1. *Read carefully.* When you summarize a passage, you must be sure you understand it fully. Read it, look up any confusing words, and discuss its meaning with others.

2. *Read with a pencil.* Whenever you read, underlining and making marginal notes can increase comprehension. Be selective; underline only main ideas. Use your own symbols and marginal comments to highlight important ideas. Good notes and underlining make later rereading quick and easy, so it pays to concentrate the first time through.

3. *Write a one-sentence paraphrase of the main idea.* If the text has a thesis statement, you can paraphrase it. If not, state what you take to be the main idea in your own words. This sentence can serve as an umbrella for everything else in the summary.

4. *Write the first draft.* Create a miniature version of the passage based only on the portions you have underlined and the marginal notes you have written. Keep this draft simple by following the order of ideas from the original. Paraphrase where possible, although parts of the first draft may still be close to the phrasing of the original.

5. *Paraphrase your first draft.* Treat your first draft like a passage to be paraphrased. Restate its ideas and information in your own style and language, quoting no more than an isolated phrase or two or perhaps a single sentence if there is an idea you cannot express as capably in your own words. Remember that a summary is a miniature essay that should express the ideas of the author not just succinctly but also smoothly and clearly. Help your readers by inserting transitions, eliminating unnecessary words, combining ideas, and clarifying any confusing syntax.

We can illustrate this procedure with an example. Suppose you have been asked to summarize the following essay on stereotyping from a book on semantics, the study of how language can affect the way we think. First, read it with care until you are certain you understand it (step 1).

After you are satisfied that you have understood the essay, go back and reread it with a pencil, underlining or paraphrasing the main ideas (step 2). Here is the passage as it was marked by one reader. Since each reader is unique, it is unlikely that you would have marked it in exactly the same way.

Stereotyping: Homogenizing People

We all carry around images of what members of particular groups are like. For instance, what image is conjured in your mind for a dope smoker, New York cab driver, black athlete, college professor, construction worker? These images are often shared by others. Typically, they stress similarities and ignore differences among members of a group. These images, then, become stereotypes—the attribution of certain characteristics to a group often without the benefit of firsthand knowledge.

Stereotypes are judgments of individuals not on the basis of direct interaction with those individuals specifically but based instead on preconceived images for the category they belong to. Stereotypes, however, are not inherently evil. Some stereotypes, when predicated upon personal experience and empirical data, can be valid generalizations about a group.

Some stereotypes are valid !?

There are several potential problems with stereotypes, however. First, these preconceived images of groups may produce a frame of reference, a perceptual set in our minds concerning the group as a whole. Then when faced with an individual from the group, the preconceived image is applied indiscriminately, screening out individual differences. Individuals become mere abstractions devoid of unique qualities, pigeon-holed and submerged in the crowd, a crowd that is thought to be homogeneous.

① The group becomes more important!

Indiscriminate application of stereotypes is particularly troublesome because stereotypes are not necessarily grounded on evidence or even direct experience. The classic study of stereotyping by Katz and Braly (1933) clearly revealed that stereotypes are often formulated in ignorance. They reflect attitudes toward labels—racial, ethnic, and others—frequently without benefit of actual contact with members of the group stereotyped. Student subjects held Turks in low esteem, yet most had never interacted with any member of this group.

A second problem with stereotypes is what general semanticists term *allness*. This is the tendency to characterize an individual or an entire group in terms of only one attribute or quality. This one characteristic becomes all that is necessary to know about a person. Once you realize that the person is a woman, or a Jew, or a Southerner, no more information is sought. This unidimensional view of a person is nothing more than a simplistic conception of an individual. You may be a Jew but also a brother, son, brilliant lawyer, charming compassionate individual, devoted father, loving husband, and so forth. Allness sacrifices complexity and substitutes superficiality. Racial and ethnic characteristics do not lend themselves to change, yet racial or ethnic labels may be the prepotent characteristic that supersedes all others. <u>In fact, allness orientation may produce exaggerated perception of group characteristics.</u> Secord et al. (1956) showed "prejudiced" and "unprejudiced" subjects several pictures of blacks and whites. The prejudiced observers exaggerated the physical characteristics of blacks such as thickness of lips and width of nose. <u>Racial labels accentuated the stereotyped differences between "races" for prejudiced (allness oriented) subjects.</u>

③

When we see stereotypes we can't see changes in people!!

A ⟨final⟩ problem associated with stereotyping is that it <u>can produce frozen evaluations.</u> Juvenile delinquents or adult felons may never shed their stigmatizing label despite "going straight." Zimbardo and Ruch (1977) summarize studies conducted at Princeton University over several decades regarding stereotypes by Princeton students of various ethnic groups. While the stereotypes did change, they tended to do so relatively slowly. In 1933, blacks were deemed superstitious by 84 percent of Princeton students, 41 percent in 1951, and 13 percent in 1967. Thirty-four years is a very long time for people to acquire an accurate image of blacks on this one item.

Summary of above

Stereotypes are thus troublesome because they are often indiscriminate, exhibit an allness orientation, and can produce frozen evaluations. Considering the pervasiveness of stereotyping in our society, one should not take it lightly. When we stereotype we define a person and this definition, superficial at best, can be quite powerful.

<u>To stereotype is to define and to define is to control,</u> especially if the definition is widely accepted regardless of its accuracy. In a male dominated society women may be stereotyped as empty-headed and illogical. The fact that the stereotype has persisted for years manifests the control men have over women, control that excludes women from executive positions and relegates them to mindless housekeeping duties. <u>Women's liberation is fundamentally the struggle to define, to reject male stereotypes of females.</u>

vicious circle

<u>Stereotypes are sometimes seductive,</u> however. When women are told repeatedly that they are stupid, they may begin believing it. A self-fulfilling prophecy may develop. Low self-esteem produced from male definitions of women as unintelligent can lead to poor performance and the consequent belief that the stereotype has merit. The stereotype is thus nurtured and perpetuated. <u>Stereotyping can thus control, insidiously imprisoning its victims in constraining roles.</u>

SUMMARY ☆

So while stereotyping isn't intrinsically evil, most stereotypes lack empirical foundations and are assertions of power and dominance over less powerful groups. Reduced to an abstraction, victims of stereotyping must struggle to define themselves or be content to accept roles others have carved out for them. It is little wonder our society has been experiencing turmoil.

—J. Dan Rothwell, *Telling It Like It Isn't* (pages 76–78)

Now write the thesis, the sentence that you have decided covers most of the material (step 3):

Thesis

Stereotypes are judgments of people based on preconceived images about a group they are supposed to belong to.

Next, a first draft might look like this (step 4):

A first draft

We all carry around images of what groups are like, and these images are often shared. They stress similarities and ignore differences. So stereotyping is giving a group certain characteristics without benefit of firsthand knowledge.

Stereotypes are judgments of individuals based on preconceived images, not on direct interaction. However, stereotypes are not inherently evil. Some are valid.

Nevertheless, there are some problems with stereotypes. When you have a preconceived image of a group, it produces a perceptual set that screens out individual differences. Indiscriminate stereotypes are not grounded on evidence and are often formulated in ignorance without actual contact. A second problem of stereotyping is allness: characterizing an individual or a group in terms of only one attribute or quality. When you realize someone is a woman, a Jew, or a Southerner, you may stop looking for other information. This is a very simplistic idea of a person. It is superficial and not complex as real people are.

A final problem with stereotypes is frozen evaluations: judgments that have stayed the same for a long time and change relatively slowly.

So we can see that stereotypes are dangerous because they are indiscriminate, are inclined toward allness, and give a frozen evaluation. They also define and control people if the stereotypes are widely accepted. Women, for example, have to struggle to reject men's stereotypes of females. Sometimes stereotypes are seductive. People believe these images, so they become self-fulfilling. An image can control its victims, imprisoning them in roles. Even though most stereotypes aren't valid, victims of stereotyping must either struggle to define themselves or accept the bad image others have made up for them.

The final step is to revise and proofread (step 5). Here you can concentrate on condensing, on avoiding repetition, and on focusing the sentences around the thesis. Because you are seeking economy, see if your first draft can be shortened. The result is a final draft that is, in effect, a summary of a summary, as in this final version:

Stereotypes are judgments of individuals based on preconceived images about a category they belong to. Although some stereotypes can be valid, they cause three problems. First, stereotypes prevent us from judging people as individuals. Second, they cause us to characterize people or groups on the basis of only one superficial attribute, a problem known as *allness*. Third, stereotypes become frozen and take years to change. If these false images are widely accepted, they can define and control people so strongly that unless the victims struggle against the stereotypes, they may come to believe them themselves (Rothwell 76–78).

The final draft

Writing Summaries

EXERCISES

1. Use the process outlined on page 144 to summarize the following passage from page A17 of a book review in the *New York Times.* The reviewer, Sarah Boxer, uses paraphrases and quotations from a book by art historian Michael Camille to explain how illuminators, artists who embellished medieval manuscripts with elaborate illustrations, often subverted the content of sacred texts. For the sake of clarity, begin your summary as follows: "A recent review of *Image on the Edge* explains author Michael Camille's theory that. . . ." Close with a parenthetical note citing Boxer.

Camille . . . tells the story of "lascivious apes, autophagic dragons, pot-bellied heads, harp-playing asses," and copulating animals populating the edges of illuminated manuscripts.

In the Middle Ages, the illuminator would do his work after the scribe was finished, Mr. Camille writes, and "that gave him a chance of undermining . . . the written word." For example, in the Rutland Psalter of 1260, the illuminator colored the manuscript so that "the letter *p* of the Latin word *conspectu* (meaning to see or penetrate visually)" turns into an arrow that flies into the posterior of a prostrate fish-man.

"The medieval image-word was, like medieval life itself, rigidly structured and hierarchical," Mr. Camille writes. "For this reason, resisting, ridiculing, overturning, and inverting it was not only possible, it was limitless." The margins of illuminated manuscripts were a playground. By the close of the thirteenth century "no text was spared the irreverent explosion of marginal mayhem."

From the look of the illuminated manuscripts, with their monkey-sucking nuns and bird-headed Jesuses, you can guess where [marginal notations] get their subversive edge. The margins, Mr. Camille writes, were the place "not only for supplementation and annotation but also for disagreement and juxtaposition—what the scholastics called disputatio" and what we might call talking back.

2. Summarize the following excerpt from pages 4–10 of Christopher Gould's article "Howard Johnson and the Standardizing of Roadside Architecture."

Much has been written about the role of Howard D. Johnson and his chain of restaurants in standardizing roadside cuisine—"The Taste of America" as it was billed in one of the company's advertising slogans. Less attention has been given to Johnson's studious efforts to appeal to hungry motorists through subtleties of architectural design. Nevertheless, Johnson's success in this regard has had an equally enduring impact on the American restaurant trade.

The Howard Johnson chain developed and refined its commercial image before the 1940 boom in tourism, opening eighty-six restaurants between 1935 and 1939. Capitalizing on the boom, the company added another seventy outlets by the end of 1941, including its $600,000 "cathedral" on Queens Boulevard, the road that led travelers to the New York World's Fair. Seating over a thousand patrons, this flagship unit was advertised as the world's largest roadside restaurant.

The interior design of Howard Johnson restaurants was celebrated as a state-of-the-art concept. One trade journal extolled the benefits of "standardized . . . interiors of light-colored wood and leather chairs, fluorescent lighting, and air conditioning" as well as the efficiency of "floor planning [so] rigidly controlled that ice cream cabinets, frankfurter grilles, garbage containers, soda fountains, dishwashers, and every other feature or piece of equipment must be placed according to a prescribed layout." Motorists were equally impressed with the layout, which was quickly adopted by competing roadside restaurants. Patrons could choose between a modest dining room, in which uniformed waitresses served full meals, and a lunch counter/take-out station that offered ice cream, hot dogs, and a few other types of simple fast food. The design permitted what one admirer has called "a merging [of] the respectability and full-meal service of the tearoom with the casual, quick-bite convenience of the soda fountain, luncheonette, and hot dog stand."

Though Howard Johnson's prototype was justly esteemed for its efficient interior design, the uniformity of its external features was equally important. In this regard, the company's founder, constantly alert to middle-class tastes and notions of homeyness, made a lasting contribution to the food-service industry, as well as to roadside architecture.

Until the 1930s, restaurants had devoted little attention to exterior design. A change, however, accompanied the desire to create corporate identities for such new chains as White Castle, Krystal, and White Tower. Located chiefly in urban areas, these restaurants were distinguished by two unusual architectural features—eye-catching, often extravagant designs suggesting the fantasy and escapism of amusement parks, and an image of impeccable cleanliness, conveyed through stark colors (especially white, black, and gray) and "hard" surfaces such as marble, porcelain, nickel, or lacquered wood.

The "vernacular" design of these early chains, though popular, was not really appropriate for roadside restaurants in smaller towns and suburban areas. First of all, local zoning ordinances prevented the construction of teapots, chili bowls, and miniature castles. Second, as marketing research has since demonstrated, stark colors and "hard" surfaces are not particularly inviting to restaurant patrons. As early as 1922, New York restaurateur William Childs recognized that since "the white, the really sanitary features, have their limitations . . . soft materials, for some purposes, are more pleasing to the senses than the hard materials."

Seeking a corporate identity for his restaurant chain, Howard Johnson muted the more extreme features of "vernacular" design without rejecting them entirely. Though the units he built before 1955 varied somewhat, their prototype was based on the "colonial" house, a staple of pre-World War II residential developments. Its defining features are familiar to most Americans over the age of fifty: white clapboards, turquoise shutters, a hipped roof topped by a stately looking cupola, and dormer windows accented with ruffled curtains and bedroom lamps. The grounds were adorned with carefully arranged shrubbery and potted flowers. Together, these features created a soft, homey atmosphere, sufficiently reserved and dignified to conform to most zoning ordinances.

In its more subtle details, however, Howard Johnson's prototype reflected some of the conventional "hard" features of contemporary chain restaurants. The most obvious was the orange roof, the firm's enduring trademark. Johnson himself sought out roofing material with a "hard" enamel finish, a stark contrast to the subdued, almost stately, residential aura of the rest of the building. Johnson's first roadside restaurant, built alongside the main highway leading to Cape Cod, was originally outfitted with asphalt shingles. Dissatisfied with their dull finish, Johnson experimented with various alternatives before finally settling on a metal substitute that provided the porcelain-enamel effect he desired. A similar touch was the paved parking lot—a rare luxury among roadside restaurants built prior to World War II. A final concession to the "hard" features of contemporary fashion was the incongruous Art Moderne lettering of the Howard Johnson sign. Each of these features contributed to an impression of cleanliness and modernity without compromising the warm, homey image of the restaurant building.

Johnson's one gesture toward fantasy and whimsicality was the weather vane placed atop the building's prim white cupola. Where one might have expected a simple monogram or perhaps some conventional icon of rural Americana, Johnson placed the company's peculiar logo—Simple Simon and the Pieman. Had it not been for this subtle, slightly rakish touch—and, of course, the metallic orange roof—the building might easily have been mistaken for a bank or a real estate office.

 ## USES OF SUMMARY

Thus far, we have said little about why a writer might summarize a text or a passage, beyond the obvious reasons of saving paper and sparing the reader any wasted time. Basically, however, summary serves most of the same purposes as paraphrase. The marginal note beside the textbook passage on page 141 shows how summary, like paraphrase, can help a reader understand and come to terms with complex and important ideas. A writer also can use summary to make a relatively difficult passage more accessible to readers who may not be familiar with its terminology and references. Our summary on page 143 of Magnus Pyke's account of European grocery shopping provides an example of that.

Summarizing an Argument

Another frequent use of summary is to demonstrate understanding of a controversial point of view or an argumentative text. Suppose you need to summarize the following excerpt from an essay about nonsexist language written by conservative columnist William Safire.

> It makes sense to substitute *worker* for *workingman* . . . , *firefighter* for *fireman,* and *police officer* for *policeman.* Plenty of women are in those occupations, and it misleads the listener or reader to retain the old form. . . .
>
> But do we need *woman actor* for *actress,* or *female tempter* for *temptress?* And what's demeaning about *waitress* that we should have to substitute *woman waiter* or the artificial *waitron?* We dropped *stewardess* largely because the occupation was being maligned—a popular book title suggesting promiscuity was *Coffee, Tea, or Me?*—a loss that also took the male *steward* out the emergency exit, and now we have the long and unnecessarily concealing *flight attendant.* We were better off with *steward* and *stewardess.*
>
> The abolition of the *-ess* suffix tells the reader or listener, "I intend to conceal from you the sex of the person in that job." Thus, when you learn that the *chairperson* or *chair* is going to be Pat Jones or Leslie Smith, or anyone not with a sexually recognizable first name like Jane or Tarzan, you will be denied the information about whether that person is a man or a woman.
>
> Ah, that's the point, say the language police, sex-eraser squad: it should not matter. But information does matter—and does it really hurt to know? What's wrong with *chairwoman* or *Congresswoman?* Let's go further: now that the anti-sexist point has been made in this generation, wouldn't it be better for the next generation to have more information rather than less?

Regardless of whether you agree with the opinions expressed here, you probably would want to attribute them to your source with an acknowledgment phrase, rather than to present them as if they were your own. Notice how the underlined phrases in the following summary do that:

> <u>Some purists argue</u> that certain forms of nonsexist language are awkward and unnecessary, contributing little if anything to gender equity. <u>These writers contend</u> that occupational titles like *flight attendant* and *waitron* are awkward or silly and that they conceal relevant information about people's identities. <u>One such critic, William Safire, believes</u> that the injustices of sexist language have been sufficiently addressed already and that some traditional job designations should be retained (10).

EXERCISE   Summarizing an Argument

The following passage appears in an editorial essay by David Cole, a professor of law at Georgetown University. Cole is disputing the claim that government officials do not threaten freedom of expression when they withhold or revoke funding for artistic exhibits that most citizens find offensive. Write a brief summary of Cole's argument and supporting evidence. Since your summary will refer to the author by name, the closing parenthetical note should indicate only that the quotation comes from page 5E of the newspaper in which it appeared. (Note: Although Cole's argument is arranged inductively, with the main idea stated in the final sentence, you may choose to arrange your summary deductively, with the main idea stated in the opening sentence.)

> The argument appears sensible. It is surely different to throw an artist in jail for his speech than to deny him a government grant. . . .
>
> But a moment's reflections shows that the conclusion that the government has a free hand to deny funding wherever it dislikes the content of speech it funds cannot be right.
>
> Virtually every form of public speech in this country is government-subsidized. The print media enjoy a multimillion-dollar subsidy in the form of second-class mailing privileges. The government gives the broadcast media free access to the airwaves, a commodity worth billions.
>
> Nonprofit advocacy organizations receive a tax exemption worth billions more. Public and private universities are subsidized through direct appropriations, financial aid to students and research grants to faculty. Every demonstration on public property is subsidized with taxpayer dollars required for security and maintenance.
>
> In light of the prevalence of government subsidies, if the state were free to deny funds to those whose speech it finds disagreeable, freedom of expression would be rendered meaningless.

Summarizing in Research Papers

Summary can serve basically the same purposes as paraphrase in research writing: to cite important facts or information, to place a topic or issue in context, or to support an interpretation or opinion. It is, of course, just as important to use parenthetical notes to identify summarized sources as paraphrased sources. The following examples illustrate contexts for using summary in research writing.

Summarizing to Cite Facts or Information

Suppose you are writing a research paper about homelessness in the United States. One of your sources, an article by David Levi Strauss titled "A Threnody for Street Kids," cites the following facts:

> "Home" has increasingly become a site of violent conflict and abuse. Half of all homes are "broken" by divorce; many more are broken by spousal abuse. Child abuse in the home is a national epidemic. Poverty kills twenty-seven children every day in America. Ozzie and Harriet are dead and the Cosbys don't live around here.
>
> Every year in the United States a million and a half kids run away from home. Many of them end up on city streets. Right now, today, there are some thirty thousand kids living on the streets of New York City. Contrary to popular belief, most of them run away not because they want to but because they have to; because even the streets are safer than where they're running from, where many of them have been physically and sexually abused by their families. Even

The original source

so, they are not running *to* anything but death. Nationwide, more than five thousand children a year are buried in unmarked graves.

A summary of these facts might prove useful in a paragraph that dispels certain myths about homelessness. Among those myths is the belief that homeless people are primarily adults who have made conscious, deliberate choices. Your summary might look like this:

<table>
<tr>
<td>A brief
summary</td>
<td>One of the most brutal facts about homelessness is the number of its victims who are minors. Driven from their families by domestic violence, huge numbers of children (30,000 in New York City alone) have taken to the streets, vainly hoping to find safety. Thousands of them die (Strauss 753).</td>
</tr>
</table>

Basically, these sentences summarize facts, while citing one statistic. Though obliged to cite your source in a parenthetical note, you probably would not name David Levi Strauss in an acknowledgment phrase, since there is nothing in the facts themselves that is uniquely his. If, on the other hand, you wanted to quote a bit, you probably would include such a phrase. A slightly longer summary, therefore, might look like this:

<table>
<tr>
<td>A longer
summary that
quotes the
source</td>
<td>One of the most brutal facts about homelessness is the number of victims who are minors. One reason is the dramatic increase in domestic violence, especially in poor neighborhoods. As journalist David Levi Strauss puts it, "Ozzie and Harriet are dead and the Cosbys don't live around here." Strauss points to some alarming facts: on any given day, thirty thousand children are homeless in New York City; thousands of homeless children die every year in the United States (753).</td>
</tr>
</table>

Summarizing to Place a Topic or Issue in Context

Suppose a member of the student government association on your campus has raised objections to Black Culture Week, arguing that such an event is unwarranted without a comparable celebration of white culture. If you wished to examine and refute this familiar argument in a research paper, you might demonstrate that most white Americans know far less about African culture than they think they do—certainly a great deal less than most African Americans know about European culture. In the course of your research, you might locate an article by Neal Ascherson titled "Africa's Lost History," which reviews a recently published book. Ascherson's article contains the following paragraph:

<table>
<tr>
<td>The original
passage</td>
<td>This is a book perfectly designed for an intelligent reader who comes to the subject of Africa reasonably fresh and unprejudiced. Unfortunately, those are still fairly uncommon qualifications in Europe. The first category of baffled consumers will be those who until yesterday spent much energy denying Africans their history. They did not quite say, like [one] Cambridge professor, that Africa had no history at all. They said that anything ancient, beautiful, or sophisticated found on the continent could have had nothing to do with the talentless loungers incapable of making a decent cup of tea or plowing in a straight line. The ruins of Great Zimbabwe had been built by Phoenicians, the Benin bronzes were probably Portuguese, and all ironwork was Arab. A more sophisticated version of this line was that although Africa had made a promising start, some unknown disaster or lurking collective brain damage had immobilized Africans halfway down the</td>
</tr>
</table>

track. This meant, among other things, that the history and archaeology of Africa belonged to the Europeans, who had dug it up and were alone able to understand it. Back to Europe it went and there, to a great extent, it remains.

A summary of this passage would allow you to place Black Culture Week in a different context from the one in which your fellow student views it. Consequently, your paper might include a paragraph like this somewhere in its introduction:

> Black Culture Week is more than just an occasion for celebrating African heritage. It is an opportunity to dispel some of the demeaning misconceptions and stereotypes that diminish respect or even curiosity among white Americans. Among these is the belief, held by many educated Europeans, that Africa has no native history and culture at all—that whatever artifacts can be found there were brought by non-Africans, who are the only people capable of understanding or appreciating them (Ascherson 26). Black Culture Week, therefore, is not so much a matter of promoting African heritage as it is a matter of correcting pervasive misinformation so that educated people can decide whether they wish to study a field that many assume to be nonexistent or unworthy of attention.

Incorporating a summary into your essay

Summarizing to Support an Interpretation or Opinion

In Chapter 3, when we talked about paraphrasing arguments, we considered the effects of various methods of attributing views to a source. Specifically, we considered the following options:

- Stating an argument with no direct reference to its source, but putting both the author's name and the appropriate page number(s) in a parenthetical note.

- Identifying the source within the summary by means of an acknowledgment phrase, leaving only page number(s) in the parenthetical note. (For example, attribution phrases that might introduce a paraphrase of Barbara Lawrence's argument appear on pages 100–01.)

- Expressing judgment about the credibility of the source in an acknowledgment phrase. (Judgmental acknowledgment phrases used in a letter to a library director are found on page 101.)

The effects of attributing an opinion to its source are equally important in the case of summary. Consider the following passage from an essay by Charles R. Lawrence, III, a professor of law at Stanford University. Lawrence makes the controversial argument that racial insults are not protected by the constitutional guarantee of free speech when they occur on college campuses.

> If the purpose of the First Amendment is to foster the greatest amount of speech, racial insults disserve that purpose. Assaultive racist speech functions as a preemptive strike. The invective is experienced as a blow, not as a proffered idea, and once the blow is struck, it is unlikely that a dialogue will follow. Racial insults are particularly undeserving of First Amendment protection because the perpetrator's intention is not to discover truth or initiate dialogue but to injure the victim. In most situations, members of minority groups realize that they are likely to lose if they respond to epithets by fighting and are forced to remain silent and submissive.

A source expressing an opinion

Courts have held that offensive speech may not be regulated in public forums such as streets where the listener may avoid the speech by moving on, but the regulation of otherwise protected speech has been permitted when the speech invades the privacy of the unwilling listener's home or when the unwilling listener cannot avoid the speech. Racist posters, fliers, and graffiti in dormitories, bathrooms, and other common living spaces would seem to clearly fall within the reasoning of these cases. Minority students should not be required to remain in their rooms in order to avoid racial assault. Minimally, they should find a safe haven in their dorm rooms and in all other common rooms that are a part of their daily routine.

I would also argue that the university's responsibility for insuring that these students receive an equal educational opportunity provides a compelling justification for regulations that insure them safe passage in all common areas. A minority student should not have to risk becoming the target of racially assaulting speech every time he or she chooses to walk across campus.

If you were arguing in favor of a campus speech code that prohibits racial insults, you could cite Lawrence to support your views. Thus, you might summarize the passage as follows:

Use of the source in an argumentative paper

The First Amendment was designed to protect the free exchange of ideas, but racial insults are designed to injure or intimidate others, to discourage rather than to promote discussion. It would be different if minority students were able to walk away from such insults, but when these insults are placed in dorms and other university buildings, offended students are compelled to endure them (Lawrence B1).

If you wanted to add authority to this opinion, you might introduce the same summary with an acknowledgment phrase—for example, "Stanford law professor Charles Lawrence concludes that . . . " or "It is the opinion of some legal experts that . . . "

If, on the other hand, you disagreed with Lawrence and saw danger in efforts to abridge free speech on college campuses, you would certainly want to precede your summary with an acknowledgment phrase that places some distance between you and Lawrence's view—for example, "Professor Charles Lawrence's views are typical of those who argue that protecting minorities must take priority over preserving unrestricted free speech." You might even consider a more judgmental acknowledgment phrase—for example, "Professor Charles Lawrence rationalizes the abridgment of free speech on college campuses by arguing that it serves to promote racial justice."

EXERCISE   ## Summarizing in Research Papers

Write a summary of each of the following passages—one that is appropriate to the given situation. Remember that you may choose to identify the source at the beginning of your summary or put the last name(s) of the author(s), along with page number(s), in a parenthetical note at the end.

a. *Source:* The following passage appears on page 5 of an article by Agis Salpukas, staff writer for the *New York Times*. The article deals with nonpolluting, renewable sources of electric power.

Situation: Enrolled in a course titled Environmental Economics, you are composing a research paper that forecasts the future of alternative sources of power. A summary of this passage will appear in your introduction.

Passage:
   [I]n the past five years, the promise of renewable power has become a distant hope. Incentives provided by state regulators and utilities have disappeared. Federal research funds have been cut by a budget-conscious Congress. The industry itself has stumbled. Kenetech's newest turbines were flawed, according to a stockholder lawsuit and some industry analysts, and the company's wind subsidiary was forced to seek bankruptcy protection.
   But while green power itself is in retreat, the grass roots support for it is still widespread. Central and South West Corporation, an electric and natural gas utility in the Southwest, recently held town meetings with some of its 1.7 million customers and found strong support for alternative energy sources. Most residents said they were willing to pay from $5 to $7 more a month to have solar or other alternatives supply part of their energy.

b. *Source:* In the following passage, music critic Paul Griffiths explains the impulses behind and the achievements of Serialism, an outgrowth of Modernism, a movement that transformed all of the arts during the first half of the twentieth century. The passage appears on page 29 of an article by Griffiths.

Situation: You are writing a research paper on modernist contributions to musical theory for a course titled Introduction to Music History. A summary of the following passage can introduce the section of your paper that addresses Serialism.

Passage:
   Serialism arose out of desires and needs to organize things in essentially different and, it was hoped, better ways. A system that grew up during the eighteenth and nineteenth centuries—a system of keys and themes, of symphonic forms and regular rhythms—had become so widespread as to seem normal. But it left a great deal out of account. In particular, it left little alternative but to regard as "primitive" any music composed before the system came into full operation or any music arising in non-Western cultures.
   Serialism changed the rules. It refused to accept [this] old system as natural and eternal, and it proposed ways of setting up new systems. Far from being proscriptive [as its critics have charged], it widened the range of what could be considered music and of how music could be made. And—this was its most revolutionary idea—it proposed that musical organization is not God-given but man-made.

c. *Source:* In the following article, published on page 10 of a California newspaper, staff writer Melinda Burns describes working and living conditions for migrant workers at a large berry farm in the Skagit Valley.

Situation: Working as a volunteer in the aftermath of a recent flood, you have become aware of the hardships endured by migrant farm workers in your region. You now wish to place what you have learned within the broader context of immigration policies and to report your findings in a research paper for a course titled Cultural Anthropology.

Passage:

About a hundred fifty Mixtecs [Indians native to the Mexican state of Oaxaca] from Santa Maria and Oxnard, including several dozen children, had been staying since June. At least one family had come all the way from Oaxaca.

The camp barracks were old and run down. . . . There were piles of trash outside the cabin doors, and the workers complained that the roofs leaked when it rained. In the collective showers, they said, the hot water ran out daily after the first twenty minutes of use. They objected to having to pay a $50 deposit for housing in such disrepair.

One young man said he had picked sixty-three pounds of blueberries in five hours that same day. At 20¢ a pound, his pay came to $12, he said.

· · ·

Alejandro Rojas, a twenty-eight-year-old Mixtec from San Juan Pias and a member of Two United Towns, a Mixtec organization in Santa Maria, told the group about recent walkouts from the strawberry fields in Santa Barbara County. More than seven hundred farm workers, most of them Mixtecs, protested in May and June for higher piece rates. Rojas said he had been fired for leading one of the walkouts, but he said it was worth it because the growers immediately raised the pickers' pay.

GUIDELINES for Effective Summarizing

The general principles set forth in this chapter can be summed up in the following guidelines for effective summarizing:

- Like paraphrasing, summarizing calls for close literal reading, but it also involves discerning main ideas—distinguishing them from minor points and illustrative examples.

- Like a paraphrase, a summary is written in your own language, although it may contain a short quotation or two—never more than a single sentence.

- Although there is no single correct way to compose a summary, one workable process is detailed on page 144.

- Summaries serve the same basic functions in research writing as paraphrases do.

 # READING SELECTION

The previous edition of *Writing, Reading, and Research* included an article by journalist Ron Suskind titled "Against All Odds." That article profiled high-school junior Cedric Jennings, an academically gifted student at one of the poorest, most dangerous urban schools in the United States. It concluded with Jennings's acceptance into a summer residential program for minority students who hope to attend Massachusetts Institute of Technology (MIT). The following article appeared in the *Wall Street Journal* four months later, after Jennings had completed the summer program. Suskind received a Pulitzer Prize in journalism for the two articles.

Class Struggle

Poor, Black, and Smart, an Inner-City Teen Tries to Survive at MIT

RON SUSKIND

In a dormitory lobby, under harsh fluorescent lights, there is a glimpse of the future: 1
a throng of promising minority high schoolers, chatting and laughing, happy and
confident.

It is a late June day, and the fifty-one teenagers have just converged here at Mass- 2
achusetts Institute of Technology for its prestigious minority summer program—a program that bootstraps most of its participants into MIT's freshman class. Already, an
easy familiarity prevails. A doctor's son from Puerto Rico invites a chemical engineer's
son from south Texas to explore nearby Harvard Square. Over near the soda machines,
the Hispanic son of two schoolteachers meets a black girl who has the same T-shirt,
from an annual minority-leadership convention.

"This is great," he says. "Kind of like we're all on our way up, together." 3

Maybe. Off to one side, a gangly boy is singing a rap song, mostly to himself. His 4
expression is one of pure joy. Cedric Jennings, the son of a drug dealer and the product of one of Washington's most treacherous neighborhoods, has worked toward this
moment for his entire life.

Cedric, whose struggle to excel was chronicled in a May 26 page-one article in [the 5
Wall Street Journal], hails from a square mile of chaos. His apartment building is surrounded by crack dealers, and his high school, Frank W. Ballou Senior High, is at the
heart of the highest-crime area in the city. Already this year, four teenagers from his
district—teens who should have been his schoolmates—were charged in homicides.
Another six are dead, murder victims themselves.

For Cedric, MIT has taken on almost mythic proportions. It represents the culmi- 6
nation of everything he has worked for, his ticket to escape poverty. He has staked
everything on getting accepted to college here, and at the summer program's end he
will find out whether he stands a chance. He doesn't dare think about what will happen if the answer is no.

"This will be the first steps of my path out, out of here, to a whole other world," 7
he had said not long before leaving Washington for the summer program. "I'll be going
so far from here, there'll be no looking back."

As Cedric looks around the bustling dormitory lobby on that first day, he finally 8
feels at home, like he belongs. "They arrive here and say, 'Wow, I didn't know there
were so many like me,' " says William Ramsey, administrative director of MIT's program. "It gives them a sense . . . that being a smart minority kid is the most normal
thing to be."

9   But they aren't all alike, really, a lesson Cedric is learning all too fast. He is one of only a tiny handful of students from poor backgrounds; most of the rest range from lower-middle-class to affluent. As he settles into chemistry class on the first day, a row of girls, all savvy and composed, amuse themselves by poking fun at "my Washington street-slang," as Cedric tells it later. "You know, the way I talk, slur my words and whatever."

10   Cedric is often taunted at his nearly all-black high school for "talking white." But now, he is hearing the flawless diction of a different world, of black students from suburbs with neat lawns and high schools that send most graduates off to college.

11   Other differences soon set him apart. One afternoon, as students talk about missing their families, it becomes clear that almost everyone else has a father at home. Cedric's own father denied paternity for years and has been in jail for almost a decade. And while many of the students have been teased back home for being brainy, Cedric's studiousness has earned him threats from gang members with guns.

12   Most worrisome, though, is that despite years of asking for extra work after school—of creating his own independent-study course just to get the basic education that students elsewhere take for granted—he is woefully far behind. He is overwhelmed by the blistering workload: six-hours each day of intensive classes, study sessions with tutors each night, endless hours more of homework.

13   Only in calculus, his favorite subject, does he feel sure of himself. He is slipping steadily behind in physics, chemistry, robotics, and English.

14   In the second week of the program, Cedric asks one of the smartest students, who hails from a top-notch public school, for help on some homework. "He said it was 'beneath him,'" Cedric murmurs later, barely able to utter the words. "Like, he's so much better than me. Like I'm some kind of inferior human being."

15   A crowd of students jostles into a dormitory lounge a few evenings later for Chinese food, soda, and a rare moment of release from studying. Cliques already have formed, there are whispers of romances, and lunch groups have crystallized, almost always along black or Hispanic lines. But as egg rolls disappear, divides are crossed.

16   A Hispanic teenager from a middle-class New Mexico neighborhood tries to teach the opening bars of Beethoven's "Moonlight Sonata" to a black youngster, a toll taker's son from Miami. An impeccably-clad black girl from an affluent neighborhood teaches some dance steps to a less privileged one.

17   Tutors, mostly minority undergraduates at MIT who once went through this program, look on with tight smiles, always watchful. The academic pressure, they know, is rising fast. Midterm exams start this week—along with all-nighters and panic. Some students will grow depressed; others will get sick from exhaustion. The tutors count heads, to see if anyone looks glum, confused, or strays from the group.

18   "They're going through so much, that a day here is like a week, so we can't let them be down in the dumps for very long," says Valencia Thomas, a graduate of this program and now a twenty-year-old sophomore at nearby Harvard University. "Their identities are being challenged, broken up and reformed. Being a minority and a high achiever means you have to carry extra baggage about who you are, and where you belong. That puts them at risk."

19   Tonight, all the students seem to be happy and accounted for. Almost.

20   Upstairs, Cedric is lying on his bed with the door closed and lights off, waiting for a miracle, that somehow, he will "be able to keep up with the others."

21   It is slow in coming.

22   "It's all about proving yourself, really," he says quietly, sitting up. "I'm trying, you know. It's all I can do is try. But where I start from is so far behind where some other kids are, I have to run twice the distance to catch up."

He is cutting back on calls to his mother, not wanting to tell her that things aren't   **23**
going so well. Barbara Jennings had raised her boy to believe that he can succeed, that
he must. When Cedric was a toddler, she quit her clerical job temporarily and went on
welfare so that she could take him to museums, read him books, instill in him the importance of getting an education—and getting out.

"I know what she'll say: 'Don't get down, you can do anything you set your mind   **24**
to,' " Cedric says. "I'm finding out it's not that simple."

Cedric isn't the only student who is falling behind. Moments later, Neda Ramirez's   **25**
staccato voice echoes across the dormitory courtyard.

"I am so angry," says the Mexican-American teen, who goes to a rough, mostly   **26**
Hispanic high school in the Texas border town of Edinburg. "I work so hard at my
school—I have a 102 percent average—but I'm realizing the school is so awful it
doesn't amount to anything. I don't belong here. My father says, 'Learn as much as
you can at MIT, do your best and accept the consequences.' I said, 'Yeah, Dad, but
I'm the one who has to deal with the failure.' " By the middle of the third week, the
detonations of self-doubt become audible. One morning in physics class, Cedric
stands at his desk, walks out into the hallway, and screams.

The physics teacher, Thomas Washington, a black twenty-four-year-old Ph.D. can-   **27**
didate at MIT, rushes after him. "I told him, 'Cedric, don't be so hard on yourself,' "
Mr. Washington recounts later. "I told him that a lot of the material is new to lots of
the kids—just keep at it."

But, days after the incident, Mr. Washington vents his frustration at how the deck   **28**
is stacked against underprivileged students like Cedric and Neda.

"You have to understand that there's a controversy over who these types of pro-   **29**
grams should serve," he says, sitting in a sunny foyer one morning after class. "If you
only took the kids who need this the most, the ones who somehow excel at terrible
schools, who swim upstream but are still far behind academically, you wouldn't get
enough eventually accepted to MIT to justify the program."

And so the program ends up serving many students who really don't need it.   **30**
Certainly, MIT's program—like others at many top colleges—looks very good. More
than half its students eventually are offered admission to the freshman class. Those
victors, however, are generally students from better schools in better neighborhoods, acknowledges Mr. Ramsey, a black MIT graduate who is the program's administrative director. For some of them, this program is little more than résumé
padding.

Mr. Ramsey, 68, had hoped it would be different. Seven years ago, when he took   **31**
over the program, he had "grand plans, to find late bloomers, and deserving kids in
tough spots. But it didn't take me three months to realize I'd be putting kids on a suicide dash."

A six-week program like MIT's, which doesn't offer additional, continuing support,   **32**
simply can't function if it is filled only with inner-city youths whose educations lag so
far behind, he says: "They'd get washed out and everything they believe in would
come crashing down on their heads. Listen, we know a lot about suicide rates up here.
I'd be raising them."

Perhaps it isn't surprising, then, that while 47 percent of all black children live in   **33**
poverty in America, only about a dozen students in this year's MIT program would
even be considered lower-middle class, according to Mr. Ramsey. Though one or two
of the neediest students like Cedric find their way to the program each year, he adds,
they tend to be long shots to make it to the next step, into MIT for college. Those few,
though, Mr. Ramsey says, are "cases where you could save lives."

34   Which is why Cedric, more than perhaps any other student in this year's program, hits a nerve.

35   "I want to take Cedric by the hand and lead him through the material," says physics instructor Mr. Washington, pensively. "But I resist. The real world's not like that. If he makes it to MIT, he won't have someone like me to help him.

36   "You know, part of it I suppose is our fault," he adds. "We haven't figured out a way to give credit for distance traveled."

37   So, within the program—like society beyond it—a class system is becoming obvious, even to the students. At the top are students like the beautifully dressed Jenica Dover, one of the girls who had found Cedric's diction so amusing. A confident black girl, she attends a mostly white high school in wealthy Newton, Mass. "Some of this stuff is review for me," she says one day, strolling from physics class, where she spent some of the hour giggling with deskmates. "I come from a very good school, and that makes all this pretty manageable."

38   Cedric, Neda, and the few others from poor backgrounds, meanwhile, are left to rely on what has gotten them this far: adrenaline and faith.

39   On a particularly sour day in mid-July, Cedric's rising doubts seem to overwhelm him. He can't work any harder in calculus, his best subject, yet he still lags behind other students in the class. Physics is becoming a daily nightmare.

40   Tossing and turning that night, too troubled to sleep, he looks out at the lights of MIT, thinking about the sacrifices he has made—the hours of extra work that he begged for from his teachers, the years focusing so single-mindedly on school that he didn't even have friends. "I thought that night that it wasn't ever going to be enough. That I wouldn't make it to MIT," he says later. "That, all this time, I was just fooling myself."

41   As the hours passed he fell in and out of sleep. Then he awoke with a jolt, suddenly thinking about Cornelia Cunningham, an elder at the Washington Pentecostal church he attends as often as four times a week with his mother. A surrogate grandmother who had challenged and prodded Cedric since he was a small boy, "Mother Cunningham," as he always called her, had died two weeks before he left MIT.

42   "I was lying there, and her spirit seemed to come to me, I could hear her voice, right there in my room, saying—just like always—'Cedric, you haven't yet begun to fight,'" he recounts. "And the next morning, I woke up and dove into my calculus homework like never before."

43   The auditorium near MIT's majestic domed library rings with raucous cheering, as teams prepare their robots for battle. Technically, this is an exercise in ingenuity and teamwork: Each three-student team had been given a box of motors, levers and wheels to design a machine—mostly little cars with hooks on the front—to fight against another team's robot over a small soccer ball.

44   But something has gone awry. The trios, carefully chosen and mixed in past years by the instructors, were self-selected this year by the students. Clearly, the lines were drawn by race. As the elimination rounds begin, Hispanic teams battle against black teams. "PUERTO RICO, PUERTO RICO," comes the chant from the Hispanic side.

45   Black students whoop as Cedric's team fights into the quarterfinals, only to lose. He stumbles in mock anguish toward the black section, into the arms of several girls who have become his friends. The winner, oddly enough, is a team led by a Caucasian boy from Oklahoma who is here because he is 1/128 Potawatomi Indian. Both camps are muted.

46   In the final weeks, the explosive issues of race and class that have been simmering since the students arrived break out into the open. It isn't just black vs. Hispanic or poor vs. rich. It is minority vs. white.

At a lunch table, over cold cuts on whole wheat, talk turns to the ultimate insult: "wanting to be white." Jocelyn Truitt, a black girl from a good Maryland high school, says her mother, a college professor, "started early on telling me to ignore the whole 'white' thing. . . . I've got white friends. People say things, that I'm trading up, selling out, but I don't listen. Let them talk."   47

Leslie Chavez says she hears it, too, in her largely Hispanic school. "If you get good grades, you're 'white.' What, so you shouldn't do that? Thinking that way is a formula for failure."   48

In an English class discussion later on the same issue, some students say assimilation is the only answer. "The success of whites means they've mapped out the territory for success," says Alfred Fraijo, a cocky Hispanic from Los Angeles. "If you want to move up, and fit in, it will have to be on those terms. There's nothing wrong with aspiring to that—it's worth the price of success."   49

Cedric listens carefully, but the arguments for assimilation are foreign to him. He knows few whites; in his world, whites have always been the unseen oppressors. "The charge of 'wanting to be white,' where I'm from," Cedric says, "is like treason."   50

A charge for which he is being called to task, and not just by tough kids in Ballou's hallways. He has had phone conversations over the past few weeks with an old friend from junior high, a boy his age named Torrance Parks, who is trying to convert Cedric to Islam.   51

"He just says I should stick with my own," says Cedric, "that I'm already betraying my people, leaving them all behind, by coming up to a big white university and all, that even if I'm successful, I'll never be accepted by whites."   52

Back in Washington, Cedric's mother, a data-input clerk at the Department of Agriculture, is worried. She hopes Cedric will now continue to push forward, to take advantage of scholarships to private prep schools, getting him out of Ballou High for his senior year, "keeping on his path out."   53

"He needs to get more of what he's getting at MIT, more challenging work with nice, hard-working kids—maybe even white kids," she says. The words of Islam, which she fears might lead toward more radical black separatism, would "mean a retreat from all that." She adds that she asks Torrance: "What can you offer my son other than hate?"   54

She is increasingly frustrated, yet unable to get her son to discuss the issue. When recruiters from Phillips Exeter Academy come to MIT to talk to the students, Cedric snubs them. "They have to wear jacket and tie there; it's elitist," he says, "It's not for me."   55

Still, in the past few weeks, Cedric has been inching forward. Perseverance finally seems to be paying off. He has risen to near the top of the group in calculus. He is improving in chemistry, adequate in robotics, and showing some potential in English. Physics remains a sore spot.   56

He also has found his place here. The clutch of middle- and upper-middle-class black girls who once made fun of him has grown fond of him, fiercely protective of him. One Friday night, when Cedric demurs about joining a Saturday group trip to Cape Cod, the girls press him until he finally admits his reason: He doesn't have a bathing suit.   57

"So we took him to the mall to pick out some trunks," says Isa Williams, the daughter of two Atlanta college professors. "Because he doesn't have maybe as many friends at home, Cedric has a tendency of closing up when he gets sad, and not turning to other people," she adds. "We want him to know we're there for him."   58

The next day, on the bus, Cedric, at his buoyant best, leads the group in songs.   59

Though he doesn't want to say it—to jinx anything—by early in the fifth week Cedric is actually feeling a shard of hope. Blackboard scribbles are beginning to make   60 sense, even on the day in late July when he is thinking only about what will follow classes: a late afternoon meeting with Prof. Trilling, the academic director. This is the meeting Cedric has been waiting for since the moment he arrived, when the professor will assess his progress and—most important—his prospects for someday getting accepted into MIT.

61   Cedric, wound tight, gets lost on the way to Prof. Trilling's office, arriving a few minutes late.

62   Prof. Trilling, who is white, ushers the youngster into an office filled with certificates, wide windows, and a dark wood desk. Always conscious of clothes, Cedric tries to break the ice by complimenting Mr. Trilling on his shoes, but the professor doesn't respond, moving right to business.

63   After a moment, he asks Cedric if he is "thinking about applying and coming to MIT."

64   "Yeah," Cedric says. "I've been wanting to come for years."

65   "Well, I don't think you're MIT material," the professor says flatly. "Your academic record isn't strong enough."

66   Cedric, whose average for his junior year was better than perfect, 4.19, thanks to several A+ grades, asks what he means.

67   The professor explains that Cedric's Scholastic Aptitude Test scores—he has scored only a 910 out of a possible 1600—are about 200 points below what they need to be.

68   Agitated, Cedric begins insisting that he is willing to work hard, "exceedingly hard," to make it at MIT. "He seemed to have this notion that if you work hard enough, you can achieve anything," Prof. Trilling recalls haltingly. "That is admirable, but it also can set up for disappointment. And, at the present time, I told him, that just doesn't seem to be enough."

69   Ending the meeting, the professor jots down names of professors at Howard University, a black college in Washington, and at the University of Maryland. He suggests that Cedric call them, that if Cedric does well at one of those colleges, he might someday be able to transfer to MIT.

70   Cedric's eyes are wide, his temples bulging, his teeth clenched. He doesn't hear Mr. Trilling's words of encouragement; he hears only MIT's rejection. He takes the piece of paper from the professor, leaves without a word, and walks across campus and to his dorm room. Crumpling up the note, he throws it in the garbage. He skips dinner that night, ignoring the knocks on his locked door from Isa, Jenica, and other worried friends. "I thought about everything," he says, "about what a fool I've been."

71   The next morning, wandering out into the foyer as calculus class ends, he finally blows. "He made me feel so small, this big," he says, almost screaming, as he presses his fingers close. " 'Not MIT material'. . . . Who is he to tell me that? He doesn't know what I've been through. This is it, right, this is racism. A white guy telling me I can't do it."

72   Physics class is starting. Cedric slips in, moving, now almost by rote, to the front row—the place he sits in almost every class he has ever taken.

73   Isa passes him a note: What happened?

74   He writes a note back describing the meeting and saying he is thinking of leaving, of just going home. The return missive, now also signed by Jenica and a third friend, tells Cedric he has worked too hard to give up. "You can't just run away," the note says, as Isa recalls later. "You have to stay and prove to them you have what it takes. . . . We all care about you and love you." Cedric folds the note gently and puts it in his pocket.

The hour ends, with a worksheet Cedric is supposed to hand in barely touched. 75
Taking a thick pencil from his bookbag, he scrawls "I AM LOST" across the blank sheet, drops it on the teacher's desk, and disappears into the crowd.

Jenica runs to catch up with him, to commiserate. But it will be difficult for her 76 to fully understand: In her meeting with Prof. Trilling the next day, he encourages her to enroll at MIT. She shrugs off the invitation. "Actually," she tells the professor, "I was planning to go to Stanford."

On a sweltering late-summer day, all three air conditioners are blasting in Cedric's 77 cramped apartment in Washington. Cedric is sitting on his bed, piled high with clothes, one of his bags not yet unpacked even though he returned home from Cambridge several weeks ago.

The last days of the MIT program were fitful. Cedric didn't go to the final banquet, 78 where awards are presented, because he didn't want to see Prof. Trilling again. But he made friends in Cambridge, and on the last morning, as vans were loaded for trips to the airport, he hugged and cried like the rest of them.

"I don't think much about it now, about MIT," he says, as a police car speeds by, 79 its siren barely audible over the air conditioners' whir. "Other things are happening. I have plenty to do."

Not really. Most days since returning from New England, he has spent knocking 80 around the tiny, spare apartment, or going to church, or plodding through applications for colleges and scholarships.

The calls from Torrance, who has been joined in his passion for Islam by Cedric's 81 first cousin, have increased. Cedric says he "just listens," and that "it's hard to argue with" Torrance.

But inside the awkward youngster, a storm rages. Not at home on the hustling 82 streets, and ostracized by high-school peers who see his ambition as a sign of "disrespect," Cedric has discovered that the future he so carefully charted may not welcome him either.

Certainly, he will apply to colleges. And his final evaluations from each MIT class 83 turned out better than he—and perhaps even Prof. Trilling—thought they would. He showed improvement right through the very last day.

But the experience in Cambridge left Cedric bewildered. Private-school scholar- 84 ship offers, crucial to help underprivileged students make up for lost years before landing in the swift currents of college, have been passed by, despite his mother's urgings. Instead, Cedric Jennings has decided to return to Ballou High, the place from which he has spent the last three years trying to escape.

"I know this may sound crazy," he says, shaking his head. "But I guess I'm sort of 85 comfortable there, at my school. Comfortable in this place that I hate."

Freewriting

In your notebook, write for ten to fifteen minutes about the summer program for minority students at MIT. You might want to draw connections to your own experiences in a college orientation program, a freshman-year seminar, or any other setting in which study skills and other strategies for academic success have been presented. You might want to consider the conflicting needs and priorities of poor and middle-class minority students or to speculate on the future that awaits Cedric, Neda, and some of the other students that Ron Suskind profiles.

Group Work

Listen carefully and take notes as each freewrite is read aloud. Try to characterize the attitudes of group members toward the MIT summer program and the minority students who participate in it. Are the members of your group unanimous in their appraisal of the program? If not, try to understand and articulate competing points of view. What future do your peers forecast for Cedric, Neda, and the other students who attended the program?

Review Questions

1. How does Cedric's family and school background differ from those of most other students in the summer program at MIT?

2. Why, according to Cedric's physics instructor, doesn't MIT restrict its summer program to underprivileged minority students?

3. Who seems to have influenced Cedric's desire to succeed academically?

4. Why does Professor Trilling believe that Cedric is "not MIT material"?

Discussion Questions

1. Of all the possible explanations for Cedric's ambition to succeed—for example, innate genius, parental encouragement, mentoring, personal effort—which do you feel are the most and the least significant?

2. Of all the barriers to Cedric's success—for example, being poor, lacking a father, living in a unsafe environment, attending an inferior school, being harassed by peers—which do you feel are most and least significant?

3. Since the *Wall Street Journal* circulates throughout North America, Cedric became a minor celebrity when Suskind's first article appeared on the front page of that newspaper several weeks before the program at MIT began. How might this have influenced the way that faculty and other students perceived Cedric and how he saw himself? Why do you suppose Suskind doesn't take this into account anywhere in his second article?

Writing

1. Write a summary of "Class Struggle" and compare it with the summary of a classmate whose educational background differs significantly from your own. In particular, see if there are major differences in what each of you takes to be the main ideas in the article. Consider, in writing, how a person's understanding of main idea might be influenced by his or her background and past experience.

2. Arrange an opportunity to observe an educational setting that you are unfamiliar with (e.g., an adult literacy class; community service instruction in an art, craft, or sports activity; a pre-kindergarten class). Report on what you learn in a profile essay like Suskind's, Brian Feagans's (Chapter 3), or Kristin Smith's (Chapter 1).

3. After locating and reading two other articles that have won Pulitzer Prizes for journalism, try to draw some inferences about the subject matter, methods of reporting, and writing style that characterize such writing. Present your findings in a short essay.

4. A year after "Class Struggle" appeared in the *Wall Street Journal,* Cedric entered Brown University as a freshman. His experiences there are related in Suskind's recent book *A Hope in the Unseen.* Write a short, informal paper speculating on the nature of those experiences. If your library has a copy of the book, read the opening and closing chapters to gauge the accuracy of your predictions.

6 Synthesizing Sources: Writing a Summary Report

In previous chapters, you worked with individual sources, paraphrasing or summarizing them in isolation. More typically, your research on a topic will lead you to consult several sources, and you will need to present the information you find in a way that combines, or *synthesizes,* those sources. If, for example, you wanted to learn more about dirigibles or about the early history of your hometown, you probably would consult books and articles. If you reported your findings, you would synthesize the information acquired from these sources.

There are several strategies for synthesizing multiple sources, and we begin with the simplest. It consists of two steps: writing separate summaries or paraphrases of the individual sources and then linking them with transitional passages. What follows is an example.

WRITING A BRIEF SUMMARY REPORT

Suppose you have been asked to report on advertising and sports. You have chosen the following articles from a list of sources provided by your instructor. As a first step toward writing your report, read each of the articles with care, searching for important ideas and underlining noteworthy information.

The Anglophile Angle*

TERRY LEFTON

1   It's an age of logo ubiquity, wherein every establishment, from the hotel where you happen to be staying to your local marina sells apparel based on logo appeal. Add some sports equity to that logo, and those with a vested interest in the organization are easily convinced that their logo is the equivalent of the New York Yankees' familiar trademark, a perennial top seller.

2   It is helpful sometimes to recall that wasn't always the case, and Wimbledon is a good place to start. The licensing history of the tennis icon shows how long-term

*This article appears on pages 28–29 of the June 6, 1999, issue of *Brandweek.*

brand management was able to transform a ramshackle licensing program erected upon a shaky legal foundation into a blue-chip equity, one that has deftly played off the non-commercial purity and prestige of the underlying property to support an extraordinary range of products, from men's suits to Japanese bento boxes, that collectively generate some $100 million in annual revenues.

Mark McCormack, founder and chairman of Cleveland-based agency IMG, recalls   3
that at his first meeting with principals from the All England Lawn Tennis and Croquet Club in 1967, he surprised them by saying that a Wimbledon highlights film might have commercial value. A little later, he suggested that foreign broadcast rights could be worth far more than the $75,000 the club was then receiving. A slightly skeptical board authorized him to sell foreign broadcast rights, but hedged its bet by making the first $75,000 of any new deals sans commission. . . .

Another revenue stream McCormack and IMG created for Wimbledon may be its   4
most creative, since it was a licensing program for a property without a logo and whose name, taken from the municipality in which the tournament is held, was largely in the public domain.

Up until the late 1970s, the club, which stages Wimbledon as the governing body   5
for tennis in England, had generally eschewed licensing as too commercial. As a result, some companies were paying to use the name, while others used it haphazardly and on products of varying quality, without much fear of retribution. Tournament officials had almost no quality control, even though legal and illegal licensees were borrowing on their equity.

McCormack and IMG suggested cleaning up the program with some licensing expertise and a dose of brand management. Once again, those in charge of tennis' top   6
tourney weren't exactly thrilled about what McCormack was proposing, but assigned IMG the rights anyway in the late 1970s, with the caveat that IMG "shouldn't spend more buying or protecting trademarks than you are going to make licensing them." IMG bought up some licensing agreements from the likes of Bancroft and Nike and shut down some others that weren't paying for use of the name. To get off the shaky legal ground of using a municipal name as a trademark, IMG later launched what today has become the well-known "flying W" logo. Using another device that is now standard, McCormack and IMG negotiated a minute or so of TV time of their own in each broadcast agreement, then used that time to push both the Wimbledon brand and its licensees, adding valuable TV exposure for the new logo. Whether it was foresight or just good fortune, the tennis boom of the 1970s and early 1980s came just after the Wimbledon trademark began to be managed as a brand. "I don't think tennis will ever see that kind of growth spurt again," said IMG licensing chief Rick Isaacson. "All of a sudden, not only playing the sport but looking like you played—the tennis lifestyle—became a big fashion statement."

With an early assist from the forces of fashion, IMG built up the Wimbledon licensing program to a point where it now brings in more than $100 million in annual   7
worldwide retail sales. That's easily bigger than any other tennis tourney's licensing revenues: by comparison, the U.S. Open generates $7 million annually. The Wimbledon universe has around forty licensees, with sales fairly evenly split between Europe, the U.S., and Japan. As you'd expect, there are a number of tennis equipment licensees, with LBH Group and Little Miss Tennis two of the larger tennis apparel licensees in the U.S. But it's the non-endemic areas that make the Wimbledon licensing program so compelling.

Hartmarx has a longstanding deal for tailored clothing, leveraging not the logo   8
but rather the cachet of the name for a brand of fine clothing, like wool blazers and pants. In the U.S., you can also buy bracelets, earrings, rings, and necklaces ranging

from $30 to $3,000 from the Continental Buying Group along with $30 to $3,000 Wimbledon blankets from Chatham. Overseas, there's an even wider assortment of Wimbledon licensed products, like chocolate, eyewear, shortbread, preserves, and teas. One could sip that tea between matches from Wedgwood's Wimbledon tea service and accompany that with some Wimbledon frozen yogurt served in some licensed Wimbledon crystal from Waterford. Most of those products could be bought at a year-round Wimbledon-branded shop at the Royal Arcade in London.

9   Japan's many Anglophiles can purchase towels and soaps, along with Wimbledon-branded bento boxes, chopsticks, coffee, and tea sets. While they are no longer on the market, Japanese fans once could even buy Wimbledon-branded wicker furniture and fishing rods. Japan is also the only place in the world where you can purchase Wimbledon tennis balls.

10   Why does Wimbledon work so well as a licensing brand? Over several weeks, officials of the tightly staffed club were not available to discuss the program, but IMG execs suggested Wimbledon's very non-commercial nature allows it to translate well to so many product categories.

11   "You've got the purity and prestige of a 120-plus-year-old event, combined with the pomp and circumstance of the royal box and the Anglophile appeal," said IMG vice president and director of fashion and apparel licensing Jeffrey Ceppos. "That means a lot to a lot of markets." McCormack still has enough affinity for Wimbledon for it to be one of the few IMG clients he continues to personally direct.

12   "I just like what it stands for," he said. "If you ask golfers what championship they dream about winning, you'd have a split between the U.S. Open, the British Open, and the Masters. If you asked a hundred tennis players, they would all say Wimbledon. It denotes tradition, heritage, prestige, quality and that British lifestyle. So if there's a company out there trying to get across any of those qualities, it fits."

Brand Builders*

Open for Business

GERRY KHERMOUCH

1   Back in 1995, Heineken decided to pull its considerable international clout out of golf sponsorships and instead beef up its exposure to tennis. Gone from its promotional calendar were such major golf events as the Heineken Dutch Open, the Australian Open, and the World Cup of Golf. Filling the vacuum the next years was an ambitious five-year sponsorship with the U.S. Tennis Association that elevated the Dutch beer brand to the top-tier status of a USTA "Corporate Champion," joining such other megabrands as IBM, Citizen, Nissan Infiniti, and Prudential Securities. Suddenly the red star and green bottle had marshalled a presence at events that include one of the highest-visibility tournaments in the country, the U.S. Open in Flushing, New York. Outsiders pegged the value of the sponsorship at about $30 million over its five-year lifetime. . . .

*This articles appears on pages 18–21 of the October 5, 1998, issue of *Brandweek*.

As for the pragmatics, while golf may be hot lately, it is a much more difficult sport for a sponsor to "own" on account of the greater diversity of activities that would have to be acquired and orchestrated to have a meaningful impact. 2

At the same time, the major U.S. brewers generally have eschewed tennis for team sports and more downscale non-team activities such as car racing, activities that are appropriate for premium beers but not necessarily for an above-premium European import like Heineken. 3

And there is a timing issue: the U.S. Open occurs during the crucial Labor Day beer-consumption period. For domestic brewers, that signals the end of the core summer selling season, but for less seasonal specialty beers like Heineken it inaugurates a fall season. 4

Tennis "is in a transition period, and we're in on the ground floor," said Heineken brand manager Scott Hunter Smith, a former Coca-Cola executive and avid tennis player, who came to the brand after the tennis commitment was established. "Yes, golf is hot, and a Tiger Woods can help you do those things. But the Williams sisters [Venus and Serena] are creating a lot of energy around tennis. And this is something Heineken can own, and do with a flair." 5

Take the most visible manifestation of Heineken's marketing against the recently concluded U.S. Open: a television spot via agency Lowe & Partners/SMS, New York, exploited a clever conceit by translating the activity of the familiar ball retrievers to Heineken's main habitat, a bar environment, where the blurred images of the young men are seen whisking away green Heineken bottles the moment they are emptied. The "Ball Boys" spot, which leverages the on-premise ubiquity that has been a key to Heineken's success through the decades, aired heavily on VH-1 and CBS coverage of the Open, as well as in six local markets, including such high-end-import meccas as Atlanta, Boston, and Chicago. As with the core campaigns of the past couple of years, the company has placed a premium on repeated images of the green bottles and red-star icon against the backdrop of urban sophisticates' watering holes. 6

Radio ads took a parallel, but not identical, tack, drawing an analogy between the one-upmanship games played between friends or ex-lovers and the blistering volleys that characterize a good U.S. Open competition. In doing so, the ads similarly act in harmony with Heineken's core campaigns, which have featured the on-premise exchanges of affluent, sometimes overly verbal members of the youthful end of Heineken's urban demo. 7

Thus, one of the radio spots employs the audio backdrop of two grunting tennis players engaged in an intense volley as two supposed buddies engage in a game of one-upmanship that grows to encompass jobs, money, material possessions, and women. 8

"I just bought a boat," one of the men casually informs his drinking buddy. "Yeah?" says the other, with a mixture of defensiveness and skepticism. 9

"Yeah. And I'm taking Rachel Novak on it this weekend." 10

"Rachel Novak? Geez, I broke up with her ages ago. You might like her, though," the other says as the sound of the winning volley is heard along with the announcement: "Game. Set. Match." Tagline: "Heineken. Proud sponsor of the U.S. Open, and grudge matches everywhere." 11

The spots, with the emphasis on more urbane wit, contrast sharply with the often broader humor of ads for domestic premium brands like Bud, Bud Light, or Miller Lite, with their talking frogs, work-shirking husbands and grunting wrestlers. "There are two kinds of fun," Smith said. "This is a classier kind of fun." 12

Not coincidentally, the USTA has been employing younger people in its own ads in a similar effort "to create change and excitement." 13

14   "They know they need to open the door and have more fun with themselves," Smith said. "Our campaign certainly helps to show that we're having fun with it."

15   Certainly, for the USTA, it's a refreshing and much needed change to have sponsors serving up active marketing communications around its events. The game's most mainstream exposure in the past decade has been through a handful of superstars in Nike or Reebok ads, and yet now the sneaker giants are reevaluating their broad endorsement rosters and media expenditures. As for corporate sponsorships, tennis has long been a destination for high-end marketers who didn't necessarily advertise to a mainstream audience, and who bought their rights more for the élan of hospitality, schmoozing in the sport's rarified air, than for active promotional use. . . .

16   "They're a terrific sponsor and partner for us," said J. Pierce O'Neil, USTA marketing director. "They truly understand the marketing power of the U.S. Open in particular, and tennis in general, and are helping us to position it as a relevant, fun and important part of the U.S. sports landscape."

Endangered Species*

LEIGH GALLAGHER

1   Which is a tougher marketing challenge—creating a brand from scratch, or bringing one back from the grave? Ask Daniel Barth, the elegant-looking president of Devanlay, the U.S. subsidiary of the French manufacturer of Lacoste apparel. Barth has the very daunting task of resurrecting Lacoste's name and its little green crocodile logo.

2   "There isn't anyone who doesn't remember the crocodile," insists Barth, 33, in a thick French accent. Unfortunately what many shoppers remember is the cheap polyester version that sold for as little as $20 at Marshalls and other discounters in the 1980s. That's when General Mills owned the brand.

3   What most consumers don't recall is the shirt's proud origins. French tennis great René Lacoste, nicknamed "Le Crocodile" because of his exceptionally long nose and speed on the court, first wore the crocodile on a white, short-sleeved tennis shirt in 1926. In 1951 he brought it to the U.S., where it became an instant hit.

4   Therein lies Barth's challenge. Devanlay, part of the French apparel maker 10 percent controlled by the Lacoste family, spent $32 million to reclaim the U.S. rights to the Lacoste name and the crocodile logo six years ago.

5   "Rescue" might be a better word. In a brand-buying spree that included outdoor-clothing maker Eddie Bauer and golf brand FootJoy, General Mills had bought the U.S. licensee for Lacoste in 1969 for $30 million. Over the next decade the cereal maker built Izod into a full line of crocodile-adorned wear, including jackets, sweaters, socks and ties. By 1982 sales reached $400 million. But fashion is not General Mills' strength.

6   Figuring knit shirts weren't much different from toasted oats, the company stopped importing the shirts from France in 1975 and began making them in Hong Kong, and the U.S. consumers started noticing changes. No more "capped" sleeves with reinforced bands around the ends. Instead of 100 percent cotton, the shirts now came in a cotton/polyester blend.

7   When sales began to slow in 1983, General Mills cut prices and relaxed its distribution policy, dumping hundreds of thousands of shirts on discounters.

*This articles appears on page 105 of the May 31, 1999, issue of *Forbes*.

By 1985 the badly overexposed croc had little cachet left. Sales had fallen to $50 **8** million. Conceding defeat, General Mills spun the Lacoste licensee off that year to shareholders as Crystal Brands, which continued to struggle. In 1993 Devanlay bought the U.S. distribution rights to the name Lacoste and the crocodile logo. (Two years later Phillips-Van Heusen bought Crystal Brands, which then included the Izod name as well as Gant shirts). But the damage to the croc had been done.

Today all Lacoste knit shirts are made in France from Swiss yarn and mother-of- **9** pearl buttons. In fifty-four colors, they sell for $69, compared with $52 for a Ralph Lauren polo shirt or $44 for a Tommy Hilfiger.

Will shoppers go for it? Barth is banking on a classic strategy: Make something in- **10** accessible and it becomes more desirable. Thus Barth is doing very little advertising— only $4 million a year—minuscule for the rag trade. But he makes sure the croc shows up on the right people, like golfer Jose Maria Olazabal and *NBC Today* show host Matt Lauer.

Barth consciously limits the distribution. Croc shirts are available in country club **11** pro shops and a few catalogs like Bullock & Jones and Ben Silver. Only a few hundred upmarket retailers like Mettlers in Florida or Bergdorf Goodman in New York carry them. Nine Lacoste shops—in places like Bal Harbour and Beverly Hills—offer the shirts, along with $500 sweater sets and $400 jackets.

Barth and his team are also banking on a new crop of consumers: shoppers in their **12** teens and twenties who missed the crocodile's first go-round. For these buyers—the same people who flock to Banana Republic for its minimalist preppy look—Barth is hoping the crocodile has just the right retro feel.

So far, so good. Devanlay turned its first profit on a 40 percent sales gain last year, **13** to $26.5 million. Barth wants to extend the crocodile franchise into footwear, eyewear, and fragrances. But he's got a lot of image-repair work to do before that can happen. "This is the real product," he says. "What you remember—but much better than you remember."

A simple strategy for your report is to summarize these sources individually and then to present the three summaries, linked with connecting comments. Writing the summaries should be easy enough, but you also want your report to have unity. Like the readings you have studied in this book, it too should have a unifying idea.

For your report to be unified, you will need to discover a theme that relates to all three sources. Certainly they all concern the commercial aspects of professional tennis. But can a single statement be made that would connect all three? To find out, you can start by paraphrasing the main idea of each source as we have done here:

- Overcoming initial reluctance, Wimbledon sponsors have garnered large profits by allowing manufacturers to affix the name and logo of the world's most prestigious tennis tournament to a wide variety of high-quality products.

- Heineken's radio and television spots during the U.S. Open target a more elite clientele than most other beer advertisements.

- Efforts to revive the once-fashionable crocodile logo popularized by tennis legend René Lacoste are complicated by memories of cheap sportswear sold by General Mills when it owned the trademark.

In search of a unifying theme, we can begin with these three observations:

- It seems wise to restrict the licensing of tennis logos to expensive, high-quality merchandise produced in relatively small volume.
- Commercials for less exclusive products like beer also target an elite clientele when they are broadcast during tennis tournaments.
- A tennis logo can quickly lose prestige and marketing appeal if it is not reserved for upscale merchandise.

From these observations, you may discern a central idea, one that can provide a unifying theme for your report. For example, you might focus on this theme: *Hoping to profit from the current enthusiasm for tennis, advertisers and promoters of the sport have learned to target an affluent clientele.*

Writing the report now becomes easier. You can begin with two or three sentences introducing the topic, state your central idea, then follow it with summaries of the three sources, as in the essay that follows. Notice too that these sources are acknowledged both by notes (within parentheses) and in a list of works cited at the end of the report. (Parenthetical notes and lists of works cited are explained near the end of this chapter.)

Pitching Tennis: Go Slow on Logos

Though less dominated by the directors of exclusive clubs, professional tennis is still surrounded by an aura of genteel sophistication. The growing popularity of the sport has not diminished the elitist appeal of Wimbledon, the U.S. Open, and other major tournaments. In fact, that appeal has become a marketable commodity. Hoping to profit from the current enthusiasm for tennis, advertisers and promoters of the sport have learned to target an affluent clientele.

Profitable marketing of the Wimbledon name and logo provides an excellent example. In 1967, members of the club that sponsors the tournament hesitantly agreed to sell foreign broadcast rights. A decade later, they approved a plan to regulate commercial use of the tournament's name and "flying W" logo. Today, as a result of those timely decisions, yearly revenues have reached $100 million. Much of this income derives from sales of tennis equipment and clothing, but growing sources of profit include jewelry, gourmet food, and premium household goods including fine linens and china. Marketers agree that a crucial ingredient of this success is the aura of prestige and integrity that surrounds Wimbledon. Despite the large profits, the public continues to perceive the tournament as uncorrupted by commercialism (Lefton 28-29).

Advertisements for less expensive goods have also been adapted to the elitist image of tennis. Heinekin, for example, a mass-marketed beer, recently became a corporate sponsor of the U.S. Open. During the tournament, however, the company's broadcast commercials differ from those of most other brewers, targeting an urbane, affluent clientele. Tournament officials regard the sponsorship as beneficial to the sport, widening its appeal to a younger audience more in tune with popular trends (Khermouch 18-21).

The fate of one trademark associated with professional tennis offers an example of what to avoid. The crocodile icon inspired by French tennis legend René Lacoste appeared on an exclusive line of sportswear long before the trademark was purchased by manufacturing conglomerate General Mills. Hoping for quick profits, the American company attached the crocodile to a cheaper line of apparel which was eventually spurned by disaffected consumers. Today, a French company, owned in part by the Lacoste family, is trying to restore the prestige of the logo with a line of expensive clothing marketed to an exclusive clientele. Success may depend upon whether wealthy customers can forget that a once prestigious trademark was compromised by its association with inferior products (Gallagher 105).

Like many other sports, tennis remains in transition. The enthusiasm aroused during the 1970s and 1980s has begun

```
to wane.  If this trend continues, promoters of the sport

may consider shedding the aura of elitism that still

surrounds it.  While that strategy may broaden its popular

appeal, it remains suspect as a commercial ploy.
```

```
                        Works Cited
Gallagher, Leigh.  "Endangered Species."  Forbes 31 May

     1999:  105.

Khermouch, Gerry.  "Brand Builders: Open for Business."

     Brandweek 5 Oct. 1998: 18-21

Lefton, Terry.  "The Anglophile Angle."  Brandweek 6 June

     1999: 28-29.
```

There are several things to note about this brief but effective synthesis of three sources. First, the report ends with a paragraph that draws a conclusion that is, in effect, an extension of the main idea stated in the opening paragraph. Second, the report is divided into several paragraphs: one to introduce the topic, one to conclude the paper, and one for each summary. Although this report could have been written as a single long paragraph, the indentations assist the reader, each one signaling a new topic. On the other hand, if the writer had used more sources or longer ones or had taken more information from each source, a greater number of paragraphs might have been appropriate.

There are, of course, other ways to synthesize the same three sources. For example, a writer might devote one paragraph to the marketing of sportswear, drawing information from Lefton and Gallagher, and another paragraph to sales of other items, drawing information from Khermouch and Lefton.

Regardless of how such a report is structured, it is called ***objective*** because it presents information from sources without any overt expression of the report writer's opinions. (In Chapter 7, we consider subjective, critical reporting, in which a writer analyzes or evaluates sources.) Nevertheless, objectivity is relative. For example, this particular report places less emphasis on the creative aspects of advertising and demographic research than the original sources. This may reflect the report writer's personal interests or recent observations, not to mention her experience with tennis and her attitudes toward the sport. Suppose, however, that the same three sources had been read and synthesized by someone very different from this writer—say, a recreation or marketing major, an ardent fan of ice hockey or professional wrestling, an investor in General Mills or one of the other companies mentioned in the articles. An objective report by the recreation major might emphasize the historical traditions of tennis and the influences of advertising on the sport. Struck by the incongruity of genteel sportsmanship and mercenary greed, the hockey fan might focus his objective report on the double standard of tennis promoters. The investor's objective report might consider which of the companies profiled in the articles are best positioned to profit from their association with professional tennis. The point is that each of these readers and, indeed, all readers unavoidably—and often unconsciously—draw connections among what they read and other texts they have encountered previously.

In short, no synthesis is ever entirely objective. Nor is any synthesis ever a completely definitive report on a topic. Consider, for example, how the writer of the foregoing synthesis might change her approach after reading the following article as a fourth source.

Corporate Ties Squeeze the Life Out of Sports*

JOE CAPPO

The older I get, the more challenging it becomes to remain a loyal fan of baseball.   **1**

Actually, this has less to do with my age than it does with the ultimate commercialization of what used to be the national pastime. The business—I hesitate to call it a sport anymore—is being run by a bunch of rich guys who have little or no regard for the tradition and dignity of baseball. This includes most of the owners and a lot of the players.   **2**

I was reminded of this when it was disclosed that Major League Baseball wants to entice corporate sponsors to put their logos on the uniforms of baseball players. This practice has not been allowed among the major sports until now.   **3**

For decades, of course, Nascar race cars and drivers' uniforms have been festooned with dozens of corporate logos, representing the investment and alliances these companies have with the racing teams. A few years back, professional tennis players started wearing discreet, but still visible, logos on their playing outfits.   **4**

In the beginning, a lot of these deals were barter arrangements. "You display my logo and I will provide you with my whole line of tennis apparel, or racing tires, or a new car, free of charge." We have since progressed to a more mercenary level, where anybody with the ability to attract a sizable number of public eyeballs is charging money to give exposure to a product, service or company.   **5**

It wasn't that long ago that college football bowl games did not have name sponsors. Now, they all do.   **6**

The movie business is loaded with this kind of guerrilla marketing, called product placement. Years ago, if a movie character was eating cereal, the producer would create an imaginary brand and package to use in the filming. "Not anymore," said an acquaintance in the movie industry. "Whenever you see a recognizable brand being used in a movie, I will guarantee you that money changed hands to get that product into the picture."   **7**

The practice has reached the point where some legislators want to require producers to list these product placements in the credits of the movies. Maybe they should run a subtitle every time there is a product placement in a movie, or sound a chime to get attention. Of course, some movies hawk so many products, it would make them sound like "The Bells of St. Mary's."   **8**

*This article appears on page 8 of the April 12, 1999, issue of *Crain's Chicago Business*.

9   Anyone being subjected to advertising should be able to tell the difference between the advertising and the programming. Most publishers go to great lengths to differentiate between the editorial product and "advertorials."

10   Don't get me wrong. Baseball has every right to put logos on team uniforms; I guess they can even force players to have logos tattooed on their foreheads. But why push things to the limit? There is nothing wrong with a little restraint, even if you pass up the chance to make a few extra bucks.

If the writer who synthesized the first three sources were to consider this article, she might draw a different conclusion. For example, she might connect the four sources with a thesis like this: "Attempting to profit from the elitism of tennis, advertisers and promoters of the sport risk alienating the individual fan."

EXERCISE   Writing a Brief Summary Report

Write a report synthesizing information found in the following three sources. Follow this procedure:

a.   Read each source with a pencil, underlining important information.

b.   Write a one-sentence summary of each source's main idea.

c.   Consider whether a theme links the three articles. If so, state that theme in a sentence that can serve as the thesis statement for your report.

d.   Write the report. Begin with your thesis statement, follow it with three summaries (in whatever order you feel is most appropriate) linked with transitional phrases if necessary, and end with a general concluding statement. For now you can omit parenthetical notes and a list of works cited, both of which are discussed later in this chapter.

A Day at the Beach*

Linda Jacobus

Ever have one of those days when the stars are all in alignment and your life just seems to fall into place no matter what you do? You call the phone company about your bill—how all those long-distance calls must be somebody else's. The phone rings once, and a real voice comes on the line to say reassuringly, "Of course, we'll take all those calls off your bill. We're very sorry for any inconvenience or emotional stress, and we'd like to give you a fifty-dollar credit on your next bill."

Or perhaps the Service Department calls to tell you that the horrible noise in your car's engine is caused by a faulty differential. Yes, it's costly to fix, but "we see you have our Platinum Care warranty package. So it won't cost you a dime. And oh yes, the car is ready and waiting for you. Can our courtesy van come pick you up?"

Well, last week I had one of those days. In fact, it was exactly the day I've just described. By noon the courtesy van had picked me up, and I was back on the road with a fifty-dollar credit on my phone. Believe me, the stars were aligned, and the sun couldn't have shone any brighter.

But then summer days by the beach are usually sunny, and that's what brings the tourists who drive below the speed limit, stopping at every red light and clogging

*This article appears on pages 6–8 of the January 2000 issue of *Tidelines*.

our already crowded streets. Unlike permanent residents, they don't realize that traffic signals in this city are timed so ingeniously that, under normal circumstances, no one ever hits more than two green lights in a row. We who live here year-round have learned to compensate for this by allowing two or three cars to pass through a red light before getting too antsy about exercising the right of way and crossing the intersection.

Another strategy that helps us get through town is the "ten-over" principle. This unwritten rule obligates everyone to exceed the speed limit by at least ten miles per hour. When everyone cooperates, we sometimes foil the traffic engineers by hitting three green lights in a row.

Imagine if you will a city of 50,000 residents swelling to, say, 100,000 for a period of three months. Then imagine the 50,000 tourists from Ohio, Pennsylvania, New Jersey, and New York in *this* city, contending with *these* driving habits. Put a freshly minted college graduate (me) behind the wheel of a bright red 1999 Nissan 300ZX.

I've just picked up my car, and, as I've said, my day just couldn't be going any better. I'm cruising back to my part-time job at a local architect's office near the beach. I've got a job interview at five with a big firm from up North. On my radio John Coltrane is riffing; the sun is radiating through the open roof; the windows are wide open; my hair is blowing in the breeze.

I approach a traffic light. It's just turned yellow—my signal to accelerate. I glance left then right. I'm in position. But wait! There stopped dead in front of me at the light is a black Jeep Wagoneer with New York tags. The driver isn't accelerating; he's just sitting there, stopped!

"Damn tourist!" I mutter.

The light turns red, and we sit there for four minutes. When it finally changes, the Jeep bolts forward, narrowly missing a car that's running the red light from the opposite direction. The driver of that car flips him off and yells an obscenity. Unwittingly, the driver of the Jeep has already violated two local rules by stopping on yellow and accelerating on green. And he's about to make matters worse by accelerating to thirty miles per hour on a street where he speed limit is forty. I'm fuming. "We're gonna miss the next light, you idiot!"

I try to pass him, but I'm blocked by a green van with a loaded luggage rack, four bicycles, a bumper sticker proclaiming that the driver's child is an honor student, and (of course) out-of-state tags. The van is also going about thirty. There's no way out. Still, however, the approaching light remains green. We're gonna make it. A glint of yellow. Brake lights. "Oh my God! He's stopping!" I wail.

The light turns green, and the black Jeep once again accelerates before the ten-count. He's lucky this time: a white Buick with Pennsylvania tags has stopped on his right, a maroon van from Ohio on his left.

And so we proceed through ten red lights in fifteen minutes; the Jeep in front of me, the green van beside me. It's almost gotten cozy by the time the van turns off, giving me room to pass.

I roar past the Jeep. Don't these people understand that the gods are on my side today? With middle finger waving I shout a cordial obscenity—some relief for my escalating road rage.

I breeze into a parking space and end the day on another high—my boss offers me a full-time position and a raise. I tell him about my interview at five. "I'll give you my answer tomorrow."

I leave for my appointment. The beachgoers have left hours earlier, and the diners haven't yet ventured out to the restaurants. I make it to the Ramada Inn twenty minutes early. I sit in my car and whine with Coltrane. A black Jeep with New York tags slides in next to me. "Oh gads! He must be following me." The driver looks to be in his forties. He's dressed in a dark grey suit, blue-striped shirt, and yellow and blue tie. He emerges and eyes my car. A glimmer of recognition.

"You like Coltrane too?" he asks. "I think we met earlier today out at the beach." I slump down in my seat, mumble something about having an appointment.

I take a few moments to regain my composure before heading to my interview. Then, after locating the banquet room that the interviewers have rented, I sit down and glance around. Ten people for one position. A gentleman comes out of an adjoining room and calls the first applicant.

Despite the embarrassing incident in the parking lot, I'm still jazzed just thinking about my day—fifty dollars, my red Z, and my boss's offer; Coltrane, sun, and summer; the way everything just falls into place. It reminds me of Ferris Bueller. No matter what he does, everything clicks.

The gentleman emerges again, then calls my name. I feel great. I follow him into the room thinking about Ferris and how certain I am that this interview is gonna click.

I look up and there sitting at the desk is the driver of the black Jeep. I'm cooked. My luck is over. I wait to get thrown out, cussed at, or lectured.

Without flinching, the man speaks. "Miss Nissan, life moves pretty fast. If you don't stop and look around once in a while, you could miss it."

I can't believe my ears! A Ferris Bueller fan! Life is sweet again.

The interview goes great, and I get the job. My new boss tells me I'll fit in nicely with the drivers in New York. Says I already have the words and gestures down pat.

Road Rage? You Want to Hear about Road Rage?*

Cory Farley

Understand, now that I am fiercely pacifist, my fighting days are long over. I yield at stop signs, ignore idiots in traffic and forgive those who trespass against me, unless they run red lights or park on the red curb at shopping centers. When those particular sinners are howling in eternal fire, I'll be roasting marshmallows.

If you want an explanation of how things get out of hand, though, I have one.

Last Sunday I ran into a supermarket for milk while my wife waited outside in the Hombre. Two women unloaded their groceries into a nearby van, then one of them gave the cart a shove. It rolled downhill and slammed into my new truck, knocking off a trim strip. A philosopher might ask if such a minor impact should begin the disassembly process on a hard-workin' truck, but sometimes these things happen. Terri got out and approached the van.

The responsible thing to do—the thing I would do and, I assume, you would do—is to apologize and give the injured party your name. The damage isn't great, but even a parking-lot ding can cost four hundred dollars to fix these days. You'd expect a cordial exchange of insurance information, at least.

"I'm sorry," one of the women—the cartshover—began. The other cut her off.

"You didn't do anything. Get in the car." Terri addressed the second woman: "I can't help noticing there's a piece of our truck on the ground. I'm pretty sure it was attached when we drove up, and. . . ."

"We didn't do anything. There's no damage." To her friend, "Get in the car." I walked up in time to see them get in their van. Terri pointed to the piece of Isuzu on the ground and began an indignant explanation. She's a teacher; she still has faith in human nature and the essential goodness of man.

Not me. I knew we were screwed. They were going to drive away, and there was nothing I could do about it. My first impulse was to restrain the women while Terri called the cops. Great idea—we could wrestle in the parking lot for hours until they got time to respond to a runaway shopping cart. Meanwhile, the first hero to come by would shoot me in the head for assaulting a woman in broad daylight.

*This article appears on page 20 of the November 2, 1998, issue of *AutoWeek*.

I considered snatching her keys and tossing them into the bushes, smashing her headlights with the four-battery rent-a-cop flashlight under my seat, using my own keys to gouge her paint as she drove off, or following her home, then sneaking back and lubing all her locks with Super Glue. But none of these things would help me, except emotionally. Society would frown on them, and my wife would find fault even with a perfectly normal reaction like kicking a dent in their door.

So they drove away, and I watched them do it. They're home free, while I have either a repair bill, an insurance claim, or a constant reminder of them for as long as I own the vehicle. I don't even care that much about the dent, to tell the truth. It's a truck; it's going to get banged up.

What I hate is the powerlessness. Terri wrote down the license number. We have a description of the van and the women, and for all the good it will do, we might as well have spent the time praying for a lottery win. There is no way, legal or extra-legal, of making them pay or making me whole. The bad guys won. In small matters like this, the bad guys nearly always win.

And that, in case you wondered, is why every so often somebody snaps and shoots up a freeway or takes a framing hammer to a BMW at an intersection. Because if you just can't flop over and take it one more time, there is nothing else you can do.

Debunking a "Trend"*

Paul Overberg

Like other [newspapers], *USA Today* had reported a "road rage" story with anecdotes and experts' claims. The premise, that this trend was growing, seemed to ring true—early project meetings ran long as we traded personal horror stories. When we tried to verify and quantify the trend, however, the reporting turned complicated.

We knew there was no real definition of road rage, and we quickly found that there weren't even good measures of its level, let alone whether it was on the rise. It was, we reasoned, the tip of a dangerous iceberg called aggressive driving: acts like running stoplights and stop signs, speeding, and recklessness.

While my colleague, Scott Bowles, started talking to police, traffic, and safety experts, I started trying to find some answers with numbers. Direct measurement seemed impossible. Aggressive driving is fleeting and elusive. I thought about counting red-light runners, for example, but scrapped the idea because it would be too hard to do nationwide.

So I fell back on indirect measures. States keep computer files on tickets and accidents, but the contents and standards vary widely. The insurance industry maintains the best crash databases, but they're private. The National Highway Traffic Safety Administration keeps detailed data on fatal crashes, but they make up just 0.5 percent of crashes reported to police.

Then I found out about NHTSA's lesser-known General Estimates System. Because of the way its approximately fifty thousand crashes are chosen each year, they make up a nationally representative sample of police-reported crashes. For each, the agency logs almost a hundred items about the circumstances, vehicles, drivers, and passengers.

It took a couple weeks to get the data from NHTSA, import twenty-seven files to database software and fix problems due to bad documentation. As I do with any new human source, I asked the data lots of questions. Over a couple weeks, I ran several hundred queries to see what they knew, check it against other sources, and make sure that I understood what they were telling me.

*This article appears on page 28 of the March-April 1999 issue of *Columbia Journalism Review.*

We checked with experts, debated, and finally worked out a definition of aggressive driving that the data could shed light on: any crash with injuries where at least one driver was cited for running a stop sign or stoplight; or speeding; or failing to yield; or reckless driving. This closely matched working definitions used by AAA (formerly the Automobile Association of America) and NHTSA.

Finally, I applied our definition to the data for 1996 and 1988, the newest and oldest available. The results were startling: aggressive driving crashes made up about 20 percent of the total in both years.

What, no trend?

I checked intervening years. Again, no trend. I tweaked the definition, running hundreds of queries to look at all the crashes in the sample, then just at higher-speed crashes, crashes with only severe or fatal injuries, crashes involving just speeding citations, hit-and-run crashes, and crashes just at traffic signals.

But the 20 percent figure remained, suggesting that our definition was solid, and that the widely reported increase in road rage was a mirage. Meanwhile, we could peg the level of aggressive driving and tally its toll, something no one else had published. The work also let us paint a portrait of aggressive driving. That led to more surprises. All else being equal, aggressive drivers were:

- Women as often as men.
- As likely to drive cars or minivans as pickups or sport-utility vehicles.
- Most prevalent in the West and South, least prevalent in the Northeast.
- Disproportionately under twenty-five, yet well-represented among the middle-aged.

The annual toll extrapolated from the sample: 1,800 deaths, 800,000 injuries, $24 billion in direct and indirect costs.

I wrote a cautious analysis for Scott and his editor, Lee Ann Ruibal. They were somewhat surprised, but Scott said it clicked with his reporting. No one could cite contrary data. Experts had begun to hedge on what could be interpreted from a key survey and a poll that had often been cited in media accounts about a road rage "epidemic." Best of all, Scott found traffic consultants who explained why our portrait made sense.

So we turned the project around completely. Instead of documenting a trend, we debunked it. But we also focused on the toll, including a page of victims' stories. We painted a detailed portrait with the data and quotes from experts and drivers. As we worked, NHTSA released the 1997 data. They didn't show a trend, either.

The project reminded me what a great tool database journalism is for challenging conventional wisdom, and for moving beyond impressions and anecdotes to get solid answers.

WRITING AN OBJECTIVE REPORT ON SOURCES

Sometimes you are asked to report not just on a particular topic (that is, on the information *in* your sources), but on the sources themselves. Such a research task can be approached in much the same way as the previously described summary report. The major difference is that a report on sources refers specifically to these sources by name. It says, in effect, "Source A says this; Source B says this; Source C says this. . . ." A report on sources can be subjective (presenting your own analysis and opinions of them), but for now we will consider just the objective report. What follows is an example.

Suppose you have been asked to report on two editorials that debate the legality of excluding gays and atheists from membership in the Boy Scouts of America. Since you will present the opinions of two other writers, rather than your own views, you should refer specifically to your sources in the report.

Before reading the following editorials, examine their titles and subtitles, which indicate that one writer supports the Boy Scouts' position and the other opposes it. Next, as you read each editorial, see how far you have to get into it before you find a statement of the author's position. Finally, read both editorials with a pencil, searching for important information and statements of opinion.

Scout's Honor*

The Boy Scouts Are under Relentless Legal Assault Because They Are an Affront to the Age

E. V. KONTOROVICH

For more than eighty years, the Boy Scouts of America have sent young boys on arduous, fortnight-long hikes; taught them to survive alone in the wilderness; and guided them through countless other physical and mental challenges that have helped transform them into mature, responsible men. But now the organization faces a challenge greater than all of these: Can it survive?   1

Recently, a New Jersey appellate court forced the Boy Scouts to give a scoutmaster post to James Dale, a gay activist and editor at *Poz*, a magazine for HIV-positive people. The divided bench overturned an old Scout policy of not allowing "avowed homosexuals" to serve as scoutmasters. What is particularly shocking about the opinion is its unabashed political expression. The court found that the Boy Scouts cannot discriminate against anyone, on any basis, because the organization is a "public accommodation," like restaurants and parks. Actually, the judges admitted that it wasn't much like a public accommodation as defined by the law, but they held that such limited definitions "would frustrate our goal of eradicating the 'cancer of discrimination' in New Jersey."   2

New Jersey is but one front in the nationwide attack on the Boy Scouts of America. Illinois was the venue of two recent defeats for the Scouts. Last year, a Chicago court ordered the reinstatement of a gay scoutmaster on the grounds of employment discrimination, despite the fact that the position is voluntary and unpaid. In February, the City of Chicago severed all its ties with twenty-eight Scout troops, to settle a suit brought by the American Civil Liberties Union.   3

The ACLU claimed that the arrangements with the Scouts violated the separation of church and state. This is an odd contention given that BSA is not a church, or a religious organization of any kind. The Boy Scouts are under relentless legal assault because they are an affront to the age. It is a nonsectarian group that simply insists that its members honor some sort of divinity in accordance with the dictates of their conscience. But   4

---

*This article appears on pages 40–42 of the April 6, 1998, issue of *National Review*.

instead of preparing to fight, several other municipalities have pre-emptively thrown the Scouts overboard.

5   The ACLU, captivated by vague emanations from the penumbra of the establishment clause, has completely forgotten the more concrete First Amendment right of free association—the right to fraternize with whomever one wants, a crucial underpinning of civil society.

6   This is a principle the California Supreme Court would do well to remember when it rules in two suits currently before it. In one, a pair of twins from Anaheim insist on retaining their membership in the Scouts despite their refusal to recite the Scout's oath, which acknowledges the existence of God. In effect, the twins' parents and supporters are using the courts to change the core credo of a voluntary organization. The California judges will also decide another suit brought by a gay scoutmaster. Arguments in similar cases will soon be heard by D.C.'s Human Rights Commission.

7   At this rate, it's no wonder that girls are starting to sue, because the Boy Scouts, by definition, discriminate against them. The California Supreme Court is considering discrimination charges brought by a teenage girl who thinks the Boy Scouts' exclusion of females is unfair because Girl Scout activities aren't as much fun. A similar suit has been filed in Florida.

8   The wave of litigation against the Scouts is not ultimately about the rights of gays, or atheists, or females. It is a challenge to the BSA's right to exist in its present form. Such an attack should not be surprising; if anything, it's odd that the Boy Scouts have hung on for so long.

9   The organization is a holdover from a vanished era. The *Boy Scout Handbook* still bears Norman Rockwell paintings of scouting activities, offered without a trace of irony. Even the BSA's by-laws talk about "character building." The Scouts' charter still calls on leaders "to teach [the boys] patriotism," and members still take an oath "to do my duty to God and my country."

10   The BSA has always been an apolitical, nonpartisan organization. But today its leaders and lawyers must defend its membership policies by saying it stands for "conservative moral views." The BSA's policies have not changed significantly since it was chartered by Congress in 1916. What has changed is the underlying society.

11   Endorsing specific, non-negotiable values has become a conservative position. The existence of the Scouts irritates the ideologues of modernity—and so hordes of litigators, the antibodies of a dissolute culture, have responded by attacking the foreign body. If the courts find in favor of the plaintiffs in the undecided cases, the meaning of the Boy Scouts will be greatly eroded. The organization will become the Gay Godless Girl/Boy Scouts of America. It is only the right to restrict membership and insist that members follow rules that can give a civic group definition.

12   In that light, consider the plaintiffs' order of battle: the ACLU; the Lambda Legal Defense Fund; the Parents, Families, and Friends of Lesbians and Gays; and the American Atheists. Yes, the American Atheists: united by common disbeliefs.

13   Fundamentally, it is meaninglessness that lies at the core of the attack on the Boy Scouts. This is a competition not between rival sets of values but between the idea of values and an antinomian moral vacuousness. The comments of plaintiffs and judges show that the intent is not just to destroy the Scouts; it is to deconstruct them.

14   For example, the Scout's oath has a clause about "keeping myself . . . morally straight," a provision the BSA says is on its face incompatible with homosexual activity. "There is nothing in [the Scout's oath] about homosexuality," says Timothy Curran, the California gay seeking reinstatement as a scoutmaster. "It says you must be 'morally straight' but you can define that any way you want." Which is precisely what New Jersey's jurisprudes chose to do.

There are tough days ahead for the Scouts, but they vow that they are in it for the 　**15** long haul; all parties agree that the U.S. Supreme Court will finally have to rule on these issues. Until then, how can one support the Scouts? Perhaps one can give their enemies a taste of their own medicine. Religious believers should join the American Atheists in droves and introduce Sunday Mass, daily prayers to Mecca, and the donning of tefillin at every meeting.

But no, that's not right—it wouldn't be in keeping with the Scouts' spirit of fair 　**16** play. Instead, the Scouts need donations to fund their ongoing appeals and fill the gap left by cowardly towns and cities.

The Bigoted Scouts of America*

BARBARA DORITY

Imagine a national organization with wide-ranging government support that contin- 　**1** ues to discriminate against persons on the basis of sexual orientation and religion. There is only one such group in the United States: the Boy Scouts of America. This huge organization (in contrast to the more liberal Girl Scouts) is making it abundantly clear that it knows exactly what it's doing and that it has no intention of changing. While the Boy Scouts did finally prohibit racially segregated units, the group doggedly clings to its loathing of atheists and homosexuals.

The BSA has the general support and encouragement of all sorts of influential in- 　**2** stitutions, most notably the United States government. In Scout Explorer programs, government employees conduct valuable and unique training classes for high-school-age youth. Agencies such as police and fire departments run Explorer Posts according to the discriminatory rules prescribed by the BSA. This results in the clearly unconstitutional activity of government employees asking children to sign an oath regarding their religious beliefs. If the child refuses to sign a statement that "America's strength lies in her trust in God," the police officer, firefighter, or member of the National Guard is required to deny that youth entrance into this tax-supported program. In effect, the Boy Scouts has enlisted the government to monitor our attitudes on religion and even to punish individuals of whom they disapprove.

Atheists and gays are by no means the only people excluded from the BSA. A few 　**3** years ago, the Muslim father of a Cub Scout was expelled from his position as a Cub Scout leader by the sponsoring organization, a Protestant church. The church felt that leadership of its Scouts should be restricted to Christians. The BSA stood behind this move, declaring that any sponsoring group could enforce whatever additional religious requirements it liked.

The Boy Scouts has spent hundreds of thousands of dollars during the past few 　**4** years defending its bigotry in courtrooms around the country. In 1996, the Pennsylvania Human Rights Commission ordered the BSA to admit an atheist as an adult leader and her child as a Scout. The organization has refused to comply, thereby committing itself to another long and unavoidably expensive court battle. Clearly, it is prepared to fight any attempt to be enlightened, with all the considerable resources at its command. Ironically, when the Scouts and its most important source of funds—the United Way—solicit donations to fund such tremendous legal expenses, they don't question the religion or sexual orientation of prospective benefactors.

*This article appears on pages 35–37 of the July-August 1998 issue of the *Humanist*.

5   Among the recent legal defeats against the BSA is one regarding the Randall twins, two young atheists from California whose family was recently named 1998 Humanist Pioneers by the American Humanist Association in recognition of their efforts to combat BSA bigotry. The Randalls filed suit when the BSA challenged the twins' membership because they refused to recite the portion of the Scout oath relating to "duty to God." The suit was based on California's Unruh Act, which forbids any California business from participating in religious and other discrimination.

6   A lower court ruled in favor of the Randalls, but the Boy Scouts appealed. The court ruled that the Randalls could work toward their Eagle badges while the litigation continued. In the meantime, the Randalls' case was combined with a similar challenge to the banning of gays. The BSA prevailed, however, when the state supreme court declared that the Boy Scouts is a "private group" and, as such, can restrict membership as it sees fit. As humanist Patrick Inniss, a Boy Scout discrimination activist, states: "This California Supreme Court decision upholding the rights of a 'private' organization to exclude anyone for apparently any reason demonstrates that, even in states with anti-discrimination laws more rigorous than federal law, the BSA is impervious to direct attack."

7   This ruling is similar to the one in Chicago's 1993 Welsh case, which established that, for the purposes of federal civil rights legislation, the BSA cannot be considered a "public accommodation." While these suits have served an important role in bringing the problem to the attention of the public, and the possibility of more legal challenges remains, we may be unable to use the law directly to force the Scouts to change.

8   However, there has been a major legal victory. In March 1998, a New Jersey appeals court ruled against the BSA in a discrimination suit involving a gay Scout. James Dale was a nineteen-year-old Eagle Scout when he was expelled in 1990 after it was discovered through a newspaper article that he was gay. He sued and lost, then appealed and won in the state's appellate court. The court ruled that the BSA is "a place of accommodation" within the meaning of the law and is, therefore, bound by the state's anti-discrimination law. BSA spokesperson Gregg Shields insists that the Scouts "has a right, as a voluntary association . . . to establish membership and leadership standards" and says the group plans to appeal this ruling to the New Jersey State Supreme Court.

9   There have also been several small victories. In April, for instance, the Boy Scouts was booted from a San Francisco charity drive that raises hundreds of thousands of dollars from city employees because of the group's stance against admitting gays. "We have a longstanding policy not to do business with groups that discriminate," said the city council in a statement, "and we feel very strongly about this." (Last year, city employees allowed $563,098 to be deducted from their paychecks and donated to charities, including the Boy Scouts.)

10   "The Boy Scouts are hated because they represent traditional morality in a Judeo-Christian context," claims Catholic League President William Donohue. What a turnaround! The Boy Scouts requires its members and leaders to be, among other things, "morally straight." It says that means it must exclude gays and atheists. Who is engaging in hatred here? "Oh, certainly not us," the BSA declares. "We're just a private, voluntary organization that insists on maintaining traditional values and freedom of association."

11   The BSA does have a huge vulnerability which we can and should exploit. No such organization can survive without the support of the community, and community standards are increasingly inclusive of all elements of society. The Boy Scouts can't survive without the government agencies, community organizations, and corporate entities that provide indispensable support.

A few breakthroughs occurred in this area in 1991 and 1992, when the Bank of   **12**
America and Levi Strauss both withdrew financial support for the Scouts. Unfortunately, these actions did not prompt other financial backers to do likewise. On April
15, 1998, at a national conference of Boy Scout sponsors and leaders, Joe Velasquez,
director of the AFL-CIO's Department of Community Services and a BSA executive
board member, eloquently summed up the situation in a statement of the union's
position—a position that humanists can certainly endorse:

> The AFL-CIO's relationship with the Boy Scouts of America has deep historical
> roots. In 1912 when the first leader of our organization, Samuel Gompers, met with
> the first leader of the Boy Scouts of America, James E. West, to talk about working to-
> gether, the Boy Scouts of America had been in existence less than two years.
> The AFL-CIO has worked with the Scouts for these 80 years because we share
> many values. . . . The BSA has always offered the labor movement an opportunity to
> help America's youth. . . . We believe it is our duty to pass those values along to our
> children, to teach them the things that are important: an understanding of service
> and personal responsibility, a love of their country, and a deep respect for the per-
> sonal dignity and individual rights of every American.

And he goes on to clearly denounce the BSA's policy of exclusion: **13**

> Because you're different from me, because you're lower than me, because you
> aren't really an individual with individual rights and personal dignity, because you're
> a member of a group I don't like or I don't understand, it follows that not only can I
> discriminate against you, I can beat you up, I can even kill you and it doesn't really
> matter because you're different from me. Is this a lesson we want to teach our young
> people? That it's okay to hate people who are different from us? To discriminate
> against them? To deny them opportunities because they're different?

Indeed, this is the crux of the matter. It's clear that this egregious situation has got   **14**
to change—now.

As in the case of the previous report, a logical step now is to formulate briefly
the main idea of each article:

- Writing in *National Review,* E. V. Kontorovich argues that lawsuits aimed at
  forcing the Boy Scouts to extend membership to gays and atheists are an
  effort to harrass the organization because of its unfashionably traditional
  idealism.
- In an editorial published in the *Humanist,* Barbara Dority contends that the
  Boy Scouts of America enjoys many forms of governmental subsidy while
  engaging in practices that are incompatible with public policies regarding
  discrimination.

Following the steps used in the exercise on pages 176–80, we can now write
the report:

```
        Can the Boy Scouts Legally Discriminate?

     E. V. Kontorovich and Barbara Dority hold sharply

differing views about recent court decisions involving the

Boy Scouts of America.  Kontorovich believes that lawsuits on
```

behalf of homosexuals and atheists who have been denied membership in the organization are part of an effort to redefine the values of scouting, undermining its commitment to religion and patriotism. He dismisses appeals to the separation of church and state as well as arguments that the Boy Scouts operate as a "public accommodation" legally barred from discrimination. He insists that every private organization has the right to define itself by deciding who it wishes to accept as members (40-42).

Dority, on the other hand, claims that the Boy Scouts of America is not a truly private organization. She points to the tax-funded contributions of police and fire departments and National Guard units, all of which support programs sponsored by the Boy Scouts. She also notes that the Scouts receive direct funding from charitable agencies, such as the United Way, which solicit contributions from homosexuals, atheists, and some of the religious minorities who have been excluded from participation in scouting activities. Given the inconsistent record of the courts, however, Dority concludes that the most effective way to challenge discrimination is to influence the government agencies, civic organizations, and companies on whose support the Boy Scouts depend (35-37).

Works Cited

Dority, Barbara. "The Bigoted Scouts of America." Humanist July-Aug. 1998: 35-37.

Kontorovich, E. V. "Scout's Honor: The Boy Scouts Are under Relentless Legal Assault Because They Are an Affront to the Age." National Review 6 Apr. 1998: 40-42.

Three things should be noted about the way this report is written. First, it lacks a concluding paragraph or statement. Although one could have been added, a short report like this does not usually require a separate conclusion, since the reader does not need to be reminded of its purpose. Conclusions are unnecessary also when you have nothing new to add to what you already have written. Second, the report is presented in two paragraphs. Since the introduction is a single sentence, the first editorial need not be introduced with a paragraph break. There is a break for the second paragraph, however, because here the reader needs to be alerted to the change in subject. Finally, the report aims to be objective, presenting the views of editorialists without commentary. When the writer says "Kontorovich believes . . . " in the first paragraph, he shows that the opinion expressed in that sentence is not necessarily that of the person writing the report. One question to ask, however, is whether the order in which the summaries are presented makes a difference. Would the report have a different effect if the editorials had been summarized in reverse order?

 ## ACKNOWLEDGING SOURCES—THE OBLIGATION OF SCHOLARSHIP

Whenever you compose a summary report or any other type of writing that relies on sources, you create something new for others to read. Although what you produce may seem less than earth-shaking in significance, you are nevertheless adding, in however small a way, to the sum of the world's knowledge. You are making a contribution to the domain of scholarship. That may sound lofty, yet it is still true that your writing makes you a member of the fellowship of scholars, past and present, subject to all the benefits and obligations of that august body.

One of the principal benefits of being a scholar is that you are entitled to read—and to use—the scholarship of others. You have a right, for example, to write a summary report based on any sources you can find. Presenting your research and ideas for others to use is in fact one of the obligations of scholarship. We must work together, sharing our findings, if humanity's search for knowledge and understanding is to progress.

Another of your obligations as a scholar is to acknowledge your sources. For example, in the summary report found on pages 172–74, the writer uses parenthetical notes and a list of works cited to identify sources of information. In the report on sources found on pages 185–86, the writer makes it clear that the ideas and opinions being presented have been expressed by others.

Whenever your writing is based on research, you should make sure readers know which ideas and discoveries are your own and which you have taken from your sources. You must give your readers accurate and complete information about what those sources are and where they can be found. Acknowledging your sources is important for two reasons:

- Credit must be given where it is due. Creators of ideas deserve to be recognized for them. Whenever you present material without acknowledging an outside source, readers assume that you are its author. When students err in this regard, they usually do so unintentionally, as a result of inexperience. However, when writers deliberately present another's work as their own, they are guilty of *plagiarism* (see pages 320–23 for a further discussion).

- Readers need to know where they can locate your sources so they can consult the original versions. This allows them not only to check the accuracy of your citations, but also to find additional material beyond what you have presented.

Besides naming them within the text itself, writers acknowledge sources in two principal ways. One is to use *notes* (such as parenthetical notes or footnotes) to credit sources of specific ideas and statements. The second way is to append a *list of works cited,* which acknowledges all the sources from which words have been quoted or from which information or ideas have been derived. A detailed discussion of lists of works cited and notes can be found in Chapters A and B in the reference section of this book. For now, however, a brief introduction should suffice.

The List of Works Cited

A writer appends a list of works cited to a research paper to identify sources. This list provides enough information for readers to identify each source and to locate it if they wish. Although this information might be presented in various ways, writers generally follow a standardized *format,* a prescribed method of listing information. Different fields have their own preferred formats. If you are writing a paper for a psychology course, for example, you may be expected to use a format different from the one you would use in a history paper. The lists of works cited for the two sample papers found in this chapter follow a format known as *MLA style,* the format prescribed by the Modern Language Association, an organization of English and foreign-language scholars. Research papers written for composition classes use this format more often than any other, and it is the one we follow throughout this book. Other widely used formats are explained in Chapters E and F in Part II of this book.

Each different type of source—a book, say, or a government document or a television program—is presented in a particular way in an MLA-style list of works cited. For now we will examine only four of the most common kinds of sources: books, articles in magazines, items in newspapers, and essays in edited anthologies or collections. Formats for other sources, as well as more detailed information about MLA-style documentation, can be found in Chapter A of Part II.

Suppose that you used a passage from a book titled *The Writings of Celia Parker Woolley* by Lee Schweninger. Here is how you would cite that source in an MLA-style list of works cited:

Author   *Title of book*

Schweninger, Lee.   The Writings of Celia Parker Woolley 1848–

1918), Literary Activist. Lewiston, NY: Mellen, 1998.

City of publication   *Publisher*   *Date*

The entry consists of three general categories of information, each of which is followed by a period. They are presented in this order:

1. *The author's name.* Give the author's last name, followed by a comma, then the author's first name, followed by middle name or initial (if either is cited in the book's title page).

2. *The complete title of the book, including any subtitle.* Capitalize the first word of the title (and of the subtitle, if there is one) and of all subsequent words except for articles (*a, an, the*), conjunctions (*and, or, but, nor*), and prepositions (*in, from, to, between,* and so on), Underline (or italicize) the title.

3. *Information about publication.*

   —*The city (and state, if the city is not a major one) in which the book was published.* Follow this with a colon.

   —*A shortened form of the publisher's name.* The shortened form always omits articles, business abbreviations (*Inc., Corp., Co.*), and words such as *Press, Books,* and *Publishers.* If the name of the publisher is that of an individual (e.g., William Morrow), cite the last name only; if it consists of more than one last name (e.g., Prentice Hall), cite only the first of them. If the name contains the words *university press,* they must be signified by the abbreviation *UP.* Follow the publisher's name with a comma.

   —*The year of publication.* End the entry with a period.

Now suppose that another source is an article from *Newsweek.* Here is how you would cite it:

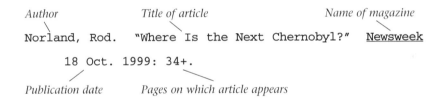

This entry consists of the same three categories of information, with only slight variations in the last two. Instead of being underlined, the title is now placed in quotation marks. Information about publication is presented as follows:

1. *The name of the magazine.* Underline (or italicize it). Do not follow it with any mark of punctuation.

2. *The publication date.* List the complete date—day, month, and year for a weekly or biweekly magazine; month(s) and year only for a monthly or bimonthly magazine; or season and year for a quarterly magazine. Abbreviate all months except May, June, and July. Follow the date with a colon.

3. *Page number(s).* List the page number(s) on which the article appears. Do not include the word *page(s)* or any abbreviation such as *pg., p.,* or *pp.* If the pages are not continuous (for example, the article from *Newsweek* cited above is printed on pages 34, 35, 36, 37, and 40), cite the number of the first page only, followed by the symbol +.

Entries for newspaper items are much the same as those for magazine articles. Following are two typical examples:

Author   *Title of article*

Leavitt, Paul.   "House Condemns Brooklyn Art Exhibit."

    USA Today 5 Oct. 1999: 8A.

Name of newspaper   *Publication date*   *Page on which article appears*

Smith, Roberta.   "Bringing America Up to Speed."   New York

    Times 24 Oct. 1999: late ed.: sec. 2: 40.

            Edition of newspaper   *Section*   *Page*

One difference between these entries and the example for magazine articles is that a section of the newspaper is cited. When the section is designated by a letter, as in the first instance, it is incorporated into the page number; when it is designated by a number, as in the second instance, it is cited separately with the abbreviation *sec.* You will also notice that the second entry cites "late ed.," since the *New York Times* appears in two separate late and national editions.

An entry for an essay in an edited anthology cites the author and title of the essay, followed by the title of the anthology and the name of its editor. Information about publication is followed by page numbers for the essay:

Author   *Title of essay*   *Title of Anthology*

Rugoff, Kathy.   "Ruth's Journey into the Fields: Feminism

    in Ozick's 'The Pagan Rabbi.' "   Women on the Edge:

    Ethnicity and Gender in Short Stories by American

    Women.   Ed. Corrine H. Dale and J. H. E. Paine.   New

    York: Garland. 129–42.

            Editors   *Pages on which essay appears*

List entries alphabetically according to the first word in each. If the author of a particular work is not named, introduce the entry for that work by title and alphabetize accordingly (ignoring the word *a, an,* or *the*). Do not number the items. Entries that occupy more than a single line must be **outdented** (the reverse of indented); that is, the first line of each entry begins at the left margin, but any subsequent lines are indented half an inch (five typed spaces). Notice how this format is applied in the following excerpt from the list of works cited in a report on the history of Delaware during the Civil War era:

Baisden, Cheryl.   "Confederate POWs Spent War Years Here."

    Air Force Times 10 Apr. 1995: 48.

"Black History Month: Church Started in Slavery." <u>Morning</u>

> <u>Star</u> [Wilmington] 26 Feb. 1997: 1D.

Chamberlain, Frances. "A Passion for Lively Regional

> History." <u>New York Times</u> 18 Oct. 1998: late ed: 14C.

Cox, James A. "Fort Delaware on the Water: A Monument to

> Rugged Rebels." <u>Civil War Times Illustrated</u> July-Aug.

> 1993: 20-26.

Essah, Patience. <u>A House Divided: Slavery and Emancipation</u>

> <u>in Delaware, 1638-1865</u>. Charlottesville: UP of

> Virginia, 1996.

Consult Chapter A of Part II for more complete information relating to lists of works cited.

A Brief List of Works Cited   **EXERCISES**

1. Suppose you have been asked to write a report on illiteracy based on the following sources. Write an MLA-style list of works cited. Be careful to follow the guidelines governing format precisely.

   a. A book by Sharon Jean Hamilton titled *My Name's Not Susan: A Life Transformed by Literacy,* published in Portsmouth, New Hampshire, by Boynton/Cook in 1995.

   b. An article by Bruce R. Joyce titled "The Great Literacy Problem and Success for All," published in the October 1999 issue of *Phi Delta Kappan,* on pages 129–31.

   c. An article by Geri Smith titled "Do Literacy and Health Spark Growth?" published in the September 29, 1999, issue of *Business Week,* on page 18.

   d. An article titled "Secret Hidden by Success: He Hid Illiteracy behind Humility and Enviable Skill," published in June 9, 1999, issue of the *Greensboro News Record,* on page 5A. No author is cited.

2. Create a list of works cited for the summary report you were asked to write for the exercise on pages 176–80.

Parenthetical Notes

A list of works cited identifies your paper's sources *in their entirety.* A ***parenthetical note***—a note placed in parentheses within your paper—identifies the *specific* location within a source from which you have taken a quotation or a bit of paraphrased information. Unlike the more complicated and cumbersome footnotes and endnotes, parenthetical notes employ a clear and efficient type of shorthand: They supply the least amount of information needed to identify a source about which more detailed information can be found in the list of works cited.

The beauty of parenthetical notes is their simplicity. MLA-style notes usually contain only two items: the author's last name and the page(s) from which the quotation or paraphrased information has been taken. For example, assume that one of your sources was Terry Lofton's article on tennis and advertising on pages 166–168. You would cite the article in your list of works cited as follows:

```
Lofton, Terry.   "The Angophile Angle."   Brandweek 6 June

     1999: 28-29.
```

Any notes within your paper need only refer the reader to this citation. To indicate that the following sentence is a paraphrase of information found on page 28 of that article, you would provide a parenthetical note:

```
In 1967, the governing board of Wimbledon hesitantly

allowed an American promoter to sell broadcasting

rights for the tournament in overseas markets

(Lofton 28).
```

The note is placed at the end of the sentence but preceding the period. Observe also that the note tells you only the *specific page* from which this idea has been taken. (In contrast, the entry in the list of works cited shows the page numbers on which the *entire article* is printed.) However, when notes refer to an article as a whole—as do the notes on page 186—then they too give all the pages on which the article appears.

When the author's name is unknown, cite instead the first word or two of the title. Suppose, for example, you wanted to paraphrase something from the second item in the list of sources concerning Delaware history. That anonymous article is cited as follows:

```
"Black History Month: Church Started in Slavery."   Morning

     Star [Wilmington] 26 Feb. 1997: 1D.
```

Your parenthetical note would look like this:

```
("Black History" 1D)
```

If your paper states the author's name (or, in the case of an anonymous article, its title), thus identifying the source, a parenthetical note provides only the page number(s). See, for example, the two notes for "Can the Boy Scouts Legally Discriminate?" on page 186. As you can see, the theory behind parenthetical notes is to provide the least information needed to identify sources,

Complete information about parenthetical notes appears in Chapter B of Part II.

Providing Parenthetical Notes

Suppose you have written a report on Delaware history during the Civil War era using the sources listed on pages 190–91. Show what the following parenthetical notes would look like:

a. A note referring to information on page 62 of Essah's book.

b. A note referring to the article in *Morning Star* as a whole.

c. A note referring to information taken from the last two pages of Cox's article.

 # READING SELECTIONS

The following articles concern the ubiquity of advertising in modern life.

Wipe Off That Milk Mustache*

FROMA HARROP

I am about to slice a banana for cereal, and what do I see on the yellow peel but a sticker that says "Got Milk?"   1

"Got milk?"   2

Got milk! The sky's still dark, the coffee isn't ready, my brain is cotton, and some-   3
one is throwing an advertisement at me. And not just any ad. "Got milk?" is the centerpiece of the highly irritating but very successful advertising campaign run by the National Dairy Council. You know, all those ads showing celebrities grinning with that white milky mustache. Yuck. Wipe your mouths.

The new millennium will see us drowning in advertisements. Ours has always   4
been a promotion-minded society, but there used to be sacred places where ads would not venture. The skins of fruit, for example. Not only bananas, but apples and pears have become canvases on which Madison Avenue can ply its craft. Movies get advertised on skins.

A menu used to be a single-purpose document: Its function was to tell us what the   5
restaurant had to offer. Just the other day I was at a nice restaurant attached to a mall (a real table-service place, not the food court). The backs of the menu's pages turned out to be advertisements for stores in the mall. This is more than annoying. It is confusing. A menu often requires making difficult choices. One doesn't want to take a commercial break between deciding to order the shrimp cocktail as appetizer and chicken parmesan as main course.

The friendly skies of United and all other airlines used to be a zone of heavenly   6
removal from the bazaar below. Sure, the in-flight magazines carried ads. You pick up a magazine and know what to expect. Now the airline screens hawk all manner of goods and services in between entertainment features. Ads appear on the paper lining the food trays.

*This article appears on page 12A of the October 18, 1999, edition of the daily newspaper *Providence Journal*.

7   A city bus is a beautiful thing, in my opinion. It needs no adornment, just a washing every now and then. First came the ads pasted to the sides of the buses. Then came the ads applied over the entire bus body. In the business, this is called a "total wrap." That includes the windows; passengers may see out, but the public outside cannot see the passengers. How can citizens interested in taking public transportation even tell that this contraption is a city bus and not the clown truck for the circus?

8   Pumping gas doesn't get any less tedious when ads pop up on screens beside the twirling dollars. The ad sequence at one of my local gas stations seemed almost a parody of American culture. First there's a weather report. Then a celebrity quiz question. Then the answer to the celebrity quiz question. Then a picture of a missing child and a number to call.

9   There is a certain charm to the jumble of flashing signs that vie for attention in Times Square. But must all America become Times Square? There are now small trucks whose purpose is nothing more than to crawl through traffic and display scrolling ads on window panels. Another new kind of advertising involves projecting giant light displays onto the sides of buildings. A twelve-thousand-watt light attached to a truck projects ads up to two hundred feet high.

10   There are ads in restroom stalls. Department stores now feature television screens that pile ads upon what might already be considered a promotional environment. Publicly funded universities name their sports arenas after products whose maker has put up money. Brand-name products advertise other brand-name products. There's a Coca-Cola Picnic Barbie: Barbie has a Coca-Cola label affixed to her vest. Her right hand holds a Frisbee advertising Coca-Cola. And in the event that anybody missed the message, her left hand grasps a bottle of Coke.

11   One of my personal favorites is Mike Cameron, who last year defied an advertising onslaught at his high school in Columbia County, Ga. Greenbrier High, incredibly, was holding a "Coke in Education Day." Coca-Cola executives appeared as guest speakers, and the students were asked to form the letters C-O-K-E for a class photo. The subversive Mr. Cameron came to school wearing a Pepsi shirt. The school actually suspended him for a day.

12   The next time I feel like a misfit for resenting the "Got milk?" banana sticker, the brave example of Mike Cameron will give me strength. I won't wonder whether I'm just too grouchy in the morning or generally lack a sense of humor. I'll just start my own campaign. The logo will read "Don't Got Bananas That Assault Me with Advertising."

Ad Nauseam*

MICHAEL J. SANDEL

1   When the Boston Red Sox installed a display of giant Coke bottles above the left field wall this season, local sportswriters protested that such tacky commercialism tainted the sanctity of Fenway Park. But ballparks have long been littered with billboards and ads. Today, teams even sell corporations the right to name the stadium: the Colorado Rockies, for example, play in Coors Field. However distasteful, such commercialism does not seem to corrupt the game or diminish the play.

*This article appears on page 23 of the September 1, 1997, issue of *New Republic*.

The same cannot be said of the newest commercial frontier—the public schools. The corporate invasion of the classroom threatens to turn schools into havens for hucksterism. Eager to cash in on a captive audience of consumers-in-training, companies have flooded teachers with free videos, posters, and "learning kits" designed to sanitize corporate images and emblazon brand names in the minds of children. Students can now learn about nutrition from curricular materials supplied by Hershey's Chocolate or McDonald's, or study the effects of the Alaska oil spill in a video made by Exxon. According to *Giving Kids the Business*, by Alex Molnar, a Monsanto video teaches the merits of bovine growth hormone in milk production, while Procter & Gamble's environmental curriculum teaches that disposable diapers are good for the earth.

Not all corporate-sponsored educational freebies promote ideological agendas; some simply plug the brand name. A few years ago, the Campbell Soup Company offered a science kit that showed students how to prove that Campbell's Prego spaghetti sauce is thicker than Ragu. General Mills distributed science kits containing free samples of its Gusher fruit snacks, with soft centers that "gush" when bitten. The teacher's guide suggested that students bite into the Gushers and compare the effect to geothermal eruptions. A Tootsie Roll kit on counting and writing recommends that, for homework, children interview family members about their memories of Tootsie Rolls.

While some marketers seek to insinuate brand names into the curriculum, others take a more direct approach: buying advertisements in schools. When the Seattle School Board faced a budget crisis last fall, it voted to solicit corporate advertising. School officials hoped to raise a million dollars a year with sponsorships like "the cheerleaders, brought to you by Reebok" and "the McDonald's gym." Protests from parents and teachers forced the Seattle schools to suspend the policy this year, but such marketing is a growing presence in schools across the country.

Corporate logos now clamor for student attention from school buses to book covers. In Colorado Springs, advertisements for Mountain Dew adorn school hallways, and ads for Burger King decorate the sides of school buses. A Massachusetts firm distributes free book covers hawking Nike, Gatorade, and Calvin Klein to almost twenty-five million students nationwide. A Minnesota broadcasting company pipes music into school corridors and cafeterias in fifteen states, with twelve minutes of commercials every hour. Forty percent of the ad revenue goes to the schools.

The most egregious example of the commercialization in schools is Channel One, a twelve-minute television news program seen by eight million students in twelve thousand schools. Introduced in 1990 by Whittle Communications, Channel One offers schools a television set for each classroom, two VCRs, and a satellite link in exchange for an agreement to show the program every day, including the two minutes of commercials it contains. Since Channel One reaches over 40 percent of the nation's teenagers, it is able to charge advertisers a hefty $200,000 per thirty-second spot. In its pitch to advertisers, the company promises access to the largest teen audience in history in a setting free of "the usual distractions of telephones, stereos, remote controls, etc." The Whittle program shattered the taboo against outright advertising in the classroom. Despite controversy in many states, only New York has banned Channel One from its schools.

Unlike the case of baseball, the rampant commercialization of schools is corrupting in two ways. First, most corporate-sponsored learning supplements are ridden with bias, distortion, and superficial fare. A recent study by Consumers Union found that nearly 80 percent of classroom freebies are slanted toward the sponsor's product. An independent study of Channel One released earlier this year found that its news programs contributed little to students' grasp of public affairs. Only 20 percent of its airtime covers current political, economic or cultural events. The rest is devoted to advertising, sports, weather, and natural disasters.

8   But, even if corporate sponsors supplied objective teaching tools of impeccable quality, commercial advertising would still be a pernicious presence in the classroom because it undermines the purposes for which schools exist. Advertising encourages people to want things and to satisfy their desires: education encourages people to reflect on their desires, to restrain or to elevate them. The purpose of advertising is to recruit consumers; the purpose of public schools is to cultivate citizens.

9   It is not easy to teach students to be citizens, capable of thinking critically about the world around them, when so much of childhood consists of basic training for a commercial society. At a time when children come to school as walking billboards of logos and labels and licensed apparel, it is all the more difficult—and all the more important—for schools to create some distance from a popular culture drenched in the ethos of consumerism.

10   But advertising abhors distance. It blurs the boundaries between places, and makes every setting a site for selling. "Discover your own river of revenue at the schoolhouse gates!" proclaims the brochure for the Fourth Annual Kid Power Marketing Conference, held last May in New Orleans. "Whether it's first-graders learning to read or teenagers shopping for their first car, we can guarantee an introduction of your product and your company to these students in the traditional setting of the classroom!" Marketers are storming the schoolhouse gates for the same reason that Willie Sutton robbed banks—because that's where the money is. Counting the amount they spend and the amount they influence their parents to spend, six- to nineteen-year-old consumers now account for $485 billion in spending per year.

11   The growing financial clout of kids is itself a lamentable symptom of parents abdicating their role as mediators between children and the market. Meanwhile, faced with property tax caps, budget cuts, and rising enrollments, cash-strapped schools are more vulnerable to the siren song of corporate sponsors. Rather than raise the public funds we need to pay the full cost of educating our schoolchildren, we choose instead to sell their time and rent their minds to Burger King and Mountain Dew.

School Daze*

Today's Kids Not Only Take Advertising's Presence in Their Classrooms for Granted, They Actually Like It.

DEBRA GOLDMAN

1   Talk about your nonconformist individuals. A couple of weeks ago, Michael Cameron, a senior at Greenbriar High School in Evans, Ga., showed up wearing a Pepsi T-shirt. During a special "Coke in Education Day," he stood out—a lone billboard for Generation Next.

2   "I wanted to mess with my friends' heads," the daring dissident told the *Wall Street Journal*. Given the school-yard mayhem wrought by kids messing with classmates these days, we're lucky a mere T-shirt was Cameron's weapon of choice. Next time, the cola wars may be fought with guns.

3   Cameron's act of defiance became a widely reported news event thanks to a vigilant principal who turned a meaningless goof—the kid doesn't even drink Pepsi—into a matter of principle. The educator, not the Coke executives (who laughed it off), en-

*This article appears on page 56 of the April 6, 1998, issue of *Adweek*.

forced brand loyalty, sentencing the rebel without a cause to a full day of in-school detention for his cheeky display of "rudeness" and "disrespect." Thus, a blatant play by the local Coke bottler to distribute Coke cards to the target market of the brand's huge summer promotion became a lesson in the traditional values teenagers are said to lack. That's educational value for you.

The most outrageous thing about Coke in Education Day, however, was not Cameron's suspension but the day itself. Only a few years ago, commercials in school, courtesy of Channel One, stirred controversy. These days, Greenbriar High simply turns its classrooms over to marketers outright. Economics class became a lesson in Coke marketing. Social science students learned about globalization from the master global marketer. Lessons concluded with the students' own salute to Coke. Obligingly outfitted in red-and-white Coke T's—do I smell a synergy with another hot educational trend, school uniforms?—they lined up to be photographed forming the word *Coke*.   **4**

Pitted against Coke as the guardian of order, Pepsi was cast in its old role as the choice of a new generation. Cameron's gesture accomplished what Pepsi's advertising no longer reliably does: give the brand, if only for a nanosecond, its old aura of youth and nonconformism. Little wonder the PepsiCo spokesman lauded Cameron as a fine young trendsetter. A lifetime's supply of Pepsi Stuff is the least the company can do for the boy.   **5**

Of course, we can learn a lot about our world by scrutinizing Coke's role in it. But I'm not sure Coke executives are the ones to teach it, especially when the lesson ends with a card-carrying student body transforming itself into a living brand logo. Surely, this is one of the creepiest public displays since the old Moscow May Day parades.   **6**

Still, this little controversy generated more bemusement than outrage. Being outraged by Coke Day is a little like being indignant about El Niño. A brand as big as Coke functions as a force of nature. Schools are just in the path of the storm.   **7**

Marketers eager to reach captive young audiences have slipped through the holes created by looser curriculum standards and the new emphasis on "relevance." The result is such pedagogical perversions as a lesson in self-esteem sponsored by Revlon, in which students are asked to contemplate "good hair days" and "bad hair days."   **8**

If you do find Coke Day shocking, chances are you're middle-aged and remember a time when school signage was provided by the pep club. The contemporary targets for these ploys, the kids themselves, not only take advertising's presence in school for granted, they like it. React, a teen-targeted Web-site-cum-Sunday-newspaper-supplement whose journalistic mission is to report back to teens what's on their own minds, asked its audience how it felt about ads in schools. A whopping four-fifths of respondents said there was nothing wrong with them. Some thought that they made school less boring. Well, duh. Hanging out in the school yard for a photo op sure beats sitting in algebra class.   **9**

Educators like Coke Day, too. There's great demand for resources that are fun and relevant among harried teachers trying to hold their students' attention. Who are the experts in creating such communications? Not educators, whose job is purportedly to teach young minds what they need to know. Marketers are the masters of the art of relevance. They're the ones with the know-how to create eye-catching posters and the budgets to produce glossy handouts with high-end production values. Plus, the stuff is free.   **10**

Besides, no one is sure what it is we need to know or what we should be teaching our kids. That's how we ended up with classes in self-esteem in the first place. With the old educational canon gone, there is only one authority qualified to decide what schools should be teaching: the students themselves. Students who don't know the Civil War from the cola wars know what they like.   **11**

The bad news for American education is that the future of the classroom belongs to those who know how to give it to them.   **12**

Freewriting

In your notebook, write for fifteen minutes in support of the claim that advertising has become too intrusive a presence in everyday life. Support what you say with personal experiences and observations, as well as any responses to specific details found in the articles by Froma Harrop, Michael Sandel, and Debra Goldman. You may look for further evidence to illustrate the ideas and arguments of these three writers, or you may develop ideas and arguments of your own. When you have completed this writing, take another fifteen minutes to refute or modify the claim that advertising has become too intrusive a presence in everyday life. Again, support what you say with personal experiences and observations, as well as any responses to details found in the three articles.

Group Work

Share both freewritings with members of your peer group by having each member read aloud as others takes notes. Try to reach some consensus about the strongest arguments in support of each position.

Review Questions

1. Why does Froma Harrop admire Mike Cameron?
2. What are Michael Sandel's two reasons for viewing commercialization as a corrupting influence on education?
3. According to Debra Goldman, how have "looser curriculum standards" contributed to the increased influence of corporations on public education?

Discussion Questions

1. Harrop views advertising as garish and ugly. Can you think of any instances in which advertising has enhanced the appearance of a building or the natural environment?
2. When school systems accept money from large corporations, are they more or less likely to receive an adequate amount of public tax-supported funding?
3. By comparing Coca-Cola T-shirts to school uniforms and a photo-op stunt to Moscow May Day parades, Goldman suggests that corporations want to suppress individualism. What are the best arguments for and against that belief?
4. Why do you suppose conservative religious leaders are sharply divided over whether to support corporate commercialism in public schools?

Writing

1. Write a brief summary report using these three sources and following the guidelines set forth in this chapter. Include a list of works cited.
2. Write an objective report on sources using the articles by Sandel and Goldman.

7 Analytical Reading and Writing

Talking with friends in the college cafeteria, you might be asked what you thought about the latest music video by a currently popular group. "I didn't like it," you might say. "It seemed repetitive. It's like I've heard and seen it all before. They've lost their edge." After some half-hearted agreement or disagreement with this appropriately vague comment, the conversation might drift to a recent party, an upcoming exam, the weather, or maybe lunch. That is the way with informal talk; it wanders almost aimlessly from here to there, rarely pausing to pursue a topic in depth.

But if the context were to change, your offhand comment could be disastrous. If, for example, you wrote that same answer on the exam for a seminar in popular culture, you would fail. In that situation, the response would not be specific enough. There is a thesis ("I didn't like it") and some support ("repetitive," "lost their edge"), but both are inappropriately thin for formal writing.

Sometimes it is difficult to make the transition from the looseness of informal spoken language to the tightness of writing. But the difference between them is significant. You rarely need much support for your ideas and opinions in conversation, but you do in writing. It is not a matter of right or wrong; it is just that each way of communicating has different conventions. As a literate member of a college community, you should know and observe these special conventions. If you were asked in the cafeteria what you thought about a recent video, a developed 500-word analysis of the cinematography would not be a smart answer. The "correct" response would be the appropriately brief one. In any situation the needs and interests of the audience should determine the ideas you will explore, the specificity of detail you will provide, and the level of language you will use.

As we noted in Chapter 4, the foundation of writing lies in the interplay between the general and the specific, the way a writer brings abstract ideas down to earth. Writers need to support general statements with appropriate details, reasons, examples, and illustrations. They are part of a special community of people who must demonstrate not only what they think, but also their reasons for thinking it. In a sense their ideas are promises to their readers, promises that they must keep by linking one idea to another. If they don't keep those promises, their readers will be disappointed. That's why good writers deliver.

Good readers also deliver. At this stage of your education, you do not want to be merely a passive consumer of ideas. If you are to be a contributing member of a college community, you must be an active, analytical reader and writer. By writing about your reading, you learn to read more carefully, and you develop more acute skills of perception. The purpose of this chapter is to explore ways for you to analyze your reading so that you can become a more informed receiver and creator of knowledge.

 ## ANALYZING THE PARTS

Whenever you analyze anything, whether it is a chess move, an automobile engine, a political theory, or a poem, you try to break down its complexity by dividing it into component parts. Then you can look at the parts individually, seeing first their detail and then examining the way they work together.

To understand anything that is complex, observers must first analyze the parts. Political scientists, for example, constantly analyze the differences between free-market and managed economies—how they produce and deliver consumer goods, what profits their industries are allowed to make, what restrictions they place on imports. Experts compare the systems by analyzing money, people, goods, laws, attitudes, and other components. They take the whole apart to see how each element works and then study the ways those elements operate together.

When you analyze a reading, you should do the same thing—consider separate aspects individually and then see how they function together as a whole. Writing is an extremely flexible medium of communication, and just as there is no set formula for writing an essay—one can write in many different ways, and the success of a work may even depend on the writer's originality—so too there is no set formula for analysis. How you view a reading depends on what it is and why you are reading it. You look for different qualities in an epic poem, a comic satire, and a scientific report. You approach a work that you read for pleasure differently than you approach a source for a research paper.

Nevertheless, there are some features common to all written works that you should consider. Every piece of writing tries to do something with concepts or information, addressing and developing a main idea in an organized sequence so that readers can understand what is being discussed. The following five aspects of a work should be considered in an analysis:

- The **purpose** for which the work was written
- The way the author has directed the work to its intended **audience**
- The **main idea** of the work
- The **development** or **support** for that idea
- The **organization** and **coherence** of the work.

We will first look at each of these five aspects individually and then see how they can be put together into a more comprehensive analysis of a reading.

Purpose

Every work must be judged in terms of what it is attempting to accomplish. You can't be upset with a zany movie for not being sufficiently philosophical or with a journal in comparative linguistics for lacking humor or with a fantasy adventure for being unrealistic.

Some writers want to change our minds; others simply want to tell us something we didn't know before. Some want to provoke us to action; others hope to entertain, cajole, shock, or educate us. As a college reader, you must be alert to these possibilities. If you misinterpret a writer's intention, the whole point may be lost; sometimes the result of such an error can be tragic—or hilarious.

Although we cannot always know exactly what an author is thinking, the general purpose of most writing is evident enough. Nevertheless, things are not always what they seem. You must be alert for satire as well as for attempts to manipulate your beliefs. You must notice the writer's biases and be wary of both slanted evidence and outright deception. Sometimes writers are candid about where they stand; but at other times you may have to read between the lines, basing your judgments about intentions on your past reading experiences and your knowledge of human nature.

In the following passage, David Sacks and Peter Thiel make no effort to conceal their bias—a disdain for the efforts of many universities to raise consciousness about issues of cultural diversity:

> "Orientation is designed to disorient you," announced Stanford professor James Adams to an auditorium of 1,600 puzzled freshmen at the beginning of the new school year. Assembled for one of many orientation-week programs on "diversity," the freshmen soon learned what he meant. A lesbian activist spoke first about "challenging your sexuality," and encouraged the seventeen- and eighteen-year-old students to "overcome" their "fears of being queer." Next, a black musician performed an electric-guitar solo as police sirens wailed in the background. He concluded his demonstration by dropping suddenly to the floor and convulsing his body in a re-enactment of the Rodney King beating.

After quoting Professor Adams's statement about the objectives of orientation at Stanford, the authors ridicule those objectives by listing the more controversial, possibly outrageous, activities involved. The authors provide various clues to signal their disregard. For example, they place the word *diversity* in quotation marks and describe the audience as "puzzled." A more subtle tactic is their reminding readers in the third sentence that some first-year students are, legally, minors. Since they are so forthright in showing their bias (and since their article was published in the conservative *National Review*), the writers cannot be accused of deception. We may choose to disagree with them—we may even dislike their methods of argument—but at least they have given us every reason to expect a presentation of their topic slanted toward their particular bias. An intelligent reader will examine Sacks and Thiel's ideas critically, aware that these are not the only possible perceptions of freshman orientation at Stanford University.

Analyzing Purpose

1. As you read the following short essay, try to decide the author's purpose in writing it:

The Mosquito Wars

Suburbanites Batten Down the Hatches

James Kaplan

The dead cow I passed last week on my running path, along the Old Croton Aqueduct in Hastings-on-Hudson, had an oversignificant look about it, like something out of David Lynch or Hitchcock: a Sign. But it wasn't, in this instance, a sign of moral rot or complacency at the heart of suburban life; it was a sign of a sickness that was thought at first to be St. Louis encephalitis but has now been reclassified as a type of West Nile virus, a disease never before seen in the Western Hemisphere, spread by mosquitoes to birds and humans. And now, apparently, moving north from Queens (had it landed at Kennedy?) to Manhattan and on to Westchester.

One of the great questions about the suburbs has always been: What's worse, for nothing to happen or for something to happen? Well, there's a lot to be said for nothing. It can make for a certain amount of edginess among overprivileged teenagers, but it beats Kosovo and East Timor, and a well-tended inner life is cheaper than lawn care. West Nile virus, however, was definitely something.

After a few cases of the virus turned up in Westchester, health officials decided to spray the county. As in Queens and Manhattan, helicopters would do the job, but, unlike the city, which used the insecticide malathion, Westchester would employ a somewhat less toxic pesticide, brand-named Anvil, a synthetic pyrethroid chemically similar to the natural bug-killing vapors emitted by chrysanthemums.

Why Anvil instead of malathion? Anvil has a slightly sinister, Wile E. Coyoteish sound to it, but apparently the stuff comes out in a finer spray, better at penetrating those lush suburban glades where mosquitoes flourish. And there is something else: malathion is said to be potentially damaging to car finishes. Who knew what kind of fuss Westchester citizens might kick up if the pearlescent coats of their Lexuses and Audis and Volvos got pitted overnight?

We would be sprayed, we were told, on Monday evening between 7:00 and 9:00. We were advised to close the windows and bring toys and pet bowls inside. We covered the sandbox. We put the Little Tikes Cozy Coupe and the Radio Flyer in the garage. We cooked dinner and joked nervously. At precisely 6:59, a police cruiser flashed around the block, its loudspeaker blaring an urgent but incomprehensible announcement: "WARGH-LMMBA-GTZABEN!" The noise Dopplered away. Something was happening.

We sat down to dinner. The baby threw his pasta around; the big boys grinned and listened for helicopter rotors. My wife and I looked at each other.

The first chopper came over at 7:47. We ran to the windows. It was a helicopter, all right, flying low: big concussions, lights flashing. Too dark to see any vapor. Back to dessert. There was a bad moment after dinner when it turned out that the eleven-year-old had switched the vent on one of the air conditioners to "Open." Outside air had been blowing in for half an hour. "I thought that meant recirculate," he said, looking worried. His younger brother, a more jovial type, laughed. "It's flower vapor!" he said.

I'm with the eleven-year-old. I worry. Initial thoughts of the Fort Knox knock-out spray scene in *Goldfinger* turned to thoughts of the crop-dusting sequence in *North by Northwest,* which turned to memories of a year ago, when we somehow managed to not go back to war with Iraq over its nerve-gas factories. All they'd have to do, I thought at the time, was send a small plane over. . . . Best to put it out of one's mind. The suburbs, after all, are the place where nothing ever happens.

Toward midnight, I spotted a big, suspicious looking mosquito flying dizzily around the bathroom. I swatted it.

2. A short column written by the chairman of a major airline introduces each issue of the company's in-flight magazine. The following column appeared in September 1999.

Staying Connected

Donald J. Carty

There's nothing like a good milestone to remind us of how far we've come, or how far we have to go. As you know, it was thirty years ago this summer that United States astronauts first walked on the moon. What a breathtaking achievement, and what a tribute to both human daring and technological progress.

Today, technological advances continue to take our breath away, in ways I for one would never have imagined thirty years ago. Keeping up with the latest technology can be fun, but it's not easy. And one of the things we're learning is that advances in one area can bump up against advances in another. Such is the case with the increasingly sophisticated navigation systems onboard our aircraft and the communication tools, including cellular phones and two-way pagers, which for some of us have become the umbilical cords connecting us with the rest of the world.

I'm often asked why we, along with the rest of the airline industry, don't permit use of cellular phones or two-way pagers in flight. The short answer is that these devices transmit and receive signals that can interfere with our aircrafts' navigation systems. This creates the possibility of distorted communications between the various onboard avionics systems, or between the cockpit and ground-based computer systems. Contrastingly, the Airfones available on most of our airplanes are specially engineered to eliminate interference with aircraft systems.

Because nothing is more important to us than safety, we've maintained a very strict policy prohibiting the use of cell phones and two-way pagers at all times on our aircraft. However, after a lot of careful study, we have now determined that we can safely relax that restriction just a bit. So going forward, approved portable electronic devices—including cell phones and two-way pagers—may be used up until five minutes prior to departure, or until the "fasten seat belts" sign is turned on. Also, in the unlikely event of a long ground delay (generally fifteen minutes or greater), the captain has the discretion to temporarily permit the use of approved electronic devices, including cell phones and two-way pagers. However, it is extremely important that when the flight crew indicates that time is up, all such devices be turned off and stowed. That doesn't just mean hanging up. Cell phones and two-way pagers may only be used on the ground and must always be turned off in flight.

As we get closer to the year 2000, new technologies will no doubt continue to challenge and amaze us—but probably not in some of the ways we once thought. At the beginning of this century, a publication called *Looking Forward* predicted that "the businessman of 1999 will take a soup pill or a concentrated-meat pill for his noonday lunch." You'll be glad to know that whether you're flying First, Business, or Coach, you will never be treated to a concentrated pill on [our] airline.

What you will be treated to is a flight crew absolutely committed to your safety. I hope you will honor their commitment by listening to and following their instructions.

We are proud to serve you, and we want you back onboard our aircraft many years to come.

> a. Several purposes are addressed in this short passage. How many can you identify?
>
> b. Do any of these purposes take priority over others? Are some in conflict with each other? Which ones are more challenging to present or justify to an audience of air passengers?
>
> c. What strategies (e.g., phrasing, order of presentation) does the writer employ to communicate information about or to elicit compliance with less welcome policies?

Audience

Although authors sometimes write mainly to express themselves, more often their purpose is to create an effect on outside readers. They usually have a particular audience in mind (for example, in writing this paragraph, we have in mind an audience of college students and their instructors), and they adjust their writing to fit the needs and interests of their intended readers. Likewise, in analyzing a work, readers must consider the audience for which it was intended and judge it on those terms.

In the following brief essay from a newsletter for fourth-graders, the writer has been attentive to the needs of young readers:

Computers Help People with Handicaps

Several million people in the U.S. are handicapped. Some can't speak or make speech signs. Some don't have the use of their arms. Today, some of these handicapped people do things they have never done before. Computers help them talk, play games, and do schoolwork.

Many handicapped people must find special ways to work computers. Some use one finger to press the keys of their computers. Other people use a pencil held in their mouth. Some use their toes.

Computers give many handicapped people a chance to do things without help from others. These people read stories on computers and play computer games. These people also use computers to turn lights on and off and to open and close doors. A handicapped person's computer can get lessons to and from a computer at a school.

Someday people with serious handicaps may be able to get jobs for the first time. Their computers will be connected to computers at places of business.

—*Weekly Reader*

Notice the clear, connected way information is presented. The short sentences, basic vocabulary, brevity, and lack of technical details all suggest the writer's awareness of audience.

It would be unfair to criticize this writer for failing to see complexity in the subject. If you were doing research on computers for a college course, you would be wise simply to look elsewhere. On the other hand, the following piece, written for an audience with special technical expertise, might be equally inappropriate as a source for a college research paper:

> Myelography and other invasive procedures designed to show disc rupture and root compression should only be employed where surgical intervention is being considered. These procedures should never be used as routine diagnostic measures. They do form an essential part of a preoperative evaluation. Myelography has two primary purposes: (1) to rule out a neurogenic cause such as nerve root tumor accounting for the clinical puncture; (2) to confirm the level of localization for the suspected disc rupture.
>
> —J. Leon Morris, "Radiologic Evaluation"

Here the assumptions about prior knowledge, the vocabulary, and the main point suggest an audience of medical specialists. Again, to criticize this piece for being dense and unreadable would be comparably unfair.

Audience, however, involves more than just the level of vocabulary and assumptions about prior knowledge. It also reflects attitudes and values that readers are expected to share. Consider, for example, the opening paragraphs of a chapter from *The Inner Bitch Guide to Men, Relationships, Dating, Etc.*, a somewhat facetious self-help manual by Elizabeth Hilts:

The inner bitch deals with men who are romantic possibilities the same way she deals with anyone—which is to say, honestly. It's just easier that way. It is vital, however, to recognize some simple truths about how men approach life.

Men, apparently, love a challenge. Theory has it that this is a basic biological fact, though I wouldn't know because I flunked basic biology. According to some people who seem to live in a parallel universe (you know who you are), this information entitles women who seek relationships with men to behave poorly.

Here's how it works in that parallel universe:

If you want a man, you have to play hard to get.

The variations in this theme are endless—don't make it "easy" for them; men are supposed to rearrange their schedules around you, but you never do the same for them; don't ever go Dutch on a date; don't call him; and the ultimate, rarely return his calls.

There's a word for this kind of behavior—***RUDE!***

Not to mention archaic, antithetical, manipulative and . . . RUDE! I mean, really, what are they thinking? This isn't behavior you'd put up with from other people, is it? If a man treated you this way, you'd have nothing to do with him, right? (The only correct answer to this question is, "Right!") Do you honestly want to indulge in rudeness yourself?

I don't think so.

The vocabulary of this passage is unpretentious; its style is informal. The writer uses contractions, asks questions, and directs a few conversational asides to the reader. Although the word *bitch* is offensive to many readers, the author probably assumes that any woman who reads a book with that word in its title will suspend judgment when it is used ironically. (Actually, Hilts connects the word with behavior that is the opposite of what overt sexists often describe as "bitchy.")

More important than vocabulary, however, are other clues that reveal the author's assumptions about her audience. For example, when she appeals to the reader's preference for honesty and ease in relationships, Hilts envisions an audience of women who are not naive or blindly romantic. Though they are not jaded or cynical, these readers are experienced, perhaps exasperated, with dating relationships and tired of self-defeating games. By proclaiming her ignorance of biology, the author appeals to an audience that resists—or distrusts—academic expertise but respects the practical advice of an experienced peer. Finally, Hilts skillfully allows readers to distance themselves from the self-defeating behavior that her book derides. Imputing this behavior to "*some people* who seem to live in a parallel universe," she slyly adds in a parenthetical aside, "you know who you are." Likewise, five paragraphs later, Hilts shifts from a judgmental third-person reference—"I mean, really, what are *they* thinking?"—to a personal appeal: "If a man treated you this way, you'd have nothing to do with him, right? . . . Do you honestly want to indulge in rudeness yourself?"

Together, these strategies establish a comfortable relationship between Hilts and her readers as forthright women, willing to defy social conventions that place them at a disadvantage in relationships. They can laugh together at past mistakes and don't mind being stigmatized as "bitches" by a culture that perpetuates self-defeating behavior viewing it as a normal part of dating.

To analyze means to take apart, but one can do this objectively only when viewing a work within the context of its intended audience. Sometimes this is little more than determining how much information and vocabulary readers are assumed to possess; at other times it is more a matter of looking for subtle clues regarding attitudes, values, interests, and experiences shared by a particular community of readers.

EXERCISES   ## Analyzing Audience

1. The following excerpts each concern the work of Joseph Eichler, a prominent California builder and developer of the post-World War II era. Use clues such as style, vocabulary, content, format, and assumed knowledge to decide if they are intended for different audiences. Which of the excerpts might include you among its targeted readers? Analyze how each text is adjusted to meet the needs of readers.

    a. People lucky enough to have been raised in California could easily overlook Eichler houses or take them for granted. Those of us who grew up in drearier climes are more likely to recognize them as the iconic designs they were.

       These low-slung, jazzy spreads, built by Joseph Eichler from the late 1940s to the early 1970s, were the avant-garde architectural expression of California dreamin'—an optimistic, middle-class, mid-century vision of the good life. . . .

       Beloved by design intelligentsia in the world's sophisticated capitals, they're nonetheless often dismissed as 1950s tract homes. But they're gaining renewed respect and delighting a new generation—thanks to a traveling exhibit of photographs and illustrations by two architects. . . .

[Eichler's] first development was probably Sunnyvale Manor I, completed in 1949. It was followed by subdivisions in Sunnyvale, Palo Alto, and Menlo Park. He soon began working with architects, developing his signature style—flat roofs, atria, open plans and walls of glass looking out at the back yard. They were considered quite avant-garde, and not for everyone. . . .

Today, Eichler [house] owners and admirers have their own San Francisco-based association, the Eichler Network, with a quarterly newsletter that's a mix of boosterism, encouragement, tips for keeping houses dry and watertight, and humor written by "Eichlerholic" Wally Fields.

—Susan Kuchinskas, "Eichler Retrospect: UC-Berkeley Exhibit Harks Back to Postwar Optimism" (review in the *San Francisco Examiner*)

b. Walking into an Eichler home is like stepping into a private oasis. Architectural features include open-beamed ceilings, glass walls, and (after 1956) atriums. The front door feels like the back: all attention is focused on an expansive wall of glass that opens to the garden. . . .

Floor plans are open with living/dining areas separated from kitchens by breakfast bars, all within view of the atrium or outdoor patio. Bedrooms and bathrooms are usually on the street side and in ells that define patio or atrium. Some feature garages, others carports with attached storage sheds.

Original construction of these post-and-beam homes included efficient systems and natural materials such as redwood tongue-and-groove siding on the exterior and redwood plywood inside. Exposed redwood beams and (later) veneered-mahogany paneling are also characteristic. Slab floors are covered in cork tiling or vinyl-asbestos flooring that allow efficient radiant heating under the floors.

Other features include wood cabinetry and grasscloth-covered closet doors that slide. Overhead lighting appears only in the kitchen. Doors are oversized to offset the high ceilings. Eichler's model homes were furnished with small Danish furniture to accentuate this overhead space.

Not content to just build houses, and in keeping with his emphasis on family life, Eichler also created neighborhoods for his homes. His developments are built around recreation areas that include community centers, nursery schools, and swimming pools. Streets discourage traffic and ensure privacy. Lots are laid out in radiating circles to create a sense of individuality despite the use of only a few house designs.

—Laura Marshall Alavosus, "California Eichlers: A Coming of Age" (article in *Old House Journal*)

c. I had never heard of Joseph Eichler until I saw his name scrawled on the corner of a fact sheet for the house my husband and I were thinking of renting just outside of Palo Alto in northern California. He was the architect, I assumed, as I wandered through the boxy post-and-beam rental that looked unprepossessing from the street. The bedrooms were on the small side, the kitchen linoleum looked shabby, and the acoustic tiles on the ceiling were ready to fall down. But the back of the L-shaped structure was practically all windows and glass doors, and the house seemed to expand into the large, inviting backyard.

That night, tired of scanning real estate ads on the Internet, I typed in "Eichler" on a whim, and came up with an entry called "The Eichler Network." Intrigued, I clicked on it and entered an entire world of Eichler, one filled with Eichler history, Eichler lore, Eichler owners sharing tips on how to keep Eichler flat-roof homes from leaking, Eichler specialists on updating Eichler kitchens and maintaining the radiant-heat floors.

Joseph Eichler, I learned, was not an architect after all. He was a businessman who had run his wife's family's dairy business. But a brush with great architecture changed his life. In 1942 Joe Eichler rented a Frank Lloyd Wright house in Hillsborough, California. He didn't even know it was a Wright house at first, but he fell in love with modern architecture. . . .

Today there are over eleven thousand Eichlers in northern California, from Marin to Sacramento to Palo Alto to San Jose. (There are another five hundred or so in southern California, in Orange County and Thousand Oaks.) . . .

But Eichlers weren't, and aren't, for everyone. When they were first being built, the houses appealed to only about 5 percent of those who came to look, estimates Catherine Munson, a longtime Eichler salesperson, who has lived in Eichlers for over forty years. "The main thing about Joe Eichler," recalls Munson, "was his integrity." At this time (prior to anti-discriminatory housing laws), most builders simply did not sell subdivision houses to non-whites, and the government did not insure home loans to African-Americans, but Eichler sales were determinedly color-blind. Says Munson, "Eichler felt, and there was the general sense, that people who bought Eichler homes tended to be more educated, sophisticated, artistic—more freethinking. He was proud of that."

—Deborah Michel, "Middle-Class Modernism" (article in *House Beautiful*)

d. I prowl the streets at night—the streets of Palo Alto, San Rafael, even San Francisco and Sunnyvale. My breath hangs in the air as I creep along the empty suburban sidewalks, stalking another one directly in my path.

Am I a thief? A kidnapper? No. More insidious than that. . . . I am an Eichlerholic!

I have a strange obsession with these wonderful homes, and have since I was a kid. I feel a tremendous surge of excitement, a burst of creative energy, whenever I'm near them.

When approached from the street at night, the Eichlers don't give up their secrets easily, of course. Open-beam ceilings seen through trapezoidal clerestory windows under the roofline, the light of the TV reflecting from the living room way in the back. A seductive glimpse of center courtyard seen through the open door. The confusion of indoor and outdoor spaces.

Sites like these lead me to wonder where my own creativity comes from. Probably from my family—a bunch of oddballs, of whom I am the oddest. But I suspect that this creativity also owes itself in no small part to living in and amongst these architectural wonders.

I was born and raised in Palo Alto, spending the first years of my life in an Eichler on Thomas Drive—a flat-top with a center courtyard. My family moved out and into a "regular home" when I was three, reinforcing through my own deprivation the magic of what I call "Eichler Vibes." I don't think these homes would have seemed quite so mysterious to me if I had lived in one all my life. That's one theory. Regardless, my fascination continues to burn.

After our move, my family continued to own the Thomas Drive house, periodically returning to clean it between tenants. And I always went along with my parents on those occasions, a chance to rekindle old memories that threatened to fade away. I remember how appropriate the house looked empty. Indeed, emptiness becomes Eichlers.

But I could still remember, sort of, what it was like to live in that house. Black Tiki masks in the atrium, my late mom scrubbing the floor and swearing: "That damn kid made a mess again!" And all the while, the strange, beautiful lighting that illuminated the middle of the house and beamed through all those skylights. And—philodendrons. Lots of philodendrons.

I recall the early 1960s as a bastion of tacky culture. I distinctly remember walking past the old Emerson console TV-radio—at the time it reached up near my shoulders—playing silly girl-group music like "It's My Party and I'll Cry If I Want to." The absurdities of television, with its Boraxo and Shake-and-Bake ads, the TV announcers blaring in their authoritative voices. Men in their stiff suits and ties, women in their goofy hoop skirts, and kids in wide-striped T-shirts. And lots and lots of Formica. How could such brilliantly designed homes have popped up in the midst of all this mediocrity?

I continued to live in Palo Alto, going to Cubberley High School for two years, until 1977. Then my family moved to Idaho, where I lived for seven years before returning to the Bay Area, to Fremont. During all that time in Idaho, and later in Fremont, something seemed to be lacking in my life, like a missing limb. There were no Eichlers to be found anywhere!

So every so often, I make time to prowl. Especially through Palo Alto. I call it "Eichler hunting." Often, when I find a favorite, I'll stand there, staring in awe, thinking, "One day, I'll own one myself!' (Yeah, right! If I can ever afford it!) Then I imagine the furniture I'll have, what plants I'll put in the atrium. When the security light flashes on, my stargazing is cut short, and I realize once again I'm a stranger of the night—in someone else's neighborhood.

I start thinking, "How odd. I'm obviously trying to connect with my past." Yet, for the longest time after my departure, I never really tried to contact the people I had known in this town. For all I knew, all of them had either passed on or moved away. Once, I realized the craziness of my behavior and knocked on the door of some friends of the family I hadn't seen in twenty years, all too long an absence. Not only did I get to relive fond memories with some old friends, but I got myself another opportunity for one more great Eichler fix.

But why do I have such an obsession with these homes? Is it just nostalgia—or is there something else going on here? Meanwhile, my family members don't share my obsession. They seem to quickly get bored with my musings about Eichlers, remembering them mostly as being small and uncomfortable. (After all, we were a family of seven and needed a lot of space!)

That's why I decided to get in touch with the *Eichler Network*. Now, as the "Eichlerholic" columnist, I have an excuse to stay on the prowl. I'm going to check out neighborhood after neighborhood. I'll visit homes at random—maybe even yours—hoping for a walk-through and looking for another story to tell. I won't be reporting about your solutions for poor window insulation and old siding, or wonder what you're going to do about those roots in the sewer. I'll leave that to the Network service pros.

Instead, I'll be looking for another Eichler Fix—and for what feelings we might have in common. Well, do we share that same passion? Is the Eichler experience something special and mystical for you too? Will I ever live in an Eichler again?

I really need to know.

—Wally Fields, "Eichlerholic" (column in the *Eichler Network* newsletter)

2. The following passage comes from a syndicated advice column for investors that appears in newspapers across America. The author, Malcolm Berko, is responding to a letter from "S. T." of Woodland Park, Colorado, who, though deeply in debt, contemplates using an inheritance of $105,000 to finance his son's college education. Try to determine any attitudes, values, interests, and experiences

shared by Berko's audience. As much as possible, connect the inferences you draw to specific details in Berko's response.

> Don't be stupid. You guys are in hock up to your earballs, and soon as you get a gift from God you're hot to trot to spend it. Suckers like you who pledge their incomes ten years hence are seldom given a second chance . . . in life. And most that do fail because they can't discipline themselves for the future. It must be genetic! . . .
>
> Forget Junior's college education. Frankly, many of today's colleges are nursery schools for teenage high school mutants. Most colleges have lowered their testing standards so that almost anyone with sixth-grade qualifications can get a degree. And the College Board in March 1994 made its SAT questions so simple that applicants with room-temperature IQs earn acceptable scores.
>
> In my opinion college degrees are fraudulent diplomas certifying an education that never happened. Today's students believe that paying four years of tuition entitles them to a degree, and so many colleges have acquiesced that we have created a new national social disease called the "dumbing down of America." Tell Junior to join the armed services. . . .

Main Idea

As you saw in Chapter 4, the central question a reader must ask about a work is what, specifically, it is about. Many writers announce their main point in a single sentence—the thesis statement. But since so many good writers develop their ideas in other ways, you cannot always expect to find a one-sentence statement of the main idea at the beginning of a text. Sometimes writers state the main idea in the middle; sometimes they put it at the end; and some other times they make their point throughout the course of a work without ever summarizing it in a single sentence. And since not every writer is a good one, sometimes writers wander from point to point without ever arriving at a focus.

Important questions to ask, then, in analyzing any text are these: (1) What is the main idea? (2) Has the writer kept to the topic, producing a unified essay about that main idea? The best advice for discovering a main idea is to read attentively and to become actively engaged in the text. Reread where necessary and read with a pencil, underlining and writing comments in the margins wherever feasible. Then try to summarize the main idea in your own words.

EXERCISES   **Analyzing the Main Idea**

1. Applying skills introduced in Chapter 4, underline important statements as you read the following essay; then state the main idea in your own words.

    Downloading Class Integrity

    Lawrence Hinman

    "Download your workload," one term paper site advertises. Across the Internet, dozens of sites have sprung up that allow students—usually for a fee ranging from

$20 to $100—to download papers and book reports from existing databases. Other sites offer customized services, offering to write book reviews, term papers, and even theses for graduate students on specific topics. Still other sites provide financial incentives for students to sell their work online.

These sites represent the tip of a virtual iceberg, an iceberg that is on a collision course with traditional methods of teaching. The Internet is forcing us to rethink our understanding of academic integrity and even to rethink the goals of education itself.

The Internet makes plagiarism easier, and this poses the most visible threat to academic integrity. Numerous sites are selling papers on the Web, and countless more are inadvertently offering them for free.

Professors often post their own work on the Internet, and it is increasingly common for students to do so as well. Coupled with sophisticated search engines, all of this makes a virtual cornucopia of material available to anyone who wants to plagiarize.

There are two responses to this challenge—external and internal. External approaches try to block access to the sites, to police student behavior on the Web in various ways. Internal approaches seek to develop the skills and motivation in students so that they will restrain themselves, even when no one is watching, from plagiarizing.

The larger threat to academic integrity, however, lies below the surface. The Internet is transforming how we teach. This is most evident in distance education, where traditional teacher-student interaction is often supplanted by computer-based instruction.

The Internet is quickly transforming what happens—and doesn't happen—in the traditional classroom, and this presents a much greater challenge.

It is not uncommon for professors to put lecture notes on a course Web site. The Internet increasingly is becoming an integral part of regular courses.

As this happens, many students feel that they hardly need to go to class. Everything they need is available on the course Web site.

Classroom education has always had a dual element. On the one hand, information gets transmitted. On the other hand, there is an engagement that occurs between teacher and students. It is in this process that academic integrity is formed. Students develop an intellectual identity, to see themselves as thinkers who take responsibility for themselves and their ideas.

As the Internet plays an increasingly prominent role in traditional undergraduate education, two paths are open to us. We can move in a direction that will make classrooms increasingly irrelevant. Insofar as we see education simply as the transmission of information, we will move naturally in this direction.

Or the Internet can be used to free classroom time for more effective interaction among professor, students, and the ideas being considered in the course—an interaction that cannot happen on the Web. The momentum of the technology, the apparent economic benefits won by cost-conscious administrators and the lack of appreciation for the central formative process of liberal education all conspire to push us toward the first path. To follow this path to its inevitable destination would be the ultimate violation of academic integrity.

2. The following is an excerpt from the opening handout in an upper-level college course. A list of class policies is not usually considered to have a main idea apart from the policies themselves. Nevertheless, do you find a theme, a central idea, running through these policies? If so, how can you summarize it?

Attendance policy: Your regular attendance is an essential requirement of the course, and attendance will be taken at each meeting. While there is no penalty for up to three absences, each absence beginning with the fourth, unless excused for a legitimate reason, will result in a one-letter lowering of your final course grade.

Students missing more than six classes (for any reason) will have missed too much of the course to receive credit for taking it and should withdraw to avoid a failing grade. Attendance will be taken at the beginning of each class. (Please do *not* submit excuses for the first three absences—no matter how noble—since none is needed.)

Late arrival: You are also required to be here on time. Late arrival causes a disruption of the class and is strongly discouraged. Consequently, three arrivals after attendance is taken will be counted as equivalent to one absence. Should you arrive late, it is *your* responsibility to check with me after class to be marked present; otherwise, you will be recorded as absent.

Reading assignments: You are expected and required to be well prepared for each class meeting. In order for you to contribute constructively to class discussions and to profit from lectures, it is essential that you have read the assignments with care. Unannounced quizzes will be frequent; results will be a significant factor in final grading decisions, since they reflect the seriousness of your participation in the course. Continuous studying and keeping up are essential; this is not a course in which students can wait until exam-time to begin studying.

Exams: Four exams will be given, after each quarter of the semester. Failure to take any of the four exams at the assigned time will result in a failing grade for the course. Make-up exams will not be given, except for a documented medical or other emergency. Any make-up will be given during the final exam period (following the final exam) and will be more difficult than the regularly scheduled exam. It is your responsibility to know the date and time of the final exam and to make advance plans accordingly. Make-up exams will *not* be given to accommodate conflicting engagements, outside jobs, or early vacations.

Course grades: Your final grade will be based principally on the four exams and a writing assignment. Passing grades on the exams and paper range from A+ (4.33) to D– (0.67). Failing grades are F (0), F– (–1.0) and F– – (–2.0). The five grades will be averaged to determine the course grade. Quiz grades will be the deciding factor when a student's average is within 0.1 of another grade. Absences in excess of six, cheating, failure to take an exam, or failure to submit the assigned paper will automatically result in a failing grade for the course. Please take note: The course grade will be determined strictly by calculation based on your performance. The professor does not "give" grades; the grade you receive in this course will be the grade you have earned for yourself.

A final observation: As you can see from the above, you are expected to be a serious, self-disciplined, conscientious student in this class, and responsibility for your actions and performance is entirely yours, not the instructor's. In the past, students who have worked conscientiously and who have consistently come to class prepared have done well in this course. Persons with poor work habits have found themselves having to repeat it.

Development

If stating an idea were enough, there would be no books or essays. Each piece of writing would consist only of a topic sentence. Of course, more is needed. Writers must explain, expand, and support their ideas. Sometimes facts or logic is called for, sometimes narration of events, and sometimes examples, illustrations, and reasons. A mathematics textbook calls for clear, step-by-step reasoning, with many examples and exercises to reinforce each lesson. New interpretations of historical events call for background information, direct evidence, and support from authoritative sources. The way that an author chooses to develop a main idea depends on the work's purpose and its intended audience.

Writers develop their ideas successfully when they support them with specific, concrete evidence. In the following excerpt, the writer answers her opening question with a series of examples.

> Who were the influential male models of appearance and behavior in turn-of-the-century America? Sports figures like boxer John L. Sullivan were important, as were businessmen and industrialists. In addition, western cowboys were also admired. They had inherited the mantle of the frontiersmen and Indian fighters after Owen Wister apotheosized their lives as cattle raisers into a saga of gunslinging drama in his 1901 novel *The Virginian*. But there were others whose image was softer and whose aggressive masculinity was countered by sophistication and humor.
>
> Cosmopolitan men of the theater, for example, were popular. This was the age, after all, when the Barrymores first rose to prominence. In the 1890s many stationery and jewelry stores displayed in their windows photos of Maurice Barrymore holding an elegant demitasse cup and saucer in his hand and garbed in full dress as in one of his famed portrayals. . . .
>
> —Lois W. Banner, *American Beauty*

In much of the writing that you do in college, you will need to conduct additional research to develop your ideas. Outside sources can provide you with the information you lack, and expert sources can lend your paper the prestige of their authority. In the following excerpt, the authors rely on research sources to support their own ideas about science classrooms:

> The design of this science classroom . . . is also based on the notion that schools are not just buildings, and that all people are life-long learners. The need for relevance in the experiences of school children and for applicability and currency in teacher-training programs is not a new one; however, these needs are not often met.
>
> In *Educating Americans for the 21st Century*, a National Science Board report, technology and an understanding of technological advances and applications were recognized as basic. While initial effects of the infusion of computers into instruction might not have produced desired results (Greenberg 107), the relevance of technology education is still apparent. Kids learn differently today, differently from the learning modes familiar to us. In the 20th century people were "paper" trained. Youngsters of the 21st century are "light" trained, i.e., comfortable with video- and computer-based material. Matching learning styles with delivery systems is crucial for success.
>
> —Richard J. Reif and Gail M. Morse, "Restructuring the Science Classroom"

The authors make their thesis about technology in classrooms more persuasive by citing support from a report of the National Science Board. Even when they cite another authority who disagrees with their contention (Greenberg), they score points by showing they are well informed and have considered all sides of the issue.

EXERCISE   ## Analyzing Development

Read each of the following passages and answer these questions: What is its main idea? What specific facts, ideas, or examples does the author present to support and develop that idea? What in the passage, if anything, helps to convince readers of the author's authority in addressing that idea? Would a different approach (for example, more citing of research sources or of personal experiences) have been more effective?

a. **LEAVE SOMETHING BEHIND**

Charles Bowden

It is a matter of honor, even though I never gave my word. It began seventeen years ago, as I stood at a counter in Organ Pipe Cactus National Monument, a little-visited backwater of the national park system on the Mexican line in Southern Arizona. Julian Hayden, then about seventy, was leaning forward and speaking to a young woman. Hayden had rolled into Arizona on a motorcycle in the 1920s, when the roads were dirt and the only way to cool the air was to wait for winter. He knew more about the deserts of southwestern Arizona and northwestern Mexico than any other man alive. He was a lean man, almost fatally handsome, and that day he was all but charming the pants off a young woman working for the Park Service. When we left, he explained to me that she was a descendant of Don Alberto Celaya, and I was stunned.

You have to know the bloodlines here to understand why. In the first decade of this century, a pleasantly crazed Norwegian named Carl Lumholtz came into the country, and in the tiny village of Sonoyta, on the edge of the great desert, Lumholtz hired a boy named Alberto Celaya to guide him into a vast wilderness, a trip that eventually became his book of the place, something he called *New Trails in Mexico.* In the 1950s, Julian Hayden started wandering the place, and Celaya as an old man became his teacher. In the low rainfall—zero to three inches a year—things have a way of staying the same here. A bone tossed aside a thousand years ago will rest next to a cigarette butt. Hayden found early-man sites that go back into a cauldron of debate—ten thousand years? Twenty thousand years? A hundred thousand years?

When Hayden entered the country, the game knew naught of man, and once, a badger waddled up and sniffed his boot and then ambled off again. I've lain on the hard ground and had bighorn sheep walk by fifteen feet away and treat me for what I am—an ungainly but apparently harmless biped. And so when Hayden flirted with the young woman, of the family Celaya, he touched a chord of knowing this unknown ground that stretched back all of the twentieth century, a kind of lineage of desert rats.

Seventeen years ago, we went into that country, my first time, into a place on the Mexican side, a place of volcanic craters and vast lavas and old intaglios left by earlier lovers and abandoned camps from back of the beyond and sleeping circles—low rock enclosures to block the wind—and old stone hammers and total silence. The tongues of lava licked north across the line into the United States, where yet more emptiness loomed, a tract of five thousand square miles without a house, a person, or a voice.

I was in. And the better part of me never came back. Julian and I became friends. The desert and I became lovers. That was the beginning of it, and now that I've bounced down some hard years, I know it will never end for me. I've got personal ties. Hundreds of miles of walking where there are no trails and damn little water. A friend is buried in the emptiness in a simple hole so that he can watch what he loved forever. I think of my friend a lot. He always figured to come back as a vulture, and when I see a buzzard wheeling overhead now, I always smile to myself. Julian himself once took me to a knoll out there where he'd scattered the ashes of two premier desert rats—Malcom Rogers and, later, Ronald Ives. And now Julian is gone, passing away peacefully in his eighty-seventh year, his head no doubt filled with the dirt and heat and silence of a thousand camps he'd made.

b. **CAN DREAMS DIAGNOSE ILLNESS?**

A Few Top Mind-Body Doctors Suggest Dreams
Can Be an Early-Warning System

Ann Japenga

Was last night's dream meaningless babble—remnants of pepperoni calzone spliced with freeze frames from *NYPD Blue*? Or, as Freud and others contended, are our nighttime visions actually trying to tell us something?

In the newest round of debate, prominent experts in mind-body medicine say dreams not only speak to us, but also send lifesaving messages. Dreams, they maintain, can warn us of serious illness long before symptoms erupt or signs appear on medical tests.

"Many physicians have been stunned by the accuracy of their patients' dreams," says Larry Dossey, M.D., an internist who popularized prayer and healing in his book *Healing Words.* His new book, *The Reinvention of Medicine,* advocates using dreams in standard medical diagnosis.

Another alternative-medicine luminary, Bernie Siegel, M.D., lectures graduating medical-school classes on the importance of listening to patients' dreams. "If we could introduce this idea in medical school, patients would not be afraid to tell us their dreams," says Siegel, a cancer surgeon and author of popular books on self-healing.

Dossey, Siegel, and other champions of dream medicine have been won over by listening to their own patients' dreams as well as by hundreds of published reports of diagnostic dreams.

Dossey tells of a patient who came to him worried because she'd had a vivid dream (diagnostic dreams are said to be more emphatic and urgent than ordinary dreams) that she had three white dots on her left ovary. Though her physical exam was normal, Dossey referred the patient for a sonogram and explained to the radiologist what they were looking for. The radiologist ridiculed the notion, but he later appeared in Dossey's office pale and shaken.

"What did you find?" Dossey asked.

"Three little white spots on her left ovary," the radiologist replied.

But Harvard Medical School dream authority J. Allan Hobson, M.D., says dream diagnosis is "scientifically unattractive" and might be explained by coincidence. "What about all the people who dream about cancer," he says, "but don't get cancer?"

Scientific evidence for dream medicine is sparse. In one of the rare studies of the topic, Russian psychiatrist Vasily Kasatkin analyzed the dreams of 1,200 subjects and found they sometimes pinpointed the precise location and severity of an illness before the malady could be medically diagnosed.

"Dreams are hard to pin down," says James Pagel, M.D., chairman of the dreams section of the American Sleep Disorders Association. "Because of that, it's still a very limited science. We don't know why people sleep, let alone why they dream."

Dossey says healers can't afford to ignore their patients' dreams. "We have to be grateful for helpful information—no matter where it comes from."

Organization and Coherence

Good writing abides by a standard of courtesy. Like good hosts, writers treat their readers well. Of course, many great poets and novelists challenge their readers by experimenting with new ways to experience time, character, and ideas. But nonfiction writers, whose purpose typically is to inform or persuade their readers, are more straightforward. They usually make their point early and stick to it. Their readers have a right to expect clarity, order, and a fair amount of logic. As one writing theorist, Kenneth Burke, has claimed, writers have a duty to take their readers by the hand, walking them through the essay and helping them see connections between ideas, sentences, and paragraphs.

An analytical reader can ask the following questions about organization and coherence: Does the writer provide indications of where the passage is heading? Can you follow the movement of ideas, or are you sometimes puzzled, lost, or taken by surprise? Is there a logic to the way the text is put together? Is there a clear link between the main idea and the support (reasons, examples, and explanations)? Is the supporting material arranged in an order that makes sense? Does the writer make the passage readable by providing transitions when new ideas are introduced?

Not every writer gives readers the help they need. The following passage leaves its readers to shift for themselves; it is so poorly organized that a reader can never be certain where it is aiming to go next. The writer builds up expectations about one topic but suddenly heads off in another direction.

> You wouldn't believe my son Jason. He was so unbelievably wild and inconsiderate yesterday I got one of my headaches. They come on with a vengeance, with no warning. I was so crazy with pain last week, it will be a miracle if my sister-in-law ever speaks to me again. I've been to specialist after specialist and none of them can find the problem. A lot of money they get paid, for what? Fancy offices and fancy diplomas so they can charge fancy fees. When I think about doctors I get another headache. My head throbs and my eyes don't focus. I don't want anything to do with people, and I'm as miserable to Jason as he usually is to me. Maybe Jason will be lucky enough to become a doctor someday and then the money will stay in the family.

This writer has given no thought to organization, writing whatever comes into his head. He leads us to think the paragraph will be about his son's behavior, but it turns into a discussion of his headaches, with frequent detours to other topics. Later we expect to learn what he said to his sister-in-law, but that topic is abandoned with no awareness of the reader's unsatisfied curiosity. The topic of doctors is introduced, then forgotten, and finally returned to at the end, with no thought for logical ordering.

In contrast, the essays in the following exercise are coherent, readable, and logical because both writers spent time thinking about how to shape their ideas for readers. They organized the movement of their thoughts by providing signposts, transitions, and examples. Coherence, however, is relative. Some readers may find one of the essays more carefully organized than the other.

Analyzing Organization

After reading each of the following essays carefully, explain as specifically as you can how the writer has organized the text. Why is the essay arranged as it is? How does the writer move from one idea to the next? How does he move between the general and the specific? What links appear between sentences and paragraphs? How does the writer guide you through the text? Do you perceive any digressions or gaps in either essay? Does one essay seem more cohesively organized than the other?

INTO THE WIND

Jim Collins

The Great Age of Sail lasted four centuries, from about 1460 to 1860. Sailing vessels dominated the world's trade routes then, and every military worth its salt was built on a powerful fleet of sailing warships. The United States was actually one of the age's last strongholds: It was only a hundred years ago, in 1899, that its tonnage under sail finally gave way to ships powered by steam.

But there is a new great age of sail underway, as anyone knows who has seen the explosion of wind surfers in Oregon's Columbia River Gorge, or looked out at a crowded Chesapeake Bay on a breezy summer day, or tried to secure a slip in Camden, Maine. The advent of durable, relatively inexpensive fiberglass hulls has resulted in literally hundreds of classes of sailboats over the past few decades. (Two of the "classics," the Sunfish and the Hobie catamaran, are standard fare at most waterfront resorts around the world.) The popularity of big races such as the America's Cup has soared. Boardsailing has been a full medal sport for the past four summer Olympics. Even wooden boat building is enjoying a resurgence. Yet the majority of sailors face the wind with only an intuitive understanding of the strange and complex forces that move a sailboat through water.

A WINDED HISTORY

What I should say, rather, is "the strange and complex forces that move a sailboat through water into the wind." Sailing with the wind (or "on the wind," with a "following wind," or "downwind") is not strange or complex at all. In terms of sailing history, sailing in the same direction as the wind has always been a no-brainer. Humankind discovered early on how to do that: Build a primitive boat and hoist a crude section of skins or cloth on a stick and hold on. The sailmaker Tom Whidden, in his book *The Art and Science of Sails,* calls sailing with the wind aft of the beam "the adult version of kite flying."

The earliest sailing ships date back at least to ancient Egypt, where drawings depict huge boats with multiple oars and a single sail. The sail would have been used only with the wind; the oars, pulled by slaves, were needed to move against it. By the time of the Greek and Roman empires, two prototypes had emerged: the slender, streamlined galley ships that used oarsmen to move into the wind; and the tublike, round cargo ships that lay deep in the water and moved awkwardly under one great sail. Sometime around the birth of Christ, a smaller mast and sail appeared in the bow, along with the occasional topsail. These bulky vessels were steered with great oars on either side of the stern. If the boats couldn't sail into the wind, they could at least sail across it ("with the wind abeam") without badly drifting. The more efficient, triangular lateen replaced the clumsy square sail around the seventh century.

Meanwhile, to the north, sailing technology was developing rapidly. Ships around Oslo, Norway, dating from 800 A.D. were discovered to have a keel and a large steering oar operated by tiller on the right side of the stern. (Which led to the term "steer-board" side, the precursor to "starboard." While we're at it, another definition of terms: Boats are commonly defined as small enough to be carried on ships. Boats generally sail in fresh water, ships in salt water.) Those Danes were among the first to set sail on the high seas, reaching North America by 1000 A.D. The advent of the fixed rudder around 1200, and the introduction of three-masted ships with smaller, more numerous, and more manageable sails, opened the seas up even further. Along with their growing knowledge of wind and navigation, captains took full-rigged ships like Columbus's *Santa Maria* from Europe across the Atlantic and beyond. The Great Age of Sail was underway. Ships got bigger and faster, their riggings and sails more refined and complex.

But a ship driven by a steam-powered paddle wheel crossed the Atlantic in 1838, and a few years later the screw-type propeller improved on the paddle wheel, and the wind was about to get knocked out of the Great Age's sails. Naval fleets soon crossed over to the new technology. Merchant sailing vessels, kept afloat by the extraordinarily fast American "clipper ships," resisted the change for a few more decades. *The Flying Cloud,* one of the most famous clippers ever built, made a Cape Horn Run from New York to San Francisco in a record eighty-nine days. In the late 1860s, though, the Suez Canal halved the distance between London and Bombay, so the sailing ships lost much of their advantage; and the compound engine cut down on the steamers' consumption of coal, allowing them to carry bulk cargo more economically. By the start of World War I, just one-fifth of the world's tonnage was under sail. By the end of World War II, sailing naval vessels had disappeared entirely; among merchant vessels only Chinese junks and Arab dhows remained. In the United States, a small number of fishermen and recreational boaters kept the craft alive. It would take a couple more technological innovations—fiberglass and lightweight, synthetic sailcloth—to snap sailing out of the doldrums.

RUNNING AGAINST THE WIND

Changes in popularity and fashion aside, the key to sailing—from full-rigged ships to sailboards—is to "tack" or move in zigzags against the wind. The best designed vessels in the world, despite all of our advances, can tack into the wind only up to the final tenth of a 360-degree circle. Much of a skipper's prowess lies in wringing every bit of efficiency out of his or her boat during the few degrees either side of that limitation. "For the racer," writes Tom Whidden, "sailing upwind has the tactical complexity of a chess match with a grand master."

In the interest of time and space (dense, formula-filled textbooks have been written), we'll ignore almost all of the complexity—the trimming of the sails, the choice of sailcloth, the sail's shape and "aspect ratio," the flex and position of the masts, the secondary sails, the design and materials of hulls and rudders and keels, why the "slot" between the mainsail and jib is misunderstood. We'll ignore the tremendous variety of boat shapes and sizes (Richard Sherman's *A Field Guide to Sailboats* lists 230 basic classes, including the Lasers I sailed in college and the C-Skows my wife Kristen grew up racing in the Midwest.) Instead, we'll focus on the basic physics that allows the paradox: using the power of the wind to move against it.

At its core, the physics is found in fluid dynamics. "A sail is like an airplane wing . . . ," the simplified explanation to sailors usually goes. On an airplane, the wind passing over the top of a curved wing has to travel a longer distance than its "brother particle" passing along the flat underside of the wing. In order for the two particles to meet at the same time at the trailing edge of the wing, the wind going over the top must travel at a greater speed. That difference in speed creates lower pressure on the top of the wing, higher on the bottom, and therefore suction or "lift." This is Bernouli's principle.

In sailing, a more complex set of forces is at work. Wind hitting the front edge of a sail moves around both the leeward and windward sides of the boat. As the wind currents reach the trailing edge of the boat, differences in pressure and resistance create a swirling "starting vortex" of air just off the boat's stern, which, like a gear in a gear train, starts a larger vortex of air circulating back around the moving boat. (Though we can't see these air currents, an analogous process happens with water moving around the keel. The starting vortex is clearly visible in the water as it sheds off the boat's track.) This circulation of airflow accentuates the speed of the air moving around the sails. The resulting low pressure pulls the boat leeward, causing the boat to "heel." The keel and the rudder channel that sideways heeling force into the direction of travel.

The first time I ever sailed an ice boat—a borrowed "DN" class made of Sitka spruce, on New Hampshire's Lake Winnipesaukee early one spring as the ice was starting to break up—that heeling sensation was intense. It lifted one of the boat's runners four feet off the ice. I urgently spilled the air out of the sail and came back to solid ice, terrified. I didn't understand the physics then. I was sailing by intuition, based on my experience on soft water. I was still trying to figure out the exaggerated heeling when I sailed past a couple of orange warning cones and smashed into frigid open water, snapping the boat's mast and damaging its deck. I'm sure it would be smoother sailing for me now, if the guy would only lend me his boat again.

GENETIC CROP RESEARCH PAYS OFF

Gregg Easterbrook

Corn that is genetically modified to include a natural insecticide, cotton that has been engineered to tolerate herbicides—if you've been reading about such new transgenic crops, you may be asking yourself, "Why do we need all this stuff?" After all, American farmers already turn out plenty of high-quality food at low prices.

Yes, it's true that most genetically modified crops now available are barely distinguishable from what they supplant, and so far they have not led to such promised advances as big reductions in the need for agricultural chemicals. And while there is no evidence that genetically engineered crops in the field have caused any harm to human health or done any damage to the environment, planting them obviously entails a risk of unwanted ecological effects.

So shouldn't the genetic engineering of crops be stopped? That is what many critics, here and in Europe, are saying. And if the current generation of crops were all that the engineering of agriculture would produce, that would be correct, because the risks, while small, would outweigh the benefits.

But the important thing to keep in mind is that the transgenic crops in the news today are just the first manifestations of a fundamental new idea. Much better versions are coming.

Initially, many new ideas seem of modest value or even appear to be a step backward. The first cell phones seemed like a niche product for millionaires. The first heart-bypass operations, statistically speaking, seemed no more effective than if the patients had refused treatment.

But the second and third generations of advances based on these ideas were spectacular. This is likely to be the pattern that genetically engineered crops will follow. The transgenic crops in the news today were conceived ten to twenty years ago. The next advances may represent the difference between those suitcase-size "portable" computers of the early 1980s and the slim laptops of today.

For example, the Rockefeller Foundation is sponsoring research on so-called golden rice, a crop designed to improve nutrition in the developing world. Breeders of golden rice are using genetics to build into the rice forms of vitamin A that the body can absorb; vitamin A deficiency is a common problem in poor countries. A second phase of the project will increase the iron content in the rice to combat anemia, which is a widespread problem among women in underdeveloped countries. Golden rice, expected to be for sale in Asia in as little as five years, may offer dramatic improvements in nutrition and health for millions of people, at just shy of zero cost to farmers and consumers.

Similar initiatives using genetic manipulation are aimed at making crops more productive by reducing their dependence on pesticides, fertilizers, and irrigation, or by increasing their resistance to plant diseases. Other projects hope to solve problems like peanut allergies by removing the genes for allergens from the plants.

Today 800 million people in poor nations are chronically undernourished, according to the United Nations, and the populations of these countries are expected to grow by an additional two billion to three billion people before the global population peaks sometime in the next century. Merely changing the way food is distributed cannot solve the need for increased agricultural output. But the second and third generations of genetically engineered crops might.

Then there are the health care possibilities. For example, the standard three-shot course required for hepatitis B inoculations in the United States alone costs about $200. There is no way people in poor nations can afford that, a reason hepatitis B is exacting a terrible toll in Africa. But researchers at Cornell University are working to transfer the genetic code for hepatitis B vaccine into bananas. If they are successful, hepatitis B inoculations could cost as little as ten cents per dose and would require no medical personnel to administer them.

This project is one reason that while skeptics in the West are looking askance at genetic engineering, the World Health Organization is having a major conference this month in Geneva to see how this technology can help improve global health.

Of course, the genetic engineering of crops must be carefully regulated. A new system of independent testing and federal oversight might be required, replacing the current hodgepodge in which the Environmental Protection Agency, the Food and Drug Administration, and the Department of Agriculture have overlapping and conflicting responsibilities.

But it would be a mistake if the underwhelming results of the first generation of transgenic crops led to laws or boycotts that blocked the second and third generations.

After all, it's the world's poorest people who would have the most to lose.

 ## WRITING A BRIEF READING ANALYSIS

Purpose, audience, main idea, development, organization and coherence—these are the most important, but by no means the only, aspects you can consider when you analyze a reading source. In addition to these general topics, each work must be considered on its own terms. Each work has its unique identity, and an analytical reader will find much in it to consider and talk about. And because readers take an active part in their reading, so too each reader's analysis will be different. It is important when you analyze a work to see it clearly, but it is also wise not to worry about being "right." In analyzing what you read, you must be willing to trust your own judgment.

Now that you have analyzed different elements of readings in isolation, you should have a better sense of how those elements work together. An analysis of the whole text should consider all five aspects. Read the following text carefully and analytically, asking yourself questions about each of the elements we have considered so far.

"Ernie's Nuns" Are Pointing the Way

MOLLY IVINS

1 Way to go, college students!

2 Reebok, the sports shoe manufacturer, admitted this week that conditions at two of its factories in Indonesia were distinctly sub-par and says its subcontractors have spent $500,000 to improve them. Reebok's actions came after a boycott of its shoes on campuses around the country coordinated by United Students against Sweatshops, a nationwide student coalition. Nice going, good win.

3 Reebok also deserves credit: In response to the boycott and criticism from human rights groups, the company commissioned a study of working conditions in its foreign factories fourteen months ago and has apparently followed up on the findings. "We hope that this will also break through and encourage more companies to do something like this," said a Reebok vice president.

4 USAS also urged students to join a new group—the Worker Rights Consortium—that will set a strict code of conduct for overseas factories that make clothes with university names.

5 USAS then pressed universities to withdraw from the Fair Labor Association . . . on grounds that the group's practices are insufficient. The specific criticisms of Fair Labor include letting manufacturers choose which plants will be monitored and giving advance notice of inspections. Another very smart move by the college students. In my day, we referred to this as "not getting co-opted by the Establishment."

6 Several human-rights groups have helped with the anti-sweatshop movement, but the bulk of the energy seems to have come from the campuses.

7 USAS has become quite sophisticated about how to guarantee independent monitoring and is also working for living wages for foreign workers, based on economic conditions in each country. These laptop activists have already had a major impact on the collegiate licensing industry and should in time be able to affect the entire apparel industry.

8 The apparel industry is—to use a word I loathe—paradigmatic, in that it is completely globalized and notoriously exploitative. Apparel manufacturers are actually design and marketing firms that "out-source" production to independent contractors all over the world. This model is increasingly copied by other industries as they seek to lower labor costs and avoid worker organizing.

9 Any Texan can get a look at the results by visiting the maquiladoras just on the other side of the Tex-Mex border. The toxic dump in Matamoras is worth a visit all on its own.

10 Tom Friedman, the *New York Times*'s foreign affairs columnist, has observed: "For many workers around the world the oppression of unchecked commissars has been replaced by the oppression of the unregulated capitalists, who move their manufacturing from country to country, constantly in search of those who will work for the lowest wages and lowest standards. To some, the Nike swoosh is now as scary as the hammer and sickle."

11   Middle-aged activists who waste time bemoaning apathy on campus could help by getting off their duffs and helping spread word about the USAS boycotts.

12   Lest you think hideous working conditions are found only in the Third World, consider the case of Big Chicken, the poultry industry in America.

13   Workers in chicken factories endure conditions that would shame Guatemala or Honduras. Many stand for hours on end in sheds that reek of manure, or chop chickens all day in cold, dark plants, or are constantly scratched by live chickens that have to be crammed into cages by the thousands.

14   The *New York Times* reported that the Rev. Jim Lewis, an Episcopal priest whose assignment is to improve the lives of poultry workers, once led a wildcat strike against a plant where a worker was fired after he had a finger cut off. The wages are so low, workers often qualify for welfare. And as Texans know from our experience with Big Chicken in East Texas, these plants are often notorious polluters as well, fouling both air and water.

15   The point of the *Times* article on Rev. Lewis was to demonstrate that hundreds of priests, ministers, and rabbis are involved in struggles to improve conditions for American workers on the bottom rungs of society.

16   This seems to me at least as newsworthy as the latest bulletin from the Christian right that Tinkie-Winkie, the purple Teletubbie, is gay or that Harry Potter books are Satanic.

If you were in a class of college students assigned to write an analysis of Molly Ivins's essay, you could begin by freewriting about each of the five elements. You might produce preliminary notes such as these:

<u>Purpose:</u> Ivins hopes to do more than provoke a response from her audience; she wants to arouse them to action. She talks about people "getting off their duffs," as if she's trying to shame them into supporting boycotts. Newspaper opinion pieces like this usually elicit a disengaged, even contemplative, response, asking readers to reconsider conventional attitudes or opinions, appealing to fairness and open-minded skepticism. But rather than urging her readers to consider new or controversial ideas, Ivins appeals to their consciences, almost shouting at them to take action. She opens her essay with an exclamation and ends it with dark sarcasm. In the few places where she adopts the more polite, sophisticated language of "think-pieces"--words like <u>paradigmatic</u> and <u>out-source</u>--she seems at pains to distance herself from it.

Audience: Ivins opens as though she were speaking
directly to college students, and she continues in that
vein throughout her first two paragraphs. But in paragraph
5 it becomes clear that she really is talking about the
actions of a specific group of students--"Another very
smart move by the college students." The word you doesn't
appear until paragraph 12: "Lest you think hideous working
conditions are found only in the Third World [. . .]." Here,
it sounds like she's talking down to her readers, the
"middle-aged activists" whom she scolded in the previous
paragraph. But in spite of her exasperation with their
laziness, Ivins exhorts these activists who share her
convictions; she isn't trying to win over hostile corporate
executives or traditional conservatives. She identifies
herself as a Texan, most notably when she says "as Texans
know from our experience," but I think that's just because
she writes a column in the Fort Worth newspaper; the issues
she deals with are international in scope, and there are
people throughout the world who share Ivins's point of
view.

Main Idea: Ivins wants readers to know that savvy,
committed activists are bringing abusive labor practices to
light and are fighting to eliminate them. Ivins says that
middle-aged, middle-class Americans who share her views ought
to support those efforts.

Development: In first seven paragraphs, Ivins presents
evidence that may have come from a single news story written
for the Associated Press or one of the other wire services.
In the next several paragraphs, she reveals knowledge of the
broader economic implications of franchizing and out-
sourcing. In paragraphs 9, 12, and 13, Ivins leads us to

believe that she has the benefit of first-hand, personal observation of inhumane working conditions in Mexico and Texas. She also quotes one article from the <u>New York Times</u> and makes reference to another.

<u>Organization and Coherence:</u> In her first five paragraphs, Ivins sounds triumphant, like she's gloating-- at last somebody's taking action! She sounds like a cheerleader: "Way to go. [. . .] Nice going, good win." The next five paragraphs place the specific event (one manufacturer's response to student activism) within a global economic context. In the following three paragraphs, Ivins alerts her audience of "middle-aged activists" to the urgency of the issue. It's not just news from some Third World country that gets brief coverage in the daily paper; it's something that well-meaning Americans permit to happen close to their own communities. Finally, Ivins talks about one particular activist, Rev. Jim Lewis--the conditions he opposes and what he's doing to change them.

These notes are a rough beginning. You would now write a draft, which you would revise and edit. Finally, your polished analysis might look like this:

Analysis: "'Ernie's" Nuns' Are Pointing the Way"

Molly Ivins, a syndicated columnist for the <u>Fort Worth Star-Telegram</u>, addresses an audience of aging Baby Boomers, many of whom were Civil Rights activists and war protestors during their college years in the 1960s and early 1970s. By applauding the commitment and savvy of today's students who have organized boycotts to improve working conditions in garment factories overseas, Ivins tries to shame her readers into action. Specifically, she upbraids them for "bemoaning apathy on campus" and enjoins them to get "off their duffs" and "spread word about the [. . .] boycotts."

Unlike most op-ed authors, Ivins does not try to appear objective or disengaged from the issue at hand. She assumes that readers share her values and political views, and she makes no effort to persuade anyone who doesn't. She appeals to our consciences rather than participating in the spirit of detached inquiry more often seen in journalistic think pieces. In fact, Ivins mocks the vocabulary of politically disengaged writing. She tries to distance herself from the word out-source by placing it in quotation marks and, when forced to use the word paradigmatic, she inserts a sarcastic aside: "to use a word I loathe."

To earn the moral authority to which Ivins lays claim, she must display knowledge of the issue--a challenging task in so short an essay. Familiarity with the focusing event that introduces the essay--the successful boycott of Reebok by United Students against Sweatshops--is a start. But many readers know that information like this is readily available through the newspaper wire services that editorial writers routinely consult. More impressive is Ivins's grasp of the economic implications of franchises and out-sourcing, a preemptive response to any notion that her views are naively idealistic. Ivins enhances her credentials with specific details about working conditions in Texas and Mexico.

Ivins's essay can be divided into three parts. In the first five paragraphs, Ivins gloats over the successful USAS boycott of Reebok. Her tone is gleeful and exultant: "Way to go. [. . .] Nice going, good win." The next five paragraphs help to establish the writer's credibility: Ivins places the boycott within a global economic context that has heroes (labor activists) and villains (greedy corporations). Then, in her final eight paragraphs, Ivins invites action. She depicts the horrible working conditions in Texas chicken factories, tells how one person is combatting the abuse, and urges her readers to join the struggle.

ASSIGNMENT   **Writing a Brief Reading Analysis**

Analyze the reading selection that follows, using this procedure:

1. Read the essay twice; underline important ideas and write comments in the margin.

2. Freewrite about each of the five elements of analysis.

3. Compose and carefully revise a draft of about three hundred to four hundred words. Begin with a description of the essay (its purpose, audience, and main idea); then analyze development, organization, and coherence. Edit your draft thoroughly.

 ## READING SELECTION

The following essay was written by a syndicated columnist for the *Washington Post* and published in November 1999.

Classroom Cheating a Serious Problem

WILLIAM RASPBERRY

1   By the time I arrived for my "Family and Community" class, I was still reeling from the results of a survey I'd just seen. A poll of more than 3,000 students listed in *Who's Who among High School Students*—the cream of our scholastic crop—revealed that 80 percent of them had engaged in academic cheating and thought cheating was commonplace. Moreover, a majority of them saw cheating as a minor infraction.

2   Surely this couldn't be correct, I thought.

3   But close to half of my Duke University students (encouragingly less than 80 percent) acknowledged some high school cheating, though all of them insisted they'd outgrown the practice since they entered college.

4   I decided to spend the bulk of the period talking about it, and the result was one of the most interesting classes of the semester.

5   We began with a discussion of honor codes and their enforcement: stiff codes (like that at the University of Virginia, where students are required to report any cheating they observe and name the cheaters on pain of expulsion), softer codes like Duke's (which requires students to report infractions but permits them, under some circum-

stances, to do so anonymously) or lax codes that amount to a no-cheating policy statement that says, in effect, don't get caught.

Most of the class—predictably—chose the middle ground. Nearly all said they would have walked away from a stolen answer sheet rather than use it to boost their college-entry SAT scores. Only a handful said they would have gone all the way and told school authorities what was being done and by whom. On the other hand, most said they were likelier to report cheating that put them at a competitive disadvantage.   6

The attitude toward reporting—and to a serious degree toward cheating—turned out to be remarkably pragmatic. Do it, or don't do it, because it works—to make life fairer, more comfortable, more predictable.   7

Then came what was for me the interesting part. The class was after all about community—about understanding and strengthening the institution that, along with family, is the foundation on which our society rests.   8

So I asked them which sort of community they'd rather live in, as students or as members of a family: one where nearly everyone adhered to the very highest ethical standards or one that embraced a middle-of-the-road live-and-let-live attitude. They were virtually unanimous in preferring the high-standard community.   9

"You'd want neighbors with higher ethical standards than your own?" I asked them. They would, but also thought it likely that they'd raise their own standards to meet the community norm. "And also lower them to meet that norm?"   10

They weren't sure, but fitting in did seem to count for something: isn't that what standards are about?   11

Then I asked them to imagine they had come up with a foolproof way of counterfeiting money. Would they be tempted? Not enough to ruin the economy, of course. Just, say, $100,000 in undetectable counterfeit. You could pay off your college loans, help out the family, get the jalopy fixed . . . and then destroy the plates. After all, you're no career criminal. Who would get hurt? Your family's better off, your debts are paid, the mechanic has a job he wouldn't have had. Maybe the trickle-down effect of your clever counterfeiting improves the entire local community.   12

And no one would do it. Ethics, they decided, wasn't only about pragmatism and getting along. Personal integrity mattered for its own sake. Who would be hurt? They would, they agreed.   13

I'm not alleging major epiphany in a single afternoon. Many of my students remain ambivalent (and unbelievably honest) about the temptation to lower their ethical standards, particularly in settings where lower standards are the norm. And if 80 percent of the brightest and best own up to cheating, those lower standards are the norm.   14

Nor is this some personal discovery of mine. Donald McCabe, the Princeton professor who conducted the survey that launched our discussion, is the founding president of the Center for Academic Integrity, a consortium of some 200 colleges and universities (including Duke, where the center is based). This group is exploring ways not merely to reverse the rising tide of academic cheating and plagiarism but, more important, to get students to embrace ethical standards as a matter of personal integrity.   15

It won't be easy, as Dr. McCabe's survey makes clear. But it's hard to think of anything more worth whatever effort it will take.   16

Freewriting

Write in your notebook for ten minutes in response to William Raspberry's essay. Among the questions you might consider are these: Do you share the author's astonishment at the results of the poll he refers to? How would you have responded to the survey and to the questions that Raspberry put to his students at Duke University? Is it likely that students can be brought to "embrace ethical standards as a matter of personal integrity"? Why or why not?

Group Work

After each member of your group has read his or her freewrite aloud, discuss the five elements of analysis detailed in this chapter (purpose, audience, main idea, development, and organization/coherence). Observe where the group is (and is not) able to reach agreement in analyzing the essay.

Review Questions

1. What are the three kinds of honor codes described in this essay?

2. What excuses or ways of rationalizing the use of counterfeit currency does Raspberry offer to his students? Why do they reject them?

3. Who belongs to the Center for Academic Integrity, and what are the organization's goals?

Discussion Questions

1. Do you suppose that Raspberry's students had any inkling that what they said in class might be referred to in their instructor's nationally syndicated column? How might such an inkling have influenced their responses to his questions and their contributions to class discussion?

2. Raspberry implies that academic cheating was once much less prevalent and that students once "embrace[d] ethical standards as a matter of personal integrity." What evidence from your own experience, observation, or reading can you cite to support or reject that belief?

3. What do you view as the chief advantages and drawbacks of each of the three types of honor codes described in this essay?

Writing

1. Using the methods presented in this chapter, write an analysis of any one of the following essays: "The Mosquito Wars," pages 202–03; "Downloading

Class Integrity," pages 210–11; "Into the Wind," pages 217–19; "Genetic Crop Research Pays Off," pages 219–20.

2. Using either Web sites or copies of school catalogs kept in the library, compare the honor code of your college or university with those of four or five comparable institutions.

8

Beginning a Research Project

Suppose you are a smoker who has finally decided to kick the habit. Knowing that your addiction will be hard to overcome, you wonder if you should try to cut down in successive stages, or if you should take the more drastic step of quitting cold turkey. Determined to succeed, you visit the library and find that people who quit all at once have the best results. You also learn that you can expect withdrawal symptoms, but that after seventy-two hours, the worst of these are over. You grit your teeth, toss your remaining cigarettes in the garbage, and resolve that you, not tobacco, will prevail.

In Chapter 1, you learned that research is another name for finding out what you need to know. In the case at hand, reading about nicotine addiction carries a clear personal benefit. However, research often helps others as well. A college *research project* is an undertaking that should not only satisfy your own curiosity but also inform anyone else who reads the paper in which you present your findings.

 ## THE RESEARCH PAPER

A *research paper* is one way to report your findings. However, the paper itself is only the final step in a project that seeks out and discovers information about a particular topic. After making your discoveries, evaluating and selecting among them, and then organizing the material you wish to report, you finally present what you have learned in a documented paper. Of course, not all research papers are alike; in years to come you probably will make frequent use of research in your writing, though not always in what you may think of as "research papers."

Although papers that draw on research can take many different forms, most fall into one of two categories. The more common of the two is the *research-based paper.* Papers of this type consist largely of information found through research; the writers of such papers present relatively few of their own opinions or discoveries. For example, a student seeking to learn whether the fearsome reputation of great white sharks is justified could write a paper based almost entirely on what she found from reading and from interviewing experts. Her own observations on the subject might play only a small part in her paper. In contrast, the *research-supported paper* presents the writer's own ideas, with research findings used to support or supplement them. Argumentative essays are frequently research-supported. For example, a student arguing for increased funding for intramural athletics could use research in part of his paper; he could demonstrate feasibility by citing published budgetary figures, and he could support his own arguments with expert testimony on the need for greater fitness. Still, his original ideas would constitute the heart of his paper.

In practice, the distinction between research-based and research-supported writing is far from absolute. It is not possible to present information in a completely impersonal or neutral way. Assume, for example, that the student writing about great white sharks tried to make her paper objective and impersonal, presenting only the facts and ideas she had learned from her reading and offering no personal opinions or speculations. Even so, the paper she wrote would be very much hers, since it was she who interpreted her sources, selected which facts and ideas to include, and shaped the material so that it represented her understanding of what great white sharks are like. Whatever type of research writing you engage in, you are expected to *think;* even research-based papers are written by human beings, not by computers.

 PRIMARY AND SECONDARY RESEARCH

We can also distinguish between types or methods of research. Most library research undertaken for college papers is *secondary research,* so called because it involves the second-hand discovery of information. Through secondary research we learn what others have previously discovered or thought about a topic. In contrast, when we make our own original discoveries, we engage in *primary research.* To give an example of primary research, an agricultural scientist might plant a standard variety of corn in one field and a new hybrid variety in another to test which provides higher yields and is more resistant to drought and disease. On the other hand, a farmer who reads a report written by that scientist to find out the best seed to plant is engaging in secondary research.

As a college student, you will have opportunities to undertake both primary and secondary research. When you conduct an experiment to test the behavior of laboratory rats or survey voter reactions to a presidential speech, you engage in primary research. When you read a history or a chemistry textbook, consult an encyclopedia, or get a printout from a computer database, you engage in secondary research.

However, not every use of a print source is secondary. Written sources can be either primary or secondary. A historian researching the slave trade in colonial America would seek sources from that era. Newspaper stories about slavery, diaries written by freed slaves and slave owners, slave auction notices and bills of sale, tracts written by abolitionists, and census figures and other records from that time are all examples of *primary sources.* In addition, the historian would consult such *secondary sources* as books and articles by other historians who have also researched and written about the slave trade.

In your upcoming research project, you may have occasion to make both secondary discoveries (in library works) and primary discoveries (by interviewing or corresponding with sources). The research you do is determined by the nature of your project and the resources at your disposal.

 # BENEFITS OF DOING RESEARCH

If research papers were not a requirement in college classes, it is doubtful that many students would have the opportunity or motivation to undertake such projects on their own. By the same token, few instructors are surprised when students, after their projects are completed, say that they were glad to have had the opportunity. Often students say they have gained more from the experience than they expected. They find that research writing can have unanticipated benefits.

Learning an Essential Skill

One aim of this book is to help you become a competent college researcher with all the tools you need to produce quality research papers. A more general—and important—aim is to give you the confidence and skills to discover and use available information about any topic that arouses your curiosity.

It is likely that you will need to write many research papers during your college career and afterward. In other classes, you may be asked to gather information on a topic and report what you discover. After college, in your professional career, you may be faced with questions that you will have to answer through research. In these cases, you will need to consult what others have written, to evaluate and select what is pertinent from this information, and to write reports on your findings.

One reason you are being asked to do one or more research projects in your current course is to give you the experience you will need to conduct future projects with confidence. Practice now will make things easier later. When you are assigned to write a research paper in an art history, marketing, or anthropology class, for example, your instructor will not have time to tutor you in the basics of research. And after you graduate, you will have no instructor at all. College students and college graduates are simply expected to have mastered these skills. Now is the time for you to become an experienced researcher.

While students in a college composition course have the opportunity to learn research skills, they are also at a disadvantage compared with other researchers. Others do research not to practice a skill but to learn about specific topics. What they are discovering is important to them, and the research process is merely a means to that end. In the composition class, however, learning about the research paper can be an end in itself, and the topic you are writing about may seem of only peripheral importance. In that regard, your research project may seem artificial to you, an exercise that is useful in teaching skills for later use but one that has no real importance of its own. This *can* happen, but it is up to you to make sure it does not. For that reason, it is essential for you to choose with care the topic that you will research and write about. Because you will be spending much time and effort on this project, you should become as involved as you can with your topic. If you pursue a topic you genuinely care about, you will gain many rewards: not only will you spend your time profitably, but you will also write a far better paper and, in the process, learn what you need to know about research methods. If you take an interest in your topic and pursue it avidly, the skills you are seeking to acquire will take care of themselves.

Contributing to Scholarship

Although competence in research and research writing are practical skills, there is yet another reason to engage in research besides its personal usefulness to you. By doing research and then making your discoveries public in a paper, you are benefiting your readers as well.

Research is at the very heart of education—it represents the cooperation that is essential to learning. Most knowledge that you have gained is a result of such cooperation. None of us would have been able to figure out the principles of algebra, to mention just one example, if we had been left entirely on our own. Fortunately, throughout the centuries, mathematicians have shared the results of their discoveries with each other and (through our school algebra classes and textbooks) with us as well. A major function of higher education is to share with students the most important thoughts and discoveries of other scholars.

School classes are not the only means by which scholars share their work with us. They also publish their findings so that we and other scholars can have access to them. To make this sharing even easier, the books and articles they produce have been gathered in a central, accessible place: the college library. Engaging in research is simply taking advantage of what other scholars have learned. Like all scholars, you have the right to read about and learn from the discoveries of others. But scholarship is more than just passively receiving the gift of knowledge. As a scholar, you play an active role. Even when you write a research-based paper reporting on the findings of others, you are still creating something new, a fresh synthesis of information, shaped with your own wisdom and insights, a *new source* that was not available to scholars before. Every research paper makes at least a modest contribution to the domain of knowledge. As a student researcher, you are fully entitled to think of yourself as a scholar engaged in a scholarly enterprise. It is for this reason that you are expected to share your findings in a written, public form.

Gaining Personal Knowledge

In traditional college research writing, the author's aim is to report findings, to share information with readers. Authors of these papers keep their writing focused on their topic, while directing attention away from themselves as authors. (The word *I* rarely appears in conventional research writing.) But while you write such a paper to inform others, no one benefits more from your project than you yourself.

Before you can inform your readers, you must first inform yourself about your topic through research. Research writing is a sharing of the knowledge you have gained.

Even the act of writing contributes to your learning. Creating a focused, unified paper forces you to see your topic in new ways. It causes you to bring together information from various sources, to make connections, to take vague ideas and make them concrete. Writing has been properly called a *learning tool;* research writers continue to gain personal knowledge while they are writing about what they have read.

On some occasions, however, personal benefit is not just a byproduct but your principal motive for conducting research. At times, you need to seek answers to questions important to you personally. Writing about such privately motivated research can be just as beneficial and worthy as carrying out conventional research projects. For that reason, one type of paper that has become increasingly popular in composition courses is the ***personal research paper.*** Unlike the standard research paper, this paper does not call for impersonal writing; as its name implies, it aims to be intensely personal. If you write a personal research paper, you should pick a topic that has real importance to you—or as one author puts it, you should let a topic pick you (Macrorie 66).† Perhaps your research will help you make a decision, such as what major or career to choose, or even which motorcycle to buy or what vacation to take. Perhaps it will just satisfy some strong curiosity. In any case, a personal research paper is a record of your quest for answers. You write your paper not only about *what* you found but also about *how* you went about finding it. The word *I* appears often in personal research writing. Even when such projects are approached with purely personal goals in mind, they provide far wider benefits. Besides being informative, they can be especially instructive because a strong motivation to find answers is the best teacher of research skills. Although personal research papers center on the writer's interest and focus on the writer's experiences, readers often find them interesting. The writer's deep involvement in the subject usually translates into lively writing.

 ## THE RESEARCH PROCESS

Like all other forms of writing, a research paper does not happen all at once. Many steps are involved. Although a research paper may seem complicated and difficult, you can learn to produce one quite capably if you take one step at a time. This and the next five chapters examine each stage in the research process. To illustrate the tasks involved, we will trace the experiences of two first-year college students as they undertake research and write papers for their composition classes. By examining the steps they follow, the problems they encounter, and the solutions they discover to overcome them, you can observe the skills that go into writing a

---

*It was also given the name "I-search paper" by Ken Macrorie in his book *The I-Search Paper,* rev. ed. (Portsmouth, NH: Boynton, 1988).

†As Chapter 6 explained, "Macrorie 66" is a form of shorthand that tells the reader that the authors are citing an idea by Ken Macrorie on page 66 of his book (identified in the preceding footnote).

research paper. The same procedure can be adapted for research writing in your other courses and in your future career.

 ## A RESEARCH ASSIGNMENT

In any given semester, students in different composition classes receive a wide variety of assignments for research projects. Some are given open-ended assignments with many options, whereas others are assigned more focused tasks, such as projects related to a particular theme the class has explored in reading and discussion.

Slade Healy and Eliza Tetirick, first-year college students enrolled in composition courses, were given different assignments by their instructors. In Slade's class, each student was asked to write a standard college research paper. Students in Eliza's class were offered the option of writing either a standard or a personal research paper. In both classes, students were asked to choose their own topics.

Following is an assignment similar to the one that students in Eliza's class received. Your own research assignment may differ from it, and your instructor may provide additional criteria for the length, scope, and format of your paper. Make careful note of any ways in which your own instructor's assignment differs from the one given here.

Research Paper	ASSIGNMENT

Investigate a question or problem that intrigues you and write an informative essay, based on your findings from research. Observe the following guidelines, depending on the option you choose or are assigned.

Option A: The Standard College Research Paper

* *Subject:* Frame your research task in the form of a question that you want your investigation to answer. You may explore any subject that arouses your curiosity and interest. You might choose a topic related to your career goals or the field you plan to major in. Perhaps a certain topic in one of your other courses has aroused your curiosity. Perhaps an event or person from recent or earlier history would be worth learning more about. Perhaps in your reading, in conversation, or in viewing a film or television documentary you have encountered a subject you would like to explore.

* *Audience:* Assume that the other members of your class are your audience. Write a paper that is appropriate for this audience—one that they will find informative and interesting.

* *Voice:* You are the author of this paper, and it should be an honest presentation of what you have learned. But remember that your readers' interests, not yours, should come first. Although sometimes research writers use the word *I* in their

papers (e.g., when they present their personal experience as a source), the focus of the paper should be on the subject matter, not on you as a person.

- *Information and opinion:* Be certain that your paper is principally based on the findings of your research rather than on personal speculation. This does not mean, however, that your paper must avoid any ideas and opinions of your own. Your paper may adopt a point of view, but if it does, you should make it clear to your readers from the beginning.

- *Length:* A typical paper is six to twelve pages long, but the length of your paper should be determined by the nature of your subject.

- *Sources:* Your paper should be based on a variety of research, including (where appropriate) such secondary sources as books, periodicals, and newspapers. If you find that additional sources are appropriate for your topic, you should also interview or correspond with experts or participants. Most papers will cite between eight and sixteen sources. In upcoming classes, you will learn how to locate appropriate sources, how to make use of what you learn from them, and how to acknowledge them in notes and in a works-cited page—that is, how to give your sources credit for their contributions to your paper.

Option B: The Personal Research Paper

Most of the guidelines for the standard research paper apply here as well, but there are some differences.

- *Subject:* You should pick a topic that is already a personal concern in your life. That is, you should seek a question you have a good reason to answer, one that can benefit you directly. Any topic that can help you make a decision or that can provide you with information that will enhance your life in some way is likely to be a good choice.

- *Voice and audience:* You should write honestly and unpretentiously about your research experience. Since your topic is of personal interest to you, the word *I* may occur often in your paper. However, you should also write so as to inform readers who may share your interest.

- *Form:* Unlike the standard paper, which is limited to the subject of the writer's research, the personal paper tells about the writer's process of discovery as well. Although no pattern for what to include and how to arrange it is right for all papers, here is a typical pattern suggested by Ken Macrorie. If you choose, your paper can follow this general outline, found in Macrorie's book *The I-Search Paper:*
  1. What I Knew (and didn't know about my topic when I started out).
  2. Why I'm Writing This Paper. (Here's where a real need should show up: The writer demonstrates that the search may make a difference in his life.)
  3. The Search [an account of the hunt, usually in chronological order; what I did first, what I did next, and so on].
  4. What I Learned (or didn't learn. A search that failed can be as exciting and valuable as one that succeeded). (Macrorie 64)

Parts 3 and 4 can be merged if it makes sense to combine your accounts of what you found and how you found it.

•   *Sources:* Interview experts, people who are likely to have the answers you want or who know where you can find answers. Consult these primary sources as well as library materials and other secondary sources.

You are also asked to keep a research notebook (explained on page 264) throughout your research project. Save all your notes, outlines, and rough drafts (more about these later), and submit them in a folder with your completed paper. Your current priority is to choose one of these options and to begin focusing on a specific topic. Use the time between now and the next class to think more about potential topics for your paper.

When their instructors announced the assignment, Slade and Eliza had a reaction typical of most first-year college students in this situation: a sinking feeling in the stomach, followed by varying degrees of anxiety. It seemed more intimidating than the papers they had written before. Although both are competent writers, they weren't sure they could do it. At least momentarily, they were afraid their deficiencies would be exposed, that they would be revealed as imposters impersonating college students.

As grim as this sounds, there is nothing unusual about what Slade and Eliza felt. All writers are apprehensive at the beginning of an assignment, especially one as unfamiliar and as complex as this research paper seemed. But despite their early fears, Slade and Eliza not only wrote their papers but also received high grades for them. Afterward they admitted that the project was not the ordeal they had expected. In fact, it was not only rewarding but also interesting, informative, and, despite much hard work, even enjoyable.

What Slade and Eliza did you can do. The trick is to divide the long project into a sequence of smaller, manageable tasks. As we examine these tasks, we will consider these two students' experiences as examples—following the progress of research from chaos to clarity, from panic to finished product. Since you will be making a similar trek, the journeys of Slade and Eliza are worth your attention.

THE FINISHED PRODUCT

Before you examine all the steps Slade and Eliza took to produce their papers, first look at where they ended up. Their polished, final drafts—the completed papers that were the result of all their work—appear on the following pages.

A Sample Standard Research Paper

First is Slade's response to option A, his research paper on social promotion in the public schools. Note that despite his impersonal voice, Slade's paper includes ideas of his own about the topic.

Jonathan Slade Healy

ENG 102

Ms. Lynne Rader

15 Nov. 1999

Social Promotion and Its Alternatives

When children fail in school, should they be promoted
to the next grade with their age group, or should they be
required to repeat the grade? Over the last hundred years,
the educational pendulum has swung between these two
approaches to student failure, and educators and
politicians continue to debate this vexing question
(American, "Passing"). After many experiments and
countless studies, the issue today is more controversial
than ever.

The practice of promoting students, regardless of how
well they perform or whether they master the subject
matter, is known as social promotion. During the early
decades of the twentieth century, poorly performing
students were regularly left back at the same grade level
on the theory that repeating the year would prepare them to
move on. By the 1930s, however, concerns about the
negative psychological effects of retention on children led
to the widespread adoption of social promotion (Adams 1-2).
In 1941 a New York Regents report concluded that "a much
wiser and more profitable procedure than non-promotion is
to adapt instruction to the needs of the pupil at all
times, and at the end of the year to advance him to the

Healy 2

next grade or class and there continue to adjust instruction to his needs" (qtd. in Rothstein 198).

In recent years, however, the pendulum has clearly been swinging once again away from social promotion and toward retention. Americans are not satisfied with the public schools, and many have blamed social promotion for students' poor performance. One Cleveland high school teacher reports: "I have students in the tenth and eleventh grades who read on a fourth-grade level. They need remediation and should never have been promoted" ("Most"). Politicians of all political viewpoints have trumpeted the ending of social promotion as their main educational goal (Wood). By last year ten states had adopted policies for ending social promotion, and the number is fast growing (Shaw 7).

Los Angeles, the nation's largest school district, will end social promotion this year. Students in grades 2, 3, 4, 5, and 8 will be evaluated on class grades and performance on test scores ("Nation's" 3). Since 1996, Chicago has required its public school students to take standardized tests in the third, sixth, and eighth grades. Those who fail must attend summer school, and if they still do not pass they must repeat the grade (Coeyman). The change in Chicago has been dramatic. Last year almost 15% of students in those grades were retained, compared to fewer than 2% in the year before the new policy (Ratnesar and Cole).

A common argument for ending social promotion is that it removes penalties when students fail to learn. As a Cleveland elementary teacher put it, "Social promotion has made me and my students less effective because we both know they will be passed regardless of what they do in the classroom all year" ("Most"). When Chicago eliminated social promotion, some students say they were motivated to work harder. Third-grader Erica Quinones, who attended summer school under the policy, intends to pass the test next time. "Instead of being in [summer] school," she says, "I could be having fun" (qtd. in Coeyman). Test scores are up since the policy was enacted, and Chicago schools report the highest math and reading scores in a decade (Ratnesar and Cole). Last year, after 4,700 eighth-graders took the summer program, the city graduated the most students to ninth grade in its history (Wood).

If ending social promotion has been so successful, why is there any controversy about making the change? For one thing, not all students have shared in the success. Tom Reece, president of the Chicago Teachers Union, says, "We are getting good results but also finding it doesn't work for everyone" (qtd. in Wood). Of the 10,000 Chicago third graders who attended summer school last year, fewer than half were promoted. Nearly a thousand were held back in third grade for a second time (Coeyman). In theory the retained students should learn the skills that they failed to learn the first time. However, some critics of

Healy 4

retention policies claim that, while social promotion does not help students, retention is even worse for them.

Professors Mary Lee Smith and Lorrie A. Shepard analyzed research studies that compared similar at-risk students, some of whom were promoted, while others were required to spend two years at the same grade level. The retained students actually did worse in school than those who were promoted (215).

While the fear of retention can motivate some students to perform, it can also have negative consequences for those who are unable to do so. Joellen Perry reports:

> Slow learners or students with attention disorders will encounter the same difficulties the second time around, while enduring the shame of repeating a grade. Educators also warn of a lingering, powerful "should be" syndrome. Years later, many retained children believe their rightful place is in the grade above. (76)

The stigma of retention can be devastating to children. In a 1980 study in which children ranked traumas, the fear of repeating a grade caused the most stress, behind only the fear of losing a parent or going blind (Perry 75). Chicago eighth-grader Corrine Murphy expressed her reaction to her school's retention policy: "If you don't pass, you stay in the same grade and people will be making fun of you" (qtd. in Coeyman).

Feelings of disgrace and loss of self-esteem may be factors in the high dropout rate among those made to repeat. Smith and Shepard report that retained students are 20% to 30% more likely to drop out of school than those who are promoted (215). Shepard says that students who repeat two grades "have a probability of dropping out of nearly 100 percent" (qtd. in Wood). This is not the result that proponents of retention hoped for.

Still another consequence of retention is the negative effects on younger children of having older children in the same classroom. Richard Rothstein, a critic of educational policies, observes: "Puberty now begins earlier than it has in the past. Putting 14-year-olds in classrooms with 11- and 12-year-olds will exacerbate the pressures these younger adolescents face." While teachers do not want socially promoted students in their classrooms, they are just as likely to object to teaching retained students who are older than the other students in their classes (197).

Most educators now believe that, by itself, neither social promotion nor retention is the solution to student failure. When Los Angeles and Chicago ended social promotion, both districts dramatically increased spending on remedial programs designed to prevent failure. Los Angeles has allocated $71 million this year for a 60-hour summer school, Saturday classes, and after-school tutoring in math and reading ("Nation's" 3). Chicago spent $24

Healy 6

million last year on summer programs and another $10
million to hire new teachers to tutor at-risk students
(Ratnesar and Cole). Identifying and dealing with student
problems is expensive, costing taxpayers as much as $1,300
per student. But it is much cheaper than the $4,000 cost
when a student repeats a grade (Wood).

According to Sandra Feldman, president of the American
Federation of Teachers, the most cost-effective approach is
to prevent failure in the first place. "What we really
need," she says, "is an intensive-care approach right from
the start, concentrating every possible resource on helping
students as soon as they start to fall behind" (qtd. in
American, "New"). Schools must provide high-quality pre-
school and kindergarten programs and well trained teachers.
In addition, they must identify struggling students in the
earliest grades, put them in small classes, and give them
solid instruction in reading. When students fail, Feldman
recommends remedial approaches that "have a good track
record but are seldom used." These include individual
tutoring, Saturday classes, and extra periods in problem
subjects (American, "New").

Smith and Shepard claim that the most effective remedy
for children performing below grade level is not retention
but promotion accompanied by remediation. They cite
research showing that tutoring, summer school, and one-on-
one help are more effective and less costly than retention
(230). When school systems use retention, they argue,

individualized instruction must also be given to retained students so that they can rejoin their age group as soon as possible (233).

Linda Darling-Hammond, executive director of the National Commission on Teaching and America's Future, claims that the quality of the teacher is the single most important factor in student performance, and she recommends directing resources to training and hiring better teachers. Low-income, minority, and special-needs students are those most often retained, and they are also the students least likely to have well qualified, effective teachers (48-49).

Educational researchers agree that the problem of student failure will be solved only through careful and costly efforts. Unfortunately, complex solutions do not lend themselves to the sound bites favored by many politicians and school boards. Until we are ready to deal seriously with the causes of failure, the educational pendulum is likely to continue to swing between social promotion and retention.

Healy 8

Works Cited

Adams, Edgar. "Alternatives to Grade-Level Retention."

    M. Ed. Thesis. U of North Carolina at Wilmington,

    1995.

American Federation of Teachers. "Passing on Failure:

    District Promotion Policies and Practices." K-12

    Educational Issues. 13 Oct. 1999 <http://www.aft.org/

    edissues/socialpromotion/Intro.htm>.

---. "New AFT Report on Social Promotion in the Schools."

    K-12 Educational Issues. 13 Oct. 1999 <http://

    www.aft.org/edissues/socialpromotion/pr90997.htm>.

Coeyman, Marjorie. "Repeating a Grade Gains Favor in

    Schools." Christian Science Monitor 6 Apr. 1999.

    MasterFILE Premier. EBSCOhost. 15 Oct. 1999 <http://

    www.epnet.com/ehost/>.

Darling-Hammond, Linda. "Avoiding Both Grade Retention and

    Social Promotion." Education Digest Nov. 1998.

    ProQuest. 14 Oct. 1999 <http://

    www.bellhowell.infolearning.com/proquest/>.

"Most Cleveland Teachers Say Social Promotion Doesn't

    Work." Sun Newspapers. 1997. 12 Oct. 1999 <http://

    www.sunnews.com/news/suburbs/metro/

    socialpromotionside.htm>.

"Nation's Largest District Ends Social Promotion."

    Curriculum Review 38.10 (1999): 3.

Perry, Joellen. "What, Mrs. Crabapple Again?" U.S. News &

    World Report 24 May 1999: 75-76.

Ratnesar, Romesh, and Wendy Cole. "Held Back." <u>Time</u> 14
    June 1999. <u>MasterFILE Premier</u>. EBSCOhost. 15 Oct.
    1999 <http://www.epnet.com/ehost/>.

Rothstein, Richard. "Where Is Lake Wobegon, Anyway?" <u>Phi
    Delta Kappan</u> Nov. 1998: 195-98.

Shaw, Donna. "Stopping Social Promotion." <u>Curriculum
    Administrator</u> 35.9 (1999): 7.

Smith, Mary Lee, and Lorrie A. Shepard. "Flunking Grades:
    A Recapitulation." <u>Flunking Grades: Research and Policies on
    Retention</u>. Ed. Lorrie A. Shepard and Mary Lee Smith. New
    York: Falmer, 1989. 214-36.

Wood, Daniel B. "California's Big Test: Holding Students
    Back." <u>Christian Science Monitor</u> 5 Feb. 1999.
    <u>MasterFILE Premier</u>. EBSCOhost. 15 Oct. 1999 <http://
    www.epnet.com/ehost/>.

A Sample Personal Research Paper

True to the nature of personal research papers, Eliza's paper on credit cards, which follows, is indeed more personal and informal than Slade's paper on social promotion. Eliza's style, however, is fully appropriate for the kind of paper she is writing.

Tetirick 1

Eliza Tetirick

ENG 102

Prof. Richard Veit

28 Oct. 1999

Giving Myself Credit:

Should I Apply for a Credit Card?

I. Why I Am Writing This Paper

"Put it on plastic," said Ellen, my roommate, as she handed her MasterCard to the clerk at Millennium Music. I had been staring at the few small bills in my wallet, debating whether I could afford a Sarah McLachlan CD, but Ellen had no hesitation. Her purchase seemed simple and painless, as if no money were involved.

Most of my friends use charge cards. Should I join the ranks of purchasers with plastic? So far I have resisted the appeals that arrive almost daily in my mailbox from card vendors, banks, even airlines and car companies. The lure of credit seems great: easy purchasing, freedom from cash, building a credit history, even free gifts. Is this right for me?

I wanted to make an informed decision, and getting this opportunity to find answers was ideal. My research has opened my eyes not just to the benefits and pitfalls of credit cards but also to the larger world of personal finance.

Tetirick 2

II. What I Knew

I now know that I was dangerously ignorant about credit and credit cards when I began my research. I knew little more than the enticing slogans I read on the envelopes sent by the credit card companies. "An extraordinary value," said one (First USA). "Special student rate," proclaimed another (First Bankcard). "The lower rate you look for plus the attention you deserve" (MBNA). "No annual fee" (American Express). "A double Cashback Bonus" (Discover).

What now surprises me most was how little I knew or thought about the consequences of getting a card. I knew that plastic is accepted for payment almost everywhere, that you buy now and pay later, that a card can get you cash at an ATM machine, and that each monthly bill requires a minimum payment. I also vaguely understood that interest is charged on the unpaid balance, but I knew almost nothing of how interest works or about the costs of revolving debt. I was unaware of the differences between one card and another or the terms they offer. I certainly did not know that the misuse of credit cards has adversely affected the lives of many students.

Sadly, I also must admit I was ignorant about most aspects of personal finance. Until arriving at college, I had never paid a monthly bill or written a check. I had worked at part-time and summer jobs, and I had spent some of my money and saved the rest for college. But I had always lived at home, and my parents handled the major family expenses.

In this state of blissful ignorance, I was seriously considering getting my first credit card. The offers were everywhere--in magazines, on campus bulletin boards, even tucked in the bag of giveaway goodies at orientation--and the arguments were persuasive if not irresistible. One offer, typical of many I received in the mail, began:

> Dear Eliza Tetirick,
>
> For most college students, everything about school is EXPENSIVE. Tuition . . . books . . . car expenses . . . even spring break!
>
> So unless you go to one of those "new age" schools that doesn't require textbooks . . . or your ideal vacation doesn't involve leaving the city limits . . . you should be carrying the College Visa from First Bankcard Center! (First Bankcard)

College is undeniably expensive, and this appeal was aimed at students in just my financial circumstances.

It was also clear from the enclosure that this company wanted my business. Its "special student offers" included discounts on brand-name merchandise, a phone card with 15 free long-distance minutes, "great Visa Rewards," and "special promotional offers." I knew that there was more to a credit card than free gifts, and I noted that "your College Visa comes with a low 7.9% APR and NO ANNUAL FEE to

Tetirick 4

help save you money." I would also get "a Low Minimum
Monthly Payment [. . .] and a 25-day Interest-Free Grace
Period" (First Bankcard). All of this sounded appealing to
me, even though at the time I did not know what "APR" stood
for--I now know it's "annual percentage rate". At this
point, it was up to me to discover if there was more to
credit cards than what I knew.

III. The Search

I had already accumulated some "sources" in a small
collection of credit card mailings and flyers, and I asked
my friends to save offers they received during the next two
weeks. I also began my search for other sources that would
give more information and a critical perspective on my
topic.

I did not know if I would find any research materials
on student credit cards, but with my very first attempt, I
hit paydirt. Using the Internet, I called up the library's
resources page to search for sources. I thought that
newspapers and magazines would offer the best bet, and I
decided to start my search with articles in the "business/
economics" category. From the menu of search engines I was
presented, I first chose the "Business NewsBank" database
of newspaper articles. In the "search for" box I entered
the key words "credit card AND student" to find articles
containing both those phrases. In seconds, a list of
articles appeared, and the very first headline was "Lead us

Tetirick 5

not into temptation: Colleges target card solicitors" from a recent issue of <u>USA Today</u>. The next two headlines were unrelated to my search, but the fourth headline was clearly relevant: "Companies Entice College Students to Take Cards Many Can Not Afford." Even before reading the articles, I knew that my personal decision would be more complicated than I had assumed. But I also knew that I had chosen a fruitful topic for my research paper. I printed out the text of the more promising articles and took notes from a few others.

The Academic Search Elite database found no results when I entered the same key words, "credit card AND student," but when I tried "credit card AND college," I got many useful article titles. Some had the full text online, and I went to the library to find the others on microfilm.

I also consulted the library's main catalog to find books on my topic. I found several government documents, but I had no luck finding recent books on credit cards. Since my topic was one of general interest, I decided to try the public library, and there I found many helpful books on personal finance.

In addition to publications, I looked for other Internet sources using the Excite search engine. The words "credit card" led me first to a news story about growing debt in America (Sanders). Interestingly, on the Web page where the article appeared there were also two credit-card ads.

Tetirick 6

Finally, when I knew enough to ask some halfway intelligent questions, I contacted Management professor Robert Keating, who generously agreed to meet with me. He answered all my questions during our interview, and I learned much from him about the pros and cons of using credit cards.

IV. What I Found

"[W]e never met a student who didn't want some extra credit," claims one card ad (First Bankcard), and if they are exaggerating, it is not by much. According to a study by Georgetown University sociologist Robert Manning, not only do 70% of college students have credit cards (Gordon), but they use them regularly. The manager of the University of California-Irvine bookstore reports that nearly two-thirds of store purchases are by credit cards (Sanders). Most students get their first cards while on campus, but 15% arrived as freshmen with cards in 1998, up from 11% just four years earlier (Frey E1).

For most students, use of cards does not present significant problems (Toloken). Larry Chiang, president of a company that markets cards to students, reports that only 4.1% of student card holders fail to pay their bills, compared with a 4.8% default rate in general. This does not necessarily mean that students are more responsible, however. According to Chiang, parents often bail out their

Tetirick 7

children, rather than have them declare bankruptcy or ruin their credit ratings (Sanders).

Not all students have such helpful parents, and many articles told of students for whom credit cards became a nightmare. As a student at the University of Southern California, Mary Hill got her first card "at a booth bedecked with school mascot Tommy Trojan." Within two years, she had 40 cards and massive debt. She filed for bankruptcy at age 22. In the next ten years, her debts caused her to be rejected by landlords and car finance companies as a bad risk, and an employer changed his mind about hiring her after running a routine check of her credit history. Only in her thirties did she finally emerge from what she called her credit "imprisonment" (Zagier B1).

Other stories came without the happy ending. Mitzi Pool had maxed out her three credit cards during her freshman year at Oklahoma Central University. She hanged herself in her dorm room, leaving her credit card bills and checkbook spread out on her bed (Gordon). Other sources also relate student suicide stories and tell of students running up credit card debts of $10,000 (Gordon), $15,000 (Fine), even $25,000 (Frey E1). "Credit is a bad thing," said Rommel Johnson, a student at Cal State Fullerton, who was forced to work three jobs simultaneously to reduce his credit debt. "It's fake money. I thought I was enhancing

Tetirick 8

my lifestyle. But I realize now that I really hocked my

future" (qtd. in Sanders).

　　With these frightening images in my mind, I needed to

know if I would be doomed to a similar fate if I got a

credit card. What I most needed was information about how

cards work. According to Finance Professor Abraham

Bertisch, "[W]hen we strip away their gold plating and

allure, major charge cards are really little more than a

revolving line of credit" (111). That is, a bank provides

the holder of a card with a fixed upper amount that may be

borrowed. If a card has a $1000 limit, that is the total

that may be charged until all or part of the balance is

paid off. The customer may then borrow again until the

upper limit is reached once again.

　　The card holder does not have to pay off the full debt

each month, but a finance charge is assessed on any unpaid

balance (Bertisch 111). Most cards have a "grace period"

of about a month on which no interest is charged, provided

the entire balance is then paid off. However, many

students fall into the trap of paying only the required

minimum on their bill each month. They are then charged

interest on the rest, which on student cards averages

between 18 and 23 percent (Fine). Bankruptcy attorney Ron

Terenzi points out that a $2500 balance would take 34 years

to pay off if one made only the minimum payments, and the

total paid would be about $10,000 (Pedone). All the

sources I read recommend paying off the entire balance each

month. They also caution against using a credit card for cash advances, except in an emergency. According to Lewis and Karen Altfest, credit cards are a poor way to borrow money. The convenience of cards "carries a high price tag, double the interest charged by many other kinds of loans" (30).

Students should also be wary of the seemingly low interest rates that some cards charge, since they can be deceptive. On the envelope of one offer I received were the words "You're pre-selected for 2.9% APR" (Discover). The smaller print inside revealed that this rate applied only to transfers of debt from other credit cards and would rise dramatically after a few months. The rate was 12.99% for purchases and 19.99% for cash advances (Discover). No wonder the experts advise students to shop around for the best offer, read the fine print, and be certain they understand the terms before accepting any card (Briles; "Credit").

Students must also be able to resist the enticements that the card marketers dangle before them. My own collection of offers included a portfolio bag, a photography book, airline bonus miles, a Sony Walkman, a "free deluxe mouse pad," and a "Looney Tunes sweatshirt"--
all for sending in an application. Booths on campus offer everything from T-shirts to chances to win airline tickets (Vickers).

Tetirick 10

If students have less money than most adults and no credit history, then why are banks so eager to offer us credit? According to Edmund Sanders, "Today's starving students are tomorrow's consumers." Banks want to build loyalty among the young. A study by Visa suggests that two-thirds of all adult credit-card holders still carry the first card they acquired (Sanders).

Many colleges and universities have become concerned about the ethics of marketing cards to students who may not be well enough informed about personal finance to handle them responsibly. According to one firm that monitors the college credit industry, between 700 and 1000 campuses have banned card marketing, and the number is growing (Toloken). Alexis Mei, president of the Student Senate at North Carolina State University, which is studying such a ban, says, "We're concerned about putting our students at risk" (qtd. in Toloken).

On the other hand, many other colleges are eager to promote card solicitation, and the reason, it seems, is profit. Marketers pay up to $600 per day for the right to set up tables on campus (Toloken). At the University of North Carolina at Chapel Hill, the bookstore puts Citibank applications into shopping bags in return for a payment (Zagier B1). Many colleges sign exclusive agreements with a marketer, in return for which they receive a dollar for each student applicant and often a percentage of purchases made on each card. Clearly, students cannot rely on others to protect them and must be well informed and extremely cautious before signing an application or using a credit card.

V. Conclusion

The principal lesson I learned from my research is that credit cards can be useful if used wisely, but they can also be extremely dangerous if misused. Had I not done this project, I might have fallen into a trap that has proved harmful and even disastrous to many other students.

I now know that credit cards can be convenient, since they don't require the user to carry around large amounts of currency. They can also give quick access to cash in an emergency. In addition, the monthly statement provides a useful record of expenses.

On the other hand, they can provide a temptation to overspend. Failure to pay off the full balance each month results in high interest penalties that greatly increase the cost of each purchase. As debt grows, some respond by obtaining additional credit cards and accumulating ever more debt in a spiral from which they may not be able to extricate themselves.

Being far better informed of the advantages and dangers of credit cards as a result of my research, I have decided to apply for a card. I compared many offers, and I have found a card that has no annual fee, provides a 28-day grace period on purchases, and charges a comparatively low

Tetirick 12

interest rate on cash advances and unpaid balances. I
expect to limit my purchases to what I can afford, but to
be safe, I am keeping my upper credit limit at $1000. As
experts advise, I will own just one card. I intend to keep
copies of my sales slips and to compare all charges with my
monthly statement. Most important, I will pay off my full
balance each month and incur no interest charges--at least,
that is my plan.

One administrator at Indiana University put the
problem of student credit cards succinctly: "We lose more
students to credit card debt than academic failure" (qtd.
in "Credit"). Thanks to what I have learned, I will make
certain I do not become another of those casualties.

Tetirick 13

Works Cited

Altfest, Lewis J., and Karen Caplan Altfest. <u>Lew Altfest</u>
<u>Answers Almost All Your Questions about Money</u>. New
York: McGraw, 1992.

American Express Centurion Bank. Mailed advertisement.
Oct. 1999.

Bertisch, Abraham M. <u>Personal Finance</u>. Fort Worth:
Dryden, 1994.

Briles, Judith. <u>Money Sense: What Every Woman Needs to</u>
<u>Know to Be Financially Confident</u>. Chicago: Moody,
1995.

"Credit Cards for Students." eStudentLoan. 12 Oct. 1999
<http://estudentloan.com/html/credit_cards.html>.

Discover Platinum. Mailed advertisement. Oct. 1999.

Fine, Andrea. "Red Ink Stains Student Wallets." <u>Christian</u>
<u>Science Monitor</u> 8 July 1999: 2. <u>Academic Search</u>
<u>Elite</u>. EBSCOhost. 12 Oct. 1999 <http://
www.epnet.com/ehost/>.

First Bankcard Center. Mailed advertisement. Oct. 1999.

First USA Platinum Visa Card. Mailed advertisement. Oct.
1999.

Frey, Carol. "Pint-Size Consumers with Full-Size Debt."
<u>News & Observer</u> [Raleigh] 11 July 1999: E1.

Gordon, Marcy. "Credit Card Firms' Tactics Decried."
Associated Press 9 June 1999. <u>NewsBank NewsFile</u>.
InfoWeb. 11 Oct. 1999 <http://infoweb9.newsbank.com>.

Keating, Robert. Personal interview. 14 Oct. 1999.

Tetirick 14

MBNA MasterCard. Mailed advertisement. Oct. 1999.

Pedone, Rose-Robin. "Co-ed Credit Crunch." <u>Long Island</u>
    <u>Business News</u> 30 Apr. 1999: 5A. <u>Business Source</u>
    <u>Elite</u>. EBSCOhost. 12 Oct 1999 <http://www.epnet.com/
    ehost/>.

Sanders, Edmund. "Young and Charged Up." <u>Orange County</u>
    <u>Register</u> 5 Sept. 1997: c1. <u>NewsBank NewsFile</u>.
    InfoWeb. 11 Oct. 1999 <http://infoweb9.newsbank.com>.

Toloken, Lisa. "Turning the Tables on Campus." <u>Credit Card</u>
    <u>Management</u> May 1999: 76-79. ProQuest. 12 Oct. 1999
    <http://proquest.umi.com>.

Vickers, Marcia. "A Hard Lesson on Credit Cards."
    <u>Business Week</u> 15 Mar. 1999: 107. <u>Academic Universe</u>.
    Lexis-Nexis. 12 Oct. 1999 <http://
    www.lexis-nexis.com/lncc/>.

Zagier, Alan Scher. "Lawmakers Strive to Limit Students'
    Credit-Card Debt." <u>News and Observer</u> [Raleigh]
    21 July 1999: B1.

Eliza's paper is about a decision that may have important consequences for her. Personal research projects also work well with less momentous topics; any question that arouses your curiosity is a worthy candidate for such a paper. Slade's project on social promotion, for example, would also have worked as a personal paper, just as Eliza could have written a standard research paper about credit cards. You might try to imagine what each of these papers would have been like if its author had chosen a different format for it.

EXERCISE   ## Analysis and Discussion

Before reading on to learn how Slade and Eliza went about researching and writing their papers, answer these questions about their final drafts:

a.   What is your impression of the strengths and weaknesses of each paper? Does each have a clear focus; that is, can you give a brief summary of its topic or central idea? Do you find it interesting? informative? clearly written? well organized? Did the author seem to do an adequate job of researching his or her topic?

b.   If you were the author's instructor, how would you respond to each paper? If you were the author, would you change it in any way to improve it?

Both Slade's paper about social promotion and Eliza's about her personal financial decision impressed their instructors and classmates, but they did not get that way all at once. Many stages involving much labor, some frustrations, and many changes preceded the final versions. The history of their creation is as informative as the papers themselves.

 ## YOUR RESEARCH SCHEDULE:
PLANNING IN ADVANCE

Writing a research paper is a labor-intensive project. Between now and the time you submit your final draft, you will be busy. You will be choosing a topic, exploring it, refining it, chasing down leads, riffling through sources, taking notes, thinking, jotting down ideas, narrowing your project's focus, doing more research and more thinking, writing a tentative draft, revising and revising again.

Obviously, a research project cannot be completed in a day or two. You need to plan now so that you have enough time to undertake each step in the process and so that you can make efficient use of your time. Like Slade Healy, you may be assigned separate deadlines for the various steps in your project. Or you may be given only the final deadline for submitting the completed paper, in which case you should establish your own intermediate deadlines for completing each stage. Slade's instructor gave the class a form much like the one shown

---

RESEARCH PROJECT

Principal Deadlines: Due Dates:

1. Research prospectus due, including a
    statement of your research topic and a
    working bibliography (see page 305):   _____

2. Note cards and preliminary outline due
    (see page 359):   _____

3. In-class editing of completed draft
    (see pages 376–377):   _____

4. Typed good draft due (see page 394):   _____

5. Final draft due (see page 394):   _____

Figure 8.1 A schedule for a research project.

in Figure 8.1, with a date for each deadline. You can use the form for recording your own schedule.

Some instructors may supply an even more detailed schedule, which may include dates for such additional activities as library orientation, additional editing sessions, and student–instructor conferences. Whatever your schedule, your instructor will certainly concur in this advice: Budget your time wisely, and get started on your project without delay.

 ## THE BENEFITS OF WORD PROCESSING

An extended discussion of the format for your completed paper appears in Chapter C of Part II. It includes settings for your word-processing program such as margins, line spacing, and justification. But the word processor itself is such a valuable tool at *every* stage of the research process that we need to give it some attention from the beginning.

Chapter 1 discussed the benefits of word processing (writing with a computer). Perhaps you have already found that word processing is the quickest and easiest way to write and that it makes you a better writer and researcher. When you compose, you can make as many changes as you wish in your writing, instantly and without mess. When you edit, you can produce a printed copy of part or all of what you have written—at the press of a button. You can easily rearrange sentences or whole sections of your paper to improve its organization. You can use the spelling-check feature to find and correct errors. Moreover, since printing a copy of your work is so easy, you can make alterations and corrections up to the last moment. And, of course, the copy you produce has a professional, error-free appearance.

Word processing also helps long before you begin the actual writing of the research paper. It can simplify and improve your work in many preliminary stages of research such as generating ideas, maintaining your working bibliography, outlining, and taking notes.

Use of the word processor has become indispensable in all areas of academic, business, and professional life. Your current research project can present an ideal opportunity for you to develop this essential skill. If you do not own a computer, your college may have computer rooms for student use. The basic operating instructions are usually not difficult, and instruction may be provided to help you get started.

 ## A RESEARCH NOTEBOOK

At the beginning of your project you may already have a clear vision—or only the vaguest notion—of what your final draft will eventually look like. Nevertheless, it is probably safe to say that your final paper will be very different from anything you currently imagine. A research project involves many discoveries, and the act of writing usually inspires us to rethink our ideas. Rather than being *assembled*, research papers typically *evolve* through a process of development and change. Prepare for an adventure in which you discover what eventually emerges on paper.

Your finished paper is the end product of that adventure, the last of several stages in the research process. What you learn during that process is probably more important in the long run than the paper itself. It was for this reason that Slade's and Eliza's instructors asked each student in their classes to keep a ***research notebook.*** At every stage of the project, researchers were expected to keep a personal record of their progress. The research notebook is like a diary. In it Slade and Eliza recorded what they were doing and what they were expected to do. They wrote about what they had found, the problems they were facing, and their plans for their next steps. Eliza used her notebook as the raw material for the "search" section of her personal research paper.

The writing you do in a research notebook should be informal, not polished. Unlike the research paper itself, the notebook is written to yourself, not to outside readers. When you are finished, you have a record of your research process. But there is also another benefit to keeping a notebook. Both Slade and Eliza found that it helped them make decisions and focus their thoughts. In addition, many of the passages both writers used in their papers came from ideas they had scribbled in their notebooks.

You should use a spiral notepad that you can carry with you when you do research, though you may also want to use your word processor (if you have one) to record some entries. You will start using your notebook from the very beginning— now—as you select and focus your research topic.

YOUR RESEARCH TOPIC

Only on rare occasions do researchers have to *choose* a topic. Such an occasion might come about for a freelance writer of magazine articles who wants to select not only a fresh subject that will interest readers and an editor but also one about which she can find enough information through interviews, legwork, and library research.

In most cases, however, researchers already have their topics before them. A situation arises that demands exploration. For example, in order for a detective novelist to write convincingly about a counterfeiting ring, he must do research to learn how counterfeiters actually operate. A historian with a theory about the causes of the Russian Revolution would have to discover the available facts about the period as well as learn what theories other historians have proposed. A lawyer writing a brief for a criminal case must research legal precedents to know how similar cases have been decided in the past and to provide herself with convincing arguments. Most researchers begin with a strong curiosity about a topic and a need to know.

As you begin your own research project, you may already have decided on a topic. Perhaps your class has been reading and talking about an interesting issue such as nuclear policy, teenage suicide, the future of the family farm, or dating practices in foreign countries. Your discussion may have raised questions in your mind, questions that you can answer only through research. Besides satisfying your own curiosity, you can perform a service for your instructor and classmates by informing them about what you have learned. For you, a research paper is a natural.

On the other hand, you may not yet have chosen a specific topic. Perhaps your instructor, like Slade's and Eliza's, has left the selection of a topic up to you. Perhaps you have been given a choice within a limited area, such as a current event, the life and views of a public figure, or your career goals. In any case, it is important for you to select a topic you can work with. Because many hundreds of topics may appeal to you, deciding on any one can be hard.

You begin with your curiosity. Your research is aimed at answering a question in your mind, at satisfying your urge to know. For that reason, it is usually helpful at the outset of a project to state your topic in the form of a *research question.* Rather than just naming a general area for your paper, such as "racial policy in the armed forces," it is often more useful to frame your project as a question to be answered, such as "How has the military dealt with discrimination?" or "How has the struggle against discrimination in the American armed forces compared with the struggle in the civilian world?" Perhaps you have formed a *hypothesis,* a theory that you would like to test. In this case your question would begin, "Is it true that . . . ?" For example, in reading about the plagues that devastated Europe during the thirteenth century, you might have speculated that in spite of modern scientific advances, the reactions of people to epidemics have not changed much in seven hundred years. If you decided to test this hypothesis through research, your question might be, "Are effects of the AIDS epidemic on our society similar to the effects of the Black Death on medieval Europe?"

Three factors are critical in framing a good research question. Your topic should have the following qualities. It should be

1. *Appealing.* This is the most crucial factor. Your research should be aimed at answering a question that genuinely arouses your curiosity or that helps you solve a problem. If you are not involved with your topic, it is unlikely that you will write an essay that will interest readers. The interest you have in your topic will also determine whether the many hours you spend on it will be rewarding or agonizing.

2. *Researchable.* You may be curious about the attitudes of college students in Japan toward religion, for example, but if you can locate only one or two sources on the subject in your local libraries, you will not be able to write a research paper about it.

3. *Narrowed.* If your question is "What is astronomy?" you will find no shortage of materials. On the contrary, you will certainly discover that your topic is too broad. You can find hundreds of books and entire journals devoted to astronomy. However, you cannot do justice to so vast a topic in a paper of a few thousand words. You will need to narrow your topic to one you can research and cover adequately. You may decide to concentrate on black holes, for example, as a more focused topic. Later on, as you continue your research and begin writing, you may narrow the topic still more, perhaps to a recent theory or discovery about black holes.

GENERATING IDEAS

Unless you already have a question in mind that you are eager to answer, or unless you are facing a pressing decision for which you need information, you will have to do some exploring and thinking about a general subject before you arrive at a properly appealing, researchable, and narrowed research question. Several techniques for stimulating ideas can help you in your selection, including brainstorming and clustering.

Brainstorming

If you were asked right now to declare some possible research topics, you might find it difficult to do so. After a few minutes of wrestling with the problem, you might finally come up with a few topics, but you might find them to be neither original nor exciting. Yet there are literally hundreds of topics that you not only would enjoy researching but also could write about well. The trick is to stimulate your mind to think of them. *Brainstorming* is one helpful technique. It is simply a way of forcing your mind to bring forth many possible topics, under the theory that one idea can lead to another and that, if enough ideas are brought forth, at least one will click.

On the day they announced the assignment, Slade's and Eliza's instructors led their classes through several activities to stimulate their thinking. Following are some examples of brainstorming exercises.

Brainstorming: Random Listing

1. We start with a light and unintimidating exercise. The following is a random list
   of concepts in no particular order and of no particular significance. Read the list
   rapidly and then, in your research notebook, begin your own list, adding as
   many items to it as you can. Give free play to your imagination. List whatever
   comes to mind without regard to whether it is serious or would make a reasonable research topic. Save those concerns for later. For now, write rapidly, and
   have some fun with your list.

surnames	water fountains	swimsuits
clowns	sea horses	salesmanship
cans	con artists	pro wrestling
lip sync	cremation	campaign buttons
lipstick	hiccups	prep schools
war paint	blueprints	sponges
juggling	Russian roulette	snuff
teddy bears	triplets	fads
cave dwellers	women's weightlifting	cavities
haircuts	chocolate	advertising jingles
ways to fasten shoes	frisbees	plastic surgery
high heels	coffins	bartending
hit men	chain letters	mirrors
cheerleaders	tanning	juke boxes
revenge	baldness	icebergs
bicycles	wigs	mermaids
televangelists	facial hair	tribal societies
silicon chips	earrings	fast food
college colors	longevity	cyclones
company logos	boomerangs	Beetle Bailey
roller skates	fuel injection	toilets
tractors	fertility	laughing
warts and birthmarks	nomads	cable cars
freckles	film editing	Mardi Gras
tattoos	spelunking	free gift with purchase

2. Because one idea leads to another in brainstorming, the ideas of other people
   can stimulate your own thinking. You can cross-fertilize your imagination by
   looking at other students' lists. After you have listed items for a few minutes, you
   can (a) exchange lists with one or more classmates or (b) join members of your
   class in calling out items (perhaps in orderly turns, perhaps randomly) as one or
   more people write them on the blackboard.

3. Stimulated by these new ideas, resume listing for another few minutes.

4. When you have finished, reread your list and circle the items that seem most
   interesting to you. What about these items stimulates your curiosity? See if

you can now pose five or six questions about them for which you would like answers.

You may be concerned that some of the topics you listed or some of the questions you posed are not particularly serious or do not seem scholarly or deep. You need not worry, since any subject that provokes your genuine interest and curiosity is worth exploring and can be given serious treatment in a research paper. The item "lipstick" in the preceding list, for example, may seem frivolous at first, but it can lead to many serious questions: What is lipstick made of (now and in the past)? How long have people been using lipstick? How has society regarded its use in earlier times? Does it symbolize anything? Is its use widespread throughout the world? Is it ever prohibited by governments or by religions? Why do American women use it but not (for the most part) American men? Such questions point to an interesting and rewarding research project. A student who pursued them would find much information. In the course of research, the student could certainly narrow the topic—perhaps to "What has society thought about lipstick?"—and write an informative, worthwhile paper.

EXERCISE   Brainstorming: Focused Listing

This brainstorming exercise is more focused than the preceding one. In your notebook, list as many ideas as you can in response to the following questions. Write rapidly, listing whatever comes to mind. List phrases, rather than complete sentences. If one topic strikes you as having possibilities as a research topic, keep listing ideas about it until you have explored it to your satisfaction. You do not need to answer every question, but do not stop listing ideas until your instructor tells you that time is up.

- What have been your favorite courses in high school and college? What topics in those courses did you find interesting? For each topic, write as many phrases associated with it as you can.

- What major are you considering? List some particular subjects you hope to explore in your major.

- What career are you considering? What specific branches of that field interest you? What jobs can you imagine yourself holding in the future? List several possibilities.

- What recent or historical events or discoveries are associated with your career interests or major field? What notable persons are associated with these areas? List some things you know about them.

- List magazine articles, books, movies, and memorable television programs that you have encountered lately. List some specific ideas or topics that they bring to mind.

- List some events or controversies that concern you. What news stories have aroused your interest or concern? What historical events have you wanted to learn more about? What do you consider the major changes that have taken place during your lifetime in world affairs? in science and technology? in the way we lead our lives? What problems face us in the future?

- What topics have you read about because you needed or wanted to learn more about them? What problems do you now need to resolve?

- What decisions will you have to make soon? Decisions about school? career? lifestyles? morality? romance? friends? family? purchases? leisure time?

- What areas are you an expert in? What are your chief interests and hobbies?

- What are some of the major gaps in your background? What should you know more about than you do?

- What notable people do you most admire? What people have had achievements that mean something to you? Think of men, women, historical figures, living people, scientists, artists, athletes, politicians. What famous people do you pity or consider villains?

Slade's class spent about fifteen minutes listing ideas for the preceding exercise. Afterward, students shared lists with classmates and discussed their ideas. They also jotted down any new ideas that came to them. Slade's list filled several pages in his notebook. Here is an excerpt from it:

```
Favorite courses

    --Psychology

            --child development/effects on development

    --History

            --JFK assination

            --Pearl Harbor

            --Vietnam War

                    --prisoners of war

                    --comparison with Gulf War

            --draft/public service

    --PE/Health

Major--Education

    --jobs available

    --salaries/benefits
```

```
--teaching

    --middle school

        --grade level?

        --concentration

Events associated with major

    --violence in schools

        --bombings, shootings, assaults on teachers

    --social promotion

    --salary increases lead to better teaching?

    --people: Maria Montessori . . .
```

Slade's list was not an orderly, logical outline, nor was it meant to be. However, this short excerpt shows his mind actively at work, listing and shaping ideas. Among the ideas he listed was social promotion, which would eventually become his paper topic. At this point, however, it was merely one of many ideas that he listed in rapid fashion. The complete list included many other ideas as well, most of which turned out to be dead ends. The excerpts shown here include "hot spots" or "centers of gravity"—ideas and phrases that engage the writer's interest.

Whereas Slade made his list in outline form, Eliza's brainstorming took the form of a series of questions. Despite their differences, both methods were equally effective in generating ideas. Here are some excerpts from Eliza's list:

```
• What will I major in? Where do my interests lie?

• Do I want to live in the dorms next year? How do most

    students pay for their apartments off campus? Does

    living off campus have benefits?

• Does having a job and being a full-time student lower

    the average student's grade-point average? . . .

• Do violent movies affect society? Does watching TV

    affect students?

• Is date rape a common occurrence? How can students guard

    against date-rape drugs?

• How much alcohol do average students consume? How much

    is too much? . . .
```

Nowhere in Eliza's list was the topic that would eventually become her paper, her decision about whether to get a credit card, but her list shows she was beginning to focus on personal issues in her life, including financial decisions. In many cases, brainstorming activities do not lead directly and immediately to a topic the writer recognizes as ideal. Instead, they open up many pathways for the writer to explore. When pursued, some of those paths will lead to still other paths for the writer to take, until eventually the right destination is reached.

Developing an Idea: Clustering

A more concentrated form of brainstorming can be called *clustering* or *mapping*. It is a technique designed to stimulate the development of many ideas related to one given idea. Slade's instructor gave his class the following exercise.

Clustering Ideas

EXERCISE

Review the lists you have made thus far and circle all the items that look promising as research topics. If you have time, ask one or two classmates to do the same thing, each using a different color ink. Finally, select one possible topic (this is not a final commitment) and write it in the center of a blank page in your notebook. Using it as a starting point, radiate from it whatever ideas come to mind. The clusterings of Slade and Eliza are shown in Figures 8.2 and 8.3.

Finally, Slade's instructor asked class members to call out questions that arose from the ideas they had listed (or new ones that occurred to them), while he wrote them on the board. Here are some typical questions offered by the students:

- What effect will the deforestation of the Amazon have on the planet?
- Is fraternity hazing a worthwhile ritual or barbaric torture?
- What motivates serial murderers?
- How are children affected by parents' divorce?
- How can you cope with the death of a family member?
- How were air bags developed?
- What treatments are available to vets to cope with tick-borne diseases?
- Is police corruption an epidemic?
- Is coral bleaching in the Caribbean an omen of environmental disaster?
- Does the Beat Generation speak to us today?
- Is Bill Gates an American hero?
- How can school teachers cope with depression in students?
- What can identical twins tell us about the effects of heredity and environment on personality?

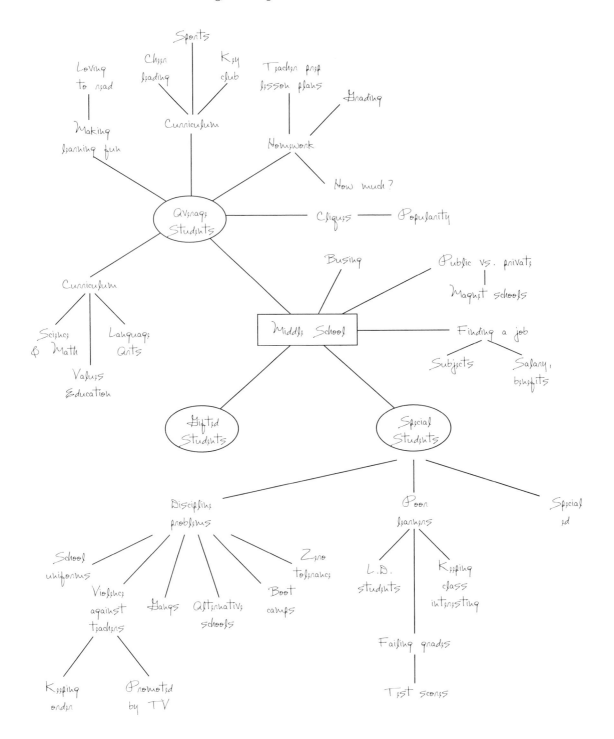

Figure 8.2 Slade's clustering.

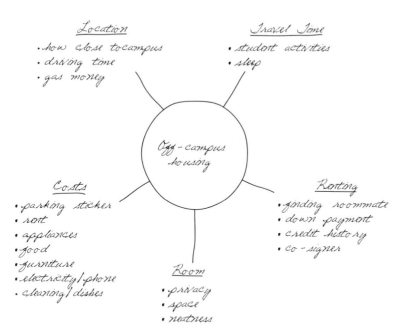

Figure 8.3 Eliza's clustering.

Prewriting exercises are not magic formulas that instantly produce perfect research topics. Instead, if all goes well, they begin a chain reaction that leads you, however circuitously, to your eventual topic. The idea-generating exercises that Slade and Eliza engaged in pointed them in helpful directions. Most of Slade's brainstorming activities centered around middle-school education, his intended career. Still, his path to his eventual topic, social promotion, was not a straight one. He had mentioned social promotion in one of his early brainstorming exercises, but he did not know at the time that he would return to it after first pursuing several other topics. In contrast, Eliza's decision to write about credit cards came more quickly than Slade's, but her discovery path involved a very sharp turn. As her clustering shows, she first centered her thoughts on a decision about off-campus housing. Soon afterwards, she changed her mind and explored a different personal decision, whether to apply for a credit card. Although the two topics may seem unrelated, Eliza reports that her thinking about an apartment caused her to consider her own credit history, which in turn sparked the idea of getting a credit card. As soon as she began to search for sources on credit cards, Eliza knew she had settled on an excellent topic for a research paper.

A research project is like a puzzle. When you begin it, you can never know how it will turn out. After all, the purpose of research is to answer questions for which you do not currently have answers. When you start, you cannot know what answers you will find. You cannot even be sure your questions are good ones. These discoveries are made only as you undertake the actual research and as you begin to write about your findings. You are almost certain to find that the research paper you end up writing will be quite different from your current expectations. What you learn along the way will cause you to change plans and go in new and often unexpected directions. You are sure to meet surprises. A good researcher must be flexible, able to adapt to whatever new ideas and information present themselves. For this reason you need not be concerned if you now have only a tentative idea of the topic for your paper. Your topic will take firmer shape (and perhaps a very different shape) as you undertake your research. The following chapters show you how to conduct research.

9 *Tools for Finding Sources*

BEGINNING YOUR RESEARCH

Having generated ideas about likely topics for papers, Slade and Eliza needed to do preliminary research to learn more about these topics and to bring their research questions into sharper focus. A visit to the library and some exploration of the resources available to them via computer were the logical next steps. From their instructors they received assignments similar to the one that follows.

Preliminary Research   ASSIGNMENT

Do some preliminary research to explore the topic you are considering.

* Learn more about your topic by reading about it in encyclopedias and other general reference sources. If the topic seems appropriate, take notes and see if you can narrow your focus to a specific question.

* See if your topic is researchable by assembling a working bibliography of about a dozen sources that you intend to consult. (Working bibliographies are further explained in Chapter 11.) Use a variety of search tools (explained in this chapter), and include books, periodicals, newspapers, and electronic media, as appropriate for your topic. If, for example, you are writing about a recent event, newspaper articles will be a significant source of information. On the other hand, if you are writing about an event from ancient history, you may not discover any newspaper sources.

* If adequate sources are not available, see if you can broaden your topic or switch to another one. If you find too many sources, read more about the subject and narrow your paper's focus within more manageable limits.

* Make sure your sources are available. Find out if the library has the periodicals and newspapers you are seeking. Check books out. If necessary, order books from other libraries through InterLibrary Loan. Ask the circulation desk to recall desired books that have been checked out by others. If most of the books are gone, however, someone else is probably writing on your topic, and the sources

you need may not become available in time. If so, avoid needless frustration by switching now to another topic.

- Do some quick reading in your sources to learn more about your topic. It might be wise to ask a professor or some other authority on your subject for suggestions about the topic and for further research sources.

- Decide what additional sources can provide valuable information for your project. Write letters to request information, if necessary. Arrange interviews in advance by setting up appointments. (Letters and interviews are discussed in Chapter 10.)

- Be sure to record your discoveries, questions, and other experiences with locating sources in your research notebook.

As they begin their first research project in college, few students are experts in using the library. Many are confused and intimidated by electronic resources such as online databases and the World Wide Web. By the time students have finished the project, however, they have learned how to find information in their library as well as to access other sources throughout the world via electronic communication.

YOUR CAMPUS LIBRARY

Your purpose in conducting a research project is not only to inform yourself about your topic by discovering information but to inform others as well by making your discoveries available in a paper. Learning is, after all, a cooperative venture, and scholars have an obligation to pass on to others what they have learned. For that reason, a wealth of important information and ideas produced by scholars has been collected and located in a convenient place for your use—your college library.

As any quick browse through the library will make abundantly clear, there are a great many potential sources out there—written about an almost unlimited number of topics. Finding information about any particular topic might seem an impossible task. Fortunately, however, the means are available for locating almost anything you are looking for. Your library offers not only *research sources* themselves, such as books and periodicals, but also *search tools*, which allow you to discover what research sources are available for your topic and to locate them. These tools include the library's book catalog, online and printed guides to periodical and newspaper sources, and reference librarians. Search tools can give you a great deal of power, allowing you to discover information on almost any topic. Of immediate interest to you, of course, is that they allow you to find sources for your research paper. This chapter, with its accompanying exercises, is intended to make you proficient in the use of various search tools.

ELECTRONIC RESOURCES

A generation ago, college students searched for books about their research topics by flipping through index cards alphabetized in drawers in a library's card catalog.

To find periodical and newspaper sources, they paged laboriously through dozens of bound indexes. The computer revolution changed all that, and today most library searches are conducted at a keyboard in front of a computer screen. Not only have searches become simpler and more convenient, but today's students have easy access to vastly more sources than did scholars just a few years ago.

Electronic searches have themselves undergone rapid change. A few years ago, the student researcher had to visit many different library terminals, each dedicated to a particular index or database. Today it is typical for a college library to have a **central information system,** a single online site from which a student can locate all of the library's holdings, find sources in any of dozens of electronic databases, and even read many sources directly on the viewing screen. Because most library information systems are accessible on the Internet, students may avail themselves of many library resources from their home computers or at computer workstations around campus.

Being able to link up with your college library from home is only a small part of the research power now available to you through computers. For example, if you wanted, you could also search the holdings of a university library in Australia, copy a file stored on a computer in Scotland, or ask a question of a scholar in Nigeria. Before we explore the various tools for locating sources, both within and outside the library, we need some general background about electronic resources. To understand electronic resources and acquire skill in using them, there is no substitute for hands-on practice, but the following can provide a useful introduction.

A collection of material that is available electronically (by computer) is generally referred to as a **database.** Databases can be classified as either portable or online. A **portable database** is one that can reside within a particular computer, such as a program on a diskette or a CD-ROM file. In contrast, an **online database** is located at a distant site, such as a host computer or another computer on a network. For you to access it, your computer must communicate with that site. A vast and ever-growing number of databases is available online. These include valuable search tools such as indexes that enable you to locate sources, electronic encyclopedias, and whole libraries of data.

Networks

To gain access to an online database, your computer terminal needs to be connected to another computer containing the database. Such an arrangement by which a number of computers can contact each other is called a **network.** Your college is likely to have its own **local network** in which most computers on campus are connected through a central computer, known as a **server.** This connectivity allows students and faculty to share files and use e-mail to communicate. Most **college library networks** are tied in with the larger campus network, providing patrons with access to library information from classroom, office, and dormitory computers. Since colleges put restrictions on who may use their network, you may need to apply for an **account** and receive an **address** and a **password.**

Smaller networks are often joined in a larger network. For example, your college library network may be joined with networks from other regional libraries, so that you can search for works in several different libraries simultaneously. The linking of libraries in such a consortium also enables students at one campus to find and borrow works owned by another campus.

Finally, networks throughout the world, most likely including your campus network, are joined together in the largest and grandest network of them all, the ***Internet.*** Originally begun by the U.S. government, this network has grown to allow computer users almost anywhere on the planet to communicate and share information. Any Internet user can send and receive messages with any other user via e-mail. For example, you could direct an inquiry about your research question to a scholar in Finland, provided you knew that person's e-mail address. You could also join one of countless ***discussion lists*** devoted to particular topics. A message sent to a list is automatically forwarded to all of its subscribers. For instance, if you were researching voting patterns of women, you might post an inquiry on the PoSciM list, which is devoted to discussion of political science issues (and maybe also to WmSt-L, a women's studies list). Other subscribers interested in your topic would be likely to reply. An index to thousands of discussion lists can be found online at www.neosoft.com/internet/paml.

Another way to follow an ongoing e-mail discussion about a particular topic is by consulting a ***newsgroup*** or a ***bulletin board.*** These are very much like actual bulletin boards, where anyone can read and post messages. Unlike discussion lists, where all items are e-mailed directly to subscribers, newsgroups and bulletin boards are "places" on the network that you can "visit" whenever you choose, but no messages are sent to your e-mail in-box.

The most popular and fastest-growing component of the Internet is the ***World Wide Web,*** which allows users to read (and create) attractive presentations of text, graphics, and sound known as ***Web pages.*** Because virtually anyone can post material on the Web, there is no limit to the variety of available presentations. For example, you can explore your college's ***home page,*** which is linked to many other Web pages containing information about its programs, faculty, and resources. You can also read electronic "magazines" (often called *zines*) on the Web or consult the Web for instant news, weather, and sports updates. The variety is so great that "surfing the Net" has become a recreational obsession for many. However, because almost anyone can post whatever they choose on the Web without oversight or restriction, much information found on Web pages is of dubious merit. Students need to take special care in evaluating material from Web sources.

USING YOUR LIBRARY'S RESEARCH TOOLS

It is worth repeating that while search tools can give you access to a vast quantity of information, the *quality* of that information varies widely. More than ever, student researchers need to use careful judgment about the reliability of their sources and the usefulness of information they encounter. Since the number of channels by which you can access research sources is so great, the following sections of this chapter will focus on those most likely to be helpful. Still, many such tools—old and new—are described, and they can seem intimidating at first. Don't allow yourself to be overwhelmed. It is not necessary for you to absorb all the information in a single sitting. Nor do you need to memorize the names of all the available reference sources and the procedures for using them. Instead, regard this chapter as a guide that you can consult whenever you need it, now and in years to come. By examining the resources that are described here one at a time and by gaining experience with their use through the practice exercises, you will soon develop a solid and confident command of the tools needed for doing college research.

Most college libraries allow you access to a great variety of resources, and you can begin your search from one convenient online screen, the home page of the library's central information system. Once you log on to this page, you are presented with a menu of choices. Different libraries set up their home pages in different ways, but most have similar features, and we will explore some typical and important research tools likely to be available through your college library's online system.

The following two menu options are a staple of most college library systems:

- *Search the library catalog.* This option allows you to find books and other items in your library's holdings.
- *Search electronic indexes and databases.* This option allows you to find articles in journals, newspapers, and other periodicals.

In addition, the menu may allow you to learn library hours, view your own library record and renew items you have borrowed, see what materials your instructor has placed on reserve, and even search catalogs at other libraries.

Finding Books and Other Library Holdings

Let us begin by examining the first of the two options just mentioned, a search of your library's catalog. The library's holdings include books, periodicals, videocassettes, sound recordings, and many other materials—and all are indexed in its online catalog. The catalog menu will present you with a number of search options, including the following:

- Author search
- Title search
- Subject search
- Keyword search
- Call number search

If you know what author or book title you are seeking, you can do an ***author search*** or a ***title search.*** Merely enter the name of the author or title, and information is displayed.

When you are engaged in a research project, you will be looking to find what books are available on a particular topic, and you will want to conduct a ***subject search*** or a ***keyword search.*** In a subject search, you enter the subject you are searching. Only particular subjects are indexed, namely the subject headings designated by the Library of Congress. Since you may not know the exact subject heading, a keyword search may be the handiest way to begin your search for books on your topic.

Doing a Keyword Search

In a keyword search, you enter one or more words that are likely to appear in a work's title, in its subject, or in catalog notes about its contents. Imagine, for example, that you are interested in researching the threat posed by so-called killer bees. If you entered "bee," you would find that dozens of works in your library are referenced by this keyword, including books about beekeeping, quilting bees, and spelling bees—and even literary works (we found one entry for the poem "What the Bee Is to the Flow'ret") and sound recordings (we found the song "Woolie Boogie Bee"). Since these are not relevant to your research, you could narrow your search by including two or more words, such as "killer bee." This would limit the search just to entries containing both of those words—not necessarily together or in that order. A keyword search for "bee killer" would produce precisely the same results as a search for "killer bee." One limitation to keyword searches is that a computer is very literal minded. If you include the word "bee," it will ignore instances of "bees" or "beehives." Most catalogs allow you to use a **wildcard symbol,** usually an asterisk, to represent optional characters. For example, if you typed "bee*," you would find instances of both "bee" and "bees," but unfortunately also of "beer," "beefeaters," and "Beethoven." Nevertheless, by a judicious choice of keywords, you can conduct a successful search. By entering the words "killer bee*" in a keyword search through our college catalog, we learned that "killer" occurred in 72 listings, "bee*" in 650 entries, but that only three entries contained both words. The results of our search are shown in Figure 9.1, in which the three titles are listed on the screen.

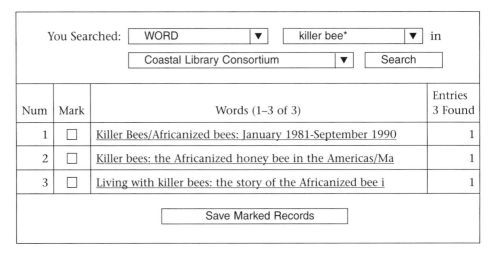

Figure 9.1 Results of a keyword search for "killer bee*" in a library catalog.

You could make a list of all the works that interest you by checking the boxes to the left of their titles. Later, when you have finished all your searches, you could ask for a display of all the works you marked. Alternatively, you could examine entries immediately. For example, if you clicked on the second title in Figure 9.1, *Killer Bees: The Africanized Honey Bee in the Americas,* you would be shown its record, part of which is reproduced in Figure 9.2. This screen gives much information about the book, including its author, title, publisher, and length (162 pages). The fact that the book was published in 1992 indicates how current it is. The fact that the book includes a ***bibliography*** tells you that you might use it to find a list of other works on the topic. The information in the boxes tells you where to go to find the book (its location and call number) and that it is available (not checked out by another patron). When a book's status is "unavailable," you can ask the circulation desk to send a ***recall notice*** to the borrower, but you would have no guarantee that it would be returned in time to meet your project's deadline.

Notice that in Figure 9.2, six different items are underlined, which means that each is a computer ***link*** to further data, and each provides a handy way to find additional sources on your topic. If you were to use your mouse to click on the author's name, "Winston, Mark L," you would be shown a list of all the holdings in the library written by that author. If you clicked on the book's call number, you would be shown a list of works with similar call numbers. Since books are numbered according to their topic, this is a handy way to see what other related books (in this case, about bees) are in your library. Finally, four different subject headings are listed. You could click on any one of them to do a subject search for this heading.

Author	<u>Winston, Mark L</u>
Title	**Killer bees: the Africanized honey bee in the Americas/Mark L.Winston**
Publisher	Cambridge, Mass.: Harvard University Press, 1992

LOCATION	**CALL#**	**STATUS**
General Collection	<u>SF538.5.A37 W56 1992</u>	AVAILABLE

Description	xiii, 162 p., [8] p. of plates: ill., maps; 22cm
Bibliography	Includes bibliography and index
Subject	<u>Africanized honeybee</u>
	<u>Africanized honeybee — America</u>
	<u>Africanized honeybee — Control</u>
	<u>Africanized honeybee — Control — America</u>
ISBN	067450352X (acid-free): $19.95

Figure 9.2 Excerpt from a book record.

It should also be noted that your search need not be limited to the holdings in your own library. A work found in another library can be borrowed by your library through an **InterLibrary Loan.** You may find it useful to check the collections of libraries likely to specialize in your subject. For example, we used our campus library's system to view the holdings at Texas A&M University, which has a large agricultural school. There we found seventeen listings under "Africanized honeybee," compared to three at the library on our campus. Similarly, if you were researching manatees, you would expect to find more works on the subject at the University of Miami than, say, at the University of North Dakota. Ask your librarian for help in searching the collections of other libraries.

EXERCISES | **Using Your Library's Central Information System**

Use your college library's online catalog to answer the following questions. Although these exercises may remind you of a scavenger hunt, they are intended to familiarize you with the resources in your library and to practice important research skills that you will use many times in the future.

1. These questions can be answered by doing an author search on your college library's catalog:

    a. How many authors with the surname Churchill have works in your library?

    b. How many author listings are there for Sir Winston Churchill (1874–1965)?

    c. View the record for one book by Sir Winston Churchill (and print it, if your computer terminal is connected to a printer). What is the book's full title? its call number? Is the book currently available in your library, or has it been checked out? In what city was the book published? by what publisher? in what year? How many pages long is the book? What subject headings could you use in a subject search to find similar works on the same topic?

2. Do a subject search, using one of the subject headings found in 1c, above. How many works does your library have on that subject? What are the title, author, and call number of one of those works (other than the Churchill book)?

3. Find an author whose last name is the same as or close to your own. Record the title and call number of one book by this author.

4. How would you use your library catalog to locate works *about,* rather than by, Sir Winston Churchill? How many works does your library have about him? Record the author, title, and call number of one such book.

5. How many books does your library have with the title (or partial title) *Descent of Man*? Who are the authors of these books?

6. Do a call number search to answer these questions: How many works are there in your library whose call numbers begin with TL789? What subject(s) are books with this number about? Record the author, title, and call number of one such book.

7. To answer this question, you may need guidance from your instructor or librarian: How can you limit your call number search to only those works (with call number TL789) that were published after 1990? How many such works are there in your library's collection? Can you limit your search to TL789 works with the word "flying" in the title? How many such works are in your library?

8. Do a keyword search to find works on your research project topic (or another topic that interests you). What subject headings do you find for these works? Use the most appropriate of these headings to do a subject search. Record information about works likely to help you in your research project.

Encyclopedias and Other General Reference Works

General reference works, books, periodicals, newspapers, and microforms are some of the resources in college libraries. Because so many sources are available, it is helpful to approach a search for information with a strategy in mind and to turn first to resources that are most likely to be of help. Before you search in particular directions, you need a broad overview of your topic. General reference works are often a good place to begin.

General reference works, such as encyclopedias and almanacs, offer information about many subjects. They are located in the reference section of your library, where they can be consulted but not checked out. Many encyclopedias, dictionaries, and almanacs are also available online or in CD-ROM format. In addition to text and pictures, some online works allow you to view film clips and hear audio as well. Another advantage of online encyclopedias is that they are frequently updated, and the latest edition is always available to you.

General encyclopedias have alphabetically arranged articles on a wide variety of subjects. *Encyclopedia Americana* and *Collier's Encyclopedia* both contain accessible articles that can provide you with helpful introductions to unfamiliar subjects. The print version of the *New Encyclopaedia Britannica* is somewhat more complicated to use in that it is divided into various sections, including the "Micropaedia," which consists of short articles and cross-references to other articles in the set, and the "Macropaedia," which consists of longer, more detailed articles. Encyclopedias published on CD-ROM disks or available online include *Encarta* and *Britannica Online.* One-volume **desk encyclopedias,** such as the *New Columbia Encyclopedia,* can be quick and handy guides to basic information about a subject. **Almanacs,** such as *Information Please Almanac, Atlas and Yearbook* and *The World Almanac & Book of Facts,* contain tables of information and are handy sources of much statistical information.

Specialized encyclopedias, restricted to specific areas of knowledge, can provide you with more in-depth information. Many such works are available—the online catalog at the university where we teach lists over a thousand works under the subject heading "Encyclopedia." By way of example, here are just a few from the beginning of the alphabet: *Encyclopedia of Adolescence, Encyclopedia of African-American Civil Rights, Encyclopedia of Aging and the Elderly, Encyclopedia of Alcoholism,*

Encyclopedia of Allergy and Environmental Illness, Encyclopedia of Amazons, Encyclopedia of American Social History, Encyclopedia of Animated Cartoons, Encyclopedia of Arms Control and Disarmament, and *Encyclopedia of Assassinations.* You can use your college catalog to locate a specialized encyclopedia dealing with your research topic. You can also browse the reference section in the appropriate stacks for your topic; sections are marked by Library of Congress call numbers (for example, BF for psychology, HV for crime, N for art, and so on).

EXERCISES | **Using General Reference Works**

1. Locate a specialized encyclopedia dealing with your research topic or another topic that appeals to you.

2. Look up that same topic in the print version of the *New Encyclopaedia Britannica* (look first in the index, which will direct you to either the "Micropaedia" or the "Macropaedia") and then in *Encyclopedia Americana* or *Collier's Encyclopedia.* Finally, if possible, consult an online or CD-ROM encyclopedia. Compare the treatment and coverage of the topic in these different works.

3. Determine if information about the same topic can also be found in a desk encyclopedia or in an almanac.

4. Finally, write a one-page account of what you discovered. In particular, what kinds of information are found in the different reference works? How do the treatments of the topic differ?

 FINDING ARTICLES: MAGAZINES, JOURNALS, AND NEWSPAPERS

Articles in magazines, journals, and newspapers are among the sources used most frequently by student researchers in composition classes, for several reasons: Articles are written on a variety of subjects; they make timely information available right up to the most recent issues; and, being relatively brief, they tend to focus on a single topic. Your college library is likely to have recent issues of hundreds of magazines and journals and of many local, national, and international newspapers. In addition, back issues of these publications are available either in bound volumes or on *microforms* (miniaturized photographic copies of the material). Many electronic indexes that you may use to find articles on your research topic allow you to view the articles directly on your screen, saving you the step of finding the article in print or on microform.

Locating Periodicals

If you are in doubt about whether your library has a magazine or journal you are looking for, you can consult a list of all the periodicals your library owns. Such a list is usually found in the library's online catalog. In most libraries, current issues of magazines and journals are shelved on open stacks; back issues are collected and bound by volume or copied onto microforms. Recent back issues, not yet bound, are sometimes available at a periodicals or service desk. If you have difficulty finding an article, ask at the periodicals or reference desk for assistance.

Microforms

As a space-saving device, many libraries store some printed materials on microforms, miniaturized photographic copies of the materials. The two principal types of microforms are *microfilm,* which comes in spools that resemble small movie reels, and *microfiche* (pronounced *MY-crow-feesh*), which comes in individual sheets of photographic film. The images they contain are so small that they can store large quantities of material. A projector is required to enlarge these images so they can be read. Most college libraries have projectors for both microfilm and microfiche. Some projectors also allow for photocopying of what appears on the projector's screen. Follow the directions on these machines or ask a librarian for assistance. Although sturdy, microforms are not indestructible, so it is important to handle them with care and to return them in the same condition as you received them.

Library Vandalism—A Crime against Scholarship

Since scholarship is a cooperative enterprise, it is essential that all scholars have access to sources. Students who steal, deface, or mutilate library materials commit a crime against the ethics of scholarship. An unforgivable sin is to tear articles from magazines, permanently depriving others of their right to read them. Many a frustrated scholar, looking for a needed source only to find it stolen, has uttered a terrible curse upon the heads of all library vandals—one that it might be wise not to incur. On the more tangible side, most states have made library vandalism a criminal offense, punishable by stiff fines and in some cases jail sentences.

Actually, there is no excuse for such vandalism. Short passages can be hand-copied. Longer excerpts, to be used for legitimate academic purposes, can be photo-copied inexpensively. Most libraries have coin-operated or debit-card photocopy machines in convenient locations. (Some photoduplication violates copyright laws; consult your instructor or librarian if you are in doubt.)

 ## USING ELECTRONIC DATABASES

Most college libraries provide links to electronic databases, which have replaced printed indexes as the most popular means for students to locate articles, electronic files, and other materials related to their research topics. These databases are either online (through an electronic connection to the database host site) or portable (stored on a CD-ROM disk). *Databases* are usually accessed through the library's central information system.

College libraries allow you access to dozens of databases, and the number is increasing at a rapid rate. In this chapter we will introduce a few of the more popular and useful databases, but you should explore your library to learn what databases are available. Most databases work in a similar way, and you need to master only a few simple principles to conduct a successful search. Once you have practiced searching one database, you should have little trouble negotiating most other databases as well. It is usually advisable to search several different databases when you are looking for articles and other information about your research topic.

A Sample Search for Periodical Sources

Your library may subscribe to several **online reference services,** such as EBSCOhost, FirstSearch, WilsonWeb, Lexis-Nexis Academic Universe, and ProQuest. Each service allows you to search a number of databases either singly or simultaneously. As an example of how you could use an online reference service, we will demonstrate a search using the EBSCOhost service. Let us imagine that you are doing a research project on college students who are binge drinkers.

Figure 9.3 shows part of the EBSCOhost menu of databases. Scrolling down the screen would reveal many other databases as well. To the left of each database is a box. As a first step in your search, you would click on the boxes of all

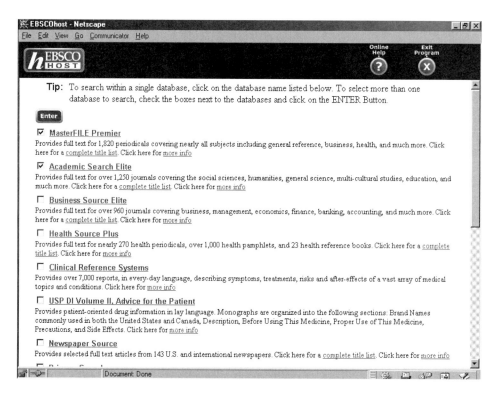

Figure 9.3 EBSCOhost menu screen with selection of databases.

the databases that might be pertinent. Let us assume you decide to search the MasterFILE Premier database (a large database of journals, magazines, and newspapers), Academic Search Elite (a database of articles in scholarly journals), and ERIC (a database of education-related journals and documents). By clicking first in those three boxes and then on the *Enter* button, you bring up the search page shown in Figure 9.4.

Tips for Successful Keyword Searches

The next step in your search is to enter **keywords** on the screen in Figure 9.4, telling the **search engine** (that's another term used to describe an online program that searches a database) what words or phrases to look for as it searches the titles and abstracts of articles. If you enter "binge drinker" in the *Find* box and then click on the *Search* button, a results list (Figure 9.5) will soon appear with a grand total of three articles—a very disappointing result.

But wait! Computers are very literal. You have asked the search engine to restrict its search just to that one phrase, greatly limiting the results. A useful tip is to use an asterisk as a **wildcard character** to find any of several related words. Entering "binge drink*" instead of "binge drinker" will broaden your search to any phrase that begins with those characters, including *binge drinker, binge drinkers,* and

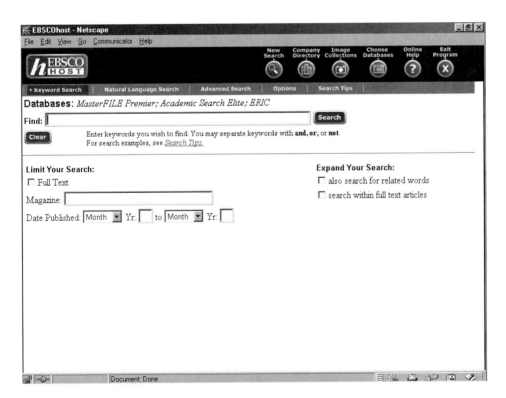

Figure 9.4 **Search page in the EBSCOhost search engine.**

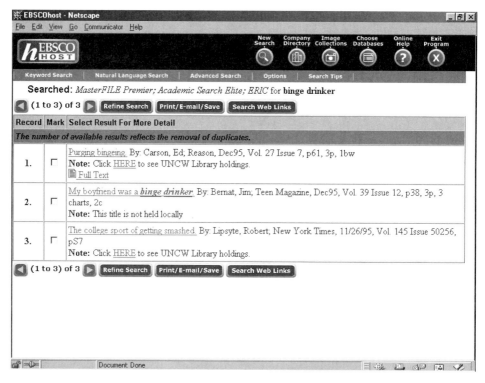

Figure 9.5 A "results list" in the EBSCOhost search engine.

binge drinking. Click on the *Search* button, and instead of three results, the search engine now reports it has found 276 items—a much more satisfactory outcome.

But perhaps a search of these keywords is still too limiting. The EBSCOhost search engine (unlike many library catalogs) assumes that two words entered side by side constitute a phrase, and it will look only for the words *binge* and *drink** when they occur next to each other, not when they are separated by other words. A solution is to conduct what is known as a **Boolean search,** using the words *AND, OR,* or *NOT.* For example, if you ask EBSCOhost to search for "binge AND drink*," it will look for articles that contain both of those words, even if they are separated from each other. That is, it would find articles that contain "binge drinkers" as well as those that contain "drinkers who go on a binge" and so on.

More is not always better, however, and now your search may be too broad. You aren't interested in binge drinking among business executives, just among college students, so a useful strategy is to refine your search further to eliminate unwanted articles. Make the search topic "binge AND drink* AND college" to eliminate any articles in which the word *college* does not appear. However, in some articles about binge drinking, the word *university* may be used instead of *college.* You can use the OR operator to search for either *college* or *university.* That is, you might have your best results if you search for the keywords "binge AND drink* AND (college OR university)." The search results that EBSCOhost returned when different keywords were entered are show in Figure 9.6. Here is a summary of how the three *Boolean operators* can work to make your search as broad or as narrow as you choose:

- The *AND* operator combines search terms so that each result contains all of the terms. For example, type *alcohol AND college* to find articles that contain both terms in each result.

- The *OR* operator combines search terms so that each result contains at least one of the terms. For example, type *alcohol OR drugs* to find results that contain either term.

- The *NOT* operator excludes terms so that each result does not contain the term that follows the NOT operator. For example, type *drugs NOT alcohol* to find results that contain the term "drugs" but not the term "alcohol."

The Next Step—Finding More Detail on Sources

In our sample search for articles about collegiate binge drinking, we used the keywords "binge AND drink* AND (college OR university)," and EBSCOhost found 166 articles (see Figure 9.7). Each result gives the article's title and publication data. The next step is to examine the most promising articles to find useful sources. You can click your mouse on the title of an article to read an *abstract* (a brief summary) of its content. Beneath the titles of the first four articles, the words "Full Text" appear. If you click on these words, you can read the entire article, on your screen. For the fifth article, only an abstract is available online. To read this article, you would have to locate the *Journal of Applied Social Psychology* in your library's microforms collection.

If you were to click on the title of the first item in Figure 9.7, "Schools Turn Off the Tap," you would see the detailed information shown in Figure 9.8. In addition to the title, author, and source of the article, this screen contains several other useful items. The abstract summarizes the article and is your best guide to

Keywords entered	Number of articles found
binge drinker	3
binge drinkers	32
binge drinking	234
binge drink*	276
binge AND drink*	308
binge AND drink* AND college	159
binge AND drink* AND (college OR university)	172

Figure 9.6 Number of articles found in an EBSCOhost search using different keywords.

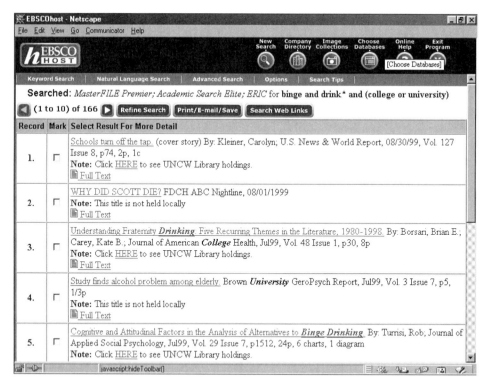

Figure 9.7 Search results for "binge and drink* and (college or university).

whether the article is likely to be a useful source for your research project. If so, you can read the full text by scrolling down the page or by clicking on "Go to Full Text" in the upper right. You can either take notes on the article immediately or print it for later use.

Another useful feature of Figure 9.8 is the "Subject(s)" heading. This article is indexed under four different subjects. If you were to click on the first subject, "DRINKING of alcoholic beverages—Universities & colleges," you would find additional articles related to that subject. The final feature in Figure 9.8, "See Articles related to," works in a similar way. A resourceful researcher will take advantage of these many ways to find useful sources.

EXERCISES   Using an Online Reference Service

1. In Figure 9.3, which of the databases shown would be your best source to find articles in academic journals? Which database(s) would you search if you were writing a paper on diet drugs? Which database(s) would be particularly useful to locate sources for a research project on student entrepreneurs who start In-

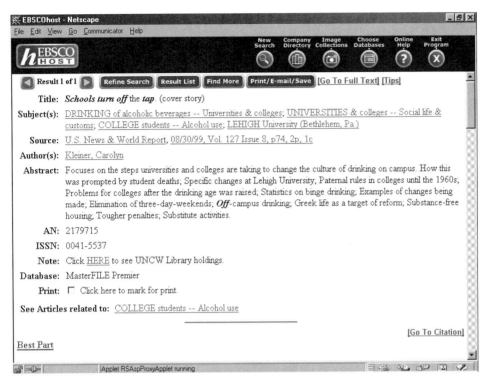

Figure 9.8 An EBSCOhost citation screen.

ternet businesses? What is the difference between the MasterFILE Premier data-base and the Newspaper Source database?

2. Figure 9.4 shows an EBSCOhost search page. If you were looking for articles about the popularity of rock music in China, what keywords would you enter in the "Find" box? Assuming that "China" or "Chin*" is one of your keywords, how could you use Boolean operators to eliminate articles about the rock group China Beach?

3. In Figure 9.4, how could you limit your search just to articles published in the year 2000? How could you ensure that search results would include only articles whose full text is available online? The search engine looks for your keywords in the titles and abstracts of articles. How could you direct the search engine to look for your keywords within the articles as well?

4. In the search results shown in Figure 9.7, who were the authors of the article "Understanding Fraternity Drinking"? In what publication did it appear? What is the length in pages of the article "Schools Turn Off the Tap"? Four of the five results are periodical articles (articles in magazines, journals, or newspapers). Which result is the transcript of an interview on a television show?

5. Figure 9.7 shows only the first 10 of 166 results. Where would you click with your mouse pointer to view the next 10 results?

6. Figure 9.9 shows a search page for WilsonWeb, another reference service. Describe what the student who has filled in the page is hoping to find from this search.

7. Figure 9.10 shows the home page of the Lexis-Nexis Academic Universe reference service. Where would you click if you wanted to find sources about the 2000 summer Olympics? Where would you click to find sources on the Supreme Court's *Roe* v. *Wade* decision on abortion?

8. Log on to your college library's central information system. Does it allow you to search for articles online? If so, which online reference services (for example, EBSCOhost, FirstSearch, Lexis-Nexis, WilsonWeb) does it allow you to search? Are there other databases you can use to search for articles?

9. Use your college library's resources to find a newspaper article about Medicare fraud published within the past year.

10. Use a different database to find an article in an academic journal about the sleeping disorder known as sleep apnea. If you can, print out the citation screen for the article; if not, copy the author, title, publication, date, and page numbers.

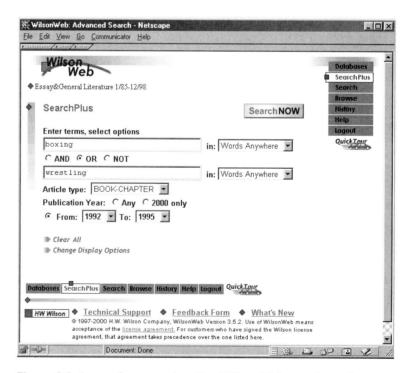

Figure 9.9 A search page using the WilsonWeb search engine.

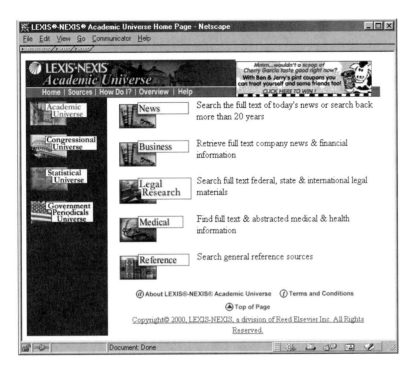

Figure 9.10 The Lexis-Nexis Academic Universe home page.

Finding Government Documents

The vast array of documents published by the U.S. government constitutes another useful resource for research in almost any field of study. Each state has at least one designated depository library that receives all documents distributed by the Government Printing Office, as well as several other partial depository libraries that receive selected government publications. Items not in your college library can usually be borrowed through the InterLibrary Loan service. Government documents are usually shelved in a special library section and identified by a special call number called a *SuDoc* number (short for the Superintendent of Documents Classification number). It is also called a *GovDoc* number by some databases. Most library catalogs do not index all their government documents along with their book holdings. To find documents and their SuDoc numbers, you need to consult one of several indexes. Although the *Monthly Catalog of U.S. Government Publications* is issued in bound volumes, most researchers find it easier to use an electronic database to locate government publications on their research topics. Several online reference services allow searches of GPO (Government Printing Office) databases. The following is an example of a search of the **GPO Monthly Catalog** index through the FirstSearch online reference service.

Imagine, for example, that you were writing a research paper on the exploration of the planet Mars. A search using the keywords "Mars exploration" would yield many documents, including one called *The Difficult Road to Mars: A Brief History of Mars Exploration in the Soviet Union.* Clicking on the title would call up on your screen the record of that publication shown in Figure 9.11. If your library has this document, it can be found in the library's government documents section by its SuDoc number NAS 1.83:1999-06-251-HQ (which in this database is called its GovDoc number).

EXERCISES   **Finding Government Documents**

1. This exercise can be undertaken by one or two students who can report their findings to the class. Find out if your college library is your state's regional depository for U.S. government documents or a partial depository. If the latter, what percentage of available government items does it receive? Where are government documents shelved in the library? How can students gain access to government documents not in your library?

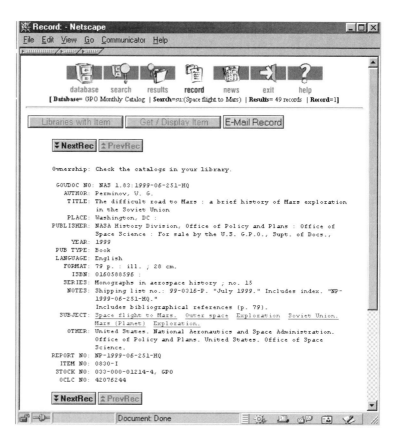

Figure 9.11 A government document record in the GPO Monthly Catalog.

2. Figure 9.11 is the record of one government document. In what year was it published? Under the heading "Subject," six different subjects are listed. Which would you click on to find additional government documents about Mars exploration?

3. Unlike the EBSCOhost online reference service, which treats a keyword entry such as "social promotion" as a phrase—that is, it will find those two words only when they appear side by side—the FirstSearch online reference service treats the keyword entry "social promotion" the same way as "social AND promotion." That is, it will look for those two words even when they are not together. If you search for "social promotion," FirstSearch will return entries such as "Barriers to the Promotion of Higher Order Thinking in Social Studies," which contains both words but has nothing to do with "social promotion" in the schools. If your library subscribes to the GPO Monthly Catalog database on FirstSearch, click on "Help" (for example, at the top right of Figure 9.11) and see if you can find how to limit your search to "social promotion" as a phrase.

4. Use a GPO index to search for government documents related to your research topic. Report on what you find.

INTERNET RESOURCES

Library sources can be accessed in systematic ways; by contrast, finding sources on the Internet is much more a hit-or-miss affair. Whereas the library's staff controls its collection and creates an index of all of the library's holdings (its online catalog), no one runs the Internet, much less controls access to it or creates a comprehensive index. The Internet is really a vast interconnected network of smaller networks, which virtually anyone can access and where virtually anyone can publish anything. Navigating the Internet and finding resources that can aid your research project require much practice, some skill, and considerable luck.

The best Internet tutorial comes from hands-on exploration, aided by your curiosity and an adventurous spirit. Here we can give only some brief information and hints to get you started.

Web Search Engines

When you seek Web sources for a research project, you will probably not know the addresses for specific files. Although no comprehensive index to the millions of Web files exists, several commercial indexes (known as *search engines*) provide access to a large number of files, either by keyword or subject searches. Among the more prominent search engines and their URL addresses are:

AltaVista	http://www.altavista.com
Ask Jeeves	http://www.ask.com
Excite	http://www.excite.com
HotBot	http://www.hotbot.com
InfoSeek	http://infoseek.go.com

Lycos   http://www.lycos.com
WebCrawler   http://webcrawler.com
Yahoo   http://www.yahoo.com

Figure 9.12 shows a HotBot search screen. If you type in a topic in the Search box, HotBot will show you a list of sites related to that topic. You can then visit one of those sites by clicking on its name. Search engines can also be used for subject searches. HotBot allows you to choose from many broad topics (for example, *arts*), then to narrow the search (perhaps to *society,* then to *history,* then to *Africa,* then to *slavery*).

A word of caution about Web documents and other Internet resources is in order. Students should evaluate them with a careful, critical eye. Find out who has created the document and how reliable or comprehensive it is. For example, if you are researching a scandal in the widget industry, you might find one or more widget Web pages. Knowing if the page is created by a widget trade organization (which would be expected to have a pro-widget bias) or by an anti-widget consumer group (with the opposite bias) is essential if you are to assess the source and determine whether and how to use it.

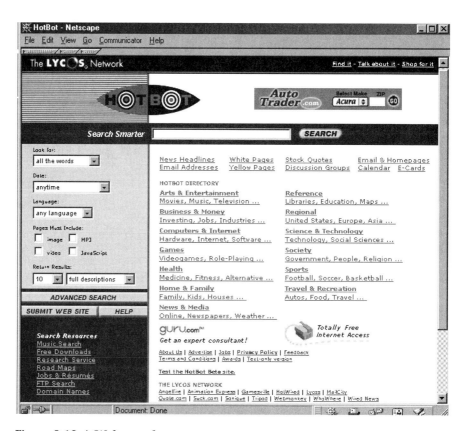

Figure 9.12 A Web search page.

Using the World Wide Web

Do the following exercises using the World Wide Web.

1. See what you can find on the Web on the following three topics: identical twins, Peru, and archery. Use one or more of the above search engines to explore these topics. Follow links from page to page as your curiosity leads you. Write a narrative describing your search and discoveries.

2. The HotBot search engine is organized around a number of topics (Arts and Entertainment, Business and Money, etc.). Select one that interests you, and continue to choose from among options until you arrive at an interesting page. Print the page (if equipment allows) or summarize its contents.

3. Use other search engines to find Web sources on your research topic.

 ## THE REFERENCE LIBRARIAN—THE MOST RESOURCEFUL RESOURCE

By far the most valuable resource in any library is the librarian, a professional who knows the library well and is an expert in locating information. Use the other resources in this chapter first, but if you become stuck or do not know where to look or cannot find the sources you need, do not hesitate to ask a librarian for help. College libraries have *reference librarians* on duty, usually at a station marked as the *reference desk.* Their job is to assist when you need help in finding sources. Reference librarians are almost always helpful, and they have aided many students with the same kinds of research problems and questions that you are likely to have.

There are some limits, however, to the services reference librarians can provide. One librarian requested that we mention some problems they are sometimes asked to solve but cannot. They cannot pick a topic for you, interpret your assignment, or answer questions about the format of your bibliographic citations. Those questions should be addressed to your instructor. The librarian's job is to assist when you need help locating library sources.

Although printed and electronic materials are of great value to researchers, they are not the only sources available. Chapter 10 discusses ways to use other sources in your research project.

10 Finding Sources outside the Library: Conducting Interviews and Writing Letters

 INTERVIEWING SOURCES

In addition to print sources, interviews with experts can provide valuable material for your paper. Because the people you interview are primary rather than secondary sources, the firsthand information they provide is exclusively yours to present—information that readers will find nowhere else. Therefore, interviewed sources can make a favorable impression, giving readers the sense that they are getting expert testimony directly and reliably. Your own reliability and credibility may also be enhanced, since you demonstrate the initiative to have extended your search beyond the usual kinds of sources.

On a college campus, professors are an accessible source of expert information. Being familiar with research in their individual fields, they also can suggest published and unpublished resources you might not have found in your library research. In her research on credit cards, Eliza Tetirick interviewed Robert Keating, a professor of management on her campus. Eliza found it invaluable to talk with someone who could answer all her questions and give expert advice.

You may also find experts living in your local community. Had she chosen to do so, Eliza could also have talked with a financial officer at the bank where she had an account.

Other valuable sources include participants and eyewitnesses. If you were researching, say, the Vietnam War or the Bosnian mission, you could interview relatives and neighbors with experience in the military. Be resourceful in considering interviewees who can contribute to your knowledge and understanding.

Conducting interviews may not be the first order of business in your research project, but because interviews require advance planning, it is important to set up appointments as early as possible—even before you are ready to conduct them. Soon after Eliza had decided on her topic, she knew she would want to talk to a business professor. She wanted to do some reading first in order to be sufficiently informed to ask intelligent questions, but she also knew that professors' time is valuable and that it would be wise to arrange an interview well in advance.

Arranging the Interview

Like every other stage in a research project, arranging interviews can lead to inevitable frustrations. For example, if you were researching a career in psychiatry, you might find it difficult to arrange an interview with a psychiatrist. After all, psychiatrists spend their days talking with patients; they may have little interest in giving up their precious free time to talk with someone else (without compensation).

When you telephone someone you don't know, be courteous and explain your purpose simply and clearly. For example, if you were calling an executive at a computer company to ask for an interview, you might say something like this:

> Hello, Ms. Smith, I'm [your name], a student at [your school]. I'm conducting a research project concerning the future of computers in the workplace. I'm particularly interested in talking to a person in the industry with your expertise, and I would like to learn your views on the topic. I wonder if I could meet with you briefly to ask you a few questions.

You can expect the person to ask you further questions about the nature of your project and about the amount of time the interview will take. If you are courteous and open and if your purposes seem serious, people are likely to cooperate with you to the extent that they are able. Be prepared to meet at a time and place convenient to the interviewee. Many interviews can be conducted in fifteen to thirty minutes. If you wish to tape-record the interview, ask for permission at the time you arrange the meeting.

Professors are usually available to students during office hours, but business people and other professionals are usually not so easy to reach. Before talking to the executive, you might have to explain your need to a receptionist or secretary, who might be reluctant to connect you. Often a letter written in advance of your telephone call can be effective in securing an interview. For example, a student who wishes to arrange an interview with a computer executive might send a letter like this one:

```
                                 202 Willow Street
                                 Wilmington, NC 28401
                                 2 March 2000

Ms. Denise Smith
Vice-President for Research and Development
CompuCosmos Corporation
Wilmington, NC 28401

Dear Ms. Smith:

        I am a student at the University of North Carolina at
Wilmington engaged in a research project concerning the
future of computer use in business offices.  I have learned
much about the topic from written sources, but I still have
some unanswered questions.  Your observations and expert
opinions would be invaluable for my report.  I know your time
```

```
is valuable, and I would be grateful if I could meet with
you for a brief interview.  I will telephone Wednesday
morning to see if I can arrange a meeting.  If you wish,
you can reach me by phone at 555-1893.
```

Sincerely,

Blair Halliday

Blair Halliday

Conducting the Interview

Some interviews may consist of a simple question or two, designed to fill specific gaps in your knowledge about your topic. Others may be extended question-and-answer sessions about a variety of topics. The success of your interviewing depends on your preparation, professionalism, and interpersonal skills. The following guidelines should be followed when you conduct an interview.

1. *Before the interview:*

   • **Be well prepared.** The most important part of the interview takes place before the questions are posed. Become as informed about your subject as you can so that you can ask the right questions. Use your reading notes to prepare questions in advance.

   • **Dress appropriately for the interview.** How you dress can influence how the interviewee behaves toward you; people are most comfortable talking with someone who dresses as they do. Business and professional people, for example, are more likely to take you seriously if you are wearing standard business attire. On the other hand, formal attire would be inappropriate when interviewing striking factory workers, who might be reluctant to speak freely with someone who looks like management.

   • **Arrive on time for your appointment.** Not only is arriving on time a matter of courtesy, but it is essential in assuring the interviewee's cooperation.

2. *During the interview:*

   • **Take careful and accurate notes.** If you intend to quote your source, you must be certain that you have copied the person's words exactly. A tape recorder can give you an accurate transcript of your interviews.

   • **Behave politely and ethically.** Be certain you have the interviewee's permission if you tape-record the conversation. If you take notes, offer to let the interviewee check the transcript later to ensure accuracy (doing so may elicit further elaborations and additional statements that you can use).

   • **Be relaxed and friendly.** People who are not accustomed to being interviewed are often nervous at first about having their comments recorded. By being friendly and relaxed, you can win their confidence and put them at ease. The most fruitful parts of interviews occur when interviewees become absorbed in what they are saying and forget they are being recorded. Begin with general questions that can be answered with ease and confidence. Later introduce more specific and pointed questions. (For experienced interviewees, these precautions may not be necessary.)

• **Make your recording as unobtrusive as possible.** Many people will not speak freely and naturally when constantly reminded that their comments are being recorded. Place the tape recorder out of the interviewee's direct line of sight. Do not write constantly during the interview; write down key phrases and facts that will allow you to reconstruct the conversation immediately after the interview.

• **Be interested in what the interviewee says.** People will speak much more freely with you if they sense that you are responsive to their comments. It is a mistake for an interviewer to read one prepared question after another, while barely listening to the interviewee's responses. Such wooden interviewing produces an uncomfortable atmosphere and strained responses.

• **Stay flexible.** Do not be a slave to your prepared questions. Listen with real curiosity to what the person says and ask further questions based on what you learn. Request explanations of what is not clear to you. Ask probing questions when a topic is raised that you would like to learn more about.

• **Let the interviewee do the talking.** Remember that it is the interviewee's ideas that you are interested in, not your own. Avoid the temptation to state your own opinions and experiences or to argue points with the interviewee.

3. *After the interview:*

• **End the interview professionally.** Check your notes and questions to determine if any gaps still need to be filled. Thank the interviewee. Ask if the person would like to check your use of statements and information for accuracy, and whether you can call again if you have further questions. Offer to send the interviewee a copy of your paper when it is completed.

• **Be fair to the source.** When you write the paper, be certain that any ideas or statements you attribute to the source are true reflections of the sound and spirit of the person's answers and comments. Be accurate in quoting the person, but eliminate slips of the tongue and distracting phrases like *uh* and *you know.*

• **Send a thank-you note.** Whether or not you send a copy of your paper to the interviewee, you should send a note expressing your appreciation for the help that the person provided.

Eliza prepared the following list of questions before she interviewed Robert Keating, a business professor who teaches at her college:

Possible Interview Questions for Professor Keating

• Are there reasons for a student to get a credit card?

• Are there reasons for a student not to get a credit card?

- Why are companies eager to give credit cards to students?
- What risks do companies face?
- What can a student do who gets in debt?
- What is APR?
- What advice do you have for students who get cards?

Although she used her prepared questions as a point of reference, Eliza found herself departing from them as she responded to Professor Keating's comments. During her interview, Eliza took notes in her research notebook. Here are some excerpts. (In a few cases we have recast them to make them clearer to other readers.)

```
Notes from the Interview with Professor Keating
-- Benefits: develop a credit rating.  "Proper use shows
   you know how to handle money."  It then allows you to
   get a bigger line of credit.
-- Why are companies eager to give cards?  For future.
   They are betting students will use same card once they
   have jobs and money to spend.
-- Isn't it a risk for the company?  Worth risk.  1-3% go
   into default.
-- They'll give students a limited line of credit.
-- Freshmen: parents may be asked to cosign.
-- APR = "annual percentage rate"
-- Rate you pay is 9.9%-22%. In North Carolina limited by
   law to 18%.
-- Big downside: inability to pay.
-- "Very hard to get rid of a bad credit rating."  There
   are some prepaid credit cards (like debit cards) that
   allow you to rehabilitate credit rating.
-- Biggest problem for students: never having dealt with
   money on their own.  Don't know how to manage it.
-- Advice: pay it all off if you can; if not, pay as much
   as you can each month.  Avoid paying late fees.
   You'll also get a bad reputation (hurts when buying
   car, downpayment on furniture).
```

After the interview with Professor Keating, Eliza reviewed her notes, expanded them while her memory of the conversation was fresh, and wrote down observations in her notebook. She then transcribed the material she thought she would use in her paper onto note cards (discussed in Chapter 11).

 ## WRITING FOR INFORMATION

It frequently happens that information helpful to your project is unavailable in the library. For example, if you were doing a project on nutrition in children's breakfast foods, you might visit a supermarket to record nutritional information and ingredients of various brands from the sides of cereal boxes. You could also write letters of inquiry to cereal manufacturers, such as the one that follows.

```
                                        November 3, 2000

Public Relations Officer
Breakfast Foods Division
General Foods Corporation
250 North Street
White Plains, NY 10625


Dear Public Relations Officer:
     As a student at [your university], I am undertaking a
research study of nutrition in breakfast cereals.  I am
particularly interested in learning if there is a market for
low-sugar cereals targeted specifically for the children's
market.  Could you please tell me the sales figures for your
low-sugar Post Crispy Critters cereal?  I would also
appreciate any additional information you could send me
related to this subject.
     I would be grateful if you could respond before [date],
the deadline for my research paper.
                              Sincerely,
                              [your signature]
                              [your name]
```

Business directories in the reference section of your library, such as *Directory of Corporate Affiliations,* can help you find company addresses. If you need further assistance, consult with the reference librarian.

It is wise to tell correspondents how you plan to use the information you are requesting. They are more likely to respond if convinced that your project will not be harmful to their interests. (Some businesses, such as tobacco or liquor companies, are understandably leery about supplying information for studies that may attack them.) You can increase your chances of getting a response by including a self-addressed stamped envelope with your letter. If time is short, a telephone call, e-mail message, or a fax may get a speedier response than a letter.

STILL OTHER SOURCES

Researchers can avail themselves of many other sources besides library materials, interviews, and letters. *Lectures, films, television programs*, and *audio recordings* are among the sources often cited in student research projects. In your paper, for example, you might quote a person who appeared in a television documentary, or you might describe an event portrayed in a news program. A song lyric or a line from movie dialogue might effectively illustrate a particular theme.

On many campuses there is a ***media center*** in which videotapes (including television documentaries), films, and various audio recordings are available. It may be housed in the library or in a separate building. Some campuses belong to a regional network of media centers that share their materials, usually with little or no charge to the borrower. If your campus has a media center, ask how you can find what sources are available on your topic and whether it is possible for you to gain access to materials from other campuses.

11

Putting Your Sources to Work

A RESEARCH PROSPECTUS

A *prospectus* is a statement of your plans for a project. During the early stages of their projects, Slade Healy and Eliza Tetirick were asked by their instructors to submit a research prospectus. Slade's class received the following assignment.

Research Prospectus   ASSIGNMENT

Bring to our next class a prospectus of your research project. It should consist of the following elements:

1. *A statement of your research question.* Your topic may be tentative at this point, so you needn't feel locked into it. In upcoming days, you may decide to alter your question or shift its focus as you conduct further research and learn more about the subject.

2. *A paragraph or two about your progress so far.* You can summarize why you chose your topic, what you already know about it, and what you hope to discover. You can also discuss any problems or successes you have had with focusing your topic and finding sources.

3. *A working bibliography* (a list of the sources you have located so far). Use the MLA format (explained in Chapter A of Part II) for your bibliography. This is a list of raw sources—sources you have not yet had much chance to examine and evaluate—so it is likely to contain some items that you will not use in your paper and therefore will not appear in the works-cited page of the final draft.

Slade and Eliza by now had a general idea of their topics. They had done some browsing in encyclopedias and other reference works, and each was beginning to assemble a list of potential sources. Following are some excerpts from Slade's research notebook, written as he was beginning his search. Slade's notes are informal, in the style of journal entries. We have edited them somewhat to make them clearer for other readers.

> On my Netscape browser, I clicked on "Search" which gives a
> list of search engines. I clicked on "Ask Jeeves" because
> I've used it before and you can ask it questions. I asked,
> "What are solutions to discipline problems in schools?" and
> miraculously it pointed me to many sources in other search
> engines. I followed a link to WebCrawler [another search
> engine] and there was much there about disruptive behavior
> and other discipline problems. I went to an Internet page
> that had quotations from teachers in Cleveland who were
> critical of school policies on discipline, testing, and
> social promotion. This caught my interest because this
> summer I tutored a fifth grade boy named Davis. Davis is
> illiterate and can recognize only short words like "to" and
> "my." I don't know how he could have been promoted to fifth
> grade when he reads on a first grade level, if that. I
> followed other links on social promotion and found an AFT [a
> teachers' union] page about it. I learned that this is a
> controversial topic. I was curious, so I then looked on the
> library's Web page and searched for articles on social
> promotion. The very first site turned up dozens of recent
> articles. Because the topic was controversial and I wanted
> to learn more and there were many sources, I thought this
> would be a good topic [. . .].

Here is another entry from Slade's notebook a few days later:

> [. . .] I found many more articles than books. [Social
> promotion] is in the news and every politician is against it.
> I found a government document about a congressional hearing
> on social promotion, but it was not very helpful [. . .].
> I have three books, including *On the Success of Failure*,
> which was against, and *Flunking Grades*, which was pro. I
> first read editorials critical of social promotion, and I
> thought everyone would be against social promotion, but I
> also read many articles critical of retention. I want to
> present the pros and cons rather than argue for one side
> [. . .].

After more searching with their college library's central information system and online databases, Slade and Eliza had settled on their topics and were ready to write their prospectuses. Slade's prospectus and working bibliography are shown in Figure 11.1. By now he had abandoned his original idea of writing about discipline problems and placed his focus on the debate about whether social promotion is the best way to help failing students.

Healy 1

Jonathan Slade Healy

Research Prospectus

1. Research question: Is social promotion or retention the best policy for coping with student failure?

2. I plan to become a middle school language arts teacher, and I want to know the best ways to cope with students who do not perform at grade level. Because I have tutored a fifth-grade student who reads on a first-grade level, I assumed that "social promotion," the policy of keeping students with their age peers even when they fail, was the cause of many of the problems with schools today. Some of the sources I have found, including many editorial writers and politicians, attack social promotion. Many others, however, such as Mary Lee Smith and Lorrie A. Shepard, argue that retention, the policy of leaving failing students back, is a worse alternative than social promotion. Because the issue is still being debated and there is no consensus, I intend to present the findings and arguments of both sides.

I have found many sources. Because the topic has been in the news lately, I found many recent newspaper and magazine articles, and many were available online. I have also found journal articles and several books. I have checked out the books. I also printed out the online articles and have found others on microfilm.

Figure 11.1 Slade's research prospectus.

Healey 2

3. Working Bibliography

American Federation of Teachers. "Passing on Failure:
    District Promotion Policies and Practices." <u>K-12</u>
    <u>Educational Issues</u>. 13 Oct. 1999 <http://www.aft.
    org/edissues/socialpromotion/Intro.htm>.

Coeyman, Marjorie. "Repeating a Grade Gains Favor in
    Schools." <u>Christian Science Monitor</u> 6 Apr. 1999.
    <u>MasterFILE Premier</u>. EBSCOhost. 15 Oct. 1999 <http://
    www.epnet.com/ehost/>.

Darling-Hammond, Linda. "Avoiding Both Grade Retention and
    Social Promotion." <u>Education Digest</u> Nov. 1998.
    ProQuest. 14 Oct. 1999 <http://
    www.bellhowell.infolearning.com/proquest/>.

"Most Cleveland Teachers Say Social Promotion Doesn't
    Work." <u>Sun Newspapers</u>. 1997. 12 Oct. 1999 <http://
    www.sunnews.com/news/suburbs/metro/
    socialpromotionside.htm>.

Shaw, Donna. "Stopping Social Promotion." <u>Curriculum</u>
    <u>Administrator</u> 35.9 (1999): 7.

Smith, Mary Lee, and Lorrie A. Shepard. "Flunking Grades:
    A Recapitulation." Ed. Lorrie A. Shepard and Mary Lee
    Smith. <u>Flunking Grades: Research and Policies on</u>
    <u>Retention</u>. New York: Falmer, 1989. 214-36.

Ratnesar, Romesh, and Wendy Cole. "Held Back." <u>Time</u> 14
    June 1999. <u>MasterFILE Premier</u>. EBSCOhost. 15 Oct.
    1999 <http://www.epnet.com/ehost/>.

Figure 11.1 *(Continued)*

Healy 3

United States. Senate. Committee on Health, Education,
　　Labor, and Pensions. <u>Hearing on Examining Legislation</u>
　　<u>on Retention and Social Promotion</u>. 106th Cong., 1st
　　sess. Washington: GPO, 1999.

Wood, Daniel B. "California's Big Test: Holding Students
　　Back." <u>Christian Science Monitor</u> 5 Feb. 1999.
　　<u>MasterFILE Premier</u>. EBSCOhost. 15 Oct. 1999 <http://
　　www.epnet.com/ehost/>.

Figure 11.1 *(Continued)*

 ## THE WORKING BIBLIOGRAPHY

A *bibliography* is a list of research sources. One of the last tasks in your search project is to type a *list of works cited* at the end of your paper—a formal bibliography or listing of all the sources you have used in writing it. But this occurs much later in the research process. For now, your task is to continue gathering sources; that is, you need to use the library databases and other research tools described in Chapter 9 to locate books and articles for your paper. The list of possible sources you draw up as you begin your search is your *working bibliography.* You add to the working bibliography during the course of your project as you discover additional sources, and you subtract from it as some sources on the list turn out not to be helpful.

A working bibliography is tentative, informal, and practical. The only requirement for a good working bibliography is that you are able to use it conveniently. Since it is for your own use—not part of the paper itself—you can record the information you need any way you like. For example, when you find a likely book from a subject citation in the library catalog, you can jot down in your notebook the key information that will enable you to locate it—perhaps only its title and call number. On the other hand, there are advantages to including more complete information in your working bibliography, as Slade did, in that you will use this information later, at the end of the project, when you type your works-cited page. Therefore, you can save considerable time by including all the information you may need later. For that reason, it is important for you to be acquainted with the standard conventions for citing sources. Those conventions are detailed in Chapter A of Part II.

Once you have completed your prospectus and have had it approved by your instructor, you are ready to put your sources to work.

 # USING YOUR WRITTEN SOURCES

The early stages of your project may have been easier than you expected. You selected a topic, did some preliminary browsing in the library, and assembled a list of sources to work with. So far so good. But now what? Is there some simple technique that experienced researchers use to get ideas and information *out* of their sources and *into* their writing?

In fact, there is a reasonably uncomplicated and orderly procedure for putting your sources to use, but it isn't exactly simple. You can't just sit down before a stack of sources, read the first one and write part of your paper, then read the second one and write some more, and so on until you are finished. Obviously, such a procedure would make for a very haphazard and disjointed paper.

You can't write your paper all at once. Because you have a substantial body of information to sort through, digest, select, and organize, you have to use good management skills in your project. Your course of action needs to consist of manageable subtasks: You need to (1) *read* your sources efficiently and selectively and (2) *evaluate* the information you find there. As you learn more about your topic, you should (3) *narrow your focus* and (4) *shape a plan* for the paper. And to make use of new ideas and information, you need to (5) *take notes* on what seems important and usable in the sources. Only then are you ready to begin the actual drafting of the paper.

This chapter examines each of these tasks in turn, but do not think of them as separate operations that you can perform one after the other. They must interact. After all, how can you know what to read and take notes on unless you have some plans for what your paper will include? On the other hand, how can you know what your paper will include until your reading reveals to you what information is available? In working on your paper, you can never put your brain on automatic pilot. As you read and learn from your sources, you must continually think about how you can use the information and how using it will fit in with (or alter) your plan for the paper.

Slade and Eliza received an assignment like the following from their instructors.

ASSIGNMENT   **Note Cards and a Preliminary Outline**

Continue your research by reading your sources, evaluating them, taking notes on note cards, narrowing your focus, and shaping a plan (a preliminary outline) for your paper. This is the most time-consuming stage of your research project, so be sure to begin working on it right away. Continue to record your experiences and observations in your research notebook.

Reading Your Sources

At this stage, you need to undertake several tasks, the first of which is to **read your sources.** A research paper should be something new, a fresh synthesis of information and ideas from many sources. A paper that is largely a summary of only one or two sources fails to do this. Become well informed about your topic by reading widely, and use a breadth of information in your paper. Most likely you have found many sources related to your topic, and the sheer volume of available material may itself be a cause for concern. Because your time is limited, you need to use it efficiently. Following are some practical suggestions for efficient reading.

- *Read only those sources that relate to your topic.* Beginning researchers often try to read too much. Do not waste valuable time reading sources that do not relate specifically to your topic. Before reading any source in detail, examine it briefly to be sure of its relevance. Chapter titles in books and section headings or even illustrations in articles may give you a sense of the work's usefulness. If you find dozens of books devoted solely to your topic, that topic probably is too broad to treat in a brief paper, and your focus should be narrowed. (Narrowing your paper's focus is discussed later in this chapter.)

- *Read each source selectively.* Do not expect to read every source from cover to cover; rather, read only those passages that relate to your topic. With a book, for example, use the table of contents in the front and the index in the back to locate relevant passages. Skim through promising sections, looking for passages relating directly to your topic—only these should you read carefully and deliberately.

- *Think as you read.* Ask yourself if what you are reading relates to your topic. Is it important and usable in your paper? Does it raise questions you want to explore further? What additional research do you need to do to answer these questions? Find new sources as needed, discard unusable ones, and update your working bibliography.

- *Read with curiosity.* Do not let your reading become a plodding and mechanical task; don't think of it as plowing through a stack of sources. Make your reading an act of exploration. You want to learn about your topic, and each source holds the potential to answer your questions. Search out answers, and if you don't find them in one source, seek them in another. There are many profitable ways for researchers to think of themselves: as explorers discovering unknown territory, as detectives following a trail of clues, as players fitting together the pieces of an intriguing puzzle.

- *Use your hand as well as your eyes when you read.* If you have photocopied an article or book chapter, underline important passages while reading, and write yourself notes in the margins. (Of course, don't do either of these things unless you own the copy; marking up material belonging to the library or to other people is a grave discourtesy.) Getting your hand into action as you read is a good way of keeping your mind active as well; writing, underlining, and note-taking force you to think about what you are reading. An article from *Business Week* that Eliza photocopied and then annotated is shown in Figure 11.2.

A HARD LESSON ON CREDIT CARDS

Parents of college students beware: The empty-nest syndrome you're experiencing may end up as empty wallet syndrome. The moment your kids step on campus, they become highly sought-after credit-card customers. To establish relationships card marketers hope will extend well beyond the college years, they are offering students everything from free T-shirts to chances to win airline tickets as enticements to sign up.

As a result, college students now have heavy card debts. Some 14% have balances of $3,000 to $7,000, and 10% owe amounts exceeding $7,000, according to Nellie Mae, a nonprofit student-loan provider in Braintree, Mass. "Students who have no history with credit are being handed it on a silver platter," says Gerri Detweiler, education adviser for Debt Counselors of America, a consumer advocacy group in Rockville, Md.

some students have big debts!

As long as they are over 18, students can get a card without asking mom or dad to co-sign. But when they get into debt trouble, they often go running to their folks for help. Jason Britton did—and then some. Now 21 and a senior at Georgetown University in Washington, Britton racked up $21,000 in debt over four years on 16 cards. "When I first started, my attitude was: 'I'll get a job after college to pay off all my debt,' " he says. He realized he dug himself into a hole when he couldn't meet the minimum monthly payments. Now, he works three part-time jobs. His parents are helping pay his tuition and loans. **PITFALLS.** Having educated himself on the pitfalls of credit, Britton now speaks to student groups on the issue. Since card issuers' pitches may be confusing, but he and experts dish out this advice:

■ Beware of *teaser rates.* Credit-card marketers may advertise a low annual percentage rate (APR), but if often jumps substantially.

Card companies give credit knowing parents will pay

example of a student in trouble

Figure 11.2 Annotation of a photocopied source.

• ***Write notes about your reading.*** Use your research notebook to "think on paper" as you read. That is, write general comments about what you have learned from your sources and the ideas you have gained for your paper. Use note cards to write down specific information that you might use in writing your paper. (Note cards are discussed in detail later in this chapter.)

Evaluating Your Sources

All sources are not equally reliable. Not all writers are equally competent; not all periodicals and publishers are equally respected; and not all statements from interviewees are equally well informed. Certainly not every claim that appears in print is true. Because you want to base your paper on the most accurate, up-to-date, and authoritative information available, you need to exercise discretion in ***evaluating your sources.*** Following are some questions you can ask about a source:

• ***Is the publication respectable?*** If you are researching flying-saucer sightings, for example, an article in an astronomy or psychology journal commands far more respect than an article like "My Baby's Daddy Came from a UFO" in a lurid supermarket tabloid. Between these two extremes are popular magazines, which cover a wide range of territory. Information that appears in a news magazine such as *Newsweek* or *U.S. News & World Report* is more likely to be accepted as balanced and well researched than information taken from a less serious publication such as *People* or *Teen*. You must use your judgment about the reliability of your sources. Because sources differ in respectability and prestige, scholars always identify their research sources so as to allow readers to make their own judgments about reliability. (Acknowledging sources is discussed in Chapter B of Part II.) As a general rule, works that identify their sources are more likely to be reliable than those that do not.

• *What are the author's credentials?* Is the author a recognized authority? An astrophysicist writing about the possibility of life in other galaxies will command more respect than, say, an amateur flying-saucer enthusiast who is a retired dentist. Expert sources lend authority to assertions you make in your paper—another reason for the standard practice of identifying your sources to your readers.

• *Is the source presenting firsthand information?* Are the writer's assertions based on primary or secondary research? For example, articles about cancer research in *Reader's Digest* or *Time* may be written with a concern for accuracy and clarity, but their authors may be reporters writing secondhand on the subject—they may not be experts in the field. You can use these sources, but be certain to consider all factors in weighing their reliability.

• *Does the source demonstrate evidence of careful research?* Does the author show by way of notes and other documentation that the statements presented are based on the best available information? Or does it appear that the author's statements derive from unsupported speculation or incomplete research? A source that seems unreliable should either not be used at all or else be cited as an example of one point of view (perhaps one that you refute using more reliable sources).

• *Is the source up-to-date?* Clearly you do not want to base your paper on information that is no longer considered accurate and complete. For example, a paper on a dynamic field such as nuclear disarmament or advances in telecommunications would be hopelessly out-of-date if it is based on five-year-old sources. If you are writing a paper on a topic about which new findings or theories exist, your research should include recent sources. Check the publication dates of your sources.

• *Does the source seem biased?* Writers have opinions that they support in their writing, but some writers are more open-minded than others. Is the author's purpose in writing to explain or to persuade? Does the author provide a balanced presentation of evidence, or are there other perspectives and evidence that the author ignores? Be aware of the point of view of the author and of the publication you are examining. An article in a magazine of political opinion such as *National Review* can be expected to take a conservative stance on an issue, just as an article in *The Nation* will express a more liberal opinion. Your own paper, even when you are making an argument for a particular viewpoint, should present evidence for all sides. If you use opinionated sources, you can balance them with sources expressing opposing points of view.

• *Do your sources consider all viewpoints and theories?* Because many books and articles are written from a single viewpoint, it is important to read widely to discover if other points of view exist as well. For example, several works have been written claiming that ancient monuments such as the pyramids are evidence of past visits to our planet by extraterrestrials. Only by checking a variety of sources might a student discover that scientists have discredited most of the evidence on which these claims are based. Students writing about such topics as astrology, subliminal advertising, Noah's flood, holistic healing, Bigfoot, or the assassination of President Kennedy should be aware that these areas are controversial and that they should seek out diverse points of view in their research so they can be fully informed and can present a complete picture of the topic to their readers.

Narrowing Your Paper's Focus

If you are like most students, the research paper assigned in your composition course may be the longest paper you have had to write, so you may feel worried about filling enough pages. Most students share that concern at this stage, but they soon find so much material that having *too much* to say (not too little) becomes their concern.

The ideal topic for your paper is one to which you can do justice—one you can write about with some thoroughness and completeness—in a paper of the length you are assigned. Most student researchers start out with a fairly broad conception of their topic and then make it more and more limited as their research and writing progress. As you learn how much information is available about your topic and as you discover through your reading what aspect most intrigues you, you should *narrow your paper's focus*—that is, bring your topic into a sharper and more limited scope.

From your first speculations about a topic until the completion of your final draft, your topic will probably undergo several transformations, usually with each new version more narrowly defined than the one before. For example, Slade Healy's clustering exercise on page 272 shows his thought processes as he was deciding on a topic. He began with the general idea of *middle schools,* since he planned to be a teacher. He then considered several general aspects of middle-school teaching, including *special students.* He then considered several specific types of special students, including *poor learners.* Next he focused more specifically on failing grades, which he later narrowed further to his ultimate topic, *social promotion.* As the following diagram indicates, his discovery of a topic moved from a more general (broader) focus to a more specific (narrower) focus.

Broader topic

Narrower topic

Middle schools

Special students

Poor learners

Failing grades

Social promotion

As another example of a topic becoming more sharply focused, a student might begin with the general concept of her major, oceanography, and narrow it through successive stages as follows:

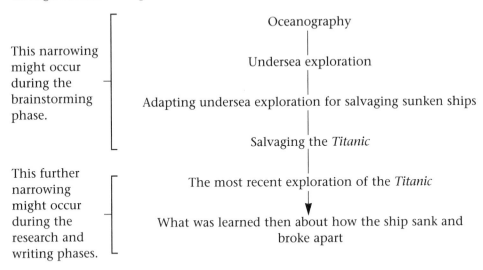

This narrowing might occur during the brainstorming phase.

Oceanography

Undersea exploration

Adapting undersea exploration for salvaging sunken ships

Salvaging the *Titanic*

This further narrowing might occur during the research and writing phases.

The most recent exploration of the *Titanic*

What was learned then about how the ship sank and broke apart

Narrowing a Topic

1. Speculate on how each of the following general topics might be successively narrowed in the course of a research project. Write each topic in your notebook, and beneath it give three or four additional topics, each more specific and more narrowly focused than the one above it. (For example, if you were given the topic *oceanography,* you might create a list something like the one above.)

   Warfare   Music   Famous people   Luxury goods

2. Now take your own research topic and make a general-to-specific list of its successive stages. First list the most general idea you started with and show how it narrowed to your present topic. Then speculate on how your topic might be narrowed even further as you complete work on your project.

Formulating and Refining a Plan

Writing is never an exact science or a tidy procedure, and the business of planning and organizing is the untidiest part of all. It would be nice if you could start by creating a full-blown outline of your paper, then take notes on the areas you have outlined, and finally write your paper from your notes, exactly as first planned. However, any writer can tell you it rarely if ever works that way.

Research papers evolve as you do research, and they continue to evolve as you write them, so it is important to remain flexible. As you learn more about your subject—as you read and take notes, and even as you begin writing—new directions will suggest themselves to you. Be prepared to adjust the focus and organization of your paper at every stage, right up to your final revision. Many a student has expected to write one paper, only to discover something quite different actually taking shape on the page. There is nothing wrong with making these changes—they are a natural part of the writing process. Writing is as much a process of discovery for the writer as it is a medium for communicating with readers.

As you start examining your sources, you may have only a hazy notion of the eventual contents of your paper, but the beginnings of a plan should emerge as you learn more and more. Shortly into your research you should be ready to pause and sketch a very general ***informal preliminary outline*** of where your paper seems to be going. Slade's first rough outline, shown in Figure 11.3, makes no pretense of being complete or final or even particularly pretty—nor should it at this stage. Slade was "thinking on paper," making sense of his own thoughts and trying to bring some vague ideas into focus. He was doing it for his own benefit, not trying to impress any outside readers. Having established some sense of his paper's parts, Slade was then able to resume reading and taking notes with greater efficiency. He now had a clearer idea of what he was looking for. He was also aware that the organization of his paper would probably change as he continued writing.

Begin with a very general outline, perhaps listing just a few of the main topics you expect your paper to include. As you continue reading, taking notes, and

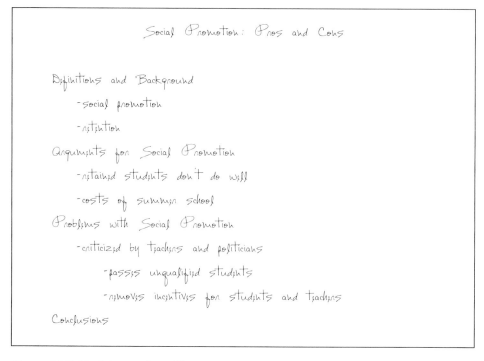

Figure 11.3 Slade's rough outline.

thinking, your outline may become more fleshed out, as you continue to refine your preliminary plans. Remember that an informal outline is an aid to you in organizing and writing your paper. It is not a part of the paper and does not need to be in any kind of polished, orderly form. A formal outline, if you do one, can be written as one of the last steps of your project. (Formal outlines are discussed in Chapter C of Part II.)

Taking Notes on Note Cards

Clearly, you cannot put into your paper everything you read in the course of your research. Some sources will be more useful than others, but still you will use only a small portion of any one source. Note-taking is a way of selecting what you can use. It is also a way of aiding your memory and storing the information and ideas you find in a convenient form for use when you write the paper.

Good notes, then, have the virtue of being both selective and accessible. You could take notes in your notebook, but a notebook is far less easy to work with than *note cards,* which have the advantage of flexibility. Unlike entries in notebooks or on long sheets of paper, notes on index cards can be easily sorted, rearranged, and weeded out. When you are ready to write, you can group note cards according to topics and arrange them in the order in which you expect to use them in the paper. This greatly simplifies the task of writing.

Besides being selective and convenient, good notes have another quality—accuracy. You are obliged as a scholar to be scrupulously accurate in reporting and acknowledging your sources. In research writing, you must quote your sources accurately and paraphrase them fairly. (Quoting and paraphrasing sources are discussed more fully in Chapter 12.) Moreover, you should give credit to sources for their contributions and make it clear to your readers which words in the paper are your own and which are taken directly from sources. You can use your sources fairly and accurately only if you write from notes that you have taken with great care.

For an example of how a writer takes notes, look first at this passage that Slade read in one of his sources, "Where is Lake Wobegon, Anyway?" an article by Richard Rothstein that appeared in *Phi Delta Kappan:*

> The effect of retention of those who do move on is equally serious. One of our concerns with contemporary American young people is their too-rapid psychosexual development. Puberty now begins earlier than it has in the past. Putting 14-year-olds in classrooms with 11- and 12-year-olds will exacerbate the pressures these younger adolescents face. Putting 16-year-olds in classrooms with 13-year-olds will do the same. While grouping children by age does cause academic problems, grouping children of varied ages together because of comparable academic skill is not a completely benign alternative. It causes other problems for teachers, parents, and children alike.
>
> Ask a seventh-grade teacher whose students are normally about 12 years old if she wants last year's sixth-graders in her class if they didn't master sixth-grade material, and she will probably say, "Certainly not." This is the kind of survey that the AFT conducted. But ask the same teacher if she wants last year's seventh graders in her class this year because they didn't master seventh-grade material, and she will just as adamantly object.[. . .]

A passage from a source

Here is the note card that Slade made for this passage:

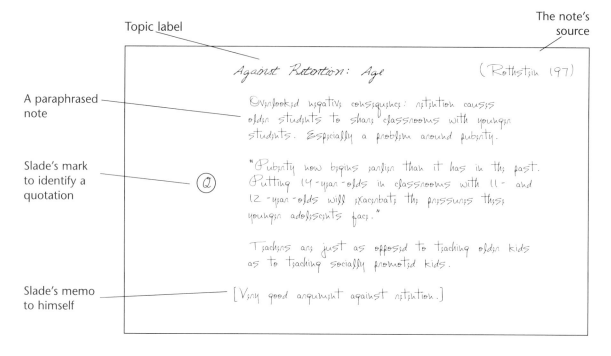

Topic label

The note's source

A paraphrased note

Slade's mark to identify a quotation

Slade's memo to himself

Later, when Slade wrote his paper, he used this card to write the following:

Slade's use of the note card in his paper

        Still another consequence of retention is the negative
effects on younger children of having older children in the
same classroom. Richard Rothstein, a critic of educational
policies, observes: "Puberty now begins earlier than it has
in the past. Putting 14-year-olds in classrooms with 11- and
12-year-olds will exacerbate the pressures these younger
adolescents face." While teachers do not want socially
promoted students in their classrooms, they are just as
likely to object to teaching retained students who are older
than the other students in their classes (Rothstein 197).

There are various systems for taking notes on cards, and you should use consistently a system that meets your needs. All good note-card systems have several features in common. In making note cards you should follow these guidelines:

- *Put no more than one unit of information on a note card.* That is, use one card for each important fact or idea. (If you try to economize by crowding many unrelated notes from a source onto a single card, you will sacrifice flexibility later when you try to sort the cards by subjects.) Some cards may contain long notes, whereas others may contain only a word or two. One source may provide you with notes on a dozen different cards, whereas another may give you only a single note (or no notes at all).

- *Label each card by topic.* A topic label helps you remember what a note card is about so that after you have finished taking notes from all your sources, you can easily arrange your cards according to topic. Slade selected the label *AGAINST RETENTION—AGE*, writing it in the upper left corner of the card. Similar labels appeared on two other cards that Slade prepared while reading different sources. When he was ready to organize his notes, Slade gathered these three cards together, discarded one of them that he knew he would not use, and arranged the remaining two in the order he was likely to use them in a first draft of his paper.

  You should consider following a procedure similar to Slade's. Whenever you take a note, consider where within your subject the information might fit and give the note a label. The label may correspond to one of the divisions in your preliminary outline. If it does not, that may suggest that the organization of your paper is developing and changing and that you need to expand or revise your outline to reflect those changes.

- *Identify the source of each note precisely.* In the upper right corner of his note card, Slade identified his note's source: *(Rothstein 197).* This is an example of a parenthetical note (explained in Chapter B of Part II), and its purpose is to tell Slade that the information on the card comes from page 197 of the article written by Rothstein. Slade had recorded the full information about that source in his working bibliography, so he needed only the author's last name to identify it.

  It is important for each note card to contain all the information you will need in order to cite its source when you write your paper—so you can give the source credit in a parenthetical note. You will find nothing more frustrating as a researcher than having to search through sources at the last minute to find a page reference for a passage that you forgot to identify on a note card. It is smart to identify each source, as Slade did, just as you will identify it in the paper itself—with a parenthetical note. For that reason, you should consult Chapter B before you begin taking notes.

- *Clearly identify the kind of information your note contains.* Three principal kinds of information can appear on note cards; you must make it clear which is which, so you do not get confused later if you use the card in writing the paper:

  –**Direct quotations.** The passage "Puberty now begins . . . " on Slade's card is quoted directly from the author, Richard Rothstein. *Any time you put a source's own words on a note card, place them within quotation marks.* Do so even if everything on the card is a quotation. It is essential that when you read a note card later, you can tell whether the words are a direct quotation or your own paraphrase of the source. For this reason, you might even use a backup procedure for identifying quotes, as Slade did. He put a circled Q next to each quotation on his cards to be doubly sure he knew these were his source's exact words.

–**Your own comments.** When you write a note from a source, it may inspire some additional thoughts of your own that you will want to jot down. You may also want to remind yourself later of how you intend to use the note in your paper. *Put your own comments in brackets.* For example, at the bottom of Slade's note card, he wrote a note to himself about where he might use the material in his paper: "[Very good argument . . .]." He placed these comments in brackets to alert himself that these were his own ideas, not those of his source.

–**Paraphrase.** Like Slade's, your cards should consist largely of paraphrases of what you have found in your sources. *Anything on a card that is not in quotation marks or in brackets is assumed to be your paraphrasing of the source.* To paraphrase, recast the source's words into your own language, using your own phrasing and style.

• *Be selective in your note-taking.* Because many beginning researchers fear they will not have enough material to use in writing their papers, they often take too many notes. When it comes time to write the paper, they soon discover that if they were to make use of every note, their paper would be dozens of pages long. In fact, for each student who cannot find enough source material for a paper, many others discover to their surprise that they have more than enough.

With experience, researchers learn to be selective, restricting their note-taking to material they stand a good chance of using. Of course, no one makes use of every note card. Especially in the early stages of reading, a researcher does not have a clear notion of what the paper will include or of what information is available. As reading continues, however, hazy notions become more substantial, and the researcher can take notes more selectively.

Figure 11.4 shows two cards that Eliza Tetirick wrote when she read the *Business Week* article, an excerpt of which is shown on page 312.

 ## AVOIDING PLAGIARISM

To ensure that you use your sources fairly and accurately, you should observe one additional guideline when you take notes: *Do your paraphrasing on the note card, not later.* If you do not intend to use a source's exact words, do not write those words on your card. (When you should and should not quote a source directly is discussed on pages 345–49.) It is wise to translate important information into your own words right after you read. This will save time and help you avoid unintentional *plagiarism*—using the source's words without quotation marks—when you begin to write from your notes. Paraphrasing and summarizing your sources now will also give you more focused notes, as well as force you to read and analyze your sources more carefully.

Since you cannot use everything in your sources, no matter how interesting, it is often necessary to boil down what you find into brief summaries of what is

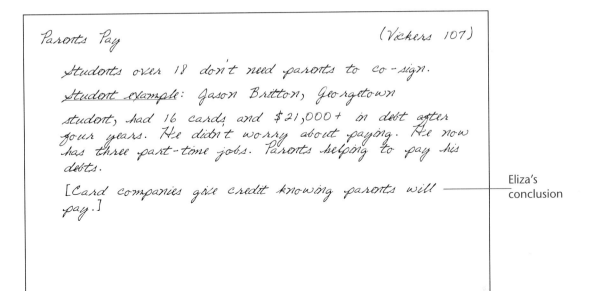

Parents Pay   (Vickers 107)

Students over 18 don't need parents to co-sign.

<u>Student example</u>: Jason Britton, Georgetown student, had 16 cards and $21,000+ in debt after four years. He didn't worry about paying. He now has three part-time jobs. Parents helping to pay his debts.

[Card companies give credit knowing parents will ——— Eliza's
pay.]   conclusion

Debt Statistics   (Vickers 107)

Many students have big debts:
14% owe $3000 - $7000
10% owe more than $7000
    —source: Nellie Mae, nonprofit student-loan
    provider.

Figure 11.4 Two additional note cards.

important. In general, the procedure for paraphrasing and summarizing a source is as follows:

1. When you have discovered a passage that you may want to use in your paper, reread it with care.

2. After you have reread it, put it aside and think about the essential idea you have learned. Then write that idea on your card in a brief version, using

your own words and style. It is often best not to look at the passage while you write the note, so as to be less likely to plagiarize the original language.

Do not forget to indicate on your note card the specific source of the paraphrase. Consider how Slade wrote the note card that appears on page 318. First, reread the exact words of his source, Richard Rothstein:

The original source

> Ask a seventh-grade teacher whose students are normally about 12 years old if she wants last year's sixth-graders in her class if they didn't master sixth-grade material, and she will probably say, "Certainly not." This is the kind of survey that the AFT conducted. But ask the same teacher if she wants last year's seventh graders in her class this year because they didn't master seventh-grade material, and she will just as adamantly object.

If Slade had written a note like the following, instead of his actual note card, he might have plagiarized the passage when he used the note card to write his paper:

A plagiarized note

> Seventh-grade teachers do not want to teach last year's sixth-graders who haven't mastered sixth-grade material. AFT's survey asked only this question. But these same teachers would object just as strenuously to having to teach last year's seventh graders who didn't master seventh-grade material.

Notice how this passage—while it selects from the original, changes some words, and rearranges phrases—relies too closely on Rothstein's original wording. In contrast, Slade's note succinctly summarizes his understanding of Rothstein's ideas in Slade's own words:

A legitimate note

> Teachers are just as opposed to teaching older kids as to teaching socially promoted kids.

Putting source information into your own words does *not* mean substituting a few synonyms now and again as you copy your source's sentence onto your note card. For example, consider how it would be possible to misuse the following sentence from the passage by Richard Rothstein, quoted earlier:

The source's words.

> One of our concerns with contemporary American young people is their too-rapid psychosexual development. Puberty now begins earlier than it has in the past. Putting 14-year-olds in classrooms with 11- and 12-year-olds will exacerbate the pressures these younger adolescents face.

A plagiarized note

> One concern we have with modern young people in America is their accelerated psychosexual growth. Puberty now has its onset earlier than it did in previous ages. If 14-year-old students are put into classes with 12-year-olds, the pressures faced by these younger children will be intensified.

Observe that this is really the Rothstein sentence with a few word substitutions (*modern* for *contemporary, growth* for *development,* and so on). Putting sources aside when you write note cards is one way to avoid this plagiarism-by-substitution. It also ensures that your paraphrase will be a genuine expression of your own understanding of a source's idea. Of course, if the exact words are particularly memorable or effective, you may wish to copy them down exactly, within quotation marks, for possible use in your paper. Notice how Slade has done this with two sentences: *"Puberty now begins earlier than it has in the past. Putting 14-year-olds in classrooms with 11- and 12-year-olds will exacerbate the pressures these younger adolescents face."* When it was time to use this note, it was clear to Slade that this was a direct quotation from his source, and he properly quoted it in his paper.

The foregoing can be summed up as follows:

GUIDELINES for Avoiding Plagiarism

1. Whenever you use ideas or information from a source but do not intend to quote the source directly, paraphrase the source. You must restate the material in your own words, using your own phrasing and style. Merely substituting synonyms for the source's words or phrases is not acceptable. Do your paraphrasing at the time you take notes.

2. Whenever you intend to use the source's words, copy those words exactly onto a note card and place them within quotation marks. To be doubly sure that you will not later mistake the author's words for your own, place a circled letter *Q* (or some other prominent device) on the card next to the quotation.

3. For any borrowed material—whether a direct quotation or your paraphrase of it—carefully note the source and page number(s) on your note card so that you can cite them in your paper.

4. In your paper, you will give full credit to the sources of all borrowed material, both those you quote directly and those you paraphrase. The only exception is for commonly available factual information. (For further guidelines, see the section "When Are Notes Needed?" in Chapter B of Part II.)

5. Observe the rules for acknowledging sources in your paper by providing acknowledgment phrases, parenthetical notes, and a list of works cited. (Further information about giving credit to sources can be found in Chapter 6 and Chapter B.)

Note Taking   EXERCISES

Following are passages that Eliza Tetirick encountered in her research into credit cards. Suppose that you were researching the same topic. Using the guidelines provided in this chapter, write notes for these sources. On your note cards, you may want to paraphrase some passages, quote others, and offer your own comments or responses. You may take more than one note from a passage.

1. The following selection is from an online article by Lucy Lazarony, "Myths about Credit Card Debt," which was posted on the CBS MarketWatch Web site. Write a note card that captures Lazarony's advice. Include a passage that you might quote in your paper.

    Pay Bill Right Away

    [. . . D]on't forget to make on-time payments on your credit cards. Mom and Dad may have advised you to hold on to your money as long as possible when paying monthly bills, but that is not a wise strategy when it comes to credit cards. The cost of being late is too high.

    Late fees on credit cards have climbed to $29, but they're only the beginning. A late payment or two will usually mean that you get slapped with an increased interest rate—20 percent more. Plus, paying late hurts your credit rating, limiting your ability to get a good loan when you need it.

    So pay your bill as soon as it arrives. If the due date falls at a time in the month when money is tight, call the card company and get it moved to another date.

2. Lisa Toloken wrote an article, "Turning the Tables on Campus," in the trade magazine *Credit Card Management.* The following passage, about "tabling," the practice by some colleges of allowing credit-card companies to set tables on campus to market cards to students, appeared on page 76.

    Although third-party marketers bear the brunt of school officials' wrath about debt-laden students, only 24% of college students receive their first card from an on-campus representative, according to The Education Resources Institute Inc. (TERI) at the Washington, D.C.-based Institute for Higher Education Policy. TERI, a nonprofit organization, is a private guarantor of student loans and engages in educational policy and research activities.

    According to TERI, 37% of students apply for their first card through the mail, apparently in response to solicitations. Thirty-six percent apply for a card after picking up a take-one application at a business. Still, tabling gives card issuers high visibility on campus. Thus, some issuers and third-party marketers are trying to keep their place on campus by directly appealing to college officials and stressing the consumer information they provide along with solicitations. Students are prime credit card candidates because marketers say consumers are loyal to the issuers who grant them their first cards, often carrying that loyalty into their prime family-building and spending years. Today, almost two-thirds of all college students have at least one credit card, with one in five having four or more cards, according to TERI.

Before reading your sources and taking notes, you should consult the following chapter, where conventions of quoting and paraphrasing are more fully explained. Chapter B of Part II demonstrates appropriate ways of acknowledging sources with parenthetical notes.

12 *Reporting on Sources: Paraphrase and Quotation*

Mostly when you *do* research on sources, you find out what other people have thought, discovered, said, or written. When you *report* on your research, you tell your readers what you have learned. The following very different passages could all be called examples of reporting on research sources.

1. My old man says he can lick your old man.
2. "If man does find the solution for world peace," wrote General George C. Marshall in 1945, "it will be the most revolutionary reversal of his record we have ever known."
3. Senator Woodling made it clear today that she would shortly declare herself a candidate for the presidency.
4. The first words ever transmitted by telephone were spoken by Bell to his assistant: "Mr. Watson, come here, I want you."
5. The Stoics argued that it was the highest wisdom to accept triumph without elation, tribulation without regret.
6. V. O. Key, Jr., a leading political scientist, offered this positive assessment of the role played by interest groups in American politics:

   > At bottom, group interests are the animating forces in the political process [. . .]. The chief vehicles for the expression of group interest are political parties and pressure groups. Through these formal mechanisms groups of people with like interests make themselves felt in the balancing of political forces. (Qtd. in Lowery 63–64)

These six passages all report on sources, since each of them communicates what has been learned from someone else. They certainly do so in different ways and with different effects. The first statement, you might guess, is spoken by one child to another, reporting on what he learned from his father. As for its authority, a listener might be wise to doubt that his father said any such thing. The last statement, in contrast, is surely an example of writing, not speech, since it has all the earmarks of a passage from a scholarly paper or article. Its very form, its direct quotation, its acknowledgment of its source and claim for his expertise (*V. O. Key, Jr., a leading political scientist*), and its careful source citation (*Qtd. in Lowery 63–64;* that is, the quotation was found on those pages in a work by Lowery) all lend it an impressive authority. The four middle passages could be either spoken or written.

There are other differences among them as well. Passages 2, 4, and 6 all present their sources' words through ***direct quotation,*** with the original language repeated in a word-for-word copy. Passages 1, 3, and 5, on the other hand, ***paraphrase*** their sources, with the source's ideas and information recast in different words. The identity of the sources in each statement is generally clear, although we are not told where the author of passage 5 learned about the Stoic philosophy; still, it is evident that the ideas presented are those of the Stoics and not the author. Of all these passages, however, only number 6 with its ***parenthetical note*** gives a careful ***citation*** of its source, the exact location from which the quotation was taken.

 ## THE CONVENTIONS OF REPORTING

Like the reporting of journalists, the reporting of scholars aims to get at and present the truth. To ensure accuracy and clarity, both types of writing follow careful rules and procedures.

Often these practices are identical in both fields. Both journalism and scholarship, for example, require that sources be acknowledged and identified. Both pay scant attention to unsupported opinions. On the other hand, both pay great respect to expert testimony. In reporting on sources, both fields observe the same time-honored conventions, including rules for paraphrasing, quoting, and even punctuating quotations. If there is one outstanding difference between scholarship and journalism, however, it is that scholarly writing, with its careful conventions of documentation, follows even more stringent procedures for identifying the precise sources from which ideas and information are taken.

This chapter is in large part devoted to these conventions. While some of it involves technicalities (e.g., does a comma go to the left or right of a quotation mark?), even they are important extensions of the care that researchers take to be accurate and truthful. While you are expected to become familiar with most of the conventions here, you should also regard this chapter as a resource that you can turn to often throughout your college career for guidance in presenting the results of your research.

 ## OPTIONS FOR PRESENTING SOURCES

Whenever you report on your research, you need to find a way of presenting to your readers what you have learned from your sources. Sometimes the appropriate method will be paraphrase; at other times, quotation. In fact, you have several options.

Imagine, for example, that in an introductory anthropology course, your instructor has assigned a research paper in which you are to analyze some aspect of American culture. You have chosen to write about the way Americans express their emotions, and in your research you come upon the following passage from page 248 of Ashley Montagu's book, *The American Way of Life*:

> To be human is to weep. The human species is the only one in the whole of animated nature that sheds tears. The trained inability of any human being to weep

is a lessening of his capacity to be human—a defect which usually goes deeper than the mere inability to cry. And this, among other things, is what American parents—with the best intentions in the world—have achieved for the American male. It is very sad. If we feel like it, let us all have a good cry—and clear our minds of those cobwebs of confusion which have for so long prevented us from understanding the ineluctable necessity of crying.

The passage expresses an interesting opinion—that American men have been trained, unnaturally, not to cry—and you want to use it in your paper. You can do so in many ways; the following are examples of your options.

Paraphrase

You can restate an author's ideas in your own words:

> Montagu claims that American men have a diminished capacity
> to be human because they have been trained by their culture
> not to cry (248).

Direct Quotation of a Sentence

You can quote an author's exact words, as in these three examples:

> In his book, The American Way of Life, Ashley Montagu writes,
> "The trained inability of any human being to weep is a
> lessening of his capacity to be human--a defect which usually
> goes deeper than the mere inability to cry" (248).

> According to Montagu, "To be human is to weep" (248).

> "If we feel like it," writes Ashley Montagu, "let us all
> have a good cry--and clear our minds of those cobwebs of
> confusion which have for so long prevented us from
> understanding the ineluctable necessity of crying" (248).

Quoting Part of a Sentence

You can incorporate part of an author's sentence into a sentence of your own:

> One distinguished anthropologist calls the American male's
> reluctance to cry "a lessening of his capacity to be human"
> (Montagu 248).

> Montagu finds it "very sad" that American men have a "trained
> inability" to shed tears (248).

Quoting Longer Passages

You can quote more than one sentence:

> Anthropologist Ashley Montagu argues that it is both
>
> unnatural and harmful for American males not to cry:
>
>> To be human is to weep [. . .]. The trained
>>
>> inability of any human being to weep is a
>>
>> lessening of his capacity to be human--a defect
>>
>> which usually goes deeper than the mere inability
>>
>> to cry [. . .]. It is very sad. (248)

In this chapter, we will study these options in some detail. We will first examine the precise methods of presenting sources through paraphrase and quotation. Afterward, we will look at strategies for using sources: when and where to use the options at our disposal. Chapter B of Part II considers the techniques for citing these sources in parenthetical notes.

 ## ACKNOWLEDGING SOURCES

Whether you paraphrase or quote an author, it is important that you make it clear that it is the author's ideas, not your own, you are presenting. This is necessary for the sake of clarity and fairness—so that the reader knows which words, ideas, and discoveries are yours and which are your source's. Parenthetical notes, which cite a page reference and, if needed, the author's name, do that. Notice, too, that each of the preceding examples makes its indebtedness to its source clear through an *acknowledgment phrase,* such as "Montagu claims that. . . ." Other acknowledgment phrases that we might have used include the following:

Acknowledgment phrases

> Ashley Montagu maintains that . . .
>
> Ashley Montagu, author of <u>The American Way of Life</u>,
>
>> says that . . .
>
> Montagu also believes that . . .
>
> Professor Montagu argues that . . .
>
> According to Ashley Montagu, the eminent
>
>> anthropologist, American men . . .

A quotation should never be placed in a paper without acknowledgment. Even a parenthetical note is not enough to identify a quotation. You must always introduce a quotation, telling your readers something about it. Avoid writing passages like this with a "naked" quotation in the middle:

```
When my grandfather died, all the members of my family--men

and women alike--wept openly.  We have never been ashamed to          Bad:
                                                                       unacknowledged
cry.  "To be human is to weep" (Montagu 248).  I am sure we            quotation

are more human, and in better mental and physical health,

because we are able to express our feelings without

artificial restraints.
```

Even though the parenthetical note identifies the source, readers find it awkward to read a quotation without knowing its origin in advance. Forcing them to skip ahead to find the note creates an undesirable interruption of the flow of the paper. These problems would not arise if the writer had used a simple phrase (e.g., *As anthropologist Ashley Montagu observed,*) to introduce the quotation:

```
When my grandfather died, all the members of my family--men

and women alike--wept openly.  We have never been ashamed to

cry.  As anthropologist Ashley Montagu observed, "To be human    Better:
                                                                  acknowledged
is to weep" (248).  I am sure we are more human, and in           quotation

better mental and physical health, because we are able to

express our feelings without artificial restraints.
```

Not only does the reader better understand the quotation's function with the introductory phrase, but the quotation has more impact as well because it has been attributed to a recognized authority.

Always give your readers enough information to identify your sources. The first time you refer to a source, give both the person's first and last names. Unless the source is a well-known figure, identify him or her so that the reader can understand why this particular person is being quoted.

```
Winston Churchill said, . . .                                    First references

Cynthia Bathurst, author of The Computer Crisis,

     believes that . . .

According to Valerie Granville, British ambassador to

     Bhutan during the Sherpa Riots, . . .

Rock star Mick Jagger gave a flip answer: . . .
```

After the first reference, the source's last name is sufficient:

```
Churchill said that . . .                                        Subsequent
                                                                 references
Later Jagger remarked, . . .
```

Although acknowledgment phrases almost always introduce quotations, they are sometimes unnecessary with paraphrased material. As a general rule, use an acknowledgment phrase when the paraphrased material represents an original idea or opinion of the source, when the source's credentials lend the material authority, or when you wish to distance yourself from opinions with which you disagree.

Acknowledgment phrase for paraphrased material

```
Anthropologist Ashley Montagu argues that crying is a

distinctively human activity--as appropriate and necessary

for males as for females (248).
```

However, an acknowledgment phrase is not needed for largely factual information, as in these passages:

No acknowledgment phrase is needed for factual information

```
At one point in his life, even Alex Haley, the author of

Roots, possessed only eighteen cents and two cans of sardines

(Powell 179).

One study has found that firstborns score better in

achievement tests that measure language and mathematics

skills (Weiss 51).
```

In such cases, the parenthetical notes provide adequate recognition of sources. (Parenthetical notes are discussed in Chapter B of Part II.) Use your best judgment about whether an acknowledgment phrase is called for with paraphrased material. When in doubt, however, provide the acknowledgment phrase. It is better to err on the side of *over-* rather than *under-*recognition of your sources.

RELYING ON EXPERTS

Besides being fair, acknowledging the contribution of a source can also add force to your own writing. In most cases, the sources you present will have greater expertise than you on the subject; a statement from one of them can command greater respect than an unsupported statement from you, a nonexpert. To illustrate this, assume that, in writing a research paper, you quote Montagu on the subject of crying and identify him to your readers as an eminent anthropologist. Could you have made the point equally effectively if instead you had written the following?

```
I think it is wrong that men in America have been brought up

to think it is not manly to cry.  Crying is natural.  Our

macho-man mentality takes a terrible toll on our emotions.
```

While you are entitled to your opinions, a reader who doubts your expertise on the subject is likely to question whether you have considered all aspects and implications of your position. After all, what reason does the reader have to trust you? However, when an expert such as Montagu is quoted, many of the doubts are removed and the statement carries greater weight.

This is not to say that experts are automatically right. Experts do not always agree with each other, and progress in humanity's quest for truth often comes as new ideas are introduced to challenge old ones. What it does mean is that experts are people who have studied their subjects thoroughly and have earned the right to be listened to with respect. Since you will not often begin with a thorough knowledge of the subjects you write about in research papers, your writing will rely heavily on what you have learned from expert sources.

 ## PARAPHRASING SOURCES

Most of the time when you present ideas or information from sources, you will paraphrase them. To *paraphrase* a statement or a piece of writing is to recast it into different words. Paraphrase is the least cumbersome way of communicating what a source has said, as well as the easiest to read. Often the source is too technical for your readers or too wordy; you can present the source's point more clearly and succinctly using your own words. When you paraphrase a source, be accurate and faithful to what your source wrote, but use your own style and phrasing. Imagine, for example, that you wished to make use of this passage as a research source:

> Nearly forty years ago Damon Runyon nearly collapsed in laughter when he covered the trial of George McManus, a gambler, who was accused of shooting Arnold Rothstein, another gambler, who thereupon died. The cause of Damon Runyon's mirth was the sight of the witnesses and jurors in the case running out into the halls during court recesses to place bets with their bookies—even as they considered the evils of gambling in the city.
> —Edwin P. Hoyt, *The Golden Rot*

You can paraphrase this information in a briefer version, using your words:

```
According to Edwin P. Hoyt, Damon Runyon was highly amused          Good

that both witnesses and jurors in a gambling trial would

place bets with their bookies during court recesses.
```

What you must *not* do is simply change a word or two while keeping the structure of the original intact:

```
Edwin P. Hoyt writes that about forty years ago Damon Runyon        Bad

almost fell down from laughing when he was a reporter for

the trial of gambler George McManus, accused of murdering

another gambler, Arnold Rothstein.
```

You can avoid word-substitution paraphrase, as well as unintentional plagiarism, if you paraphrase from memory rather than directly from the original copy. Chapters 3 and 11 describe the best method as follows: *Read the passage so that you understand it; then put it aside, and write your recollection of its meaning on a note card, in your own words.* Be certain to observe the guidelines for avoiding plagiarism (see page 323).

| EXERCISE | **Paraphrasing a Source** |

Imagine that each of the following is a source for a research project. Write a paraphrase of important information from each quotation as you would on a note card. Then write it as you would in the paper itself, giving credit to your source with a suitable acknowledgment phrase. *(Note:* You do not need to present all of the information from each passage in either your paraphrases or your acknowledgments.)

a. *Source:* Linus Pauling. He won Nobel Prizes for both Chemistry (1954) and Peace (1962).

    Quotation:
    Science is the search for truth—it is not a game in which one tries to beat his opponent, to do harm to others. We need to have the spirit of science in international affairs, to make the conduct of international affairs the effort to find the right solution, the just solution of international problems, not the effort by each nation to get the better of other nations, to do harm to them when it is possible.

b. *Source:* Edwin P. Hoyt. This quotation is from his book, *The Golden Rot: A Somewhat Opinionated View of America,* published in 1964.

    Quotation:
    Let there be no mistake, the pressures on government for destruction of wilderness areas will grow every time the nation adds another million in population. The forest service has been fighting such pressures in the West for fifty years. Any national forest visitor can gauge the degree of success of the "multiple use program" of the forest service very nicely by taking a fishing rod and setting out to catch some trout. He will find mile after mile of the public waters posted by private landowners who do not allow fishing or hunting on their property—or on the government property they lease. Inevitably this includes the best beaver dams and open stretches of water along the streams.

c. *Source:* Marvin Harris. He is an anthropology professor and author of several books on human behavior throughout the world.

    Quotation:
    The trouble with the "confessions" is that they were usually obtained while the accused witch was being tortured. Torture was routinely applied until the witch confessed to having made a pact with the Devil and having flown to a sabbat [a witches' meeting]. It was continued until the witch named the other people who were present at the sabbat. If a witch attempted to retract a confession, torture was applied even more intensely until the original confession was reconfirmed. This left a person accused of witchcraft with the choice of dying once and for all at the stake or being returned repeatedly to the torture chambers. Most people opted for the stake. As a reward for their cooperative attitude, penitent witches could look forward to being strangled before the fire was lit.

d. *Source:* Jessica Mitford. She was a well-known muckraker, an investigative journalist who specialized in exposing scandals and abuses.

    Quotation:
    True, a small minority of undertakers are beginning to face the facts and to exhibit more flexibility in their approach to customers, even to develop some understanding and respect for people who as a matter of principle do not want the full funerary

treatment ordinarily prescribed by the industry. But the industry as a whole, and par-ticularly the association leaders, are unable to come to grips with the situation that confronts them today because their whole operation rests on a myth: the assump-tion that they have the full and unqualified backing of the vast majority of the Amer-ican people, that the costly and lavish funeral of today, with all its fabulous trimmings, is but a reflection of American insistence on "the best" in all things. It is particularly hard for them to grasp the idea that a person who has lived well or even luxuriously might *prefer* the plainest disposition after death.

 ## QUOTING SOURCES

In research writing, sources are quoted less often than they are paraphrased, but quotation is more complicated and requires more explanation.

Punctuating Quotations

The conventions of punctuation have driven many a student nearly to distraction. They seem arbitrary and often illogical. If you were to set about tinkering with the rules of punctuating, you could very likely make some worthwhile improvements in the current system. Nonetheless, the system as it stands is well established and unlikely to change. Your consolation is that, even if it is complicated, it can be mastered, and it does serve its purpose of giving readers helpful signals that make reading easier. In the case of quotations, punctuation makes it clear just which passages are your own and which belong to your sources.

The following are the most important punctuation conventions for present-ing sources. You should learn these guidelines and follow them carefully.

1. *Use double quotation marks (" ") before and after a source's words when you copy them directly.*

> At the Battle of Trafalgar, Admiral Nelson exhorted his
>
> fleet: "England expects every man to do his duty."
>
> The phrase "bats in the belfry" was coined by the writer
>
> Eden Phillpotts.

Double quotation marks

2. *Use single quotation marks (' ') before and after quoted material when it occurs within other quoted material—that is, when it occurs inside double quotation marks.*

> Charles and Mary Beard contend that the American government
>
> was not established as a <u>democracy</u>: "The Constitution did not

contain the word or any word lending countenance to it, except possibly the mention of 'We, the people,' in the preamble."

Single
quotation
marks

We used this example earlier in the chapter: "According to Ashley Montagu, 'To be human is to weep.' "

3. *Indent a quotation that takes up more than four lines in your paper.* In typing, indent one inch (ten spaces) from the left margin. Do not indent any additional spaces from the right margin. If you are quoting a single paragraph or less, do not indent the first line of the quotation any additional spaces:

The millionaire Andrew Carnegie believed that free enterprise and private charity, not government social programs, offered the best solution to the problem of poverty:

Indent the left margin one inch (10 spaces). Do not indent the right margin.

> Thus is the problem of Rich and Poor to be solved. The law of accumulation will be left free; the laws of distribution free. Individualism will continue, but the millionaire will be but a trustee of the poor; entrusted for a season with a great part of the increased wealth of the community, but administering it for the community far better than it could or would have done for itself.

However, if the indented quotation consists of two or more paragraphs, indent the first line of each paragraph an additional quarter inch or three spaces:

Florence Nightingale questioned the unequal treatment of men and women in Victorian England:

Indent paragraphs an additional quarter inch (three spaces)

> Now, why is it more ridiculous for a man than for a woman to do worsted work and drive out every day in the carriage? Why should we laugh if we see a parcel of men sitting around a drawing room table in the morning, and think it all right if they were women?

```
        Is man's time more valuable than woman's?

        Or is the difference between man and woman this,

        that women have confessedly nothing to do?
```

These passages demonstrate other guidelines as well:

- **An indented quotation is never placed within quotation marks.** Quotation marks are unnecessary since the indenting already makes it clear that the passage is a quotation.

- **When typing, do not skip extra lines before or after an indented quotation.** The entire paper, including such quotations, is double-spaced.

4. *Accuracy is essential in quoting a source.*

- **Copy a quoted passage exactly as it is printed.** The only exception is for obvious typographical errors, which you should correct. Otherwise, make no changes in a quoted passage, even if you disagree with its wording or punctuation. For example, if you, rather than Andrew Carnegie, had been the author of the quotation on page 334, you might have used a colon or dash after the word *poor* instead of a semicolon. But since Carnegie used a semicolon, that is the way it must appear when you copy it.

- **Insert *[sic]*, the Latin word meaning "thus," in brackets, immediately after an apparent error.** Do so only if you feel it necessary to identify it as your source's error, not your error in copying the passage.

```
The régime posted a proclamation on every streetcorner:

"Amnesty will be granted all mutineers who lay down their

arms.  Die-heart [sic] traitors who persist in rebellion

will be shot."
```

This device should be used only rarely. Avoid using *sic* to belittle a source with whom you disagree.

5. *Use punctuation to separate a quotation from an acknowledgment phrase or sentence.*

- **Use a comma (,) or colon (:) when the phrase comes before the quotation. A comma is preferred when the introduction is not a complete sentence:**

```
Jacques Delille wrote, "Fate chooses our relatives, we

choose our friends."

As Al Jolson remarked, "You ain't heard nothin' yet, folks."
```

The introduction is not a complete sentence

- **A colon is preferred when the introduction is a complete sentence:**

The introduction is a complete sentence

Edmund Burke believed that sadism is a component of human nature: "I am convinced that we have a degree of delight and that no small one, in the real misfortunes and pains of others."

Colon

The last words in Act II are spoken by Hamlet: "The play's the thing / Wherein I'll catch the conscience of the King."

- **Use a colon to introduce an indented quotation:**

From his jail cell Martin Luther King wrote about the law:

> An unjust law is a code that a numerical or power majority group compels a minority group to obey but does not make binding on itself. This is <u>difference</u> made legal. By the same token, a just law is a code that a majority compels a minority to follow and that it is willing to follow itself. This is <u>sameness</u> made legal.

- **However, no punctuation is needed when a quotation is a continuation of the introductory sentence:**

No colon

According to the Library Bill of Rights, libraries are forums for information and ideas, and they have

> [. . .] the responsibility to provide [. . .] all points of view on all questions and issues of our times, and to make these ideas and opinions available to anyone who needs or wants them, regardless of age, race, religion, national origin, or social and political views.

- **Use a comma when the acknowledgment phrase comes after the quotation, unless the quotation ends in a question mark or exclamation point:**

Comma

"When you have nothing to say, say nothing," wrote Charles Caleb Colton.

But:

"Who can refute a sneer?" asked William Paley.	No Comma

- When the acknowledgment phrase is inserted within a quoted sentence, begin and end it with commas:

"Politics," said Bismarck, "is not an exact science."	Commas

- Use no punctuation at all (other than quotation marks) when you make quoted words part of your own sentence:

Robert E. Rogers's advice to the Class of 1929 at MIT was to "marry the boss's daughter."	No comma

The word *that* incorporates a quotation that follows it into your sentence. Note carefully the difference in punctuation among the following three sentences:

–Quotation treated as an independent sentence:

Henry Ford said, "History is more or less bunk."	Comma

–Quotation incorporated into the sentence:

Henry Ford said that "history is more or less bunk."	No comma

–Quotation paraphrased:

Henry Ford said that history is nonsense.	No comma

6. *Capitalize the first word of a quotation when it is treated as an independent sentence. Do not capitalize it when it is incorporated into your own sentence.*

Margaret Hungerford gave us the famous saying, "Beauty is in the eye of the beholder."	Uppercase letter
Like Margaret Hungerford, many psychologists believe that "beauty is in the eye of the beholder."	Lowercase letter

7. *The trickiest rules apply to punctuation at the close of a quotation. Refer to the following examples whenever necessary.*

- Commas and periods are always placed inside a closing quotation mark:

"From the sublime to the ridiculous is but a step," wrote Napoleon.	Comma inside the quotation mark
Martin Joseph Routh offered timeless advice over a century ago: "You will find it a very good practice always to verify your references, sir."	Period inside the quotation mark

Period inside single and double quotation marks

Judge Learned Hand wrote, "I should like to have every court begin, 'I beseech ye in the bowels of Christ, think that we may be mistaken.' "

- Colons (:), semicolons (;), and dashes (—) are placed outside closing quotation mark:

Colon outside the quotation mark

"Blood, toil, tears and sweat": these were the sacrifices Churchill promised to his country.

On his deathbed, O. Henry said, "Turn up the lights--I

Semicolon outside the quotation mark

don't want to go home in the dark"; then he expired.

- Questions marks (?) and exclamation points (!) go inside the closing quotation mark when they belong to the quotation, but outside when they do not:

Question mark belongs to quotation

Macbeth asked, "What is the night?"

Question mark does not belong to quotation

Who said, "Cowards die many times before their deaths"?

Exclamation point belongs to quotation

Colonel Sidney Sherman first shouted, "Remember the Alamo!"

Exclamation point does not belong to quotation

How dare you respond, "No comment"!

- For punctuation following a parenthetical note, see pages 463–64 or the quick reference guide on the inside back cover.

8. Follow these conventions for quoting poetry:

- Use a slash (/) with a space before and after it to divide quoted lines of poetry:

Space, slash, space

Ogden Nash wrote, "Candy / Is dandy / But liquor / Is quicker."

- Longer passages of poetry are indented:

Emily Dickinson wrote:

> "Faith" is a fine invention
>
> When Gentlemen can see--
>
> But Microscopes are prudent
>
> In an Emergency.

Indent the left margin 10 spaces

Like other indented passages, poetry is not placed within quotation marks. The word *"Faith"* is in quotation marks because Dickinson punctuated it that way in her poem.

Punctuating Quotations

1. The following passages that appear in brackets are quotations, printed with their original capitalization and punctuation. Remove the brackets and add whatever punctuation is necessary. Make whatever additions and changes are necessary to put each sentence into proper form.

   a. Anne Morrow Lindbergh wrote [The wave of the future is coming and there is no fighting it.].

   b. Rachel Carson was among the first to warn against the pollution of the environment [As crude a weapon as the cave man's club, the chemist's barrage has been hurled against the fabric of life.].

   c. [Gentlemen of the old régime in the South would say, "A woman's name should appear in print but twice—when she marries and when she dies."] wrote Arthur Wallace Calhoun in 1918.

   d. [Gentlemen] wrote Anita Loos [always seem to remember blondes.].

   e. How many students today believe with James B. Conant that [He who enters a university walks on hallowed ground.]?

   f. William Morris called this a [golden rule] [Have nothing in your houses that you do not know to be useful, or believe to be beautiful.]; a rather different conception of what a house should be is presented by a statement of architect Le Corbusier [A house is a machine for living in.].

   g. Freud never underestimated the role of religion in human culture [If one wishes to form a true estimate of the full grandeur of religion, one must keep in mind what it undertakes to do for men. It gives them information about the source and origin of the universe, it assures them of protection and final happiness amid the changing vicissitudes of life, and it guides their thoughts and motions by means of precepts which are backed by the whole force of its authority.].

   h. Poverty is not portrayed as romantic in Keats's poem "Lamia"
   [Love in a hut, with water and a crust,
   Is—Love, forgive us!—cinders, ashes, dust.]

   i. Gloating on his pact with the devil, Doctor Faustus asked [Have not I made blind Homer sing to me?].

   j. [We was robbed!] shouted manager Joe Jacobs into the microphone in 1932, when the decision went against his fighter, Max Schmeling.

2. Create sentences that incorporate quotations according to the following guidelines.

   a. Use this quotation by Mark Twain in a sentence that begins with an acknowledgment phrase:
   Man is the only animal that blushes. Or needs to.

   b. Use the following quotation by Havelock Ellis in a sentence that ends with an acknowledgment phrase:
   The place where optimism most flourishes is the lunatic asylum.

c. Use the following quotation by George Santayana in a sentence with an acknowledgment phrase inserted within it:

Fanaticism consists in redoubling your efforts when you have forgotten your aim.

d. Incorporate a paraphrase of this quotation into a sentence that acknowledges its author, Congressman Grimsley Buttersloop:

My opponents have accused me of embezzlement, drinking, fooling around, and falling asleep during committee meetings. The only thing they haven't accused me of is not loving my country, and that they can never do.

e. When you quote the following, let the reader know that its author, Frank Winslow, deliberately misspelled the word *souperior* in a letter to his aunt, Martha Fleming:

All I can say of your clam chowder is that it was positively souperior.

Altering Quotations

Sometimes when you write about your research you will want to use a quotation that does not precisely fit. Either it lacks a word or a phrase that would make its meaning clear to your readers, or else it contains too much material—unnecessary words that are not relevant to your point. For example, imagine that you found this quotation from a person named Vanessa O'Keefe:

I absolutely long to prove to the world, as I said in an interview yesterday, that a perpetual motion machine is not an impossibility.

Assume you wanted to introduce it with the phrase *Vanessa O'Keefe announced that she. . . .* Fortunately, there are methods that allow you to alter such a quotation to fit your needs. By using them, you can write:

```
Vanessa O'Keefe announced that she "absolutely long[ed] to

prove to the world [. . .] that a perpetual motion machine

is not an impossibility."
```

As you can see, you can make certain alterations in quotations to suit your needs. When you do so, however, you must obey these two guidelines:

1. You must make it completely clear to your readers precisely what changes you have made.

2. Your alterations must not distort the meaning or essential phrasing of a quotation or make it appear to say something other than what the author intended.

The following methods may be followed to alter quotations:

Adding to Quotations: Brackets [ ]

Whenever a word, phrase, or suffix needs to be added to a quotation to make its meaning clear, you may insert it within **brackets**. Brackets are most commonly used to explain a reference. For example, it would not be evident to a reader of this quotation that it was the United States that José Martí was referring to as "the monster":

> I have lived in the monster and I know its insides; and my
>
> sling is the sling of David.

By using brackets when you quote this sentence, you can make the reference clear:

> In a letter to Manuel Mercado, Martí wrote, "I have lived in
>
> the monster [the United States] and I know its insides; and
>
> my sling is the sling of David."

Insertion in brackets

Similarly, you can insert modifiers in brackets. The following insertion makes it clear which frontier is being referred to:

> Churchill said, "That long [Canadian-American] frontier
>
> from the Atlantic to the Pacific Oceans, guarded only by
>
> neighborly respect and honorable obligations, is an example
>
> to every country and a pattern for the future of the
>
> world."

Another use for brackets is to provide brief translations of foreign or archaic words:

> Chaucer wrote, "A fol [fool] can not be stille."

Unusual terms may also require explanation. For example, if you used the following quotation in writing about doctors performing unnecessary operations, you might need to explain the term *arthroscopic surgery* to your readers.

> According to Dr. Robert Metcalf, who teaches orthopedic
>
> surgery at the University of Utah, the problem exists in his
>
> field as well: "There's considerable concern that
>
> arthroscopic surgery [a technique for repairing damaged
>
> knees] is being overutilized and is sometimes being done in a
>
> manner damaging to healthy cartilage."

When the unclear term is a simple pronoun, you can replace it altogether with the noun it refers to. For example, in the following quotation, instead of "They [the Americans] are the hope of the world," you can write:

> Baron de l'Aulne expressed a more favorable opinion in 1778:
>
> "[The Americans] are the hope of the world."

Instead of brackets, however, sometimes the simplest solution is to incorporate the unclear portion into your own sentence:

```
Writing about Americans in 1778, Baron de l'Aulne expressed

the more favorable opinion that "they are the hope of the

world."
```

Or better still:

```
In 1778, Baron de l'Aulne expressed the more favorable

opinion that Americans are "the hope of the world."
```

The best rule is to use brackets when they provide the simplest way of making the source's meaning clear to your readers. As you can see, bracketing is a useful tool that can solve several writing problems. At the same time, it should not be overused. As with other devices, when brackets appear again and again in a paper, readers will find them distracting.

Subtracting from Quotations: Ellipsis Dots [. . .]

You can omit irrelevant parts of a quotation and replace them with ***ellipsis dots***, three typed periods separated by spaces and placed within brackets. The part you omit can be a word, a phrase, one or more sentences, or even a much longer passage. As with everything you place within brackets, there is one important condition: You must not distort the author's meaning or intentions.

Good writers edit their writing, paring away what is unnecessary, off the point, or distracting. Quotations are used most effectively when you select them carefully and when you keep only the pertinent parts and omit what is not needed. As an example, consider again the passage by Ashley Montagu quoted earlier:

> To be human is to weep. The human species is the only one in the whole of animated nature that sheds tears. The trained inability of any human being to weep is a lessening of his capacity to be human—a defect which usually goes deeper than the mere inability to cry. And this, among other things, is what American parents—with the best intentions in the world—have achieved for American males. It is very sad. If we feel like it, let us all have a good cry—and clear our minds of those cobwebs of confusion which have for so long prevented us from understanding the ineluctable necessity of crying.

As interesting as this passage is, you might be best able to make your point if you quote only parts of it. For example:

```
Anthropologist Ashley Montagu argues that it is both

unnatural and harmful for American males not to weep:

     To be human is to weep. [. . .] The trained

     inability of any human being to weep is a lessening
```

Ellipses dots indicate a deletion

```
of his capacity to be human--a defect which usually

goes deeper than the mere inability to cry. [. . .]

It is very sad.
```

Whole sentences have been removed from the passage and replaced with ellipses. Parts of a sentence can also be omitted, as follows:

```
Montagu feels that "the trained inability [. . .] to weep is

a defect which usually goes deeper than the mere inability

to cry."
```

As with brackets, there is a danger in overusing ellipses. Not only can they become distracting to the reader, but they can also defeat your purpose in quoting, as with this monstrosity:

```
Montagu feels that "the [. . .] inability [. . .] to weep is

a defect which [. . .] goes deeper than the [. . .] inability

to cry."
```

The preceding sentence makes so many changes in the original quotation that it can no longer be said to communicate Montagu's phrasing, and the point of using direct quotation is lost. Paraphrase would make much more sense; for example:

```
Montagu feels that the inability to cry is a more significant

defect than might be realized.
```

Ellipsis dots are not needed when it is already obvious that the passage you have quoted is only a part of the original:

```
A man's inability to cry, according to Montagu, is a

"lessening of his capacity to be human."
```

Ellipsis dots are
not needed

You should use ellipses, however, when it is not obvious that you are quoting only a portion of the source's complete sentence:

```
Montagu wrote, "The trained inability of any human being

to weep is a lessening of his capacity to be human

[. . .]."
```

When the omission comes at the front of a quoted sentence, you may capitalize the first word if you put the first letter in brackets:

```
Montagu offered this advice: "[L]et us all have a good cry

[. . .]."
```

Using Brackets and Ellipsis Dots

1. The following is part of the transcript of a reporter's interview with a political candidate, Paul Shawn. Read it and comment on the quotations that follow.

    Q: Your opponent, Darla Stowe, says you hunger for money. Is that true?

    A: If you mean, do I want to earn enough for my family to live decently, then yes, I hunger for money. I think that's true of almost everyone. But I hunger for other things as well: peace, justice, brotherhood, and national prosperity.

    Q: Your opponent also says you are using this race as a stepping-stone to higher office. Is this true?

    A: Actually, I'm quite certain I have no more desire for higher office than she has.

    Which of the following quotations can be justified on the basis of this interview? Explain why each of them is fair or unfair, and discuss its use of brackets, ellipses, and paraphrase.

    a. Paul Shawn says he "hunger[s] for [. . .] peace, justice, brotherhood, and national prosperity."

    b. Shawn admitted, "[Y]es, I hunger for money."

    c. Shawn's opponent accuses him of using this race to seek further political advancement, but he responds, "I have no more desire for higher office [. . .]."

    d. Shawn believes that a "hunger for money" is "true of almost everyone."

    e. Quick in responding to an opponent's accusation, Shawn retorted that he has "no more desire for higher office than [Darla Stowe] has."

    f. While admitting he has the same interest as most people in earning a comfortable living for his family, Shawn says he has other goals as well: "peace, justice, brotherhood, and national prosperity."

2. Use quotations from the following passages according to the instructions given for each. Introduce each quotation with an acknowledgment phrase.

    a. *Quotation:*
        I always dreamed of it as being a kind of earthly paradise where no troubles ever intruded.
        Speaker: Linnea Aycock
        Instructions: (1) Introduce the quotation with the acknowledgment phrase *Linnea Aycock said,* and use brackets to show that Aycock is talking about Tahiti. (2) Write another version, this time quoting only part of her sentence. Without using brackets, show that she is talking about Tahiti.

    b. *Quotation:*
        Our inspiration was a cartoon that appeared in a children's magazine.
        Speaker: A NASA scientist
        Instruction: Use brackets to indicate that the cartoon inspired the design of a new space helmet.

    c. *Quotation:*
        My generation never thought of college in terms of making ourselves employable. It was OK to be interested in Plato or T. S. Eliot or Freud, but never in IBM or General Mills. It was easy then to regard jobs with contempt since there were so

many of them. It is very different with today's job-conscious generation. The response to Shakespeare now is likely to be, "How will he help me in my job?"
Writer: Ronni Jacobsen
Instruction: Quote two or three sentences that communicate the main idea of this passage. Use ellipsis dots to represent what you omit.

d. *Quotation:*
My message to all you students is that hard work and self-discipline are the keys—and you should never forget this—to success in your college and business careers.
Speaker: Cyrus T. Pierpont
Instruction: Begin with *Cyrus T. Pierpont told students that.* Omit unnecessary parts of the quotation, including the first eight words and the part that is surrounded by dashes. Although it is not necessary, you can change *your* to *their.*

e. *Quotation:*
If idiots drive motor vehicles when they are drunk, this should happen: they should lose their licenses and be sent to jail—for 90 days or longer.
Speaker: Sergeant Robert Symmes
Instruction: Introduce the quotation with the words *Sergeant Robert Symmes said that.* Alter the quotation by deleting the word *if,* inserting *who* after *idiots,* omitting *this should happen:,* and making whatever other changes are necessary.

WHEN TO QUOTE AND WHEN TO PARAPHRASE

One of the questions beginning research writers often ask their instructors is: "How many quotations should I put in my paper?" Their uncertainty is not usually allayed by the appropriate answer: "It depends." What it depends on are the circumstances of the individual case—and your own good judgment. While there is no easy answer to the question, some useful guidelines can help you decide how to use your sources.

1. *Do not overquote.* In fact, do not quote very much at all. Most beginning researchers quote far too much in their papers. Quotations should be saved for special occasions, and with good reason: Readers find papers that are filled with quotation after quotation unpleasant and hard to read. (By now you are probably tired of reading quotations in this chapter!) When they encounter a great many quotations, readers will often skim them or skip them entirely. No one likes to read a passage like this:

"Early [Roman] amphitheaters," according to Fredericks,   Bad (too many quotations)
"were temporary wooden structures that often collapsed under
the weight of spectators, with the result of great loss of
life" (40). Bennett reports:

    The most famous of all buildings of this kind was
    the Flavian Amphitheater in Rome. Also called the

> Colosseum because of its size, it was begun by the
> emperor Vespasian and dedicated by his son Titus
> in A.D. 80. [. . .] After the 6th century it was
> used as a fortress and a quarry. (101)

Fredericks says, "Although accounts of the time report it held more than 80,000 spectators, modern estimates place its capacity at 50,000" (42). The architectural historian Anne Ramsey wrote:

> Structurally and functionally, the Roman Colosseum
> has been rivaled by no comparably sized arenas
> until the most recent age. Even today it remains a
> model of planning for rapid crowd access and exit
> and for unobstructed spectator sight lines. (17–18)

Of these four quotations, piled one upon the other, all but the last, which expresses the opinion of an authority, should be rephrased in the writer's own words. The passage then becomes much more readable:

Better

> The first Roman amphitheaters were temporary structures
> built of wood. Because they could not long support the great
> crowds who attended the spectacles, they often collapsed in
> terrible disasters (Fredericks 40). Later they were replaced
> by permanent facilities, the most famous of which was the
> Flavian Amphitheater, better known as the Colosseum. Begun
> by the emperor Vespasian, it was dedicated in A.D. 80 by his
> son, Titus. It served as a sports and gladiatorial arena
> with a capacity of 50,000 spectators until the sixth century.
> It was then allowed to deteriorate, being used occasionally
> as a fortress and frequently stripped of its stone for use in
> other buildings (Bennett 101). Nevertheless, it survived and
> remains today one of the most widely admired Roman buildings.
> Architectural historian Anne Ramsey writes:

>> Structurally and functionally, the Roman
>> Colosseum has been rivaled by no comparably sized

```
arenas until the most recent age. Even today it
remains a model of planning for rapid crowd
access and exit and for unobstructed spectator
sight lines.   (17-18)
```

The rule can be restated as follows: *If you have a choice between quoting and paraphrasing a source, paraphrase it.*

2. *Always paraphrase a source, except when a direct quotation is needed.* You should paraphrase most of your sources most of the time, especially under the following conditions.

- **Paraphrase if the source provides factual information.** Avoid quotations like the following:

```
The collapsing of bridges was a considerable problem in     Unnecessary
                                                            quotation
the past: "In the latter half of the 19th century,

American bridges were failing at the rate of 25 or more

per year!" (Worth 29).
```

Instead, state this factual information in your own words:

```
A century ago American bridges were far more dangerous     Better

than today, collapsing at an annual rate of 25 or more

(Worth 29).
```

- **Paraphrase if you can say it more briefly or clearly in your own words.**

```
Sun worshiper Andrea Bergeron claims that "Solists face     Wordy

grave and persistent discrimination, not the least of which

is that which prohibits a fair hearing for our beliefs.

Because our beliefs are not traditional we are dismissed

as cultists" (202).
```

Very likely, you would need nothing more elaborate than this brief paraphrase to make your point:

```
Andrea Bergeron feels that she and her fellow Solists (sun     Better

worshipers) are discriminated against and their religious

views are not taken seriously (202).
```

3. *Quote a source directly when the source's words work better than your own.* If you use them sparingly, quotations can be effective in your research writing. Use them in the following cases:

• **Quote when the source's words are phrased in a particularly eloquent or memorable way.** Paraphrase could not do justice to the following quotations:

General Patton wrote, "A pint of sweat will save a gallon of blood" (987).

In 1947, physicist J. Robert Oppenheimer expressed the unease felt by many scientists about their role in developing the atom bomb: "In some sort of crude sense which no vulgarity, no humor, no overstatement can quite extinguish, the physicists have known sin; and this is a knowledge which they cannot lose" (1055).

You may not always find it easy to decide whether a statement from a source is so well phrased that it should be presented to readers directly. Use your best judgment. In cases where you are in doubt, the wisest course is to paraphrase.

• **Quote when you are writing about the source or the source's words:**

Ginter was never modest in his self-descriptions: "When I was born 42 years ago to a family of humble asparagus farmers, none suspected I would one day be the world's leading transcriber of baroque music for the banjo" (37).

The advertisement promised "luxury villas with a spectacular ocean view," but only by leaning far out the windows of our ancient bungalow could we gain even a distant glimpse of the sea.

Victor Hugo called Jean Henri Fabre "the Homer of the Insects" with good reason. Few naturalists wrote such vivid metaphors as Fabre does in this description of the praying mantis:

> To judge by the term <u>Prègo-Diéu</u>, we should look
> to see a placid insect, deep in pious
> contemplation; and we find ourselves in the

```
presence of a cannibal, of a ferocious spectre
munching the brain of a panic-stricken victim.
(Qtd. in Lynch and Swanzey 51)
```

- **Quote when the source is an expert whose exact words will lend authority to a claim that you make:**

```
Paratrupus schusterensis, the common swamp frogwort, is
a delicacy among scavenger gourmets. Florence Demingo,
author of A Field Guide to Edible Weeds, exclaims: "Ah,
the frogwort!  No other plant offers such a thrill to the
palate while fortifying the liver with such potent dosages
of Vitamin B-8" (188).
```

```
The public is often outraged when technicalities decide
the outcome of important court cases, but as Justice Felix
Frankfurter observed in 1943, "The history of liberty has
largely been the history of the observance of procedural
safeguards" (37).
```

```
As anthropologist Ashley Montagu observed, "To be human is
to weep" (248).
```

Usually, however, you can paraphrase an authority with the same good results:

```
Florence Demingo, author of A Field Guide to Edible Weeds,
finds the frogwort both tasty and rich in Vitamin B-8 (188).
```

And one final consideration for quotation in research papers:

- **Do not restrict your quoting to already quoted material.** Many students quote only passages that appear within quotation marks in their sources; that is, they quote writers they have found quoted by other writers. It never occurs to them to quote their sources directly. Of course, you should not overquote, but on the other hand, do not be afraid to quote your sources themselves. If, for example, you were using this very paragraph as a research source, you could quote from it:

```
Veit, Gould, and Clifford advise, "Do not restrict your
quoting to already quoted material" (349).
```

EXERCISE | Judging When to Paraphrase and Quote

Decide if any of the quotations in the following passages should instead have been paraphrased by the writers. For those quotations, write a paraphrase that could be substituted for the inappropriate quotation. Omit any notes that you decide are unnecessary.

a. Pott's disease is "tuberculosis caries of the vertebrae, resulting in curvature of the spine. It was named after the physician who described it, Percival Pott (1714–88)" (Gleitman 110).

b. Geologists and seismologists are uncertain how to interpret the cryptic note found in McPhilibar's hand after the cave-in: "Major discover [sic]—8th strata, fault line demarcation—earthquake predictor. Eureka!" (Donnelly 192).

c. Harris argues that the animal-powered agriculture of India is not necessarily a problem to be corrected:

> To convert from animals and manure to tractors and petrochemicals would require the investment of incredible amounts of capital. Moreover, the inevitable effect of substituting costly machines for cheap animals is to reduce the number of people who can earn their living from agriculture [. . .]. Less than 5 percent of U.S. families now live on farms, as compared with 60 percent about a hundred years ago. If agribusiness were to develop along similar lines in India, jobs and housing would soon have to be found for a quarter of a billion displaced peasants. (12)

d. Humans are not entirely logical creatures. Often we take our guidance from emotional and spiritual voices within us. As the philosopher Pascal observed, "The heart has its reasons which reason knows nothing of" (40).

e. "The word *ain't*," says Phillips, "has generated its share of controversy" (64). Frelling writes, "*Ain't* is widely accepted in casual conversation. It is rarely used in formal discourse and in writing" (6). A controversy arises especially over its use as a contraction for *am not.* Dwight Macdonald speaks in its behalf, noting that "there is no other workable contraction, for *amn't* is unpronounceable and *aren't* is ungrammatical" (144). Theodore Bernstein, on the other hand, says, "There can be no doubt that *ain't I* is easier to say than *aren't I* and *amn't I,* and sounds less stilted than *am I not.* Nevertheless, what should be not always is" (13–14).

 ## A FURTHER NOTE ON PLAGIARISM

Undoubtedly, the most often repeated exhortation in this book is your obligation as a scholar to acknowledge your sources. The message is so important that we don't want to risk its being missed. Feel free to make use of sources (after, all, that is what research is all about), but give them full credit when you do so. Failure to acknowledge a source, thereby making someone else's work appear to be your own, is plagiarism.

The most glaring cases of plagiarism are deliberate acts of cheating: students handing in papers that they did not write or copying articles from magazines and passing them off as their own work. These are dishonest acts that rank with library vandalism as among the most serious breaches of the code of scholarship. They are dangerous as well, since penalties for them are understandably severe, and instructors are much better than most plagiarists realize at spotting work that is not a student's own.

A less serious offense, but also one to be avoided, is an unintentional act of plagiarism. Most of the time when students plagiarize, they do so innocently, unaware that they are violating the rules of scholarship. They copy a sentence or two from an article, not knowing that they should either quote or paraphrase it. They change a few words in copying a sentence, sincerely believing that they are paraphrasing it. They do not provide a parenthetical note because they do not know that one is needed. They are not trying to cheat; they are not even aware that they are cheating. It is just that no one ever told them to do otherwise. Perhaps when they were in the fifth grade, they wrote papers that consisted of copying out passages from encyclopedia articles. That may have gone unreprimanded in grade school. It is never tolerated in college.

There is certainly no need to plagiarize, because you are allowed to use sources provided that you acknowledge them. In fact, there is no advantage in it either: Papers based on expert sources, fairly acknowledged, are what is wanted of scholars. They are exactly what instructors are looking for.

 ## PRACTICE WITH USING SOURCES

The first part of this chapter—in which you learned to paraphrase and quote individual sources—can be compared to the on-the-ground instruction given to would-be parachutists. It is essential background, but the real learning doesn't take place until the first jump. In the rest of this chapter, we intend to push you out of the plane. Your jump will involve taking a selection of sources and using them to write a brief research-based essay.

Writing a Brief Objective Research Essay

When you do research, you have a purpose in mind: You are seeking to learn more about a certain topic and, often, to inform others about what you have discovered. As an example to illustrate the process involved in a brief research project, imagine that you have been assigned to report briefly to your political science class on a controversy surrounding the Constitution's Bill of Rights. Let's suppose that, having narrowed your topic, you decide to review the "Schillinger case." Here are excerpts from five (fictitious) sources that you have discovered in your research:

The following is a news article from the *Essex Herald-Journal,* 5 August 2000, on page 6:

State Seeks to Force Cancer Treatment

State authorities have asked the courts to grant them custody over the 13-year-old daughter of a clergyman so that she can receive the anti-cancer treatment doctors say she needs to stay alive.

The Rev. and Mrs. Paul Schillinger and their daughter, Cathy, are members of the Children of Prophecy church, which rejects all medical treatment and relies on faith to cure ailments. The Schillingers are contesting the state's attempt to force Cathy to undergo chemotherapy. Doctors say that she suffers from leukemia and will die within six months without treatment.

Claiming in his brief to the court that "the first duty of the state is to protect its citizens," State's Attorney J. Walker Dodson says he is "reluctantly" undertaking the action to save the girl's life.

At a press conference outside the courthouse, Cathy Schillinger affirmed her own opposition to the state's action. "I know there is a better place waiting for me in heaven. If God calls me, I am ready to die," she said.

If the court rules in favor of the state, the girl will be placed in Memorial Hospital until the course of treatments can be completed.

A ruling is expected later this month.

This excerpt is from an article by Cathy's father, the Rev. Paul Schillinger, "Leave Our Daughter Alone," printed on page 20 of the *Lexington Post,* 9 August 2000:

> . . . I know in my heart I am doing God's will. He holds the power of life and death, and if in His infinite goodness and wisdom He wants us to live we will live, and if He wants us to die we will die. No state and no court can say otherwise. The judge and the doctors are trying to play God, and they are committing a damnable blasphemy. My daughter is willing to die if she must, because she knows there is a better place for her waiting in heaven.

The following is an excerpt from page 67 of the September/October 2000 issue of *American Religion.* It appeared in an article by Mark Signorelli, "A Church-State Battle over Child Custody," printed on pages 65–67:

> Interviewed outside court, State's Attorney Dodson said, "Cathy Schillinger's life is in imminent danger, and only this action can save her. If it were her father or any other adult, we would not intervene. But Cathy is a minor, not yet able to make an informed decision about a complicated matter, nor is there evidence that she fully understands the issues involved. It is our policy not to interfere with the parents' raising of their children as they see fit unless the child is abused or in danger. Here the child's right to life takes priority."

This is a letter to the editor of *National News Weekly,* appearing in the 16 August 2000 edition, on page 17:

> Dear Editor:
>
> Once again our fundamental American rights and freedoms are being trampled by the very government that was established to protect them. Freedom of religion and the right of parents to raise their children in their own beliefs and values mean nothing to the prosecutors. As a neighbor, I have known the Schillingers for years. They are a loving family, and the parents want Cathy to live. But they and Cathy believe that medical treatment is sinful, and the government must respect that. People must respect the beliefs of others, even if they do not agree with them.
>
> Helen Bridgeman

This is the first sentence from a front-page article in the 17 August 2000 *Essex Herald-Journal.* The headline is "Girl's Death Ends State Attempt at Custody":

> The state's effort to gain custody over 13-year-old Cathy Schillinger was made moot this morning when the girl died of leukemia in her sleep.

No one can read about this case without having an opinion, very likely a strong emotional one. You probably also recognize with the rational part of your brain that the issues here are complicated ones with profound implications and that there is much to be considered on both sides before you can reach a wise decision about their merits.

You can use these sources to write either *subjectively* or *objectively* about the case; that is, you can express your opinion, or you can simply present information to the reader without offering views of your own. As an example of the difference between objective and subjective writing, note that the reporter who was the author of the first source wrote objectively. By reading that article you cannot tell the reporter's personal feelings about the case. On the other hand, there is nothing objective about Helen Bridgeman's letter to the editor. You know exactly where she stands. She and the reporter were clearly writing for two different purposes.

Often it is wise to write objectively about a controversial matter before expressing an opinion. This ensures that you at least examine the merits of both sides before rushing in with a judgment.

In this imaginary paper, let's assume that you have decided first to present the facts from the case objectively and afterward to draw subjective conclusions from what you have found. For this earlier part of the paper, then, you will write a brief objective report on the Schillinger case, informing your readers of the nature of the case and the issues involved.

How do you begin writing an objective report from the five sources that you have discovered? They consist of two tersely written news stories, quotations from some of the principal participants on opposing sides, and an opinion from an outside reader. All of them might offer material you can use. But what do you do with them?

Unlike the summary reports you produced in Chapter 6, you cannot simply summarize each source individually and then present the summaries one after the other. Instead you must interweave your materials. Since you have important statements from participants, you will also want to quote some of their words. You will need, then, to select material from your sources and produce a synthesis. Here is how one student, Keith Pearsall, Jr., wrote a report from these five excerpts:

> The Schillinger case, another prominent instance of conflicting rights and freedoms, involved a 13-year-old girl with leukemia. On one side of the case stood the girl and her parents, who rejected all medical treatment on religious grounds. On the other stood the state, which sought to force the medical care doctors say she needed to remain alive ("State" 6). Parental and religious rights were in conflict with the right to life itself and with the obligation to protect minors.

Keith's paraphrase of a source

Keith's thesis statement

One question that is raised by the case is the extent to which parents have the right to raise their children in their own religious beliefs and practices. The father of the girl, a minister in the Children of Prophecy church, believed that God alone "holds the power of life and death, [. . .] and if He wants us to die we will die." The minister also believed that in seeking to counteract the divine will, the state was committing a "damnable blasphemy" (Schillinger 20). The daughter, Cathy, subscribed to her parents' beliefs and expressed her willingness to die if necessary rather than undergo treatment they believed to be sinful ("State" 6).

According to State's Attorney J. Walker Dodson, on the other hand, the issue was not one of religious freedom but of the state's "first duty [. . .] to protect its citizens" (qtd. in "State" 6). Dodson argued that the girl was too young to make an informed decision about a matter of vital interest to her and that the state was obliged to protect her right to life (Signorelli 67).

Legal questions in this controversial case have still not been answered, since the girl died before the courts could reach a decision.

Quoting a source directly (margin note)

A note for paraphrased material (margin note)

A note for a quotation (margin note)

No note for widely available information (margin note)

Keith has taken five sources and from them has written something that is new and his own. The report is objective, since nowhere are Keith's opinions evident, but he still remains in control throughout. He is aware of the point of the entire report, and he shapes it with several of his own sentences. For example, the last sentence of the first paragraph and the sentence following it are topic sentences, expressing his summary of the main ideas of the passage.

In his handling of sources, Keith avoids three mistakes often made by inexperienced research writers; that is, he observes three important rules:

1. *Don't just quote.*

2. *Don't just quote quotations.*

3. *Don't just note quotations.*

Examples from Keith's report can demonstrate what the rules mean:

Don't Just Quote

Many beginning researchers quote too much, tediously stringing together one quotation after another. Keith avoids that mistake. His three direct quotations all make perfect sense in his report. In addition, he selects only the words from his sources that are most relevant, and he introduces them so that the reader always knows who is being quoted and why. More often than quoting, however, Keith paraphrases his sources. For example, in the first three sentences of his report and the last sentence of his second paragraph, he has rephrased material from his sources into his own words. The result is a clear, readable, effective report.

Don't Just Quote Quotations

Some students quote only material that appeared within quotation marks in their sources. It never occurs to them to quote the sources themselves. Note that Keith does both: The first source contains quotations, and Keith uses them in his report. Although the second source does not quote any other authors, Keith quotes from it as well. This may seem obvious, but many students are unaware of this valuable way researchers can use their sources.

Don't Just Note Quotations

Another mistake made by inexperienced research writers is to give parenthetical notes only for direct quotations. Notice that Keith provides notes not only for sources he has quoted, but also for sources he has paraphrased, such as his citation of the first source in his opening paragraph.

Not every source you use will receive mention in notes. Each of the sources played a role in Keith's writing of the report, but only three of them are noted in parentheses. The fourth source, the neighbor's letter, gave Keith some general ideas, but since it did not provide him with any specific information, he decided not to paraphrase it or quote from it. Therefore, it did not receive a note. Although the fifth source, the mention of Cathy's death in a news story, did contain the information used in Keith's last paragraph, that information is so readily available (found in news accounts throughout the country) that acknowledgment is not necessary.

Because Keith quoted or paraphrased only three of his five sources (and cited them in parenthetical notes), he omitted the two other sources from his list of works cited, which follows:

Works Cited

Schillinger, Paul. "Leave Our Daughter Alone." <u>Lexington</u>
<u>Post</u> 9 Aug. 2000: 20.

Signorelli, Mark. "A Church-State Battle over Child
Custody." <u>American Religion</u> Sept./Oct. 2000: 65-67.

"State Seeks to Force Cancer Treatment." <u>Essex Herald-</u>
<u>Journal</u> 5 Aug. 2000: 6.

Writing an Objective Research Essay

Imagine that in writing a paper about how Americans have kept track of time through the years, you discovered the following (purely fictitious) sources. Part of your paper will concern a recent proposal to change our current time zones. Use these sources to write a brief objective report on what you have learned. Acknowledge your sources with parenthetical notes and provide the list of works cited that you would include in your final paper.

1. This news story appeared last year in the May 22 issue of *Birmingham Star-News* in section B, page 4. Dina Waxman wrote the article under the headline, "Parent Tells Dangers of Time Zone Change."

   Congressional hearings on a proposal to have all the country's clocks tell the same time continued today with testimony from a parents' group opposed to the plan.

   The proposal, put forth by Edna Odom of Muscatine, Iowa, would eliminate the four time zones that now divide the country. She would replace them with a single nationwide zone.

   Testifying against Odom's plan was Floyd Rugoff, president of the Eureka, California, PTA. He argued that it would endanger schoolchildren, who would travel to or from school in darkness.

   Under the proposal, clocks in the Eastern zone would be set back one and a half hours, while Pacific zone clocks would be set ahead by the same period. Central and Mountain zone clocks would receive half-hour adjustments. Alaska and Hawaii would be exempt from the proposal.

   In his testimony Rugoff said, "In December it's already dark in the morning when children leave for school. If we change, California children won't see the sunrise until 8:30, and in New England it will have set by the time children come home from school. We're going to see a big increase in accidents involving children."

2. These excerpts are from Edna Odom's article, "It's About Time," in *Future and Change* magazine. It appeared in last year's January issue on pages 76 to 78.

   If all of the country operated by the same clock, businesses would reap an enormous advantage. Communication from coast to coast would be simplified. Now, with four time zones, companies operating from nine to five on the two coasts have only five working hours in common, and only three if you remove the two lunch hours. Under my proposal, if an executive in Tucson needs to reach her main office in New York at 4 P.M., she can call and get through. The way it is now, the time in the East would be 7 P.M., and she'd have to wait until Monday morning for the New York office to reopen. Television networks, airlines, and neighboring communities that now straddle time zones would all reap enormous benefits. [page 77]

   . . . It isn't as if we were being asked to switch day with night. An hour and a half change isn't that big. The claims of opponents are vastly exaggerated. We already move the clocks an hour twice each year, and everyone adjusts easily. There is nothing that says that the sun has to be overhead at noon. If it's dark at 6 A.M., why can't a farmer milk the cows at 8 instead? Schools could open later or earlier to accord with the sunlight. Why are people so hidebound? If the human race isn't flexible enough to make small adjustments, heaven help us when a major catastrophe strikes. [page 78]

3.   "Farmer Ticked by Time Scheme" is the headline for an article that appeared without byline last May 23 on page 24 of the *Riverside Ledger*:

> In his testimony against the OUT (Odom Unified Time) proposal, farmer Duane Wentworth of Millinocket, Maine, argued that the proposal would wreak havoc with livestock producers.
>
> "Animals operate by the sun, not the clock," he said, "and we can't convince them otherwise. If we have to get up at 4 in the morning to tend them, we'll be eating lunch at 9 and going to bed by 8. We'll be out of sync with the rest of the country."

Writing a Brief Subjective Research Essay

Not all writing is objective writing; sometimes your purpose is to express your own opinion in order to convince others. Chapter 14 considers argumentative writing in detail, but here we will take a brief look at how writers can use research sources to support and strengthen an argument. Of course, you are always free to offer an opinion without any outside support at all, but the support of experts can greatly help your case. By taking your facts from sources, you also show your readers that you have gone to the trouble of researching the issue, and you make yourself seem more worthy of their trust. When you quote or paraphrase authorities in support of your opinions, those opinions seem much more impressive than they otherwise would.

For a brief example of how subjective writing can be supported by sources, imagine that you are arguing your own views on the unified time zone plan that was introduced in the exercise above. You can use those sources effectively to support your argument:

> Edna Odom's proposal to synchronize all the nation's clocks within a single time zone may seem attractive at first glance, but closer inspection of the scheme reveals serious flaws. Although Odom rightly points out the benefits to TV networks and airlines of eliminating time zone differences, she is too quick to dismiss her plan's opponents as "hidebound" and its problems as "exaggerated" (77–78).
>
> The proposed change would have the most impact on the two coasts, where clocks would be altered by an hour and a half from current settings. While Odom sees this as small, the effects would be considerable for farmers and schoolchildren, to take only two examples. Since livestock regulate their lives by the sun, farmers on the east coast would need to rise as early as 4 A.M. to tend animals at sunrise ("Farmer" 24). And as the president of a California PTA chapter observed in testifying before Congress, it would be dark in winter as western children traveled to school and as eastern children returned home from school. He predicted that the number of auto accidents involving children pedestrians would increase sharply (Waxman 4).
>
> A principal advantage that Odom claims for her scheme is that it would aid communication by standardizing business schedules. But she also recommends that schools and other institutions adjust their opening and closing times to conform with the sun (77–78). She can't have it both ways. If California schools open according to the sun, three hours after New York schools, parents will demand

that businesses where they work do likewise, and the uniformity that Odom promises will be lost.

While it would be wonderful if time were the same in all parts of the country—and of the world, for that matter—the fact is that the sun refuses to cooperate. Any proposal that is based on human wishes, without regard for the realities of nature, is doomed to certain failure. Imperfect as our current time system is, it is at least preferable to the alternative.

The list of works cited for this essay would be the same one that you listed for the objective essay in the exercise.

The writer of this essay argues the case against the plan. The sources he uses buttress his arguments and lend it authority. For example, because he has supported it with sources, readers are more likely to accept his claim that the plan would hurt farmers and schoolchildren; the reader can see that this is not just the writer's unfounded speculation.

Notice that the writer has used sources to help make his point. At the same time, he has not been a slave to the sources. While he takes several arguments from sources, much of the language and thought behind the paper is entirely his own. His introduction and conclusion are original, and in the third paragraph he has applied his own logical twist to turn Edna Odom's argument against her.

Sources, in other words, are tools that require the ingenuity of writers to make use of them. There is nothing in the three sources that led inevitably to this paper. In fact, another writer with different views about time zones could use them to write an equally effective paper supporting Edna Odom's proposal.

EXERCISE   ## Writing Subjective Research Essays

1. Write a subjective essay arguing your views on the Schillinger case. Use the five sources found on pages 351–52 to support your essay. Acknowledge your sources in notes and include a list of works cited.

2. Write a subjective essay that argues in favor of Edna Odom's time zone proposal. Support your position, using the sources in the exercise on pages 356–57.

13 *Writing and Revising the Research Paper*

GETTING ORGANIZED

Once Slade Healy and Eliza Tetirick had gathered material from their sources and taken notes on index cards, they were ready for the next step: the actual writing of their papers. While writing proved less time-consuming than source-gathering, it was no less important, and, like earlier stages of the research process, it consisted of several substeps. Slade and Eliza each received an assignment similar to the following for the first of these substeps:

Preparing to Write   ASSIGNMENT

Do the following before our next class meeting in preparation for writing your first draft:

- Complete your note-taking on index cards.

- Formulate a thesis statement; that is, state in a sentence or two your concept of the main idea of your paper.

- Sort your note cards by topic.

- Prepare an updated informal working outline for your first draft.

- Put new topic titles on your note cards as necessary, arrange them in the order suggested by your outline, and put aside (but do not discard) the ones you do not expect to use.

Formulating a Thesis Statement

When Slade began his project, he was afraid he would not have enough to say about his topic. However, halfway through his first source, he had fifteen cards' worth of notes. Aware that he was taking too many notes, Slade concluded that he would need to be more selective. Like almost every other student researcher, he found that a shortage of material would not be a problem for him after all. He sharpened his focus and began to take fewer but more carefully chosen notes. Even so, he ended up taking notes on over a hundred cards, several dozen more than he would end up using.

When Slade began his search for sources, the topic he had in mind was a broad one, the problem of failing students in public schools. He began to take notes, but before long he saw that his original topic was leading in too many different directions that were far too diverse for one research paper. His topic, he realized, needed to be more specific, and he soon narrowed it to social promotion, a decision made easier by the abundance of sources he found on that topic.

Slade's expectation at this point was that he would write about the benefits school districts gained as they abandoned the practice of social promotion and began to make failing students repeat the grade. To his surprise, he found many other sources that were critical of the alternative policy. Informed opinion, he discovered, was divided. As is usually the case in research, Slade found contradictory evidence and an absence of clear-cut patterns. Because of these mixed opinions, Slade did not become entirely sure of his paper's thesis until he was well into an early draft of the paper itself. He was then able to formulate a ***thesis statement***, a brief summary of what he expected to be his main focus:

Thesis: Many schools are abandoning social promotion and

replacing it with a policy of retaining failing students, but

experts are divided over which policies are in students' best

interests.

Slade's thesis statement might be criticized for failing to take a definitive stand, but his purpose in the paper was not to argue for one side or another but to present a balanced view of his research findings. Being balanced and fair, however, does not mean being unable to analyze or draw conclusions, and the final draft of Slade's paper made it clear that many of his sources (and, apparently, Slade himself) had concluded that solutions to failure were far more complex and costly than replacing one simple policy with another.

Student writers are sometimes misled by the advice to *start* a research project with a thesis that is clear, unified, and restricted. Like an outline, a thesis ought to assist the process of searching, thinking, and composing; it should never become a straightjacket. As we have seen, Slade's preliminary research caused him to narrow his focus and shift his point of view. For Eliza, once she settled on her topic, formulating a thesis statement presented little difficulty. She simply expressed in plain language the goals of her project:

Thesis: I want to find out the benefits and pitfalls for

students of getting a credit card so that I can decide

whether or not to do so myself.

As we have seen, premature commitment to a thesis can become a hindrance to thorough, objective inquiry. Nevertheless, many writers prefer to develop a cohesive theme during the early stages of research. They have found that keeping such a theme in view—often in the form of a preliminary thesis statement—can help focus their work. If you have difficulty finding such a focus, try the following procedure:

Tips for Formulating a Thesis Statement

1. ***Think about your project in general terms.*** In your notebook, write a quick informal paragraph describing what you expect your paper to say and do. It may help to respond to these questions: What main topic have your efforts become focused on? What question(s) have you been trying to answer? What have you learned from your research? Do you now have a point of view about your topic— a conclusion or insight that you want to express in your paper?

2. ***Make your general idea specific.*** Review the paragraph you have written, and see if you can summarize its main idea in a single sentence.

As you continue your work, you should think often about how each part of your paper supports your focus. Be prepared to eliminate any sections that stray from the main topic. You may, of course, adjust your focus as you proceed with your project. In the final draft of his paper, Slade introduced his readers to his subject with this summary of his thesis:

```
When children fail in school, should they be promoted to the
next grade with their age group, or should they be required
to repeat the grade?  Over the last hundred years, the
educational pendulum has swung between these two approaches
to student failure, and educators and politicians continue to
debate this vexing question.
```

Sorting Your Note Cards

With an evolving conception of his topic, Slade recorded in his notes material that he thought was usable. While his note cards were a distillation of all he had learned from his reading, they still represented a formidable mass of data. He now had to select and arrange his cards into an order he could use. He read through them and sorted them by topic.

Since Slade had written a topic label at the top of each note card, he was able to group many of his cards together by subject. He found that most of his cards fell into a half dozen general categories: "history of social promotion," "statistics— pro," "statistics—con," "psychological effects on children," and so on. As he sorted he also set aside many discards—notes it was now clear he could not use. There were also many strays—single cards that did not fit conveniently into categories with any others. Slade had to decide if these belonged in his paper and, if so, how he might use them. In some cases, he would not know for sure until the actual writing.

Even with a good plan and a working outline, the final form of a paper can rarely be predicted in advance. Like Slade, you might follow this procedure:

1. ***Read through and sort your note cards.*** Sorting your cards into piles on a large table or on the floor can be helpful. Be sure you sort the cards by *topic* (not by any other principle, such as by source). Some piles will contain note cards from several different sources.

2. ***When your cards are sorted, think about how they can be used and arranged.*** Write about your ideas in your research notebook; think as you write, using the opportunity to work out ideas for organizing your paper. But do not be dismayed if you encounter loose ends at this stage. You will make many further decisions about your paper's organization as you write it.

3. ***Put aside any cards you do not expect to use.***

The best way to create an organizational plan for a paper is to think first in terms of the most general categories. Slade wrote this about his project in his research notebook:

> Most of the news stories talk of the ~~trend~~ tide away from
> social promotion. The Internet has dozens of quotes from
> Cleveland teachers, nearly all ~~complaining about~~ saying
> social promotion has been a disaster. [. . .] Longer
> articles talk more about costs with plenty of statistics.
> Chicago spends millions of dollars on summer schools, which
> were needed because of the new policy of failing students.
> There is more to the matter than just a ~~stupid~~ failed policy
> being replaced. I can give statistics, but I also want to
> talk about the reasons for and against. Introduce with
> explanation of social promotion, nature of debate, History?
> [. . .] Undecided: include section on voluntary retention of
> young children for social reasons, not academic reasons?
> Include trade schools as alternative for failing students?

Slade did not yet have a clear organization in mind for his paper, but we can see his mind working here—even making decisions as he wrote. He was confident he had good materials to work with, and he had enough ideas for a least a tentative organization that he could try out.

Updating Your Outline

Having thought about the parts of his paper and how he might put those parts together, Slade needed a clearer idea—a diagram of what his paper might look like. That is, he needed an *informal working outline*, an updated plan for organizing his paper.

When you create an outline, the headings you use will correspond, in theory, to the topic labels on your note cards. In reality, though, you will need to make adjustments to both the cards and the outline as a clear conception of the shape of your paper gradually forms in your mind. Try to put your ideas on paper in a handy visual form: A working outline is nothing more than a way of making these ideas visible and concrete.

Checking and rechecking his note cards, Slade developed the parts of an outline and, after several revisions, created an informal scheme, shown in Figure 13.1, to use in writing his first draft. Although some of the details would change in the final version of his paper, Slade found this outline helpful as he wrote, especially in getting started.

During his next class, Slade showed his outline and note cards to the other students in his editing group. He discussed his plans, received suggestions, and—even more valuable—answered questions. Explaining and defending his outline helped Slade notice strengths and weaknesses in his plan. An added benefit of the session was that it familiarized everyone in each editing group with classmates' projects.

 ## WRITING THE FIRST GOOD DRAFT

Having a tentative plan for organizing their papers, Slade and Eliza received an assignment like the following from their instructors:

Writing the Paper ASSIGNMENT

You are now ready to write a careful draft of your paper. Do so, and revise it until you are satisfied that it is as clearly written, well organized, interesting, and as informative as you can make it. Be sure to document your sources carefully with parenthetical notes and include an updated list of works cited. You should also consult the guidelines for editing and revising on pages 373–376.

Research Writing: General Guidelines

Slade soon discovered that his outline was only a starting point. In fact, he made changes in his organization from almost the moment he began his actual writing. He encountered difficulties with his opening, and, as his rough drafts would show, he went through at least six versions of the introductory section before he felt ready

Jonathan Slade Healy

Thesis and Working Outline

Ending Social Promotion: The Pros and Cons

Thesis: Many schools are abandoning social promotion and replacing it with a policy of retaining failing students, but experts are divided over which policies are in students' best interests.

Introduction

    Explanation of terms: social promotion and retention

    Brief history

    Thesis: controversial problem

Examples

    Changes in Chicago, Los Angeles, New Orleans, New York

Problems with social promotion

    Students not learning

    Bad morale for students and teachers

Problems with retention

    Academic: mixed results

    Social

        Psychological problems

        Problems caused by mixing age groups

Conclusion

    Issue complicated, not simple

    Many steps needed to deal with failure

Figure 13.1 Slade's thesis and working outline.

to move on. His preliminary outline rapidly became obsolete, but it had served its purpose. It had forced Slade to think about his paper as a whole—about how the individual parts might work together. Once he had made the outline, his concept of what he would accomplish in his writing became considerably less vague.

Although later parts of his draft went more smoothly, Slade discovered there is more to writing a paper than following a plan. Certainly, it is not just a matter of first writing about note 1, then about note 2, and so on throughout the paper. It will help to consider the following guidelines in writing your paper:

1. *Keep your goals in mind.* Novices can easily be overwhelmed by the procedures and details of research writing. Because of the many steps—all the procedures for assembling a list of sources and making note cards, outlines, and parenthetical notes—it is easy to lose sight of what a research paper is really about. The goal of your research is to learn something, to discover truth. In writing your paper, your goal is to present what you have learned so that your readers can also become informed. It follows that your writing should be readable and honest, informative and interesting. Never lose sight of these important goals as you write. Do not be blinded by procedures for their own sake.

2. *Remember that principles of good writing apply to research writing, too.* Like any other type of paper, a research paper should be clear and lively, not stodgy and pompous. It should be written so it can be read with enjoyment and without difficulty. Quotations and other source material should be neatly integrated into your writing so they are not obtrusive or awkward.

Like any other author, you have a responsibility to make the reader's job easier. Use topic sentences to help the reader know what to expect. Provide paragraph breaks to signal changes in topic or emphasis. Where appropriate, use transitional words and phrases (such as *on the other hand, also, for example,* and *consequently*) to make clear the relationship between successive sentences and paragraphs.

3. *Most of your paper should be you, not your sources.* While your sources may provide you with most of the information that you present in your paper, *you* are the one writing it. Write in your own voice. Your research paper should communicate what you have to say—just like any other paper you write. Remember, too, that your use of sources is simply a means to the goal of informing your readers; it is not an end in itself. Don't let your paper become simply a vehicle for presenting sources. Don't let your sources get in the way of clear writing.

4. *Don't be a slave to your note cards and outline.* Whenever you use a note from one of your cards, think about how it contributes to the point you are making. If a note isn't useful, don't include it. If it isn't clear, explain it. If you realize that your paper would be improved by adding new topics or rearranging your outline, by all means do so.

5. *Don't rely too heavily on one or two sources.* Inevitably, a few of your sources will have proved more helpful than the rest, and you will rely on these more than the others in writing your paper. Remember, however, that it is not your paper's purpose to restate what has already been said by another source or

two. A research paper should present something new, a fresh synthesis of information and ideas from many sources. A paper that is largely a summary of only one or two sources fails to do this. A variety of sources should make substantial contributions to your paper. On the other hand, the opposite extreme—where it becomes an end in itself to squeeze in material from every source you find—should also be avoided. Let common sense guide you between these two extremes.

Some Practical Writing Tips

Following are some practical tips on the act of writing itself:

Don'i Put Your Writing Off

Although the pressure of an impending deadline may stimulate great energy, it is unwise to begin writing your paper the night before it is due. You will produce a far better paper if you allow time for careful writing and revision. Start writing as soon as possible. Finishing ahead of your deadline will allow you the valuable opportunity to put the paper aside for a day or so, at which time you can take it up again, read it with fresh eyes, and gain new perspectives for improving it further.

Adopt Methods That Work for You

All writers are different. Use your past experience to decide what writing practices give you the best results.

Write in a place you find comfortable. A quiet library setting may free you from distractions and give you ready access to additional sources. On the other hand, you may prefer sitting at your computer keyboard at home, benefiting from the advantages of word processing. Or perhaps settling into a comfortable easy chair, writing with a pad on your lap and with your note cards on a table by your side, may allow you to do your best work.

Find ways to overcome obstacles. When you get stuck in your writing, perhaps it may help you to pause for a snack or a brief break to recharge your mental batteries— or you may find it best to shift gears, perhaps rereading what you have written or redirecting your attention to another part of the paper.

Adopt Positive Attitudes

Recognize that writing is hard work. Good writers work hard enough to make it *look* easy. Don't be discouraged by the snags that inevitably arise, and be prepared to give your project the time and energy it deserves.

Be persistent in writing. During the hard work of writing, writers are often visited with thoughts of more pleasant things they could be doing. At such times it is tempting to put down the pen or turn off the computer, promising yourself to resume writing later. Such temptations pose stern challenges to one's character and moral fiber. To be a successful writer is to develop self-discipline and to continue when one would rather not. As with any discipline you develop (from quitting smoking to mastering the cello to training for a triathlon), it is important to set realistic goals and to stick with them. At each writing session, set a goal of writing a certain number of pages or working for a certain number of hours—and meet it faithfully. Writing isn't usually fun, although at times it can be. But writing *is* very satisfying, especially when you know you have worked hard and produced a work you are proud of.

Have confidence in yourself. Even if this is your first research project, there is no reason to think you can't achieve admirable results. Remember, there are no secret formulas that others know and you don't. A paper is nothing more complicated than this: You have learned some information and are simply explaining it to readers who are much like yourself. Keep that in mind, tell your story clearly, let your own interest in the topic come through—and you will write a successful paper.

Getting Started

By the time you are ready to write, the hardest work should be behind you. You have plenty to say, as well as a plan for how you want to say it. You have a stack of note cards, arranged in the order in which you expect to use them. Once you are a page or two into your writing, the work should start to flow more smoothly. After students get past the initial unfamiliarity of working with source material, they usually find research writing little different from any other kind. In fact, because they are so well prepared, it is often easier.

Frequently, the most difficult part is simply getting started. In writing his first draft, Slade began by composing his opening section. He assumed that not all his readers would be familiar with the controversy about social promotion, so he decided to begin by introducing terms and giving some background. After many drafts, he produced this version:

The practice of promoting students, regardless of whether they have mastered the subject matter, is known as "social promotion." The alternative, leaving students back to repeat the grade, is known as "retention." In the early twentieth century, poorly performing students were regularly retained on the theory that repeating the year would prepare them to move on. By the 1930s, however, concerns about the psychological effects of retention on children led to many schools adopting social promotion (Adams 1-2). Since then, many experiments have been tried, and many studies have been conducted, but the issue remains as controversial today as it was then.

An early draft of Slade's opening

As he revised his paper in subsequent drafts, Slade realized that the definitions with which he began made his opening less than exciting, and he decided that he could better engage his readers' interest if he acquainted them with his paper's theme from the very beginning. He decided to wait until the second paragraph before introducing a (shorter) definition of social promotion and a (longer) account of the history of the controversy. The final version of his opening can be seen on page 238.

Struggling with an opening is not uncommon. Often it is best to wait until after you have drafted the body of a paper before even attempting to write the beginning. Writers sometimes waste time by overlooking the fact that the parts of a paper do not have to be written in the order in which they are to be read. If you are having difficulty getting started or are unsure about where to begin, start with a section that especially interests you or that seems easiest to write. Once you are successfully under way, composing the rest of the paper may be easier.

Writing the Opening

After you have written a draft of the body of your paper, you are in a better position to see what type of opening is most effective. An introductory section can serve many purposes: to inform readers of what your paper is about and where it is going, to generate interest, and to create a smooth transition into the body of the paper. There are many ways to begin a research paper; the following strategies are among those most frequently used:

Option 1: Begin with a Summary of the Paper's Main Idea

The purpose of beginning with a summary of the main idea is to tell your readers immediately what the paper is about. A version of your thesis statement will figure prominently in the opening, which serves as a summary of the entire paper to come.

This is the way Slade opened the final draft of his paper:

```
When schoolchildren fail in school, should they be

promoted to the next grade with their age group, or should

they be required to repeat the grade?  Over the last hundred

years, the educational pendulum has swung between these two

approaches to student failure, and educators and politicians

continue to debate this vexing question (American,

"Passing").  After many experiments and countless studies,

the issue today is more controversial than ever.
```

In his first sentence, Slade sets forth the question his paper will seek to answer, and he ends the paragraph with a sentence that succinctly states his thesis. The readers' job is made easier because Slade has given them a clear expectation of what will follow in the paper.

Option 2: Begin with Background

Because your readers may not be well informed about your topic, you can provide them with a brief overview. The background you provide may include a history of the topic or a summary of occurrences leading up to the events you describe. For example, Slade might have opened his paper with this historical summary:

> During the early decades of the twentieth century, students who performed poorly in the public schools were regularly left back at the same grade level on the theory that repeating the year would prepare them to move on. That policy changed in the 1930s, however, when many educators expressed concerns about the negative psychological effects of retention on children (Adams 1-2). In 1941 a New York State report concluded that "a much wiser and more profitable procedure than non-promotion is to adapt instruction to the needs of the pupil at all times, and at the end of the year to advance him to the next grade or class and there continue to adjust instruction to his needs" (qtd. in Rothstein). This was the beginning of "social promotion," the policy of promoting students no matter how well they performed. In recent years, however, many have questioned the wisdom of social promotion, and a debate continues to rage about which policy better serves our students.

In this paragraph, the historical summary leads into a clear statement of the paper's thesis in the final sentence.

Option 3: Begin with an Interesting Anecdote

Starting with a specific story not only can capture your readers' interest immediately but also can be used to lead into your thesis statement. Eliza began her personal research paper with an anecdote from her own experience:

> "Put it on plastic," said Ellen, my roommate, as she handed her MasterCard to the clerk at Millennium Music. I had been staring at the few small bills in my wallet,

> debating whether I could afford a Sarah McLachlan CD, but
> Ellen had no hesitation. Her purchase seemed simple and
> painless, as if no money were involved.
>
>   Most of my friends use charge cards. Should I join the
> ranks of purchasers with plastic?

Traditional research papers also can begin with anecdotes. For example, Slade could have opened his paper with a story:

>   Chicago eighth-grader Lashawnda Walker watched her
> classmates move on to high school a year ago. Because she
> scored below her grade level on the Iowa Basic Skills reading
> test, Lashawnda was required to attend summer school. Her
> score improved on the retake but not enough to let her
> graduate. After a second year in the eighth grade, she was
> dismayed when she came up a few points short of a passing
> score and was sent to summer school once again. "I feel
> really bad that I didn't make it," she said. "I think about
> that test all the time." Lashawnda is one of the human
> faces affected by Chicago's widely heralded new policy to end
> "social promotion," the practice of advancing students to the
> next grade regardless of their level of skill or achievement
> (Ratnesar and Cole).

Option 4: Begin by Explaining Your Purpose for Writing

A personal research paper often begins with a section headed "Why I Wrote This Paper" or "What I Wanted to Find Out." Instead of beginning with an anecdote, Eliza could have gone directly to a statement of her purpose:

>   Most of my friends use charge cards. Should I join the
> ranks of purchasers with plastic? So far I have resisted
> the appeals that arrive almost daily in my mailbox from card
> vendors, banks, even airlines and car companies. The lure of
> credit seems great: easy purchasing, freedom from cash,
> building a credit history, even free gifts. Is this right
> for me?

Many scientific papers also begin by stating specifically what is to come in the rest of the paper. Conventional research papers, however, generally avoid direct statements by the author about purpose. A rule of thumb in writing for the liberal arts is that papers should avoid talking about themselves. That is, they should not contain statements such as "In this paper I will . . . " or "The rest of this paper will examine. . . ." (Note how the other sample beginnings make the theme evident without any such statements.) The personal research paper is an exception to this rule.

Writing the Conclusion

The one section of the research paper that can be even more troublesome than the opening is the conclusion. After all, once you have said what you have to say, what else remains to be done? Fortunately, it is not as hopeless as that. The principal purpose of a conclusion is not to say something new but to draw the ends of the paper together and to leave the reader with a satisfying sense of closure. Simply put, an ending should feel to the reader like an ending.

One strategy, appropriate for a long paper, is to tie together what you have written by summarizing the paper's content. This may be effective if you can summarize the paper in a fresh and insightful way. A summary serves no purpose, however, if it merely rehashes what has already been made evident to the alert reader.

Often an effective way of ending a research paper and allowing your readers to put what they have read into perspective is to assess (draw conclusions from) what you have learned. In an informative paper, the ending is the most appropriate place to offer your own observations and insights about your topic.

In his final paragraph, Slade not only summarized his paper in a fresh way, but he also drew a conclusion about his topic:

> Educational researchers agree that the problem of
> student failure will be solved only through careful and
> costly efforts. Unfortunately, complex solutions do not lend
> themselves to the sound bites favored by many politicians and
> school boards. Until we are ready to deal seriously with
> the causes of failure, the educational pendulum is likely to
> continue to swing between social promotion and retention.

Slade also helped his readers get a sense of closure by ending with the same image with which he began his paper—the pendulum swinging back and forth.

Eliza's ending was less conventional than Slade's but no less effective. In her concluding paragraph, she didn't summarize but instead introduced something new—a quotation that brought the paper's topic into focus:

> One administrator at Indiana University put the problem
> of student credit cards succinctly: "We lose more students to

```
credit card debt than academic failure" (qtd. in "Credit").

Thanks to what I have learned, I will make certain I do not

become another of those casualties.
```

Her final sentence plays off that quotation and succinctly states her conclusion—that she has gained the wisdom from her research to make a sound decision.

A word of caution: Strategies such as these are offered as helpful possibilities, not as rules or boundaries. Good writing resists formulas, and good writers continually find original ways of achieving their goals. Adopt whatever strategies work for you, and consider new approaches. That is the best way to extend your range as a writer.

Giving Your Paper a Title

Giving your paper a title may be the final stage of your project. Ideally, your title should both indicate to your readers what your paper is about and arouse their interest. In his first draft, Slade gave his paper the title "Coping with Failure in School." A classmate who read the draft remarked that from the title he expected it to be about advice to college students. Slade later considered several more informative titles, including "Social Promotion vs. Retention in Public Schools" and "Social Promotion, Retention, and Alternative Approaches to Student Failure." He finally settled for the simpler "Social Promotion and Its Alternatives." Eliza chose a much more playful title: "Giving Myself Credit: Should I Apply for a Credit Card?" She fully intended both meanings of the phrase *giving myself credit:* the paper is about giving herself a financial line of credit but also about giving herself the authority to make a sound decision.

Arresting, clever, or witty titles are not easy to create—and not always desirable, as there is a fine line between originality and cuteness. Start with a simple, direct title that captures your theme. If later on you are inspired with a better choice, fine, but if not, no one should object to a plain but clear title.

EDITING AND REVISING

Writers differ in their work habits. Eliza is a constant reviser. Composing, rearranging, and editing at the keyboard of her word processor, Eliza tends to write a little, pause to read what she has produced, make changes, and then move on. Slade, on the other hand, is more of an all-at-once reviser: He generally writes long passages straight through, forging ahead while ideas are still fresh in his mind. Only after he has written several pages will Slade pause to reread and make changes.

Because of their different work habits, Eliza and Slade produced very different kinds of preliminary drafts. Slade wrote several complete drafts, each more polished than the previous one. Eliza, on the other hand, emerged with something very close to a final draft after having gradually reached the concluding section of her paper. To call Eliza's final paper a single "perfect" draft, however, would be very misleading. Since Eliza was constantly rereading, revising, and editing earlier parts of her paper, these parts had actually gone through several drafts by the time she reached her conclusion. Her success was due partly to productive work habits and partly to the fact that Eliza kept the structure of her paper clearly in view from the outset.

Both writers achieved success by using methods that worked for them. You, too, should feel free to adopt practices that work for you. Basically, though, you can be an effective editor of your own work if you approach it like a reader. Put aside what you have written for a day or more until you can read it with a fresh perspective. Put yourself in your readers' place, trying to anticipate whether they will find it clear, readable, and effective. You may find it helpful to consult the checklist that begins below, considering each question as if you were responding to a paper someone else has written.

Reworking Your Paper

After completing preliminary drafts, both writers put aside what they had written for a while, then came back and reread them with a pencil in hand. A page from Eliza's early draft in which she made particularly extensive changes appears in Figure 13.2. Although Eliza makes handwritten corrections on pages composed at a word processor, other writers prefer working entirely on paper, while still others make all their revisions directly at the computer keyboard.

Checklist for Editing and Revising

Topic, Focus, and Support

- Is it clear what the topic of the paper is? Does the writer provide a thesis statement or otherwise make it evident, early in the paper, what the paper is about? Is any further help needed for the reader to see the paper's point?
- Is the topic adequately narrowed—that is, neither too broad nor too limited for the writer to do it justice in a paper of this length?
- Has the writer kept the promises made by the thesis statement? That is, does the paper remain focused on its thesis? Does it stick to the point?
- Is the thesis supported with a variety of details or evidence?
- Is this support clear and convincing?
- In reading the paper, have you learned what you were expecting to learn from it? What questions remain in your mind? What needs to be developed more? What seems to be missing?

Audience, Style, and Readability

- Is the writing style appropriate for its intended audience? What passages do you have trouble understanding?
- Does the paper read smoothly and easily? Does the paper's use of sources and quotations ever become distracting or interrupt the smooth flow of your reading?

Tetirick 1

Eliza Tetirick

Editing draft

                    Giving Myself Credit:
                                    credit
            Should I Apply for a Card?

                                        staring at the few small bills on my wallet

I. Why I Am Writing This Paper
                                            Ellen,
        "Put it on plastic," said my roommate, ~~Ellen~~ as she
                                at Millenium Music.
handed her MasterCard to the clerk. I had been debating
                Sarah McLachlan   *Her*
whether I could afford a CD, but Ellen's purchase seemed so
and painless   *had no hesitation.*
simple, as if no money were involved.

        Should I join the ranks of purchasers with plastic?
So far I have been resisting the appeals ~~from banks~~ that
                                                airlines and
            from banks card vendors, banks, even car companies
arrive almost daily in my mailbox. The lure of credit
                            freedom from   building a credit history
cards seems great: easy purchasing, ~~no~~ cash ~~to carry,~~ even
free gifts. (Most of my friends use charge cards.) Is this
right for me?

        I wanted to make an informed decision, and the
                                            getting this
opportunity to find answers was ideal. ~~I found out much~~
                                                            larger
My search has   *the benefits and pitfalls of   also   the world of*
~~that~~ opened my eyes not just to credit cards but to ~~much~~
~~about~~ personal finance.

II. What I Knew

    I now know that, (when I began my research,) I was
about credit + credit cards
    dangerously ignorant. I knew little more (about credit and
                                enticing
(credit cards) than the slogans that were found on the
envelopes sent by the credit card vendors. "An

- Is the paper free from awkward phrasing, misspellings, typographical errors, and other mechanical flaws?

- Does the paper conform to MLA format (see Chapter C in Part II)?

Organization

- Is the paper organized in a way that makes sense? Can you understand why topics come where they do in the paper? Could any parts be rearranged for greater logic and clarity? Are there passages in different parts of the paper that should be brought together?

- Does the paper begin with a helpful general introduction to the topic? Can you tell from the introduction where the paper is going? Does the paper capture your interest right from the beginning? Could it be made more lively and interesting?

- Does the writer provide smooth and helpful transitions between subjects? Can you always tell how the part you are reading fits into the paper as a whole?

- Does the paper end with a satisfying conclusion?

Use of Sources

- Is the paper based on a variety of sources? Is the use of sources balanced, or is most of the information taken from only one or two sources?

- Is most of the information from sources paraphrased, rather than quoted directly? Are quotations used excessively? When sources are quoted, is there a reason for doing so? (See pages 345–49 for the proper use of quotations.)

- Does the writer avoid "naked quotations"? That is, is each quotation introduced by a phrase or sentence? When sources are referred to in the paper, are they adequately identified in acknowledgment phrases? That is, are you given enough information about them so that you can tell who they are and whether they are experts on the subject? (See pages 328–30).

- Are sources documented? Does the paper credit its sources within parenthetical notes? Does it credit paraphrased material as well as direct quotations? (Consult the Quick Reference Guides on the inside covers of this book.)

- Does the writer avoid overnoting (unnecessary notes for commonly available information) as well as undernoting (paraphrasing a source's ideas without providing a note)?

- Is it clear what each note refers to? That is, can you tell what information goes with what note?

- Are the sources listed in a works-cited page following the paper? Are the number and types of sources adequate for the paper?

- Does each note provide the least amount of information needed to refer you to the works-cited page and to identify the specific pages being referenced by the note?

- Except for longer, indented passages, are the notes placed inside the sentences with the period after, not before, the note?
- Does the punctuation in each note and in each entry in the works-cited page follow the prescribed format exactly? (Check the Quick Reference Guides on the inside covers.) Are items in the works-cited page listed in alphabetical order? Has the writer remembered that these items should not be numbered in MLA format?

Getting Advice from Other Readers

No matter how good a job writers do at editing their own writing, they can always benefit from outside help as well. Writers become so closely involved with their work that they can lose the ability to observe it from the reader's perspective. For that reason, good editing often requires advice from a reader who can point out flaws and possibilities that have escaped the writer's notice.

When he was satisfied with his revisions, Slade brought his printed paper to class for editing. (Students in Eliza's class met with partners outside of class time to edit each other's papers.) Slade and his classmates were given the following assignment:

ASSIGNMENT   **Group Editing**

Read the papers written by members of your editing group and offer them the most helpful advice you can give.

Your Role as Editor

- Read each paper with care and interest, as if it were written with you as its intended audience.
- In responding to the paper, think of yourself as a friend trying to help, not as a judge providing a grade or evaluation.

The Editing Procedure

Read each paper at least twice, first for a general impression, then for specific details.

- The first time, read it straight through to gain a general impression. Do not stop to ask questions or write comments. When you have completed your first reading, pause to write a paragraph or two about the paper in general, including the following:

  –State what the paper's main idea seems to be.
  –Describe your general reaction to the paper. What did you learn from it?
  –Tell the author how the paper worked for you. Where was the best writing in the draft? Did the paper develop as you expected it to? As you were reading, did questions arise in your mind that the author answered or failed to answer? Did you ever have trouble following it?
  –Ask any other questions and make any other general comments about the paper as a whole.

- Now read the paper a second time, paying greater attention to specifics. Pause at any time to write comments, according to the following guidelines:

  –Write comments, questions, or ideas in pencil in the margins of the paper. Put checkmarks by passages that you want to talk with the writer about.

  –Point out the paper's strengths (note passages you especially like) as well as weaknesses, but be honest. You will not be much help to the author if you say that everything is wonderful when you think the paper might be improved. You are not insulting the writer by offering ideas to improve it. Specific suggestions are much more helpful than vague comments like "?" or "Needs work."

  –If you are in doubt about an editing or proofreading matter, consult with your instructor.

- Finally, talk with the paper's author. Explain your comments. Describe your response to the paper, what problems or questions you had while reading it, and what suggestions you have for making it better.

Slade received editing suggestions from the two other students in his editing group. The following pages show the comments of Angela, one of his peers.

Healy 1

Jonathan Slade Healy

Editing draft

From your title,) was expecting advice to students.

Coping with Failure in School

The practice of promoting students, regardless of whether they have mastered the subject matter, is known as "social promotion." The alternative, leaving students back to repeat the grade, is known as "retention." In the early twentieth century, poorly performing students were regularly retained on the theory that repeating the year would prepare them to move on. By the 1930s, however, concerns about the psychological effects of retention on children led to many schools adopting social promotion (Adams 1-2). Since then, many experiments have been tried, and many studies have been conducted, but the issue remains as controversial today as it was then.

It took me a while to realize you weren't writing about college students

Are definitions the best way to start?

I'm curious about these effects

In recent years, politicians have campaigned against social promotion (Wood), and the pendulum has swung back toward retention. Americans are dissatisfied with the public schools, and many have blamed social promotion as a factor in students' poor performance. One Cleveland high school teacher reports, "I have students in the tenth and eleventh grades who read on a fourth-grade level. They need remediation and should never have been promoted" ("Most"). An elementary teacher said, "Social promotion has made me and my students less effective because we both know they will be passed regardless of what they do in the classroom all year" ("Most"). When social promotion is

)like this image.

These quotations are effective and make the problem seem real.

Healy 2

eliminated, some students say they are motivated to work harder. Third-grader Erica Quinones, who attended summer school under the policy, intends to pass the test next time. "Instead of being in [summer] school," she says, "I could be having fun" (qtd. in Coeyman).

In 1996, Chicago became one of many districts to eliminate social promotion. I~~t~~ requires its public school students to take standardized tests in the third, sixth, and eighth grades. Students who fail then take summer school, but they must repeat the grade if they still cannot pass (Coeyman). Last year almost 15% of students in those grades were retained, compared to less than 2% in the year before the new policy (Ratnesar and Cole). Of the 10,000 Chicago third graders who attended summer school last year, fewer than half were promoted. Nearly a thousand students who had already been held back in third grade were retained for a second time (Coeyman). However, the city did graduate the most students to ninth grade in its history (Wood).

Wow! could this be an argument that the new policy isn't working?

To make the new policy work, Chicago spent $24 million last year on summer programs and another $10 million to hire new teachers to tutor at-risk students (Ratnesar and Cole). Los Angeles, another city that has ended social promotion, is spending $71 million this year for a 60-hour summer school, Saturday classes, and after-school tutoring in math and reading ("Nation's" 3).

I'm confused. Are you saying that retention is too expensive? Or does this mean that they need to spend money to help students?

I like it that you give both sides.

Not everyone is in favor of eliminating promotion, and some educators argue that retention does more harm than good. *Are they teachers!* Mary Lee Smith and Lorrie A. Shepard analyzed research studies that compared students who were promoted with students who were required to spend two years at the same grade level. <u>The retained students actually did worse in school than those who were promoted</u> (215). *But weren't the promoted students smarter! Or did they compare similar students?*

While a retention policy can motivate some students to perform, it can also have negative consequences for those unable to do so. Joellen Perry writes "Slow learners or students with attention disorders will encounter the same difficulties the second time around, while enduring the shame of repeating a grade. Educators also warn of a lingering, powerful 'should be' syndrome. Years later, many retained children believe their rightful place is in the grade above"(76). The stigma of retention can be devastating to children. In a 1980 study in which children ranked traumas, the fear of repeating a grade caused the most stress, behind only the fear of losing a parent or going blind (Perry 75). Chicago eighth-grader Corrine Murphy expressed her reaction to her school's retention policy by saying, "If you don't pass, you stay in the same grade and people will be making fun of you" (qtd. in Coeyman).

Indent the long quote!

This is a powerful argument.

The quote reinforces the point well.

Feelings of disgrace and loss of self-esteem may be factors in the high dropout rate among those made to repeat. Smith and Shepard report that retaining students

Healy 4

"increases the probability of [their] eventually dropping out of school by 20% to 30%" (215). Shepard says that students who repeat two grades "have a probability of

Well said

dropping out of nearly 100 percent" (qtd. in Wood). This is not the outcome proponents of retention hoped for.

Still another consequence of retention is the effect on younger children of having older, retained children in the same classroom. Richard Rothstein, a critic of educational policies, observes:

A good point

> Puberty now begins earlier than it has in the
> past. Putting 14-year-olds in classrooms with
> 11- and 12-year-olds will exacerbate the
> pressures these younger adolescents face [. . .].
> While grouping children by age does cause
> academic problems, grouping children of varied
> ages together because of comparable academic
> skill is not a completely benign alternative. It
> causes other problems for teachers, parents, and
> children alike. (197)

Most educators now believe that the solution to the problem of failure does not lie in either social promotion or retention. Sandra Feldman, president of the American Federation of Teachers, said that "neither social promotion nor holding kids back without help is a successful strategy for improving learning. What we really need is an intensive-care approach right from the start, concentrating every possible resource on helping students as soon as they

Can you change it so the quote doesn't repeat the previous sentence!

Healy 5

start to fall behind" (qtd. in American, "New"). Feldman

says that a "five-point program" is needed for ending

social promotion:

First, pre-school and kindergarten children need high-

quality programs. If this cannot be provided for all

children, then the focus should be on the poorest school

districts in the country.

Second, we need to need to "develop rigorous grade-by-

grade standars for students." Teachers need a set of

standards if they are to make sound judgments and to know

right away when students are having problems.

Third, Feldman says, all elementary teachers must be

properly trained in teaching reading. This is not always

the case, and school districts must make this training a

priority.

Fourth, we have to catch the problem students early in

their careers. Feldman says, "The most cost-effective

remedial program is one that prevents students from failing

in the first place."

Fifth, schools should use approaches that have been

tried and proven effective. These include individual

tutoring, Saturday classes, and "double dosing," which

means an extra period in the problem subject (American,

"Passing").

In addition, a report by the AFT (American Federation

of Teachers) says that if we want to eliminate social

promotion, we have to do the following:

[handwritten note in left margin: These are good points, but it seems like a list.]

[handwritten editing marks: "d" inserted in "standars" and caret below]

Healy 6

-- Place well-trained teachers in every classroom by developing policies to attract and retain the best teachers in schools with high-risk student populations.

-- Make it a top priority to provide all teachers with opportunities to learn how to teach students to read.

-- Learn from schools and districts that have successfully implemented research-based reforms. ("New")

Educational researchers agree that social promotion may not be successful, but simply keeping students back is not the answer either. Real solutions to the problem of student failure will require careful and costly solutions. Unfortunately, complex solutions do not lend themselves to the sound bites favored by many politicians and school boards.

Slade, you made me interested in the topic. I was never left back, but I had friends who were (in kindergarten). I now have an understanding of the arguments pro and con. In fact, I really like the way you presented both sides without favoring one over the other.

I marked some places where I wasn't sure if information was supposed to support or oppose social promotion. You did a nice job of giving both facts and quotations from real people.

— Angela

Slade found Angela's comments valuable because they revealed another reader's response to his paper as well as useful ideas for improving it. Several of Angela's remarks highlight what worked well for her ("These quotations are effective and make the problem seem real"). Others inform Slade about a passage she found unclear ("It took me a while to realize you weren't writing about college students"). Remarks that specify her difficulty are particularly useful ("I'm confused. Are you saying that retention is too expensive? Or does this mean that they need to spend money to help students?") In some of her comments Angela responds on a personal level to what Slade is saying ("Wow! Could this be an argument that the new policy *isn't* working?"). Angela's longer commentary at the end of Slade's paper includes a personal response ("I was never left back . . . "), but it also summarizes her response and makes helpful suggestions.

Note that Angela's comments are framed in a positive and unintrusive way. When she offers suggestions, she does so in the form of questions, making it clear that the paper belongs to Slade and that final editing decisions rest with him ("Are definitions the best way to start?"). Even when she notes a minor formatting error, she asks rather than tells ("Indent the long quote?"), and it is clear that Angela's goal is to be as helpful to Slade as possible as he undertakes his revision. Her comments are constructive, useful, and confidence-building.

In addition to responding to the valuable suggestions of his classmates and instructor, Slade discovered other ways to improve his paper over the next week. Each time he reread his draft, Slade noticed new possibilities of revising it. He spent many hours rephrasing, clarifying, and even rearranging sections of the paper, until he was ready to submit the polished draft that you read in Chapter 8, which is reprinted, with annotations, on the following pages.

Healy 1

Jonathan Slade Healy

ENG 102

Ms. Lynne Rader

15 Nov. 1999

The title is not underlined or placed within quotation marks.

The writer introduces the reader to the paper's topic right away. For other opening strategies, see pages 368–71.

Social Promotion and Its Alternatives

When children fail in school, should they be promoted to the next grade with their age group, or should they be required to repeat the grade? Over the last hundred years, the educational pendulum has swung between these two approaches to student failure, and educators and politicians continue to debate this vexing question (American, "Passing"). After many experiments and countless studies, the issue today is more controversial than ever.

The practice of promoting students, regardless of how well they perform or whether they master the subject matter, is known as social promotion. During the early decades of the twentieth century, poorly performing students were regularly left back at the same grade level on the theory that repeating the year would prepare them to move on. By the 1930s, however, concerns about the negative psychological effects of retention on children led to the widespread adoption of social promotion (Adams 1-2). In 1941 a New York Regents report concluded that "a much wiser and more profitable procedure than non-promotion is to adapt instruction to the needs of the pupil at all times, and at the end of the year to advance him to the

The writer clarifies a term for the reader and provides historical background.

A parenthetical note is used to identify the source of paraphrased material.

Healy 2

next grade or class and there continue to adjust
instruction to his needs" (qtd. in Rothstein 198).

When one
source is
quoted in
another source,
give the source
where the
quotation was
found.

In recent years, however, the pendulum has clearly
been swinging once again away from social promotion and
toward retention. Americans are not satisfied with the
public schools, and many have blamed social promotion for
students' poor performance. One Cleveland high school
teacher reports: "I have students in the tenth and eleventh
grades who read on a fourth-grade level. They need
remediation and should never have been promoted" (qtd.in

Notes for
electronic
sources
do not
give page
references.

"Most"). Politicians of all political viewpoints have
trumpeted the ending of social promotion as their main
educational goal (Wood). By last year ten states had
adopted policies for ending social promotion, and the
number is fast growing (Shaw 7).

Notes for print
sources give
the page(s)
where the
information
was found.

Los Angeles, the nation's largest school district,
will end social promotion this year. Students in grades 2,
3, 4, 5, and 8 will be evaluated on class grades and
performance on test scores ("Nation's" 3). Since 1996,
Chicago has required its public school students to take
standardized tests in the third, sixth, and eighth grades.

A note for an
anonymous
work gives the
first word or
two of the title.

Those who fail must attend summer school, and if they still
do not pass they must repeat the grade (Coeyman). The
change in Chicago has been dramatic. Last year almost 15%
of students in those grades were retained, compared to fewer
than 2% in the year before the new policy (Ratnesar and
Cole).

Healy 3

A common argument for ending social promotion is that it removes penalties when students fail to learn. As a Cleveland elementary teacher put it, "Social promotion has made me and my students less effective because we both know they will be passed regardless of what they do in the classroom all year" (qtd. in "Most"). When Chicago eliminated social promotion, some students say they were motivated to work harder. Third-grader Erica Quinones, who attended summer school under the policy, intends to pass the test next time. "Instead of being in [summer] school," she says, "I could be having fun" (qtd. in Coeyman). Test scores are up since the policy was enacted, and Chicago schools report the highest math and reading scores in a decade (Ratnesar and Cole). Last year, after 4,700 eighth-graders took the summer program, the city graduated the most students to ninth grade in its history (Wood).

If ending social promotion has been so successful, why is there any controversy about making the change? For one thing, not all students have shared in the success. Tom Reece, president of the Chicago Teachers Union, says, "We are getting good results but also finding it doesn't work for everyone" (qtd. in Wood). Of the 10,000 Chicago third graders who attended summer school last year, fewer than half were promoted. Nearly a thousand were held back in third grade for a second time (Coeyman). In theory the retained students should learn the skills that they failed to learn the first time. However, some critics of

The writer presents benefits of ending social promotion.

The writer then presents costs associated with ending social promotion.

Healy 4

retention policies claim that, while social promotion does not help students, retention is even worse for them.

An acknowledgment phrase marks the beginning of a passage.

Professors Mary Lee Smith and Lorrie A. Shepard analyzed research studies that compared similar at-risk students, some of whom were promoted, while others who were required to spend two years at the same grade level. The retained students actually did worse in school than those who were promoted (215).

A note marks the end of the passage.

While the fear of retention can motivate some students to perform, it can also have negative consequences for those who are unable to do so. Joellen Perry reports:

Longer quotations are indented one inch or ten spaces. No quotation marks are used.

> Slow learners or students with attention disorders will encounter the same difficulties the second time around, while enduring the shame of repeating a grade. Educators also warn of a lingering, powerful "should be" syndrome. Years later, many retained children believe their rightful place is in the grade above. (76)

A note following an indented quotation comes after the period.

The stigma of retention can be devastating to children. In a 1980 study in which children ranked traumas, the fear of repeating a grade caused the most stress, behind only the fear of losing a parent or going blind (Perry 75). Chicago eighth-grader Corrine Murphy expressed her reaction to her school's retention policy: "If you don't pass, you stay in the same grade and people will be making fun of you" (qtd. in Coeyman).

Other notes come before the period.

Healy 5

Feelings of disgrace and loss of self-esteem may be factors in the high dropout rate among those made to repeat. Smith and Shepard report that retained students are 20% to 30% more likely to drop out of school than those who are promoted (215). Shepard says that students who repeat two grades "have a probability of dropping out of nearly 100 percent" (qtd. in Wood). This is not the result that proponents of retention hoped for.

The writer integrates part of a quotation into his own sentence.

    Still another consequence of retention is the negative effects on younger children of having older children in the same classroom. Richard Rothstein, a critic of educational policies, observes: "Puberty now begins earlier than it has in the past. Putting 14-year-olds in classrooms with 11- and 12-year-olds will exacerbate the pressures these younger adolescents face." While teachers do not want socially promoted students in their classrooms, they are just as likely to object to teaching retained students who are older than the other students in their classes (197).

    Most educators now believe that, by itself, neither social promotion nor retention is the solution to student failure. When Los Angeles and Chicago ended social promotion, both districts dramatically increased spending on remedial programs designed to prevent failure. Los Angeles has allocated $71 million this year for a 60-hour summer school, Saturday classes, and after-school tutoring in math and reading ("Nation's" 3). Chicago spent $24

Having shown the limitations of social promotion and retention, the writer now presents the alternatives.

Healy 6

million last year on summer programs and another $10
million to hire new teachers to tutor at-risk students
(Ratnesar and Cole). Identifying and dealing with student
problems is expensive, costing taxpayers as much as $1,300
per student. But it is much cheaper than the $4,000 cost
when a student repeats a grade (Wood).

According to Sandra Feldman, president of the American
Federation of Teachers, the most cost-effective approach is
to prevent failure in the first place. "What we really
need," she says, "is an intensive-care approach right from
the start, concentrating every possible resource on helping
students as soon as they start to fall behind" (qtd. in
American, "New"). Schools must provide high-quality pre-
school and kindergarten programs and well trained teachers.
In addition, they must identify struggling students in the
earliest grades, put them in small classes, and give them
solid instruction in reading. When students fail, Feldman
recommends remedial approaches that "have a good track
record but are seldom used." These include individual
tutoring, Saturday classes, and extra periods in problem
subjects (American, "New").

Smith and Shepard claim that the most effective remedy
for children performing below grade level is not retention
but promotion accompanied by remediation. They cite
research showing that tutoring, summer school, and one-on-
one help are more effective and less costly than retention
(230). When school systems use retention, they argue,

Acknowledgment
phrases identify
sources not
familiar to the
reader and
establish them
as authorities.

Only the page
number is
given in a note
when the
authors' names
are identified
in the text.

Healy 7

individualized instruction must also be given to retained students so that they can rejoin their age group as soon as possible (233).

Linda Darling-Hammond, executive director of the National Commission on Teaching and America's Future, claims that the quality of the teacher is the single most important factor in student performance, and she recommends directing resources to training and hiring better teachers. Low-income, minority, and special-needs students are the students most often retained, and they are also those least likely to have well qualified, effective teachers (48–49).

Educational researchers agree that the problem of student failure will be solved only through careful and costly efforts. Unfortunately, complex solutions do not lend themselves to the sound bites favored by many politicians and school boards. Until we are ready to deal seriously with the causes of failure, the educational pendulum is likely to continue to swing between social promotion and retention.

The writer ends by summing up and drawing conclusions from his research.

Healy 8

Works Cited

Adams, Edgar. "Alternatives to Grade-Level Retention."
    M. Ed. thesis. U of North Carolina at Wilmington,
    1995.

American Federation of Teachers. "Passing on Failure:
    District Promotion Policies and Practices." <u>K-12
    Educational Issues</u>. 13 Oct. 1999 <http://www.aft.org/
    edissues/socialpromotion/Intro.htm>.

---. "New AFT Report on Social Promotion in the Schools."
    <u>K-12 Educational Issues</u>. 13 Oct. 1999 <http://
    www.aft.org/edissues/socialpromotion/pr90997.htm>.

Coeyman, Marjorie. "Repeating a Grade Gains Favor in
    Schools." <u>Christian Science Monitor</u> 6 Apr. 1999.
    <u>MasterFILE Premier</u>. EBSCOhost. 15 Oct. 1999 <http://
    www.epnet.com/ehost/>.

Darling-Hammond, Linda. "Avoiding Both Grade Retention and
    Social Promotion." <u>Education Digest</u> Nov. 1998.
    ProQuest. 14 Oct. 1999 <http://
    www.bellhowell.infolearning.com/proquest/>.

"Most Cleveland Teachers Say Social Promotion Doesn't
    Work." Sun Newspapers. 1997. 12 Oct. 1999 <http://
    www.sunnews.com/news/suburbs/metro/
    socialpromotionside.htm>.

"Nation's Largest District Ends Social Promotion."
    <u>Curriculum Review</u> 38.10 (1999): 3.

Perry, Joellen. "What, Mrs. Crabapple Again?" <u>U.S. News &
    World Report</u> 24 May 1999: 75-76.

Sources are listed in alphabetical order.

Hyphens indicate a second article by the same author

Sources are not numbered.

Give the date when you consulted an electronic source (see Chapter 9).

Healy 9

Ratnesar, Romesh, and Wendy Cole. "Held Back." <u>Time</u> 14
    June 1999. <u>MasterFILE Premier</u>. EBSCOhost. 15 Oct.
    1999 <http://www.epnet.com/ehost/>.

Rothstein, Richard. "Where Is Lake Wobegon, Anyway?" <u>Phi
    Delta Kappan</u> Nov. 1998: 195-98.

Shaw, Donna. "Stopping Social Promotion." <u>Curriculum
    Administrator</u> 35.9 (1999): 7.

Smith, Mary Lee, and Lorrie A. Shepard. "Flunking Grades:
    A Recapitulation." <u>Flunking Grades: Research and
    Policies on Retention</u>. Ed. Lorrie A. Shepard and Mary
    Lee Smith. New York: Falmer, 1989. 214-36.

Wood, Daniel B. "California's Big Test: Holding Students
    Back." <u>Christian Science Monitor</u> 5 Feb. 1999.
    <u>MasterFILE Premier</u>. EBSCOhost. 15 Oct. 1999
    <http://www.epnet.com/ehost/>.

Give the online location of an electronic database used to access a source (see Chapter 9).

**TYPING AND PROOFREADING
YOUR POLISHED DRAFT**

Slade and Eliza benefited from the comments and suggestions they received from classmates in their editing groups and from their instructors. They made further revisions in their papers and submitted them in polished form, in accordance with the assignment they had been given, which follows.

ASSIGNMENT   **Submitting Your Portfolio**

Submit the following items in your folder:

- Your typed polished draft.
- All earlier drafts and outlines.
- Your note cards in two packets:
  –those you used in your paper, in the order you used them.
  –those you wrote but did not use.
- Your research notebook.

When you prepare your final draft, be sure that you observe formatting conventions described in Chapter C of Part II, along with any others your instructor may specify. Before you submit your paper, read it through several times, slowly and carefully, looking for errors. Look for typing mistakes, misspellings, missing words, punctuation problems, and any other surface errors that may have escaped your notice in earlier readings. It is especially useful to have a friend proofread the paper as well, because by now you have become so familiar with what you have written that you may have difficulty noticing surface details.

Neatly cross out a minor error with a single line and write the correction above it. Never erase, and do not use correction fluid for making handwritten changes. Any page with a major error or numerous minor errors should be reprinted.

After proofreading their final drafts, Slade and Eliza brought them to class, where their instructors gave them one final assignment:

ASSIGNMENT   **Final Proofreading**

Read the final drafts of the other students in your editing group. Do not mark on their papers, but if you find an error, point it out to the author so that it can be corrected.

At last, Slade and Eliza submitted their final drafts. For both, the project had been difficult but rewarding work. Like their classmates, they had struggled with the previously unfamiliar process of research and research writing. They had uncovered and managed a large body of research materials. From these sources, they had created essays that had substance, form, and interest—essays they were proud of. They had also learned a great deal, not only about their particular topics, but also about research, about college scholarship, and even about the meaning of an education itself. It is likely that after the hard work of your own research project is completed, you too, like Slade, Eliza, and many thousands of other students before you, will feel a well-deserved sense of satisfaction with what you have accomplished.

14 *Argument: Reading, Writing, and Research*

You don't have to be hostile or arrogant to be effective at argument. You don't even have to be an expert or have first-hand experience with your topic. In fact, in writing a college-level argument, you should avoid sounding overly confident, too sure you have found the truth. You are expected to be reasonable, fair-minded, and logical. In a strange way, that may be a relief, since you don't have the pressure of needing to win at all costs. Unlike a debater, to whom winning is everything, a writer in a serious argument is above mere victory. The goal is something more important and valuable—the honest search for truth in a world where there are often competing truths. Of course, you always want to make your case convincing enough to have an impact on your audience but you "win" in argumentative writing when you are fair, thorough, and clear. The challenge of writing an argument is to place ideas in a public forum to see if they stand up under scrutiny. College students argue a position not to trick or outmaneuver others, but to test the validity of ideas. That is the intellectual and ethical excitement of argument.

Of course, not all efforts to persuade others take that perspective. Advertisements, for example, are usually concerned not with discovering truth but with selling products. In some cases, ethics and fairness play little part in their attempt to influence consumers to buy.

If you think of argument as a straight line or continuum, at one end would be the rigorous logic and impersonal language of the physical sciences—for example, a geologist trying to convince colleagues that her experiments reverse accepted theories of beach erosion. At the other end might be a richly colored photograph of a dream-like, misty lake that tries to persuade us that mystery and romance await the user of a new shampoo. The two extremes of this continuum would look like this:

Logical reasoning ⟷ *Emotional appeal*

 ## EMOTIONAL APPEAL

Although emotional persuasion is not a primary concern in this chapter, we begin by considering the techniques of advertisements. At times their strategies seem obvious. But even though we recognize that ads are designed to manipulate us, they are still effective. They succeed because their creators know that they will be viewed casually on billboards or in magazines and rarely analyzed in college classes. In the right context, these ads evidently appeal to consumers, since people spend billions of dollars on products that are not necessities.

By studying advertising methods, we become aware of how ads and other forms of emotional appeal motivate people to do and believe what their creators want them to. Awareness is the only defense against manipulation.

The advertisement in Figure 14.1 provides an example of this type of persuasion. Like most other magazines ads, it is concerned more with stimulating and satisfying emotional desires than with describing the specific features of a product. In fact, the advertisement illustrates a formula developed by Hugh Rank, an analyst of advertising and propaganda. First comes *attention-getting*. When they first see this ad, most people will notice a sleek, speeding automobile; next, they will see a high-tech instrument panel alongside a section of soft leather upholstery. Second comes *confidence-building*. Since "the new Lincoln LS is engineered to encourage rapid travel," one might conclude that speeding is a safe, responsible way

Figure 14.1

to operate such a vehicle. Third comes *desire-stimulating*. The Lincoln's interior is so luxurious that it "practically begs you and your passengers to linger." Fourth comes *urgency-stressing*. Since the paradox of speed and power alongside serene, luxurious comfort is "a conundrum that could require years of driving to solve," the consumer is advised to "get started." Finally comes *response-seeking*. The reader is encouraged to consult the Lincoln Web site or call a toll-free number.

Not every ad illustrates Rank's formula quite so clearly. However, many ads emphasize the emotional appeal of a product while providing little if any information about ingredients, specifications, or the like. Ads are subject to testing and research so that the emotions and the desires they evoke coincide with what usually motivates the consumer. As you study the following ads, try to decide whether you are part of the audience that the ad makers had in mind.

EXERCISE | **Emotional Appeal**

Look carefully at the advertisements on the following pages (Figures 14.2 and 14.3). Be as observant and perceptive as you can, and freewrite for five to ten minutes about each. What audience do the advertisers have in mind, and what responses are they seeking to stimulate? How does each advertiser expect people to be persuaded by the appeal? Is one ad more logical than the other? Is emotional appeal a component of both ads? Now try to envision ads that seek the same results without any recourse to emotional appeals. How would they differ from the ads pictured here? Would they be more or less effective in achieving the advertisers' goals?

 LOGICAL ARGUMENT

In contrast to emotional appeal, most serious argument relies on factual data and logic. Sometimes the logic is presented in a tightly organized pattern, as in the following passage written by a noted biologist who argues for the conservation of wilderness areas.

> For species on the brink, from birds to fungi, the end can come in two ways. Many, like the Moorean tree snails, are taken out by the metaphorical equivalent of a rifle shot—they are erased but the ecosystem from which they are removed is left intact. Others are destroyed by a holocaust, in which the entire ecosystem perishes.
>
> The distinction between rifle shots and holocausts has special merit in considering the case of the spotted owl *(Strix occidentalis)* of the United States, an endangered form that has been the object of intense national controversy since 1988. Each pair of owls requires about 3 to 8 square kilometers of coniferous forest more than 250 years old. Only this habitat can provide the birds with both enough large hollow trees for nesting and an expanse of open understory for the effective hunting of mice and other small mammals. Within the range of the spotted owl in western Oregon and Washington, the suitable habitat is largely

THINK OF US AS A GROWTH

STOCK IN PINSTRIPES.

Today, it seems you have a choice of two very different types of stocks: The solid, dependable, long-term investments. Or dynamic-growth stocks, fueled by new technologies. But what if you could have the best of both worlds? By-combining Bell Atlantic with GTE, we seek to offer shareholders just that. How? The merger will create one of the world's premier telecommunications companies, with extraordinary bandwidth. Immediately, this will create a huge growth opportunity by matching GTE's national resources with Bell Atlantic's extensive and data-hungry customer base in the Northeast. We'll also offer a widely diverse range of products and services, including local, long distance, wireless and Internet solutions. The result will be an entirely new dimension of value for our investors. The opportunities will be there. Never have we been so well equipped to capitalize on them.

www.mergerinfo.com

Figure 14.2

Figure 14.3

confined to twelve national forests. The controversy was engaged first within the U.S. Forest Service and then the public at large. It was ultimately between loggers, who wanted to continue cutting the primeval forest, and environmentalists determined to protect an endangered species. The major local industry around the owl's range was affected, the financial stakes were high, and the confrontation was emotional. Said the loggers: "Are we really expected to sacrifice thousands of jobs for a handful of birds?" Said the environmentalists: "Must we deprive future generations of a race of birds for a few more years of timber yield?"

Overlooked in the clamor was the fate of an entire habitat, the old-growth coniferous forest, with thousands of other species of plants, animals, and microorganisms, the great majority unstudied and unclassified. Among them are three rare amphibian species, the tailed frog and the Del Norte and Olympic salamanders. Also present is the western yew, *Taxus brevifolia,* source of taxol, one of the most potent anticancer substances ever found. The debate should be framed another way: what else awaits discovery in the old-growth forests of the Pacific Northwest?

The cutting of primeval forest and other disasters, fueled by the demands of growing human populations, are the overriding threat to biological diversity everywhere. But even the data that led to this conclusion, coming as they do mainly from vertebrates and plants, understate the case. The large, conspicuous organisms are the ones most susceptible to rifle shots, to overkill and the introduction of competing organisms. They are of the greatest immediate importance to man and receive the greater part of his malign attention. People hunt deer and pigeons rather than sowbugs and spiders. They cut roads into a forest to harvest Douglas fir, not mosses and fungi.

Not many habitats in the world covering a kilometer contain fewer than a thousand species of plants and animals. Patches of rain forest and coral reef harbor tens of thousands of species, even after they have declined to a remnant of the original wilderness. But when the *entire* habitat is destroyed, almost all of the species are destroyed. Not just eagles and pandas disappear but also the smallest, still uncensused invertebrates, algae, and fungi, the invisible players that make up the foundation of the ecosystem. Conservationists now generally recognize the difference between rifle shots and holocausts. They place emphasis on the preservation of entire habitats and not only the charismatic species within them. They are uncomfortably aware that the last surviving herd of Javan rhinoceros cannot be saved if the remnant woodland in which they live is cleared, that harpy eagles require every scrap of rain forest around them that can be spared from the chainsaw. The relationship is reciprocal: when star species like rhinoceros and eagles are protected, they serve as umbrellas for all the life around them.

—Edward O. Wilson, *The Diversity of Life*

Even though conservation can be an emotional topic, Professor Wilson appeals to reason. His voice is calm, logical, and confident. A reader may well be convinced that he has authority and reason on his side.

To say that an argument is based on logical reasoning, however, is not to say that the argument is necessarily "right." Two opponents can argue opposite sides of a complex issue, each using logical reasoning in support of his or her position. For example, a proponent of logging in the forests that Edward O. Wilson is seeking to protect could develop an argument based on the economic consequences to the logging industry and to the people and communities that rely on it for their livelihoods. A reader would have to weigh the arguments of both sides in deciding which, on balance, has made the more persuasive case.

 ## BALANCED, CREDIBLE ARGUMENT

Both the creators of the ads and the scientist who wrote the piece on species extinction have undoubtedly succeeded in making at least some people see things their way—in the first case, primarily through an appeal to emotion, and in the other case, primarily through reasoned argument. Most serious argumentative writing uses some of both; it relies on sound reasoning (sometimes called *logos*), but it also recognizes that our minds are more than calculating machines, that they respond to emotional appeals *(pathos)* as well. Consequently, classical rhetoricians understood that effective arguments rely on appeals of both kinds.

The focus of this chapter is somewhere between the extremes of logic and emotion, on the kind of persuasive essays you will read and write in your college courses. In college reading you will analyze the strategies and tactics of arguments, and in your writing you will take positions on topics that are open to debate. You will be required to support your ideas by assembling evidence based on your own logic and experience and on the logic and experience of others. In doing so, you will need to deal with those who disagree with you by noting the strengths and weaknesses of their positions. And throughout, you will want to sound like a person whom readers can believe and trust.

This introduces the third element of argumentation—*ethos* or *persona*. Writers use ethical appeals to persuade the reader by projecting an image of credibility and trustworthiness. This credibility must be earned. It is very difficult to convince someone whom you have alienated through shoddy research, arrogance, or bad writing. As Aristotle pointed out long ago, the persona or personality that the writer projects matters at least as much as the substance and validity of the argument. Readers have to trust you before they will accept your claims. You can inspire trust only by being a careful thinker and writer. For intelligent readers, the credibility of the writer is crucial.

But even if you are reasonable and well prepared, your argument still may not change the minds of those who have strong psychological, social, political, or religious reasons for believing the way they do. After all, the scientific evidence for the dangers of cigarette smoking is impressive, yet millions continue to puff their health away. Even though the surgeon general seems to have won the debate over the hazards of smoking, logic is still not enough to persuade legions of smokers. Atheists and believers rarely change their minds in debates with each other, and sports fans seldom agree with the referee when a close call goes against their team. The old warning not to argue about religion, politics, and sports is sound advice. Apparently there is little hope of changing the minds of those with an emotional commitment to a different outlook. But among open-minded, reasonable people searching for the truth, there are innumerable ideas open to debate. In fact, without intellectual dispute, the life of the mind would be greatly impoverished.

INFORMAL ANALYSIS OF ARGUMENTS

Intelligent readers try to be on the lookout for false promises and manipulative language in advertisements. It is usually easy enough to see what advertisers are up to. But it is not always easy to see through questionable arguments that appear to be logical. That takes more concentration and more time. In college classrooms, professors and students continually put forth their ideas and positions on a wide variety of topics. Textbooks too are full of arguments, usually sound—but not always. Unless you want to be the victim of half-baked ideas and sloppy thinking, you must develop your skills as a reader of arguments. One reasonable tactic in analyzing the soundness of an argument is to take it apart, dividing it into its component elements. Doing this makes the analysis manageable.

Most arguments can be considered in terms of five elements. By asking questions about these, you can get to the heart of an argument:

- *Purpose:* What *audience* does the writer have in mind; that is, whom is the writer trying to persuade? What is the author's reason for wanting to persuade those people? What might their position be on this issue?

- *Thesis* (sometimes called an *assertion* or *proposition*): What is the main idea that the writer is trying to persuade the reader to accept or act on? Is the writer's position direct and clear? Is the thesis presented as the only reasonable position?

- *Evidence:* What kinds of information does the writer cite to support the thesis? What specific arguments does the author present? Is the evidence sound; that is, is it authoritative, believable, and sufficient? Does it rely on logic or emotion? How is the evidence arranged? Does it convince you?

- *Refutation:* Are the positions of opposing sides presented fairly? Would the opposing sides agree with the writer's understanding of their position? Does the writer show the opposing arguments to be invalid? Are there opposing arguments that the writer has overlooked?

- *Persona:* What is the writer's attitude? Is it hostile, cheerful, irate, reasonable, sarcastic? Does the writer sound believable? Is the writer obviously biased or arguing from a narrow perspective? Does the language used add to the credibility of the author, or is it too offensive or aggressive? Do you trust this person to be fair and open-minded?

Questions in these five areas can be applied to any written argument, and they offer a valuable way of analyzing the writer's methods and the effectiveness of her presentation. If you are interested in exploring your own ideas about a passage you are reading, your analysis does not need to be a formal paper. You can answer these questions in informal notes or freewriting.

To illustrate informal analysis of an argument, read the following editorial published in *The Nation,* a magazine of opinion with a liberal slant. The author, Roger W. Bowen, is president of the State University of New York (SUNY), New Paltz.

The Price of Democracy

ROGER W. BOWEN

1   A 1998 ruling by the U.S. Court of Appeals for the Seventh Circuit, if it is not reversed by the Supreme Court this autumn, will undermine democratic student government and seriously harm the already fragile sense of community in public institutions of higher education across the nation. The case, *Board of Regents v. Southworth,* involves a suit against the University of Wisconsin by several self-described conservative students who are unhappy because a portion of their mandated student fees is being used to support eighteen student groups whose activities run counter to the plaintiffs' ideological, political, or religious beliefs. Among the groups are Amnesty International; the Lesbian, Gay, Bisexual, and Transgender Campus Center; and the Campus Women's Center. The Court of Appeals struck down the university's fee policy as violating the plaintiffs' First Amendment rights.

2   At first blush the principle informing *Southworth,* taxpayer choice, is an appealing one. The conservative Wisconsin plaintiffs have argued that whoever pays the piper should get to call the tune. By this logic, whether mandated student fees or government taxes are at issue, the payer should have the right to determine how his or her money will be spent by the governing authority.

3   Many years ago I argued in a *New York Times* op-ed that taxpayers should have the right to determine how their total tax payment is distributed to the various levels of government. I advocated paying to my village that which I owed to the federal government. My motivation for wanting a change in the rules was simple: I had lost confidence in the federal government's ability to use my hard-earned tax dollars wisely; I felt that my local government was, if not wiser, then at least more accessible and therefore potentially more receptive to my views.

4   The similarity between that view and *Southworth* is deceptive. Despite the apparent agreement on the principle of taxpayer sovereignty, the conservative Wisconsin students' position involves the right not to subsidize any organization espousing principles they dislike. I was not seeking a tax reduction; the conservative Wisconsin students are; they want the fight to reduce their fees and hence their overall support for a university they voluntarily attend. A comparable approach, if applied to my scheme, would be a taxpayer's right to deduct monies from any government function not meeting with the taxpayer's approval—a line-item veto.

5   Choice is one thing, veto power something else entirely. Democratically elected governments, including student governments, are disinclined to relinquish such powers to individual members of the community. To do so would destroy state sovereignty in the name of libertarianism. Government would not just cease to be effective, it might cease to be.

6   Equally destructive is the damage inflicted on the sense of community. Universities and nation-states are something more than their constituent parts. They are communities whose members accept some loss of freedom in exchange for certain benefits—some tangible, some not—and who appreciate that the common good is best advanced if all members' differences are respected. If a community is to work, pluralism in all its crazy messiness must be accepted, even celebrated.

7   The Wisconsin litigants, like many on the right in today's culture wars, do not, it seems, so much want membership in a community as they want ownership. Ownership for them is the right to retain control over some portion of the dues that signify

community membership and which, if paid in their entirety, would make them full members. Partial membership is what *Southworth* makes possible.

The academy has always been racy, unconventional and intellectually daring, all traits inimical to conservative values. Paradoxically, this means that conservatives may feel out of place in the academy, but it does not change the fact that their voice is central to the academy's intellectual vibrancy. Without conservatives as full members, yin lacks yang, conversation becomes sterile, debate can become monotonal, and learning may be reduced to mindless absorption of orthodoxy. The academy needs—indeed, depends upon—thinking conservatives who courageously challenge the dominant liberal ethos. This happens occasionally in ways that create stronger community. A recent example is the 1995 University of Virginia case *Rosenberger v. University of Virginia,* in which a group of conservative religious students successfully challenged the university's refusal to provide funding for a Christian student publication.

In that case the conservative Virginia students, unlike those in Wisconsin, did not say that they wanted to opt out of paying mandated fees for student organizations whose values they disliked; rather, they only wanted university funding for their own activity, a religious newspaper, to be equitably (not equally) provided from these same mandated student fees. Virginia's Christian students sought full membership in a pluralistic community. Wisconsin's student conservatives seek exactly the opposite by arguing that they are under no obligation to support "speech with which they disagree," in the words of the court ruling. This argument is dangerous. In matriculating at Wisconsin, all students, whether they know this or not, enter into a moral compact defined in terms of the university's charter or mission statement. If Wisconsin's resembles SUNY, New Paltz's, and I suspect it does, then it includes a statement of principles reflective of democracy's values, chief of which is the right of free expression as central to the academic enterprise.

Regrettably, the Wisconsin conservative students lack democratic dispositions; they ask not for a fair distribution of the community's wealth to advance their own interests but instead wish to deny other groups their fair share. This profoundly negative act will, I hope, be seen by the Supreme Court as weakening democracy, the community and the academy, and for those reasons be overturned. If the Court decides otherwise, will it be only a matter of time before conservatives request a partial tuition refund, calculated on the basis of the number of objectionable words and/or ideas uttered by liberal faculty members in the classroom? Or, writ large, will I be permitted in the future to withhold that portion of my federal taxes going to the Pentagon?

8

9

10

Following is an example of how the questions on page 403 might be used to analyze Roger Bowen's argument. The responses are written as brief notes, developed extemporaneously:

<u>Purpose:</u> Bowen appeals to readers who share his

political values and convictions. He disputes the ostensibly

logical argument that people shouldn't have to subsidize

an organization committed to an agenda to which they are

strongly opposed. He wants to reassure readers with liberal views that supporting the "establishment" in this particular case is not incompatible with democratic principles, including respect for diversity and individualism. As a university president, Bowen probably has a vested interest in the debate, since the current court ruling could cause a bureaucratic nightmare for public institutions like SUNY, New Paltz.

Thesis: Bowen opens with a statement of his position and an assessment of what's at stake. In other parts of his essay, however, Bowen acknowledges the logical appeal of contrary points of view--at least on the surface--and he tries to refute them.

Evidence: In his introduction, Bowen demonstrates his knowledge of the Southworth case. But in following paragraphs, he relies more on abstract logic and reasoning, until paragraph 8, where he refers to another court decision. In his last three paragraphs, Bowen calls on his authority as a university administrator to offer pronouncements about the guiding principles of an academic community. The last two sentences of the essay introduce an emotional appeal: if the Southworth ruling is sustained, the ideals of academic life will be compromised. Bowen's prediction that students may ask for refunds based on their exposure to liberal views is probably facetious.

Refutation: In paragraphs 2-3, Bowen concedes that the court ruling may seem reasonable, acknowledging that he himself once adopted an ostensibly similar position in regard to federal taxes. But in paragraphs 4-5 he distinguishes his former position (in favor of redirecting tax payments) from the argument presented in the Southworth case (in favor of avoiding an assessment). The distinction, he claims, is one of choice vs. veto power.   Since an appeals court has ruled in favor of the conservative students, their case must have <u>some</u> merit; so Bowen tries to show that he has considered this before rejecting their position.   He also anticipates that some people may accuse him of inconsistency, if not hypocrisy.   He tries to deflect those charges by asserting the value of conservative dissent within the academy and by referring to the Rosenberger case, in which conservative students adopted a position that he considers stronger.

<u>Persona:</u>   Though he opens with a sense of urgency, presenting the court ruling as a threat to the ideals of a university, Bowen is at pains to avoid a combative stance. Acknowledging the logic of the students' argument and his own vulnerability to charges of inconsistency, Bowen appeals to the better instincts of his readers--a shared commitment to rational, fair-minded inquiry and debate.   He also makes prominent use of the word "community," a term with positive connotations of cooperation and equality.

Informal Analysis of Argument   EXERCISES

1. Two different approaches to argumentation are *Aristotelian* and *Rogerian*, named for the classical philosopher and rhetorician Aristotle and the modern humanist psychologist Carl Rogers.

   Using the Aristotelian approach, you try to influence the reader by citing authorities and presenting overwhelming evidence in support of your views. You diminish and silence the opposition by assembling an irrefutable case. You project confidence in the rightness of your position and assume that all reasonable people will agree with you. You win; the opposition loses.

   A Rogerian approach tries to listen to the opposition to see where they are coming from, what their values and assumptions are. According to this view of argument, one side does not have to be all wrong; there are various reasonable positions. Typically, you try to paraphrase your opponents' views in a way that they can accept. You try to engage them in dialogue, accepting a partial solution. You try to enlist mutual respect, not achieve victory. In Rogerian argument, the writer assumes that there are many truths.

a. What elements of each appeal do you find in Roger Bowen's essay?

b. What might you change in Bowen's essay to make it more Rogerian or more Aristotelian?

2. You are now ready to analyze an argument yourself. Keeping in mind the previous example, read the following editorial by Doug Henwood, a contributing editor for *The Nation,* the same magazine in which Roger Bowen's essay was published. After reading the editorial, respond to the questions on page 403, which concern the five elements of argument.

Next: Debtors' Prison?

Doug Henwood

Almost from the first, American law has been fairly kind to debtors. We've long had indulgent bankruptcy laws for businesses and people, thanks to the influence of populism and a feeling even among policy-makers that if we wanted economic growth, we needed risk-takers, and if we wanted risk-takers, we had to spare them the worst consequences of what, in retrospect, may look like reckless borrowing.

All that may change. This past spring, the House passed an extremely severe bill—one actually written by a law firm for the credit industry—that would clamp down on the ability of individuals to have their debts erased by filing for bankruptcy. A Senate committee has passed a slightly softer bill that's waiting to get to the Senate floor. The Administration has expressed reservations about both bills, but you never know what the President will sign, especially when financiers have strong opinions on an issue.

Currently, most people filing for bankruptcy have two options: chapter 7, which allows for the "discharge" (cancellation) of certain kinds of debts, and chapter 13, which prescribes an installment payment program, so that people can try to pay off their debts without being harassed by collection agents. (Debts that can't be discharged include taxes, child support payments and federal loans.) Only about a third of filers take the chapter 13 route, and of those who do, about two-thirds fail to meet their repayment schedule (while their debts continue to compound). Despite that sorry record, the reform bills would force more people into repayment schemes. The effect would be, in the words of Ken Klee, a UCLA law professor who, as a House staffer, wrote much of the 1978 bankruptcy code, to turn the federal bankruptcy courts into "publicly funded collection agencies," supervising household budgets and assuring that debts are serviced.

The most odious feature of the proposed tightening is that chapter 7 would be means-tested—a first in U.S. history. Details vary between the bills, but the effect would be to close off the chapter 7 option to filers with incomes above the national average, ignoring all geographical and personal variations among filers.

It's hardly as if the industry is troubled. Credit cards are twice as profitable to banks as their other lines of business. That's not surprising, given the economics of the industry: The banks borrow money at rates under 6 percent interest and turn around and lend it to their credit card customers at around 15 percent. No wonder they mailed out more than three billion solicitations last year! Though rising delinquency rates have cooled their ardor a bit over the last year, issuers had been targeting what the industry calls "subprime" borrowers—less affluent people desperate for a little help in making ends meet. Unfortunately, it's hard to make ends meet when you're paying 15 percent or more on your borrowed money.

The industry, led by its most visible advocate, Federal Reserve chairman Alan Greenspan, has a simple explanation for the fact that personal bankruptcy rates were at an all-time high in 1998 and have fallen off only a bit since then: a loss of a sense of shame. In other words, people don't think twice about running up their credit cards and then going bust. There's no evidence that this is the case. Rigorous studies of actual bankrupts, like those by Elizabeth Warren of Harvard Law School and sociologist Teresa Sullivan, vice president of the University of Texas, show that people who go bust typically go from being merely burdened to being in crisis when something happens to interrupt their income, like loss of a job, divorce (especially hellish for women) or a health problem. Most people who file for bankruptcy do so as a last resort and find the whole process leading up to it emotionally difficult.

    Should this bill become law, it would represent a major triumph of money in politics. The credit industry showered politicians with $21 million in contributions during the 1997–98 election cycle and untold millions more in lobbying and PR. Decency has no money on its side; all it has is the potential for citizens, debtors or not, to call, write or e-mail their legislators.

WRITING A CRITIQUE OF AN ARGUMENT

As you probably noticed in the previous section, analyzing another writer's arguments is an effective way to understand how ideas are put together. But it can also help you analyze and clarify your own positions on an issue and can provide you with the motivation and ideas to write arguments of your own. All good *writers* of arguments must first be good *readers* of arguments.

    Before writing an argument, it is useful to engage in a serious kind of reading analysis—composing a **critique.** A critique is a more formal and objective look at an argument than the informal, subjective analysis described in the previous section, but it does include your own opinions. You begin a critique by answering the same questions, but you try to move beyond these personal responses, becoming more analytical, more detached. After your initial reaction, you try to stand back and look carefully at what the writer has said. Above all, you want to be fair in your judgment.

    Critiquing does not mean finding fault. It means weighing the good parts against the bad, arriving at a balanced view. Of course, it might turn out that a particular argument is, in your judgment, not very sound. That's fine. All you can do is make a sincere effort to analyze its strengths and weaknesses. Your purpose is first to search for the truth and then to write a clearly organized evaluation of the writer's whole argument. Not only does critiquing arguments help you see more clearly what writers are saying; it also directly prepares you to write competent and cogent arguments yourself.

    The following procedure can be used whenever you write a critique of an argument. Notice how the dialogue that develops between you and the writer can lead naturally into a written critique.

Procedure for Writing a Critique

Preparation

1. Read the passage twice. The second time read with a pencil, underlining important ideas and writing comments in the margin.

2. Respond to the passage subjectively. Freewrite for five minutes, recording any personal response you have: agreement, anger, bewilderment, thoughtfulness, or any other reaction.

3. Respond objectively. Write a brief summary of the passage. Do not insert any of your own ideas.

Analysis

Think through your analysis before writing by responding informally to the questions on page 403. Ask questions about these five elements:

1. Purpose
2. Thesis
3. Evidence
4. Refutation
5. Persona

Writing the Critique

1. Begin the first paragraph with a brief objective summary of the argument and with a thesis statement that presents your judgment of the reading.

2. Support your thesis by analyzing the important evidence presented in the passage.

3. Comment on any of the five elements in your analysis that you consider noteworthy.

Revision

Reread and edit your paper. Ask others to read it. Consider their suggestions as you revise it. Prepare your polished draft and proofread the computer-printed (or typed) copy with care.

To observe how this procedure can help you compose a critique, read the following article by Michelle Cottle, published in the *New Republic,* a magazine of opinion. Cottle disputes the perception that violence in the workplace is a growing menace in the United States. After reading the article, observe how one writer uses the recommended sequence to critique Cottle's argument.

Workplace Worrywarts

The Rise of the "Going Postal" Industry

MICHELLE COTTLE

1   Look over at the colleague toiling in the next cubicle. Is he a white man in his thirties or forties? Does he seem stressed out? Does he suffer from low self-esteem? Do people

suspect he's experiencing personal problems—tiffs with the wife, attitude from the kids? If so, you should start being really, really nice to this guy, because he fits the profile of someone at risk to go berserk one day soon and start blowing away his coworkers like a character in a Tarantino flick.

Don't take my word for it: I learned these tips from a new newsletter called *Workplace Violence Briefings: News You Need to Know.* For $195 a year, you too can receive a monthly dose of anxiety-inducing stats, headlines, and snippets such as "Routine HR Activities Can Trigger Violence" and "Why the Risk of Workplace Violence Will Increase." Also included are quickie articles on prevention: "Watch for These Subtle Warning Signs of Impending Violence," "Similarities in the Backgrounds of Those Who Erupt in Violence," "How to Say 'No' Diplomatically." Most valuable of all, the newsletter provides contact info for myriad experts in the now white-hot field of workplace violence prevention.

It was bound to happen. In response to growing fear of high-profile workplace tragedies—the most sensational recent example being [the] Atlanta massacre, in which day trader Mark Barton went on a shooting spree that left nine dead and thirteen wounded—a cottage industry of consultants has sprung up, pledging to protect your organization from a similar fate. While such rampages may seem frighteningly random, consultants insist they are able to employ a variety of tools to identify and defuse potentially bloody situations: employee background checks, profiles to screen out unbalanced job applicants, manager training to help spot on-the-edge employees, security systems to keep out angry people with weapons, and so on. Costs vary depending on what you want and how many employees will participate: basic training videos are a few hundred dollars, while comprehensive programs and security systems can easily hit six figures.

Companies of every size and flavor are signing on: Mazda, CalTrans, the city of San Francisco, the state of New Jersey—even the U.S. Air Force. Some clients want help addressing an existing "situation"—a disgruntled ex-employee or friction among coworkers. Others simply hope to guard against the chaos they're seeing on television; most consultants say that in the wake of media events such as Columbine and Atlanta, demand for their services rises dramatically.

Such a response is understandable—but unfortunate. Many prevention programs are a monumental waste. Sure, there's a chance your organization can reduce—though never eliminate—the risk of "an incident." But, for the vast majority of businesses, the additional margin of safety will not be worth the necessary investment of time, money, and emotional energy. And that doesn't even factor in the intangible social cost of promoting the idea that employers are somehow responsible for shielding us against not only foreseeable hazards such as shoddy equipment or toxic substances but also the most irrational, unpredictable tendencies of our fellow man.

Forget what you think you know from the media. There is no epidemic of deadly workplace violence; in fact, fatalities are down almost 20 percent from 1992. Last year, the Bureau of Labor Statistics put the total number of workplace homicides at 709—just seven more than the number of workers killed by falling from a roof, scaffold, or other lofty perch. Still, if that figure makes you nervous, there are basic steps you can take to safeguard your person. Number one: Don't drive a taxi. Cabbies have long endured the highest death rate of any occupation: between 1990 and 1992, forty-one of every 100,000 were killed on the job. You should also steer clear of jobs at liquor stores or gas stations. More than 75 percent of workplace homicides in this country occur during the commission of another crime, such as robbery. Referred to as Type I violence, these attacks are perpetrated by strangers seeking money, not coworkers seeking vengeance.

7   Other employees at increased risk of violence are police officers, prison guards, security guards, and health care workers. They face what the state of California calls Type II violence, "an assault by someone who is either the recipient or the object of a service provided by the affected workplace or the victim" (e.g., getting injured or killed while trying to restrain a violent convict or mental patient).

8   Obviously, we don't want to downplay these dangers. There are concrete precautions that employers can and should take to improve worker safety in high-risk fields: installing security cameras, additional lighting, bulletproof partitions, lock-drop safes, and panic buttons. Similarly, the Occupational Safety and Health Administration (OSHA) has violence-prevention guidelines for the health-care industry.

9   More and more, however, what companies are angsting about—and what consultants are focusing on—is Type III violence, which consists not only of coworker rampages but also of instances in which domestic discord spills over into the workplace, and a crazed husband storms into the office itching to teach his woman (and anyone else who crosses his path) a brutal lesson. "Companies are looking to prevent the sensational stuff," says Richard Fascia, president of Jeopardy Management Group in Cranston, Rhode Island.

10   For consultants, the advantages of specializing in Type III violence prevention are clear. Although Type III episodes occur far less frequently than do other types, their random nature means that essentially any organization is a candidate for prevention counseling. ("Everyone needs it—absolutely," says Dana Picore, a Los Angeles cop-turned-consultant.) Moreover, while the owner of the corner liquor store might be loath to drop big bucks on violence prevention, the management of a large accounting firm might not even blink at the cost. Thus, instead of targeting the industries hardest hit by violence, the market is becoming saturated with employment attorneys, clinical psychologists, and retired law enforcement agents clamoring to advise you on how to keep the Mark Bartons at bay. There has been "an explosion of training, an explosion of consultants," says Joseph A. Kinney, president of the National Safe Workplace Institute, a consulting firm in Charlotte, North Carolina.

11   So why should we care if some hysterical human-resources managers fall for the latest consulting craze? Put aside the practical matter that there are almost certainly better ways to spend corporate (or government) resources. In a broader sense, this trend just isn't healthy: bringing in a high-paid consultant to talk at length about what to do if a colleague decides to try a little target shooting in the executive washroom is just as likely to exacerbate our collective fears as to alleviate them. "If we have big programs to counter a danger, then the danger must be large—or so our reasoning goes," says Barry Glassner, a professor of sociology at the University of Southern California and the author of *The Culture of Fear.* "The more programs we have and the bigger they get, the bigger the problem seems. . . . [I]n fact, we're living in about the safest time in human history."

12   Consultants counter that they're concerned with preventing not only homicides but also the more common eruptions of low-level violence: shouting matches in the boardroom, abusive language, fistfights on the loading dock. But it's clearly the sensational killings they want employers to think of. The website of one Sacramento consultant features graphics depicting bullet holes and exploding bombs and cautions: "We often hire the person that kills us. It is the killer in our ranks that we must address. . . ." Another firm's ad sucks you in with the words "HE'S GOT A GUN!" in bold red letters.

13   Then, of course, there are the two words guaranteed to make any manager's blood run cold: *legal liability.* Consultants note that, while they cannot guarantee you a violence-free work environment, they can protect you from lawsuits if something does occur. They are quick to cite the "general duty" clause of the Occupational Safety and

Health Act, which requires employers to guard against "recognized hazards" in the workplace. All Safety Training's website shrieks, "If you have employees, you have a Workplace Violence problem! Because you are required to provide a safe workplace, you can be held liable, and your costs can run into the MILLIONS of dollars!"

But this threat, too, is wildly overstated. OSHA has no specific guidelines on the Type III violence most companies fear. The agency has issued safety recommendations for high-risk workplaces, such as late-night retail establishments, but it is exceedingly vague about what it expects from, say, brokerage firms. "It's very rare that workers are able to sue employers for workplace violence," says Charles Craver, a professor of employment law at George Washington University. Because of the broad immunity workers'-comp laws provide employers, "in most assault-type cases, the recourse against an employer is solely workers' compensation," he explains. There are rare exceptions—if, for example, there's proof that an employer deliberately injured workers or that the company negligently brought someone on board whom they knew, or suspected, to be prone to violent behavior. But the burden of proof is high. As long as a company behaved with "reasonable care," says Craver, the suit will likely go nowhere.

14

This is not to imply that consultants are preying on our fear simply to make a fast buck. Many of them got into the field after years in law enforcement and are painfully aware of the dark side of human nature. They speak movingly of the tragedies they have witnessed on the job and of lives shattered by violence. But do we really want to adopt their understandably paranoid perspective in our workplaces? This seems an unreasonably high price to pay to combat what is, in reality, a blessedly marginal danger.

15

Here is a freewritten response to Michelle Cottle's article:

Cottle pooh-poohs the popular belief that workplace violence has reached epidemic proportions. Writers for magazines like the New Republic often display skepticism of widely held views and disdain for conventional wisdom. I kind of admire that stance because, in this case, a writer who scoffs at our fears of violence or questions the reactions of people who have been affected by violence will be suspected of insensitivity. So I see Cottle as kind of gutsy. However, I find myself irritated by her heavy sarcasm and mocking tone. I resist her assertion that safety carries a self-evident price tag--her confidence that a cool-headed reckoning of costs and benefits can lead us to a fair, cheap, and easy solution to the problem. She belittles her opposition, dismissing their fears as hysterical. Frankly, I'm even inclined to mistrust her use of statistics and

First response: freewriting

expert opinion. Near the end of her article, she seems concerned mainly with the bottom line for employers: Don't worry, you won't get sued.

This freewriting explores an initial, subjective response. The following objective summary provides perspective:

An objective
summary

> Michelle Cottle argues that experts in the field of violence prevention are exaggerating the dangers posed by employees who carry personal stress into the workplace. Cottle suggests that consulting firms exploit fears aroused by the Columbine massacre and the shooting spree in an Atlanta office building. She also implies that these firms offer false hope that random, irrational acts of violence can be anticipated and prevented. Cottle distinguishes violence that occurs in dangerous working environments, like liquor stores and prisons, from violence caused by stress and other factors affecting the personal lives of mentally unstable employees. She claims that some consultants have used scare tactics to persuade companies to waste time and money on services of dubious value.

An informal analysis of the article helps prepare the writer to draft a formal critique:

Informal
analysis

> Purpose: Cottle tries to persuade employers that irrational violence is, by its very nature, random and unpredictable. She urges them not to overestimate the likelihood that this type of violence will erupt in any given workplace and warns of the scare tactics that consulting agencies use to market their services as an effective deterrent to violence. She argues that the advertising claims of consultants are misleading, that the costs of their services exceed any plausible benefit, and that they deliberately exaggerate dangers in hopes of gaining

clients. She ridicules the fear of violence, characterizing it as the "hysterical" response of "worrywarts" influenced by a current "craze." However, Cottle is so derisive of both the fear of violence and the methods of consultants that it is not completely clear whether she is more committed to persuading readers than she is in winning an argument by belittling her opponents.

Thesis: Cottle states her thesis in paragraph 5: "Many prevention programs are a monumental waste," adding that "for the vast majority of businesses, the additional margin of safety will not be worth the investment of time, money, and emotional energy."

Evidence: Cottle quotes the newsletters and advertising literature of consulting agencies, comparing their exaggerated claims to data provided by the U.S. Bureau of Labor Statistics (from which she also derives the classifications of violence discussed in paragraphs 6-10). Is this fair? Advertising, in general, appeals to the emotions and rarely provides thorough, objective facts about products or services. For example, does anyone expect TV ads for children's cereal to offer detailed, reliable information about nutrition or preservatives? (Perhaps Cottle would argue that consultants, many of whom are former police officers, ought to uphold a higher standard of ethics.) She seeks to buttress her criticism of consultants by quoting two university professors (Glassner and Craver), though the first quotation sounds like it may have been taken out of context. However, she undermines the appearance of fairness and objectivity by introducing one quotation from a consulting firm's brochure with the word shrieks.

<u>Refutation:</u>   Cottle seems more concerned with destroying the arguments of her opponents than with affirming her own point of view. The first instance of refutation appears in paragraph 5 when she concedes that fear of violence is "understandable--but unfortunate." She also acknowledges that organizations <u>can</u> reduce safety risks, though she adds that the possibility of violence is never eliminated. But she dismisses these reservations by arguing that the cost of any "additional margin of safety" far outweighs the benefits. In her next paragraph, Cottle anticipates and refutes the argument that news reports offer proof of any rise in workplace violence: "Forget what you think you know from the media." (A familiar ploy: "the media" are constantly blamed for exaggerating problems while overlooking the "real" story.) In paragraph 8, Cottle deflects accusations of insensitivity by saying, "Obviously, we don't want to downplay" the risk of Types I and II violence. But she cleverly uses this concession to trivialize Type III violence, the kind that "companies are <u>angsting</u> about" (another derisive phrase). In paragraph 11, Cottle addresses the why-should-we-care argument. In this case, her tactic is to pass over or "put aside" a supposedly stronger argument in support of her position (there are better ways to spend money than to hire consultants) in favor of a simpler, presumably irrefutable assertion (validating fears of violence "isn't healthy"). It's as if she's saying, "Let me save time here." Also, any skeptics inclined to quibble are served warning that she's holding more powerful ammunition in reserve. Cottle then refutes the claim that consultants may alleviate less ominous types of workplace stress by citing the emotional appeals found in some of their

advertisements.   (But does this really prove that consultants
<u>can't</u> help companies reduce the likelihood of verbal abuse
and fistfights?)   Concluding her argument, Cottle adopts the
"I'm-not-saying-that . . . " strategy: "This is not to imply
that consultants are preying on our fear simply to make a
fast buck."   Though she seems to acknowledge the sincerity of
"many" consultants, Cottle asks readers whether "we really
want to adopt their understandably paranoid perspective."
(Are "paranoid" views <u>ever</u> understandable?   Isn't this
another instance of loaded diction?)

   <u>Persona:</u>   Cottle relies on some of the emotional appeals
that she imputes to consultants.   Her language is inflated.
"Hysterical" personnel managers are falling prey to a
momentary "craze"; advertisements for consulting services
"shriek"; former law enforcement officers are "paranoid";
attorneys and clinical psychologists "clamor" to offer their
services.   She tries to belittle consultants, portraying them
as hucksters who hope to "suck you in" with "quickie" answers
and describing their services as a new "cottage industry" in
"the now white-hot field of workplace violence prevention."
On the other hand, when Cottle refers to acts of violence,
she uses understatement and euphemism--words like "situation"
and "incident," placed in quotation marks as if to distance
herself from popular jargon.   In paragraph 6, she adopts a
condescending tone: among the "basic steps you can take to
safeguard your person" is not to drive a taxi.   In other
words, causes and remedies are so self-evident that no one
needs to hire a consultant to recognize what they are.

Having developed some ideas, the writer is ready to draft her critique. Notice that she begins objectively with a summary and explanation of Cottle's argument, then examines its persuasiveness, and finally expresses reservations and disagreement.

Michelle Cottle, writing for the New Republic, argues that news reports often sensationalize the menace of deranged office employees and thereby exaggerate the danger of workplace violence. Fears aroused by these reports play into the hands of consultants who offer programs aimed at minimizing the risk of violence perpetrated by stressed-out workers. Cottle believes that hiring these consultants wastes money and jeopardizes employee morale by propagating the mistaken belief that workplace violence has reached epidemic proportions. While Cottle may be correct in claiming that violence is sensationalized, she weakens her argument by adopting a contentious stance, ridiculing the fears of employers and attributing greedy opportunism to consultants.

To show how consulting agencies exploit fears of workplace violence, Cottle cites ominous headlines from a trade publication which she derides as "a monthly dose of anxiety-inducing stats, headlines, and snippets." She acknowledges, however, that these scare tactics fuel a demand for programs, often expensive, that are supposed to anticipate and prevent seemingly random acts of violence. Cottle finds this demand "understandable--but unfortunate" because it causes companies to waste money and encourages workers to blame employers for hazards that no one can foresee. She also contends that the fear-mongering of consultants has obscured a statistical decline in workplace violence and diverted attention from the more preventable hazards of truly dangerous work like driving a taxi or working in a liquor store or a prison. Cottle distinguishes between reasonable efforts to enhance the security of workers who are logical targets of crime and futile attempts to avoid violence brought on by stress or mental illness. She concludes that consultants exaggerate the danger of these random, unpredictable events and mislead employers about their responsibility to prevent them.

Cottle is most persuasive when she supports her case with data provided by the Bureau of Labor Statistics. However, the fact that 709 homicides occurred on the job last year is not reassuring, even though it is "just" seven more deaths than were caused by falling. Cottle responds to this objection glibly: persons troubled by the statistic should consider the risks of driving a cab or working in a liquor store--as if concern for the personal safety of office workers were unjustified so long as anyone else has to face greater danger. Police officers, prison wardens, security guards, and others who perform hazardous work usually enter their careers conscious of the risks; persons who choose other fields of work cannot be blamed for wanting to avoid comparable, or even lesser, dangers.

More troublesome are the logical fallacies in Cottle's argument. Having argued that office work is safer than many other types of employment, Cottle sets up a false dilemma: "instead of targeting the industries hardest hit by crime," consultants are exploiting a "market saturated with employment attorneys, clinical psychologists, and retired law enforcement agents clamoring to advise" companies about the less urgent needs of office workers. Shouldn't we find ways to improve everyone's security? A similar fallacy appears in Cottle's quotation from Barry Glassner's book The Culture of Fear, which blames programs designed to remedy problems for increasing public perception of those problems. Assuring modern workers that they live "in about the safest time in human history" is hardly different from telling coal miners and factory workers of the nineteenth century that, compared to the Middle Ages, they lived during a time of extraordinary comfort, security, and opportunity.

Another weakness in Cottle's argument is the assumption that we can calculate the value of safety. When Cottle says that any "additional margin of safety will not be worth the necessary investment of time, money, and emotional energy," she speaks for employers; workers might hold a different view. Later, disputing claims that safety programs reduce the risk of liability, Cottle offers reassurance in Professor Craver's statement that employees are not likely to win lawsuits involving workplace violence. If the danger has been so irresponsibly exaggerated, why does Cottle go to such pains to show that companies are not liable?

Finally, Cottle seems too intent on overwhelming opponents in a debate that need not end with a triumphant victor and a silenced loser. She alienates uncommitted readers by denigrating the field of consulting as a "craze" or "a cottage industry" in a "white-hot field," consultants as opportunists who "clamor" and "shriek," managers of human resources as "hysterical," and much of the public as "worrywarts." Readers who come to the article with little prior knowledge are offered a polarized view in which the author concedes only that her opponents are "understandably paranoid." Most fair-minded readers will recognize that few issues are quite so clear-cut.

You may not agree with this critique. Although the writer attempts to weigh the strengths and weaknesses of "Workplace Worrywarts," she is influenced by what she considers an unfair presentation of opposing arguments and is alienated by Cottle's combative, Aristotelian approach to argument. Note that the critique acknowledges these subjective responses (biases, perhaps), yet strives to be fair and logical, and that some of the writer's irritation, expressed in the informal analysis, is removed or modulated in the critique. Any analysis of an argument should be rigorous and balanced, but in writing a critique, you should be clear about your own views. An issue worth debating has more than one side, and not everyone can be brought to the same position. Another reader might find Cottle's argument valid and therefore view this critique as unduly harsh. A critique of an argument balances objective and subjective judgments. You might want to try your own critique of Cottle's essay.

Writing a Critique of an Argument   **EXERCISES**

1. How successful is this critique of Michelle Cottle's argument? Has the writer been fair in her judgments? Are her arguments reasonable? Did she miss something that you would have commented on?

   Which writer do you find more convincing, Cottle or the author of the critique? Is there a part of each writer's opinion that makes sense to you? How might each be made more persuasive?

2. Now it is your turn. Use the procedures presented in this section to compose a polished written critique of the following essay by Katha Pollitt, a political columnist who writes about legal issues. Use your own ideas to evaluate the author's arguments. Remember that a critique is not necessarily an attack on another person's argument; you may find yourself agreeing with someone whose writing you critique. Your critique should address whatever successes and flaws you find in the text you analyze.

Polymaritally Perverse

Katha Pollitt

I've always vowed I would never be one of those people—and you know who you are!—who cancel their ACLU* membership in a fit of pique over a single issue. So I'll just say that I was surprised to learn recently that the organization has a policy opposing laws against polygamy: "The ACLU believes that criminal and civil laws prohibiting or penalizing the practice of plural marriage violate constitutional protections of freedom of expression and association, freedom of religion, and privacy for personal relationships among consenting adults." A footnote explains that "plural marriage" is a gender-neutral term.

Unfortunately, in the real world, it's not. The ACLU policy was set back in 1991 in response to a child-custody case in Utah, where at least 25,000 fundamentalist Mormons still follow the path of Brigham Young, husband of twenty-seven, and where "plural marriage" means only one thing—polygyny, or one man with multiple wives. Depending on whom you talk to, polygyny is either openly tolerated in Utah—until this year no one had been arrested for it in half a century—or severely stigmatized. Polygyny became a hot topic there last year, when a sixteen-year-old girl belonging to the secretive Kingston Order sought to leave her "marriage"—she was her uncle's fifteenth "wife"—and was beaten unconscious by her father. After a major brouhaha—Republican Governor Mike Leavitt seemed surprised to learn that polygyny was illegal—the uncle was convicted of incest, and the father of child abuse.

*American Civil Liberties Union

Polygyny itself was never at issue. The girl, who had been pulled out of school in the seventh grade, is now in protective custody, catching up on her education and being a teenager.

The girl's story is not uncommon, says Carmen Thompson, a former polygynous wife who directs Tapestry of Polygamy (www.polygamy.org), an eighteen-month-old volunteer organization that assists women in flight from polygynous marriages. Tapestry has aided some three hundred "refugees" just since the start of this year, and their stories are hair-raising: incest, abuse, children who have no birth certificates and are never sent to school, threats of "blood atonement" (death) made to fleeing wives. This reality recedes from view, though, when you put on libertarian glasses. Then the important testimony comes from Elizabeth Joseph, poster girl for "feminist polygamy." As she put it in a *New York Times* op-ed, you get to have your career, a co-wife watches your kids, and the children have a strong paternal authority figure. A feminist touting the virtues of patriarchal dads makes me a bit suspicious, but in any case, Joseph, a lawyer and radio-station operator who isn't a Mormon and who entered her "marriage" with one man and seven other women as a mature adult, is hardly a typical polygynous wife.

Consider the phrase "consenting adult." After much *Sturm und Drang,* Utah raised the age of consent last year from fourteen to sixteen—fifteen with the permission of a judge, who is barred by law from asking questions that might uncover coercion. Girls cannot refuse to be "home schooled," and school authorities don't insist that such schooling means math and history and English and science, with progress measured by tests. Instead, they look the other way when girls are pulled from school to work for free in clan businesses, as was the Kingston girl, while awaiting the summons to marry.

One Utah Civil Liberties Union board member said my arguments were "ethnocentric." Leaving aside the appropriateness of the term, nobody would argue that cultural diversity is an absolute value overriding every other consideration. No one I spoke with at the ACLU had a problem with rejecting religious or cultural defenses of child abuse, domestic violence or female genital mutilation. "Violence is different," ACLU director Ira Glasser told me. But if the ACLU is going to draw a line at all, why only there? Why not see polygyny as a human rights violation, a contract so radically inegalitarian—he has fifteen wives, each wife has one-fifteenth of a husband; she can have no more mates, he can have as many as he likes—that it ought to be illegal? That some women may find this arrangement acceptable doesn't mean the law should permit it, any more than the law should let people work for a dollar an hour, or sell their kidneys, or clean houses off the books and wind up with no Social Security.

So what is the ACLU doing? Outside Utah, plural marriage is not an issue. But gay marriage is. Every person I spoke with connected the two issues, on the grounds that if you accept restrictions on the legal definition of marriage in the one case, you have no standing to argue against such restrictions in the other. "So if polygyny is the price of gay marriage, you're willing to pay it?" I asked Glasser. Yes, he replied. But except for the fact that neither one is included in the legal definition of marriage, plural marriage and gay marriage have little in common. Two same-sexers are entering into the same contract as two heteros. That's why people who argue gay marriage will "threaten marriage" can never say exactly what the threat is. But plural marriage is fundamentally different. It would redefine all marriage contracts, because every marriage would be legally open to the addition of more partners.

Of course, as Glasser and others were quick to point out, monogamous marriage is also often exploitative and harmful to women, and fifteen-year-old girls can be pushed into monogamous marriage too. Right! But those facts suggest that there's something amiss with the whole strategy of trying to expand the marital population. Shouldn't the real libertarian position be that marriage itself has to go? There's something deeply contradictory about accepting the state's right to privilege married people while denying it the right to decide who those people will be and to define what marriage is.

In a world where the age of consent was, say, thirty, where teenage girls had real autonomy, where all women were well educated and able to support themselves and their children, and where people were less isolated and easily trapped, the libertarian position would make more sense. Polygyny, I suspect, would be a rarity—and maybe marriage too.

 # WRITING AN ARGUMENTATIVE RESEARCH ESSAY

In writing a critique, you were responding to another writer's argument. You expressed either your agreement or disagreement with the writer—or a little of both. In any case your response could not help but take an argumentative form. Still, you were reacting, not presenting your own original argument. This section will discuss how you can write an argument of your own, perhaps even one that others will want to critique and respond to. In particular it will focus on writing an argumentative essay that is also a research paper—that is, one that uses sources to inform its argument, giving it authority and credibility.

Dozens of books are devoted exclusively to the complexities of argumentative writing. The subject has a long scholarly tradition that goes all the way back to Aristotle's *Rhetoric*, a study of argument that is still used as a text to teach theories and tactics for persuading audiences. The scholarly field of rhetorical argument is valuable, but in this chapter we can delve into only a few basic principles.

Arguments take so many forms—writers can find so many different ways to persuade their readers—that it would be impossible to give you an easy formula for argumentative writing. We can give suggestions, however, and some general advice that you can follow to write effective arguments. Like other types of academic writing, an argumentative research paper can seem intimidating if you have had little experience in writing one before. You will find, nonetheless, that you can argue effectively and persuasively. As you did when you critiqued the arguments of others, you need to pay attention to the principal elements that make up an argument. The following sections discuss important ideas that should be considered whenever you write an argument.

Purpose

The best advice of all is to have a real reason for wanting to persuade others and to keep that goal in mind as you write. Argue about a topic you care about and believe in. Argue because you feel it is important for others to learn the truth. Argue to make the world a better place. Without that commitment, argument becomes an empty exercise, offering little prospect for success or satisfaction from it. If you care about your argument, however, it can be an exciting, important activity—and one at which you are likely to succeed.

Although commitment is important, it is also important to retain an open mind and to be willing to be persuaded yourself when better ideas and new information are presented to you. The purpose of college writing, as we have suggested, is not to win a contest or to wield power; rather, it is to test ideas in a sincere search for truth. To that end, you must be honest and fair, but it is also your duty to present the views you believe in as effectively as you can.

Thesis

Although at times writers of arguments feel they can be most effective if they disguise their actual objectives, as a college writer you should make your thesis clear to your readers. State your point in a sentence or two, early in your paper.

Not every thesis is worth arguing. The thesis you write about should meet the following criteria:

- It should be **controversial.** You should address an idea about which reasonable people can disagree. You would waste your time arguing that pollution is wrong, because reasonable people would be unlikely to dispute that thesis. You could, however, argue for or against outlawing internal-combustion automobiles, because you will find reasonable and informed people on both sides of that controversy.

- It should be **arguable.** Argue a position that is open to objective analysis. It is futile to argue about a matter of purely individual taste, like whether racquetball is a more exciting sport than tennis. You cannot profitably dispute likes and dislikes. But you might argue that "racquetball promotes cardiovascular fitness more effectively than tennis does." Research can examine this question, evidence can be gathered, and readers can draw conclusions based on objective criteria.

- It should be **clearly defined.** Words and phrases like *freedom, law and order, murder,* and *obscenity* may be perfectly clear to you, but friendships and even lives have been lost over different interpretations of "obvious" terms. You may want to argue that "pornography should not be shown on television," but if you do, you will have to make very clear what you mean by pornography and to suggest some reasonable method of testing whether a show is pornographic or not.

Audience

Write your argument with your audience in mind. Who is it that you want to persuade? What people do you expect to be reading your argument? What do your readers expect from you and you from them? Why might they ignore you, and what can you do to avoid that? The tone of your writing, the language you use, and the sophistication of your evidence must all be adjusted to the interests, values, and education of your readers. What might appeal to first-year college students might fail miserably with students in either junior high or graduate school.

Because of those differences, arguments must be tailor-made for specific audiences; one size does not fit all.

It is not dishonest to write in different ways for different readers. Sometimes it is important to withhold an idea or reason that you believe but that you know will offend or alienate your readers. Mature people know enough not to speak everything that is on their minds. If diplomats at the United Nations said exactly what they thought of each other, there would be few civilized discussions. You cannot get people even to listen to your argument if you threaten them or make them feel defensive. If you are writing to readers who disagree with you, try to understand their point of view, to view reality from their perspective. Not only will this allow you to examine the issue more fully and clearly, but it will help you present your argument in a way that will be most effective with this audience.

Persona

As a writer of arguments, you must be acutely aware of how you sound to your audience. When you write, you want to project a certain image, one that is appropriate to the situation at hand. You might take on the role of a concerned environmentalist, a crusading member of the student senate, or a frustrated commuter campaigning for additional student parking places. Each of these different personas can be adopted sincerely at various times by the same writer. Being your true self means being flexible and honest.

Regardless of how well thought out and researched your arguments are, you must still appear trustworthy enough to be believed. In order to establish a believable persona, it is important to maintain a reasonable tone. Extreme statements and emotional rhetoric work fine at pep rallies or in sermons to the already converted, but they can repel both those who disagree with you and the undecided. You should resist the temptation to belittle the opposition or to engage in name-calling. Shocking audiences may help the writer feel better, but it rarely presents the writer as balanced and fair. Readers need to feel rapport with the writer before they will alter their opinions.

Evidence

In presenting support for your thesis, you can appeal to your readers' emotions, as most advertising does, or to their reason, as participants in scientific debate strive to do. Argumentative writing often contains both kinds of appeals. What you should avoid, on the one hand, is the kind of emotional appeal that ignores reasoning, aiming only at your readers' fears and insecurities. On the other hand, you should avoid a persona so coldly impersonal that your essay may as well have been written by a computer.

You are the author of your own argument, and the ideas you present are a reflection of your own mind. If you are to win your readers' regard in an argumentative essay, your own voice and thoughts should come through. On the other hand, it is also important to win your readers' trust through the authority of your evidence. Research can help. Not only can sources supply you with support for your thesis, but they can also lend their expert authority to your writing and convince your readers that you have studied the subject carefully enough to be trusted. Library research may be most appropriate when you are arguing about a controversy that has received public attention, such as gun control or drunk-driving laws. Observation, interviews, or questionnaires may be appropriate in researching a local issue or an original proposal, such as your plan to improve food services in the campus cafeteria.

Opposition

Remember that any point worth arguing about will have an opposing point of view. You must admit that in your essay. And you must do so in a way that will be fair to your opponents. People do not cooperate or alter their positions when they feel threatened; they become defensive and rigid. It increases your credibility when you admit that those who differ with you are reasonable people. You should also realize that your readers will think of the counterarguments to your position, and it is good strategy to anticipate their objections and to refute them. Experienced writers do so briefly, since they realize that they don't have to devastate the other side. Let the reader see that you know the issue is complex, and then give a reasonable, brief response to opposing arguments. You will seem more trustworthy if you not only defend your position but also acknowledge the opposing view.

Organization

You can organize your essay in many ways, but you may find the following very general arrangement to be helpful, particularly in your first attempts at argumentative writing:

1. *Introduction:* Provide background information so that your readers are informed about the controversy; then state your thesis.
2. *Evidence:* Offer support for your thesis. (This is the longest part of your essay.)
3. *Opposition:* Acknowledge and refute opposing points of view.
4. *Conclusion:* Draw conclusions from the evidence so as to restate the point of your thesis.

You are now ready to research and write an argumentative essay.

Writing an Argumentative Essay   ASSIGNMENT

Write an argumentative essay in support of a thesis that you believe in. It can be about a national controversy, such as mercy killing or nuclear weapons policy; about a local issue, such as your school's new requirements for graduation; or about your own proposals for making the world a better place. Support your thesis with evidence from your own reasoning and research. You can invent a purpose and an audience for your essay if you choose. For example, you can write it in the form of a letter to the college Board of Trustees, petitioning members to provide greater support for the women's intramural program. Acknowledge your sources with parenthetical notes and provide a list of works cited.

 A SAMPLE ARGUMENTATIVE RESEARCH PAPER

Following is an argumentative research essay written by a first-year college student named Donna Bullock. Donna wrote on the topic of whether school uniforms are an effective remedy to violence and other threats to the safety and education of American school children. You may not agree with Donna's conclusions, but notice how she has used research to explore ideas and bolster her opinions. The result is a paper with great credibility. As readers, we cannot dismiss Donna's opinions as uninformed; instead, we note the care she has used to research the topic, and we are obliged to treat her presentation with respect.

Bullock 1

Donna Bullock

English 102

Prof. Sylvia Wintermoots

17 March 2000

School Uniforms: Panacea or Placebo?

On April 20, 1999, two members of a teenage clique known as the Trenchcoat Mafia gunned down thirteen of their classmates at Columbine High School in Littleton, Colorado. A week later, a Canadian youth, following their example, shot two fellow students at Taber High School in Alberta Province. Together, these incidents refueled controversy over school uniforms as an effective way to combat violence and other threats to the safety and education of American school children (Bergman).

A national debate was sparked in 1994 when Long Beach, California, became the first large public school district in the United States to require uniforms. In subsequent years, schools in that city reported a dramatic decline in violent crime: from 2,087 incidents the year before uniforms were mandated to 196 in 1998 (McLean). Whether school uniforms deserve full credit for this decline or whether they fit into a more complex system of correlations remains unclear. It is also uncertain whether most other school districts could expect similar results. However, President Clinton contributed to the growing enthusiasm for uniforms

> The writer introduces her topic with a focusing event.

> The writer provides background.

Bullock 2

by declaring in his 1996 State of the Union Address: "If it means teenagers will stop killing each other over designer jackets, then our public schools should be able to require their students to wear uniforms" (qtd. in Wilkins 19).

When the issue is cast in these terms, uniforms present an obvious appeal. Wearing uniforms is a small sacrifice when lives are at stake, and, in the aftermath of the Columbine tragedy, many Americans are anxious to embrace any plausible deterrent to further violence. On the other hand, initial reactions to tragic events are often simplistic, provoking hasty measures that may preclude more effective remedies. When schools adopt uniforms as a quick fix, they disregard more complex explanations of violence and may easily overlook strategies more likely to prevent it.

The writer states her thesis.

Advocates of school uniforms advance a number of persuasive claims, the most compelling of which involve reductions in crime. Schools in Long Beach, for example, witnessed not only a 90 percent decrease in violent crime, but also a 69 percent decline in vandalism and a 90 percent reduction in suspensions (Chatterjee 14), along with a dramatic increase in school attendance (Dyrli 7). Similar results have been recorded at Riverside Park Academy in Montreal, where drug use and vandalism almost disappeared after a uniform policy was imposed in 1992 (McLean). Some educational experts believe that school uniforms reduce

The writer presents arguments that she will later challenge.

Bullock 3

victimization (Scherer) and gang-related violence (Loesch),
supporting their views with the testimony of teachers,
school administrators, parents, and students. Says Heather
Kimberly, a recent graduate of Columbine High School and
current student teacher:

> I see uniforms as the only answer [. . .]. Ever
> since we were in elementary school, people picked
> on people's clothes: they were too dirty or the
> wrong style. Besides, if everyone wore blue
> shirts and dark pants, no one would have known
> what gangs they belonged to. A lot of school
> boards around here are getting uniforms on the
> next ballot. (Qtd. in McLean)

Still other benefits are attributed to school uniforms.
Less costly than other types of clothing, uniforms obscure
socioeconomic distinctions among students while making
intruders more conspicuous. Proponents argue that uniforms
improve school spirit and eliminate distractions that
interfere with learning. One Virginia parent came to
support uniforms after observing the provocative attire of
girls attending a local high school. Responding to a
Newsweek article about school uniforms, she declared:

> Let's face it, there is absolutely no way that a
> young man can focus on academics when he's
> surrounded by young women so inappropriately

Bullock 4

dressed. And as for the young ladies, how on earth can they complete their schoolwork when they have to concentrate on pulling down their skirts, pulling up the straps on their tank tops and trying to walk in those awful shoes--not to mention worrying about whether or not their clothes came from Target or Bloomingdale's?
(Schreiner 19)

Presented with these claims along with the pervasive belief that public education is under siege, many Americans view school uniforms as a sovereign remedy. According to one recent poll, 68 percent of New Jersey parents would prefer sending their children to schools that require uniforms ("Lives" 38). The New York City school district, the nation's largest, recently mandated uniforms for the elementary grades, and thirty-seven states allow schools to adopt similar policies. Legislators in Kansas are considering legislation that would mandate uniforms in all public schools ("How").

However, despite the momentum toward mandating uniforms, critics continue to voice reservations. They point out, for example, that the highly touted policy adopted by Long Beach public schools was accompanied by other reforms--including a character-education program and increased monitoring of school hallways--that may have

The writer presents arguments to refute the claims of school uniform proponents played larger roles in reducing crime ("How"; Wilkins 19). Critics reject the claim that school uniforms thwart gangs, since students often exhibit affiliation through hairstyles, fashion accessories, and other adornments. Says Julia Wilkins, a special-education teacher from Buffalo:

> It seems a lot simpler to just have a general rule against gang-related garb in schools. This could be more easily achieved by forbidding the wearing of any nonessential accessories, such as bandannas and pagers, rather than implementing a whole school uniform to combat the problem. (20)

Equally dubious is the claim that school uniforms are a wholesome alternative to extravagant displays of high fashion. A recent headline in Business Week proclaims that when schools require uniforms "Haute Couture Hits the Playground." The article reports how trendy fashion lines like Esprit de Corps and DKNY have entered the market for school uniforms, selling white shirts for thirty dollars and plain skirts for more than forty dollars (Reiss and McNatt 6). And since uniforms can't be worn for after-school activities such as sports, parents may actually have to spend more money.

The most persuasive evidence that benefits of school uniforms have been exaggerated appears in a 1998 study published by David Brunsma and Kerry Rockquemore in the

Bullock 6

Journal of Educational Research. Using data gathered in the National Educational Longitudinal Study of 1998, the authors conclude that "student uniforms have no direct effect on substance abuse, behavioral problems, or attendance." In fact, contrary to recent claims, they report "a negative effect of uniforms on student academic achievement." The authors go on to concede, however, that "[u]niform policies may indirectly affect school environment and student outcomes by providing a visible and public symbol of commitment to school improvement and reform" (53).

In the foregoing statement, Brunsma and Rockquemore present the most responsible view of the issue. Few critics reject school uniforms as a futile response to problems that plague public education. Instead, they view extravagant claims skeptically and urge school officials to take a more holistic view. Uniforms, they argue, are most likely to bring improvements when accompanied by other measures.

Unfortunately, the most zealous advocates of school uniforms often adopt a more combative stance. Journalist Ted Byfield, for instance, dismisses opponents as "60s person[s, . . .] flake educators and newspaper columnists of that vintage who sense, one hopes correctly, that yet another monument to their revolution is about to be dismantled." (44) Undoubtedly, a few critics of school uniforms exemplify the position that Byfield ridicules,

The writer rejects extreme positions on both sides of the issue.

Bullock 7

resting their case entirely on issues of free expression and civil liberties. For instance, one indignant subscriber to Newsweek, denouncing school uniforms as a "delusion that has captured the imagination of education-policy makers," argues that "[i]nstead of focusing on encouraging creativity, nurturing academic talent or making schools an environment of openness where students can express themselves, we are turning our schools into conformity factories" (Hunt 19). Both of these writers engage in polarized thinking and contribute little to rational debate.

   The wise approach is to proceed cautiously. Granting the importance of free expression, we cannot ignore the success of Long Beach and other school systems that have adopted uniform policies. Every freedom is subject to limitation, especially when some greater good is involved. Nevertheless, concerns about civil liberties cannot be cast aside. The recent expulsion of five students for wearing armbands to protest their school's uniform policy provides sobering evidence. Overruling school officials, a Louisiana judge declared that "state-operated schools may not be enclaves of totalitarianism" (qtd. in "A Fashion" B6). No matter what benefits uniform policies may bring, they will undermine education whenever students, parents, and school officials will not, or cannot, exercise the intellectual independence of educated people in a free society.

Bullock 40

Works Cited

Bergman, Brian. "Tragedy in Taber." <u>Maclean's</u> 10 May 1999:

    20–23. <u>MasterFILE Premier</u>. EBSCOhost. 8 Jan. 2000

    <http://ehostvgw1.epnet.com/ehost1/>.

Brunsma, David L., and Kerry A. Rockquemore. "Effects of

    Student Uniforms on Attendance, Behavior Problems,

    Substance Use, and Academic Achievement." <u>Journal of</u>

    <u>Educational Research</u> 92 (1998): 53–62.

Byfield, Ted. "One Gutsy Proposal." <u>Alberta</u>

<u>Report/Newsmagazine</u>

    28 June 1999: 44. <u>MasterFILE Premier</u>. EBSCOhost.

    8 Jan. 2000 <http://ehostvgw1.epnet.com/ehost1/>.

Chatterjee, Camille. "Uniform Improvements." <u>Psychology</u>

    <u>Today</u> Sept.–Oct. 1999: 14.

Dyrli, Odvard Egil. "Largest School System Adopts Student

    Uniforms." <u>Curriculum Administrator</u> 34.3 (1998): 7.

"A Fashion Statement." <u>Times-Picayune</u> [New Orleans] 22 Dec.

    1999: B6.

"How Do Clothes Affect the Classroom?" <u>News and Observer</u>

    [Raleigh, NC] 19 Dec. 1999: A 31. <u>Proquest Newspapers</u>.

    ProQuest. 10 Jan. 2000 <http://proquest.umi.com/

    pqdweb>

Hunt, Michael. Letter. <u>Newsweek</u> 25 October 1999: 19.

"The Lives of a Fruitcake, Student Princes, Etc." <u>Adweek</u> 6

    Dec. 1999: 38.

Bullock 41

Loesch, Paul C. "A School Uniform Program That Works."
Principal 74.4 (1995): 28–30.

McLean, Candis. "Uniformly Mysterious." Alberta Report/
Newsmagazine 14 June 1999: 39. MasterFILE Premier.
EBSCOhost. 8 Jan. 2000 <http://ehostvgw1.epnet.com/
ehost1/>.

Reiss, Tammy, and Robert McNatt. "Haute Couture Hits the
Playground." Business Week 17 Aug. 1998: 6.

Scherer, Marge. "School Snapshot: Focus on African American
Culture." Educational Leadership 49.4 (1991): 17–19.

Schreiner, Sharon. Letter. Newsweek 25 Oct. 1999: 19.

Wilkins, Julia. "School Uniforms: The Answer to Violence in
American Schools or a Cheap Educational Reform?"
Humanist Mar.–Apr. 1999: 19–22.

Critiquing an Argumentative Essay

Using the procedure outlined on pages 409–10, critique Donna Bullock's essay "School Uniforms: Panacea or Placebo?" In particular, consider the following: Donna resists a widely held point of view. Are her arguments sufficient to make others consider her position? If you did not begin the essay in agreement with Donna, were your views altered as you read her arguments? What kinds of arguments and evidence does she use to make her case? Does she give a fair presentation of opposing arguments? Does she seem interested in fair play? Does she use her research effectively? What kind of persona does she project? Does her style contribute to the effectiveness of her argument?

PART II

Research Paper
Reference Handbook

A   *List of Works Cited (MLA Format)*

A *list of works cited,* placed at the end of a research paper, identifies all of the sources you have quoted, paraphrased, or referred to. A *working bibliography* is a list of possible sources that you draw up as you begin your research and that you revise and update throughout your research project. You should provide your readers with citations of your sources to give the authors rightful credit for their contributions to your work and to allow your readers the opportunity to consult your sources directly. Consequently, it is important that you cite sources with care.

 BIBLIOGRAPHIC FORMATS

A list of works cited is expected to conform to a certain *bibliographic format*—a prescribed method of listing source information. Every academic field, such as English, sociology, or mathematics, has a preferred format that dictates not only what information about sources should be in the list of works cited but also how it should be arranged and even punctuated.

Unfortunately, each format has its own quirks and peculiarities. Which one you use will depend on the academic discipline in which you are working. If you are writing a paper for a psychology course, for example, you may be required to use a different format than you would use in a chemistry paper. The research papers in Part I follow the *Modern Language Association (MLA) format,* which is widely used in humanities courses (courses in such fields as literature, history, philosophy, theology, languages, and the arts), and it is frequently accepted for use in other courses as well. Two other formats widely used in the social and applied sciences—that of the *American Psychological Association (APA)* and the *numbered references* system—are presented in Chapters E and F. Fortunately, you do not need to memorize the details of these various formats. However, it is important that you know they exist, that you know how to find and use them, and that you follow whatever format you use with care. These chapters can serve as a reference guide to the various bibliographic formats you may encounter throughout your college career.

GENERAL GUIDELINES—MLA FORMAT

The following general guidelines apply to MLA-style bibliographies. Notice how Slade Healy followed the format in his working bibliography on pages 308–09 and in his list of works cited on pages 392–93.

1.   *What to include?* Slade's working bibliography listed the sources he had discovered during the preliminary stages of his project. He had not yet examined all of them, and some he would not use in his paper. Later, in his list of works cited, he would include only the sources he used in writing the paper. You should include a source in your list of works cited if you have quoted or paraphrased from it or if you have made reference to it. Do not list a work if you consulted it but did not make use of it in writing the paper.

2.   *In what order?* Sources are presented in alphabetical order, *not* in the order in which they are used in the paper. Do not number the items in your list.

3.   *What word first?* Each entry begins with the author's last name. When a work is anonymous—that is, when no author's name is given—the title is listed first. If the first word is *a, an,* or *the,* put that word first, but use the next word of the entry to determine its place within alphabetical order.

4.   *What format for titles?* In typed or handwritten papers, titles of longer works, such as books and magazines, are <u>underlined</u> to represent the *italics* used in printing. Do not underline the period that follows a title. Titles of shorter works, such as articles and book chapters (which are published as subparts of longer works), are printed within quotation marks (" "). Thus in Figure A.1 we observe that the article "Pint-Size Consumers with Full-Size Debt" was published in the newspaper *News & Observer.*

5.   *What format for publishers?* Publishers' names are shortened in MLA style. If a publishing firm is named after several persons, only the first is used (e.g., *Houghton* instead of *Houghton Mifflin Co.).* Omit first names (write *Knopf* instead of *Alfred A. Knopf, Inc.),* and omit words such as *Books, Press,* and *Publishers.* Use the abbreviation *UP* to represent *University Press* (e.g., *Indiana UP, U of Michigan P,* and *UP of Virginia).* When questions arise, use your judgment about identifying a publisher accurately. For example, you may write *Banner Books* to distinguish it from *Banner Press.*

6.   *What margins?* The first line of each entry begins at the left margin (one inch from the left edge of the page). The second and all following lines are indented one-half inch (five spaces if typewritten). In other words, each entry is "*out*dented" (also called a *hanging indent),* the reverse of the way paragraphs are *in*dented. The purpose is to make it easy for readers to find the first word of the entry so they can quickly locate individual items from a long list.

7.   *What spacing?* Double-space throughout, both within and between entries. Do not skip extra lines between entries.

```
                                                    Tetirick 13

                           Works Cited

Altfest, Lewis J., and Karen Caplan Altfest.  Lew Altfest

     Answers Almost All Your Questions about Money.  New

     York: McGraw, 1992.

American Express Centurion Bank.  Mailed advertisement.

     Oct. 1999.

Frey, Carol.  "Pint-Size Consumers with Full-Size Debt."

     News & Observer [Raleigh] 11 July 1999: E1.

Gordon, Marcy.  "Credit Card Firms' Tactics Decried."

     Associated Press 9 June 1999.  NewsBank NewsFile.

     InfoWeb.  11 Oct. 1999 <http://infoweb9.newsbank.com>.

Keating, Robert.  Personal interview.  14 Oct. 1999.
```

Figure A.1 Sample Works Cited page.

8. *What punctuation?* Punctuation conventions, however inexplicable they may seem, should be observed with care. Follow the models in this book whenever you create a list of works cited, paying close attention to periods, commas, parentheses, underlining, quotation marks, and spaces. In MLA style, most entries have three principal components, each one followed by a period: the author, the title, and the publication information. The most common oversight is to omit the period at the end of each entry.

9. *What heading?* Informal bibliographies do not require any special heading. A formal list of works cited, except in short papers with few sources, should begin on a separate page at the end of your paper. Center the heading

```
                    Works Cited
```

(or *Bibliography,* if you prefer) and double-space (skip one line within and between entries). Do not skip an extra line between the heading and the first entry.

Citing Electronic Sources

Not many years ago, students who wrote research papers encountered almost all of their written sources in print form. Today, many research sources are likely to be gathered electronically. These might include a newspaper article retrieved from an online database, an entry from an encyclopedia on CD-ROM, a Web page on the Internet, even a Shakespeare play stored on some distant computer. As with other sources, you are expected to cite electronic sources so as to give credit to their authors and to allow your readers to retrieve and consult them directly.

A problem peculiar to electronic sources, particularly online sources, is that many of them are subject to being updated without notice or moved to another electronic address or even withdrawn altogether, so that someone seeking to consult a source next week may not find it in exactly the same form as another person who consulted it last week—or perhaps may not find it at all. In contrast, a printed work, such as a book, can be cited in the certainty that others who consult it will be able to find exactly the same text that you encountered. Although thousands of copies may be printed, all of them have the same words on the same pages. A book may be updated (for example, the book you are now reading has been updated four times since its initial publication), but each update is identified with a new edition number. (This is the fifth edition of *Writing, Reading, and Research.*)

Being able to identify electronic sources accurately is not a great problem with ***portable electronic sources*** such as software programs on CD-ROM or diskette, which, like books, are identified with edition or version numbers. ***Online sources*** such as World Wide Web pages and some databases, however, are subject to frequent updating and revision. For such sources, it may not be possible to provide a citation that will allow others to consult the source in exactly the same form it took when you consulted it. In your citation of such sources, you should give information that is as adequate as possible, as well as the date when you consulted the source. Consult the models that follow for citing both portable and online electronic sources.

 ## MODEL ENTRIES—MLA FORMAT

You are likely to encounter many different kinds of sources in your research. When you compile a list of works cited using MLA style, you should find the appropriate model for each source from the samples that follow and copy its format with care. If you still have questions about a source you wish to list, consult the *MLA Handbook for Writers of Research Papers,* fifth edition, which can be found in the reference section of most college libraries, or ask your instructor for assistance.

Examine the following model entries and read the explanatory notes. For quick reference later on, you can consult the model MLA citations printed on the inside front and back covers.

Sources in Books

Citations for books have three main divisions:

```
Author's name.  The title of the book.  Publication
    information.
```

For the ***author's name,*** list the last name first, followed by a comma, followed by the author's other names. Abbreviations such as *Ph.D.* and titles such as *The Rev.* are omitted from citations. The ***book title*** is underlined. List the full title, including any subtitle. When there is a subtitle, place a colon immediately following the main title and then list the subtitle. ***Publication information*** is cited in this format:

```
City of publication: publisher, year of publication.
```

You can find this information on the book's title page and its copyright page (usually the page following the title page). Use the shortened version of the ***publisher's name.*** If the ***year of publication*** is not recorded on the title page, use the most recent year on the copyright page. If more than one ***city of publication*** is listed, give the first. If the city is not widely known, you can also list the state (using standard post office abbreviations—two capital letters, no periods) or foreign country.

A Book with One Author

```
Naipaul, V. S.  Between Father and Son: Family Letters.

     New York: Knopf, 2000.

Wheelock, Arthur K., Jr.  Vermeer and the Art of Painting.

     New Haven: Yale UP, 1995.
```

In the Naipaul example, a colon is placed between the book's title and its ***subtitle.*** Publishers' names are abbreviated: *Knopf* stands for Alfred A. Knopf, Inc.; *UP* is the standard abbreviation for University Press, as in *Yale UP.* However, you may give the publisher's name in a more complete form, particularly if you are in doubt (*Hill & Wang* rather than *Hill,* to avoid confusion with Ernest Hill Publishing or Lawrence Hill Books).

A Book with Two or Three Authors

```
Cunningham, William G., and Paula A. Cordeiro.  Educational

     Administration: A Problem-Based Approach.  Boston:

     Allyn, 2000.

Reid, Jo Anne, Peter Forrestal, and Jonathan Cook.  Small

     Group Learning in the Classroom.  Portsmouth, NH:

     Heinemann, 1990.
```

The first book is written by William Cunningham and Paula Cordeiro. Note that only Cunningham's name is inverted (last name listed first), since only the first author's last name is used to determine the work's alphabetized placement in the list of sources. Cunningham's name is listed before Cordeiro's, because that is the order in which their names appear on the title page. Do not rearrange the authors' names alphabetically. This same principle applies for listing authors of magazine articles and other works. You may use the state abbreviation when you consider it helpful in identifying the city of publication (*Portsmouth, NH*).

A Book with More Than Three Authors

Courtois, Stéphane, et al.   The Black Book of Communism:

Crimes, Terror, Repression.   Cambridge, MA: Harvard

UP, 1999.

Courtois is one of six authors of this book. The term *et al.* is a Latin abbreviation meaning "and others." It is not underlined or italicized in lists of works cited. You may also list all of the authors, if you consider it desirable to acknowledge them by name.

Two or More Works by the Same Author

Asimov, Isaac.   Adding a Dimension.   New York: Discus,

1975.

---.   "Fifty Years of Astronomy."   Natural History Oct.

1985: 4+.

---.   The New Intelligent Man's Guide to Science.   New York:

Basic, 1965.

Asimov, Isaac, and John Ciardi.   A Grossery of Limericks.

New York: Norton, 1981.

The first three works (two books and a magazine article) are written by the same author, Isaac Asimov. The fourth work is written by Asimov and another author. When you have used more than one work by the same author, your works-cited list should arrange the works alphabetically by title. (In our example *Adding* comes before *Fifty*, which comes before *New.*) Replace the author's name for all but the first work with three hyphens followed by a period. The reader can then see at a glance that the author is represented more than once and is alerted not to confuse one work with another. Use hyphens only when works have identical authors; notice that Asimov's name is not replaced for the fourth work, since its authors (Asimov and Ciardi) are not identical with the author of the first three works (Asimov alone).

A Book in a Later Edition

Popenoe, David.   Sociology.   11th ed.   Boston: Prentice,

2000.

Popenoe's book is in its eleventh edition.

A Book in a Series

Matthee, Rudolph P. <u>The Politics of Trade in Safavid Iran:</u>

   <u>Silk for Silver, 1600–1730</u>. Cambridge Studies in

   Islamic Civilization. New York: Cambridge UP, 2000.

Matthee's book is one of several books published by Cambridge University Press in a series entitled Cambridge Studies in Islamic Civilization.

A Book Published in More Than One Volume

When an author gives different titles to individual volumes of a work, list a specific volume this way:

Brinton, Crane, John B. Christopher, and Robert Lee Wolff.

   <u>Prehistory to 1715</u>. Vol. 1 of <u>A History of</u>

   <u>Civilization</u>. 6th ed. 2 vols. Englewood Cliffs, NJ:

   Prentice, 1984.

When individual volumes are not titled, cite the book this way:

Messenger, Charles. <u>For Love of Regiment: A History of</u>

   <u>British Infantry, 1660–1993</u>. 2 vols. Philadelphia:

   Trans-Atlantic, 1995.

If you use only one of these volumes, cite it this way:

Messenger, Charles. <u>For Love of Regiment: A History of</u>

   <u>British Infantry, 1660–1993</u>. Vol. 1. Philadelphia:

   Trans-Atlantic, 1995.

A Book with a Translator or Editor

Ramos, Julio. <u>Divergent Modernities: Culture and Politics in</u>

   <u>Nineteenth-Century Latin America</u>. Trans. John D.

   Blanco. Durham: Duke UP, 1999.

Shakespeare, William. <u>Henry V</u>. Ed. T. W. Craik. New York:

   Routledge, 1995.

Ramos's book was translated into English by Blanco. Craik edited this edition of the Shakespeare play. Compare how editors are cited in a book written by a single author (the Shakespeare example) with how they are cited in a book consisting of a collection of shorter works by various authors (the following example).

An Anthology of Shorter Works by Different Authors

> Stimpson, Catherine R., and Ethel Spector Person, eds.
>
>   Women: Sex and Sexuality. Chicago: U of Chicago P,
>
>   1980.

Stimpson and Person edited this book, an anthology of essays by various writers. It should be noted that occasions when you refer to such a collection *as a whole* in your research will be relatively rare. More frequently, you will use material from an *individual work* in the collection, and you will cite that specific work (rather than the collection as a whole) in your list of works cited, as in the following examples.

A Work from an Anthology

> Leifer, Myra. "Pregnancy." Women: Sex and Sexuality. Ed.
>
>   Catherine R. Stimpson and Ethel Spector Person.
>
>   Chicago: U of Chicago P, 1980. 212-23.
>
> Lichtheim, George. "The Birth of a Philosopher." Collected
>
>   Essays. New York: Viking, 1973. 103-10.
>
> Rushdie, Salman. "A Pen against the Sword: In Good Faith."
>
>   Newsweek 12 Feb. 1990: 52+. Rpt. in One World, Many
>
>   Cultures. Ed. Stuart Hirschberg. New York:
>
>   Macmillan, 1992. 480-96.

Leifer's article "Pregnancy" is one of the essays in the collection *Women: Sex and Sexuality* edited by Stimpson and Person. The Lichtheim book in the example does not have an editor; Lichtheim is the author of all the essays in the book. Rushdie's article originally appeared in *Newsweek;* the person who wrote this listing found it in Hirschberg's book, where it had been **reprinted** (*rpt.*). Note also that the **page numbers** on which the essays appear within the books are listed. In listing page numbers, omit all but the last two digits of the final page number, unless they are different from those of the first page. For example, you would write: 5–7, 377–79 (not –9 or –379), 195–208, 1006–07 (not –7 or –1007), and 986–1011.

Citing Several Essays from the Same Collection

If several essays are cited from the same collection, you can save space by using **cross-references.** First, include the entire collection as one of the items in your list of works cited, as follows:

```
Stimpson, Catherine R., and Ethel Spector Person, eds.

     Women: Sex and Sexuality.  Chicago: U of Chicago P,

     1980.
```

Then you are free to list each article you refer to in your paper, followed by an abbreviated reference to the collection—just the last names of the editors and the pages on which the articles appear, as follows:

```
Baker, Susan W.  "Biological Influences on Human Sex and

     Gender."  Stimpson and Person 175-91.

Diamond, Irene.  "Pornography and Repression: A

     Reconsideration."  Stimpson and Person 129-33.

Leifer, Myra.  "Pregnancy."  Stimpson and Person 212-23.
```

A Book Published before 1900

```
Nightingale, Florence.  Notes on Nursing: What It Is, and

     What It Is Not.  New York, 1860.
```

The publisher's name may be omitted for works published before 1900.

A Paperback or Other Reprinted Book

```
Horwitz, Tony.  Confederates in the Attic: Dispatches from

     the Unfinished Civil War.  1998.  New York: Vintage,

     1999.
```

The book was originally published (in hardcover, by a different publisher) in 1998.

A Work Written by a Group or Government Agency

```
Sotheby's.  Nineteenth Century European Paintings, Drawings

     and Watercolours.  London: Sotheby's, 1995.

United States.  Department of Justice.  Office of Juvenile

     Justice and Delinquency Prevention.  Cross-Age

     Teaching.  Washington: GPO, 1999.
```

Cite the group as author, even when it is also the publisher, as in the Sotheby's example. The book on nineteenth-century painting is attributed to Sotheby's, the British auction house, rather than to individual authors. For a work produced by a government agency, first state the name of the government (for example, *United States*), followed by the agency (and subgroup, if any) authoring the work.

An Online Book

> Irving, David. <u>Hitler's War</u>. New York: Viking, 1977. 20
>
> Jan. 2000 <http://www.focal.org/books/hitler/HW.pdf>.
>
> Robinson, Kenneth. <u>Beyond the Wilderness</u>. Online Originals,
>
> 1998. 21 Dec. 1999 <http://www.onlineoriginals.com/
>
> beyondsy.html>.
>
> Wollstonecraft, Mary. <u>Vindication of the Rights of Women</u>.
>
> 1792. <u>Project Bartleby</u>. Ed. Steven H. van Leeuwen.
>
> 13 Feb. 2000 <http://www.bartleby.com/144/index.html>.

For an online book that first appeared in print, such as Irving's book, provide standard information for the print source of the reproduced text, if available. Then provide the date you consulted the online work, immediately followed (no period) by the online address, within brackets. If an online address cannot fit all on one line, you can break it following a slash (/), but do not use a hyphen to show the break. Robinson's book did not first appear in print. Wollstonecraft's book, originally published in 1792, was reproduced online by a scholarly project called Project Bartleby. Because electronic sources vary widely, you may need to use your judgment about how best to identify your source. For a periodical or newspaper article that has been reproduced online, see the section on pages 454–55, "A Printed Article Reproduced Online."

A Work on CD-ROM or Diskette

> Merritt, Frederick S., M. Kent Loftin, and Jonathan T.
>
> Ricketts. <u>Standard Handbook for Civil Engineers</u>. 4th
>
> ed. CD-ROM. New York: McGraw, 1999.

Treat a work published in an electronic medium like a print work, but state the medium (in this case, *CD-ROM*).

An Article in an Encyclopedia or Other Reference Work

> Brandon, James R. "East Asian Arts." <u>Encyclopaedia</u>
>
> <u>Britannica: Macropaedia</u>. 15th ed. 1998.
>
> "Wellstone, Paul." <u>Who's Who in America</u>. 54th ed. 2000.
>
> "Yokel." <u>The Shorter Oxford English Dictionary</u>. 1973.

The *Britannica* is a printed encyclopedia. Pages need not be listed for reference works whose entries are arranged alphabetically (and can therefore easily be found). In many reference works, such as *Who's Who in America,* no authors are named for individual entries. Publishers need not be cited for well-known reference books. Provide publisher information for ***lesser-known reference works:***

> Hames, Raymond. "Yanomamö." <u>South America</u>. Vol. 7 of
>
>   <u>Encyclopedia of World Cultures</u>. Boston: Hall, 1994.

Electronic reference works are cited as follows:

> "Latitude and Longitude." <u>Britannica Online</u>. 28 Feb. 2000
>
>   <http://search.eb.com/bol/topic?xref=7843>.
>
> "Yokel." <u>Oxford English Dictionary</u>. 2nd. ed. CD-ROM.
>
>   Oxford: Oxford UP, 1992.

The "Latitude and Longitude" entry was consulted through the online version of the *Encyclopaedia Britannica*. Because many online reference works upgrade entries regularly, give the date when you consulted the source, immediately followed by the online address in brackets.

Sources in Periodicals and Newspapers

Entries for different types of periodical and newspaper sources are explained in the following section. Periodical entries are also summarized in Figure A.2.

An Article in a Magazine

> Block, Toddi Gutner. "Riding the Waves." <u>Forbes</u> 11 Sept.
>
>   1995: 182+.
>
> Lynn, Jacquelyn. "Hidden Resources." <u>Entrepreneur</u> Jan.
>
>   2000: 102-08.
>
> Robinson, Ann. "Gifted: The Two-Faced Label." <u>The Gifted</u>
>
>   <u>Child Today</u> Jan./Feb. 1989: 34-36.

This format is used for all weekly, biweekly, monthly, or bimonthly periodicals, except for scholarly journals. The Lynn article appears on pages 102 through 108. The Block article is not printed on continuous pages; it begins on page 182 and is continued farther back in the magazine. For such articles, only the first page is listed, immediately followed by a plus sign (+). Although some magazines may show a volume or issue number on the cover, these are not needed in the entry. Names of months, except for May, June, and July, are abbreviated. Note that there is no punctuation between the periodical's name and the publication date. For a magazine article that has been reproduced on an electronic database (and which

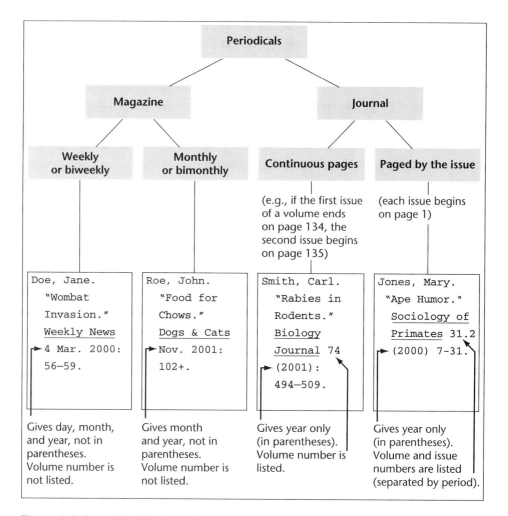

Figure A.2 Periodical listings for an MLA Works Cited list.

you do not consult in its original print version), see the section on pages 454–55, "A Printed Article Reproduced Online." For an article published online only, see "An Article Published Online (Not Reproduced)" on page 456.

An Article in a Journal

```
Reese, Hayne W.   "Some Contributions of Philosophy to
     Behavioral Sciences."   Journal of Mind and Behavior 20
     (1999): 183–210.
```

Journals are usually scholarly publications and are typically published three or four times yearly. Each year begins a new volume. The volume number (20 in this case) is included in the entry for a journal article. It is not necessary to include the seasonal designation (Winter, Spring, and so on). Pages in many journals are numbered according to the volume, not the issue. For example, if the Winter issue of volume 20 of *Journal of Mind and Behavior* ended on page 110, the Spring issue would begin on page 111. The paging of the next volume (21) would begin again with page 1. Some journals, however, begin each issue on page 1; for these, add a period and the issue number following the volume number, as follows:

Green, Anna. "Returning History to the Community: Oral

History in a Museum Setting." <u>Oral History Review</u> 24.2

(1997): 53-72.

The number 24.2 tells you that the article appeared in volume 24, issue 2, of *Oral History Review*. Periodical listings are also shown in the chart on page 452. For a journal article that has been reproduced in an electronic database (and which you do not consult in its original print version), see the section on pages 454–55, "A Printed Article Reproduced Online."

An Article in a Newspaper

Constable, Pamela. "Afghan Hijack Drama Ends Peacefully."

<u>Washington Post</u> 1 Jan. 2000: A21.

Kaufman, Leslie, and Saul Hansell. "Holiday Lesson in Online

Retailing." <u>New York Times</u> 2 Jan. 2000, natl. ed.:

sec. 3: 1+.

Ranii, David. "New AIDS Drug Is Step Closer to Approval."

<u>News and Observer</u> [Raleigh] 7 Nov. 1995: 1D+.

The article *The* is omitted from citations of newspapers such as the *Washington Post*. When the newspaper's name does not include the city (e.g., *News and Observer*), provide the city name in brackets; however, do not give a city for national newspapers like the *Wall Street Journal* and *USA Today*. Number pages as they appear in your source. The number on the page of the newspaper where the Constable article appears is A21 (that is, page 21 of section A), while the newspaper where the Ranii article appeared has the section and page numbers reversed (it begins on page 1D). When both the section and pages are numbered, present them as in the third example (*sec. 3: 1+*). Because the *New York Times* publishes two different editions (called the late and the national editions), it is necessary to specify which edition you used. For a newspaper article that has been reproduced on an electronic database (and which you do not consult in its original print version), see the section on pages 454–55, "A Printed Article Reproduced Online."

An Editorial

"Replace Unfair Tax Law." Editorial. <u>USA Today</u> 28 Aug.

1995: 12A.

A Letter to the Editor

Sadler, David. Letter. <u>U.S. News & World Report</u> 3-10 Jan.

2000: 7.

A Review

Bickerton, Derek. "Life without Father." Rev. of <u>The</u>

<u>Emperor's Embrace: Reflections on Animal Families and</u>

<u>Fatherhood</u>, by Jeffrey Moussaieff Masson. <u>New York</u>

<u>Times Book Review</u> 2 Jan. 2000: 5.

Glenn, Kenny. Rev. of <u>Man on the Moon</u> [film]. <u>Premiere</u>

Jan. 2000: 20.

Rev. of <u>Going to the Territory</u>, by Ralph Ellison. <u>Atlantic</u>

Aug. 1986: 91.

Stearns, David Patrick. Rev. of <u>The Well-Tempered Clavier</u>,

by J. S. Bach [CD]. Angela Hewitt, piano. <u>Stereophile</u>

Dec. 1999: 173+.

The first and third reviews are of books; the second is of a film; the fourth is of a music recording on CD. Information in review listings appears in this order: the reviewer's name; the title of the review; the work reviewed; its author; performers and performance information, if applicable; and the publication information. Notice that only the first review was published under a title. In the third review, Ralph Ellison is the author of the book reviewed; the review itself is published anonymously. If the medium of the reviewed work is not obvious, it can be added in brackets after the name of the work (for example, *[CD]*).

A Printed Article Reproduced Online

When you consult a magazine, journal, or newspaper article that has been reproduced online, provide information as you would for its original print version, or as much as is available. Then give the date when the database was consulted, immediately followed (no period) by the online address.

"Doctors Striving to Preempt Diabetes." <u>Boston Globe</u> 1 Jan.

2000: A3. 15 Jan. 2000 <http://www.boston.com/

dailyglobe2/001/nation/Doctors_striving_to_preempt_

diabetes+.shtml>.

Eddy, Melissa. "Experts Worry about Economic Collapse in

Bosnia." <u>News and Observer on the Web</u> 1 Jan. 2000. 2

Jan. 2000 <http://www.nandotimes.com/24hour/nao/business/

story/0,2257,500148948-500180852-500736195-0,00.html>.

Mazurek, Robert Henry. "Under the Ice." <u>Popular Science</u>

Jan. 2000: 28. ProQuest. 14 Feb. 2000 <http://

proquest.umi.com>.

Yue, Lorene. "Economists Expect Federal Reserve to Leave Rates

Unchanged." <u>Detroit Free Press</u> 20 Dec. 1999. <u>Newspaper</u>

<u>Source</u>. EBSCOhost. 14 Jan. 2000 <http://www.epnet.com>.

The first two articles were accessed via the online versions of the publications in which they appeared in print. The second two articles were reproduced by an online reference service. The anonymous "Doctors" article was originally published in the *Boston Globe* newspaper on January 1, 2000. It was consulted online on January 15, 2000. No pages are listed for the Eddy and Yue articles, because the online versions did not list the pages on which the original print articles appeared. The Yue article was found on the Newspaper Source database and was accessed through the EBSCOhost online reference service. For online sites that are available to all, such as the *Boston Globe* and *News and Observer* sites, you should give the complete address at which the article was found. For online reference services such as ProQuest and EBSCOhost that are accessible only through libraries that subscribe to the service, you can give just the home page site for the service. Online addresses that do not fit on one line should be broken, without an inserted hyphen, after a slash.

A Printed Article Reproduced on CD-ROM or Microform

Diamond, Nina L. "Dolphin Sonar: A Biologist and Physicist

Team Up to Find the Source of Sound Beams." <u>Omni</u> July

1994: 24. <u>Popular Periodicals Standard</u>. CD-ROM.

NewsBank. Oct. 1995.

Sipe, Cynthia L., and Anne E. Roder. "Mentoring School-Age

Children: A Classification of Programs." <u>Public/Private</u>

<u>Ventures Mentor</u> Spring 1999. <u>ERIC</u>. Microfiche. ED

431 070.

The Diamond article was accessed through the Popular Periodicals Standard database on CD-ROM. For a CD-ROM database that is periodically updated, give the publication date. The Sipe article was indexed in the ERIC database and reproduced on microfiche. For microfiche, give the identifying number in the collection's files—in this case, *ED 431 070.*

An Article Published Online (Not Reproduced)

"Phythian, Nicholas. "Ivory Coast Calm, Deposed President

Leaves." <u>Reuters</u>. <u>Yahoo! News</u> 26 Dec. 1999. 26 Dec.

1999 <http://dailynews.yahoo.com/h/nm/19991226/ts/

ivorycoast_leadall_8.html>.

West, Alden. "Camping With Wolves." <u>Dynamic Patterns</u> 5 May

1999. 28 Jan. 2000 <http://www.dynamicpatterns.com/

webzine/non-fiction/west_camping_wolves.html>.

Unlike the preceding examples, these two articles did not first appear in print form. The article by Phythian is a news story from the Reuters news agency and appeared as an online news listing. It was consulted on the same day that it was posted (December 26). The West article appeared in *Dynamic Patterns,* an online "zine." It was consulted January 28, 2000, several months after its electronic publication (May 5, 1999).

Other Sources

An Audio Recording

Dickinson, Dee. <u>Creating the Future: Perspectives on</u>

<u>Educational Change</u>. Audiocassette. Minneapolis:

Accelerated Learning Systems, 1991.

Mahler, Gustav. Symphony No. 7. Michael Tilson Thomas,

cond. London Symphony Orch. CD. RCA Victor, 1999.

Shuster, George N. Jacket notes. <u>The Poetry of Gerard</u>

<u>Manley Hopkins</u>. LP. Caedmon, n.d.

Audio recordings vary greatly in type and purpose, so do not hesitate to exercise judgment about what information is important. In general, label each recording by medium (CD, audiocassette, LP, and so on), although the label is optional for compact discs, which are assumed to be the standard audio medium. For a musical recording, list first the name of the composer, or performer, or conductor, depending on what aspect of the recording you are emphasizing. Recordings are produced by print-media publishers as well as traditional record companies, with the line separating them increasingly blurred; list either the manufacturer and year (as in the second example) or city, publisher, and year (as in the first example). Cite jacket or liner notes as in the third example. When a date is unavailable, as in the last example, use *n.d.* for "no date."

Computer Software

Atoms, Symbols and Equations. Vers. 2.1. Software. 18 Jan.

2000 <http://ourworld.compuserve.com/homepages/RayLec/

atoms.htm>.

Twain's World. CD-ROM. Parsippany, NJ: Bureau Development,

1993.

The first example is of software downloaded from the Internet; the second is software published on CD-ROM. The boundary between pure software and a book or other work that is published in an electronic medium is not a distinct one. See also "A Work on CD-ROM or Diskette" above.

A Film or Video Recording

All the Pretty Horses. Dir. Billy Bob Thornton. Screenplay

by Cormac McCarthy. Sony, 2000.

For a film, give the title, the director, the distributor, and the year of release. You may include other information you consider pertinent, such as the screenwriter and principal performers. For a film viewed on videocassette, DVD, or videodisc, provide that same information, but also identify the medium, the distributor, and the video release date:

The Little Foxes. Dir. William Wyler. Perf. Bette Davis,

Herbert Marshall, and Dan Duryea. MGM, 1941.

Videocassette. Embassy, 1985.

Cite a non-theatrical video as follows:

The Classical Hollywood Style. Program 1 of The American

Cinema. Prod. New York Center for Visual History.

Videocassette. Annenberg/CPB, 1995.

A Government Document

See "A Work Written by a Group or Government Agency" on page 449.

A Lecture

> Granetta, Stephanie. Class lecture. English 315.
>
> > Richardson College. 7 Apr. 2000.
>
> Kamenish, Eleanor. "A Tale of Two Countries: Mores in France
>
> > and Scotland." Public lecture. Friends of the Public
> >
> > Library. Louisville, 16 Apr. 2000.

A Pamphlet

> Golden Retriever Club of America. <u>Prevention of Heartworm</u>.
>
> > n.p.: GRCA, 2000.
>
> <u>Who Are the Amish?</u> Aylmer, Ont.: Pathway, n.d.

Pamphlets are treated like books. Use these abbreviations for unknown information: *n.p.* for both "no place" and "no publisher," *n.d.* for "no date," and *n. pag.* for "no pagination" (when the source lacks page numbers). Because pamphlets vary widely, you should exercise judgment to make your listing clear.

A Personal Interview

> Keating, Robert. Personal interview. 14 Oct. 1999.

A Television or Radio Program

> <u>The Crossing</u>. Dir. Robert Harmon. Screenplay by Sherry
>
> > Jones and Peter Jennings. History Channel. 1 Jan. 2000.
>
> Silberner, Joanne. Report on Internet drug sales. <u>All</u>
>
> > <u>Things Considered</u>. National Public Radio. 28 Dec. 1999.

An Unpublished Essay

> Tetirick, Eliza. "Giving Myself Credit: Should I Apply for a
>
> > Credit Card?" Essay written for Prof. Richard Veit's
> >
> > English 102 class. Fall semester 1999.

An Unpublished Letter or E-Mail

> Colbert, Stanley. Letter to author. 5 Mar. 2000.
>
> Wilkes, Paul. E-mail to author. 29 Dec. 1999.

An Unpublished Questionnaire

```
Questionnaire conducted by Prof. Barbara Waxman's English 102

    class.   Feb. 2000.
```

Citation for a project or paper written for a college class need be no more formal than this. An essay meant for wider circulation, however, would need to include the title of the course and the name of the college. Common sense is your best guide in these matters.

A List of Works Cited   EXERCISE

This exercise practices many types of bibliographic entries. Imagine that (in a temporary lapse from sanity) you have written a paper called "The Shoelace in History" and you have made use of the following sources. Compile your list of works cited, paying close attention to proper MLA format.

As a first step, circle the word in each of the following items that would begin the listing. Second, order the entries alphabetically. Third, put each listing in proper MLA form. (*Warning:* Some listings contain irrelevant information that you will not use in your works-cited list.) Finally, prepare the finished list.

1. The book *Sandals in Greece and Rome* was written by Sally Parish and published in 1997 by Wapiti Press in Omaha.

2. You found Walter Kelly's article "Shoelaces" on page 36 of volume 12 of the 1994 edition of *Encyclopedia of Haberdashery,* published in New York by the Buster Green Company.

3. During World War II, Fiona Quinn wrote *Knit Your Own Shoelaces* as part of the Self-Reliance Series printed in Modesto, California, in 1942 by Victory Press.

4. On page 36 of its July 23, 1977, edition, *Time* magazine published "Earth Shoes Unearthed in Inca Ruins." No author is given.

5. Two days ago, using the Internet, you consulted an online book by Imelda Markoz, *Never Too Many Shoes.* Two years ago, it had appeared in print, published by Converse Press in Wichita. You found the book at the address http://www.shoebooks.umanila.edu.

6. Constance Jowett translated a book by Max Philador and Elisaveta Krutsch, *Shoelaces in Africa and the Far East 1800–1914.* It was published in 1999 by Vanitas Publishers, Inc. Cities listed on the title page for Vanitas are Fort Worth, Texas; Chicago; Amsterdam; and Sydney, Australia.

7. On January 5 of this year Louise K. Frobisher wrote you a letter about her father's shoelace research.

8. You found volume 3 of Fiona Quinn's six-volume work of 1950: *The Shoe in the English-Speaking World,* published by S. T. Bruin & Sons of Boston.

9. On pages 711 and 712 of volume 17 of the *Indiana Journal of Podiatry* (November 1974) appears an essay, "Solving the Loose Shoe Problem" by Earl Q. Butz.

10. Leon Frobisher, Werner Festschrift, Ella Fitsky, and Ian McCrimmer published the twelfth edition of *Shoemaking with a Purpose* in 1996. The publisher, Hooton-Muffin of Boston, has published editions of the book since 1939.

11. The Society of Legwear Manufacturers wrote a book, *Laces, Gaiters, and Spats,* in 1901. Provolone-Liederkranz Publishers, Ltd., of Toronto reprinted it in 1955.

12. Mr. O. Fecteau and Ms. Mary Facenda edited a 1993 anthology, *An Ethnography of Footwear,* published in New Orleans by Big Muddy Publications. You found an article on pages 70–81, "Footloose and Sandal-Free," by J. R. R. Frodobaggins.

13. Norman Zimmer thoroughly explores "The Shoelace Motif in Finno-Latvian Sonnet Sequences" in the Fall 1993 edition (volume 43), pages 202 through 295, of a scholarly journal called *PMLA.*

14. Theodore and Louisa Mae Quinn edited a book written by their mother, Fiona Quinn, shortly before her death. The book, *Old Laces and Arsenic,* is published by Capra Press of Los Angeles. Copyright dates given are 1947, 1952, and 1953.

15. In the February 4, 1968, *Hibbing Herald* newspaper, the article "Lace, Lady, Lace" appeared under Robert Dylan's byline. A week ago today, you printed out a copy of the article online in the MasterFile Premier database by using the EBSCOhost search engine. EBSCOhost's home page is http://www.epnet.dome/ehost/.

16. You draw on information from a television exposé, "The Shoelace Coverup," which appeared last Sunday on the CBS show *60 Minutes*. Leslie Stahl is the narrator.

17. *Dog's Life* is a monthly magazine published in Atlanta. In volume 16, number 3, of that publication (whose date is August 2000), Walter Kelly's article "Little Laces for Little People" appeared. It began on pages 32 to 37 and continued on pages 188 and 189. You found it using the ProQuest reference service (home page: http://www.bellhowell.infolearning.com/proquest/).

18. You used the World Wide Web to read an article, "Tasteless Laces" by M. R. Blackwell. It appeared this year in the January issue of *Cyberlace,* which calls itself "the e-zine for the well shod." The address of the article is http://www.knotco.edu/cyberlace/notaste.html.

Congratulations. Having completed this exercise, you are now prepared for almost any situation that you may face as you prepare lists of sources in the future.

Remember, for quick reference, consult the summary of MLA bibliographic models on the inside front covers.

Parenthetical Notes (MLA Format)

Research writing has two principal devices for giving detailed information about sources: lists of works cited and notes. The former is a *general*, alphabetized list of all the sources you used in your writing. A ***note***, in contrast, acknowledges the *specific* location within a source of a *specific* quotation or bit of information in your paper. For example, if you quoted this very sentence in a paper you were writing, you would include the fifth edition of *Writing, Reading, and Research* in your list of works cited. A note, however, would also be needed with the quotation to tell your readers that it came from page 461 of this book.

 TYPES OF NOTES

Notes are of three principal kinds: parenthetical notes, footnotes, and endnotes. Parenthetical notes are by far the simplest kind of notes to use, and they are the standard method for documenting sources in MLA style. Footnotes and endnotes, however, are sometimes used by scholars in such fields as history, theology, and the fine arts. The following case illustrates the differences among these three types of notes.

Imagine that you included the following source in your list of works cited:

Sternberg, Robert J., and Todd I. Lubart. <u>Defying the Crowd:</u>
<u>Cultivating Creativity in a Culture of Conformity</u>. New
York: Free, 1995.

A works-cited listing

Suppose you made use of the following passage about the invention of Post-it® Notes, which appeared on page 4 of that book:

> Consider, for example, the Post-its on which many people jot reminders of things they need to get done. These "stick-ums" were created when an engineer at the 3M Company ended up doing the opposite of what he was supposed to. He created a weak adhesive, rather than the strong one that was the goal of his working division. But instead of throwing out the weak adhesive, he redefined the problem he was trying to solve: namely, to find the best use for a very weak adhesive. . . . Some of the greatest discoveries and inventions happen when people do just the opposite of what they have been told to do!

A passage from that source

461

Assume you paraphrased material from this passage in your paper as follows:

Your
paraphrase
of the source

```
Creativity consists in seeing possibilities where others
see only dead ends.  For example, the discovery of a weak
adhesive by an engineer who was actually looking for a
strong adhesive led to the invention of Post-it® Notes.
```

It is your obligation to identify the specific source you used in writing this paraphrase. Here it is done with a ***parenthetical note:***

```
Creativity consists in seeing possibilities where others
see only dead ends.  For example, the discovery of a weak
adhesive by an engineer who was actually looking for a
strong adhesive led to the invention of Post-it® Notes
(Sternberg and Lubart 4).
```

A parenthetical
note

The note tells your readers that you discovered this information on page 4 of the Sternberg and Lubart book, the complete citation for which can be found in your list of works cited.

By contrast, if you use the footnote or endnote system, you mark your paraphrase with a raised number:

```
Creativity consists in seeing possibilities where others
see only dead ends.  For example, the discovery of a weak
adhesive by an engineer who was actually looking for a
strong adhesive led to the invention of Post-it® Notes.[1]
```

Reference to
a footnote or
endnote

The raised number refers the reader to the following note:

A footnote or
endnote

```
    [1] Robert J. Sternberg and Todd I. Lubart, Defying the
Crowd: Cultivating Creativity in a Culture of Conformity (New
York: Free, 1995), 4.
```

As a ***footnote,*** it would be typed at the bottom of the page on which the reference appeared. As an ***endnote,*** it would be typed in a list of notes at the end of the paper.

Unless you are using a word processor that automatically formats and arranges your footnotes for you, you will find endnotes easier to type than footnotes. Both, however, involve redundancy; notice that the sample footnote repeats all the information already found in the works-cited listing. In contrast, parenthetical notes are far simpler and more economical than either footnotes or endnotes. In this chapter, we will focus on the MLA parenthetical style, but a full discussion of footnotes and endnotes can be found in Chapter D, and still other styles of notation are explained in Chapters E and F.

PARENTHETICAL NOTES

The rationale for parenthetical notes is that a note should give the least amount of information needed to identify a source—and give it within the paper itself; readers who want to know more can consult the list of works cited for further information. Different academic fields use slightly different formats for parenthetical notes. We consider here one general-purpose format, but you should be aware that papers written for other classes may require some adjustment in their note form. Always ask your instructor for format information if you are in doubt.

In the style used here as a model—the MLA style—a note is placed in the paper at the point where it is needed to identify a source. A typical note consists of two bits of information, in this format: (author pages). That is, the author's last name and the pages from which the information is taken are placed in parentheses. Here is an example of how a parenthetical note is used with a quotation:

> One textbook defines <u>false arrest</u> as "an intentional,
>
> unlawful, and unprivileged restraint of a person's liberty,
>
> either in prison or elsewhere, whereby harm is caused to
>
> the person so confined" (Wells 237).

Observe that the note follows the quotation and that the period is placed *after* the parentheses, not at the end of the quotation. In other words, the note is treated as a part of the sentence. If a quotation ends with a question mark or exclamation point, add a period after the note, as follows:

> Schwitzer taped a quotation from Thoreau to the wall above
>
> his desk: "I have never yet met a man who was quite awake.
>
> How could I have looked him in the face?" (Johnson 65).

Period follows the note

If the author's name already appears in your sentence, it can be omitted from the note. For example:

> Wells writes that "a false arrest or false imprisonment is an
>
> intentional, unlawful, and unprivileged restraint of a
>
> person's liberty, either in prison or elsewhere, whereby harm
>
> is caused to the person so confined" (237).

For a longer, indented quotation, the note can be placed immediately following the acknowledgment phrase, as follows:

> Historians of the last century maintained a firm belief in
>
> human progress, according to British historian Edward Hallett
>
> Carr (324):
>
> > The liberal nineteenth-century view of history had
> >
> > a close affinity with the economic doctrine of

```
laissez-faire--also the product of a serene and
self-confident outlook on the world.  Let everyone
get on with his particular job, and the hidden hand
would take care of the universal harmony.
```

Alternatively, the note can be placed at the quotation's end, as in this example:

```
Although the earth is a small planet in a remote corner of a
minor galaxy, there are reasons for arguing its importance:
          One should not be impressed too much by mere
     quantity; great dimensions and heavy mass have no
     merit by themselves; they cannot compare in value
     with immaterial things, such as thoughts, emotions,
     and other expressions of the soul.  To us the earth
     is the most important of all celestial bodies,
     because it has become the cradle and seat of our
     spiritual values.  (Öpik 9)
```

Period precedes the note in an indented quotation

Notice one oddity of the parenthetical style: When a note is placed after an indented quotation, it follows the final period. (In the other cases we have seen, the period follows the parenthetical note.)

Many students mistakenly assume that notes are used only for quotations, but they are used for paraphrased ideas and information as well. For example:

Note for paraphrased material

```
John Huston's first movie, The Maltese Falcon, is a faithful
adaptation of Dashiell Hammett's novel (Fell 242).
```

Fell's book is the source of the information, but the sentence is not a direct quotation. This point is important and needs to be stressed: *Use notes whenever you make use of a source's ideas and information, whether you quote the source's words directly or paraphrase them.* Since your research paper will contain more paraphrasing than direct quotation, most of your parenthetical notes will follow information written in your own phrasing.

The beauty of parenthetical notes is their simplicity: They provide the *least* amount of information needed to identify a source from the list of works cited, and the same form is used whether the source is a book, a periodical, or a newspaper. Only a few special cases require any variation from this standard form.

Some Special Cases

Notes should be as unobtrusive as possible; therefore, they should contain the least information needed to identify the source. In the following special cases, you will have to include additional information in your notes.

Works with No Author

For works where no author is given, substitute the title (the item that comes first in the entry for that work in the list of works cited; remember that the point of notes is to refer your readers to the list of works cited if further information is needed). For example, consider a note for an anonymous article listed like this:

```
"An Infant's Cries May Signal Physiological Defects."

    Psychology Today June 1974: 21-24.
```

A parenthetical note referring to this article might look like this:

```
("An Infant's" 22)
```

Notice that when a title is long, only the first word or two should be given in the note, with no ellipsis dots. Also notice another difference: The list of works cited locates the complete text of the article, pages 21 through 24, whereas the note lists only page 22. The reason is that a list of works cited gives *all* the pages on which an article appears, whereas a note refers to the *specific* page or pages from which a quotation or piece of information is taken.

Works with Two or More Authors

Notes for works with multiple authors list their names just as they appear in your list of works cited. (You can find the works-cited entries for these two sources on pages 445 and 446.)

```
(Reid, Forrestal, and Cook 52-54)

(Courtois et al. 112)
```

Two or More Works by the Same Author

When two or more works by the same author appear in your list of works cited, add the first word or two from the title to your note to distinguish one work from another. For example, if your paper uses both a book by Isaac Asimov, *Adding a Dimension,* and a magazine article by him, "Happy Accidents," notes for those two sources might look like this:

```
(Asimov, Adding 240-43)

(Asimov, "Happy" 68)
```

Two Authors with the Same Last Name

When two authors with the same last name are cited in a paper, include their first names in notes so as to distinguish between them. For example:

```
(George Eliot 459)

(T. S. Eliot 44)
```

A Multivolume Work

If you are citing a book published in more than one volume, you do not need to list the volume number in the note if it is shown in the list of works cited.

Take, for example, the following entry:

```
Agus, Jacob Bernard.  The Meaning of Jewish History.

        2 vols.  London: Abelard, 1963.  Vol. 2.
```

Since your list of works cited shows that only this one volume is used in your paper, your notes should not list the volume number. For example:

```
(Agus 59)
```

If, on the other hand, your paper uses more than one volume of a work, each note needs to specify the volume as well, as in these examples:

```
(Agus 1: 120)

(Agus 2: 59)
```

Reference to an Entire Work

When you refer to a work as a whole, rather than to a specific passage, no page numbers are needed, as in this example, which refers readers to three different sources found in the list of works cited:

```
At least three full-length biographies of Philbin have been

written since his death (Brickle; Baskin; Tillinghast).
```

More often, when a work as a whole is referred to, the author's name is mentioned in the paper itself, so no note is needed. For example:

```
Fermin's book on wine-making is sold only by mail-order.
```

Reference to More Than One Work

Sometimes a note needs to refer to more than one work. You can list multiple sources in a note, separated by semicolons:

```
Broadwell's controversial theory about the intelligence of

lizards has been disputed by eminent herpetologists

(Matsumoto 33; Vanderhooten 7; Crambury 450).
```

Reference to Discontinuous Pages

When you have taken source material from discontinuous pages of a work, list the pages, separated by commas:

```
(Witanowski 47, 103)
```

A Source without Pages

Many sources, such as recordings, television programs, and interviews, have no pages. For example, suppose you have conducted an interview for your paper and have this entry in your list of works cited:

```
Philcox, Arthur C.   Personal interview.   17 Oct. 2000.
```

Information from the interview can be cited simply with the interviewee's name:

```
During World War II, children in Hadleyville played at being

civil defense spotters on the levee, searching the skies for

German aircraft (Philcox).
```

If the interviewee's name appears in the passage, no note at all is needed, as shown here:

```
Retired teacher Arthur Philcox says that ballpoint pens did

not replace fountain pens in Hadleyville's grade schools

until the mid-1950s.
```

References with Other Forms of Page Numbering

Page references in parenthetical notes should use the same numbering system as in the text being referred to. For example a reference to pages with Roman numbering would look like this:

```
(Bullock iv-viii)
```

Reference to a newspaper article uses the system employed by that newspaper:

```
(Carlton B17-B18)
```

An Electronic Source

Some electronic texts look much like their printed versions, and the text appears on numbered pages. An example is David Irving's book *Hitler's War,* which you would list on a works-cited page like this:

```
Irving, David.   Hitler's War.   New York: Viking, 1977.   20

     Jan. 2000 <http://www.focal.org/books/hitler/HW.pdf>.
```

Because page numbers are visible on screen, you would cite a reference to this book as you would to any other—for example:

```
(Irving 166)
```

Some works, however, display no page numbers on screen, such as Kenneth Robinson's online book *Beyond the Wilderness.* Consequently, a parenthetical note referring to that work as a whole or to any part of the work would simply be:

```
(Robinson)
```

The same is true for periodical articles that you have not consulted in their original print forms but only as reproductions, without page numbers, in an electronic database. For example, the newspaper article in the following works-cited listing was consulted online through the Newspaper Source database, where it was reproduced without page numbers:

Yue, Lorene.   "Economists Expect Federal Reserve to Leave

Rates Unchanged."   <u>Detroit Free Press</u> 20 Dec. 1999.

<u>Newspaper Source</u>.   EBSCOhost.   14 Jan. 2000 <http://

www.epnet.com>.

Since it was consulted online and not in its original print form, a parenthetical note would not list page references:

(Yue)

One Source Cited in Another

Sometimes you wish to quote a source whom you have found quoted in *another* source. In such a case, your note should cite the actual source from which you take the material you are using. Imagine, for example, that in reading a book by an author named Robinson, you encounter a quotation from an article by another author named Amoros. Robinson provided a note (*Amoros 16*), to cite the quotation's location in Amoros's article. However, unless you actually then go to Amoros's article to look up the quotation, you would list Robinson as your source, preceded by *qtd. in* (an abbreviation for "quoted in"):

Quoting a print source found in another source

Amoros writes that "successful politicians, like successful

actors and teachers, always stay in character" (qtd. in

Robinson 199).

Also use *qtd. in* for notes when the person being quoted was an interview source. For example, if Robinson had interviewed and then quoted someone named Reese, you would give Robinson as your source for the Reese quotation:

Quoting an interview source found in another source

Reese said, "The secret to life is learning how to write off

your losses" (qtd. in Robinson 208).

However, if you paraphrased Reese, you would omit *qtd. in:*

Paraphrasing one source found in another source

Reese believes that people should not dwell on past setbacks

(Robinson 208).

Once you have practiced citing sources in your own research writing, you will quickly become familiar with the techniques involved. Observe the way notes are used in the works that you read, as in Slade's and Eliza's papers on pages 238–61. In writing your own research papers, refer to the Quick Reference Guide on the inside back covers of this book as needed, and use this chapter for fuller explanations. When unusual situations arise and you are uncertain how to cite a source, the wisest course may be to improvise, guided by your common sense. Always keep in mind that the purpose of notes is to acknowledge your sources in a clear, brief, consistent, and unobtrusive way.

Using Parenthetical Notes

Assume that the following passages are all taken from the same research paper. Parenthetical notes have been omitted, but information about their sources is given in brackets following each passage. First, write the list of works cited that would appear at the end of the paper (assuming that these are the paper's only sources). Second, insert parenthetical notes in the passages.

1. The world's most advanced bicycle was invented in 1977 by

    Swiss inventor Ugo Zwingli.

    [You discovered this information on page 33 of Vilma Mayer's book, *101 Offbeat Ideas,* published by the Phantom Company of Chicago in 1994.]

2. When he first encountered Zwingli's invention, cyclist

    Freddie Mercxx exclaimed: "This will either revolutionize

    road racing or set it back a hundred years!"

    [Mercxx wrote this on page 44 of his column, "New Products," which appeared on pages 44 and 45 of the November 1978 *Cyclist's World.*]

3. According to Rupert Brindel, president of the International

    Bicycle Federation, "The cycling world was in a tizzy about

    the Zwingli frame. Supporters called it 'the bike of the

    future,' while detractors said it removed the <u>sport</u> from the

    sport of cycling."

    [You found this in Melba Zweiback's book, *Two Wheels,* on page 202. She is quoting from Brindel's article, "The Zwingli Fiasco," which appeared on page 22 of the *Sporting Times* newspaper, April 13, 1993. *Two Wheels* was published in Montreal by Singleday in 2000.]

4. Zwingli had discovered a revolutionary way to reinforce

    tissue paper. The result was a frame so lightweight that

    it would actually gain speed while coasting uphill.

    [This too was taken from Mayer's book, page 36.]

5. In his <u>Memoirs</u>, Zwingli wrote, "I was overjoyed by how strong

    the tissue-paper frame was. The first prototype held up well

    under every test--until the first rainstorm."

[He wrote *Memoirs* in 1988; the quotation is from the bottom of page 63 and the top of page 64. Zigurat Press of Zurich published it.]

6. Zwingli's bicycle was a mere curiosity until the following

year, when he made his second brilliant discovery:

waterproof tissue paper.

[You paraphrased this from "And Now: Non-Absorbent T.P.," an anonymous brief article on page 416 of the July 1978 *Applied Chemistry Bulletin* (volume 28), a journal with continuous paging.]

7. The twin brother of Freddie Mercxx, also a world-class

cyclist, wrote:

> With all other bicycles, the strongest and fittest
>
> cyclist wins the race. With the Zwingli bike, the
>
> lightest racer wins. I'm tired of being wiped off
>
> the track by skinny guys on tissue paper.

[Otto Mercxx wrote this in a letter to his brother dated 28 January 1980.]

8. The fate of the Zwingli bicycle was sealed in 1985 when it

was outlawed for competition by a vote of 70 to 3 of the

International Bicycle Federation.

[You found this information on page 54 of Melba Zweiback's magazine article, "IBF Disposes of Tissue Paper 10-Speed," published on pages 54, 55, and 56 of the August 1985 *Newsmonth*.]

9. Although the following week's Tour de Finland race was marred

by protests from newly unemployed lightweight riders, the

cycling world soon returned to normal.

[This information appeared on page C17 of the *New York Times-News-Post* newspaper dated August 22, 1980, in an article by Greg LeMoon under the headline "Featherweight Furor in Finland." You read the article last Tuesday in the AllSports-News online database, using the BOSCOworld online reference service at http://www.BOSCO.com.]

When Are Notes Needed?

It is your privilege as a scholar to make use of the scholarship of other people in your writing. It is your obligation as a scholar to make it clear to your readers which words and ideas in your writing are your own and which ones came from your sources. The general rule for when notes are needed is this: *Provide notes for all quotations; provide notes for all paraphrased information that is not commonly available knowledge.* The examples that follow illustrate this rule.

A frequent mistake made by beginning scholars is to give notes only for quotations. Remember that you need to acknowledge your debts to your sources, whether you quote their exact words or only borrow their ideas. You should give a note for information you have used, even if you have phrased it in words entirely your own. For example, assume you are writing an article on the Black Death, the plague that devastated medieval Europe, and one of your sources is Barbara Tuchman's book *A Distant Mirror.* Imagine that you found this passage on page 94:

> . . . Although the mortality rate was erratic, ranging from one fifth in some places to nine tenths or almost total elimination in others, the overall estimate of modern demographers has settled—for the area extending from India to Iceland—around the same figure expressed in Froissart's casual words: "a third of the world died." His estimate, the common one at the time, was not an inspired guess but a borrowing of St. John's figure for mortality from plague in Revelation, the favorite guide to human affairs in the Middle Ages.
>
> A third of Europe would have meant about 20 million deaths. No one knows how many died. Contemporary reports were an awed impression, not an accurate count.

If you wrote any of the following sentences based on this passage, you would need to give credit to Tuchman in a note.

    It is widely accepted that about one third of Europe's
    population died from the Black Death (Tuchman 94).

    Although a mortality of 20 million Europeans is usually
    accepted for the Black Death, no accurate figures exist to
    confirm this estimate (Tuchman 94).

    Even if the usual mortality estimate of one third of Europe
    (Tuchman 94) is not accepted, the Black Death still exacted a
    horrendous toll of the population.

None of these passages is a direct quotation, but since they are based on your source, they require notes. In the first two examples, by placing the note at the end of the sentence, you signal that all the information is from Tuchman's book. In the third example, by placing the note in the middle of the sentence, you indicate that only the material preceding the note is from that source.

You do not need to note information from a source if it is widely available and generally accepted. For example, you might have learned this information in an encyclopedia or almanac: *Oklahoma became a state in 1907*. Although you did not know this fact before you looked it up, it is such common information that it is in effect public property, and you need not acknowledge a source in a note. The facts on the Black Death in Tuchman's article, on the other hand, represent her own research findings, and she deserves full acknowledgment when her ideas are used.

The distinction being drawn here may not always be an obvious one. As is often the case with research writing, your best practice is to let common sense be your guide. You can usually tell when information is public property and when a source deserves credit for it in a note. But when you are in doubt, the safest course is to provide the note.

How Many Notes Are Enough?

In writing a research paper, you are creating something new, even if almost all the ideas and information in it are from your sources. At the very least, your contribution is to synthesize this information and to present it in a fresh way. For this reason your research paper will be based on a variety of sources. A long paper based on only one or two sources serves little purpose since it does nothing new. Consequently, your research papers are likely to have a number of notes, indicating the contributions of your various sources.

Sometimes you will have to use many notes to acknowledge a complex passage that is developed, quite legitimately, from several different sources. For example:

```
Herbal folk remedies have been imported to the West with
mixed results.  An East African tea seems to be effective
against cholera ("Nature's" 6), while moxibustion, a Chinese
remedy for diarrhea, is still largely untested ("Burning"
25).  A Chinese arthritis medicine called "Chuifong
Toukuwan," on the other hand, is a positive danger to
health (Hunter 8).
```

The second sentence requires two notes because it is based on two separate sources.

On the other hand, there can be a danger in overloading your paper with notes. One reason the format of notes is so brief is to keep them from getting in the way of what you are saying in the paper. When a paper is filled with note after note, even brief notes call attention to themselves, and they distract and annoy readers. With notes—as with quotations, brackets, and ellipsis dots—there can be too much of a good thing. Avoid passages like this in your writing:

Bad (too many notes)

```
In 1948, Isaac Stork ran for president (McCall 80) on the
Anti-Vice ticket (Sullivan 42).  His platform included a
prohibition on all sweetened or alcoholic beverages (McCall
80), fines for wearing brightly colored outfits (Stokes 124),
and the clothing of naked cats, dogs, and horses (McCall 81).
```

The notes here are annoying, not only because they interrupt the passage so often but also because they are unnecessary. It is evident that the writer has done some research and is eager to show off. The writer is deliberately juggling three sources, all of which contain the same information. The first sentence would seem to state commonly available information that does not require acknowledgment. Information in the second sentence might also be considered public property, but to be safe, the writer might provide a single joint note after the final sentence like this:

```
. . . cats, dogs, and horses (McCall 80-81; Stokes 124).
```

Judging When Notes Are Needed   EXERCISE

Imagine that it is some time in the near future and that you are writing a brief research report. Imagine too that, having found the following six passages in your research, you have then written the report that follows them. What remains for you to do is to supply notes for the report.

1. Horseradish (*Armoracia lapathifolia*), a plant of the mustard family, is grown for its pungent, white fleshy root. [*Source:* Elizabeth Silverman's book, *Common Plants of North America,* page 208.]

2. I first met Mr. Finnahey when I stopped by his farm to get forms filled out for his medical benefits. When I asked him his age, he said, "I forget the exact year I was born. It was the same year the Brooklyn Bridge was built." Naturally I didn't believe him since he didn't look a day over 40, and his wife, Becky, was 26. Imagine my surprise when he brought out his birth certificate. [*Source:* social worker Marlys Davenport, quoted on page 35 of a newspaper article written by Lester Grady.]

3. The Brooklyn Bridge was built in 1883. [*Source:* an anonymous article in *Encyclopedia Galactica,* volume 4, page 73.]

4. When I arrived to examine Julius Finnahey, he was eating a lunch of peanut butter and horseradish sandwiches. "Best thing for you," he said. "I eat 'em every day—always have." This was my first clue to the cause of his longevity. My research into his diet led to a discovery that may provide humans of the future with lifetimes lasting perhaps two centuries. [*Source:* Chester Vinneman writing on page 19 of his article, "Radish-Legume Combination Slows the Aging Process," in the *New England Medical Report.*]

5. Chester Vinneman discovered that the combination of the trace element *vinnemanium,* which occurs in the common horseradish root, with amino acids in the common peanut retards the decay of the cell wall lining in human tissue. To Vinneman, the increased longevity which his discovery will provide is a mixed blessing: "I find the prospect both thrilling and frightening. The questions and problems that it raises stagger the mind." [*Source:* an unsigned article, "Life Everlasting Now a Reality?" in *Timely* magazine, page 78, continued on page 80.]

6. Chester Vinneman won the Nobel Prize for medicine for his discovery of the miracle age retardant. He is a professor of biochemistry at the University of Manitoba. [*Source: Who's Who,* page 993.]

Here is a section of your report, which is based on the preceding list of sources. Supply the appropriate parenthetical notes.

```
    Important discoveries are often the result of chance

occurrences.  If it had not been for a routine inquiry by
```

social worker Marlys Davenport, Chester Vinneman might never
have won the Nobel Prize for medicine. It was Davenport who
confirmed Julius Finnahey's amazing statement that he was
born in 1883, "the year the Brooklyn Bridge was built."

Professor Vinneman made the connection between
Finnahey's extraordinary youthfulness and his diet of
peanut butter and horseradish sandwiches. Horseradish
(<u>Armoracia lapathifolia</u>) was not previously thought to have
benefits beyond the flavor of its pungent root. Through
extensive tests, however, Vinneman discovered a previously
unreported trace element in horseradish, which he named
<u>vinnemanium</u>. This element, when combined with amino acids
such as those found in peanuts, prevents human cell walls
from decaying.

Vinneman predicts that as the result of his discovery,
human lifetimes may extend in the future to as many as two
centuries. He finds the prospect of such longevity "both
thrilling and frightening. The questions and problems
that it raises stagger the mind." It remains to be
seen how wisely humankind will cope with greatly extended
lives.

Finally, explain why you placed notes where you did and why you provided notes
for some statements and not others.

How Much Material Can One Note Cover?

A parenthetical note comes after borrowed material, but how can a writer make
clear *how much* of the preceding material is referred to by the note? The following
passage illustrates the problem:

Haagendaz was considered one of Denmark's premier eccentrics.
He continually wore the same heavy woolen sweater, regardless
of the occasion or season. Former colleagues attest that he

```
worked in near darkness, and he reportedly kept exotic

spiders and beetles as pets (Noland 18).
```

The extent of the reference is not clear. Is Noland the source for all three examples of Haagendazs's eccentricities or just the latter two (or the last one)? The ambiguity could be avoided, perhaps, by placing a note after each paraphrased sentence. But the paper would then be overloaded with notes, and readers would find it annoying to meet with identical notes sentence after sentence.

A somewhat clearer way to define a long borrowed passage is to mark its beginning with an acknowledgment phrase. For example:

```
Noland reports that Haagendazs was considered one of

Denmark's premier eccentrics.  He continually wore the same

heavy woolen sweater, regardless of the occasion or season.

Former colleagues attest that he worked in near darkness,

and he reportedly kept exotic spiders and beetles as pets

(18).
```

The acknowledgment phrase marks the beginning of the borrowed passage.

The note marks the end of the passage.

Here it is clear that the entire passage is taken from page 18 of a work by Noland. However, acknowledgment phrases are not commonly used with factual information, and an excess of acknowledgment phrases can be as distracting to readers as an excess of parenthetical notes. Alas, some ambiguity in the scope of your references is probably unavoidable. Rely on your judgment about whether a borrowed passage is adequately marked, but if you are in doubt, supply the acknowledgment phrase. You may also ask your instructor for advice.

Judging When Borrowed Material Is Adequately Marked

EXERCISE

Examine the parenthetical notes in the research papers by Slade and Eliza on pages 238–61. For each parenthetical note, is it clear how much material is borrowed from the source? If not, can you suggest a way to make it clearer?

 INFORMATION FOOTNOTES

Even when you use parenthetical notes to acknowledge sources, you can still use footnotes to supply information that you feel does not belong in the text of your paper. To mark an *information footnote,* place a raised asterisk (*) in the place where you invite the reader to consult the note, like this:

```
. . . domesticated animals such as dogs, cats,* and . . .
```

At the bottom of the same page, type ten underline bars and present your footnote on the next line, beginning with a raised asterisk, like this:

---

      * Witherspoon does not classify the common house cat as

a "domesticated" animal but as a "wild" animal that merely

"coexists" with humans (16).

Typing footnotes can be cumbersome. Fortunately, most word-processing programs can place footnotes automatically at the bottom of the proper page.

If you use a second information footnote on the same page, mark it with a double asterisk (**) or dagger (†). You should, however, use information footnotes rarely. Almost always when you have something to tell your readers, it is better to say it within the paper itself. This is in line with the general rule that anything that interrupts the reader or makes reading more difficult should be avoided.

C *Research Paper Format (MLA Style)*

 FORMAT FOR YOUR POLISHED DRAFT

The polished draft of your paper should be printed (using word processing software on a computer). A neatly handwritten paper may be allowed in rare cases, but only a printed or typed paper presents a professional appearance. When you are communicating with others, appearance counts. Although the paper's appearance does not alter the content of your writing, it most certainly does affect the way your writing is received. Instructors try to be as objective as possible in judging student work, but they are still swayed, like all other humans, by appearances. Computer-printed or typed papers give the impression of more serious, careful work, and they are certainly more inviting and easier to read. In the professional world, reports and correspondence are always computer-printed or typed; anything less would be unthinkable. There is no reason to treat your college writing with any less respect.

Computer word processing offers the greatest benefits for composing, revising, copyediting, and printing your paper. With a word processor, you can make additions, deletions, corrections, and rearrangements of passages easily and at any time. The spell-check feature can identify errors in spelling and typing that you might otherwise miss. And, of course, the finished product has a polished, professional appearance.

Use a typewriter only if a computer is unavailable. Most writers find it difficult to compose on a typewriter; it is easier to make changes and corrections in handwritten drafts. But once they have completed a draft, writers find it advantageous to type it. Typing your paper forces you to read it slowly and carefully. For many writers, some of their best ideas for polishing and revising their work come during typing. If you have not learned keyboarding skills, you would be well advised to do so at the earliest opportunity; you will be greatly handicapped if you lack direct access to either a computer or a typewriter.

When you print or type your paper, follow the format exemplified by one of the sample papers shown in Chapter 8. In particular, pay attention to the following conventions.

Format for Computer-Printed or Typed Papers

The following are standard format guidelines for research papers. Individual instructors may wish to modify some of them according to their preferences. Check with your instructor if you have questions about the required format.

Paper

For computer printing, use plain white, heavyweight, 8½ × 11-inch paper. If you type, use good-quality, non-see-through, nonoily, nonerasable, 20-pound, 8½ × 11-inch paper. Print on one side of the paper only.

Ink

Use only black ink. Replace the cartridge in your printer if it no longer produces a dark copy.

Type Font

For computer-printed papers, a laser, inkjet, or dot matrix printer with correspondence-quality type is best. If your software allows you a choice of fonts, choose Courier, a monospaced font; your instructor may also allow a proportional-space font. Never use a fancy typeface such as script or italic.

Spacing

Double-space (leave every other line blank) throughout the paper. This includes indented quotations and the list of works cited, which are also double-spaced. Do not skip additional lines between paragraphs.

Margins

Leave one-inch margins at the top, bottom, and sides of each page of the paper. The right margin does not need to be straight; do not divide words with hyphens just to achieve a straighter margin. For computer-printed papers, a justified right margin is not desirable; that is, do not have the computer insert extra spaces between words so as to make the right margin straight.

    If you wish, you can adjust the bottom margin of any page to avoid a *widow line* or an *orphan*—the typesetting terms for stranded lines. An orphan is the first line of a new paragraph at the bottom of a page; a widow is the last line of a paragraph at the top of a page. To avoid widows and orphans, do not type the first line of a new paragraph at the bottom of a page but begin it instead at the top of the following page. Also, do not begin a new page with the last line of a paragraph; if necessary, type that line at the bottom of the preceding page. Notice how Slade Healy avoided an orphan at the bottom of page 388.

Indenting

Indent one-half inch (five spaces) before beginning each new paragraph. Indent long quotations one inch (ten spaces) from the left margin; do not indent from

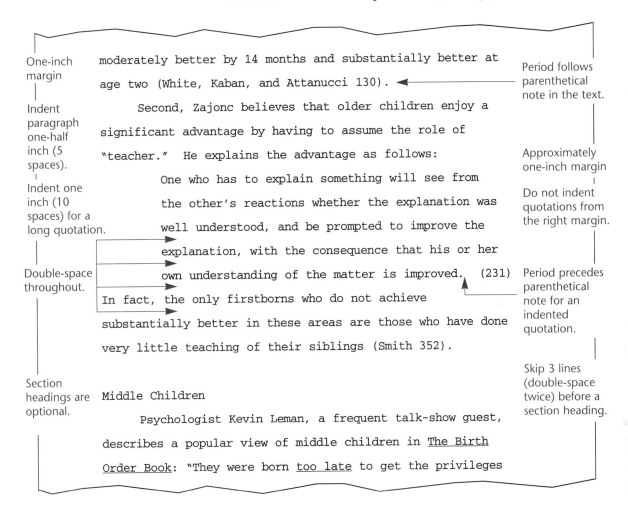

Figure C.1 **Format for the spacing and margins in a research paper.**

the right margin. (For additional directions, see pages 333–35.) Figure C.1 shows an excerpt from a research paper demonstrating how margins and indentions should be handled.

The First Page

The format of your first page should resemble that of Slade's paper in Figure C.2.

- *Page identification.* Your last name and the page number go at the top of the first page and each subsequent page. If you are using a standard word-processing program with a "header" feature, you can have it automatically put this header at the upper right of each page. Number the first page of the paper as page 1, even if you use a cover page. Do not precede the page number with *p.* or *page.*

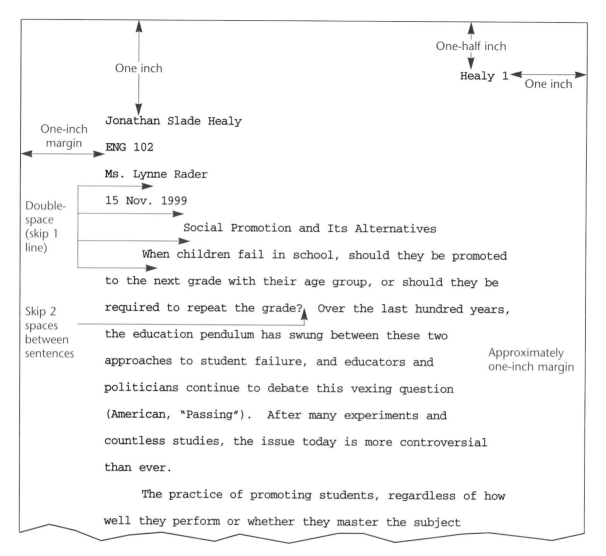

Figure C.2 Format for the first page.

- *Author information.* Type your full name, course information, and the date in the upper-left corner of the first page, about one inch from the top of the paper. If you use an automatic header for the page identification, the author information goes on the first line of the paper itself, immediately below the header. A separate cover page is needed only for lengthy reports (see page 484.

- *Title.* Double-space again (skip a line), and center the title. Only the first letter of each important word in the title should be capitalized; do not capitalize a word such as *the* (article), *and* (conjunction), or *of* (preposition) unless it is the first word of the title or the first word following a colon. Do not underline the title or enclose it in quotation marks. Of course, you should use standard punctuating conventions for titles of works that you include within your own titles. For example:

`The Depiction of Old Age in `<u>`King Lear`</u>

`and in "The Love Song of J. Alfred Prufrock"`

- *Body*. Double-space following the title, and begin your paper. Skip two spaces between sentences. (Notice how Slade skipped two spaces following each period that ends a sentence, each question mark, and each exclamation point in his paper.)

Subsequent Pages

The format of subsequent pages is shown in Figure C.3. If you use an automatic header, have the computer automatically place your last name and page number at the top right of each page. If not, type this information at the top right, and then double-space twice (skip three lines); the first line of text should begin one inch from the top of the page.

Tables and Figures

You can include *tables*—the presentation of data in columns—and *figures*—drawings, graphs, photographs, or other inserts—in your paper. Tables and figures can be either of your own creation or copied from a source (and duly acknowledged). A sample page from a research paper that includes a table is shown in Figure C.4. Figure C.5 shows a figure that the writer photocopied from a source he acknowledged.

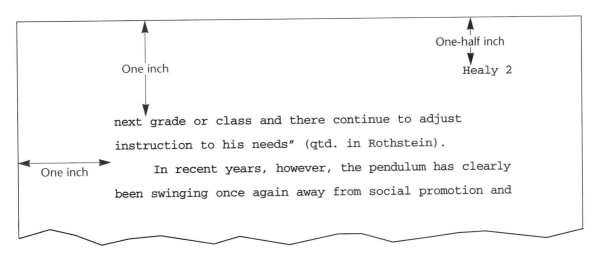

Figure C.3 Format for subsequent pages.

Reagan 8

Other statistics show that although the number of medical students in their thirties and forties is increasing, one's chances of being admitted to medical school decrease with age, as Table 1 demonstrates:

The table is referred to within the paper.

Quadruple-space before and after each table or figure.

Each table or figure is given a number and a label.

Table 1

Percentages of Men and Women Accepted by Medical Schools (1989)[a]

Raised lower-case letters are used for footnotes within tables and figures.

Age	Men	Women
21–23	73	67
24–27	58	55
28–31	49	53
32–34	46	51
35–37	41	46
38 and over	27	34

Double-space throughout the table.

Each line of a table begins at the left margin (it is not centered).

Source: Plantz, Lorenzo, and Cole 115

[a] The chart is based on data gathered by the American Medical Association.

The table ends with the source and footnotes (if any).

I have learned that there are many criteria other than age that medical schools consider when reviewing applications.

The paper resumes following the table.

Figure C.4 Sample page with table.

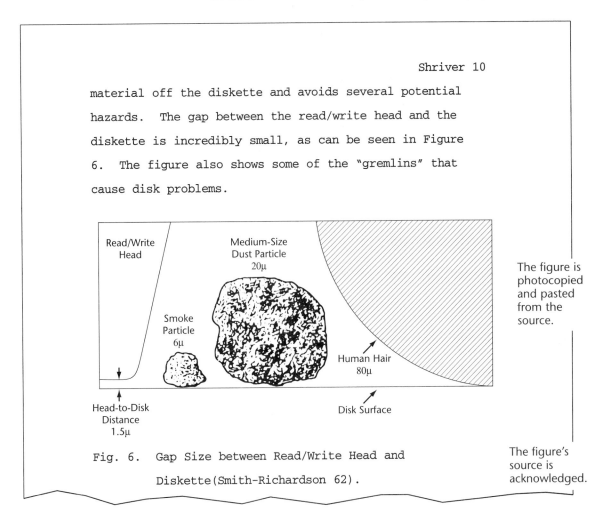

Figure C.5 **Sample page with a figure.**

Observe the following guidelines when you include tables and figures:

1. All tables and figures should be referred to within the paper (e.g., "Table 1 shows the variation among . . . ," " . . . as can be seen in Figure 6," and so on). Place the table or figure as close as possible following its mention in the paper.

2. Tables and figures should be numbered consecutively (Table 1, Table 2, Table 3, . . . ; Figure 1, Figure 2, . . .). Each table should be given a clear explanatory label on the following line, and each figure should have an explanatory caption typed on the same line and placed below the figure. Each line begins at the left margin; it is not centered.

3. Double-space throughout, but skip three lines (double-space twice) both before and after a table or figure.

4. Lines may be drawn across the page (as in Figure C.4, for example) to set a table or figure apart from the rest of the paper.

5. A table or figure may be photocopied from a source and pasted onto your page (see Figure C.5). You may then wish to photocopy the entire page again.

6. If the table or figure is taken from a source, acknowledge the source on a line following the table or figure.

7. If you use footnotes (as in Figure C.4), assign them raised lowercase letters (a, b, c, and so on) and place the notes below the table or figure (and source citation, if given).

List of Works Cited

Begin the list of works cited on a new page. (The exception is a very brief list, which you can begin after skipping three lines from the end of the text.)

- *Title.* Center the title *Works Cited* (or *Bibliography*) about one inch from the top of the page; that is, skip three lines following the page number.
- *Spacing.* Double-space between the title and the first entry and throughout the list. Do not skip additional lines between entries.
- *Entries.* Follow the guidelines in Chapter A. Remember to "outdent" each entry; that is, begin each entry at the left margin and indent the second and subsequent lines one-half inch (five spaces). List items in alphabetical order. Do not number your entries. The list of works cited should include only works that you quoted or paraphrased in writing the paper, not works you consulted but did not use.

Refer to Figure C.6 for a sample works-cited page.

Fastening the Paper

Fasten your paper with a paper clip in the upper left-hand corner. Do not staple or rivet pages together or place your paper in a cover unless you are requested to do so by your instructor.

Title Page

A title page is standard only for a book-length report, a paper with multiple chapters, or a paper with preliminary material such as a formal outline or preface. If you use a title page, it should follow the format shown in Figure C.7.

Title-page information is typed in the center of the page. Center each line, and leave equal space above and below the typed material. Most word-processing programs can automatically center material on a page from top to bottom. If you type, you can use this formula to determine the number of lines to skip from the top of the page before typing the first line:

1. Count the number of lines of text that will appear on your title page, including skipped lines. (Eliza Tetirick's title information takes up 17 lines in the example.)

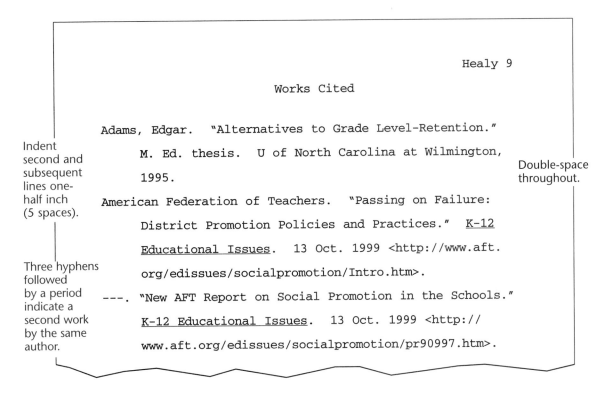

Indent second and subsequent lines one-half inch (5 spaces).

Double-space throughout.

Three hyphens followed by a period indicate a second work by the same author.

Healy 9

Works Cited

Adams, Edgar. "Alternatives to Grade Level-Retention."
    M. Ed. thesis. U of North Carolina at Wilmington,
    1995.

American Federation of Teachers. "Passing on Failure:
    District Promotion Policies and Practices." K-12
    Educational Issues. 13 Oct. 1999 <http://www.aft.
    org/edissues/socialpromotion/Intro.htm>.

---. "New AFT Report on Social Promotion in the Schools."
    K-12 Educational Issues. 13 Oct. 1999 <http://
    www.aft.org/edissues/socialpromotion/pr90997.htm>.

Figure C.6 Sample Works Cited page.

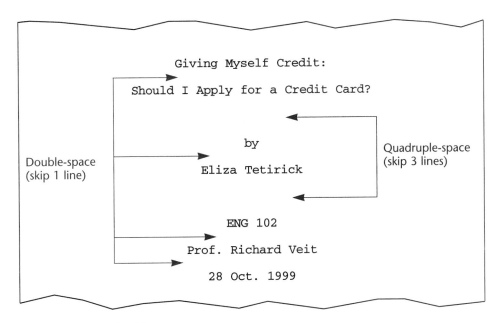

Double-space (skip 1 line)

Quadruple-space (skip 3 lines)

Giving Myself Credit:

Should I Apply for a Credit Card?

by

Eliza Tetirick

ENG 102

Prof. Richard Veit

28 Oct. 1999

Figure C.7 Sample title page.

2. Subtract that number from 66, the total number of lines on a typical page, to get the number of unused lines. (In Eliza's case, 66 – 17 = 49.)

3. Divide that number in half. (Half of 49 is 24½.)

4. Skip that number of lines (in Eliza's case, 24 or 25) from the top of the page, and begin typing.

To center each line from left to right, count the number of characters (letters, spaces, and punctuation) in the line (Eliza's first line, *Giving Myself Credit:*, consists of 21 characters). Backspace half that many spaces from the center of your paper (10 or 11 spaces) and begin typing. If you use a title page, do not repeat title information on the following page. Number the following page as page 1.

Typing Errors

Correction tape is preferable to white correction fluid for removing errors as you type. Never use an eraser. If you use a computer, use the spell-check feature and proofread to make your paper as error-free as possible before you print your final draft.

Errors Discovered during Proofreading

Neatly cross out a minor error with a single line, and write the correction above it. Never erase, and do not use correction fluid for making handwritten changes. Any page with a major error or numerous minor errors should be retyped.

Format for Handwritten Papers

Most of the guidelines for typed and computer-generated papers also apply to handwritten papers, with the following adjustments. Consult your instructor to determine if handwritten papers are acceptable.

Paper

Use lined, non-see-through 8½ × 11-inch loose-leaf paper. Never use sheets torn or cut from a spiral notebook. Paper should be college ruled (3½ lines per inch) and have a left margin line. Write on only one side of each sheet of paper.

Pen

Use a fine-point pen with dark blue or black ink. Never use a pen that smudges or that leaves small ink blotches when touched to the page.

Handwriting

Write in a neat, clear hand. Hard-to-read, distractingly fancy, or slovenly handwriting detracts from the effectiveness of your presentation. If you have difficulty with your handwriting, you would be wise to have your paper typed. Do not make your writing excessively large or leave excessive space between words. Handwritten papers with only a few words on each line are unpleasant to read because they demand constant eye movement.

Margins

Leave about a one-inch margin from the top and from the left of each page. That is, begin each page on the second line, and begin each line at the red margin line. Do not leave space for right and bottom margins, unless requested to do so by your instructor. The title and page numbers are placed as in typed papers.

Spacing

Single-space your paper unless you are requested by your instructor to double-space.

Errors

Handwritten papers should be error-free. Neatly cross out a minor error with a single line, and write the correction above it. Never erase or use correction fluid to make corrections. Any page with a major error or numerous minor errors should be recopied.

Excerpts from a handwritten paper are shown in Figures C.8 and C.9.

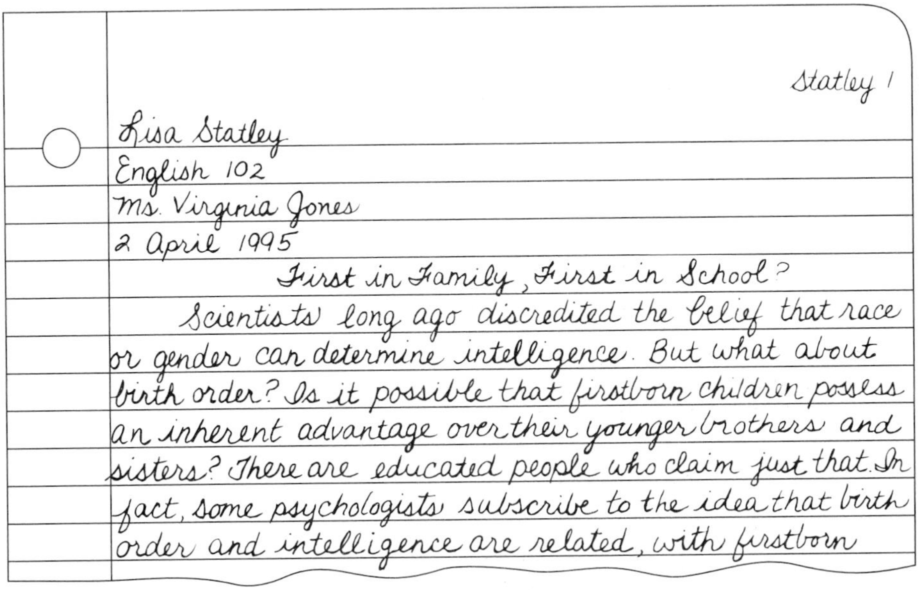
Statley 1

Lisa Statley
English 102
Ms. Virginia Jones
2 April 1995

First in Family, First in School?

Scientists long ago discredited the belief that race or gender can determine intelligence. But what about birth order? Is it possible that firstborn children possess an inherent advantage over their younger brothers and sisters? There are educated people who claim just that. In fact, some psychologists subscribe to the idea that birth order and intelligence are related, with firstborn

Figure C.8 Sample first page of a handwritten paper.

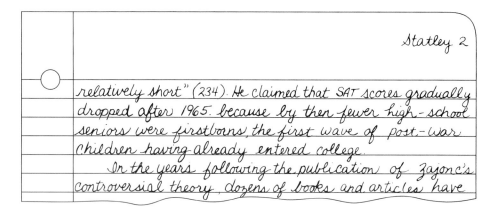

Figure C.9 Subsequent page from a handwritten paper.

 A FORMAL OUTLINE

The general, *informal outlines* that Slade Healy used in writing his early drafts (see pages 316 and 364) helped him organize his research materials. The length and complexity of a research paper require writers to have a plan for arranging it—one that is general and flexible enough so that they can develop and alter it as they discover new ideas.

Informal outlines are valuable, but most writers—both beginners and professionals alike—find it difficult and limiting to create a detailed, formal outline *before* they write. As you have now read many times in this book, writing is a learning process. Writers rarely know exactly how a paper will turn out before they write it. Even the best-prepared writers are usually surprised by the final form their writing takes. This occurs because our minds are actively at work when we write, and writing stimulates new thoughts that can take our writing in unforeseen directions.

Although a *formal outline* is limited in usefulness when it is prepared before you begin writing, it *can* be useful as part of the revision process—when it is written *after* you have completed a preliminary draft. As a scaled-down map of your paper, the formal outline allows you to see its organization with clarity. It can point out the flaws of your arrangement and suggest new possibilities. Some instructors require that a printed, formal outline be included as a part of the research paper to make sure that their students have considered organization carefully. The detailed formal outline that Slade submitted with his paper is printed on the following page.

Social Promotion and Its Alternatives

I.   Introduction
     A. Controversy: promotion or retention?
     B. History
        1. Early 20th century: retention
        2. 1930s and 1940s: social promotion

II. Today: swing of pendulum
     A. Criticism of social promotion
        1. Teachers' objections
        2. Politicians' platforms
     B. Examples of new policies
        1. Los Angeles
        2. Chicago

III. Effects of new policies
     A. Benefits
        1. Motivation
        2. Higher test scores
        3. More students graduating
     B. Negative effects
        1. Educational: poor performance by retained
           students
        2. Psychological
           a. "Should be" syndrome
           b. Stigma of retention
           c. Loss of self-esteem
        3. Social: older students in classroom

IV. Complex solutions needed
     A. Remedial programs
        1. Los Angeles
        2. Chicago
     B. Preventive programs
        1. Better teacher training
        2. Smaller classes

V.   Conclusion: Complex solutions needed for a
     complex problem

An outline can be as detailed—or as general—as you wish. Slade's outline is reasonably complete, but he could have made it either shorter or longer if he wished. Compare it to this excerpt from a less detailed version of Slade's outline:

I.   Introduction

    A. Controversy: promotion or retention?

    B. History

II. Today: swing of pendulum

    A. Criticism of social promotion

    B. Examples of new policies

III. Effects of new policies

    A. Benefits

        1. Motivation

        2. Higher test scores

        3. More students graduating

    B. Negative effects

        1. Educational

        2. Psychological

        3. Social

IV. Complex solutions needed

    A. Remedial programs

    B. Preventive programs

V.   Conclusion

On the other hand, a more detailed outline might expand section IV, "Complex solutions needed," as follows:

IV. Complex and costly solutions needed

    A. Remedial programs

        1. Costs for systems

            a. Los Angeles: $71 million

                (1) Summer school

                (2) Saturday programs

                (3) After-school tutoring

            b. Chicago

                (1) Summer programs: $24 million

```
        (2) New teachers: $10 million

    2. Costs per student: $1300

  B. Preventive programs . . .
```

When you are revising your paper, a detailed outline can help you see how each part fits into the whole. When you have difficulty in creating an outline, the cause is often a problem with the organization of your paper. Your attempts to create a logical outline can often suggest a workable rearrangement of material within your paper. For example, before Slade created his formal outline, he had placed the benefits and costs of the new Chicago policy together in a single section. Only when he created his outline did he decide that a more effective organization would have the costs of a retention policy placed alongside other problems with eliminating social promotion.

On the other hand, a writer should not be a slave to a rigidly symmetrical outline. In the final analysis, the nature of your material and not form-for-form's-sake should determine your outline. For that reason, Slade's sections II, III, and IV are similar but not precisely parallel in their structure.

Standard Numbering System

Formal outlines usually follow the format that Slade used. Notice that each major part of Slade's outline is divided into subparts. These subparts are indented and marked with numbers and letters, following this *standard system:*

Paper Title

 I. First major part of the paper
  A. First subpart of I
  B. Second subpart of I
   1. First subpart of B
   2. Second subpart of B
 II. Second major part
  A. First subpart of II
   1. First subpart of A
   2. Second subpart of A
  B. Second subpart of II
   1. First subpart of B
   2. Second subpart of B
 III. Third major part
  A. First subpart of III
   1. First subpart of A
   2. Second subpart of A
   3. Third subpart of A

  B. Second subpart of III

   1. First subpart of B

   2. Second subpart of B

    a. First subpart of 2

    b. Second subpart of 2

    c. Third subpart of 2

   3. Third subpart of B

Decimal System

The *decimal system* is also widely used for outlines, particularly for scientific papers.

  1. First major part

  2. Second major part

   2.1 First subpart of 2

   2.2 Second subpart of 2

    2.2.1 First subpart of 2.2

    2.2.2 Second subpart of 2.2

     2.2.2.1 . . .

     2.2.2.2 . . .

3. . . .

  3.1 . . .

  3.2 . . .

  3.3 . . .

Some instructors who assign formal outlines require, in the interest of symmetry, that whenever a part is to have subparts, there must be at least two of them; that is, they prefer that there not be a part 1 without at least a part 2, and so on. For example, they would find level B1a in the following to be faulty because it is the only entry on its level (there is no B1b):

  B. Negative effects

   1. Educational

    a. Poor performance by retained students

   2. Psychological

    a. "Should be" syndrome

    b. Stigma of retention . . .

It should be stressed that not everyone objects to lone subparts. For those who do, the preceding can easily be adjusted by incorporating the subpart into the part above it:

B. Negative effects

    1. Educational: poor performance by retained students

    2. Psychological . . .

Formal Outlines

1. Following are the parts of an outline for an argumentative paper. They appear in the proper order, but they have not been numbered or indented. Number them according to the *standard system* for outlining.

The Case against Saturday Morning Cartoons

Introduction
Background: description of current situation
Thesis: harm to children by Saturday morning cartoon shows
Counterarguments (those favoring these shows)
Positive-benefit arguments
Benefit to parents: babysitting
Benefits to children
Cartoon violence a harmless outlet for children's aggression
Children taught about life from cartoons
Free-market arguments
Programming determined by ratings, sponsors
Children's viewing up to parents, not networks
Censorship dangerous to our way of life
Refutation of counterarguments
Refutation of positive-benefit arguments
Damage to parents: deprived of interaction with their children
Damage to children
Shown only violent solutions to problems
Shown only the worst aspects of life
Refutation of free-market arguments
Morality, not only profits, a responsibility of networks
Parents unable to judge and screen all programming
Voluntary controls, not censorship, requested
Additional argument: danger to society of children's viewing
A nation of antisocial zombies
A nation of viewers, not doers
Conclusion: a call for reform

2. Renumber the preceding outline entries using the decimal system.

Topic and Sentence Outlines

The preceding formal outlines are examples of *topic outlines,* in which all the parts consist of phrases rather than complete sentences. In a *sentence outline,* the parts consist of complete sentences. For example:

> I. Policies for coping with student failure are controversial.
>   A. Educators have debated whether to socially promote or to retain failing students.
>   B. The pendulum has swung back and forth in the 20th century.
>   1. In the early decades, retention was the norm.
>   2. During the 1930s and 1940s, social promotion became the preferred policy.
> II. Today the pendulum is swinging once again toward retention. . . .

You can use either the topic or sentence outline method, but whichever you choose, be certain that you follow it consistently.

Like some of the other steps in research writing, the details of outline-writing may strike you as complicated—as undoubtedly they are—but they do serve a purpose. Use your informal and formal outlines to help you organize, write, and revise your paper. But remember that an outline is a tool to help you produce a better paper and not an end in itself. It is important at all times to remember the central goal of your research writing: to communicate what you have discovered in an effective way. Like all parts of the research process, the outline will work best and be of most help to you if you approach it with common sense.

EXERCISE | ### Sentence Outlines

1. Continue revising Slade Healy's outline on page 489 to make it a sentence outline.

2. Rewrite the outline in the preceding exercise (on page 493) to make it a sentence outline. Each line of the outline should be a complete sentence.

D Footnotes and Endnotes

Scholars in the fields of art, dance, history, music, religion, and theater often use footnotes and endnotes, instead of parenthetical notes, to document sources. Although it should not be necessary for you to memorize the details of the format, you should know how to use this chapter as a reference guide whenever you need to write footnotes or endnotes. When you do, consult it carefully and be certain to follow the format exactly, paying special attention to the mechanics of arrangement and punctuation.

Figure D.1 shows how a portion of Slade Healy's research paper would have looked if he had used footnotes instead of parenthetical notes. (Compare it with his use of parenthetical notes on pages 243–44.) The excerpt in Figure D.2 shows what his "Notes" page would have looked like if he had used endnotes.

Footnotes and endnotes serve the same purpose as parenthetical notes—to identify and give credit to your sources for their specific contributions to your paper. In the same place in your paper where you would put a parenthetical note, put a raised number to refer your readers to the note. Number your notes consecutively throughout the paper, starting with number 1. For footnotes, type each note at the bottom of the same page where the reference occurs. For endnotes, type all notes, in numerical order, on a separate page following the paper but preceding the list of works cited.

SAMPLE FOOTNOTES AND ENDNOTES

The models in this chapter show the footnote/endnote format for works cited in Chapter A on pages 441–60. Note that complete information about a source is required only the first time it is cited in a note. Subsequent notes use an abbreviated format. (See sample footnote 28 in Figure D.1.)

Sources in Books

A Book with One Author

> [1] V. S. Naipaul, <u>Between Father and Son: Family Letters</u> (New York: Knopf, 2000) 52–54.

Healy 7

to prevent failure in the first place.   "What we really
need," she says, "is an intensive-care approach right from
the start, concentrating every possible resource on helping
students as soon as they start to fall behind."[25]   Schools
must provide high-quality pre-school and kindergarten
programs and well trained teachers.   In addition, they must
identify struggling students in the earliest grades, put
them in small classes, and give them solid instruction in
reading.   When students fail, Feldman recommends remedial
approaches that "have a good track record but are seldom
used."   These include individual tutoring, Saturday
classes, and extra periods in problem subjects.[26]

Smith and Shepard claim that the most effective remedy
for children performing below grade level is not retention
but promotion accompanied by remediation.   They cite
research showing that tutoring, summer school, and one-on-
one help are more effective and less costly than
retention.[27]   When school systems use retention, they argue,
individualized instruction must also be given to retained

[25]Qtd. in American Federation of Teachers, "New AFT
Report on Social Promotion in the Schools," K-12
Educational Issues, 13 Oct. 1999 <http://www.aft.org/
edissues/socialpromotion/pr90997.htm>.

[26]American, "New."

[27]Mary Lee Smith and Lorrie A. Shepard, "Flunking
Grades: A Recapitulation," ed. Lorrie A. Shepard and Mary

Marginal notes:

Notes are numbered consecutively throughout the paper. The numbers are superscripts (raised slightly above the line).

Double-space twice (skip 3 lines).

Double-space within and between footnotes.

Figure D.1 Sample pages from a paper that uses footnotes.

Healy 8

students so that they can rejoin their age group as soon as possible.[28]

Linda Darling-Hammond, executive director of the National Commission on Teaching and America's Future, claims that the quality of the teacher is the single most important factor in student performance, and she recommends directing resources to training and hiring better teachers. Low-income, minority, and special-needs students are the students most often retained, and they are also the students least likely to have well qualified, effective teachers.[29]

Educational researchers agree that the problem of student failure will be solved only through careful and costly efforts. Unfortunately, complex solutions do not lend themselves to the sound bites favored by many politicians and school boards. Until we are ready to deal seriously with the causes of failure, the educational pendulum is likely to continue to swing between social promotion and retention.

Lee Smith, _Flunking Grades: Research and Policies on Retention_ (New York: Falmer, 1989) 230.

[28]Smith and Shephard 233.

[29]Linda Darling-Hammond, "Avoiding Both Grade Retention and Social Promotion," _Education Digest_ Nov. 1998, ProQuest, 14 Oct. 1999: 48–49 <http://www.bellhowell.infolearning.com/proquest/>.

After the first reference to a source (see footnote 27), the abbreviated form is used.

A line drawn on the page signals that the first footnote beneath it is continued from the previous page.

Figure D.1 *(Continued)*

Healy 9

Notes

[1] American Federation of Teachers, "Passing on Failure: District Promotion Policies and Practices," <u>K-12 Educational Issues</u>, 13 Oct. 1999 <http://www.aft.org/edissues/socialpromotion/Intro.htm>.

[2] Edgar Adams, "Alternatives to Grade Level Retention," Ed.D. thesis, U of North Carolina at Wilmington, 1995, 1-2.

[3] Qtd. in Rothstein, Richard, "Where Is Lake Wobegon, Anyway?" <u>Phi Delta Kappan</u> Nov. 1998, 198.

[4] "Most Cleveland Teachers Say Social Promotion Doesn't Work," <u>Sun Newspapers</u>, 1997, 12 Oct. 1999 <http://www.sunnews.com/news/suburbs/metro/socialpromotionside.htm>.

[5] Daniel B. Wood, "California's Big Test: Holding Students Back," <u>Christian Science Monitor</u> 5 Feb. 1999, <u>MasterFILE Premier</u>, EBSCOhost, 15 Oct. 1999 <http://www.epnet.com/ehost/>.

[6] Donna Shaw, "Stopping Social Promotion," <u>Curriculum Administrator</u> 35.9 (1999): 7.

[7] Marjorie Coeyman, "Repeating a Grade Gains Favor in Schools," <u>Christian Science Monitor</u> 6 Apr. 1999, <u>MasterFILE Premier</u>, EBSCOhost, 15 Oct. 1999 <http://www.epnet.com/ehost/>.

[8] Romesh Ratnesar and Wendy Cole, "Held Back," <u>Time</u> 14 June 1999, <u>MasterFILE Premier</u>, EBSCOhost, 15 Oct. 1999 <http://www.epnet.com/ehost/>.

Figure D.2 Sample notes page from a paper that uses endnotes.

Footnotes/endnotes differ from works-cited entries in several particulars: The first line of each footnote/endnote is indented; the authors first (not last) name comes first; the publisher and date are enclosed in parentheses; and commas (not periods) separate major items. Also, unlike works-cited entries (but like parenthetical notes), footnotes/endnotes give the specific page or pages in the source from which the cited information is taken.

Second and Subsequent References—All Sources

After a work has been cited in one note, you do not need to repeat all the same information in subsequent notes that refer to that same source. For second and subsequent references to a source, footnotes/endnotes should contain the least amount of information needed to identify the source (usually the author and page number).

> [2] Naipaul 109.

A Book with Two or Three Authors

> [3] William G. Cunningham and Paula A. Cordeiro, Educational Administration: A Problem-Based Approach (Boston: Allyn, 2000) 88.
>
> [4] Jo Anne Reid, Peter Forrestal, and Jonathan Cook Small Group Learning in the Classroom (Portsmouth, NH: Heinemann, 1990) 110.

A Book with More Than Three Authors

> [5] Stéphane Courtois, et al., The Black Book of Communism: Crimes, Terror, Repression, (Cambridge, MA: Harvard UP, 1999) 248-49.

A Book in a Later Edition

> [6] David Popenoe, Sociology, 11th ed. (Boston: Prentice, 2000) 55-58.

A Book in a Series

> [7] Rudolph P. Matthee, The Politics of Trade in Safavid Iran: Silk for Silver, 1600-1730, Cambridge Studies in Islamic Civilization (New York: Cambridge UP, 2000) 303.

A Book Published in More Than One Volume

Volumes individually titled:

   [8] Crane Brinton, John B. Christopher, and Robert Lee Wolff, <u>Prehistory to 1715</u>, Vol. 1 of <u>A History of Civilization</u>, 6th ed., 2 vols. (Englewood Cliffs, NJ: Prentice, 1984) 303.

Volumes not individually titled:

   [9] Charles Messenger, <u>For Love of Regiment: A History of British Infantry, 1660–1993</u>, vol. 1 (Philadelphia: Trans-Atlantic, 1995) 388.

A Book with a Translator or Editor

   [10] Julio Ramos, <u>Divergent Modernities: Culture and Politics in Nineteenth-Century Latin America</u>, trans. John D. Blanco (Durham: Duke UP, 1999) 97–99.

   [11] William Shakespeare, <u>Henry V</u>, ed. T. W. Craik (New York: Routledge, 1995) 88.

A Work from an Anthology

   [12] Myra Leifer, "Pregnancy," <u>Women: Sex and Sexuality</u>, ed. Catherine R. Stimpson and Ethel Spector Person (Chicago: U of Chicago P, 1980) 215.

   [13] George Lichtheim, "The Birth of a Philosopher," <u>Collected Essays</u> (New York: Viking, 1973) 103–04.

   [14] Salman Rushdie, "A Pen against the Sword: In Good Faith" <u>Newsweek</u> 12 Feb. 1990: 52+, rpt. in <u>One World, Many Cultures</u>, ed. Stuart Hirschberg (New York: Macmillan, 1992) 480.

A Book Published before 1900

   [15] Florence Nightingale, <u>Notes on Nursing: What It Is, and What It Is Not</u> (New York, 1860) 27.

A Paperback or Other Reprinted Book

[16] Tony Horwitz, <u>Confederates in the Attic: Dispatches from the Unfinished Civil War</u> (1998; New York: Vintage, 1999) 177.

A Work Written by a Group or Government Agency

[17] Sotheby's, <u>Nineteenth Century European Paintings, Drawings and Watercolours</u> (London: Sotheby's, 1995) 164.

[18] United States: Department of Justice: Office of Juvenile Justice and Delinquency Prevention, <u>Cross-Age Teaching</u> (Washington: GPO, 1999) 44.

An Online Book

[19] David Irving, <u>Hitler's War </u>(New York: Viking, 1977), 20 Jan. 2000 <http://www.focal.org/books/hitler/HW.pdf>.

[20] Kenneth Robinson, <u>Beyond the Wilderness</u>, Online Originals, 1998, 21 Dec. 1999 <http://www.onlineoriginals.com/beyondsy.html>.

[21] Mary Wollstonecraft, <u>Vindication of the Rights of Women</u>, 1792, <u>Project Bartleby</u>, ed. Steven H. van Leeuwen, 13 Feb. 2000 <http://www.bartleby.com/144/index.html>.

A Work on CD-ROM or Diskette

[22] Frederick S. Merritt, M. Kent Loftin, and Jonathan T. Ricketts, <u>Standard Handbook for Civil Engineers</u>, 4th ed., CD-ROM (New York: McGraw, 1999).

An Article in an Encyclopedia or Other Reference Work
A well-known reference work:

[23] James R. Brandon, "East Asian Arts," <u>Encyclopaedia Britannica: Macropaedia</u>, 15th ed., 1998.

[24] "Wellstone, Paul," <u>Who's Who in America</u>, 54th ed., 2000.

[25] "Yokel," <u>The Shorter Oxford English Dictionary</u>, 1973.

A lesser-known reference work:

> [26] Raymond Hames, "Yanomamö," <u>South America</u>, Vol. 7 of <u>Encyclopedia of World Cultures</u> (Boston: Hall, 1994).

An electronic reference work:

> [27] "Latitude and Longitude," <u>Britannica Online</u>, 28 Feb. 2000 <http://search.eb.com/bol/topic?xref=7843>.

> [28] "Yokel," <u>Oxford English Dictionary</u>, 2nd. ed., CD-ROM (Oxford: Oxford UP, 1992).

Sources in Periodicals and Newspapers

An Article in a Magazine

> [29] Toddi Gutner Block, "Riding the Waves," <u>Forbes</u> 11 Sept. 1995: 182.

> [30] Jacquelyn Lynn, "Hidden Resources," <u>Entrepreneur</u> Jan. 2000: 105.

> [31] Ann Robinson, "Gifted: The Two-Faced Label," <u>The Gifted Child Today</u> Jan./Feb. 1989: 34–35.

An Article in a Journal

Pages numbered continuously throughout a volume:

> [32] Hayne W. Reese, "Some Contributions of Philosophy to Behavioral Sciences," <u>Journal of Mind and Behavior</u> 20 (1999): 183–210.

Each issue begins on page 1:

> [33] Anna Green, "Returning History to the Community: Oral History in a Museum Setting," <u>Oral History Review</u> 24.2 (1997): 60.

An Article in a Newspaper

> [34] Pamela Constable, "Afghan Hijack Drama Ends Peacefully," <u>Washington Post</u> 1 Jan. 2000: A21.

[35] David Ranii, "New AIDS Drug Is Step Closer to Approval," <u>News and Observer</u> [Raleigh] 7 Nov. 1995: 1D+.

[36] Leslie Kaufman and Saul Hansell, "Holiday Lesson in Online Retailing," <u>New York Times</u> 2 Jan. 2000, natl. ed.: sec. 3: 1, 12.

An Editorial

[37] "Replace Unfair Tax Law," editorial, <u>USA Today</u> 28 Aug. 1995: 12A.

A Letter to the Editor

[38] David Sadler, letter, <u>U.S. News & World Report</u> 3–10 Jan. 2000: 7.

A Review

[39] Derek Bickerton, "Life without Father," Rev. of <u>The Emperor's Embrace: Reflections on Animal Families and Fatherhood</u>, by Jeffrey Moussaieff Masson, <u>New York Times Book Review</u> 2 Jan. 2000: 5.

[40] Kenny Glenn, rev. of <u>Man on the Moon</u> [film], <u>Premiere</u> Jan. 2000: 20.

[41] Rev. of <u>Going to the Territory</u>, by Ralph Ellison, <u>Atlantic</u> Aug. 1986: 91.

[42] David Patrick Stearns, rev. of <u>The Well-Tempered Clavier</u>, by J. S. Bach [CD], Angela Hewitt, piano, <u>Stereophile</u> Dec. 1999: 173.

A Printed Article Reproduced Online

[43] "Doctors Striving to Preempt Diabetes," <u>Boston Globe</u> 1 Jan. 2000: A3, 15 Jan. 2000 <http://www.boston.com/dailyglobe2/001/nation/Doctors_striving_to_preempt_diabetes+.shtml>.

[44] Melissa Eddy, "Experts Worry about Economic Collapse in Bosnia," News and Observer on the Web 1 Jan. 2000, 2 Jan. 2000 <http://www.nandotimes.com/24hour/nao/business/story/0,2257,500148948-500180852-500736195-0,00.html>.

[45] Robert Henry Mazurek, "Under the Ice," Popular Science Jan. 2000: 28, ProQuest, 14 Feb. 2000 <http://proquest.umi.com>.

[46] Lorene Yue, "Economists Expect Federal Reserve to Leave Rates Unchanged," Detroit Free Press 20 Dec. 1999, Newspaper Source, EBSCOhost, 14 Jan. 2000 <http://www.epnet.com>.

A Printed Article Reproduced on CD-ROM or Microform

[47] Nina L. Diamond, "Dolphin Sonar: A Biologist and Physicist Team Up to Find the Source of Sound Beams," Omni July 1994: 24, Popular Periodicals Standard, CD-ROM, NewsBank, Oct. 1995.

[48] Cynthia L. Sipe and Anne E. Roder, "Mentoring School-Age Children: A Classification of Programs," Public/Private Ventures Mentor Spring 1999, ERIC, Microfiche, ED 431 070.

An Article Published Online (Not Reproduced)

[49] Nicholas Phythian, "Ivory Coast Calm, Deposed President Leaves," Reuters, Yahoo! News 26 Dec. 1999, 26 Dec. 1999 <http://dailynews.yahoo.com/h/nm/19991226/ts/ivorycoast_leadall_8.html>.

[50] Alden West, "Camping With Wolves," Dynamic Patterns 5 May 1999, 28 Jan. 2000 <http://www.dynamicpatterns.com/webzine/non-fiction/west_camping_wolves.html>.

Other Sources

An Audio Recording

[51] Dee Dickinson, <u>Creating the Future: Perspectives on Educational Change</u>, Audiocassette (Minneapolis: Accelerated Learning Systems, 1991).

[52] Gustav Mahler, Symphony No. 7, Michael Tilson Thomas, cond., London Symphony Orch., CD, RCA Victor, 1999.

[53] George N. Shuster, jacket notes, <u>The Poetry of Gerard Manley Hopkins</u>, LP, Caedmon, n.d.

Computer Software

[54] <u>Atoms, Symbols and Equations</u>, Vers. 2.1, software, 18 Jan. 2000 <http://ourworld.compuserve.com/homepages/RayLec/atoms.htm>.

[55] <u>Twain's World</u>, CD-ROM (Parsippany, NJ: Bureau Development, 1993).

A Film or Video Recording

[56] <u>All the Pretty Horses</u>, dir. Billy Bob Thornton, screenplay by Cormac McCarthy, Sony, 2000.

[57] <u>The Little Foxes</u>, dir. William Wyler, perf. Bette Davis, Herbert Marshall, and Dan Duryea, MGM, 1941, videocassette, Embassy, 1985.

[58] <u>The Classical Hollywood Style</u>, program 1 of <u>The American Cinema</u>, prod. New York Center for Visual History, videocassette, Annenberg/CPB, 1995.

A Government Document

See "A Work Written by a Group or Government Agency" on page 501.

A Lecture

[59] Stephanie Granetta, class lecture, English 315, Richardson College, 7 Apr. 2000.

[60] Eleanor Kamenish, "A Tale of Two Countries: Mores in France and Scotland," public lecture, Friends of the Public Library, Louisville, 16 Apr. 2000.

A Pamphlet

[61] Golden Retriever Club of America, <u>Prevention of Heartworm</u> (n.p.: GRCA, 2000) 2.

[62] <u>Who Are the Amish?</u> (Aylmer, Ont.: Pathway, n.d.).

A Personal Interview

[63] Robert Keating, personal interview, 14 Oct. 1999.

A Television or Radio Program

[64] <u>The Crossing</u>, dir. Robert Harmon, screenplay by Sherry Jones and Peter Jennings, History Channel, 1 Jan. 2000.

[65] Joanne Silberner, report on Internet drug sales, <u>All Things Considered</u>, National Public Radio, 28 Dec. 1999.

An Unpublished Essay

[66] Eliza Tetirick, "Giving Myself Credit: Should I Apply for a Credit Card?" essay written for Prof. Richard Veit's English 102 class, fall semester 1999.

An Unpublished Letter or E-Mail

[67] Stanley Colbert, letter to author, 5 Mar. 2000.

[68] Paul Wilkes, e-mail to author, 29 Dec. 1999.

An Unpublished Questionnaire

[69] Questionnaire conducted by Prof. Barbara Waxman's English 102 class, Feb. 2000.

E   *APA Format*

 FORMATS OTHER THAN MLA

Although you will use the MLA parenthetical or footnote/endnote format to acknowledge sources in papers that you write for humanities courses (such as research papers in a composition class), other disciplines may require you to use different formats. Since many journals establish their own conventions for documenting sources, you are also likely to encounter various other formats when you conduct library research. A glance through scholarly journals in your college library will show you that dozens of different formats are in use—usually varying only in minor ways from MLA format or the formats described in this chapter.

Although it is not practical to describe all the different formats here, you should be familiar with the most commonly used formats for citing sources. It is probably unnecessary for you to memorize the details of any of them, but when you use a particular format you should be prepared to model your own references carefully on sample entries, such as those in this chapter. Note the ways in which these formats differ from MLA format and pay close attention to the information that is presented in each entry, the order in which it is presented, and the punctuation used to denote and separate items.

Two principal formats, besides the MLA, are in wide use among scholars. The APA format (described in this chapter) gives special prominence to the source's publication date in all citations. In the numbered references format (described in the following chapter), each source is assigned a number in the list of works cited; each note in the paper refers to a source by its assigned number.

 APA STYLE

Next to the MLA style, the most common format for documenting sources is that of the American Psychological Association—*APA style.* This format (or a variation of it) is widely used for course papers and journal articles in psychology but also in many other disciplines in both the social and natural sciences. Although APA format differs in many particulars from MLA format, the main difference is the prominence its citations give to the source's publication date. In fields where new theories and discoveries are constantly challenging past assumptions, readers must know if a writer's sources are up-to-date. Note how the date is featured in the following sample APA citations. Parenthetical notes in APA style always include the date, as in the following:

```
    . . . tendency of creative people to be organized (Sternberg

    & Lubart, 1995, p. 246).
```

Following is the listing for that same source, as it appears in the reference page (list of works cited). Notice that the date is given in parentheses immediately following the author's name.

```
    Sternberg, R. J., & Lubart, T. I. (1995). Defying the

        crowd: Cultivating creativity in a culture of

        conformity. New York: Free Press.
```

The particulars of APA reference style are explained in the following sections.

APA Bibliographic Citations (Reference List)

At the end of the paper, all sources are listed on a separate page, under the title *References* (not *Works Cited*). Like the MLA format, the APA also arranges works alphabetically, according to the first word in each item. See, for example, Figure E.1 on page 509.

In addition to the prominence given to publication dates, bibliographic citations in APA style differ from MLA listings in three principal ways:

1. In APA style, only the author's last name is given in full. Initials are used for first and middle names. Thus, an author who would be listed in MLA style as *Sternberg, Robert J.* is listed as *Sternberg, R. J.* in APA style.

2. Except for proper names, only the first word of the work's title (and, if there is a subtitle, the first word following the colon) is capitalized. Thus, a book title that would be listed in MLA style as *Defying the Crowd: Cultivating Creativity in a Culture of Conformity* is listed in APA style as *Defying the crowd: Cultivating creativity in a culture of conformity*.

3. Titles of periodical articles (and other works shorter than book-length) are not enclosed in quotation marks as they are in MLA style.

Other differences can be seen in the following sample entries.

Model Entries

Punctuation following underlined text is also underlined in APA style.

Social Promotion and Its Alternatives

6

References

Author's last names and first initials are given.

Adams, E. (1995). <u>Alternative to grade level retention.</u> Unpublished doctoral dissertation, University of North Carolina at Wilmington.

Two works by the same author in the same year are labeled *a* and *b*.

American Federation of Teachers. (1997a). Passing on failure: District promotion policies and practices. Retrieved on October 13, 1999 from K-12 Educational Issues on the World Wide Web: http://www.aft.org/ edissues/socialpromotion/Intro.htm

American Federation of Teachers. (1997b). New AFT report on social promotion in the schools. Retrieved on October 13, 1999 from K-12 Educational Issues on the World Wide Web: http://www.aft.org/edissues/ socialpromotion/pr90997.htm

Titles are capitalized according to the rules for sentence capitalization.

Article titles are not placed in quotation marks.

Online sources are cited in this format.

Figure E.1 Sample APA References page.

A Book

Naipaul, V. S. (2000). <u>Between father and son: Family letters.</u> New York: Knopf.

A Book in a Later Edition

Popenoe, D. (2000). <u>Sociology</u> (11th ed.). Boston: Prentice Hall.

APA style presents the ***names of publishers*** in a more complete form. For example, it uses *Prentice Hall* instead of *Prentice.* As in MLA style, words such as *Press, Publishers,* and *Company* are omitted.

A Book with a Translator

> Ramos, J. (1999). <u>Divergent modernities: Culture and</u>
>
>   <u>politics in nineteenth-century Latin America</u> (J. D.
>
>   Blanco, Trans.). Durham: Duke University Press.
>
>   (Original work published 1997).

A parenthetical reference to this work would give both dates: (Ramos, 1997/1999, p. 22).

A Book with an Editor

> Chapman, G. (1990). <u>Teaching young playwrights</u> (L. Barrett,
>
>   Ed.). Portsmouth, NH: Heinemann.

An Anthology of Shorter Works by Different Authors

> Stimpson, C. R., & Person, E. S. (Eds.). (1980). <u>Women:</u>
>
>   <u>Sex and sexuality.</u> Chicago: University of Chicago Press.

APA style does not abbreviate university presses (compare *U of Chicago P* in MLA style).

A Work from an Anthology

> Baker, S. W. (1980). Biological influences on human sex
>
>   and gender. In C. R. Stimpson & E. S. Person, (Eds.),
>
>   <u>Women: Sex and sexuality</u> (pp. 175–191). Chicago:
>
>   University of Chicago Press.

An article's title is not enclosed within quotation marks as in MLA style. ***Page numbers*** are preceded by ***p.*** (for *page*) or ***pp.*** (for *pages*). Do not abbreviate page numbers; for example, write *pp. 175–191,* not *175–91.*

An Online Book

> Robinson, K. (1998). <u>Beyond the wilderness.</u> Retrieved
>
>   December 21, 1999 from Online Originals on the World Wide
>
>   Web: http://www.onlineoriginals.com/beyondsy.html

Online sources include a sentence in this format:

```
Retrieved on [retrieval date] from [source] on the World Wide
    Web: [Web address]
```

Unlike MLA style, APA style does not place the Web address within angle brackets or follow it with a period.

An Article in a Magazine

```
Block, T. G. (1995, September 11). Riding the waves.
    Forbes, 182, 184.
Lynn, J. (2000, January). Hidden resources. Entrepreneur,
    102-108.
```

Titles of magazines and other periodicals are treated exactly as in MLA style. They are underlined, and every important word is capitalized. Dates are listed in full, with the year first. Months are not abbreviated. If an article does not appear on continuous pages, all page numbers are listed.

An Article in a Journal

A journal whose pages are numbered continuously throughout a volume:

```
Reese, H. W. (1999). Some contributions of philosophy to
    behavioral sciences. Journal of Mind and Behavior, 20,
    183-210.
```

A journal, every issue of which begins on page 1:

```
Green, A. (1997). Returning history to the community:
    Oral history in a museum setting. Oral History Review,
    24(2), 53-72.
```

For journal articles (unlike newspaper articles), neither *p.* nor *pp.* is used.

An Article in a Newspaper

```
Constable, P. (2000, January 1). Hijack drama ends
    peacefully. The Washington Post, p. A21.
Kaufman, L., & Hansell, S. (2000, January 2). Holiday lesson
    in online retailing. The New York Times, national
    edition, section 3, pp. 1, 12.
```

A Printed Article Reproduced Online

> Doctors striving to preempt diabetes (2000, January 1).
>
>   Boston Globe, p. A3. Retrieved January 2, 2000 from
>
>   the World Wide Web: http://www.boston.com/dailyglobe2/
>
>   001/nation/Doctors_striving_to_preempt_diabetes+.shtml
>
> Eddy, M. (2000, January 1). Experts worry about economic
>
>   collapse in Bosnia. News and Observer on the Web.
>
>   Retrieved January 2, 2000 from the World Wide Web:
>
>   http://www.nandotimes.com/24hour/nao/business/story/
>
>   0,2257,500148948-500180852-500736195-0,00.html
>
> Mazurek, R. H. (2000, January). Under the ice. Popular
>
>   Science, p. 28. Retrieved February 14, 2000 from
>
>   ProQuest database on the World Wide Web: http://
>
>   proquest.umi.com
>
> Yue, L. (1999, December 20). Economists expect Federal
>
>   Reserve to leave rates unchanged. Detroit Free Press.
>
>   Retrieved January 14, 2000 from the EBSCOhost database
>
>   (Newspaper Source) on the World Wide Web: http://
>
>   www.epnet.com

A Personal Interview or E-Mail

Personal communication is not included in an APA reference list. However, a parenthetical note (see pp. 513–14) is used and takes the following form: (R. Keating, personal communication, October 14, 1999)

An Anonymous Work

> L. A. crix nix short pix dis. (1992, November 30).
>
>   Variety, p. 44.

A Book with Two or Three Authors

> Cunningham, W. G., & Cordeiro, P. A. (2000). Educational
>
>   administration: A problem-based approach. Boston:
>
>   Allyn & Bacon.

APA citations of works with multiple authors differ form MLA citations in three ways:

1. Initials and last names of all authors (not just the first author) are inverted.
2. All authors are listed by name (*et al.* is not used in bibliographic listings for works with multiple authors, although it is used in parenthetical notes for works with more than six authors).
3. An ampersand (&) is used in place of the word *and* before the last author's name.

Two or More Works by the Same Author, Different Years

```
Irvin, E. (1998). New . . .

Irvin, E. (2000, May). Lessons . . .
```

When two or more works have the same author(s), arrange the works chronologically (not alphabetically, as in MLA style). The earliest work is listed first.

Two or More Works by the Same Author, Same Years

```
Bushman, D. (2000a). Development . . .

Bushman, D. (2000b). Reduced . . .
```

When the author(s) have two or more works in the same year, arrange the works alphabetically by title. Place lowercase letters (*a, b, c,* and so on) immediately after the year.

A Work Written by a Group or Government Agency

```
Sotheby's (1995). Nineteenth century European paintings,

    drawings and watercolours. London: Author.

U.S. Department of Justice, Office of Juvenile Justice and

    Delinquency Prevention. (1999). Cross-age teaching.

    Washington, DC: U.S. Government Printing Office.
```

Use *Author* for the publisher when the author and the publisher are the same.

Other Sources

Treatment of other sources, as well as detailed information about APA format, can be found by consulting the latest edition of the *Publication Manual of the American Psychological Association.* You can find the book in the reference section of most college libraries.

Notes in APA Style

Parenthetical notes in APA format are handled similarly to the MLA method, but with three notable differences:

1. The year of publication is included in the note.
2. All items are separated by commas.
3. Page numbers are preceded by the abbreviation *p.* or *pp.*

When a work is referred to as a whole, no page numbers are needed:

```
In a study of reaction times (Sanders, 2000), . . .
```

Only the year is needed when the author's name appears in the sentence:

```
Sanders (2000) studied reaction times . . .
```

Include pages when the source can be located more specifically:

```
" . . . not necessary" (Galizio, 1998, p. 9).
```

Give the first word or two from the title when the author's name is unknown. Book titles are underlined; periodical titles in notes (unlike in the reference list) are enclosed in quotation marks; all important words are capitalized (also like reference-list citations):

```
. . . the book (Culture, 1999).

. . . the article ("US policy," 1996).
```

Only the year, not the complete date, is given in notes referring to periodical articles.

For a work with six or fewer authors, the note lists all authors' last names:

```
(Andrulis, Beers, Bentley, & Gage, 1997)
```

However, only the first author's name is given for a work with more than six authors:

```
(Sabella et al., 2000)
```

When the reference list cites two or more works written by the same author in the same year, use lowercase letters to differentiate them, as in reference-list citations:

```
(Bushman, 2000a)

(Bushman, 2000b)
```

These two notes cite different works by Bushman, both written in 2000.

When a note refers to more than one work, list the references alphabetically and separate them with a semicolon:

```
(Earle & Reeves, 1999; Kowal, 2000)
```

Sample Pages in APA Style

Any paper written using MLA format can also be written in APA format. For example, Slade Healy could have used APA style for his paper on social promotion.

A cover page is typically used for APA papers. The cover page is numbered as page 1, and a shortened version of the title is placed above the page number on each page, as in Figure E.2.

The title is repeated on the opening page of the paper, numbered as page 2. Compare Figures E.3 and E.4 with pages from Slade's MLA-style paper on pages 480–81. Compare Figure E.1 with Slade's list of works cited on page 485.

Social Promotion and Its Alternatives

1

Social Promotion and Its Alternatives

Jonathan Slade Healy

English 102

November 15, 1999

Figure E.2 Sample APA cover page.

Social Promotion and Its Alternatives

2

Social Promotion and Its Alternatives

When children fail in school, should they be promoted
to the next grade with their age group, or should they be
required to repeat the grade? Over the last hundred years,
the education pendulum has swung between these two
approaches to student failure, and educators and politicians

Figure E.3 Sample APA opening page.

Social Promotion and Its Alternatives

6

of losing a parent or going blind (Perry, 1999, p. 75).

Chicago eighth-grader Corrine Murphy expressed her reaction

to her school's retention policy: "If you don't pass, you

stay in the same grade and people will be making fun of

you" (Coeyman, 1999).

Feelings of disgrace and loss of self-esteem may be

factors in the high dropout rate among those made to

repeat. Smith and Shepard report that retained students

are 20 to 30 percent more likely to drop out of school than

those who are promoted (1989, p. 215). Shepard says that

APA parenthetical notes include the work's date. Page numbers are preceded by p. or pp.

Figure E.4 Sample APA notes.

F *Format Featuring Numbered References*

Another common bibliographic format uses ***numbered references*** to identify sources. Variations on this format are used most widely in fields such as mathematics, computer science, finance, and other areas in the applied sciences.

Sources are assigned a number in the references page (list of works cited) and are referred to in the paper by that number rather than by the author's name. Items in the references list can be arranged either in alphabetical order or in the order in which references occur within the paper. Figure F.1 shows how the reference list at the end of Slade Healy's paper might have looked if he had used this style. In this case, the references are numbered in the order in which they first appear in the paper.

Here is how the first four sentences with notes in Slade's paper would have appeared if he had used the numbered references style:

```
Over the last hundred years, the education pendulum has

swung between these two approaches to student failure, and

educators and politicians continue to debate this vexing

question [1].

By the 1930s, however, concerns about the negative

psychological effects of retention on children led to the

widespread adoption of social promotion [2, pp. 1-2].

In 1941 a New York Regents report concluded that "a much

wiser and more profitable procedure than non-promotion is to

adapt instruction to the needs of the pupil at all times,

and at the end of the year to advance him to the next grade

or class and there continue to adjust instruction to his

needs" [qtd. in 3, p. 198].
```

Healy 8

References

1. American Federation of Teachers. "Passing on Failure: District Promotion Policies and Practices." K-12 Educational Issues. 13 Oct. 1999 <http://www.aft.org/edissues/socialpromotion/Intro.htm>.

2. Adams, Edgar. "Alternatives to Grade Level Retention." Dissertation. U of North Carolina at Wilmington, 1995.

3. Rothstein, Richard. "Where Is Lake Wobegon, Anyway?" Phi Delta Kappan Nov. 1998: 195-98.

4. Most Cleveland Teachers Say Social Promotion Doesn't Work." Sun Newspapers. 1997. 12 Oct. 1999 <http://www.sunnews.com/news/suberbs/metro/socialpromotionside.htm>.

Figure F.1 Sample list with numbered references.

The last note—[qtd. in 3, p. 198]—refers to the third work in Slade's reference list, the article by Richard Rothstein. Later in his paper, when Slade again refers to Rothstein's article, he uses the same reference number:

> While teachers do not want socially promoted students in their classrooms, they are just as likely to object to teaching retained students who are older than the other students in their classes [3, p. 197].

Apart from the use of reference numbers, there is no uniform style for citing bibliographic sources in this format. Individual items in the bibliography could follow the principles of MLA format, APA format, or yet some other format. If you are required to use numbered references for a course paper, be sure to check with your instructor for specific format details.

Another characteristic of papers using this format is that citation of page references is far less common than in either MLA or APA style. Usually, sources are referred to in the paper solely by their reference numbers, which are usually written within brackets:

`Smith and Gurganus [6] showed that . . .`

Often even the authors' names are omitted:

`Other examples of this approach are [1,4,5]. In 1996, [3]`

`analyzed . . .`

Instead of brackets, alternative formats that use numbered references place them either within parentheses:

`Fort (7) disputes the findings of Byington (3) . . .`

or as raised numbers:

`It has been demonstrated`[1] `that artifacts that occur . . .`

The raised number *1* in the preceding example refers not to a footnote or endnote but directly to the first source in the references list.

Index

Credits

Pages 5–6   From "Against the Grain" by David Bartholomae in *Writers on Writing* (T. Waldrep, ed.). New York: Random House, 1985. Reproduced with permission of The McGraw Hill Companies.

Page 31   From *All American Music* by John Rockwell.

Page 32   From "American Visionary," by Allan Ulrich in the *San Francisco Examiner* (Sept. 5, 1999). Reprinted with permission.

Pages 35–36   Genius in Changing Numbers by Gene Weingarten, © 1999, *The Washington Post*. Reprinted with permission.

Pages 38–40   Reprinted with the permission of The Free Press, an imprint of Simon & Schuster, from *Passionate Attachments: Thinking About Love* by Willard Gaylin, M.D., and Ethel Person, M.D. Copyright © 1988 by Friends of Columbia Analytic Center, Inc.

Page 45   Excerpt from "I'm Not Sick, I'm Just in Love" by Katherine Davis from *Newsweek*, July 17, 1995. © 1995, Newsweek, Inc. All rights reserved. Reprinted by permission.

Page 59   Jenny Hung, "Surviving a Year of Sleepless Nights," From *Newsweek*, Sept. 20, 1999, © 1999 Newsweek, Inc. All rights reserved. Reprinted by permission.

Pages 67–68   From *Abnormal Psychology: Current Perspectives*, Fifth Edition, by R. R. Bootzin and J. R. Acocella. New York: Random House, 1993. Reproduced with permission of The McGraw-Hill Companies.

Pages 70–72   Jerry Adler, "The Truth about High School," From *Newsweek*, May 10, 1999, © 1999 Newsweek, Inc. All rights reserved. Reprinted by permission.

Pages 72–73   Excerpt from *The Sound of Mountain Water* by Wallace Stegner. Copyright © 1969 by Wallace Stegner. Reprinted by permission of Doubleday, a division of Bantam Doubleday Dell Publishing Group, Inc.

Pages 75–76   Christopher John Farley and Patrick Dawson, "Sorry, No Vacancies," *Time*, Aug. 7, 1999: 34–35. © Time, Inc. Reprinted with permission.

Pages 77–78   Excerpt from *Zen and the Art of Motorcycle Maintenance* by Robert Pirsig. Copyright © 1974 by Robert M. Pirsig. Reprinted by permission of William Morrow and Company, Inc.

Pages 82–85   Nicholas Lemann, "Buffaloed," *New Yorker*, Sept. 13, 1999. Reprinted by permission of International Creative Management, Inc. © 1999 Nicholas Lemann.

Pages 97–98   Anthony Brode, "Lucky Goldilocks," reproduced by permission of Punch, Ltd.

Page 99   "Loveliest of Trees, the Cherry Now" by A. E. Housman from *The Collected Poems of A. E. Housman*. Copyright © 1939, 1940, 1965 by Henry Holt and Company, Inc. Copyright © 1967, 1968 by Robert Symons. Reprinted by permission of Henry Holt and Company, Inc.

Pages 105–114   Brian Feagans, "On the Fringe," *Sunday Star-News*, Dec. 27, 1998. © 1998, Wilmington Star-News, Inc. Used by permission.

Page 121   "Magnet Campus Allows High-IQ High-Schoolers to Thrive, reprinted in the *Sunday Star-News*, Feb. 11, 1996. © *Daily News of Los Angeles*.

Page 123   Sarah Boxer, "In Fine Print, Punctuation to Puncture Pedants with," *The New York Times*, Sept. 4, 1999. © The New York Times Inc. All rights reserved. Reprinted with permission.

Pages 125–26   Daniel McGuinn, "The Big Score," From *Newsweek*, Sept 6, 1999, © 1999 Newsweek, Inc. All rights reserved. Reprinted by permission.

Page 126   Jeff Giles, "Inner City to Ivy League," From *Newsweek*, June 15, 1998, © 1998 Newsweek, Inc. All rights reserved. Reprinted by permission.

Page 129   "Goodbye, Di," From *Newsweek*, Sept. 6, 1999, © 1999 Newsweek, Inc. All rights reserved. Reprinted by permission.

Page 129   Molly Ivins, "Ernies Nuns' Are Pointing the Way," *Fort Worth Star-Telegram*, Oct. 21, 1999, and "www.mollybooks.yea!," *Fort Worth Star-Telegram*, Dec. 22, 1998. Reprinted by permission.

Page 129   David Brooks, "Conscientious Consumption," *New Yorker*, Nov. 23, 1998: 46–47. Reprinted by permission.

Pages 131–38   Fred Fedler, "An Enduring Hoax: H. L. Mencken's Fraudulent History of the White House Bathtub," *Media Hoaxes*. Ames, Iowa: Iowa State University Press, pp. 118–28. Reprinted by permission.

Pages 145–46   "Stereotyping: Homogenizing People" in *Telling It Like It Isn't* by Dan Rothwell. Reprinted by permission of the author.

Pages 147–48   Sarah Boxer, "In Fine Print, Punctuation to Puncture Pedants with," *The New York Times*, Sept. 4, 1999. © The New York Times Inc. All rights reserved. Reprinted with permission.

Page 150   William Safire, "On Language: The Concealment of Sex," *The New York Times Magazine*, Jan. 1, 1995. Reprinted by permission.

Pages 151–52   David Levi Strauss, "A Threnody for Street Kids," *The Nation*, June 1, 1992: 752–54. Reprinted with permission from the June 1, 1992 issue of *The Nation*.

Page 155   Agis Salpukis, "Green Power Wanes, but Not at the Grass Roots," *The New York Times*, Mar. 9, 1997. Reprinted by permission.

Page 155   Paul Griffiths, "Surviving the Siege, but Barely," *The New York Times*, Aug. 17, 1997. Reprinted by permission.

Pages 155–56   Melinda Burns, "For Migrant Workers, the Bad Old Days Have Never Died," *San Francisco Examiner*, Sept. 5, 1999: 10. Reprinted with permission.

Pages 157–63   "Against All Odds" by Ron Suskind. Reprinted by permission of *The Wall Street Journal*, © 1994 Dow Jones & Company, Inc. All Rights Reserved Worldwide.

Pages 166–68   Terry Lefton, "The Anglophile Angle," *Brandweek*, Oct. 5, 1998: 18–21. © 1998/99 ASM

Parenthetical Notes (MLA Style): Quick Reference Guide

Detailed information on parenthetical notes can be found on pages 461–76.

PURPOSE
Use a note to identify the specific source location for a specific idea, piece of information, or quotation in your paper.

FORMAT
Give the specific page reference, preceded by the *least* amount of information needed to identify the source in your list of works cited.

PLACEMENT
Place the note following the passage.

MODEL ENTRIES

Standard Reference
Give the author and page(s):

    A fear of thunder is common among dogs (Digby 237).

Author Identified in the Passage
Omit the author's name in the note:

    Digby noted that dogs are often terrified of thunder (237).

An Anonymous Work (Unidentified Author)
Use the first word or two from the title:

    ("An infant's" 22)

A Work with Two or Three Authors

    (Reid, Forrestal, and Cook 48-49)

A Work with More Than Three Authors

    (Courtois et al. 112)

Two or More Works by the Same Author
Add the first word(s) from the title:

    (Asimov, Adding 240-43)
    (Asimov, "Happy" 68)

Two Authors with the Same Last Name
Include the authors' first names:

    (George Eliot 459)
    (T. S. Eliot 44)

A Multivolume Work
The volume number precedes the page number(s):

    (Agus 2: 59)

Exception: Omit the volume number if only one volume is identified in your list of works cited:

    (Agus 59)